RULES OF DEBIT AND CREDIT

TEMPORARY ACCOUNTS

 W9-BHX-787

Withdrawals
(Sole Proprietorship/Partnership)

Debit	Credit
+	−
Increase	Decrease
Normal Balance	

Example: Linda Carter, Withdrawals

Revenue

Debit	Credit
−	+
Decrease	Increase
	Normal Balance

Examples: Fees Income
Sales

Contra Revenue

Debit	Credit
+	−
Increase	Decrease
Normal Balance	

Examples: Sales Discounts
Sales Returns and Allowances

Cost of Goods Sold

Debit	Credit
+	−
Increase	Decrease
Normal Balance	

Examples: Purchases
Freight In

Contra Cost of Goods Sold

Debit	Credit
−	+
Decrease	Increase
	Normal Balance

Example: Purchases Discounts
Purchases Returns and Allowances

Expenses

Debit	Credit
+	−
Increase	Decrease
Normal Balance	

Examples: Advertising Expense
Utilities Expense
Rent Expense

eleventh edition

College Accounting

Chapters 1–13

McGraw-Hill's HOMEWORK MANAGER  PLUS™

online

THE COMPLETE SOLUTION

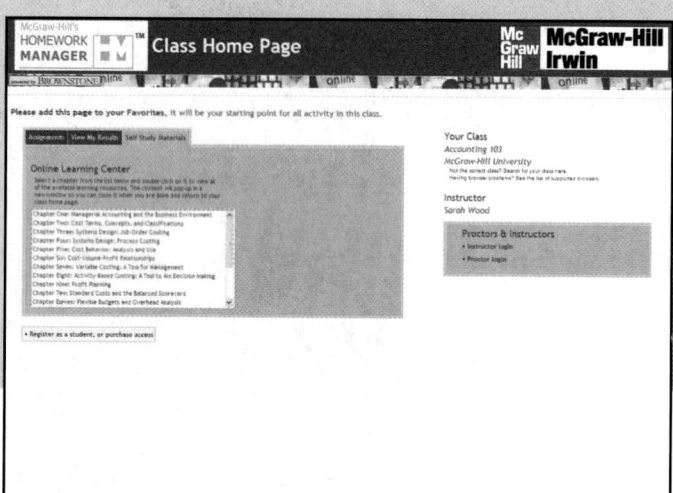

McGraw-Hill's
Homework Manager

™ This online homework management solution contains the textbook's end-of-chapter material. Now you have the option to build assignments from static and algorithmic versions of the text problems and exercises, or build self-graded quizzes from the additional questions provided in the online test bank.

Features:

- Assigns book-specific problems/exercises to students
- Provides integrated test bank questions for quizzes and tests
- Automatically grades assignments and quizzes, storing results in one grade book
- Dispenses immediate feedback to students regarding their work

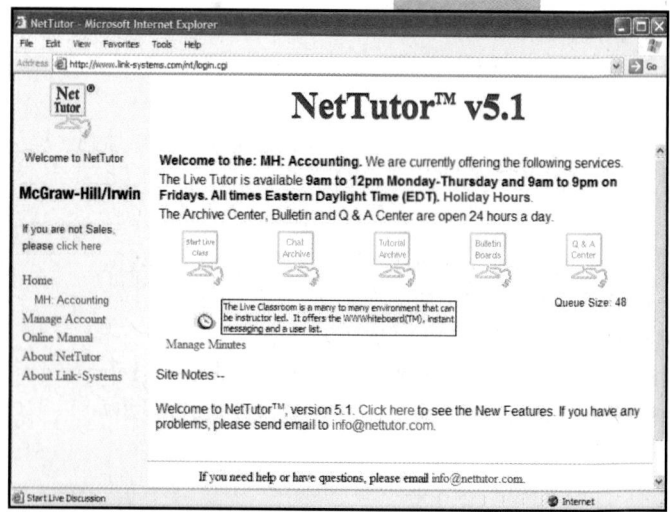

NetTutor

NetTutor™ Only available through Homework Manager Plus, NetTutor connects students with qualified tutors online. Students can submit questions online for a response within 24 hours, explore archived questions, or engage in a real-time tutoring session online.

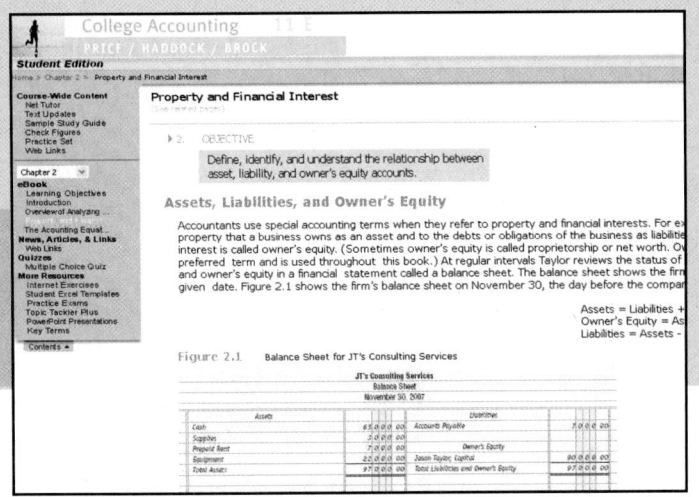

Interactive Online Version
of the Textbook

In addition to the textbook, students can rely on this online version of the text for a convenient way to study. The interactive content is fully integrated with Homework Manager to give students quick access to relevant content as they work through problems, exercises, and practice quizzes.

Features:

- Online version of the text is integrated with Homework Manager

- Students referred to appropriate sections of online book as they complete an assignment or take a practice quiz

- Direct link to related material that corresponds with the learning objective within the text.

McGraw-Hill's Homework Manager Plus combines the power of Homework Manager with the latest interactive learning technology to create a comprehensive, fully integrated online study package. Students working on assignments in Homework Manager can click a simple hotlink and instantly review the appropriate material in the Interactive Online Textbook. Net-Tutor rounds out the package by offering live tutoring with a qualified expert in the course material.

By including Homework Manager Plus with your textbook adoption, you're giving your students a vital edge as they progress through the course and ensuring that the help they need is never more than a mouse click away. Contact your McGraw-Hill representative or visit the book's website to learn how to add Homework Manager Plus to your adoption.

HOMEWORK **MANAGER**
HELPS YOU EFFICIENTLY

McGraw-Hill's
HOMEWORK
MANAGER  ™

Problems and exercises from the book, as well as questions from the test bank, have been integrated into Homework Manager to give you a variety of options as you deliver assignments and quizzes to students via the web. You can choose from static or algorithmic questions and have the graded results automatically stored in your grade book online.

Have you ever wished that you could assign a different set of problems to each of your students, individualizing their educational experience? The algorithmic question capabilities of Homework Manager give you the opportunity to do so. The problem-making function inserts new numbers and data from an endless supply into the set question structure. Each student will have a different answer while learning the same principles from the text. This also enables the students to master concepts by revisiting the same questions with different data.

Assign coursework online.

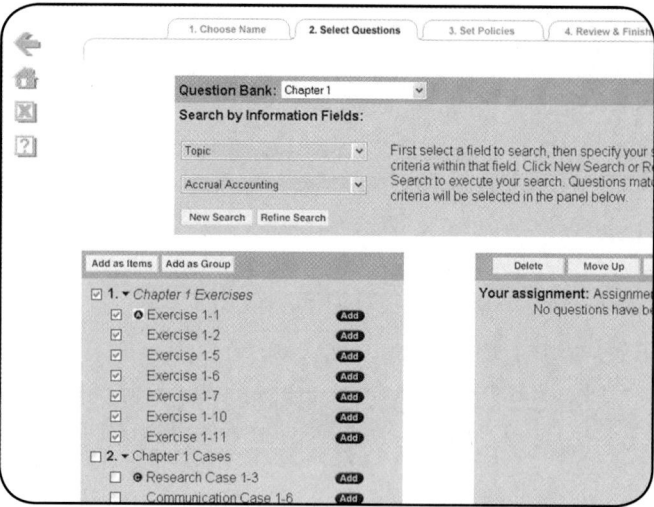

MANAGE YOUR CLASS.

Control how content is presented.

Homework Manager gives you a flexible and easy way to present course work to students. You determine which questions to ask and how much help students will receive as they work through assignments. You can determine the number of attempts a student can make with each problem or provide hints and feedback with each question. The questions can also be linked to an online version of the text for quick and simple reference while completing an assignment.

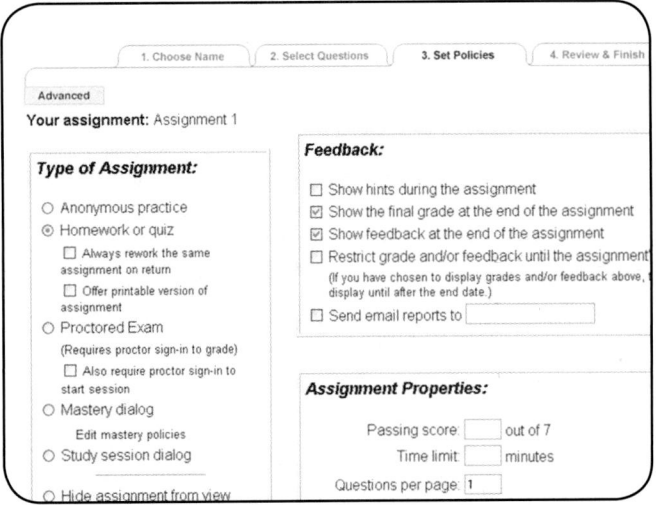

Track student progress.

Assignments are graded automatically, with the results stored in your private grade book. Detailed results let you see at a glance how each student does on as assignment or an individual problem. You can even see how many attempts it took them to solve it. You can monitor how the whole class does on each problem, and even determine where individual students might need extra help.

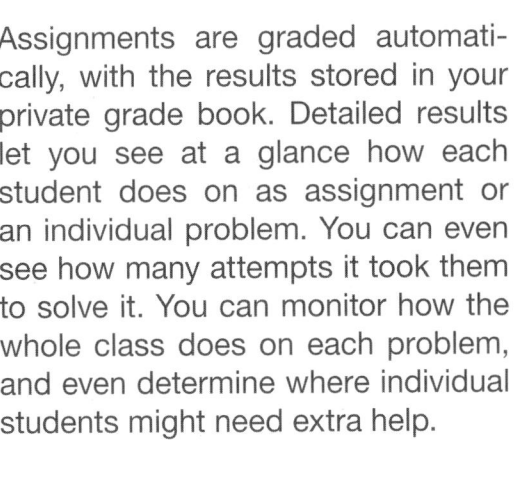

PROFESSORS CAN ALLOW
HOMEWORK **MANAGER**
TO GIVE STUDENTS HELPFUL FEEDBACK

Auto-grading and feedback.

Question 1: *Score 6.5/8*

Your response	Correct response
Exercise 2-1: Using Cost Terms [LO2, LO5, LO7] Following are a number of cost terms introduced in the chapter:	**Exercise 2-1: Using Cost Terms [LO2, LO5, LO7]** Following are a number of cost terms introduced in the chapter:

Period cost	Fixed cost		Period cost	Fixed cost
Variable cost	Prime cost		Variable cost	Prime cost
Opportunity cost	Conversion cost		Opportunity cost	Conversion cost
Product cost	Sunk cost		Product cost	Sunk cost

Your response	Correct response
Choose the cost term or terms above that most appropriately describe the costs identified in each of the following situations. A cost term can be used more than once.	Choose the cost term or terms above that most appropriately describe the costs identified in each of the following situations. A cost term can be used more than once.
1. Crestline Books, Inc., prints a small book titled *The Pocket Speller* . The paper going into the manufacture of the book would be called direct materials and classified as a Product cost (6%). In terms of cost behavior, the paper could also be described as a Product cost (0%) with respect to the number of books printed.	1. Crestline Books, Inc., prints a small book titled *The Pocket Speller* . The paper going into the manufacture of the book would be called direct materials and classified as a Product cost. In terms of cost behavior, the paper could also be described as a variable cost with respect to the number of books printed.
2. Instead of compiling the words in the book, the author hired by the company could have earned considerable fees consulting with business organizations. The consulting fees forgone by the author would be called Opportunity cost (6%).	2. Instead of compiling the words in the book, the author hired by the company could have earned considerable fees consulting with business organizations. The consulting fees forgone by the author would be called Opportunity cost.
3. The paper and other materials used in the manufacture of the book, combined with the direct labor cost involved, would be called Prime cost (6%).	3. The paper and other materials used in the manufacture of the book, combined with the direct labor cost involved, would be called Prime cost.
4. The salary of Crestline Books' president would be classified as a Product cost (0%), and the salary will appear on the income statement as an expense in the time period in which it is incurred.	4. The salary of Crestline Books' president would be classified as a Period cost, and the salary will appear on the income statement as an expense in the time period in which it is incurred.
5. Depreciation on the equipment used to print the book would be classified by Crestline Books as a Product cost (6%). However, depreciation on any equipment used by the company in selling and administrative activities would be classified as a Period cost (6%). In terms of cost behavior, depreciation would probably be classified as a Fixed cost (6%) with respect to the number of books printed.	5. Depreciation on the equipment used to print the book would be classified by Crestline Books as a Product cost. However, depreciation on any equipment used by the company in selling and administrative activities would be classified as a Period cost. In terms of cost behavior, depreciation would probably be classified as a Fixed cost with respect to the number of books printed.
6. A Product cost (6%) is also known as an inventoriable cost,	6. A Product cost is also known as an inventoriable cost, since

Immediately after finishing an assignment, students can compare their answers side-by-side with the detailed solutions. Students can try again with new numbers to see if they have mastered the concept.

eleventh edition

College Accounting
Chapters 1–13

JOHN ELLIS PRICE, Ph.D., CPA
Professor of Accounting and Vice Provost
University of North Texas–Dallas Campus
Dallas, Texas

M. DAVID HADDOCK, JR., Ed.D., CPA
Professor of Accounting and Associate Vice-President for Academic Affairs
Chattanooga State Technical Community College
Chattanooga, Tennessee

HORACE R. BROCK, Ph.D., CPA
Distinguished Professor of Accounting Emeritus
College of Business Administration
University of North Texas
Denton, Texas

**McGraw-Hill
Irwin**

Boston   Burr Ridge, IL   Dubuque, IA   Madison, WI   New York   San Francisco   St. Louis
Bangkok   Bogotá   Caracas   Kuala Lumpur   Lisbon   London   Madrid   Mexico City
Milan   Montreal   New Delhi   Santiago   Seoul   Singapore   Sydney   Taipei   Toronto

The McGraw·Hill Companies

McGraw-Hill
Irwin

COLLEGE ACCOUNTING

Chapters 1-13

Published by McGraw-Hill/Irwin, a business unit of The McGraw-Hill Companies, Inc., 1221 Avenue of the Americas, New York, NY, 10020. Copyright © 2007 by The McGraw-Hill Companies, Inc. All rights reserved. No part of this publication may be reproduced or distributed in any form or by any means, or stored in a database or retrieval system, without the prior written consent of The McGraw-Hill Companies, Inc., including, but not limited to, in any network or other electronic storage or transmission, or broadcast for distance learning.

Some ancillaries, including electronic and print components, may not be available to customers outside the United States.

This book is printed on acid-free paper.

4 5 6 7 8 9 0 DOW/DOW 0 9 8 7

ISBN-13:   978-0-07-302992-4 (student edition)
ISBN-10:   0-07-302992-0 Chapters 1-32 (student edition)
ISBN-13:   978-0-07-321537-2 (instructor edition)
ISBN-10:   0-07-321537-6 Chapters 1-32 (instructor edition)
ISBN-13:   978-0-07-319682-4
ISBN-10:   0-07-319682-7 Chapters 1-25
ISBN-13:   978-0-07-319680-0 (student edition)
ISBN-10:   0-07-319680-0 Chapters 1-13 (student edition)
ISBN-13:   978-0-07-321538-9 (instructor edition)
ISBN-10:   0-07-321538-4 Chapters 1-13 (instructor edition)

Editorial director: *Brent Gordon*
Publisher: *Stewart Mattson*
Developmental editor II: *Sarah Wood*
Marketing manager: *Marc Chernoff*
Media producer: *Greg Bates*
Senior project manager: *Susanne Riedell*
Lead production supervisor: *Michael R. McCormick*
Senior designer: *Mary E. Kazak*
Senior photo research coordinator: *Jeremy Cheshareck*
Photo researcher: *Teri Stratford*
Senior media project manager: *Rose M. Range*
Senior supplement producer: *Carol Loreth*
Cover design: *Eric Kass/Lodge Design*
Cover image: *Wilhelm Scholz/Getty Images*
Interior design: *Amanda Kavanagh/Ark Design Studio*
Typeface: *10.5/12 Times Roman*
Compositor: *Cenveo*
Printer: *R. R. Donnelley*

The Library of Congress has cataloged the single volume edition of this work as follows:
Price, John Ellis.
    College accounting / John Ellis Price, M. David Haddock, Jr., Horace R. Brock—11th ed.
      p. cm.
    "Chapters 1–32."
    Includes index.
    ISBN-13: 978-0-07-302992-4
    ISBN-10: 0-07-302992-0 (alk. paper)
    1. Accounting. I. Haddock, M. David. II. Brock, Horace R. III. Title.
HF5635.B8542 2007
657'.044—dc22   2005052297

www.mhhe.com

About the Authors

JOHN ELLIS PRICE is professor of accounting and vice provost of the University of North Texas (UNT) Dallas Campus. Dr. Price has previously held positions of professor and assistant professor, as well as chair and dean, at the University of North Texas, Jackson State University, and the University of Southern Mississippi. Dr. Price has also been active in the Internal Revenue Service as a member of the Commissioner's Advisory Group for two terms, and as an Internal Revenue agent.

Professor Price is a certified public accountant who has twice received the UNT College of Business Administration's Outstanding Teaching Award, and the university's President's Council Award. Majoring in accounting, he received his BBA and MS degrees from the University of Southern Mississippi, and his Ph.D. in accounting from the University of North Texas.

Dr. Price is a member of the Mississippi Society of Certified Public Accountants, the American Accounting Association, the American Taxation Association (serving as past chair of the Subcommittee on Relations with the IRS and Treasury), and currently acts as chair of the American Institute of Certified Public Accountants Minority Initiatives and is a member of the Foundation Trustees.

M. DAVID HADDOCK, JR., is currently professor of accounting and associate vice president for academic affairs at Chattanooga State Technical Community College in Tennessee. Over the past 30+ years, Professor Haddock has served in faculty and administrative roles at Auburn University at Montgomery, the University of Alabama in Birmingham, West Georgia College, and Chattanooga State Technical Community College. He received a teaching excellence award from the University of Texas in 1991.

Professor Haddock was elected vice president of the Tennessee Society of Certified Public Accountants in 2005 after serving on the board of directors and as the Chattanooga TSCPA chapter president.

HORACE BROCK is director of International Programs in the Institute of Petroleum Accounting, and is distinguished professor emeritus from the University of North Texas. At UNT, he served as chairman of the Department of Accounting and was also director of international programs and director of oil and gas programs for UNT's Professional Development Institute. His teaching experience includes visiting professorships at Ohio State University, University of Arkansas, and Arizona State University.

Professor Brock's professional activities include being chairman of, and consultant to, the Financial Accounting Standards Board's Task Force on Accounting for the Extractive Industries, and serving on the FASB task force on disclosures in the financial reports of petroleum companies. He has been a member of the SEC's Oil and Gas Accounting Committee, and presently he is a member of the AICPA's Task Force to Revise the Accounting and Auditing Guide for Oil and Gas Producing Companies.

Motivating Your

Just as motivation and dedication are required to be a successful runner, learning accounting takes dedication and practice. For many students, the material covered in this text is the first exposure to accounting and the first step to a new or better career. Our market research has shown that motivating students is the number 1 teaching challenge for instructors. Those students who are motivated to master the accounting cycle and analyze transactions will be on their way to success in this course.

College Accounting, 11th edition, by Price, Haddock, and Brock, will help inspire your students to achieve success in this course. Its readability, clear step-by-step examples, and proven problem material keep students involved and engaged in class, motivating them to complete the practice needed to master the key concepts of accounting.

Most importantly, College Accounting helps your students succeed by providing clarity, relevance, and strong technology support.

Students to Succeed

Clarity

Students and instructors continue to praise *College Accounting* for its readability. The authors' writing style and clear step-by-step examples make key concepts easy to grasp. Features like the **Business Transaction Analysis Model** make it easy for students to see how to analyze business transactions. The Important and Recall margin elements provide students with the definitions of key terms and concepts.

Relevance

Most students lose motivation when they don't see the relevance of accounting. *College Accounting* shows students how the accounting concepts they are studying are applied at real world companies, such as **Yahoo, Coca-Cola,** and **Wal-Mart,** and why they are important. The Managerial Application and Accounting On the Job boxes give students the opportunity to apply the concepts they have learned to real world scenarios and develop critical thinking and problem solving skills. Students also like to know why what they are studying is important to them. Each section objective is accompanied by an explanation of why it is important.

Technology

The 11th edition of *College Accounting* provides unparalleled technology aides that will help your students. **McGraw-Hill's Homework Manager**™ and **McGraw-Hill's Homework Manager Plus**™ let instructors assign, collect, and grade algorithmically generated homework online, and give students the ability to work with an electronic version of the textbook. Students will also benefit from **Topic Tackler,** a multimedia tutorial focusing on the most difficult topic in each chapter. **NetTutor**™, provides students with live online tutoring. And our new **Algorithmic Test Bank** lets instructors create exam questions with fresh numbers every time.

Motivate Your Students to Get Running with Price/Haddock/Brock!

What's New to the

- Updated illustrations, examples, and problems throughout the text.

- **New Continuation problems** in the end-of-chapter material that carry over from one problem to another and from one chapter to another, reinforcing learning objectives.

- Updated, more thought-provoking Self Reviews.

- Coverage on **contemporary trends in banking,** such as debit cards and online banking, as well as discussion of bank fraud and identity theft have been added in Chapter 9.

- Coverage of the **Sarbanes Oxley Act** and discussion of the following organizations has been included in Chapter 14: The American Institute of Certified Public Accountants (AICPA), Federal and State Agencies Other Than the SEC, Other Organizations in the United States, and The International Accounting Standards Board.

- Based on reviewer feedback, Chapter 15 has been reorganized so that first the allowance method is fully explained and then the direct charge-off method is covered in order to minimize students' confusion between the two.

- Chapter 18 has been updated to clarify that fair market value method is a financial accounting procedure and the income tax method is an income tax procedure. In the 11th edition, the discussion of impairment has been placed following the discussion of depletion. This edition also reflects the rules of FASB Statement 142, calling for amortizing costs of limited-life tangibles and the application of impairment tests in lieu of amortization of unlimited-life intangibles.

- Early retirement of bonds section in Chapter 22 has been rewritten to improve students' understanding.

- The discussion of variance analysis of manufacturing overhead in Chapter 31 has been rewritten to give the student an overall approach.

- **Topic Tackler Plus** is a complete multimedia tutorial focusing on the most problematic areas in the college accounting course.

Eleventh Edition

- **McGraw-Hill's Homework Manager™** is a web-based supplement that duplicates problem structures directly from the end-of-chapter material in the textbook, using algorithms to provide a limitless supply of online self-graded practice and assignment problems. The algorithmic test bank is also included in Homework Manager™. **McGraw-Hill's Homework Manager Plus™** allows students to link directly to an online version of the text and web resources when working on the problem.

- **NetTutor™** allows tutors and students to communicate with each other in a variety of ways, including interactive online tutorials, a Q&A Center that allow students to receive answers to questions within 24 hours of submission, and a searchable archive of previously asked questions.

- **ALEKS® for the Accounting Cycle** uses an innovative adaptive questioning system to provide guided learning to each and every student.

- **Algorithmic Test Bank** enables instructors to create countless versions of the same problem, ensuring unique versions or quizzes or tests.

- **Carol Yacht's General Ledger** software helps students master every aspect of the general ledger, from inputting receipts to calculating ratios for analysis. Tied to select end-of-chapter material, it allows students to solve problems using a generic general ledger system or Peachtree templates. Students receive a free copy of the educational version of Peachtree Complete, the same software relied upon by thousands of firms throughout the world.

What makes Price/Haddock/Brock

College Accounting provides your students with engaging pedagogical tools designed to help them learn and master the material.

CHAPTER OPENER:

Brief features about real-world companies allow students to see how the chapter's information and insights apply to the world outside the classroom. Thinking Critically questions stimulate thought on the topics to be explored in the chapter.

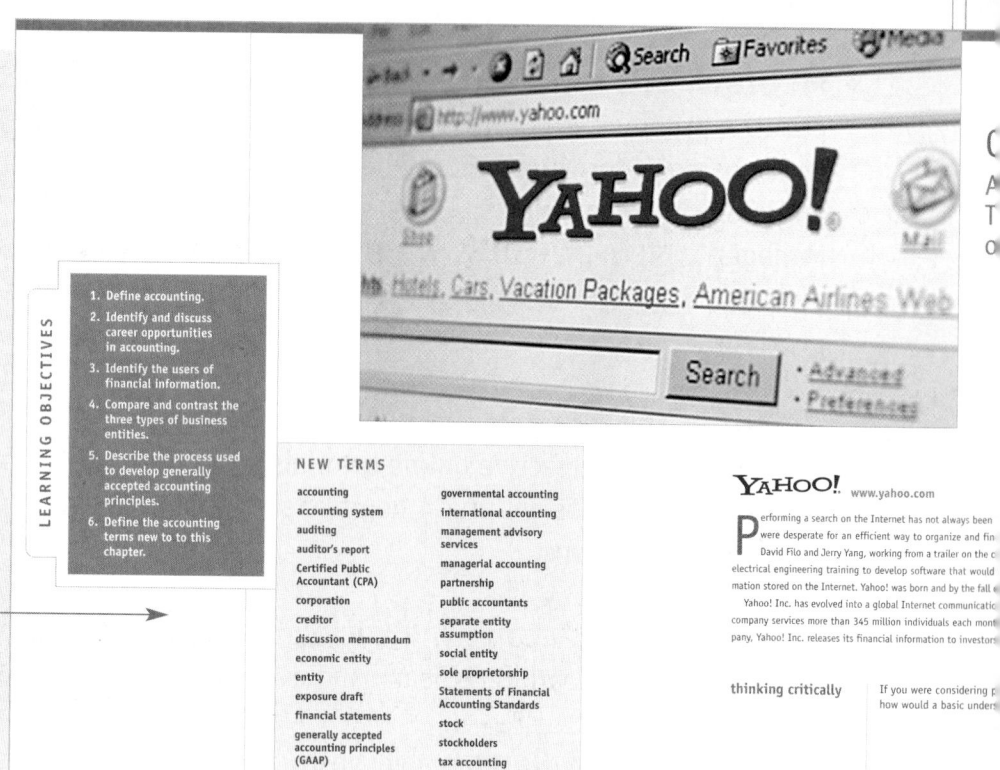

LEARNING OBJECTIVES

1. Define accounting.
2. Identify and discuss career opportunities in accounting.
3. Identify the users of financial information.
4. Compare and contrast the three types of business entities.
5. Describe the process used to develop generally accepted accounting principles.
6. Define the accounting terms new to this chapter.

NEW TERMS

accounting	governmental accounting
accounting system	international accounting
auditing	management advisory services
auditor's report	managerial accounting
Certified Public Accountant (CPA)	partnership
corporation	public accountants
creditor	separate entity assumption
discussion memorandum	social entity
economic entity	sole proprietorship
entity	Statements of Financial Accounting Standards
exposure draft	stock
financial statements	stockholders
generally accepted accounting principles (GAAP)	tax accounting

YAHOO! www.yahoo.com

Performing a search on the Internet has not always been [...] were desperate for an efficient way to organize and fin[...] David Filo and Jerry Yang, working from a trailer on the c[...] electrical engineering training to develop software that would [...] mation stored on the Internet. Yahoo! was born and by the fall [...] Yahoo! Inc. has evolved into a global Internet communicatio[...] company services more than 345 million individuals each month[...] pany, Yahoo! Inc. releases its financial information to investors[...]

thinking critically If you were considering p[...] how would a basic unders[...]

Section 1

SECTION OBJECTIVES

▶ 1. **Define accounting.**
WHY IT'S IMPORTANT
Business transactions affect many aspects of our lives.

▶ 2. **Identify and discuss career opportunities in accounting.**
WHY IT'S IMPORTANT
There's something for everyone in the field of accounting. Accounting professionals are found in every workplace from public accounting firms to government agencies, from corporations to nonprofit organizations.

▶ 3. **Identify the users of financial information.**
WHY IT'S IMPORTANT
A wide variety of individuals and businesses depend on financial information to make decisions.

LEARNING OBJECTIVES: Appearing in the Chapter Opener and within the margins of the text, Learning Objectives alert students to what they should expect as they progress through the chapter. Many students question why they are studying a learning objective, which is why we explain **"Why It's Important."**

such a powerful learning tool?

BUSINESS TRANSACTION ANALYSIS MODELS: Instructors say mastering the ability to properly analyze transactions is critical to success in this course. Price's step-by-step transaction analysis illustrations show how to identify the appropriate general ledger accounts affected, determine debit or credit activity, present the transaction in T-account form, and record the entry in the general journal.

THE BOTTOM LINE: Appear in the margins alongside select transactions and concepts in the text. These visuals offer a summary of the effects of these transactions—the end result—on the financial statements of a business.

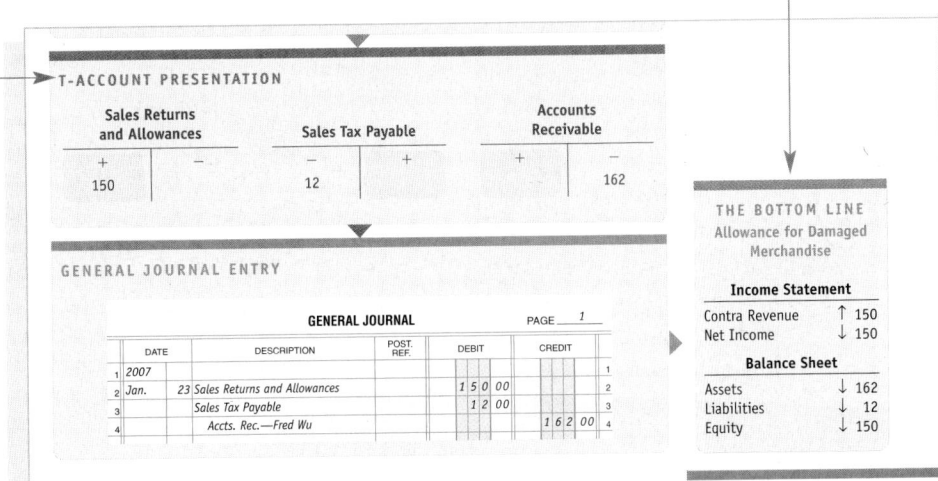

T-ACCOUNT PRESENTATION

Sales Returns and Allowances		Sales Tax Payable		Accounts Receivable	
+	−	−	+	+	−
150		12			162

GENERAL JOURNAL ENTRY

GENERAL JOURNAL   PAGE ___1___

	DATE	DESCRIPTION	POST. REF.	DEBIT	CREDIT	
1	2007					1
2	Jan.	23 Sales Returns and Allowances		1 5 0 00		2
3		Sales Tax Payable		1 2 00		3
4		Accts. Rec.—Fred Wu			1 6 2 00	4

THE BOTTOM LINE
Allowance for Damaged Merchandise

Income Statement

Contra Revenue	↑ 150
Net Income	↓ 150

Balance Sheet

Assets	↓ 162
Liabilities	↓ 12
Equity	↓ 150

recall

Debits = Credits
No matter how many accounts are affected by a transaction, total debits must equal total credits.

RECALL AND IMPORTANT!: **Recall** is a series of brief reinforcements that serve as reminders of material covered in *previous* chapters that are relevant to the new information being presented. **Important!** draws students' attention to critical materials introduced in the *current* chapter.

ACCOUNTING ON THE JOB <<

HOSPITALITY AND TOURISM

Industry Overview

Hospitality is the world's largest industry, accounting for more jobs, sales, and tax revenue than any other industry. The hospitality industry, also known as the travel or tourism industry, is composed of hotels, restaurants, institutional food service, cruise lines, arenas, travel agencies, meeting and convention centers, sport complexes, resorts, parks, clubs, spas, and tourism-related transportation. In the United States, the hospitality industry's employment growth is twice that of any other industry. Hospitality is forecasted to become the nation's largest industry by the year 2010.

Career Opportunities

- State Tourism Bureau Director
- Director of Resort Contracts and Purchasing
- Executive Chef
- Travel Technology Specialist
- Tour Promotions Manager
- Vice President of Hotel Operations
- Airport Passenger Services Supervisor
- Catering Director

Preparing for a Hospitality and Tourism Career

- Gain expertise in database administration or programming. Hotels, spas, golf courses, and airlines use sophisticated computerized systems to track reservations and memberships.

- Obtain an associate's or bachelor's degree in hotel, restaurant, and institutional management or a degree in hospitality and tourism management. Core course requirements include database management, electronic spreadsheets, and accounting.

- Enroll in an advanced internship program. The Disney College Program offers specialties in marketing, hotel management, finance, and communications. Marriott International offers paid internships from 8 to 16 weeks in duration. Opportunities exist in accounting and finance, catering, front office, human resources, sales, and culinary arts.

- Receive training on the latest Worldspan computer reservation system developed by Delta, TWA, and Northwest Airlines.

THINKING CRITICALLY

What skills and education might be required for the position of hotel general manager with a major hotel chain such as Marriott International?

INTERNET APPLICATION

Visit the Web site of a trade organization such as the Travel Industry Association of America to learn about potential career paths within the industry. Describe the purpose of the association. What resources are offered on the site?

ACCOUNTING ON THE JOB AND COMPUTERS IN ACCOUNTING:

features provide research opportunities in the realms of careers, business technologies, and software.

MANAGERIAL IMPLICATIONS <<

FINANCIAL INFORMATION

- Managers of a business make sure that the firm's accounting system produces financial information that is timely, accurate, and fair.
- Financial statements should be based on generally accepted accounting principles.
- Each year a publicly traded company must submit financial statements, including an independent auditor's report, to the SEC.
- Internal reports for management need not follow generally accepted accounting principles but should provide useful information that will aid in monitoring and controlling operations.
- Financial information can help managers to control present operations, make decisions, and plan for the future.
- The sound use of financial information is essential to good management.

THINKING CRITICALLY

If you were a manager, how would you use financial information to make decisions?

MANAGERIAL IMPLICATIONS:

Puts your student in the role of a manager and asks them to apply the concepts learned in the chapter.

INTERNATIONAL INSIGHTS: Accounting issues that provide connections to the global world of business.

International INSIGHTS

Business Etiquette

In Japan, business cards are always offered with two hands. The receiver should accept the card with two hands, study it, and bow slightly before placing it into a shirt or jacket pocket. Placing the card near the heart shows respect for both the person and the company.

SELF REVIEW:

Each section concludes with a Self Review that includes questions, multiple choice exercises, and an analysis assignment. A Comprehensive Self-Review appears at the end of each chapter. Answers are provided at the end of the chapter.

Section 1: **Self Review**

QUESTIONS

1. What does the term "accounts payable" mean?

2. What is a business transaction?

3. Describe a transaction that increases an asset and the owner's equity.

EXERCISES

4. Maria Sanchez purchased a computer for $2,500 on account for her business. What is the effect of this transaction?

a. Cash decrease of $2,500 and owner's equity increase of $2,500.

b. Equipment increase of $2,500 and cash increase of $2,500.

c. Equipment decrease of $2,500 and accounts payable increase of $2,500.

d. Equipment increase of $2,500 and accounts payable increase of $2,500.

5. Carolyn Carter began a new business by depositing $50,000 in the business bank account. She wrote two checks from the business account: $6,000 for office furniture and $2,000 for office supplies. What is her financial interest in the company?

a. $42,000

b. $44,000

c. $48,000

d. $50,000

ANALYSIS

6. Import Specialty Co. has no liabilities. The asset and owner's equity balances are as follows. What is the balance of "Supplies"?

Cash	$24,000
Office Equipment	$16,000
Supplies	????
Mireya Cortez, Capital	$45,000

(Answers to Section 1 Self Review are on page 53.)

Price's abundant end-of-chapter material

Problem Sets A and B, Challenge Problems, and Mini-Practice Sets conclude with an **Analyze** question asking the student to evaluate each problem critically.

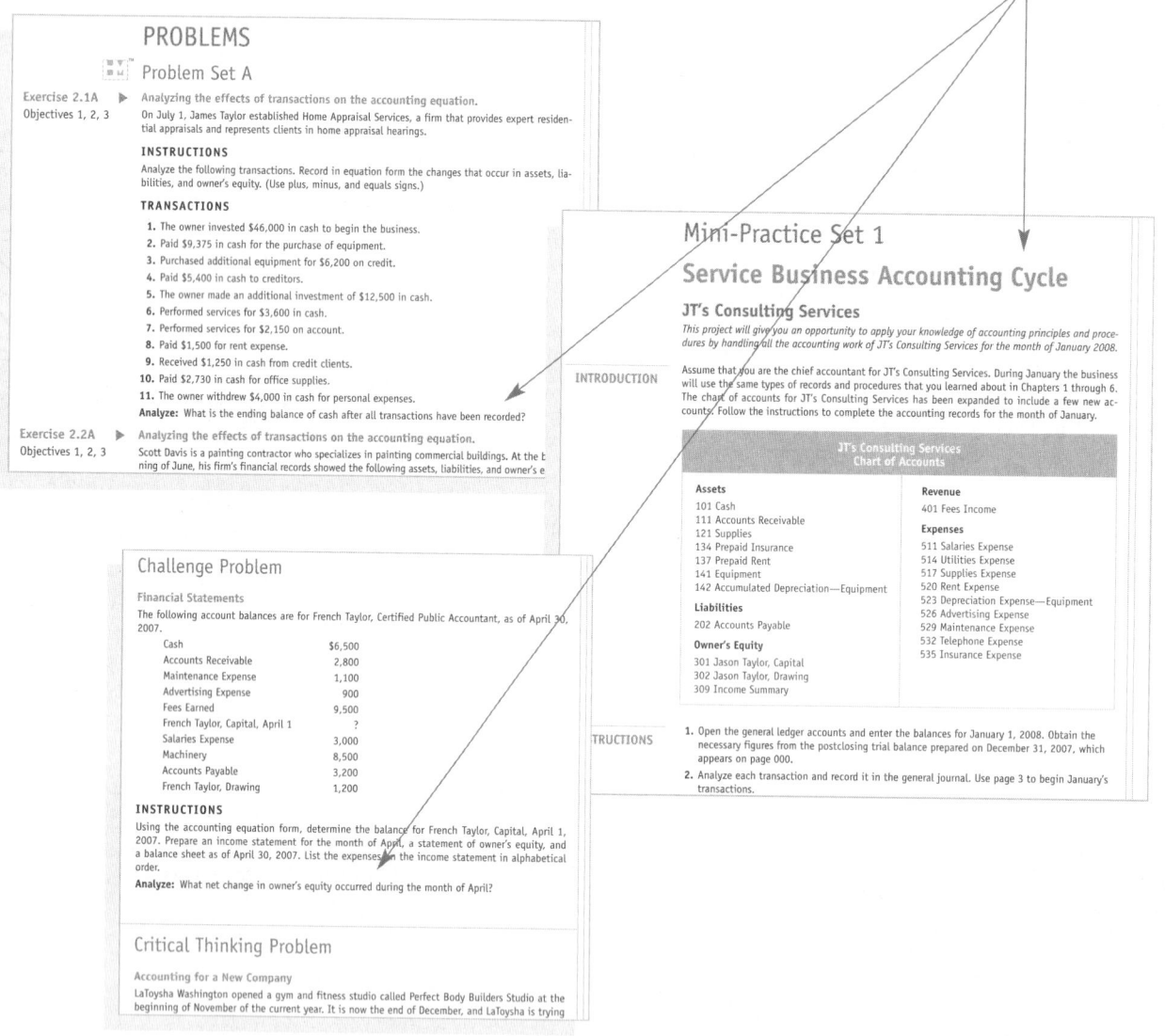

PROBLEMS

Problem Set A

Exercise 2.1A
Objectives 1, 2, 3

▶ Analyzing the effects of transactions on the accounting equation.

On July 1, James Taylor established Home Appraisal Services, a firm that provides expert residential appraisals and represents clients in home appraisal hearings.

INSTRUCTIONS

Analyze the following transactions. Record in equation form the changes that occur in assets, liabilities, and owner's equity. (Use plus, minus, and equals signs.)

TRANSACTIONS

1. The owner invested $46,000 in cash to begin the business.
2. Paid $9,375 in cash for the purchase of equipment.
3. Purchased additional equipment for $6,200 on credit.
4. Paid $5,400 in cash to creditors.
5. The owner made an additional investment of $12,500 in cash.
6. Performed services for $3,600 in cash.
7. Performed services for $2,150 on account.
8. Paid $1,500 for rent expense.
9. Received $1,250 in cash from credit clients.
10. Paid $2,730 in cash for office supplies.
11. The owner withdrew $4,000 in cash for personal expenses.

Analyze: What is the ending balance of cash after all transactions have been recorded?

Exercise 2.2A
Objectives 1, 2, 3

▶ Analyzing the effects of transactions on the accounting equation.

Scott Davis is a painting contractor who specializes in painting commercial buildings. At the beginning of June, his firm's financial records showed the following assets, liabilities, and owner's e

Challenge Problem

Financial Statements

The following account balances are for French Taylor, Certified Public Accountant, as of April 30, 2007.

Cash	$6,500
Accounts Receivable	2,800
Maintenance Expense	1,100
Advertising Expense	900
Fees Earned	9,500
French Taylor, Capital, April 1	?
Salaries Expense	3,000
Machinery	8,500
Accounts Payable	3,200
French Taylor, Drawing	1,200

INSTRUCTIONS

Using the accounting equation form, determine the balance for French Taylor, Capital, April 1, 2007. Prepare an income statement for the month of April, a statement of owner's equity, and a balance sheet as of April 30, 2007. List the expenses on the income statement in alphabetical order.

Analyze: What net change in owner's equity occurred during the month of April?

Critical Thinking Problem

Accounting for a New Company

LaToysha Washington opened a gym and fitness studio called Perfect Body Builders Studio at the beginning of November of the current year. It is now the end of December, and LaToysha is trying

Mini-Practice Set 1

Service Business Accounting Cycle

JT's Consulting Services

This project will give you an opportunity to apply your knowledge of accounting principles and procedures by handling all the accounting work of JT's Consulting Services for the month of January 2008.

INTRODUCTION

Assume that you are the chief accountant for JT's Consulting Services. During January the business will use the same types of records and procedures that you learned about in Chapters 1 through 6. The chart of accounts for JT's Consulting Services has been expanded to include a few new accounts. Follow the instructions to complete the accounting records for the month of January.

JT's Consulting Services	
Chart of Accounts	
Assets	**Revenue**
101 Cash	401 Fees Income
111 Accounts Receivable	
121 Supplies	**Expenses**
134 Prepaid Insurance	511 Salaries Expense
137 Prepaid Rent	514 Utilities Expense
141 Equipment	517 Supplies Expense
142 Accumulated Depreciation—Equipment	520 Rent Expense
	523 Depreciation Expense—Equipment
Liabilities	526 Advertising Expense
202 Accounts Payable	529 Maintenance Expense
	532 Telephone Expense
Owner's Equity	535 Insurance Expense
301 Jason Taylor, Capital	
302 Jason Taylor, Drawing	
309 Income Summary	

INSTRUCTIONS

1. Open the general ledger accounts and enter the balances for January 1, 2008. Obtain the necessary figures from the postclosing trial balance prepared on December 31, 2007, which appears on page 000.
2. Analyze each transaction and record it in the general journal. Use page 3 to begin January's transactions.

Preparing a trial balance and an income statement.

Using the account balances from Exercise 3.5, prepare a trial balance and an income statement for Antique Restorations. The trial balance is for December 31, 2007, and the income statement is for the month ended December 31, 2007.

◀ Exercise 3.6
Objectives 5, 6

CONTINUING ▶▶▶
Problem

Preparing a statement of owner's equity and a balance sheet.

From the trial balance and the net income or net loss determined in Exercise 3.6, prepare a statement of owner's equity and a balance sheet for Antique Restoration as of December 31, 2007.

◀ Exercise 3.7
Objective 6

CONTINUING ▶▶▶
Problem

Problems that build off of earlier problems in the text are noted with a continuation icon.

helps develop problem solving skills.

Business Connections

Reinforce chapter materials from practical and real-world perspectives:

Managerial Focus: Applies accounting concepts to business situations.

Ethical Dilemma: Provides the opportunity for students to discuss ethics in the workplace, formulate a course of action for certain scenarios, and support their opinions.

Streetwise: Questions from the Real World: Students are asked to research various components of the Home Depot Annual Report and answer questions related to content, presentation, and meaning.

Financial Statement Analysis: A brief excerpt from a real-world annual report and questions that lead the student through an analysis of the statement, concluding with an Analyze Online activity where students research the company's most recent financial reports on the Internet.

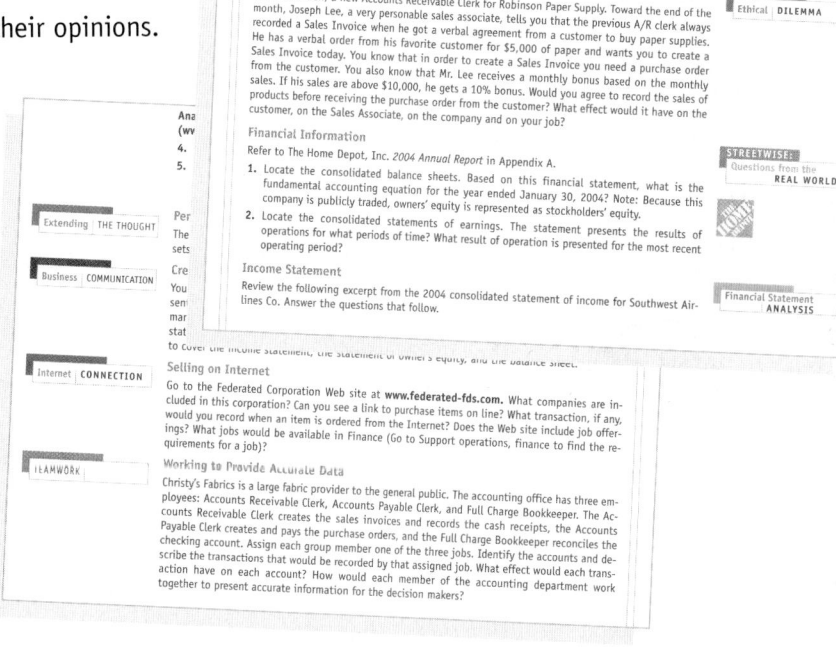

Extending the Thought: Activities build on chapter concepts and present new issues and situations, asking students to recall and apply learned information.

Business Communication: These activities hone students' interpersonal skills through the preparation of a variety of business communication formats such as memos, oral presentations, outlines, and more.

Team Work: Each chapter contains a collaborative learning activity to prepare students for team-oriented projects and work environments.

Internet Connection: These activities give students the opportunity to conduct online research about major companies, accounting trends, organizations, and government agencies.

The Eleventh Edition brings accounting concepts to life with relevant real-world businesses.

Yahoo!	KB Home
American Eagle Outfitters	McCormick & Company
Southwest Airlines	Circuit City Stores Inc.
Johnson & Johnson	The Coca-Cola Company
Adobe	Kinder Morgan Energy Partners
Caterpillar	Sara Lee Corporation
Wal-Mart	Conoco Phillips
Boeing	McDonald's Corporation
DuPont	3M
Carnival Corporation	UPS
CSX Corporation	Dole Food Co.
Pier 1 Imports	The Walt Disney Co.
Amazon.com	Eastman Kodak Co.
H&R Block	Alcoa
Dell Inc.	Goodrich Corp.
Ikea	Cisco
Safeway	Avery Dennison Corp.
Mattel, Inc.	Alcoa
Goodyear	Harley-Davidson
Fed Ex	Navistar International

Technology Tools

ONLINE LEARNING CENTER

www.mhhe.com/price11e

For instructors, Price/Haddock/Brock's Online Learning Center contains the Instructor's Resource Manual, PowerPoint slides, Solutions Manual, Excel Templates tied to the end-of-chapter material, and Practice Set answer keys. Links to professional resources are also available.

In addition, for students and instructors, there are check figures, articles tied to end-of-chapter material, and McGraw-Hill's Homework Manager (see below). Instructors can pull all of this material into their PageOut course syllabus or use it as part of another online course management system.

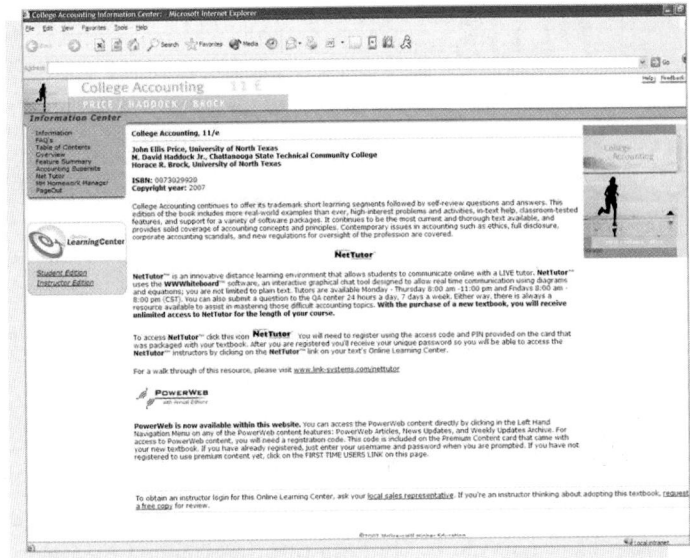

The student section of the site also includes (in addition to the elements mentioned above) new Topic Tackler Plus content (see page W-17), self-quizzes, learning objectives, auto narrated PowerPoint slides, chapter outlines, and digital flashcards.

Course management systems containing the OLC content are available in WebCT and Blackboard cartridges.

McGRAW-HILL'S HOMEWORK MANAGER™
ISBN-13: 9780073226033 (ISBN-10: 0073226033)

McGraw-Hill's Homework Manager™ is an online homework management solution that contains the textbook's end-of-chapter material. Instructors have the option to build assignments from static and algorithmic versions of the end-of-chapter material or build self-graded quizzes from the test bank.

Features:
• Assigns book-specific problems/exercises to students
• Provides integrated testbank questions for quizzes and tests
• Automatically grades assignments and quizzes and stores results in one gradebook

Learn more about McGraw-Hill's Homework Manager by referring to the opening pages of this text.

Technology Tools (continued)

McGRAW-HILL'S HOMEWORK MANAGER PLUS™
ISBN-13: 9780073226019 (ISBN-10: 0073226017)

McGraw-Hill's Homework Manager Plus™ gathers all of *College Accounting's* online student resources under one convenient access point. Combining the power and flexibility of McGraw-Hill's Homework Manager with other proven technology tools, McGraw-Hill's Homework Manager Plus provides the best possible value for the student eager to embrace the full benefits of online study and review.

In addition to McGraw-Hill's Homework Manager, students may also access:

NetTutor™

Available through McGraw-Hill's Homework Manager Plus, NetTutor connects students with qualified tutors online. Students can work with an online tutor in real time, or post a question to be answered within 24 hours. Homework Manager Plus adopters receive unlimited tutoring time on NetTutor. NetTutor may also be bundled with the text separately from McGraw-Hill's Homework Manager Plus.

Interactive Online Version of the Textbook

In addition to the textbook, students can rely on this online version of the text for a convenient way to study. This interactive web-based textbook contains hotlinks to key definitions and real company websites, and is integrated with Homework Manager to give students quick access to relevant content as they work through problems, exercises, and practice quizzes.

ALEKS for the Accounting Cycle provides a detailed, guided overview through every stage of the accounting cycle. Aleks Math Prep for Accounting provides coverage of the basic math skills needed to succeed. ALEKS (Assessment and LEarning in Knowledge Spaces) delivers precise, qualitative diagnostic assessments of students' knowledge, guides them in the selection of appropriate new study material, and records their progress toward mastery of curricular goals in a robust classroom management system.

ALEKS interacts with the student much as a skilled human tutor would, moving between explanation and practice as needed, correcting and analyzing errors, defining terms and changing topics on request. By sophisticated modeling of a student's knowledge state for a given subject, ALEKS can focus clearly on what the student is most ready to learn next. When students focus on exactly what they are ready to learn, they build confidence, and a learning momentum that fuels success.

For more information, visit the ALEKS website at www.business.aleks.com.

CAROL YACHT'S GENERAL LEDGER AND PEACHTREE COMPLETE 2006 CD-ROM

Carol Yacht's General Ledger Software is McGraw-Hill/Irwin's custom-built general ledger package. Carol Yacht's General Ledger can help your students master every aspect of the general ledger, from inputting sales and cash receipts to calculating ratios for analysis or inventory valuations.

Carol Yacht's General Ledger allows students to review an entire report, and then double-click any single transaction to review or edit it. The report will then be updated on the fly to include the revised figures. When it comes to learning how an individual transaction affects the outcome of an entire report, no other approach matches that of Carol Yacht's General Ledger.

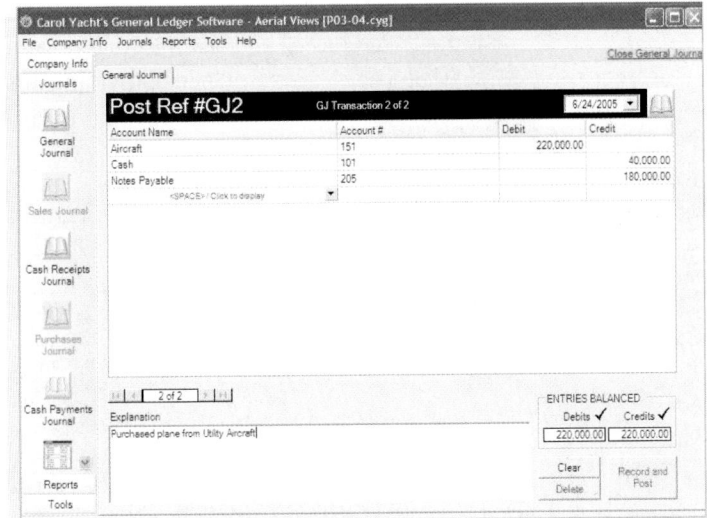

Also on Carol Yacht's General Ledger CD, students receive the educational version of Peachtree Complete 2006, along with templates containing data for many of the text exercises and problems. Familiarity with Peachtree Complete will be essential for students entering the job market, and Carol Yacht's Peachtree templates that accompany College Accounting 11/e makes sure they get plenty of practice.

Students can use Carol Yacht's General Ledger to solve numerous problems from the textbook; the data for these problems is already included on the Carol Yacht's General Ledger CD-ROM. You can even populate Carol Yacht's General Ledger with your own custom data.

Technology Tools (continued)

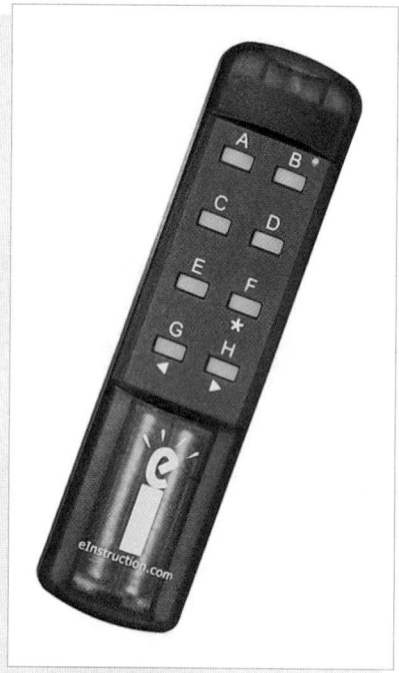

CPS CLASSROOM PERFORMANCE SYSTEM

This is a revolutionary system that brings ultimate interactivity to the classroom. CPS is a wireless response system that gives you immediate feedback from every student in the class. CPS units include easy-to-use software for creating and delivering questions and assessments to your class. With CPS you can ask subjective and objective questions, then every student simply responds with their individual, wireless response pad, providing instant results. CPS is the perfect tool for engaging students while gathering important assessment data.

PAGEOUT

PageOut is McGraw-Hill's unique point-and-click course Website tool. With PageOut you can post your syllabus online, assign McGraw-Hill Online Learning Center or eBook content, add links to important off-site resources, and maintain student results in the online grade book. PageOut is free for every McGraw-Hill/Irwin user and, if you're short on time, we even have a team ready to build your site from scratch!

COURSE CARTRIDGES

McGraw-Hill has course cartridges for all platforms provided to adopters for FREE and services to help you actually manage and teach your online course, as well as run and maintain the software. To see how these platforms can assist your online course, visit www.mhhe.com/support. And remember: all Price digital content is easily incorporated into any online course management system.

Instructor Supplements

INSTRUCTOR CD-ROM
ISBN-13: 9780073203454 (ISBN-10: 0073203459)

This all-in-one resource incorporates the Test Bank, PowerPoint® Slides, Instructor's Resource Guide, Solutions Manual, Teaching Transparency Masters, and Spreadsheet Application Template Software.

INSTRUCTOR'S RESOURCE GUIDE
ISBN-13: 9780073203461 (ISBN-10: 0073203467)

This supplement contains extensive chapter-by-chapter lecture notes, along with useful suggestions for presenting key concepts and ideas, to help with classroom presentation. The lecture notes coordinate closely with the PowerPoint Slides, making lesson planning even easier.

INSTRUCTOR'S EDITION
Chapters 1-13 ISBN-13: 9780073215389 (ISBN-10: 0073215384)
Chapters 1-32 ISBN-13: 9780073215372 (ISBN-10: 0073215376)

This special edition contains several types of marginal annotations to help you plan your lessons: Teaching Tips, Extending the Content, and Check Figures.

SOLUTIONS MANUAL
Chapters 1-13 ISBN-13: 9780073030463 (ISBN-10: 0073030465)
Chapters 1-32 ISBN-13: 9780073030487 (ISBN-10: 0073030481)

This supplement contains completed step-by-step calculations to all assignment and Study Guide material, as well as a general discussion of the Thinking Critically questions that appear throughout the text.

SOLUTIONS TRANSPARENCIES
Chapters 1-13 ISBN-13: 9780073203416 (ISBN-10: 0073203416)
Chapters 14-25 ISBN-13: 9780073203423 (ISBN-10: 0073203424)
Chapters 26-32 ISBN-13: 9780073203430 (ISBN-10: 0073203432)

These transparencies feature completed step-by-step calculations to all assignment material. Masters of these transparencies are available in the Solutions Manual.

TEST BANK (PRINT VERSION)
ISBN-13: 9780073258690 (ISBN-10: 0073258695)

This comprehensive Test Bank includes more than 2,000 true/false, multiple choice, and completion questions and problems.

ALGORITHMIC-DIPLOMA TESTBANK (FROM BROWNSTONE)
ISBN-13: 9780073258706 (ISBN-10: 0073258709)

New to the eleventh edition this computerized testbank is an algorithmic problem generator enabling instructors to create similarly structured problems with different values, which allows every student to be assigned a unique quiz or test. The user-friendly interface gives faculty the ability to easily create different versions of the same test, change the answer order, edit or add questions, and even conduct online testing.

EZ TEST
EZ Test is available on the Instructor CD-Rom.

McGraw-Hill's EZ Test is a flexible and easy-to-use electronic testing program. The program allows instructors to create tests from book specific items. It accommodates a wide range of question types, plus instructors may add their own questions. Multiple versions of the test can be created and any test can be exported for use with course management systems such as WebCT, BlackBoard, or PageOut. EZ Test Online is a new service and gives you a place to easily administer your EZ Test created exams and quizzes online. The program is available for Windows and Macintosh environments.

MICROSOFT EXCEL TEMPLATES

Prepared by Jack Terry of ComSource Associates, Inc., these Excel templates offer solutions to the Student version. Only available on the Instructor CD and the text's Web site.

CHECK FIGURES

These provide key answers for selected problems and cases. They are available on the text's Web site.

PRACTICE SET ANSWER KEY

Available on the text's Web site, this includes solutions to the Action Video and Home Team Advantage Practice Sets.

CAROL YACHT'S GENERAL LEDGER AND PEACHTREE COMPLETE 2006
ISBN-13: 9780073196831 (ISBN-10: 0073196835)
GL Software developed by Jack E. Terry, ComSource Associates, Inc.
Peachtree templates prepared by Carol Yacht

The CD-ROM includes fully functioning versions of McGraw-Hill's own General Ledger Application software as well as Peachtree Complete 2006. Problem templates are included that allow you to assign text problems for working in either Yacht's General Ledger or Peachtree 2006.

Student Supplements

STUDY GUIDE/WORKING PAPERS

Chapters 1-13 ISBN-13: 9780073203485 (ISBN-10: 0073203483)
Chapters 14-25 ISBN-13: 9780073030586 (ISBN-10: 0073030589)
Chapters 1-32 ISBN-13: 9780073030593 (ISBN-10: 0073030597)

This study aid summarizes essential points in each chapter, tests students' knowledge using self-test questions, and contains forms that help students organize their solutions to homework problems.

MICROSOFT EXCEL TEMPLATES

Prepared by Jack Terry of ComSource Associates, Inc., this spreadsheet-based software uses Excel to solve selected problems in the text, which are identified in the margin of the text with an appropriate icon. The Student Excel Templates are only available on the text's Web site.

TOPIC TACKLER PLUS DVD

ISBN-13: 9780073203478 (ISBN-10: 0073203475)

The Topic Tackler DVD helps students master difficult concepts in managerial accounting through a creative, interactive learning process. Designed for study outside the classroom, this multimedia delves into chapter concepts with graphical slides and video clips centered around engaging exercises designed to put students in control of their learning of accounting topics.

ACTION VIDEO PRACTICE SET

ISBN-13: 9780073196848 (ISBN-10: 0073196843)

Action Video Productions is a sole proprietorship, service business that uses source documents, a general journal, a general ledger, worksheets, and a filing system to provide students with a usable practice set. The strength of this set is the use of source documents in conjunction with the daily business activities. This set can be completed after Chapter 6 of College Accounting.

HOME TEAM ADVANTAGE PRACTICE SET

ISBN-13: 9780073196855 (ISBN-10: 0073196851)

Home Team Advantage is a sole proprietorship, merchandising business that uses source documents, special journals, a general ledger, a subsidiary ledger, a worksheet, accounting forms, and a filing system for student use. This very realistic retail business will give a student accounting practice where merchandise inventory and the cost of goods sold become an integral part of the income statement. This set can be completed after Chapter 13.

Acknowledgments

The authors are deeply grateful to the following accounting educators for their ongoing involvement with *College Accounting*. The efforts of these knowledgeable and dedicated instructors provide the authors with valuable assistance in meeting the changing needs of the college accounting classroom.

Shawn Abbott, College of the Siskiyous
Karen Alexander, College of the Albemarle
Cheryl Baron, Ridgewater College
Anna Boulware, St. Charles Community College
Sharon Breeding, Central Kentucky Technical College
Dreama Cathey, Tennessee Technology Center
Gerald Caton, Yavapai College
Juanita Clobes, Gateway Technical College
Catherine Collins, Waubonsee Community College
Susan Davis, Green River Community College
Doris Donovan, Dodge City Community College
Michael Farina, Cerritos College
Daniel J. Gibbons, Waubonsee Community College
Scott Gibson, Decker College
Chad M. Grooms, Gateway Community and Technical College
Jeff Henderson, Bryman College
David Juriga, St. Louis Community College
Dmitriy Kalyagin, Chabot College
Deanna King, Ivy Tech Community College of Indiana
Christine Kloezeman, Glendale Community College
Patty Kolarik, Hutchinson Community College
John F. Mayhorne, Yorktowne Business Institute, Inc.
Noel McKeon, Florida Community College-Downtown Campus
Wanda Metzgar, Boise State University
Sharon Mumaugh, Sawyer College
Donna L. Occhifinto, The Cittone Institute
Stephen Pan, Las Vegas College
Linda Paul, Baton Rouge Community College
Margaret Pollard, American River College
Verlindsey Stewart, J.F. Drake State Technical College
William J. Stibrany, Lehigh Valley College
Domenico A. Tavella, B.S.B.A., M.B.A., Pittsburgh Technical Institute
Sherri Walls, Vatterott College
Sheila Wiley, Louisiana Technical College-Shelby Jackson Campus
Linda Whitten, Skyline College

Thank You . . .

WE ARE GRATEFUL for the outstanding support from McGraw-Hill/ Irwin. In particular, we would like to thank Brent Gordon, Editorial Director; Stewart Mattson, Publisher; Sarah Wood, Developmental Editor; Marc Chernoff and Melissa Larmon, Marketing Managers; Susanne Riedell, Senior Project Manager; Michael McCormick, Production Supervisor; Mary Kazak, Senior Designer; Carol Loreth, Senior Supplement Producer; Rose Range, Senior Media Project Manager; Jeremy Cheshareck, Photo Research Coordinator; and Greg Bates, Media Producer.

Finally, we would like to thank Barbara Schnathorst, Beth Woods, and Kawonza Carter, for working so hard to ensure an error-free eleventh edition as well as Michael Farina, Christine Kloezeman, and Joanne Butler for their contributions.

John Price • M. David Haddock • Horace Brock

Brief Contents

1	Accounting: The Language of Business	3
2	Analyzing Business Transactions	22
3	Analyzing Business Transactions Using T Accounts	54
4	The General Journal and the General Ledger	94
5	Adjustments and the Worksheet	131
6	Closing Entries and the Postclosing Trial Balance	164
7	Accounting for Sales and Accounts Receivable	198
8	Accounting for Purchases and Accounts Payable	246
9	Cash Receipts, Cash Payments, and Banking Procedures	282
10	Payroll Computations, Records, and Payments	338
11	Payroll Taxes, Deposits, and Reports	376
12	Accruals, Deferrals, and the Worksheet	414
13	Financial Statements and Closing Procedures	454

Contents

CHAPTER 1 **Accounting: The Language of Business** 3

Section 1 **What Is Accounting?** 4

The Need for Financial Information 4
Accounting Defined 4
Accounting Careers 5
Users of Financial Accounting 6
Section 1 Self Review 9

Section 2 **Business and Accounting** 10

Types of Business Entities 10
Generally Accepted Accounting Principles 12
Section 2 Self Review 14

Chapter Review and Applications 15

Chapter Summary 15
Glossary 16
Comprehensive Self Review 17
Discussion Questions 17
Problem 18
Business Connections 18
Answers to Self Reviews 20

CHAPTER 2 **Analyzing Business Transactions** 22

Section 1 **Property and Financial Interest** 24

Beginning with Analysis 24
Assets, Liabilities, and Owner's Equity 28
Section 1 Self Review 29

Section 2 **The Accounting Equation and Financial Statements** 30

The Fundamental Accounting Equation 30
The Income Statement 35
The Statement of Owner's Equity and the Balance Sheet 37
The Importance of Financial Statements 40
Section 2 Self Review 40

Chapter Review and Applications 41

Chapter Summary 41
Glossary 42
Comprehensive Self Review 42

CONTENTS

Discussion Questions	42
Exercises	43
Problems	46
Business Connections	51
Answers to Self Reviews	53

CHAPTER 3   Analyzing Business Transactions Using T Accounts   **54**

Section 1 Transactions That Affect Assets, Liabilities, and Owner's Equity	**56**
Asset, Liability, and Owner's Equity Accounts	56
Account Balances	62
Section 1 Self Review	**64**
Section 2 Transactions That Affect Revenue, Expenses, and Withdrawals	**65**
Revenue and Expense Accounts	65
The Drawing Account	69
The Rules of Debit and Credit	71
The Trial Balance	71
Financial Statements	74
Chart of Accounts	75
Permanent and Temporary Accounts	75
Section 2 Self Review	**76**
Chapter Review and Applications	**77**
Chapter Summary	77
Glossary	78
Comprehensive Self Review	78
Discussion Questions	79
Exercises	80
Problems	82
Business Connections	90
Answers to Self Reviews	92

CHAPTER 4   The General Journal and the General Ledger   **94**

Section 1 The General Journal	**96**
Journals	96
The General Journal	96
Section 1 Self Review	**104**
Section 2 The General Ledger	**105**
Ledgers	105
Correcting Journal and Ledger Errors	109
Section 2 Self Review	**111**

Chapter Review and Applications   112

    Chapter Summary   112

    Glossary   113

    Comprehensive Self Review   113

    Discussion Questions   113

    Exercises   114

    Problems   116

    Business Connections   126

    Answers to Self Reviews   128

CHAPTER 5   **Adjustments and the Worksheet**   131

Section 1 **The Worksheet**   132

    The Trial Balance Section   132

    The Adjustments Section   133

    Section 1 Self Review   138

Section 2 **Financial Statements**   139

    The Adjusted Trial Balance Section   139

    The Income Statement and Balance Sheet Sections   140

    Preparing Financial Statements   142

    Journalizing and Posting Adjusting Entries   145

    Section 2 Self Review   147

    Chapter Review and Applications   148

       Chapter Summary   148

       Glossary   149

       Comprehensive Self Review   149

       Discussion Questions   149

       Exercises   150

       Problems   152

       Business Connections   160

       Answers to Self Reviews   161

CHAPTER 6   **Closing Entries and the Postclosing Trial Balance**   164

Section 1 **Closing Entries**   166

    The Closing Process   166

    Section 1 Self Review   171

Section 2 **Using Accounting Information**   175

    Preparing the Postclosing Trial Balance   175

    Interpreting the Financial Statements   176

    The Accounting Cycle   178

    Section 2 Self Review   180

Chapter Review and Applications   **181**

    Chapter Summary   **181**

    Glossary   **181**

    Comprehensive Self Review   182

    Discussion Questions   **182**

    Exercises   **182**

    Problems   **185**

    Business Connections   **193**

    Answers to Self Reviews   195

MINI-PRACTICE SET 1

Service Business Accounting Cycle   196

JT's Consulting Services

CHAPTER 7

Accounting for Sales and Accounts Receivable   198

Section 1 **Merchandise Sales**   **200**

  Special Journals and Subsidiary Ledgers   200

  The Sales Journal   200

  Section 1 Self Review   **206**

Section 2 **Accounts Receivable**   **207**

  The Accounts Receivable Ledger   207

  Sales Returns and Allowances   208

  Schedule of Accounts Receivable   214

  Section 2 Self Review   **215**

Section 3 **Special Topics in Merchandising**   **216**

  Credit Sales for a Wholesale Business   216

  Credit Policies   218

  Sales Taxes   222

  Section 3 Self Review   **226**

Chapter Review and Applications   **227**

    Chapter Summary   **227**

    Glossary   **228**

    Comprehensive Self Review   228

    Discussion Questions   **229**

    Exercises   **229**

    Problems   **233**

    Business Connections   **242**

    Answers to Self Reviews   244

CHAPTER 8   Accounting for Purchases and Accounts Payable   246

Section 1 **Merchandise Purchases**   **248**

Accounting for Purchases   248
Section 1 Self Review   **255**

Section 2 **Accounts Payable**   **256**

The Accounts Payable Ledger   256
Purchases Returns and Allowances   257
Schedule of Accounts Payable   259
Determining the Cost of Purchases   259
Internal Control of Purchases   261
Section 2 Self Review   **263**

Chapter Review and Applications   264
Chapter Summary   **264**
Glossary   **264**
Comprehensive Self Review   265
Discussion Questions   **265**
Exercises   **266**
Problems   **266**
Business Connections   **278**
Answers to Self Reviews   **280**

CHAPTER 9   Cash Receipts, Cash Payments, and Banking Procedures   282

Section 1 **Cash Receipts**   **284**

Cash Transactions   284
The Cash Receipts Journal   284
Section 1 Self Review   **290**

Section 2 **Cash Payments**   **291**

The Cash Payments Journal   291
The Petty Cash Fund   296
Internal Control over Cash   298
Section 2 Self Review   **300**

Section 3 **Banking Procedures**   **301**

Writing Checks   301
Endorsing Checks   301
Preparing the Deposit Slip   303
Handling Postdated Checks   303

CONTENTS

Reconciling the Bank Statement	303
Adjusting the Financial Records	307
Internal Control of Banking Activities	309
Section 3 Self Review	**310**
Chapter Review and Applications	**311**
Chapter Summary	**311**
Glossary	**312**
Comprehensive Self Review	**313**
Discussion Questions	**313**
Exercises	**314**
Problems	**316**
Business Connections	**333**
Answers to Self Reviews	**335**

CONTENTS

CHAPTER 10	Payroll Computations, Records, and Payment	**338**
	Section 1 Payroll Laws and Taxes	**340**
	Who Is an Employee?	340
	Federal Employee Earnings and Withholding Laws	340
	State and Local Taxes	341
	Employer's Payroll Taxes and Insurance Costs	341
	Employee Records Required by Law	343
	Section 1 Self Review	**344**
	Section 2 Calculating Earnings and Taxes	**345**
	Computing Total Earnings of Employees	345
	Determining Pay for Hourly Employees	346
	Determining Pay for Salaried Employees	352
	Recording Payroll Information for Employees	352
	Section 2 Self Review	**354**
	Section 3 Recording Payroll Information	**355**
	Recording Payroll	355
	Paying Employees	356
	Individual Earnings Records	358
	Completing January Payrolls	359
	Section 3 Self Review	**361**
	Chapter Review and Applications	**362**
	Chapter Summary	**362**
	Glossary	**362**
	Comprehensive Self Review	**363**
	Discussion Questions	**363**
	Exercises	**363**
	Problems	**366**
	Business Connections	**373**
	Answers to Self Reviews	**374**

CHAPTER 11   Payroll Taxes, Deposits, and Reports   **376**

Section 1 **Social Security, Medicare, and Employee Income Tax**   **378**

Payment of Payroll Taxes   378
Wage and Tax Statement, Form W-2   387
Annual Transmittal of Wage and Tax Statements, Form W-3   387
Section 1 Self Review   **389**

Section 2 **Unemployment Tax and Workers' Compensation**   **390**

Unemployment Compensation Insurance Taxes   390
Internal Control over Payroll Operations   398
Section 2 Self Review   **399**

Chapter Review and Applications   400
   Chapter Summary   **400**
   Glossary   **400**
   Comprehensive Self Review   401
   Discussion Questions   **401**
   Exercises   **402**
   Problems   **403**
   Business Connections   **411**
   Answers to Self Reviews   412

CHAPTER 12   Accruals, Deferrals, and Worksheets   **414**

Section 1 **Calculating and Recording Adjustments**   **416**

The Accrual Basis of Accounting   416
Using the Worksheet to Record Adjustments   416
Section 1 Self Review   **427**

Section 2 **Completing the Worksheet**   **428**

Preparing the Adjusted Trial Balance Section   428
Preparing the Balance Sheet and Income Statement Sections   429
Calculating Net Income or Net Loss   432
Section 2 Self Review   **433**

Chapter Review and Applications   434
   Chapter Summary   **434**
   Glossary   **434**
   Comprehensive Self Review   435
   Discussion Questions   **435**
   Exercises   **436**
   Problems   **438**
   Business Connections   **449**
   Answers to Self Reviews   451

CONTENTS

CONTENTS

CHAPTER 13   **Financial Statements and Closing Procedures**   454

Section 1 **Preparing the Financial Statements**   **456**

The Classified Income Statement   456
The Statement of Owner's Equity   459
The Classified Balance Sheet   459
Section 1 Self Review   **461**

Section 2 **Completing the Accounting Cycle**   **462**

Journalizing and Posting the Adjusting Entries   462
Journalizing and Posting the Closing Entries   465
Preparing a Postclosing Trial Balance   467
Interpreting the Financial Statements   468
Journalizing and Posting Reversing Entries   469
Review of the Accounting Cycle   473
Section 2 Self Review   **475**

Chapter Review and Applications   **476**

Chapter Summary   **476**
Glossary   **476**
Comprehensive Self Review   **477**
Discussion Questions   **478**
Exercises   **479**
Problems   **483**
Business Connections   **493**
Answers to Self Reviews   **495**

MINI-PRACTICE SET 2   **Merchandising Business Accounting Cycle**   496

Bargain Buys

Appendix A Excerpts from The Home Depot, Inc., *2004 Annual Report*   A-1
Appendix B Combined Journal   B-1
Glossary   G
Credits   C
Index   I-1

College
Accounting

LEARNING OBJECTIVES

1. Define accounting.

2. Identify and discuss career opportunities in accounting.

3. Identify the users of financial information.

4. Compare and contrast the three types of business entities.

5. Describe the process used to develop generally accepted accounting principles.

6. Define the accounting terms new to this chapter.

NEW TERMS

accounting	governmental accounting
accounting system	international accounting
auditing	management advisory services
auditor's report	
Certified Public Accountant (CPA)	managerial accounting
corporation	partnership
creditor	public accountants
discussion memorandum	separate entity assumption
economic entity	social entity
entity	sole proprietorship
exposure draft	Statements of Financial Accounting Standards
financial statements	
generally accepted accounting principles (GAAP)	stock
	stockholders
	tax accounting

Chapter 1
Accounting:
The Language
of Business

YAHOO!® www.yahoo.com

Performing a search on the Internet has not always been easy. In the early 1990s computer users were desperate for an efficient way to organize and find information on the Internet. In 1994 David Filo and Jerry Yang, working from a trailer on the campus of Stanford University, used their electrical engineering training to develop software that would help them locate and categorize information stored on the Internet. Yahoo! was born and by the fall of 1994 had received over 1 million hits.

Yahoo! Inc. has evolved into a global Internet communications, commerce, and media company. The company services more than 345 million individuals each month worldwide. As a publicly owned company, Yahoo! Inc. releases its financial information to investors, owners, and managers quarterly.

thinking critically

If you were considering purchasing stock in Yahoo! Inc., how would a basic understanding of accounting assist you?

Section 1

SECTION OBJECTIVES

▶ **1. Define accounting.**

WHY IT'S IMPORTANT

Business transactions affect many aspects of our lives.

▶ **2. Identify and discuss career opportunities in accounting.**

WHY IT'S IMPORTANT

There's something for everyone in the field of accounting. Accounting professionals are found in every workplace from public accounting firms to government agencies, from corporations to nonprofit organizations.

▶ **3. Identify the users of financial information.**

WHY IT'S IMPORTANT

A wide variety of individuals and businesses depend on financial information to make decisions.

TERMS TO LEARN

accounting
accounting system
auditing
certified public accountant (CPA)
financial statements
governmental accounting
management advisory services
managerial accounting
public accountants
tax accounting

What Is Accounting?

Accounting provides financial information about a business or a nonprofit organization. Owners, managers, investors, and other interested parties need financial information in order to make decisions. Because accounting is used to communicate financial information, it is often called the "language of business."

The Need for Financial Information

Suppose a relative leaves you a substantial sum of money and you decide to carry out your lifelong dream of opening a small sportswear shop. You rent space in a local shopping center, purchase fixtures and equipment, purchase goods to sell, hire salespeople, and open the store to customers. Before long you realize that, to run your business successfully, you need financial information about the business. You probably need information that provides answers to the following questions:

- How much cash does the business have?
- How much money do customers owe the business?
- What is the cost of the merchandise sold?
- What is the change in sales volume?
- How much money is owed to suppliers?
- What is the profit or loss?

As your business grows, you will need even more financial information to evaluate the firm's performance and make decisions about the future. An efficient accounting system allows owners and managers to quickly obtain a wide range of useful information. The need for timely information is one reason that businesses have an accounting system directed by a professional staff.

Accounting Defined

Accounting is the process by which financial information about a business is recorded, classified, summarized, interpreted, and communicated to owners, managers, and other interested parties. An **accounting system** is designed to accumulate data about a firm's financial affairs, classify the data in a meaningful way, and summarize it in periodic reports called **financial statements**. Owners and managers obtain a lot of information from financial statements. The accountant

- establishes the records and procedures that make up the accounting system,

▶ **1. OBJECTIVE**

Define accounting.

4

- supervises the operations of the system,
- interprets the resulting financial information.

Most owners and managers rely heavily on the accountant's judgment and knowledge when making financial decisions.

Accounting Careers

▶ 2. OBJECTIVE
Identify and discuss career opportunities in accounting.

Many jobs are available in the accounting profession, and they require varying amounts of education and experience. Bookkeepers and accountants are responsible for keeping records and providing financial information about the business. Generally bookkeepers are responsible for recording business transactions. In large firms bookkeepers may also supervise the work of accounting clerks. Accounting clerks are responsible for recordkeeping for a part of the accounting system—perhaps payroll, accounts receivable, or accounts payable. Accountants usually supervise bookkeepers and prepare the financial statements and reports of the business.

Newspapers and Web sites often have job listings for accounting clerks, bookkeepers, and accountants:

- Accounting clerk positions usually require one to two accounting courses and little or no experience.
- Bookkeeper positions usually require one to two years of accounting education plus experience as an accounting clerk.
- Accountant positions usually require a bachelor's degree but are sometimes filled by experienced bookkeepers or individuals with a two-year college degree. Most entry-level accountant positions do not have an experience requirement. Both the education and experience requirements for accountant positions vary according to the size of the firm.

Accountants usually choose to practice in one of three areas:

- public accounting
- managerial accounting
- governmental accounting

PUBLIC ACCOUNTING

Public accountants work for public accounting firms. Public accounting firms provide accounting services for other companies. Usually they offer three services:

- auditing
- tax accounting
- management advisory services

The largest public accounting firms in the United States are called the "Big Four." The "Big Four" are Deloitte & Touche, Ernst & Young, KPMG, and PricewaterhouseCoopers.

Many public accountants are **certified public accountants (CPAs)**. To become a CPA, an individual must have a certain number of college credits in accounting courses, demonstrate good personal character, pass the Uniform CPA Examination, and fulfill the experience requirements of the state of practice. CPAs must follow the professional code of ethics.

Auditing is the review of financial statements to assess their fairness and adherence to generally accepted accounting principles. Accountants who are CPAs perform financial audits.

Tax accounting involves tax compliance and tax planning. *Tax compliance* deals with the preparation of tax returns and the audit of those returns. *Tax planning* involves giving advice to clients on how to structure their financial affairs in order to reduce their tax liability.

Management advisory services involve helping clients improve their information systems or their business performance.

ABOUT
ACCOUNTING

Accounting Services
The role of the CPA is expanding. In the past, accounting firms handled audits and taxes. Today accountants provide a wide range of services, including financial planning, investment advice, accounting and tax software advice, and profitability consulting. Accountants provide clients with information and advice on electronic business, health care performance measurement, risk assessment, business performance measurement, and information system reliability.

MANAGERIAL ACCOUNTING

Managerial accounting , also referred to as *private accounting*, involves working for a single business in industry. Managerial accountants perform a wide range of activities, including

- establishing accounting policies,
- managing the accounting system,
- preparing financial statements,
- interpreting financial information,
- providing financial advice to management,
- preparing tax forms,
- performing tax planning services,
- preparing internal reports for management.

GOVERNMENTAL ACCOUNTING

Governmental accounting involves keeping financial records and preparing financial reports as part of the staff of federal, state, or local governmental units. Governmental units do not earn profits. However, governmental units receive and pay out huge amounts of money and need procedures for recording and managing this money.

Some governmental agencies hire accountants to audit the financial statements and records of the businesses under their jurisdiction and to uncover possible violations of the law. The Securities and Exchange Commission, the Internal Revenue Service, the Federal Bureau of Investigation, and Homeland Security employ a large number of accountants.

▶ 3. OBJECTIVE

Identify the users of financial information.

Users of Financial Information

The results of the accounting process are communicated to many individuals and organizations. Who are these individuals and organizations, and why do they want financial information about a particular firm?

OWNERS AND MANAGERS

Assume your sportswear shop is in full operation. One user of financial information about the business is you, the owner. You need information that will help you evaluate the results of your operations and plan and make decisions for the future. Questions such as the following are difficult to answer without financial information:

- Should you drop the long-sleeved pullover that is not selling well from the product line, or should you just reduce the price?
- How much should you charge for the denim jacket that you are adding to the product line?
- How much should you spend on advertising?
- How does this month's profit compare with last month's profit?
- Should you open a new store?

SUPPLIERS

A number of other people are interested in the financial information about your business. For example, businesses that supply you with sportswear need to assess the ability of your firm to pay its bills. They also need to set a credit limit for your firm.

BANKS

What if you decide to ask your bank for a loan so that you can open a new store? The bank needs to be sure that your firm will repay the loan on time. The bank will ask for financial information prepared by your accountant. Based on this information, the bank will decide whether to make the loan and the terms of the loan.

TAX AUTHORITIES

The Internal Revenue Service (IRS) and other state and local tax authorities are interested in financial information about your firm. This information is used to determine the tax base:

- Income taxes are based on taxable income.
- Sales taxes are based on sales income.
- Property taxes are based on the assessed value of buildings, equipment, and inventory (the goods available for sale).

The accounting process provides all of this information.

Regulate

REGULATORY AGENCIES AND INVESTORS   *—Read*

If an industry is regulated by a governmental agency, businesses in that industry have to supply financial information to the regulating agency. For example, the Federal Communications Commission receives financial information from radio and television stations. The Securities and Exchange Commission (SEC) oversees the financial information provided by publicly owned corporations to their investors and potential investors. Publicly owned corporations trade their shares on stock exchanges and in over-the-counter markets. Congress passed the Securities Act of 1933 and the Securities Exchange Act of 1934 in order to protect those who invest in publicly owned corporations.

The SEC is responsible for reviewing the accounting methods used by publicly owned corporations. The SEC has delegated this review to the accounting profession but still has the final say on any financial accounting issue faced by publicly owned corporations. If the SEC does not agree with the reporting that results from an accounting method, the SEC can suspend trading of a company's shares on the stock exchanges.

> Major changes are in store for the regulatory environment in the accounting profession with the passage of the Public Company Accounting Reform and Investor Protection Act of 2002 (also known as the Sarbanes-Oxley Act) that was signed into law by President Bush on August 2, 2002. The Act is the most far-reaching regulatory crackdown on corporate fraud and corruption since the creation of the Securities and Exchange Commission in 1934.

The Sarbanes-Oxley Act was passed in response to the wave of corporate accounting scandals starting with the demise of Enron Corporation in 2001, the arrest of top executives at WorldCom and Adelphia Communications Corporation, and ultimately the demise of Arthur *—accounting firm* Andersen, an international public accounting firm formerly a member of the "Big Five." Arthur Andersen was found guilty of an obstruction of justice charge after admitting that the firm destroyed thousands of documents and electronic files related to the Enron audit engagement. As a result of the demise of Arthur Andersen, the "Big Five" are now the "Big Four."

The Act significantly tightens regulation of financial reporting by publicly held companies and their accountants and auditors. The Sarbanes-Oxley Act creates a five-member Public Company Accounting Oversight Board. The Board will have investigative and enforcement powers to oversee the accounting profession and to discipline corrupt accountants and auditors. The Securities and Exchange Commission will oversee the Board. Two members of the Board will be certified public accountants, to regulate the accountants who audit public companies, and the remaining three must not be and cannot have been CPAs. The chair of the Board may be held by one of the CPA members, provided that the individual has not been engaged as a practicing CPA for five years.

Major provisions of the bill include rules on consulting services, auditor rotation, criminal penalties, corporate governance, and securities regulation. The Act prohibits accountants from offering a broad range of consulting services to publicly traded companies that they audit and requires accounting firms to change the lead audit or coordinating partner and the reviewing partner for a company every five years. Additionally, it is a felony to "knowingly" destroy or create documents to "impede, obstruct or influence" any existing or contemplated federal investigation. Auditors are also required to maintain all audit or review work papers for five years. Criminal penalties, up to 20 years in prison, are imposed for obstruction of justice and the Act raises the maximum sentence for defrauding pension funds to 10 years.

Chief executives and chief financial officers of publicly traded corporations are now required to certify their financial statements and these executives will face up to 20 years in prison if they "knowingly or willfully" allow materially misleading information into their financial statements. Companies must also disclose, as quickly as possible, material changes in their financial position. Wall Street investment firms are prohibited from retaliating against analysts who criticize investment-banking clients of the firm. The Act contains a provision with broad new protection for whistle blowers and lengthens the time that investors have to file lawsuits against corporations for securities fraud.

By narrowing the type of consulting services that accountants can provide to companies that they audit, requiring auditor rotation, and imposing stiff criminal penalties for violation of the Act, it appears that this new legislation will significantly help to restore public confidence in financial statements and markets and change the regulatory environment in which accountants operate.

CUSTOMERS

Customers pay special attention to financial information about the firms with which they do business. For example, before a business spends a lot of money on a mainframe computer, the business wants to know that the computer manufacturer will be around for the next several years in order to service the computer, replace parts, and provide additional components. The business analyzes the financial information about the computer manufacturer in order to determine its economic health and the likelihood that it will remain in business.

FIGURE 1.1

Users of Financial Information

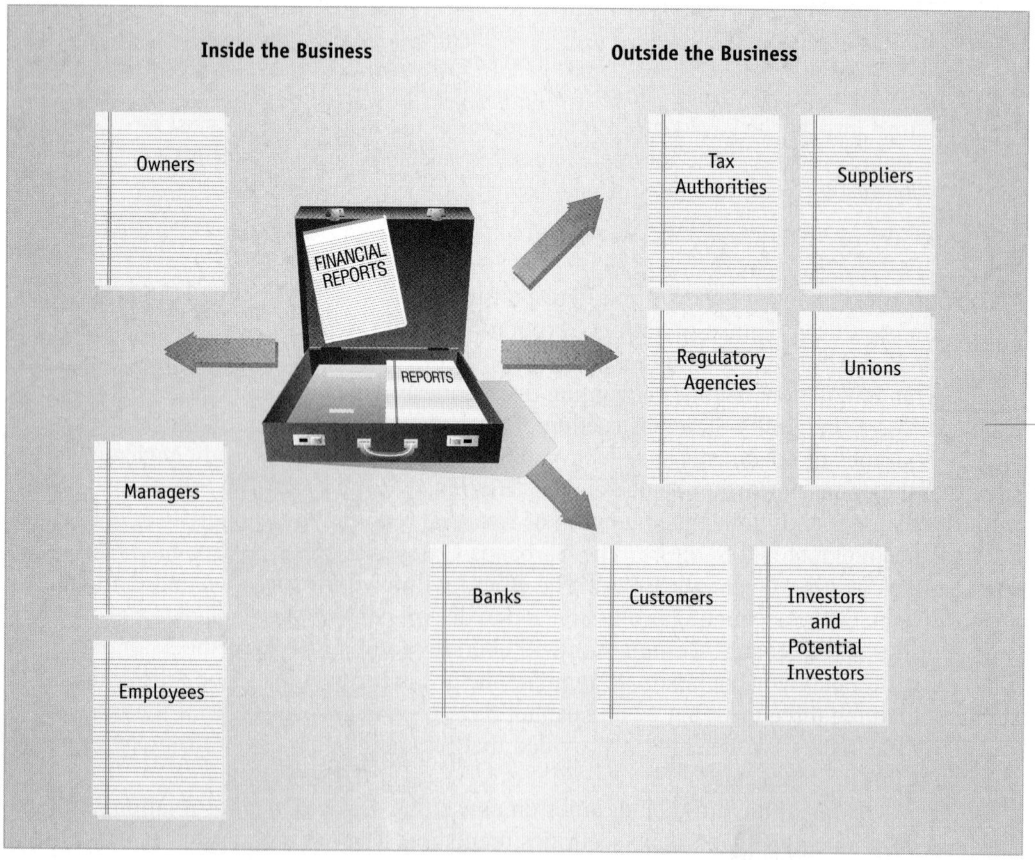

EMPLOYEES AND UNIONS

Often employees are interested in the financial information of the business that employs them. Employees who are members of a profit-sharing plan pay close attention to the financial results because they affect employee income. Employees who are members of a labor union use financial information about the firm to negotiate wages and benefits.

Figure 1.1 illustrates different financial information users. As you learn about the accounting process, you will appreciate why financial information is so important to these individuals and organizations. You will learn how financial information meets users' needs.

Section 1: Self Review

QUESTIONS

1. Why is accounting called the "language of business"?

2. What are financial statements?

3. What are the names of three accounting job positions?

EXERCISES

4. Which organization has the final say on financial accounting issues faced by publicly owned corporations?

  a. Internal Revenue Service

  b. U.S. Treasury Department

  c. Federal Trade Commission

  d. Securities and Exchange Commission

5. One requirement for becoming a CPA is to pass the

  a. State Board Examination

  b. Uniform CPA Examination

  c. SEC Accounting Examination

  d. Final CPA Examination

ANALYSIS

6. The owner of the sporting goods store where you work has decided to expand the store. She has decided to apply for a loan. What type of information will she need to give to the bank?

(Answers to Section 1 Self Review are on page 20.)

Section 2

SECTION OBJECTIVES

▶ **4. Compare and contrast the three types of business entities.**

WHY IT'S IMPORTANT

Each type of business entity requires unique legal and accounting considerations.

▶ **5. Describe the process used to develop generally accepted accounting principles.**

WHY IT'S IMPORTANT

Accounting professionals are required to use common standards and principles in order to produce reliable financial information.

TERMS TO LEARN

auditor's report
corporation
creditor
discussion memorandum
economic entity
entity
exposure draft
generally accepted accounting principles (GAAP)
international accounting
partnership
separate entity assumption
social entity
sole proprietorship
Statements of Financial Accounting Standards
stock
stockholders

The accounting process involves recording, classifying, summarizing, interpreting, and communicating financial information about an economic or social entity. An **entity** is recognized as having its own separate identity. An entity may be an individual, a town, a university, or a business. The term **economic entity** usually refers to a business or organization whose major purpose is to produce a profit for its owners. **Social entities** are nonprofit organizations, such as cities, public schools, and public hospitals. This book focuses on the accounting process for businesses, but keep in mind that nonprofit organizations also need financial information.

Types of Business Entities

The three major legal forms of business entity are the sole proprietorship, the partnership, and the corporation. In general the accounting process is the same for all three forms of business. Later in the book you will study the different ways certain transactions are handled depending on the type of business entity. For now, however, you will learn about the different types of business entities.

SOLE PROPRIETORSHIPS

A **sole proprietorship** is a business entity owned by one person. The life of the business ends when the owner is no longer willing or able to keep the business going. Many small businesses are operated as sole proprietorships.

The owner of a sole proprietorship is legally responsible for the debts and taxes of the business. If the business is unable to pay its debts, the **creditors** (those people, companies, or government agencies to whom the business owes money) can turn to the owner for payment. The owner may have to pay the debts of the business from personal resources, including personal savings. When the time comes to pay income taxes, the owner's income and the income of the business are combined to compute the total tax responsibility of the owner.

It is important that the business transactions be kept separate from the owner's personal transactions. If the owner's personal transactions are mixed with those of the business, it will be difficult to measure the performance of the business. The term **separate entity assumption** describes the concept of keeping the firm's financial records separate from the owner's personal financial records.

PARTNERSHIPS

A **partnership** is a business entity owned by two or more people. The partnership structure is common in businesses that offer professional services, such as law firms, accounting firms, architectural firms, medical practices, and dental practices. At the beginning of the partnership,

10

two or more individuals enter into a contract that details the rights, obligations, and limitations of each partner, including

- the amount each partner will contribute to the business,
- each partner's percentage of ownership,
- each partner's share of the profits,
- the duties each partner will perform,
- the responsibility each partner has for the amounts owed by the business to creditors and tax authorities.

The partners choose how to share the ownership and profits of the business. They may share equally or in any proportion agreed upon in the contract. When a partner leaves, the partnership is dissolved and a new partnership may be formed with the remaining partners.

Partners are individually, and as a group, responsible for the debts and taxes of the partnership. If the partnership is unable to pay its debts or taxes, the partners' personal property, including personal bank accounts, may be used to provide payment. It is important that partnership transactions be kept separate from the personal financial transactions of the partners.

▶ 4. OBJECTIVE
Compare and contrast the three types of business entities.

> Under the Limited Liability Partnership Act of most states, a Limited Liability Partnership (LLP) may be formed. An LLP is a general partnership that provides some limited liability for all partners. LLP partners are responsible and have liability for their own actions and the actions of those under their control or supervision. They are not liable for the actions or malfeasance of another partner. Except for the limited liability aspect, LLPs generally have the same characteristics, advantages, and disadvantages as any other partnership.

CORPORATIONS

A **corporation** is a business entity that is separate from its owners. A corporation has a legal right to own property and do business in its own name. Corporations are very different from sole proprietorships and partnerships.

Stock, issued in the form of stock certificates, represents the ownership of the corporation. Corporations may be *privately* or *publicly* owned. Privately owned corporations are also called *closely held* corporations. The ownership of privately owned corporations is limited to specific individuals, usually family members. Stock of closely held corporations is not traded on an exchange. In contrast, stock of publicly owned corporations is bought and sold on stock exchanges and in over-the-counter markets. Most large corporations have issued (sold) thousands of shares of stock.

An owner's share of the corporation is determined by the number of shares of stock held by the owner compared to the total number of shares issued by the corporation. Assume that Alicia Martinez owns 300 shares of Sample Corporation. If Sample Corporation has issued 1,000 shares of stock, Martinez owns 30 percent of the corporation (300 shares ÷ 1,000 shares = 0.30 or 30%). Some corporate decisions require a vote by the owners. For Sample Corporation, Martinez has 300 votes, one for each share of stock that she owns. The other owners have 700 votes.

important!

Separate Entity Assumption
For *accounting* purposes all forms of business are considered separate entities from their owners. However, the corporation is the only form of business that is a separate *legal* entity.

> Subchapter S Corporations, also known as S corporations, are entities formed as corporations which meet the requirements of Subchapter S of the Internal Revenue Code to be treated essentially as a partnership so the corporation pays no income tax. Instead, shareholders include their share of corporate profits, and any items that require special tax treatment, on their individual income tax returns. Otherwise, S corporations have all of the characteristics of regular corporations. The advantage of the S corporation is that the owners have limited liability and avoid double taxation.

Characteristic	Type of Business Entity		
	Sole Proprietorship	**Partnership**	**Corporation**
Ownership	One owner	Two or more owners	One or more owners, even thousands
Life of the business	Ends when the owner dies, is unable to carry on operations, or decides to close the firm	Ends when one or more partners withdraw, when a partner dies, or when the partners decide to close the firm	Can continue indefinitely; ends only when the business goes bankrupt or when the stockholders vote to liquidate
Responsibility for debts of the business	Owner is responsible for firm's debt when the firm is unable to pay	Partners are responsible individually and jointly for firm's debts when the firm is unable to pay	Stockholders are not responsible for firm's debts; they can lose only the amount they invested

TABLE 1.1

Major Characteristics of Business Entities

One of the advantages of the corporate form of business is the indefinite life of the corporation. A sole proprietorship ends when the owner dies or discontinues the business. A partnership ends on the death or withdrawal of a partner. In contrast, a corporation does not end when ownership changes. Some corporations have new owners daily because their shares are actively traded (sold) on stock exchanges.

Corporate owners, called **stockholders** or *shareholders*, are not personally responsible for the debts or taxes of the corporation. If the corporation is unable to pay its bills, the most stockholders can lose is their investment in the corporation. In other words, the stockholders will not lose more than the cost of the shares of stock.

The accounting process for the corporate entity, like that of the sole proprietorship and the partnership, is separate from the financial affairs of its owners. Usually this separation is easy to maintain. Most stockholders do not participate in the day-to-day operations of the business.

Table 1.1 summarizes the business characteristics for sole proprietorships, partnerships, and corporations.

Generally Accepted Accounting Principles

The Securities and Exchange Commission has the final say on matters of financial reporting by publicly owned corporations. The SEC has delegated the job of determining proper accounting standards to the accounting profession. However, the SEC sometimes overrides decisions the accounting profession makes. To fulfill its responsibility, the accounting profession has developed, and continues to develop, **generally accepted accounting principles (GAAP)**. Generally accepted accounting principles must be followed by publicly owned companies unless they can show that doing so would produce information that is misleading.

THE DEVELOPMENT OF GENERALLY ACCEPTED ACCOUNTING PRINCIPLES

Generally accepted accounting principles are developed by the Financial Accounting Standards Board (FASB), which is composed of seven full-time members. The FASB issues **Statements of Financial Accounting Standards**. The FASB develops these statements and, before issuing them, obtains feedback from interested people and organizations.

First, the FASB writes a **discussion memorandum** to explain the topic being considered. Then public hearings are held where interested parties can express their opinions, either orally or in writing. The groups that consistently express opinions about proposed FASB statements

important!

GAAP

The SEC requires all publicly owned companies to follow generally accepted accounting principles. As new standards are developed or refined, accountants interpret the standards and adapt accounting practices to the new standards.

MANAGERIAL IMPLICATIONS <<

FINANCIAL INFORMATION

- Managers of a business make sure that the firm's accounting system produces financial information that is timely, accurate, and fair.
- Financial statements should be based on generally accepted accounting principles.
- Each year a publicly traded company must submit financial statements, including an independent auditor's report, to the SEC.
- Internal reports for management need not follow generally accepted accounting principles but should provide useful information that will aid in monitoring and controlling operations.
- Financial information can help managers to control present operations, make decisions, and plan for the future.
- The sound use of financial information is essential to good management.

THINKING CRITICALLY

If you were a manager, how would you use financial information to make decisions?

---

are the SEC, the American Institute of Certified Public Accountants (AICPA), public accounting firms, the American Accounting Association (AAA), and businesses with a direct interest in a particular statement.

The AICPA is a national association for certified public accountants. The AAA is a group of accounting educators. AAA members research possible effects of a proposed FASB statement and offer their opinions to the FASB.

After public hearings, the FASB releases an **exposure draft**, which describes the proposed statement. Then the FASB receives and evaluates public comment about the exposure draft. Finally, FASB members vote on the statement. If at least four members approve, the statement is issued. The process used to develop GAAP is shown in Figure 1.2 on page 14.

Accounting principles vary from country to country. **International accounting** is the study of the accounting principles used by different countries. In 1973, the International Accounting Standards Committee (IASC) was formed. Recently, the IASC's name was changed to the International Accounting Standards Board (IASB). The IASB deals with issues caused by the lack of uniform accounting principles. The IASB also makes recommendations to enhance comparability of reporting practices.

THE USE OF GENERALLY ACCEPTED ACCOUNTING PRINCIPLES

Every year publicly traded companies submit financial statements to the SEC. The financial statements are audited by independent certified public accountants (CPAs). The CPAs are called *independent* because they are not employees of the company being audited and they do not have a financial interest in the company. The financial statements include the auditor's report. The **auditor's report** contains the auditor's opinion about the fair presentation of the operating results and financial position of the business. The auditor's report also confirms that the financial information is prepared in conformity with generally accepted accounting principles. The financial statements and the auditor's report are made available to the public, including existing and potential stockholders.

Businesses and the environment in which they operate are constantly changing. The economy, technology, and laws change. Generally accepted accounting principles are changed and refined as accountants respond to the changing environment.

International INSIGHTS

Standards

In 1999 the FASB chairman offered the IASC three guiding principles for its work:

1. Identify a common mission or objective for all parties involved in the process.
2. Develop an accepted and trusted process for creating the standards.
3. Develop standards that achieve high quality.

▶ **5. OBJECTIVE**

Describe the process used to develop generally accepted accounting principles.

Topic Tackler

PLUS

FIGURE 1.2 | **The Process Used by FASB to Develop Generally Accepted Accounting Principles**

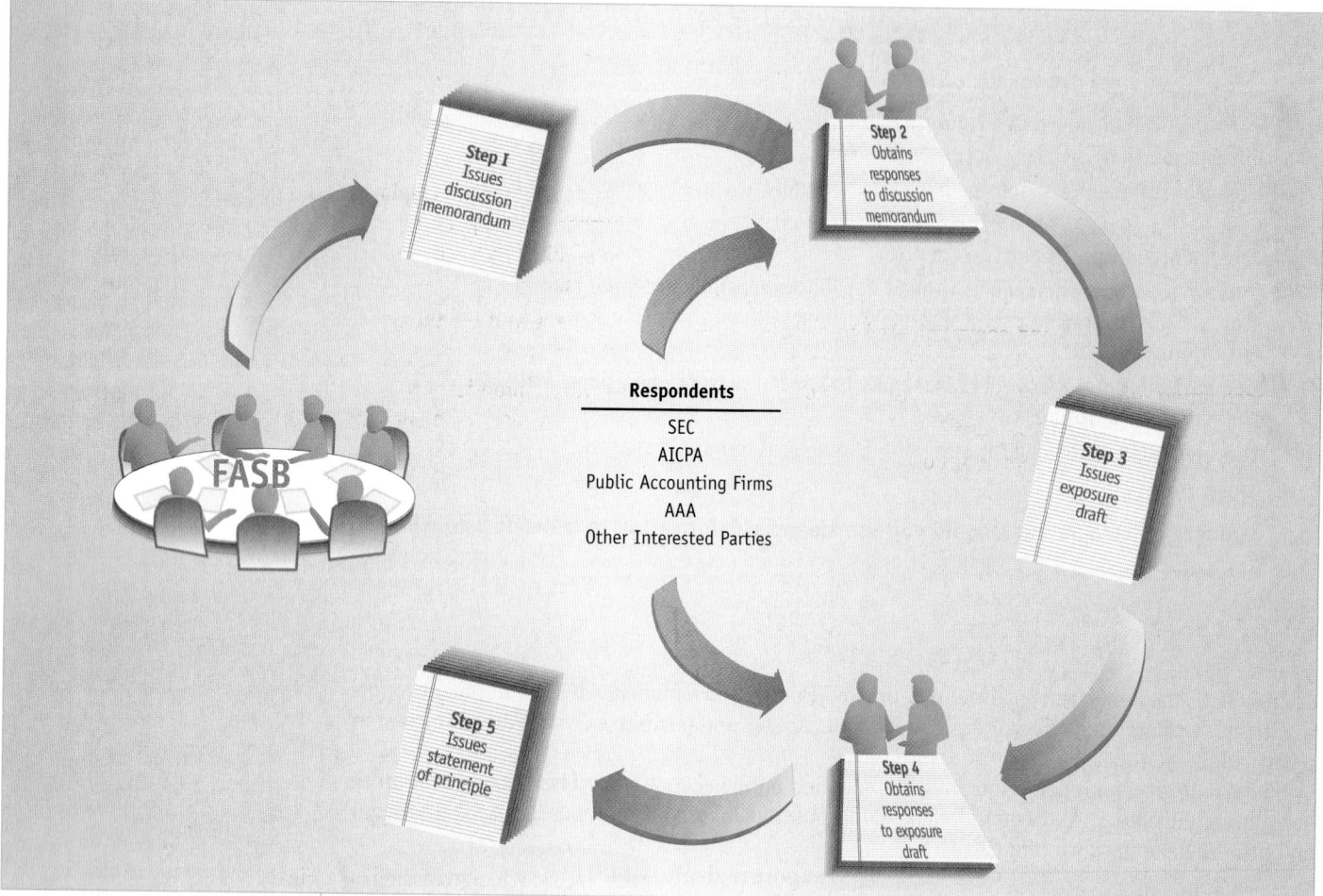

Section 2: **Self Review**

QUESTIONS

1. Why are generally accepted accounting principles needed?

2. How are generally accepted accounting principles developed?

3. What are generally accepted accounting principles?

EXERCISES

4. A nonprofit organization such as a public school is a(n)

   a. economic entity

   b. social entity

   c. economic unit

   d. social unit

5. An organization that has two or more owners who are legally responsible for the debts and taxes of the business is a

   a. corporation

   b. sole proprietorship

   c. partnership

   d. social entity

6. You plan to open a business with two of your friends. You would like to form a corporation, but your friends prefer the partnership form of business. What are some of the advantages of the corporate form of business?

(Answers to Section 2 Self Review are on page 20.)

REVIEW   ## Chapter Summary

Accounting is often called the "language of business." The financial information about a business is communicated to interested parties in financial statements.

Learning Objectives

1 Define accounting.

Accounting is the process by which financial information about a business is recorded, classified, summarized, interpreted, and communicated to owners, managers, and other interested parties. Accurate accounting information is essential for making business decisions.

2 Identify and discuss career opportunities in accounting.

- There are many job opportunities in accounting.

- Accounting clerk positions, such as accounts receivable clerk, accounts payable clerk, and payroll clerk, require the least education and experience.

- Bookkeepers usually have experience as accounting clerks and a minimum of one to two years of accounting education.

- Most entry-level accounting positions require a college degree or significant experience as a bookkeeper.

- Accountants usually specialize in one of three major areas.

- Some accountants work for public accounting firms and perform auditing, tax accounting, or management advisory functions.

- Other accountants work in private industry where they set up and supervise accounting systems, prepare financial reports, prepare internal reports, or assist in determining the prices to charge for the firm's products.

- Still other accountants work for government agencies. They keep track of public funds and expenditures, or they audit the financial records of businesses and individuals to determine whether the records are in compliance with regulatory laws, tax laws, and other laws. The Securities and Exchange Commission, the Internal Revenue Service, the Federal Bureau of Investigation, and Homeland Security employ many accountants.

3 Identify the users of financial information.

All types of businesses need and use financial information. Users of financial information include owners and managers, employees, suppliers, banks, tax authorities, regulatory agencies, and investors. Nonprofit organizations need similar financial information.

4 Compare and contrast the three types of business entities.

- A sole proprietorship is owned by one person. The owner is legally responsible for the debts and taxes of the business.

- A partnership is owned by two or more people. The owners are legally responsible for the debts and taxes of the business.

- A corporation is a separate legal entity from its owners.

- Note that all three types of business entities are considered separate entities for accounting purposes.

5 Describe the process used to develop generally accepted accounting principles.

- The SEC has delegated the authority to develop generally accepted accounting principles to the accounting profession. The Financial Accounting Standards Board handles this task. A series of steps used by the FASB includes issuing a discussion memorandum, an exposure draft, and a statement of principle.

- The SEC oversees the Public Company Accounting Oversight Board that was created by the Sarbanes-Oxley Act. The Board regulates financial reporting by accountants and auditors of publicly held companies.

- Each year firms that sell stock on stock exchanges or in over-the-counter markets must publish audited financial reports that follow generally accepted accounting principles. They must submit their reports to the Securities and Exchange Commission. They must also make the reports available to stockholders.

6 Define the accounting terms new to this chapter.

GLOSSARY

Accounting (p. 4) The process by which financial information about a business is recorded, classified, summarized, interpreted, and communicated to owners, managers, and other interested parties

Accounting system (p. 4) A process designed to accumulate, classify, and summarize financial data

Auditing (p. 5) The review of financial statements to assess their fairness and adherence to generally accepted accounting principles

Auditor's report (p. 13) An independent accountant's review of a firm's financial statements

Certified public accountant (CPA) (p. 5) An independent accountant who provides accounting services to the public for a fee

Corporation (p. 11) A publicly or privately owned business entity that is separate from its owners and has a legal right to own property and do business in its own name; stockholders are not responsible for the debts or taxes of the business

Creditor (p. 10) One to whom money is owed

Discussion memorandum (p. 12) An explanation of a topic under consideration by the Financial Accounting Standards Board

Economic entity (p. 10) A business or organization whose major purpose is to produce a profit for its owners

Entity (p. 10) Anything having its own separate identity, such as an individual, a town, a university, or a business

Exposure draft (p. 13) A proposed solution to a problem being considered by the Financial Accounting Standards Board

Financial statements (p. 4) Periodic reports of a firm's financial position or operating results

Generally accepted accounting principles (GAAP) (p. 12) Accounting standards developed and applied by professional accountants

Governmental accounting (p. 6) Accounting work performed for a federal, state, or local governmental unit

International accounting (p. 13) The study of accounting principles used by different countries

Management advisory services (p. 5) Services designed to help clients improve their information systems or their business performance

Managerial accounting (p. 6) Accounting work carried on by an accountant employed by a single business in industry

Partnership (p. 10) A business entity owned by two or more people who are legally responsible for the debts and taxes of the business

Public accountants (p. 5) Members of firms that perform accounting services for other companies

Separate entity assumption (p. 10) The concept of keeping a firm's financial records separate from the owner's personal financial records

Social entity (p. 10) A nonprofit organization, such as a city, public school, or public hospital

Sole proprietorship (p. 10) A business entity owned by one person who is legally responsible for the debts and taxes of the business

Statements of Financial Accounting Standards (p. 12) Accounting principles established by the Financial Accounting Standards Board

Stock (p. 11) Certificates that represent ownership of a corporation

Stockholders (p. 12) The owners of a corporation; also called shareholders

Tax accounting (p. 5) A service that involves tax compliance and tax planning

Comprehensive **Self Review**

1. What is the purpose of the auditor's report?
2. How is the ownership of a corporation different from that of a sole proprietorship?
3. What is the purpose of accounting?
4. What does the accounting process involve?
5. What are the three types of business entities?

(Answers to Comprehensive Self Review are on page 21.)

Discussion Questions

1. What types of people or organizations are interested in financial information about a firm, and why are they interested in this information?
2. What is the function of the Securities and Exchange Commission?
3. What are the three types of business entities, and how do they differ?
4. Why is it important for business records to be separate from the records of the business's owner or owners? What is the term accountants use to describe this separation of personal and business records?
5. What is the purpose of the Financial Accounting Standards Board?
6. What groups consistently offer opinions about proposed FASB statements?
7. What are the three major areas of accounting?
8. What types of services do public accountants provide?
9. What is tax planning?
10. What are the major functions or activities performed by accountants in private industry?
11. What led to the passage of the Public Company Accounting Reform and Investor Protection Act of 2002?
12. What is the purpose of the Public Company Accounting Oversight Board?

PROBLEM

Critical Thinking Problem

Which Type of Business Entity?

Mary Amos has worked for a national chain of women's clothing stores since graduating from college five years ago. She has held several positions with the company and is currently manager of several stores in her area.

Over the past five years, Mary has observed that many women shop at one store for outfits and another for shoes, jewelry, and other accessories. Mary believes there is an unmet demand for a women's store that sells complete outfits from head to toe. Mary has always dreamed of owning her own store and believes her idea of a "one stop shop" for women would be well received in the marketplace, especially with women executives who have limited time for shopping. Mary's store would sell an array of women's clothes, shoes, jewelry, and accessories for business, social, and leisure functions. Mary has discussed her idea with a number of people in the industry, including sales associates in other women's clothing stores, and has conducted a marketing survey to test the viability of her plans. On the basis of analyses of her discussions and the data from the marketing survey, Mary believes that her plans are sound and that there is a high probability that she will be successful should she pursue her dream.

A new upscale shopping mall is opening nearby and Mary has decided that now is the time to take the plunge into business for herself. Mary plans to open her business under the name of The Style Shop in the new mall.

One of the things that Mary must decide in the process of transforming her idea to reality is the form of ownership for her new business. Should it be organized as a sole proprietorship, a partnership, or a corporation?

What advice would you give Mary? What advantages and disadvantages are there to each choice? The following diagram will help you organize your thoughts.

Business Entity	Advantages	Disadvantages
Sole Proprietorship		*come after personal belonging*
Partnership		
Corporation		

BUSINESS CONNECTIONS

Managerial | FOCUS

Know Accounting

1. Why is it important for managers to have financial information?

2. Do you think a manager will obtain enough financial information to control operations effectively if the manager simply reads a set of financial statements once a year? Why or why not?

3. The owner of a small business commented to a friend that he did not see the need for an accounting system in his firm because he closely supervises day-to-day operations and knows exactly what is happening in the business. Would you agree with his statement? Why or why not?

4. This chapter listed a number of questions that the owner or manager of a firm might ask when trying to evaluate the results of the firm's operations and its financial position. If you were an owner or manager, what other questions would you ask to judge the firm's performance, control operations, make decisions, and plan for the future?

5. The major objective of most businesses is to earn a profit. What other objectives might a business have? How can financial information help management to achieve these objectives?

6. Many business owners and managers are not accountants. Why is it useful for such people to have a basic knowledge of accounting?

7. Are international accounting standards important to management? Why or why not?

8. Why is the separate entity assumption important to a manager?

To Tell or Not to Tell

AEC Computers is in the process of signing a large contract with a circuit board supplier, Gerald Bown's Electronics. At a party you overhear two individuals stating that a few of Mr. Bown's checks were returned by the bank. As a friend of Mr. Bown's son, you are afraid to mention this fact to your President because it would cancel the contract. What should you do?

Ethical | DILEMMA

Information

Refer to The Home Depot, Inc. *2004 Annual Report* in Appendix A.

1. Review the letter written by Bob Nardelli, President and Chief Executive Officer. To what audiences is the letter directed? Describe the types of financial information presented in the letter. Why would this information be important to readers?

2. Information provided in a company's annual report can also include nonfinancial strategies for merchandising, customer service, or new ventures. Based on the letter presented from The Home Depot, Inc.'s president and CEO, describe three successful strategies that the company implemented in 2004.

STREETWISE:
Questions from the
REAL WORLD

Notes to Financial Statements

Within a company's annual report, a section called "Notes to Consolidated Financial Statements" offers general information about the company along with detailed notes related to its financial statements. An excerpt from American Eagle Outfitters, Inc.'s, "Notes to Consolidated Financial Statements," *2003 Annual Report*, is presented below.

Financial Statement
ANALYSIS

AMERICAN EAGLE
OUTFITTERS
ae.com

> The Company designs, markets, and sells its American Eagle brand of relaxed, casual clothing for 15- to 25-year-olds in its United States and Canadian retail stores. We also operate via the Internet at **ae.com** as well as through our catalog business. The American Eagle brand provides high quality merchandise at affordable prices. American Eagle's collection offers modern basics like jeans, cargo pants, and graphic Ts as well as a stylish assortment of cool accessories, outerwear, and footwear. The Bluenotes brand targets a slightly younger demographic, offering a more urban/suburban, denim-driven collection for 12- to 22-year-olds. The Company operates retail stores located primarily in regional enclosed shopping malls in the United States and Canada.

Analyze:

1. Would American Eagle Outfitters, Inc., be considered an economic entity or a social entity? Why?

2. What types of merchandise does this company sell?

3. Who are the potential users of the information presented? Why would this information be helpful to these users?

Analyze Online: On the American Eagle Outfitters, Inc., Web site **(www.ae.com)**, review the *Company Overview* section. Click on About AE, then click on AE Investment Info.

4. What age consumer does the company target?

5. What types of merchandise does the company offer? Has the merchandise selection changed from the merchandise described in the *2003 Annual Report*?

6. What information is offered to the shareholder on the Web site?

Independent Auditor

A certified public accountant (CPA) who audits a company's financial statements must be independent. What is meant by "independent" in this sense? Why is it important? What situations or factors might affect a CPA's independence?

Extending | THE THOUGHT

Business | COMMUNICATION

Memo

As the manager of the accounting department, you have been asked by the human resources director to help prepare a job description for a job opening in your department. The company wishes to fill the position of bookkeeper. The heading of your memo should include the following:

Date:

To:

From:

Subject:

The body of your memo should include the job responsibilities, and the training and experience necessary for the position.

TEAMWORK

Determining Information

Palfreyman Mattress Company is planning to expand into selling bedroom furniture. This expansion will require a loan from the bank. The bank has requested financial information. Discuss, in a group, the information the bank would require. What information, if any, would you not provide the bank?

Internet | CONNECTION

FASB—What Is It?

Go to the FASB Web site at **www.FASB.org**. The FASB pronouncements are listed. How many FASB pronouncements are currently listed? How are they listed?

Answers to Self Reviews

Answers to Section 1 Self Review

1. The results of the accounting process—financial statements—communicate essential information about a business to concerned individuals and organizations.
2. Periodic reports that summarize the financial affairs of a business.
3. Clerk, bookkeeper, and accountant.
4. **d.** Securities and Exchange Commission
5. **b.** Uniform CPA Examination
6. Current sales and expenses figures, anticipated sales and expenses, and the cost of the expansion.

Answers to Section 2 Self Review

1. GAAP help to ensure that financial information fairly presents a firm's operating results and financial position.
2. FASB develops proposed statements and solicits feedback from interested individuals, groups, and companies. FASB evaluates the opinions received and votes on the statement.
3. Accounting standards that are changed and refined in response to changes in the environment in which businesses operate.
4. **b.** social entity
5. **c.** partnership
6. The shareholders are not responsible for the debts and taxes of the corporation. Corporations can continue in existence indefinitely.

Answers to Comprehensive Self Review

1. To obtain the objective opinion of a professional accountant from outside the company that the statements fairly present the operating results and financial position of the business and that the information was prepared according to GAAP.

2. A sole proprietorship is a business entity owned by one person. A corporation is a separate legal entity that has a legal right to own property and do business in its own name.

3. To gather and communicate financial information about a business.

4. Recording, classifying, summarizing, interpreting, and communicating financial information about a business.

5. Sole proprietorship, partnership, and corporation.

CHAPTER 1: Review and Applications

LEARNING OBJECTIVES

1. Record in equation form the financial effects of a business transaction.

2. Define, identify, and understand the relationship between asset, liability, and owner's equity accounts.

3. Analyze the effects of business transactions on a firm's assets, liabilities, and owner's equity and record these effects in accounting equation form.

4. Prepare an income statement.

5. Prepare a statement of owner's equity and a balance sheet.

6. Define the accounting terms new to this chapter.

NEW TERMS

accounts payable	income statement
accounts receivable	liabilities
assets	net income
balance sheet	net loss
break even	on account
business transaction	owner's equity
capital	revenue
equity	statement of owner's equity
expense	
fair market value	withdrawals
fundamental accounting equation	

Chapter 2
Analyzing Business Transactions

 www.southwest.com

Rollin King and Herb Kelleher started their airline business as many entrepreneurs do, with one simple notion. They felt if they could get passengers to their destinations on time, at the lowest possible fares, and make sure they had a good time doing it, customers would respond. And respond they have.

Today, Southwest Airlines flies more than 70 million passengers a year all across the country. In an economy where most major airlines struggle to stay out of bankruptcy, Southwest has flourished, thanks to its focused philosophy of low fares and its commitment to its Employees and Customers. Its business strategy of operating high-frequency point-to-point service routes and eliminating the costs associated with hub routes has been imitated by United's Ted® and Delta's Song®. Herb Kelleher and Colleen Barrett, Southwest's fun-loving leaders, established a culture that encourages Employees to have fun. Consistently voted as one of the top places to work, Southwest Employees participate in Employee chili cook-offs, paper airplane contests, and dance competitions—many of these contests take place in-fight to the delight of passengers.

thinking critically | How does a happy workforce contribute to a company's net profit or bottom line?

Section 1

Property and Financial Interest

SECTION OBJECTIVES

▶ 1. **Record in equation form the financial effects of a business transaction.**

WHY IT'S IMPORTANT

Learning the fundamental accounting equation is a basis for understanding business transactions.

▶ 2. **Define, identify, and understand the relationship between asset, liability, and owner's equity accounts.**

WHY IT'S IMPORTANT

The relationship between assets, liabilities, and owner's equity is the basis for the entire accounting system.

TERMS TO LEARN

accounts payable
assets
balance sheet
business transaction
capital
equity
liabilities
on account
owner's equity

The accounting process starts with the analysis of business transactions. A **business transaction** is any financial event that changes the resources of a firm. For example, purchases, sales, payments, and receipts of cash are all business transactions. The accountant analyzes each business transaction to decide what information to record and where to record it.

Beginning with Analysis

Let's analyze the transactions of JT's Consulting Services, a firm that provides a wide range of accounting and consulting services. Jason Taylor, CPA, has a master's degree in accounting. He is the sole proprietor of JT's Consulting Services. Tennille Brisbane, the office manager, has an associate's degree in business and has taken 12 semester hours of accounting. The firm is located in a large office complex.

Every month JT's Consulting Services bills clients for the accounting and consulting services provided that month. Customers can also pay in cash when the services are rendered.

STARTING A BUSINESS

Let's start from the beginning. Jason Taylor obtained the funds to start the business by withdrawing $90,000 from his personal savings account. The first transaction of the new business was opening a checking account in the name of JT's Consulting Services. The separate bank account helps Taylor keep his financial interest in the business separate from his personal funds.

When a business transaction occurs, it is analyzed to identify how it affects the equation *property equals financial interest.* This equation reflects the fact that in a free enterprise system, all property is owned by someone. In this case Taylor owns the business because he supplied the property (cash).

Use these steps to analyze the effect of a business transaction:

1. Describe the financial event.
   - Identify the property.
   - Identify who owns the property.
   - Determine the amount of increase or decrease.
2. Make sure the equation is in balance.

▶ 1. **OBJECTIVE**

Record in equation form the financial effects of a business transaction.

Property	=	Financial Interest

BUSINESS TRANSACTION

Jason Taylor withdrew $90,000 from personal savings and deposited it in a new checking account in the name of JT's Consulting Services.

ANALYSIS

a. The business received $90,000 of *property* in the form of cash.

b. Taylor had an $90,000 *financial interest* in the business.

Note that the equation *property equals financial interest* remains in balance.

Property		=	Financial Interest
	Cash	=	Jason Taylor, Capital
(a) Invested cash	+**$90,000**		
(b) Increased equity			+**$90,000**
New balances	$90,000	=	$90,000

An owner's financial interest in the business is called **equity**, or **capital**. Jason Taylor has $90,000 equity in JT's Consulting Services.

PURCHASING EQUIPMENT FOR CASH

The first priority for office manager Tennille Brisbane was to get the business ready for opening day on December 1.

BUSINESS TRANSACTION

JT's Consulting Services issued a $10,000 check to purchase a computer and other equipment.

ANALYSIS

c. The firm purchased new property (equipment) for $10,000.

d. The firm paid out $10,000 in cash.

The equation remains in balance.

Property				=	Financial Interest
	Cash	+	Equipment	=	Jason Taylor, Capital
Previous balances	$90,000			=	$90,000
(c) Purchased equipment		+	**$10,000**		
(d) Paid cash	−**10,000**				
New balances	$80,000	+	$10,000	=	$90,000

Notice that there is a change in the composition of the firm's property. Now the firm has cash and equipment. The equation shows that the total value of the property remains the same, $90,000. Jason Taylor's financial interest, or equity, is also unchanged. Note that property (Cash and Equipment) is equal to financial interest (Jason Taylor, Capital).

These activities are recorded for the business entity JT's Consulting Services. Jason Taylor's personal assets, such as his personal bank account, house, furniture, and automobile, are kept separate from the property of the firm. Nonbusiness property is not included in the accounting records of the business entity.

PURCHASING EQUIPMENT ON CREDIT

Brisbane purchased additional office equipment. Office Plus, the store selling the equipment, allows JT's Consulting Services 60 days to pay the bill. This arrangement is called buying **on account** . The business has a *charge account*, or *open-account credit*, with its suppliers. Amounts that a business must pay in the future are known as **accounts payable** . The companies or individuals to whom the amounts are owed are called *creditors*.

BUSINESS TRANSACTION

 *no cash has been paid yet.*

JT's Consulting Services purchased office equipment on account from Office Plus for $12,000.

ANALYSIS

e. The firm purchased new property (equipment) that cost $12,000.
f. The firm owes $12,000 to Office Plus.
The equation remains in balance.

	Property			=	Financial Interest		
	Cash	+	Equipment	=	Accounts Payable	+	Jason Taylor, Capital
Previous balances	$80,000	+	$10,000	=			$90,000
(e) Purchased equip.		+	12,000				
(f) Incurred debt					+$12,000		
New balances	$80,000	+	$22,000	=	$12,000	+	$90,000

Office Plus is willing to accept a claim against JT's Consulting Services until the bill is paid. Now there are two different financial interests or claims against the firm's property—the creditor's claim (Accounts Payable) and the owner's claim (Jason Taylor, Capital). Notice that the total property increases to $102,000. Cash is $80,000 and equipment is $22,000. Jason Taylor, Capital stays the same; but the creditor's claim increases to $12,000. After this transaction is recorded, the left side of the equation still equals the right side.

When Ben Cohen and Jerry Greenfield founded Ben & Jerry's Homemade Ice Cream, Inc., in 1978, they invested $8,000 of their own funds and borrowed funds of $4,000. The equation *property equals financial interest* is expressed as

Property	=	Financial Interest
cash	=	creditors' claims
		+ owners' claims
$12,000	=	$ 4,000
		+ 8,000
		$12,000

PURCHASING SUPPLIES

Brisbane purchased supplies so that JT's Consulting Services could start operations. The company that sold the items requires cash payments from companies that have been in business less than six months.

ABOUT ACCOUNTING

History

For as long as people have been involved in business, there has been a need for accounting. The system of accounting we use is based upon the works of Luca Pacioli, a Franciscan monk in Italy. In 1494, Pacioli wrote about the bookkeeping techniques in practice during his time.

BUSINESS TRANSACTION

JT's Consulting Services issued a check for $3,000 to Office Supplies, Inc. to purchase office supplies.

ANALYSIS

g. The firm purchased office supplies that cost $3,000.

h. The firm paid $3,000 in cash.
The equation remains in balance.

	Property					=	Financial Interest		
	Cash	+	Supplies	+	Equipment	=	Accounts Payable	+	Jason Taylor, Capital
Previous balances	$80,000			+	$22,000	=	$12,000	+	$90,000
(g) Purchased supplies		+	$3,000						
(h) Paid cash	−3,000								
New balances	$77,000	+	$3,000	+	$22,000	=	$12,000	+	$90,000

Notice that total property remains the same, even though the form of the property has changed. Also note that all of the property (left side) equals all of the financial interests (right side).

PAYING A CREDITOR

Brisbane decided to reduce the firm's debt to Office Plus by $5,000.

BUSINESS TRANSACTION

JT's Consulting Services issued a check for $5,000 to Office Plus.

ANALYSIS

i. The firm paid $5,000 in cash.

j. The claim of Office Plus against the firm decreased by $5,000.
The equation remains in balance.

	Property					=	Financial Interest		
	Cash	+	Supplies	+	Equipment	=	Accounts Payable	+	Jason Taylor, Capital
Previous balances	$77,000	+	$3,000	+	$22,000	=	$12,000	+	$90,000
(i) Paid cash	−5,000								
(j) Decreased debt							−5,000		
New balances	$72,000	+	$3,000	+	$22,000	=	$7,000	+	$90,000

RENTING FACILITIES

In November Brisbane arranged to rent facilities for $3,500 per month, beginning in December. The landlord required that rent for the first two months—December and January—be paid in advance. The firm prepaid (paid in advance) the rent for two months. As a result, the firm obtained the right to occupy facilities for a two-month period. In accounting this right is considered a form of property.

BUSINESS TRANSACTION

JT's Consulting Services issued a check for $7,000 to pay for rent for the months of December and January.

ANALYSIS

k. The firm prepaid the rent for the next two months in the amount of $7,000.

l. The firm decreased its cash balance by $7,000.

The equation remains in balance.

	Property						=	Financial Interest		
	Cash	+	Supplies	+	Prepaid Rent	+	Equipment	=	Accounts Payable	+	Jason Taylor, Capital
Previous balances	$72,000	+	$3,000			+	$22,000	=	$7,000	+	$90,000
(k) Paid cash	−7,000										
(l) Prepaid rent					+$7,000						
New balances	$65,000	+	$3,000	+	$7,000	+	$22,000	=	$7,000	+	$90,000

Notice that when property values and financial interests increase or decrease, the total of the items on one side of the equation still equals the total on the other side.

Property		=	Financial Interest	
Cash	$65,000		Accounts Payable	$ 7,000
Supplies	3,000		Jason Taylor, Capital	90,000
Prepaid Rent	7,000			
Equipment	22,000			
Total	$97,000	=	Total	$97,000

> The balance sheet is also called the *statement of financial position*. Caterpillar Inc., reported assets of $36.4 billion, liabilities of $30.4 billion, and owners' equity of $6.0 billion on its statement of financial position at December 31, 2003.

▶ 2. OBJECTIVE
Define, identify, and understand the relationship between asset, liability, and owner's equity accounts.

Assets, Liabilities, and Owner's Equity

Accountants use special accounting terms when they refer to property and financial interests. For example, they refer to the property that a business owns as **assets** and to the debts or obligations of the business as **liabilities** . The owner's financial interest is called **owner's equity** . (Sometimes owner's equity is called *proprietorship* or *net worth*. Owner's equity is the preferred term and is used throughout this book.) At regular intervals Taylor reviews the status of the firm's assets, liabilities, and owner's equity in a financial statement called a **balance sheet** . The balance sheet shows the firm's financial position on a given date. Figure 2.1 shows the firm's balance sheet on November 30, the day before the company opened for business.

JT's Consulting Services
Balance Sheet
November 30, 2007

Assets					Liabilities				
Cash	65	0 0 0	00		Accounts Payable	7	0 0 0	00	
Supplies	3	0 0 0	00						
Prepaid Rent	7	0 0 0	00		Owner's Equity				
Equipment	22	0 0 0	00		Jason Taylor, Capital	90	0 0 0	00	
Total Assets	97	0 0 0	00		Total Liabilities and Owner's Equity	97	0 0 0	00	

FIGURE 2.1   **Balance Sheet for JT's Consulting Services**

The assets are listed on the left side of the balance sheet and the liabilities and owner's equity are on the right side. This arrangement is similar to the equation *property equals financial interest.* Property is shown on the left side of the equation, and financial interest appears on the right side.

The balance sheet in Figure 2.1 shows

- the amount and types of property the business owns,
- the amount owed to creditors,
- the owner's interest.

This statement gives Jason Taylor a complete picture of the financial position of his business on November 30.

Section 1: **Self Review**

QUESTIONS

1. What does the term "accounts payable" mean?
2. What is a business transaction?
3. Describe a transaction that increases an asset and the owner's equity.

EXERCISES

4. Maria Sanchez purchased a computer for $2,500 on account for her business. What is the effect of this transaction?

   a. Cash decrease of $2,500 and owner's equity increase of $2,500.

   b. Equipment increase of $2,500 and cash increase of $2,500.

   c. Equipment decrease of $2,500 and accounts payable increase of $2,500.

   d. Equipment increase of $2,500 and accounts payable increase of $2,500.

5. Carolyn Carter began a new business by depositing $50,000 in the business bank account. She wrote two checks from the business account: $6,000 for office furniture and $2,000 for office supplies. What is her financial interest in the company?

   a. $42,000
   b. $44,000
   c. $48,000
   d. $50,000

ANALYSIS

6. Import Specialty Co. has no liabilities. The asset and owner's equity balances are as follows. What is the balance of "Supplies"?

Cash	$24,000
Office Equipment	$16,000
Supplies	????
Mireya Cortez, Capital	$45,000

(Answers to Section 1 Self Review are on page 53.)

Section 2

The Accounting Equation and Financial Statements

SECTION OBJECTIVES

▶ **3. Analyze the effects of business transactions on a firm's assets, liabilities, and owner's equity and record these effects in accounting equation form.**

WHY IT'S IMPORTANT

Property will always equal financial interest.

▶ **4. Prepare an income statement.**

WHY IT'S IMPORTANT

The income statement shows the results of operations.

▶ **5. Prepare a statement of owner's equity and a balance sheet.**

WHY IT'S IMPORTANT

These financial statements show the financial condition of a business.

TERMS TO LEARN

accounts receivable
break even
expense
fair market value
fundamental accounting equation
income statement
net income
net loss
revenue
statement of owner's equity
withdrawals

The word *balance* in the title "balance sheet" has a special meaning. It emphasizes that the total on the left side of the report must equal, or balance, the total on the right side.

The Fundamental Accounting Equation

In accounting terms the firm's assets must equal the total of its liabilities and owner's equity. This equality can be expressed in equation form, as illustrated here. The amounts are for JT's Consulting Services on November 30.

Assets	=	Liabilities	+	Owner's Equity
$97,000	=	$7,000	+	$90,000

The relationship between assets and liabilities plus owner's equity is called the **fundamental accounting equation**. The entire accounting process of analyzing, recording, and reporting business transactions is based on the fundamental accounting equation.

If any two parts of the equation are known, the third part can be determined. For example, consider the basic accounting equation for JT's Consulting Services on November 30, with some information missing.

	Assets	=	Liabilities	+	Owner's Equity
1.	?	=	$7,000	+	$90,000
2.	$97,000	=	?	+	$90,000
3.	$97,000	=	$7,000	+	?

In the first case, we can solve for assets by adding liabilities to owner's equity ($7,000 + $90,000) to determine that assets are $97,000. In the second case, we can solve for liabilities by subtracting owner's equity from assets ($97,000 − $90,000) to determine that liabilities are $7,000. In the third case, we can solve for owner's equity by subtracting liabilities from assets ($97,000 − $7,000) to determine that owner's equity is $90,000.

▶ **3. OBJECTIVE**

Analyze the effects of business transactions on a firm's assets, liabilities, and owner's equity and record these effects in accounting equation form.

Topic Tackler

PLUS

EARNING REVENUE AND INCURRING EXPENSES

important!
Revenues increase owner's equity.
Expenses decrease owner's equity.

JT's Consulting Services opened for business on December 1. Some of the other businesses in the office complex became the firm's first clients. Taylor also used his contacts in the community to identify other clients. Providing services to clients started a stream of revenue for the business. **Revenue**, or *income,* is the inflow of money or other assets that results from the sales of goods or services or from the use of money or property. A sale on account does not increase money, but it does create a claim to money. When a sale occurs, the revenue increases assets and also increases owner's equity.

An **expense**, on the other hand, involves the outflow of money, the use of other assets, or the incurring of a liability. Expenses include the costs of any materials, labor, supplies, and services used to produce revenue. Expenses cause a decrease in owner's equity.

A firm's accounting records show increases and decreases in assets, liabilities, and owner's equity as well as details of all transactions involving revenue and expenses. Let's use the fundamental accounting equation to show how revenue and expenses affect the business.

SELLING SERVICES FOR CASH

During the month of December, JT's Consulting Services earned a total of $26,000 in revenue from clients who paid cash for accounting and bookkeeping services. This involved several transactions throughout the month. The total effect of these transactions is analyzed below.

ANALYSIS

m. The firm received $26,000 in cash for services provided to clients.

n. Revenues increased by $26,000, which results in a $26,000 increase in owner's equity. The fundamental accounting equation remains in balance.

	Assets						= Liabilities +		Owner's Equity		
	Cash	+ Supplies	+	Prepaid Rent	+ Equipment	=	Accounts Payable	+	Jason Taylor, Capital	+	Revenue
Previous balances	$65,000	+ $3,000	+	$7,000	+ $22,000	=	$7,000	+	$90,000		
(m) Received cash	+26,000										
(n) Increased owner's equity by earning revenue										+	$26,000
New balances	$91,000	+ $3,000	+	$7,000	+ $22,000	=	$7,000	+	$90,000	+	$26,000
				$123,000					$123,000		

Notice that revenue amounts are recorded in a separate column under owner's equity. Keeping revenue separate from the owner's equity will help the firm compute total revenue more easily when the financial statements are prepared.

SELLING SERVICES ON CREDIT

JT's Consulting Services has some charge account clients. These clients are allowed 30 days to pay. Amounts owed by these clients are known as **accounts receivable**. This is a new form of asset for the firm—claims for future collection from customers. During December JT's Consulting Services earned $9,000 of revenue from charge account clients. The effect of these transactions is analyzed on page 32.

ANALYSIS

o. The firm acquired a new asset, accounts receivable, of $9,000.

p. Revenues increased by $9,000, which results in a $9,000 increase in owner's equity. The fundamental accounting equation remains in balance.

▼

	Assets							=	Liab.	+	Owner's Equity		
	Cash	+	Accts. Rec.	+	Supp.	+	Prepaid Rent	+	Equip.	=	Accts. Pay.	+	Jason Taylor, Capital	+	Rev.
Previous balances	$91,000				+ $3,000	+	$7,000	+	$22,000	=	$7,000	+	$90,000	+ $26,000
(o) Received new asset—accts. rec.		+ $9,000												
(p) Increased owner's equity by earning revenue														+ 9,000
New balances	$91,000	+ $9,000	+	$3,000	+	$7,000	+	$22,000	=	$7,000	+	$90,000	+ $35,000

$132,000 $132,000

COLLECTING RECEIVABLES

During December JT's Consulting Services received $4,000 on account from clients who owed money for services previously billed. The effect of these transactions is analyzed below.

ANALYSIS

q. The firm received $4,000 in cash.

r. Accounts receivable decreased by $4,000.

The fundamental accounting equation remains in balance.

▼

	Assets							=	Liab.	+	Owner's Equity		
	Cash	+	Accts. Rec.	+	Supp.	+	Prepaid Rent	+	Equip.	=	Accts. Pay.	+	Jason Taylor, Capital	+	Rev.
Previous balances	$91,000	+ $9,000	+	$3,000	+	$7,000	+	$22,000	=	$7,000	+	$90,000	+ $35,000
(q) Received cash	+4,000													
(r) Decreased accounts receivable		−4,000												
New balances	$95,000	+ $5,000	+	$3,000	+	$7,000	+	$22,000	=	$7,000	+	$90,000	+ $35,000

$132,000 $132,000

In this type of transaction one asset is changed for another asset (accounts receivable for cash). Notice that revenue is not increased when cash is collected from charge account clients. The revenue was recorded when the sale on account took place (see entry (**p**)). Notice that the fundamental business accounting equation, *assets equal liabilities plus owner's equity,* stays in balance regardless of the changes arising from individual transactions.

PAYING EMPLOYEES' SALARIES

So far Taylor has done very well. His equity has increased by the revenues earned. However, running a business costs money, and these expenses reduce owner's equity.

During the first month of operations, JT's Consulting Services hired an accounting clerk. The salaries for the new accounting clerk and the office manager are considered an expense to the firm.

BUSINESS TRANSACTION

In December JT's Consulting Services paid $7,000 in salaries for the accounting clerk and Tennille Brisbane.

ANALYSIS

s. The firm decreased its cash balance by $7,000.

t. The firm paid salaries expense in the amount of $7,000, which decreased owner's equity.

The fundamental accounting equation remains in balance.

	Assets					=	Liab.	+	Owner's Equity		
	Cash +	Accts. Rec. +	Supp. +	Prepaid Rent +	Equip. =		Accts. Pay. +	J. Taylor, Capital +	Rev.	−	Exp.
Previous balances	$95,000 +	$5,000 +	$3,000 +	$7,000 +	$22,000 =		$7,000 +	$90,000 +	$35,000		
(s) Paid cash	−7,000										
(t) Decreased owner's equity by incurring salaries exp.											− $7,000
New balances	$88,000 +	$5,000 +	$3,000 +	$7,000 +	$22,000 =		$7,000 +	$90,000 +	$35,000	−	$7,000
			$125,000						$125,000		

Notice that expenses are recorded in a separate column under owner's equity. The separate record of expenses is kept for the same reason that the separate record of revenue is kept—to analyze operations for the period.

PAYING UTILITIES EXPENSE

At the end of December, the firm received a $500 utilities bill.

BUSINESS TRANSACTION

JT's Consulting Services issued a check for $500 to pay the utilities bill.

ANALYSIS

u. The firm decreased its cash balance by $500.

v. The firm paid utilities expense of $500, which decreased owner's equity.

The fundamental accounting equation remains in balance.

	Assets					=	Liab. +		Owner's Equity		
	Cash +	Accts. Rec. +	Supp. +	Prepaid Rent +	Equip. =		Accts. Pay. +	J. Taylor, Capital +		Rev. −	Exp.
Previous balances	$88,000 +	$5,000 +	$3,000 +	$7,000 +	$22,000 =		$7,000 +	$90,000 +		$35,000 −	$7,000
(u) Paid cash	−500										
(v) Decreased owner's equity by utilities exp.											+500
New balances	$87,500 +	$5,000 +	$3,000 +	$7,000 +	$22,000 =		$7,000 +	$90,000 +		$35,000 −	$7,500

$124,500 $124,500

EFFECT OF OWNER'S WITHDRAWALS

On December 30, Taylor withdrew $4,000 in cash for personal expenses. **Withdrawals** are funds taken from the business by the owner for personal use. Withdrawals are not a business expense but a decrease in the owner's equity.

BUSINESS TRANSACTION

Jason Taylor wrote a check to withdraw $4,000 cash for personal use.

ANALYSIS
w. The firm decreased its cash balance by $4,000.
x. Owner's equity decreased by $4,000.
The fundamental accounting equation remains in balance.

	Assets					=	Liab. +		Owner's Equity		
	Cash +	Accts. Rec. +	Supp. +	Prepaid Rent +	Equip. =		Accts. Pay. +	J. Taylor, Capital +		Rev. −	Exp.
Previous balances	$87,500 +	$5,000 +	$3,000 +	$7,000 +	$22,000 =		$7,000 +	$90,000 +		$35,000 −	$7,500
(w) Withdrew cash	−4,000										
(x) Decreased owner's equity								−4,000			
New balances	$83,500 +	$5,000 +	$3,000 +	$7,000 +	$22,000 =		$7,000 +	$86,000 +		$35,000 −	$7,500

$120,500 $120,500

SUMMARY OF TRANSACTIONS

Figure 2.2 on page 35 summarizes the transactions of JT's Consulting Services through December 31. Notice that after each transaction, the fundamental accounting equation is in balance. Test your understanding by describing the nature of each transaction. Then check your results by referring to the discussion of each transaction.

	Cash	+	Accts. Rec.	+	Supp.	+	Prepaid Rent	+	Equip.	=	Accts. Pay.	+	J. Taylor, Capital	+	Rev.	−	Exp.
(a) & (b)	+90,000												+ 90,000				
Balances	90,000									=			90,000				
(c) & (d)	−10,000						+ 10,000										
Balances	80,000						+ 10,000			=			90,000				
(e) & (f)									+ 12,000		+ 12,000						
Balances	80,000								+ 22,000	=	12,000	+	90,000				
(g) & (h)	−3,000				+ 3,000												
Balances	77,000				+ 3,000				+ 22,000	=	12,000	+	90,000				
(i) & (j)	−5,000										−5,000						
Balances	72,000				+ 3,000				+ 22,000	=	7,000	+	90,000				
(k) & (l)	−7,000						+ 7,000										
Balances	65,000				+ 3,000	+	7,000	+	22,000	=	7,000	+	90,000				
(m) & (n)	+26,000													+	26,000		
Balances	91,000				+ 3,000	+	7,000	+	22,000	=	7,000	+	90,000	+	26,000		
(o) & (p)		+	9,000											+	9,000		
Balances	91,000	+	9,000	+	3,000	+	7,000	+	22,000	=	7,000	+	90,000	+	35,000		
(q) & (r)	+4000	−	4,000														
Balances	95,000	+	5,000	+	3,000	+	7,000	+	22,000	=	7,000	+	90,000	+	35,000		
(s) & (t)	−7,000															−	7,000
Balances	88,000	+	5,000	+	3,000	+	7,000	+	22,000	=	7,000	+	90,000	+	35,000	−	7,000
(u) & (v)	−500															+	500
Balances	87,500	+	5,000	+	3,000	+	7,000	+	22,000	=	7,000	+	90,000	+	35,000	−	7,500
(w) & (x)	−4,000												− 4,000				
Balances	$83,500	+	$5,000	+	$3,000	+	$7,000	+	$22,000	=	$7,000	+	$86,000	+	$35,000	−	$7,500

Assets = $120,500   Liab. + Owner's Equity = $120,500

FIGURE 2.2   Transactions of JT's Consulting Services Through December 31, 2007

The Income Statement

To be meaningful to owners, managers, and other interested parties, financial statements should provide information about revenue and expenses, assets and claims on the assets, and owner's equity.

The **income statement** shows the results of business operations for a specific period of time such as a month, a quarter, or a year. The income statement shows the revenue earned and the expenses of doing business. (The income statement is sometimes called a *profit and loss statement* or a *statement of income and expenses*. The most common term, income statement, is used throughout this text.) Figure 2.3 shows the income statement for JT's Consulting Services for its first month of operation.

▶ **4. OBJECTIVE**
Prepare an income statement.

FIGURE 2.3

Income Statement for JT's
Consulting Services

JT's Consulting Services
Income Statement
Month Ended December 31, 2007

Revenue			
Fees Income			3 5 0 0 0 00
Expenses			
Salaries Expense	7 0 0 0 00		
Utilities Expense	5 0 0 00		
Total Expenses		7 5 0 0 00	
Net Income		2 7 5 0 0 00	

recall

Financial Statements
Financial statements are
reports that summarize a
firm's financial affairs.

The income statement shows the difference between income from services provided or goods sold and the amount spent to operate the business. **Net income** results when revenue is greater than the expenses for the period. When expenses are greater than revenue, the result is a **net loss**. In the rare case when revenue and expenses are equal, the firm is said to **break even**. The income statement in Figure 2.3 shows a net income; revenue is greater than expenses.

The three-line heading of the income statement shows *who, what,* and *when.*

- Who—the business name appears on the first line.
- What—the report title appears on the second line.
- When—the period covered appears on the third line.

The third line of the income statement heading in Figure 2.3 indicates that the report covers operations for the "Month Ended December 31, 2007." Review how other time periods are reported on the third line of the income statement heading.

Period Covered	Third Line of Heading
Jan., Feb., Mar.	Three-Month Period Ended March 31, 2007
Jan. to Dec.	Year Ended December 31, 2007
July 1 to June 30	Fiscal Year Ended June 30, 2007

Note the use of single and double rules in amount columns. A single line is used to show that the amounts above it are being added or subtracted. Double lines are used under the final amount in a column or section of a report to show that the amount is complete. Nothing is added to or subtracted from an amount with a double line.

> Some companies refer to the income statement as the *statement of operations*. American Eagle Outfitters, Inc. reported $1.5 billion in sales on consolidated statements of operations for the fiscal year ended January 29, 2004. American Eagle Outfitters, Inc. was ranked as the sixteenth fastest-growing company in the United States by *Fortune* magazine in September 2000.

The income statement for JT's Consulting Services does not have dollar signs because it was prepared on accounting paper with ruled columns. However, dollar signs are used on income statements that are prepared on plain paper, that is, not on a ruled form.

The Statement of Owner's Equity and the Balance Sheet

▶ **5. OBJECTIVE**
Prepare a statement of owner's equity and a balance sheet.

The **statement of owner's equity** reports the changes that occurred in the owner's financial interest during the reporting period. This statement is prepared before the balance sheet so that the amount of the ending capital balance is available for presentation on the balance sheet. Figure 2.4 on page 38 shows the statement of owner's equity for JT's Consulting Services. Note that the statement of owner's equity has a three-line heading: *who, what,* and *when.*

- The first line of the statement of owner's equity is the capital balance at the beginning of the period.
- Net income is an increase to owner's equity; net loss is a decrease to owner's equity.
- Withdrawals by the owner are a decrease to owner's equity.
- Additional investments by the owners are an increase to owner's equity.
- The total of changes in equity is reported on the line "Increase in Capital" (or "Decrease in Capital").
- The last line of the statement of owner's equity is the capital balance at the end of the period.

International INSIGHTS

Business Etiquette

In Japan, business cards are always offered with two hands. The receiver should accept the card with two hands, study it, and bow slightly before placing it into a shirt or jacket pocket. Placing the card near the heart shows respect for both the person and the company.

ACCOUNTING ON THE JOB «

HOSPITALITY AND TOURISM

Industry Overview

Hospitality is the world's largest industry, accounting for more jobs, sales, and tax revenue than any other industry. The hospitality industry, also known as the travel or tourism industry, is composed of hotels, restaurants, institutional food service, cruise lines, arenas, travel agencies, meeting and convention centers, sport complexes, resorts, parks, clubs, spas, and tourism-related transportation. In the United States, the hospitality industry's employment growth is twice that of any other industry. Hospitality is forecasted to become the nation's largest industry by the year 2010.

Career Opportunities

- State Tourism Bureau Director
- Director of Resort Contracts and Purchasing
- Executive Chef
- Travel Technology Specialist
- Tour Promotions Manager
- Vice President of Hotel Operations
- Airport Passenger Services Supervisor
- Catering Director

Preparing for a Hospitality and Tourism Career

- Gain expertise in database administration or programming. Hotels, spas, golf courses, and airlines use sophisticated computerized systems to track reservations and memberships.
- Obtain an associate's or bachelor's degree in hotel, restaurant, and institutional management or a degree in hospitality and tourism management. Core course requirements include database management, electronic spreadsheets, and accounting.
- Enroll in an advanced internship program. The Disney College Program offers specialties in marketing, hotel management, finance, and communications. Marriott International offers paid internships from 8 to 16 weeks in duration. Opportunities exist in accounting and finance, catering, front office, human resources, sales, and culinary arts.
- Receive training on the latest Worldspan computer reservation system developed by Delta, TWA, and Northwest Airlines.

THINKING CRITICALLY

What skills and education might be required for the position of hotel general manager with a major hotel chain such as Marriott International?

INTERNET APPLICATION

Visit the Web site of a trade organization such as the Travel Industry Association of America to learn about potential career paths within the industry. Describe the purpose of the association. What resources are offered on the site?

FIGURE 2.4

Statement of Owner's Equity for JT's Consulting Services

JT's Consulting Services
Statement of Owner's Equity
Month Ended December 31, 2007

Jason Taylor, Capital, December 1, 2007			90000 00
Net Income for December	27500 00		
Less Withdrawals for December	4000 00		
Increase in Capital		23500 00	
Jason Taylor, Capital, December 31, 2007		113500 00	

If Jason Taylor had made any additional investments during December, this would appear as a separate line on Figure 2.4. Additional investments can be cash or other assets such as equipment. If an investment is made in a form other than cash, the investment is recorded at its fair market value. **Fair market value** is the current worth of an asset or the price the asset would bring if sold on the open market.

The ending balances in the asset and liability accounts are used to prepare the balance sheet.

	Assets					=	Liab.	+	Owner's Equity		
	Cash +	Accts. Rec. +	Supp. +	Prepaid Rent +	Equip. =		Accts. Pay. +	J. Taylor, Capital +	Rev. −	Exp.	
New balances	$83,500 +	$5,000 +	$3,000 +	$7,000 +	$22,000 =		$7,000 +	$86,000 +	$35,000 −	$7,500	
			$120,500						$120,500		

The ending capital balance from the statement of owner's equity is also used to prepare the balance sheet. Figure 2.5 on page 39 shows the balance sheet for JT's Consulting Services on December 31, 2007.

The balance sheet shows

- Assets—the types and amounts of property that the business owns,
- Liabilities—the amounts owed to creditors,
- Owner's Equity—the owner's equity on the reporting date.

In preparing a balance sheet, remember the following.

- The three-line heading gives the firm's name (who), the title of the report (what), and the date of the report (when).
- Balance sheets prepared using the account form (as in Figure 2.5) show total assets on the same horizontal line as the total liabilities and owner's equity.
- Dollar signs are omitted when financial statements are prepared on paper with ruled columns. Statements that are prepared on plain paper, not ruled forms, show dollar signs with the first amount in each column and with each total.
- A single line shows that the amounts above it are being added or subtracted. Double lines indicate that the amount is the final amount in a column or section of a report.

Figure 2.6 on page 39 shows the connections among the financial statements. Financial statements are prepared in a specific order:

- income statement
- statement of owner's equity
- balance sheet

important!

Financial Statements
The balance sheet is a snapshot of the firm's financial position on a specific date. The income statement, like a movie or video, shows the results of business operations over a period of time.

JT's Consulting Services
Balance Sheet
December 31, 2007

Assets					Liabilities				
Cash	8	3 5 0 0	00		Accounts Payable		7 0 0 0	00	
Accounts Receivables		5 0 0 0	00						
Supplies		3 0 0 0	00						
Prepaid Rent		7 0 0 0	00		Owner's Equity				
Equipment	2 2	0 0 0	00		Jason Taylor, Capital	1 1 3	5 0 0	00	
Total Assets	1 2 0	5 0 0 0 0			Total Liabilities and Owner's Equity	1 2 0	5 0 0	00	

FIGURE 2.5   Balance Sheet for JT's Consulting Services

Step 1: Prepare the Income Statement

JT's Consulting Services
Income Statement
Month Ended December 31, 2007

Revenue							
Fees Income					3 5 0 0 0	00	
Expenses							
Salaries Expense	7 0 0 0	00					
Utilities Expense	5 0 0	00					
Total Expenses					7 5 0 0	00	
Net Income					2 7 5 0 0	00	

Step 2: Prepare the Statement of Owner's Equity

JT's Consulting Services
Statement of Owner's Equity
Month Ended December 31, 2007

Jason Taylor, Capital, December 1, 2007					9 0 0 0 0	00	
Net Income for December	2 7 5 0 0	00					
Less Withdrawals for December	4 0 0 0	00					
Increase in Capital					2 3 5 0 0	00	
Jason Taylor, Capital, December 31, 2007					1 1 3 5 0 0	00	

Step 3: Prepare the Balance Sheet

FIGURE 2.6

Process for Preparing Financial Statements

Net income (or loss) is transferred to the statement of owner's equity.

The ending capital balance is transferred to the balance sheet.

JT's Consulting Services
Balance Sheet
December 31, 2007

Assets					Liabilities				
Cash	8	3 5 0 0	00		Accounts Payable		7 0 0 0	00	
Accounts Receivables		5 0 0 0	00						
Supplies		3 0 0 0	00						
Prepaid Rent		7 0 0 0	00		Owner's Equity				
Equipment	2 2	0 0 0	00		Jason Taylor, Capital	1 1 3	5 0 0	00	
Total Assets	1 2 0	5 0 0 0 0			Total Liabilities and Owner's Equity	1 2 0	5 0 0	00	

MANAGERIAL IMPLICATIONS

ACCOUNTING SYSTEMS

- Sound financial records and statements are necessary so that businesspeople can make good decisions.
- Financial statements show
  - the amount of profit or loss,
  - the assets on hand,
  - the amount owed to creditors,
  - the amount of owner's equity.
- Well-run and efficiently managed businesses have good accounting systems that provide timely and useful information.
- Transactions involving revenue and expenses are recorded separately from owner's equity in order to analyze operations for the period.

THINKING CRITICALLY

If you were buying a business, what would you look for in the company's financial statements?

Net income from the income statement is used to prepare the statement of owner's equity. The ending capital balance from the statement of owner's equity is used to prepare the balance sheet.

The Importance of Financial Statements

Preparing financial statements is one of the accountant's most important jobs. Each day millions of business decisions are made based on the information in financial statements.

Business managers and owners use the balance sheet and the income statement to control current operations and plan for the future. Creditors, prospective investors, governmental agencies, and others are interested in the profits of the business and in the asset and equity structure.

Section 2: **Self Review**

QUESTIONS

1. What information is included in the financial statement headings?

2. What are withdrawals and how do they affect the basic accounting equation?

3. If an owner gives personal tools to the business, how is the transaction recorded?

EXERCISES

4. What information is contained on the income statement?

   a. revenues and expenses for a period of time

   b. revenue and expenses on a specific date

   c. assets, liabilities, and owner's equity for a period of time

   d. assets, liabilities, and owner's equity on a specific date

5. Caldwell Interior Designs has assets of $80,000 and liabilities of $25,000. What is the owner's equity?

   a. $55,000   **c.** $25,000

   b. $80,000   **d.** $15,000

ANALYSIS

6. Nelson Hardware had revenues of $45,000 and expenses of $23,000. How does this affect owner's equity?

(Answers to Section 2 Self Review are on page 53.)

REVIEW   Chapter Summary

Accounting begins with the analysis of business transactions. Each transaction changes the financial position of a business. In this chapter, you have learned how to analyze business transactions and how they affect assets, liabilities, and owner's equity. After transactions are analyzed and recorded, financial statements reflect the summarized changes to and results of business operations.

Learning Objectives

1 Record in equation form the financial effects of a business transaction.

The equation *property equals financial interest* reflects the fact that in a free enterprise system all property is owned by someone. This equation remains in balance after each business transaction.

2 Define, identify, and understand the relationship between asset, liability, and owner's equity accounts.

The term *assets* refers to property. The terms *liabilities* and *owner's equity* refer to financial interest. The relationship between assets, liabilities, and owner's equity is shown in equation form.

Assets	=	Liabilities	+	Owner's Equity
Owner's Equity	=	Assets	−	Liabilities
Liabilities	=	Assets	−	Owner's Equity

3 Analyze the effects of business transactions on a firm's assets, liabilities, and owner's equity and record these effects in accounting equation form.

1. Describe the financial event.
   - Identify the property.
   - Identify who owns the property.
   - Determine the amount of the increase or decrease.
2. Make sure the equation is in balance.

4 Prepare an income statement.

The income statement summarizes changes in owner's equity that result from revenue and expenses. The difference between revenue and expenses is the net income or net loss of the business for the period.

An income statement has a three-line heading:
- who
- what
- when

For the income statement, "when" refers to a period of time.

5 Prepare a statement of owner's equity and a balance sheet.

Changes in owner's equity for the period are summarized on the statement of owner's equity.
- Net income increases owner's equity.
- Added investments increase owner's equity.
- A net loss for the period decreases owner's equity.
- Withdrawals by the owner decrease owner's equity.

A statement of owner's equity has a three-line heading:
- who
- what
- when

For the statement of owner's equity, "when" refers to a period of time.

The balance sheet shows the assets, liabilities, and owner's equity on a given date.

A balance sheet has a three-line heading:
- who
- what
- when

For the balance sheet, "when" refers to a single date.

The financial statements are prepared in the following order.

1. Income Statement
2. Statement of Owner's Equity
3. Balance Sheet

6 Define the accounting terms new to this chapter.

Glossary

Accounts payable (p. 26) Amounts a business must pay in the future

Accounts receivable (p. 31) Claims for future collection from customers

Assets (p. 28) Property owned by a business

Balance sheet (p. 28) A formal report of a business's financial condition on a certain date; reports the assets, liabilities, and owner's equity of the business

Break even (p. 36) A point at which revenue equals expenses

Business transaction (p. 24) A financial event that changes the resources of a firm

Capital (p. 25) Financial investment in a business; equity

Equity (p. 25) An owner's financial interest in a business

Expense (p. 31) An outflow of cash, use of other assets, or incurring of a liability

Fair market value (p. 38) The current worth of an asset or the price the asset would bring if sold on the open market

Fundamental accounting equation (p. 30) The relationship between assets and liabilities plus owner's equity

Income statement (p. 35) A formal report of business operations covering a specific period of time; also called a profit and loss statement or a statement of income and expenses

Liabilities (p. 28) Debts or obligations of a business

Net income (p. 36) The result of an excess of revenue over expenses

Net loss (p. 36) The result of an excess of expenses over revenue

On account (p. 26) An arrangement to allow payment at a later date; also called a charge account or open-account credit

Owner's equity (p. 28) The financial interest of the owner of a business; also called proprietorship or net worth

Revenue (p. 31) An inflow of money or other assets that results from the sales of goods or services or from the use of money or property; also called income

Statement of owner's equity (p. 37) A formal report of changes that occurred in the owner's financial interest during a reporting period

Withdrawals (p. 34) Funds taken from the business by the owner for personal use

Comprehensive **Self Review**

1. If one side of the fundamental accounting equation is decreased, what will happen to the other side? Why?

2. What effect do revenue and expenses have on owner's equity?

3. What is the difference between buying for cash and buying on account?

4. In what order are the financial statements prepared? Why?

5. Describe a transaction that will cause Accounts Payable and Cash to decrease by $500.

(Answers to Comprehensive Self Review are on page 53.)

Discussion Questions

1. Describe the effects of each of the following business transactions on assets, liabilities, and owner's equity.

   a. Bought equipment on credit.

b. Paid salaries to employees.

c. Sold services for cash.

d. Paid cash to a creditor.

e. Bought furniture for cash.

f. Sold services on credit.

2. What information does the income statement contain?

3. How is net income determined?

4. What information is shown in the heading of a financial statement?

5. Why does the third line of the headings differ on the balance sheet and the income statement?

6. What information does the statement of owner's equity contain?

7. How does net income affect owner's equity?

8. What are assets, liabilities, and owner's equity?

9. What information does the balance sheet contain?

10. What is the fundamental accounting equation?

11. What is revenue?

12. What are expenses?

APPLICATIONS

Exercises

Completing the accounting equation.

The fundamental accounting equation for several businesses follows. Supply the missing amounts.

◀ **Exercise 2.1**
Objective 1, 2

Assets	=	Liabilities	+	Owner's Equity
1. $48,500	=	$9,750	+	$?
2. $39,400	=	$8,850	+	$?
3. $24,900	=	$?	+	$19,900
4. $?	=	$1,875	+	$15,750
5. $15,650	=	$?	+	$11,475

Determining accounting equation amounts.

Just before Carter Laboratories opened for business, Tracy Lynn, the owner, had the following assets and liabilities. Determine the totals that would appear in the firm's fundamental accounting equation (Assets = Liabilities + Owner's Equity).

◀ **Exercise 2.2**
Objectives 1, 2

Cash	$18,100
Laboratory Equipment	40,500
Laboratory Supplies	2,750
Loan Payable	6,900
Accounts Payable	4,475

Exercise 2.3

Objectives 1, 2, 3

▶ **Determining balance sheet amounts.**

The following financial data is for the dental practice of Dr. Donna Wells when she began operations in July. Determine the amounts that would appear in Dr. Wells's balance sheet.

1. Owes $9,500 to the Jones Equipment Company.
2. Has cash balance of $3,250.
3. Has dental supplies of $1,470.
4. Owes $1,675 to Ace Furniture Supply.
5. Has dental equipment of $12,900.
6. Has office furniture of $2,750.

Exercise 2.4

Objectives 1, 2, 3

▶ **Determining the effects of transactions on the accounting equation.**

Indicate the impact of each of the transactions below on the fundamental accounting equation (Assets = Liabilities + Owner's Equity) by placing a "+" to indicate an increase and a "−" to indicate a decrease. The first transaction is entered as an example.

	Assets	=	Liabilities	+	Owner's Equity
Transaction 1	+				+

TRANSACTIONS

1. Owner invested $30,000 in the business.
2. Purchased $12,000 supplies on account.
3. Purchased equipment for $9,500 cash.
4. Paid $1,500 for rent (in advance).
5. Performed services for $3,200 cash.
6. Paid $525 for utilities.
7. Performed services for $4,100 on account.
8. Received $1,650 from charge customers.
9. Paid salaries of $2,700 to employees.
10. Paid $2,000 to a creditor on account.

Exercise 2.5

Objectives 1, 2, 3

▶ **Determining the effects of transactions on the accounting equation.**

EZ Quick Copy had the transactions listed below during the month of April. Show how each transaction would be recorded in the accounting equation. Compute the totals at the end of the month. The headings to be used in the equation follow.

Assets			=	Liabilities	+	Owner's Equity			
Cash +	Accounts Receivable +	Equipment	=	Accounts Payable	+	Inez Owens, Capital	+	Revenue	− Expenses

TRANSACTIONS

1. Inez Owens started the business with a cash investment of $25,000.
2. Purchased equipment for $8,500 on credit.
3. Performed services for $1,050 in cash.
4. Purchased additional equipment for $1,800 in cash.
5. Performed services for $2,275 on credit.
6. Paid salaries of $1,975 to employees.
7. Received $1,100 cash from charge account customers.
8. Paid $4,500 to a creditor on account.

Identifying transactions.

◀ **Exercise 2.6**
Objectives 1, 2, 3

The following equation shows the effects of a number of transactions that took place at Maple Street Auto Repair Company during the month of August. Describe each transaction.

		Assets			=	Liabilities +		Owner's Equity			
	Cash +	Accounts Receivable +	Equipment =			Accounts Payable +	Inez Owens, Capital +		Revenue	–	Expenses
Bal.	$40,000 +	$3,000 +	$32,000 =			$19,000 +	$56,000 +		0	–	0
1.	+5,000								+$5,000		
2.	−3,800		+3,800								
3.	−1,900					−1,900					
4.	−3,350										−$3,350
5.	+750	−750									
6.		+6,000							+6,000		
7.	−2,050										−2,050

Computing net income or net loss.

◀ **Exercise 2.7**
Objective 4

Flores Computer Maintenance and Repair Shop had the following revenue and expenses during the month ended June 30. Did the firm earn a net income or incur a net loss for the period? What was the amount?

Fees for computer repairs	$19,800
Advertising expense	2,650
Salaries expense	9,050
Telephone expense	325
Fees for printer repairs	2,775
Utilities expense	550

Computing net income or net loss.

◀ **Exercise 2.8**
Objective 4

On December 1 Rosa Vasquez opened a speech and hearing clinic. During December her firm had the following transactions involving revenue and expenses. Did the firm earn a net income or incur a net loss for the period? What was the amount?

Paid $1,300 for advertising.

Provided services for $1,150 in cash.

Paid $350 for telephone service.

Paid salaries of $1,050 to employees.

Provided services for $1,250 on credit.

Paid $175 for office cleaning service.

Preparing an income statement.

◀ **Exercise 2.9**
Objective 4

At the beginning of September, Stanley Neal started Neal's Investment Services, a firm that offers advice about investing and managing money. On September 30, the accounting records of the business showed the following information. Prepare an income statement for the month of September 2007.

Cash	$16,050	Fees Income	$36,400
Accounts Receivable	1,500	Advertising Expense	2,750
Office Supplies	1,200	Salaries Expense	7,500
Office Equipment	18,250	Telephone Expense	350
Accounts Payable	2,350	Withdrawals	4,000
Stanley Neal, Capital, September 1, 2007	12,850		

CHAPTER 2: Review and Applications

Exercise 2.10

Objective 5

CONTINUING >>>
Problem

▶ **Preparing a statement of owner's equity and a balance sheet.**

Using the information provided in Exercise 2.9, prepare a statement of owner's equity and a balance sheet for Neal's Investment Services as of September 30, 2007.

PROBLEMS

 ## Problem Set A

Problem 2.1A

Objectives 1, 2, 3

▶ **Analyzing the effects of transactions on the accounting equation.**

On July 1, James Taylor established Home Appraisal Services, a firm that provides expert residential appraisals and represents clients in home appraisal hearings.

INSTRUCTIONS

Analyze the following transactions. Record in equation form the changes that occur in assets, liabilities, and owner's equity. (Use plus, minus, and equals signs.)

TRANSACTIONS

1. The owner invested $46,000 in cash to begin the business.
2. Paid $9,375 in cash for the purchase of equipment.
3. Purchased additional equipment for $6,200 on credit.
4. Paid $5,400 in cash to creditors.
5. The owner made an additional investment of $12,500 in cash.
6. Performed services for $3,600 in cash.
7. Performed services for $2,150 on account.
8. Paid $1,500 for rent expense.
9. Received $1,250 in cash from credit clients.
10. Paid $2,730 in cash for office supplies.
11. The owner withdrew $4,000 in cash for personal expenses.

Analyze: What is the ending balance of cash after all transactions have been recorded?

Problem 2.2A

Objectives 1, 2, 3

▶ **Analyzing the effects of transactions on the accounting equation.**

Scott Davis is a painting contractor who specializes in painting commercial buildings. At the beginning of June, his firm's financial records showed the following assets, liabilities, and owner's equity.

Cash	$15,880	Accounts Payable	$4,100
Accounts Receivable	7,200	Scott Davis, Capital	50,850
Office Furniture	16,900	Revenue	21,390
Auto	27,050	Expenses	9,310

INSTRUCTIONS

Set up an accounting equation using the balances given above. Record the effects of the following transactions in the equation. (Use plus, minus, and equals signs.) Record new balances after each transaction has been entered. Prove the equality of the two sides of the final equation on a separate sheet of paper.

TRANSACTIONS

1. Performed services for $2,675 on credit.
2. Paid $600 in cash for a new office chair.

3. Received $2,800 in cash from credit clients.

4. Paid $320 in cash for telephone service.

5. Sent a check for $750 in partial payment of the amount due creditors.

6. Paid salaries of $3,900 in cash.

7. Sent a check for $350 to pay electric bill.

8. Performed services for $4,850 in cash.

9. Paid $920 in cash for auto repairs.

10. Performed services for $4,450 on account.

Analyze: What is the amount of total assets after all transactions have been recorded?

Preparing a balance sheet.

Rodriguez's Equipment Repair Service is owned by Jorge Rodriguez.

◀ **Problem 2.3A**
Objective 5
eXcel

INSTRUCTIONS

Use the following figures to prepare a balance sheet dated February 28, 2007. (You will need to compute the owner's equity.)

Cash	$16,650	Equipment	$38,500
Supplies	2,690	Accounts Payable	11,500
Accounts Receivable	6,100		

Analyze: What is the net worth, or owner's equity, at February 28, 2007 for Rodriguez's Equipment Repair Service?

Preparing an income statement, a statement of owner's equity, and a balance sheet.

◀ **Problem 2.4A**
Objectives 4, 5
eXcel

The following equation shows the transactions of Cotton Cleaning Service during March. The business is owned by Jerry Cotton.

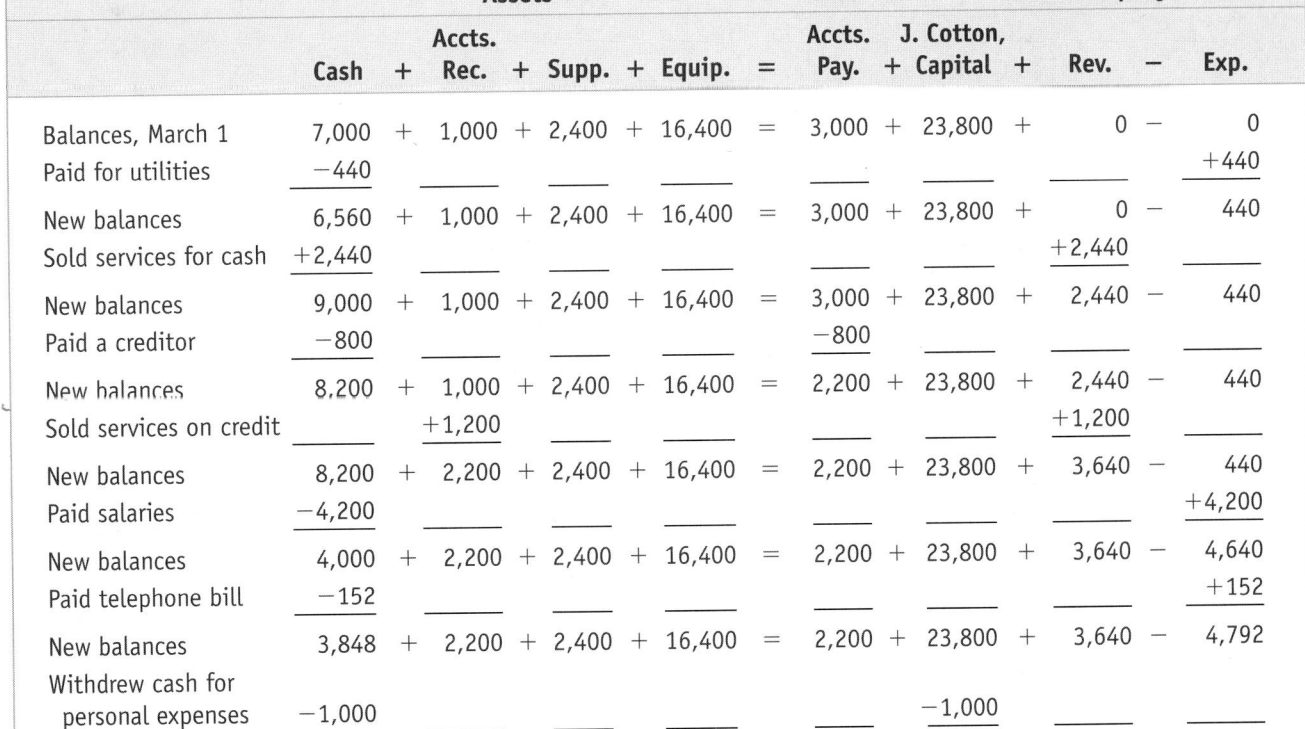

	Assets				=	Liab. +		Owner's Equity		
	Cash	+ Accts. Rec.	+ Supp.	+ Equip.	=	Accts. Pay.	+ J. Cotton, Capital	+ Rev.	−	Exp.
Balances, March 1	7,000	+ 1,000	+ 2,400	+ 16,400	=	3,000	+ 23,800	+ 0	−	0
Paid for utilities	−440									+440
New balances	6,560	+ 1,000	+ 2,400	+ 16,400	=	3,000	+ 23,800	+ 0	−	440
Sold services for cash	+2,440							+2,440		
New balances	9,000	+ 1,000	+ 2,400	+ 16,400	=	3,000	+ 23,800	+ 2,440	−	440
Paid a creditor	−800					−800				
New balances	8,200	+ 1,000	+ 2,400	+ 16,400	=	2,200	+ 23,800	+ 2,440	−	440
Sold services on credit		+1,200						+1,200		
New balances	8,200	+ 2,200	+ 2,400	+ 16,400	=	2,200	+ 23,800	+ 3,640	−	440
Paid salaries	−4,200									+4,200
New balances	4,000	+ 2,200	+ 2,400	+ 16,400	=	2,200	+ 23,800	+ 3,640	−	4,640
Paid telephone bill	−152									+152
New balances	3,848	+ 2,200	+ 2,400	+ 16,400	=	2,200	+ 23,800	+ 3,640	−	4,792
Withdrew cash for personal expenses	−1,000						−1,000			
New balances	2,848	+ 2,200	+ 2,400	+ 16,400	=	2,200	+ 22,800	+ 3,640	−	4,792

INSTRUCTIONS

Analyze each transaction carefully. Prepare an income statement and a statement of owner's equity for the month. Prepare a balance sheet for March 31, 2007. List the expenses in detail on the income statement.

Analyze: In order to complete the balance sheet, which amount was transferred from the statement of owner's equity?

Problem Set B

Problem 2.1B
Objectives 1, 2, 3

▶ **Analyzing the effects of transactions on the accounting equation.**

On September 1, Mireya Cortez opened Self Images Tutoring Service.

INSTRUCTIONS

Analyze the following transactions. Use the fundamental accounting equation form to record the changes in property, claims of creditors, and owner's equity. (Use plus, minus, and equals signs.)

TRANSACTIONS

1. The owner invested $9,000 in cash to begin the business.
2. Purchased equipment for $4,000 in cash.
3. Purchased $1,500 of additional equipment on credit.
4. Paid $750 in cash to creditors.
5. The owner made an additional investment of $1,500 in cash.
6. Performed services for $1,080 in cash.
7. Performed services for $780 on account.
8. Paid $650 for rent expense.
9. Received $550 in cash from credit clients.
10. Paid $775 in cash for office supplies.
11. The owner withdrew $1,000 in cash for personal expenses.

Analyze: Which transactions increased the company's debt? By what amount?

Problem 2.2B
Objectives 1, 2, 3

▶ **Analyzing the effects of transactions on the accounting equation.**

Sherrye Cravens owns Cravens' Consulting Service. At the beginning of September, her firm's financial records showed the following assets, liabilities, and owner's equity.

Cash	$9,500	Accounts Payable	$2,500
Accounts Receivable	3,000	Sherrye Cravens, Capital	12,450
Supplies	3,200	Revenue	13,000
Office Furniture	6,000	Expenses	6,250

INSTRUCTIONS

Set up an equation using the balances given above. Record the effects of the following transactions in the equation. (Use plus, minus, and equals signs.) Record new balances after each transaction has been entered. Prove the equality of the two sides of the final equation on a separate sheet of paper.

TRANSACTIONS

1. Performed services for $2,000 on credit.
2. Paid $720 in cash for utilities.
3. Performed services for $2,500 in cash.

4. Paid $400 in cash for office cleaning service.

5. Sent a check for $1,200 to a creditor.

6. Paid $480 in cash for the telephone bill.

7. Issued checks for $3,500 to pay salaries.

8. Performed services for $2,800 in cash.

9. Purchased additional supplies for $500 on credit.

10. Received $1,500 in cash from credit clients.

Analyze: What is the ending balance for owner's equity after all transactions have been recorded?

Preparing a balance sheet.

◀ **Problem 2.3B**
Objective 5

Samuel Hawkins is opening a tax preparation service on December 1, which will be called Hawkins' Tax Service. Samuel plans to open the business by depositing $12,000 cash into a business checking account. The following assets will also be owned by the business: furniture (fair market value of $4,000), and a computer and printer (fair market value of $4,800). There are no outstanding debts of the business as it is formed.

INSTRUCTIONS

Prepare a balance sheet for December 1, 2007, for Hawkins' Tax Service by entering the correct balances in the appropriate accounts. (You will need to use the accounting equation to compute owner's equity.)

Analyze: If Hawkins' Tax Service had an outstanding debt of $4,000 when the business was formed, what amount should be reported on the balance sheet for owner's equity?

Preparing an income statement, a statement of owner's equity, and a balance sheet.

◀ **Problem 2.4B**
Objectives 4, 5

The equation below shows the transactions of Kathryn Price, Attorney and Counselor of Law, during August. This law firm is owned by Kathryn Price.

	Assets				**=**	**Liab. +**		**Owner's Equity**		
		Accts.				Accts.	K. Price,			
	Cash	+ Rec.	+ Supp.	+ Equip.	=	Pay.	+ Capital	+ Rev.	−	Exp.
Balances, Aug. 1	3,600	900	+ 2,700	+ 5,000	=	600	+ 11,600	+ 0	−	0
Paid for utilities	−300									−300
New balances	3,300 +	900	+ 2,700	+ 5,000	=	600	+ 11,600	+ 0	−	300
Sold services for cash	+3,000							+3,000		
New balances	6,300 +	900	+ 2,700	+ 5,000	=	600	+ 11,600	+ 3,000	−	300
Paid a creditor	−300					−300				
New balances	6,000 +	900	+ 2,700	+ 5,000	=	300	+ 11,600	+ 3,000	−	300
Sold services on credit		+2,400						+2,400		
New balances	6,000 +	3,300	+ 2,700	+ 5,000	=	300	+ 11,600	+ 5,400	−	300
Paid salaries	−2,700									+2,700
New balances	3,300 +	3,300	+ 2,700	+ 5,000	=	300	+ 11,600	+ 5,400	−	3,000
Paid telephone bill	−300									+300
New balances	3,000 +	3,300	+ 2,700	+ 5,000	=	300	+ 11,600	+ 5,400	−	3,300
Withdrew cash for personal expenses	−600						−600			
New balances	2,400 +	3,300	+ 2,700	+ 5,000	=	300	+ 11,000	+ 5,400	−	3,300

INSTRUCTIONS

Analyze each transaction carefully. Prepare an income statement and a statement of owner's equity for the month. Prepare a balance sheet for August 31, 2007. List the expenses in detail on the income statement.

Analyze: In order to complete the statement of owner's equity, which amount was transferred from the income statement?

Challenge Problem

Financial Statements

The following account balances are for French Taylor, Certified Public Accountant, as of April 30, 2007.

Cash	$6,500
Accounts Receivable	2,800
Maintenance Expense	1,100
Advertising Expense	900
Fees Earned	9,500
French Taylor, Capital, April 1	?
Salaries Expense	3,000
Machinery	8,500
Accounts Payable	3,200
French Taylor, Drawing	1,200

INSTRUCTIONS

Using the accounting equation form, determine the balance for French Taylor, Capital, April 1, 2007. Prepare an income statement for the month of April, a statement of owner's equity, and a balance sheet as of April 30, 2007. List the expenses on the income statement in alphabetical order.

Analyze: What net change in owner's equity occurred during the month of April?

Critical Thinking Problem

Accounting for a New Company

LaToysha Washington opened a gym and fitness studio called Perfect Body Builders Studio at the beginning of November of the current year. It is now the end of December, and LaToysha is trying to determine whether she made a profit during her first month of operations. You offer to help her and ask to see her accounting records. She shows you a shoe box and tells you that every piece of paper pertaining to the business is in that box.

As you go through the material in the shoe box, you discover the following:

a. A receipt from Adams Properties for $4,000 for November's rent on the exercise studio.

b. Bank deposit slips totaling $3,680 for money collected from customers who attended exercise classes.

c. An invoice for $25,000 for exercise equipment. The first payment is not due until December 31.

d. A bill for $1,050 from the maintenance service that cleans the studio. LaToysha has not yet paid this bill.

e. A December 19 parking ticket for $100. LaToysha says she was in a hurry that morning to get to the studio on time and forgot to put money in the parking meter.

f. A handwritten list of customers and fees for the classes they have taken. As the customers attend the classes, LaToysha writes their names and the amount of each customer's fee on the list. As customers pay, LaToysha crosses their names off the list. Fees not crossed off the list amount to $1,200.

g. A credit card receipt for $400 for printing flyers advertising the grand opening of the studio. For convenience, LaToysha used her personal credit card.

h. A credit card receipt for $400 for two warm-up suits LaToysha bought to wear at the studio. She also put this purchase on her personal credit card.

Use the concepts you have learned in this chapter to help LaToysha.

1. Prepare an income statement for the first month of operation of Perfect Body Builders Studio.

2. How would you evaluate the results of LaToysha's first month of operation?

3. What advice would you give LaToysha concerning her system of accounting?

BUSINESS CONNECTIONS

Interpreting Results

1. How does an accounting system help managers control operations and make sound decisions?

2. Why should managers be concerned with changes in the amount of creditors' claims against the business?

3. Is it reasonable to expect that all new businesses will have a net income from the first month's operations? From the first year's operations?

4. After examining financial data for a monthly period, the owner of a small business expressed surprise that the firm's cash balance had decreased during the month even though there was substantial net income. Do you think that this owner is right to expect cash to increase whenever there is a net income? Why or why not?

To Record or Not to Record

You are Sarineh, a new Accounts Receivable Clerk for Robinson Paper Supply. Toward the end of the month, Joseph Lee, a very personable sales associate, tells you that the previous A/R clerk always recorded a Sales Invoice when he got a verbal agreement from a customer to buy paper supplies. He has a verbal order from his favorite customer for $5,000 of paper and wants you to create a Sales Invoice today. You know that in order to create a Sales Invoice you need a purchase order from the customer. You also know that Mr. Lee receives a monthly bonus based on the monthly sales. If his sales are above $10,000, he gets a 10% bonus. Would you agree to record the sales of products before receiving the purchase order from the customer? What effect would it have on the customer, on the Sales Associate, on the company and on your job?

Financial Information

Refer to The Home Depot, Inc. *2004 Annual Report* in Appendix A.

1. Locate the consolidated balance sheets. Based on this financial statement, what is the fundamental accounting equation for the year ended January 30, 2005? Note: Because this company is publicly traded, owners' equity is represented as stockholders' equity.

2. Locate the consolidated statements of earnings. The statement presents the results of operations for what periods of time? What result of operations is presented for the most recent operating period?

Income Statement

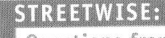

Review the following excerpt from the 2004 consolidated statement of income for Southwest Airlines Co. Answer the questions that follow.

Southwest Airlines Co. Consolidated Statement of Income Years Ended December 31,			
	2004	**2003**	**2002**
Operating Revenues: (in millions)			
Passenger	$6,280	$5,741	$5,341
Freight	117	94	85
Other	133	102	96
Total operating revenues	6,530	5,937	5,522
Net Income	$313	$442	$241

Analyze:

1. Although the format for the heading of an income statement can vary from company to company, the heading should contain the answers to who, what, and when. List the answers to each question for the statement presented above.

2. What three types of revenue are reflected on this statement?

3. The net income of $313,000,000 reflected on Southwest Airlines Co.'s consolidated statement of income for 2004 will be transferred to the next financial statement to be prepared. Net income is needed to complete which statement?

Analyze Online: Find the *Investor Relations* section of the Southwest Airlines Co. Web site (**www.southwest.com**) and answer the following questions.

4. What total operating revenues did Southwest Airlines Co. report for the most recent quarter?

5. Find the most recent press release posted on the Web site. Read the press release, and summarize the topic discussed. What effect, if any, do you think this will have on company earnings? Why?

Personal Financial Statements

The balance sheet for an individual is called a "statement of financial condition." What kinds of assets and liabilities would appear on a statement of financial condition?

Creating an Outline

You are a senior accountant for a mid-size apparel corporation. You have been asked to give a presentation on the basics of financial statements to the managers of the marketing, advertising, manufacturing, and sales departments. Each manager needs to understand what each financial statement presents and why each is important. Prepare an outline for your presentation. Be sure to cover the income statement, the statement of owner's equity, and the balance sheet.

Selling on Internet

Go to the Federated Corporation Web site at **www.federated-fds.com.** What companies are included in this corporation? Can you see a link to purchase items on line? What transaction, if any, would you record when an item is ordered from the Internet? Does the Web site include job offerings? What jobs would be available in Finance (Go to Support operations, finance to find the requirements for a job)?

Working to Provide Accurate Data

Christy's Fabrics is a large fabric provider to the general public. The accounting office has three employees: Accounts Receivable Clerk, Accounts Payable Clerk, and Full Charge Bookkeeper. The Accounts Receivable Clerk creates the sales invoices and records the cash receipts, the Accounts Payable Clerk creates and pays the purchase orders, and the Full Charge Bookkeeper reconciles the checking account. Assign each group member one of the three jobs. Identify the accounts and describe the transactions that would be recorded by that assigned job. What effect would each transaction have on each account? How would each member of the accounting department work together to present accurate information for the decision makers?

Answers to **Self Review**

Answers to Section 1 Self Review

1. Amounts that a company must pay to creditors in the future.
2. A financial event that changes the resources of the firm.
3. An example is the initial investment of cash in a business by the owner.
4. **d.** Equipment is increased by $2,500 and accounts payable is increased by $2,500.
5. **d.** $50,000
6. $5,000

Answers to Section 2 Self Review

1. The firm's name (who), the title of the statement (what), and the time period covered by the report (when).
2. Funds taken from the business to pay for personal expenses. They decrease the owner's equity in the business.
3. As an additional investment by the owner recorded on the basis of fair market value.
4. **a.** revenue and expenses for a period of time
5. **a.** $55,000
6. $22,000 increase

Answers to Comprehensive Self Review

1. The opposite side of the accounting equation will decrease because a decrease in assets results in a corresponding decrease in either a liability or the owner's equity.
2. Revenue increases owner's equity. Expenses decrease owner's equity.
3. Buying for cash results in an immediate decrease in cash; buying on account results in a liability recorded as accounts payable.
4. The income statement is prepared first because the net income or loss is needed to complete the statement of owner's equity. The statement of owner's equity is prepared next to update the change in owner's equity. The balance sheet is prepared last.
5. The payment of $500 to a creditor on account.

CHAPTER 2: Review and Applications

LEARNING OBJECTIVES

1. Set up T accounts for assets, liabilities, and owner's equity.

2. Analyze business transactions and enter them in the accounts.

3. Determine the balance of an account.

4. Set up T accounts for revenue and expenses.

5. Prepare a trial balance from T accounts.

6. Prepare an income statement, a statement of owner's equity, and a balance sheet.

7. Develop a chart of accounts.

8. Define the accounting terms new to this chapter.

NEW TERMS

account balance	footing
accounts	normal balance
chart of accounts	permanent account
classification	slide
credit	T account
debit	temporary account
double-entry system	transposition
drawing account	trial balance

Chapter 3
Analyzing Business Transactions Using T Accounts

$\mathcal{Johnson}\text{-}\mathcal{Johnson}$ www.jnj.com

Johnson & Johnson opened its doors in 1886 with 14 employees in an old wallpaper factory. The Johnson Brothers, Robert Wood, James Wood, and Robert Mead Johnson recognized the critical need for improved antiseptic surgical procedures. The Company designed a soft, absorbent dressing that could be mass-produced and shipped in quantity to hospitals.

Throughout the 1900s, Johnson & Johnson broadened its offerings through new product development and diversification. Today Johnson & Johnson has become a worldwide family of 200 companies, marketing health care products throughout the world. The company's more than 111,000 employees are engaged in producing products that serve a broad segment of medical needs. They range from baby care, first aid, and hospital products to prescription pharmaceuticals, diagnostics, and products relating to family planning, dermatology, and feminine hygiene. With consecutive sales increases for over 70 years, the company's sales exceeded $47 billion and net earnings for 2004 were $8.5 billion.

thinking critically | How might the accountants at Johnson & Johnson have recorded the company's first sales transaction in the 1880s? What effect did this transaction have on the fundamental accounting equation?

Section 1

Transactions That Affect Assets, Liabilities, and Owner's Equity

In this chapter you will learn how to record the changes caused by business transactions. This recordkeeping is a basic part of accounting systems.

SECTION OBJECTIVES

▶ **1. Set up T accounts for assets, liabilities, and owner's equity.**

WHY IT'S IMPORTANT

The T account is an important visual tool used as an alternative to the fundamental accounting equation.

▶ **2. Analyze business transactions and enter them in the accounts.**

WHY IT'S IMPORTANT

Accountants often use T accounts to help analyze and classify business transactions.

▶ **3. Determine the balance of an account.**

WHY IT'S IMPORTANT

Accurate account balances contribute to a reliable accounting system.

TERMS TO LEARN

account balance
accounts
classification
footing
normal balance
T account

Asset, Liability, and Owner's Equity Accounts

The accounting equation is one tool for analyzing the effects of business transactions. However, businesses do not record transactions in equation form. Instead, businesses establish separate records, called **accounts** , for assets, liabilities, and owner's equity. Use of accounts helps owners and staff analyze, record, classify, summarize, and report financial information. Accounts are recognized by their **classification** as assets, liabilities, or owner's equity. Asset accounts show the property a business owns. Liability accounts show the debts of the business. Owner's equity accounts show the owner's financial interest in the business. Each account has a name that describes the type of property, the debt, or the financial interest.

Accountants use T accounts to analyze transactions. A **T account** consists of a vertical line and a horizontal line that resemble the letter **T.** The name of the account is written on the horizontal (top) line. Increases and decreases in the account are entered on either side of the vertical line.

The following are T accounts for assets, liabilities, and owner's equity.

ASSETS		=	LIABILITIES		+	OWNER'S EQUITY	
+	−		−	+		−	+
Record increases	Record decreases		Record decreases	Record increases		Record decreases	Record increases

RECORDING A CASH INVESTMENT

Asset accounts show items of value owned by a business. Jason Taylor invested $90,000 in the business. Tennille Brisbane, the office manager for JT's Consulting Services, set up a *Cash* account. Cash is an asset. Assets appear on the left side of the accounting equation. Cash increases appear on the left side of the **Cash** T account. Decreases are shown on the right side. Brisbane entered the cash investment of $90,000 **(a)** on the left side of the **Cash** account.

T accounts normally do not have plus and minus signs. We show them to help you identify increases (+) and decreases (−) in accounts.

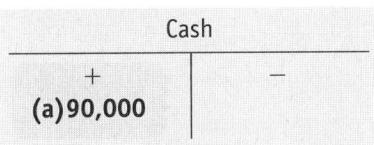

Tennille Brisbane set up an account for owner's equity called **Jason Taylor, Capital.** Owner's equity appears on the right side of the accounting equation (Assets = Liabilities + Owner's Equity). Increases in owner's equity appear on the right side of the T account. Decreases in owner's equity appear on the left side. Brisbane entered the investment of $90,000 **(b)** on the right side of the **Jason Taylor, Capital** account.

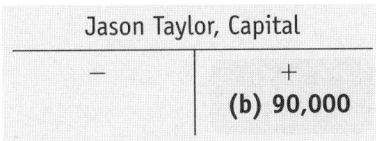

Use these steps to analyze the effects of the business transactions:

1. Analyze the financial event.
   - Identify the accounts affected.
   - Classify the accounts affected.
   - Determine the amount of increase or decrease for each account.
2. Apply the left-right rules for each account affected.
3. Make the entry in T-account form.

▶ 1. OBJECTIVE
Set up T accounts for assets, liabilities, and owner's equity.

recall

The Accounting Equation
Assets = Liabilities + Owner's Equity

▶ 2. OBJECTIVE
Analyze business transactions and enter them in the accounts.

BUSINESS TRANSACTION

Jason Taylor withdrew $90,000 from personal savings and deposited it in the new business checking account for JT's Consulting Services.

ANALYSIS
a. The asset account, **Cash,** is increased by $90,000.
b. The owner's equity account, **Jason Taylor, Capital,** is increased by $90,000.

LEFT-RIGHT RULES
LEFT Increases to asset accounts are recorded on the left side of the T account. Record $90,000 on the left side of the **Cash** T account.

RIGHT Increases to owner's equity accounts are recorded on the right side of the T account. Record $90,000 on the right side of the **Jason Taylor, Capital** T account.

T-ACCOUNT PRESENTATION

Cash		Jason Taylor, Capital	
+	−	−	+
(b) 90,000			(b) 90,000

RECORDING A CASH PURCHASE OF EQUIPMENT

Tennille Brisbane set up an asset account, *Equipment,* to record the purchase of a computer and other equipment.

BUSINESS TRANSACTION

JT's Consulting Services issued a $10,000 check to purchase a computer and other equipment.

ANALYSIS

c. The asset account, *Equipment,* is increased by $10,000.

d. The asset account, *Cash,* is decreased by $10,000.

LEFT-RIGHT RULES

LEFT   Increases to asset accounts are recorded on the left side of the T account. Record $10,000 on the left side of the *Equipment* T account.

RIGHT Decreases to asset accounts are recorded on the right side of the T account. Record $10,000 on the right side of the *Cash* T account.

T-ACCOUNT PRESENTATION

Equipment			Cash	
+	−		+	−
(c) 10,000				**(d)** 10,000

Let's look at the T accounts to review the effects of the transactions. Brisbane entered $10,000 **(c)** on the left (increase) side of the *Equipment* account. She entered $10,000 **(d)** on the right (decrease) side of the *Cash* account. Notice that the *Cash* account shows the effects of two transactions.

Equipment		Cash	
+	−	+	−
(c) 10,000		**(a)** 90,000	**(d)** 10,000

RECORDING A CREDIT PURCHASE OF EQUIPMENT

Liabilities are amounts a business owes its creditors. Liabilities appear on the right side of the accounting equation (Assets = Liabilities + Owner's Equity). Increases in liabilities are on the right side of liability T accounts. Decreases in liabilities are on the left side of liability T accounts.

BUSINESS TRANSACTION

The firm bought office equipment for $12,000 on account from Office Plus.

ANALYSIS

e. The asset account, *Equipment,* is increased by $12,000.

f. The liability account, *Accounts Payable,* is increased by $12,000.

LEFT-RIGHT RULES

LEFT Increases to asset accounts are recorded on the left side of the T account. Record $12,000 on the left side of the *Equipment* T account.

RIGHT Increases to liability accounts are recorded on the right side of the T account. Record $12,000 on the right side of the *Accounts Payable* T account.

important!

For liability T accounts
- right side shows increases,
- left side shows decreases.

T-ACCOUNT PRESENTATION

Equipment		Accounts Payable	
+	−	−	+
(e) 12,000			(f) 12,000

Let's look at the T accounts to review the effects of the transactions. Brisbane entered $12,000 **(e)** on the left (increase) side of the *Equipment* account. It now shows two transactions. She entered $12,000 **(f)** on the right (increase) side of the *Accounts Payable* account.

Equipment		Accounts Payable	
+	−	−	+
(c) 10,000			(f) 12,000
(e) 12,000			

> The balance sheet of Avery Dennison Corporation at January 1, 2005, showed machinery and equipment balances of $1.38 billion.

RECORDING A CASH PURCHASE OF SUPPLIES

Tennille Brisbane set up an asset account called *Supplies.*

BUSINESS TRANSACTION

JT's Consulting Services issued a check for $3,000 to Office Supplies Inc. to purchase office supplies.

ANALYSIS

g. The asset account, *Supplies,* is increased by $3,000.

h. The asset account, *Cash,* is decreased by $3,000.

LEFT-RIGHT RULES

LEFT Increases to asset accounts are recorded on the left side of the T account. Record $3,000 on the left side of the *Supplies* T account.

RIGHT Decreases to asset accounts are recorded on the right side of the T account. Record $3,000 on the right side of the *Cash* T account.

T-ACCOUNT PRESENTATION

Supplies		Cash	
+	−	+	−
(g) 3,000			**(h)** 3,000

Brisbane entered $3,000 **(g)** on the left (increase) side of the *Supplies* account and $3,000 **(h)** on the right (decrease) side of the *Cash* account.

Supplies		Cash	
+	−	+	−
(g) 3,000		**(a)** 90,000	**(d)** 10,000
			(h) 3,000

Notice that the *Cash* account now shows three transactions: the initial investment by the owner (a), the cash purchase of equipment (d), and the cash purchase of supplies (h).

RECORDING A PAYMENT TO A CREDITOR

On November 30 the business paid $5,000 to Office Plus to apply against the debt of $12,000 shown in *Accounts Payable.*

COMPUTERS IN ACCOUNTING <<

HARDWARE AND SOFTWARE: A WORKING PARTNERSHIP

When you arrive at work and turn on your computer, many processes happen behind the scenes. Computers are made up of hardware and software. *Hardware* includes a CPU (central processing unit), disk drives, memory, monitor, keyboard, and printer. *Software* makes computer hardware perform tasks. Without software, a computer can do nothing. Software programs come in two basic types: system software and application software.

System software controls the operation of the application software and coordinates the activities of the hardware. Think of your system software as the air-traffic controller of your computer. Popular operating systems include MacOS, Windows, Unix, and Linux.

Application software tells your computer to perform a task. A word processing application such as Microsoft Word has the tools to create, edit, and format text. Spreadsheet applications such as Microsoft Excel or Lotus 1-2-3 organize numbers and words into meaningful columns and rows. Software applications are developed to create efficient and fast ways to convert

data into meaningful information. Accounting applications such as Peachtree Accounting and AccuBooks convert data into meaningful information.

Accounting software application programs range from simple and inexpensive to sophisticated and costly. These applications provide tools to enter business transactions and automatically transfer the details to the appropriate accounts. Standardized financial statements and reports can be generated using simple menus. From start to finish, these applications help the accountant maintain accurate records and provide management a wide variety of financial reports.

THINKING CRITICALLY

What software applications have you used? What suggestions would you make for improvement to these applications?

INTERNET APPLICATION

Use an Internet search engine to find accounting software applications. Choose two applications suitable for small businesses and write a brief review of each product. Based on your research, which product do you prefer? Why?

BUSINESS TRANSACTION

JT's Consulting Services issued a check in the amount of $5,000 to Office Plus.

ANALYSIS
i. The asset account, *Cash,* is decreased by $5,000.

j. The liability account, *Accounts Payable,* is decreased by $5,000.

LEFT-RIGHT RULES
LEFT   Decreases to liability accounts are recorded on the left side of the T account. Record $5,000 on the left side of the *Accounts Payable* T account.

RIGHT   Decreases to asset accounts are recorded on the right side of the T account. Record $5,000 on the right side of the *Cash* T account.

T-ACCOUNT PRESENTATION

Accounts Payable		Cash	
−	+	+	−
(j) 5,000			**(i)** 5,000

Let's look at the T accounts to review the effects of the transactions. Brisbane entered $5,000 **(i)** on the right (decrease) side of the *Cash* account. She entered $5,000 **(j)** on the left (decrease) side of the *Accounts Payable* account. Notice that both accounts show the effects of several transactions.

Cash		Accounts Payable	
+	−		
(a) 90,000	(d) 10,000	**(j) 5,000**	(f) 12,000
	(h) 3,000		
	(i) 5,000		

RECORDING PREPAID RENT

In November JT's Consulting Services was required to pay the December and January rent in advance. Brisbane set up an asset account called *Prepaid Rent.*

BUSINESS TRANSACTION

JT's Consulting Services issued a check for $7,000 to pay rent for the months of December and January.

ANALYSIS
k. The asset account, *Prepaid Rent,* is increased by $7,000.

l. The asset account, *Cash,* is decreased by $7,000.

LEFT-RIGHT RULES

LEFT   Increases to asset accounts are recorded on the left side of the T account. Record $7,000 on the left side of the *Prepaid Rent* T account.

RIGHT   Decreases to asset accounts are recorded on the right side of the T account. Record $7,000 on the right side of the *Cash* T account.

▼

T-ACCOUNT PRESENTATION

Prepaid Rent			Cash		
+		−		+	−
(k) 7,000					(l) 7,000

Let's review the T accounts to see the effects of the transactions. Brisbane entered $7,000 **(k)** on the left (increase) side of the *Prepaid Rent* account. She entered $7,000 **(l)** on the right (decrease) side of the *Cash* account.

Notice that the *Cash* account shows the effects of numerous transactions. It shows initial investment (a), equipment purchase (d), supplies purchase (h), payment on account (i), and advance rent payment (l).

Prepaid Rent			Cash		
+		−	+		−
(k) 7,000			(a) 90,000		(d) 10,000
					(h) 3,000
					(i) 5,000
					(l) 7,000

▶ **3. OBJECTIVE**

Determine the balance of an account.

Account Balances

An **account balance** is the difference between the amounts on the two sides of the account. First add the figures on each side of the account. If the column has more than one figure, enter the total in small pencil figures called a **footing** . Then subtract the smaller total from the larger total. The result is the account balance.

- If the total on the right side is larger than the total on the left side, the balance is recorded on the right side.
- If the total on the left side is larger, the balance is recorded on the left side.
- If an account shows only one amount, that amount is the balance.
- If an account contains entries on only one side, the total of those entries is the account balance.

Let's look at the *Cash* account for JT's Consulting Services. The left side shows $90,000. The total of the right side is $25,000. Subtract the footing of $25,000 from $90,000. The result is the account balance of $65,000. The account balance is shown on the left side of the account.

Cash		
+		−
(a) 90,000		(d) 10,000
		(h) 3,000
		(i) 5,000
		(l) 7,000
		25,000 ← Footing
Bal. 65,000		

Usually account balances appear on the increase side of the account. The increase side of the account is the **normal balance** of the account.

The following is a summary of the procedures to increase or decrease accounts and shows the normal balance of accounts.

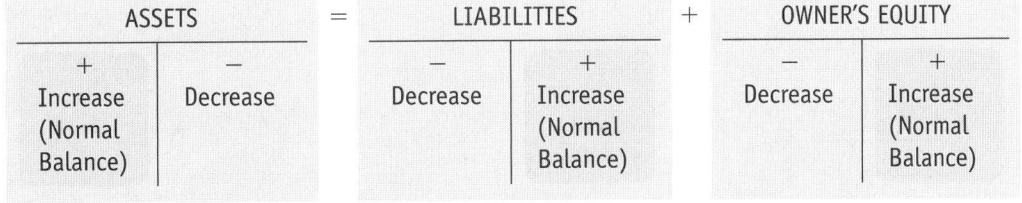

ASSETS		=	LIABILITIES		+	OWNER'S EQUITY	
+	−		−	+		−	+
Increase (Normal Balance)	Decrease		Decrease	Increase (Normal Balance)		Decrease	Increase (Normal Balance)

Figure 3.1 shows a summary of the account balances for JT's Consulting Services.
Figure 3.2 shows a balance sheet prepared for November 30, 2007.
In equation form the firm's position after these transactions is:

Assets							=	Liabilities	+	Owner's Equity
Cash	+	Supp.	+	Prepaid Rent	+	Equip.	=	Accounts Payable	+	Jason Taylor, Capital
$65,000	+	$3,000	+	$7,000	+	$22,000	=	$7,000	+	$90,000

ASSETS

Cash

+	−
(a) 90,000	(d) 10,000
	(h) 3,000
	(i) 5,000
	(l) 7,000
	25,000
Bal. 65,000	

Supplies

+	−
(g) 3,000	

Prepaid Rent

+	−
(k) 7,000	

Equipment

+	−
(c) 10,000	
(e) 12,000	
Bal. 22,000	

=

LIABILITIES

Accounts Payable

−	+
(j) 5,000	(f) 12,000
	Bal. 7,000

+

OWNER'S EQUITY

Jason Taylor, Capital

−	+
	(b) 90,000

FIGURE 3.1

T-Account Balances for JT's Consulting Services

ABOUT ACCOUNTING

Law Enforcement
The FBI and other law enforcement agencies recruit accountants to investigate criminal conduct. Perhaps the most famous use of accounting by law enforcers is the conviction of Al Capone for tax evasion after he could not be jailed for his ties to organized crime.

JT's Consulting Services
Balance Sheet
November 30, 2007

Assets		Liabilities	
Cash	6 5 0 0 0 00	Accounts Payable	7 0 0 0 00
Supplies	3 0 0 0 00		
Prepaid Rent	7 0 0 0 00	Owner's Equity	
Equipment	2 2 0 0 0 00	Jason Taylor, Capital	90 0 0 0 00
Total Assets	9 7 0 0 0 00	Total Liabilities and Owner's Equity	97 0 0 0 00

FIGURE 3.2 | **Balance Sheet for JT's Consulting Services.**

Notice how the balance sheet reflects the fundamental accounting equation.

Section 1: **Self Review**

QUESTIONS

1. What is meant by the "normal balance" of an account? What is the normal balance side for asset, liability, and owner's equity accounts?

2. Increases are recorded on which side of asset, liability, and owner's equity accounts?

3. What is a footing?

EXERCISES

4. Foot and find the balance of the **Cash** account.

Cash	
+	−
13,000	5,000
9,000	1,500
	1,250
	1,175

a. 12,050

b. 13,075

c. 14,750

d. 22,000

5. The Nelson Company purchased new computers for $5,400 from Office Supplies, Inc., to be paid in 30 days. Which of the following is correct?

a. **Equipment** is increased by $5,400. **Cash** is decreased by $5,400.

b. **Equipment** is decreased by $5,400. **Accounts Payable** is increased by $5,400.

c. **Equipment** is increased by $5,400. **Accounts Payable** is increased by $5,400.

d. **Equipment** is increased by $5,400. **Accounts Payable** is decreased by $5,400.

ANALYSIS

6. From the following accounts, show that the fundamental accounting equation is in balance. All accounts have normal balances.

Cash—$7,700

Accounts Payable—$5,000

Euline Hawkins, Capital—$15,000

Equipment—$10,000

Supplies—$2,300

(Answers to Section 1 Self Review are on page 92.)

Transactions That Affect Revenue, Expenses, and Withdrawals

Let's examine the revenue and expense transactions of JT's Consulting Services for December to see how they are recorded.

Revenue and Expense Accounts

Some owner's equity accounts are classified as revenue or expense accounts. Separate accounts are used to record revenue and expense transactions.

RECORDING REVENUE FROM SERVICES SOLD FOR CASH

During December the business earned $26,000 in revenue from clients who paid cash for bookkeeping, accounting, and consulting services. This involved several transactions. Tennille Brisbane entered $26,000 **(m)** on the left (increase) side of the asset account **Cash.**

Cash		
	+	−
Bal.	65,000	
(m)	**26,000**	

How is the increase in owner's equity recorded? One way would be to record the $26,000 on the right side of the **Jason Taylor, Capital** account. However, the preferred way is to keep revenue separate from the owner's investment until the end of the accounting period. Therefore, Brisbane opened a revenue account for **Fees Income.**

Brisbane entered $26,000 **(n)** on the right side of the **Fees Income** account. Revenues increase owner's equity. Increases in owner's equity appear on the right side of the T account. Therefore, increases in revenue appear on the right side of revenue T accounts.

SECTION OBJECTIVES

▶ **4. Set up T accounts for revenue and expenses.**

WHY IT'S IMPORTANT

T accounts help you understand the effects of all business transactions.

▶ **5. Prepare a trial balance from T accounts.**

WHY IT'S IMPORTANT

The trial balance is an important check of accuracy at the end of the accounting period.

▶ **6. Prepare an income statement, a statement of owner's equity, and a balance sheet.**

WHY IT'S IMPORTANT

Financial statements summarize the financial activities and condition of the business.

▶ **7. Develop a chart of accounts.**

WHY IT'S IMPORTANT

Businesses require a system that allows accounts to be easily identified and located.

TERMS TO LEARN

chart of accounts
credit
debit
double-entry system
drawing account
permanent account
slide
temporary account
transposition
trial balance

▶ **4. OBJECTIVE**

Set up T accounts for revenue and expenses.

Topic Tackler

PLUS

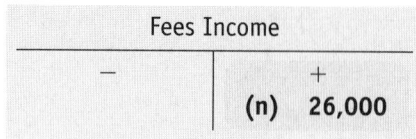

The right side of the revenue account shows increases and the left side shows decreases. Decreases in revenue accounts are rare but might occur because of corrections or transfers.

Let's review the effects of the transactions. Brisbane entered $26,000 **(m)** on the left (increase) side of the **Cash** account and $26,000 **(n)** on the right (increase) side of the **Fees Income** account.

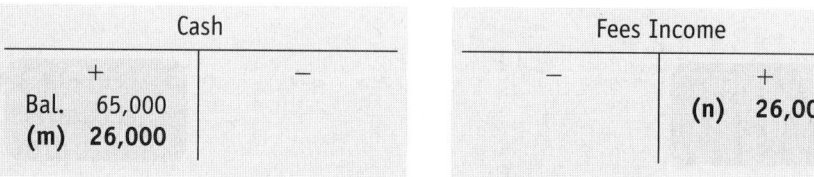

At this point the firm needs just one revenue account. Most businesses have separate accounts for different types of revenue. For example, sales of goods such as clothes are recorded in the revenue account **Sales.**

RECORDING REVENUE FROM SERVICES SOLD ON CREDIT

In December JT's Consulting Services earned $9,000 from various charge account clients. Brisbane set up an asset account, **Accounts Receivable.**

ANALYSIS

o. The asset account, **Accounts Receivable,** is increased by $9,000.

p. The revenue account, **Fees Income,** is increased by $9,000.

LEFT-RIGHT RULES

LEFT   Increases to asset accounts are recorded on the left side of the T account. Record $9,000 on the left side of the **Accounts Receivable** T account.

RIGHT   Increases in revenue appear on the right side of the T account. Record $9,000 on the right side of the **Fees Income** T account.

T-ACCOUNT PRESENTATION

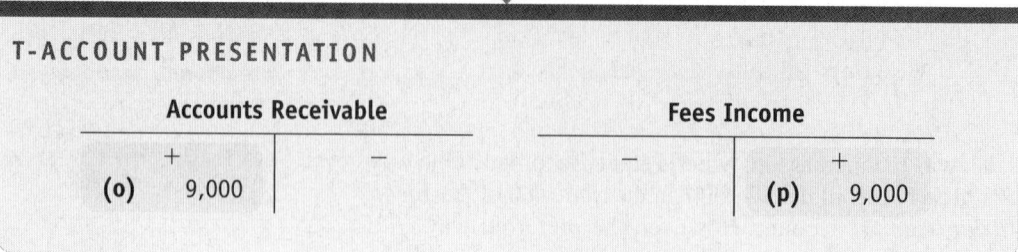

Let's review the effects of the transactions. Brisbane entered $9,000 **(o)** on the left (increase) side of the **Accounts Receivable** account and $9,000 **(p)** on the right (increase) side of the **Fees Income** account.

Accounts Receivable		
+		−
(o) 9,000		

Fees Income		
−		+
		(n) 26,000
		(p) 9,000

RECORDING COLLECTIONS FROM ACCOUNTS RECEIVABLE

Charge account clients paid $4,000, reducing the amount owed to JT's Consulting Services.

ANALYSIS

q. The asset account, **Cash,** is increased by $4,000.

r. The asset account, **Accounts Receivable,** is decreased by $4,000.

LEFT-RIGHT RULES

LEFT   Increases to asset accounts are recorded on the left side of the T account. Record $4,000 on the left side of the **Cash** T account.

RIGHT   Decreases to asset accounts are recorded on the right side of the T account. Record $4,000 on the right side of the **Accounts Receivable** T account.

T-ACCOUNT PRESENTATION

Cash		
+		−
(q) 4,000		

Accounts Receivable		
+		−
		(r) 4,000

Let's review the effects of the transactions. Brisbane entered $4,000 **(q)** on the left (increase) side of the **Cash** account and $4,000 **(r)** on the right (decrease) side of the **Accounts Receivable** account. Notice that revenue is not recorded when cash is collected from charge account clients. The revenue was recorded when the sales on credit were recorded (p).

Cash		
+		−
Bal. 65,000		
(m) 26,000		
(q) 4,000		

Accounts Receivable		
+		−
(o) 9,000		(r) 4,000

RECORDING AN EXPENSE FOR SALARIES

Expenses decrease owner's equity. Decreases in owner's equity appear on the left side of the T account. Therefore, increases in expenses (which are decreases in owner's equity) are recorded on the left side of expense T accounts. Decreases in expenses are recorded on the right side of the T accounts. Decreases in expenses are rare but may result from corrections or transfers.

recall

Expense
An expense is an outflow of cash, the use of other assets, or the incurring of a liability.

BUSINESS TRANSACTION

In December JT's Consulting Services paid $7,000 in salaries.

ANALYSIS

s. The asset account, *Cash,* is decreased by $7,000.

t. The expense account, *Salaries Expense,* is increased by $7,000.

LEFT-RIGHT RULES

LEFT Increases in expenses appear on the left side of the T account. Record $7,000 on the left side of the *Salaries Expense* T account.

RIGHT Decreases in asset accounts are recorded on the right side of the T account. Record $7,000 on the right side of the *Cash* T account.

T-ACCOUNT PRESENTATION

Salaries Expense			Cash	
+	−		+	−
(t) 7,000				(s) 7,000

International INSIGHTS

Electricity

Accountants who travel with laptop computers should know the voltage used at their destinations. Power in the United States is 110 volts, but in most other countries it is 220 volts.

Brisbane entered $7,000 **(s)** on the right (decrease) side of the *Cash* T account.

Cash			
+		−	
Bal.	65,000	(s)	7,000
(m)	26,000		
(q)	4,000		

How is the decrease in owner's equity recorded? One way would be to record the $7,000 on the left side of the *Jason Taylor, Capital* account. However, the preferred way is to keep expenses separate from owner's investment. Therefore, Brisbane set up a *Salaries Expense* account.

To record the salary expense, Brisbane entered $7,000 **(t)** on the left (increase) side of the *Salaries Expense* account. Notice that the plus and minus signs in the *Salaries Expense* account show the effect on the expense account, not on owner's equity.

Salaries Expense		
+		−
(t) 7,000		

Most companies have numerous expense accounts. The various expense accounts appear in the Expenses section of the income statement.

RECORDING AN EXPENSE FOR UTILITIES

At the end of December, JT's Consulting Services received a $500 bill for utilities. Brisbane set up an account for *Utilities Expense.*

BUSINESS TRANSACTION

JT's Consulting Services issued a check for $500 to pay the utilities bill.

ANALYSIS

u. The asset account, *Cash,* is decreased by $500.

v. The expense account, *Utilities Expense,* is increased by $500.

LEFT-RIGHT RULES

LEFT Increases in expenses appear on the left side of the T account. Record $500 on the left side of the *Utilities Expense* T account.

RIGHT Decreases to asset accounts are recorded on the right side of the T account. Record $500 on the right side of the *Cash* T account.

T-ACCOUNT PRESENTATION

Utilities Expense		Cash	
+	−	+	−
(v) 500			(u) 500

Let's review the effects of the transactions.

Utilities Expense		Cash	
+	−	+	−
(v) **500**		Bal. 65,000	(s) 7,000
		(m) 26,000	(u) **500**
		(q) 4,000	

The Drawing Account

In sole proprietorships and partnerships, the owners generally do not pay themselves salaries. To obtain funds for personal living expenses, owners make withdrawals of cash. The withdrawals are against previously earned profits that have become part of capital or against profits that are expected in the future.

Since withdrawals decrease owner's equity, withdrawals could be recorded on the left side of the capital account. However, the preferred way is to keep withdrawals separate from the owner's capital account until the end of the accounting period. An owner's equity account called a **drawing account** is set up to record withdrawals. Increases in the drawing account (which are decreases in owner's equity) are recorded on the left side of the drawing T accounts.

BUSINESS TRANSACTION

Jason Taylor wrote a check to withdraw $4,000 cash for personal use.

ANALYSIS

w. The asset account, *Cash,* is decreased by $4,000.

x. The owner's equity account, *Jason Taylor, Drawing,* is increased by $4,000.

LEFT-RIGHT RULES

LEFT   Increases to drawing accounts are recorded on the left side of the T account. Record $4,000 on the left side of the *Jason Taylor, Drawing* T account.

RIGHT   Decreases to asset accounts are recorded on the right side of the T account. Record $4,000 on the right side of the *Cash* T account.

T-ACCOUNT PRESENTATION

Jason Taylor, Drawing		Cash	
+	−	+	−
(x) 4,000			(w) 4,000

Let's review the transactions. Brisbane entered $4,000 (**w**) on the right (decrease) side of the asset account, *Cash,* and $4,000 (**x**) on the left (increase) side of *Jason Taylor, Drawing.* Note that the plus and minus signs show the effect on the drawing account, not on owner's equity.

Jason Taylor, Drawing		Cash	
+	−	+	−
(x) 4,000		Bal. 65,000	(s) 7,000
		(m) 26,000	(u) 500
		(q) 4,000	(w) 4,000

Figure 3.3 shows a summary of the relationship between the capital account and the revenue, expense, and drawing accounts.

FIGURE 3.3

The Relationship Between Owner's Equity and Revenue, Expenses, and Withdrawals

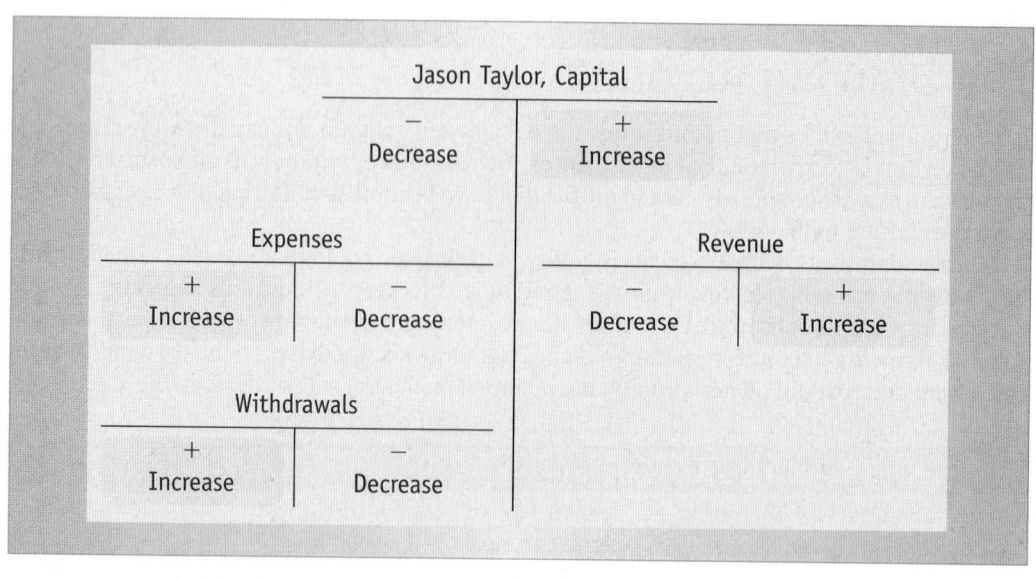

important!

Normal Balances

Debit:	*Credit:*
Asset	Liability
Expense	Revenue
Drawing	Capital

ASSET ACCOUNTS		LIABILITY ACCOUNTS		OWNER'S CAPITAL ACCOUNT	
Debit	Credit	Debit	Credit	Debit	Credit
+	–	–	+	–	+
Increase Side (Normal Bal.)	Decrease Side	Decrease Side	Increase Side (Normal Bal.)	Decrease Side	Increase Side (Normal Bal.)

OWNER'S DRAWING ACCOUNT		REVENUE ACCOUNTS		EXPENSE ACCOUNTS	
Debit	Credit	Debit	Credit	Debit	Credit
+	–	–	+	+	–
Increase Side (Normal Bal.)	Decrease Side	Decrease Side	Increase Side (Normal Bal.)	Increase Side (Normal Bal.)	Decrease Side

FIGURE 3.4 | **Rules for Debits and Credits**

The Rules of Debit and Credit

Accountants do not use the terms *left side* and *right side* when they talk about making entries in accounts. Instead, they use the term **debit** for an entry on the left side and **credit** for an entry on the right side. Figure 3.4 summarizes the rules for debits and credits. The accounting system is called the **double-entry system** . This is because each transaction has at least two entries— a debit and a credit.

After the December transactions for JT's Consulting Services are recorded, the account balances are calculated. Figure 3.5 on page 72 shows the account balances at the end of December. Notice that the fundamental accounting equation remains in balance (Assets = Liabilities + Owner's Equity).

The Trial Balance

Once the account balances are computed, a trial balance is prepared. The **trial balance** is a statement that tests the accuracy of total debits and credits after transactions have been recorded. If total debits do not equal total credits, there is an error. Figure 3.6 on page 72 shows the trial balance for JT's Consulting Services. To prepare a trial balance, perform the following steps:

1. Enter the trial balance heading showing the company name, report title, and closing date for the accounting period.
2. List the account names in the same order as they appear on the financial statements.
   - Assets
   - Liabilities
   - Owner's Equity
   - Revenue
   - Expenses
3. Enter the ending balance of each account in the appropriate Debit or Credit column.
4. Total the Debit column.
5. Total the Credit column.
6. Compare the total debits with the total credits.

FIGURE 3.5   **End-of-December 2007 Account Balances**

| | ASSETS | = | LIABILITIES | + | OWNER'S EQUITY |

Cash

Bal.	65,000	(s)	7,000
(m)	26,000	(u)	500
(q)	4,000	(w)	4,000
	95,000		11,500
Bal.	83,500		

Accounts Payable

| Bal. | 7,000 |

Jason Taylor, Capital

| | Bal. | 90,000 |

Accounts Receivable

| (q) | 9,000 | (r) | 4,000 |
| Bal. | 5,000 | | |

Jason Taylor, Drawing

| (x) | 4,000 | |

Supplies

| Bal. | 3,000 | |

Fees Income

	(n)	26,000
	(p)	9,000
	Bal.	35,000

Prepaid Rent

| Bal. | 7,000 | |

Salaries Expense

| (t) | 7,000 | |

Equipment

| Bal. | 22,000 | |

Utilities Expense

| (v) | 500 | |

FIGURE 3.6

Trial Balance

recall

Financial Statement Headings

The financial statement headings answer three questions:

Who—the company name

What—the report title

When—the date of, or the period covered by, the report

JT's Consulting Services
Trial Balance
December 31, 2007

ACCOUNT NAME	DEBIT					CREDIT				
Cash	83	5	0	0	00					
Accounts Receivable	5	0	0	0	00					
Supplies	3	0	0	0	00					
Prepaid Rent	7	0	0	0	00					
Equipment	22	0	0	0	00					
Accounts Payable						7	0	0	0	00
Jason Taylor, Capital						90	0	0	0	00
Jason Taylor, Drawing	4	0	0	0	00					
Fees Income						35	0	0	0	00
Salaries Expense	7	0	0	0	00					
Utilities Expense		5	0	0	00					
Totals	132	0	0	0	00	132	0	0	0	00

MANAGERIAL IMPLICATIONS <<

FINANCIAL STATEMENTS

- Recording entries into accounts provides an efficient method of gathering data about the financial affairs of a business.
- A chart of accounts is usually similar from company to company; balance sheet accounts are first, followed by income statement accounts.
- A trial balance proves the financial records are in balance.
- The income statement reports the revenue and expenses for the period and shows the net income or loss.
- The statement of owner's equity shows the change in owner's equity during the period.
- The balance sheet summarizes the assets, liabilities, and owner's equity of the business on a given date.
- Owners, managers, creditors, banks, and many others use financial statements to make decisions about the business.

THINKING CRITICALLY:
What are some possible consequences of not recording financial data correctly?

UNDERSTANDING TRIAL BALANCE ERRORS

If the totals of the Debit and Credit columns are equal, the financial records are in balance. If the totals of the Debit and Credit columns are not equal, there is an error. The error may be in the trial balance, or it may be in the financial records. Some common errors are

- adding trial balance columns incorrectly;
- recording only half a transaction—for example, recording a debit but not recording a credit, or vice versa;
- recording both halves of a transaction as debits or credits rather than recording one debit and one credit;
- recording an amount incorrectly from a transaction;
- recording a debit for one amount and a credit for a different amount;
- making an error when calculating the account balances.

FINDING TRIAL BALANCE ERRORS

If the trial balance does not balance, try the following procedures.

1. Check the arithmetic. If the columns were originally added from top to bottom, verify the total by adding from bottom to top.
2. Check that the correct account balances were transferred to the correct trial balance columns.
3. Check the arithmetic used to compute the account balances.
4. Check that each transaction was recorded correctly in the accounts by tracing the amounts to the analysis of the transaction.

Sometimes you can determine the type of the error by the amount of the difference. Compute the difference between the debit total and the credit total. If the difference is divisible by 2, a debit might be recorded as a credit, or a credit recorded as a debit.

If the difference is divisible by 9, there might be a transposition. A **transposition** occurs when the digits of a number are switched (357 for 375). The test for a transposition is

▶ 5. OBJECTIVE
Prepare a trial balance from T accounts.

$$\begin{array}{r} 375 \\ -357 \\ \hline 18 \end{array} \qquad 18/9 = 2$$

Also check for slides. A **slide** occurs when the decimal point is misplaced (375 for 37.50). We can test for a slide in the following manner.

$$\begin{array}{r} 375.00 \\ -37.50 \\ \hline 337.50 \end{array} \qquad 337.50/9 = 37.50$$

▶ **6. OBJECTIVE**

Prepare an income statement, a statement of owner's equity, and a balance sheet.

Financial Statements

After the trial balance is prepared, the financial statements are prepared. Figure 3.7 shows the financial statements for JT's Consulting Services. The amounts are taken from the trial balance. As you study the financial statements, note that net income from the income statement is used on the statement of owner's equity. Also note that the ending balance of the *Jason Taylor, Capital* account, computed on the statement of owner's equity, is used on the balance sheet.

FIGURE 3.7

Financial Statements for JT's Consulting Services

JT's Consulting Services
Income Statement
Month Ended December 31, 2007

Revenue		
Fees Income		35 0 0 0 00
Expenses		
Salaries Expense	7 0 0 0 00	
Utilities Expense	5 0 0 00	
Total Expenses		7 5 0 0 00
Net Income		2 7 5 0 0 00

JT's Consulting Services
Statement of Owner's Equity
Month Ended December 31, 2007

Jason Taylor, Capital, December 1, 2007		90 0 0 0 00
Net Income for December	27 5 0 0 00	
Less Withdrawals for December	4 0 0 0 00	
Increase in Capital		23 5 0 0 00
Jason Taylor, Capital, December 31, 2007		113 5 0 0 00

JT's Consulting Services
Balance Sheet
December 31, 2007

Assets		Liabilities	
Cash	83 5 0 0 00	Accounts Payable	7 0 0 0 00
Accounts Receivable	5 0 0 0 00		
Supplies	3 0 0 0 00		
Prepaid Rent	7 0 0 0 00	Owner's Equity	
Equipment	22 0 0 0 00	Jason Taylor, Capital	113 5 0 0 00
Total Assets	120 5 0 0 00	Total Liabilities and Owner's Equity	120 5 0 0 00

Chart of Accounts

A **chart of accounts** is a list of all the accounts used by a business. Figure 3.8 shows the chart of accounts for JT's Consulting Services. Each account has a number and a name. The balance sheet accounts are listed first, followed by the income statement accounts. The account number is assigned based on the type of account.

Asset Accounts	100–199	Revenue Accounts	400–499
Liability Accounts	200–299	Expense Accounts	500–599
Owner's Equity Accounts	300–399		

Notice that the accounts are not numbered consecutively. For example, asset account numbers jump from 101 to 111 and then to 121, 137, and 141. In each block of numbers, gaps are left so that additional accounts can be added when needed.

Permanent and Temporary Accounts

The asset, liability, and owner's equity accounts appear on the balance sheet at the end of an accounting period. The balances of these accounts are then carried forward to start the new period. Because they continue from one accounting period to the next, these accounts are called **permanent accounts** or *real accounts*.

Revenue and expense accounts appear on the income statement. The drawing account appears on the statement of owner's equity. These accounts classify and summarize changes in owner's equity during the period. They are called **temporary accounts** or *nominal accounts* because the balances in these accounts are transferred to the capital account at the end of the accounting period. In the next period, these accounts start with zero balances.

JT'S CONSULTING SERVICES Chart of Accounts	
Account Number	**Account Name**
Balance Sheet Accounts	
100–199	**ASSETS**
101	Cash
111	Accounts Receivable
121	Supplies
137	Prepaid Rent
141	Equipment
200–299	**LIABILITIES**
202	Accounts Payable
300–399	**OWNER'S EQUITY**
301	Jason Taylor, Capital
Statement of Owner's Equity Account	
302	Jason Taylor, Drawing
Income Statement Accounts	
400–499	**REVENUE**
401	Fees Income
500–599	**EXPENSES**
511	Salaries Expense
514	Utilities Expense

▶ 7. OBJECTIVE
Develop a chart of accounts.

FIGURE 3.8

Chart of Accounts

important!

Balance Sheet Accounts
The amounts on the balance sheet are carried forward to the next accounting period.

important!

Income Statement Accounts
The amounts on the income statement are transferred to the capital account at the end of the accounting period.

Section 2: **Self Review**

QUESTIONS

1. What is a transposition? A slide?

2. What is the increase side for *Cash; Accounts Payable;* and *Jason Taylor, Capital?*

3. What is a trial balance and what is its purpose?

EXERCISES

4. Which account has a normal debit balance?

   a. *Fees Income*

   b. *M. J., Drawing*

   c. *M. J., Capital*

   d. *Accounts Payable*

5. The company owner took $2,000 cash for personal use. What is the entry for this transaction?

   a. Debit *Cash* and credit *Gloria Bahamon, Capital.*

   b. Debit *Gloria Bahamon, Capital* and credit *Cash.*

   c. Debit *Gloria Bahamon, Drawing* and credit *Cash.*

   d. Debit *Cash* and credit *Gloria Bahamon, Drawing.*

ANALYSIS

6. Describe the errors in the Davis Interiors trial balance.

Davis Interiors
Trial Balance
December 31, 2007

	DEBIT	CREDIT
Cash	15 000 00	
Accts. Rec.	10 000 00	
Equip.	7 000 00	
Accts. Pay.		15 000 00
M. Davis, Capital		22 000 00
M. Davis, Drawing		10 000 00
Fees Income	14 000 00	
Rent Exp.	2 000 00	
Supplies Exp.	2 000 00	
Telephone Exp.	5 000 00	
Totals	55 000 00	47 000 00

(Answers to Section 2 Self Review are on page 92.)

REVIEW | Chapter Summary

In this chapter, you have learned how to use T accounts to help analyze and record business transactions. A chart of accounts can be developed to easily identify all the accounts used by a business. After determining the balance for all accounts, the trial balance is prepared to ensure that all transactions have been recorded accurately.

Learning Objectives

1 Set up T accounts for assets, liabilities, and owner's equity.

T accounts consist of two lines, one vertical and one horizontal, that resemble the letter **T.** The account name is written on the top line. Increases and decreases to the account are entered on either the left side or the right side of the vertical line.

2 Analyze business transactions and enter them in the accounts.

Each business transaction is analyzed for its effects on the fundamental accounting equation, Assets = Liabilities + Owner's Equity. Then these effects are recorded in the proper accounts. Accounts are classified as assets, liabilities, or owner's equity.

- Increases in an asset account appear on the debit, or left, side because assets are on the left side of the accounting equation. The credit, or right, side records decreases.

- An increase in a liability account is recorded on the credit, or right, side. The left, or debit, side of a liability account is used for recording decreases.

- Increases in owner's equity are shown on the credit (right) side of an account. Decreases appear on the debit (left) side.

- The drawing account is used to record the withdrawal of cash from the business by the owner. The drawing account decreases owner's equity.

3 Determine the balance of an account.

The difference between the amounts recorded on the two sides of an account is known as the balance of the account.

4 Set up T accounts for revenue and expenses.

- Revenue accounts increase owner's equity; therefore, increases are recorded on the credit side of revenue accounts.

- Expenses are recorded on the debit side of the expense accounts because expenses decrease owner's equity.

5 Prepare a trial balance from T accounts.

The trial balance is a statement to test the accuracy of the financial records. Total debits should equal total credits.

6 Prepare an income statement, a statement of owner's equity, and a balance sheet.

The income statement is prepared to report the revenue and expenses for the period. The statement of owner's equity is prepared to analyze the change in owner's equity during the period. Then the balance sheet is prepared to summarize the assets, liabilities, and owner's equity of the business at a given point in time.

7 Develop a chart of accounts.

A firm's list of accounts is called its chart of accounts. Accounts are arranged in a predetermined order and are numbered for handy reference and quick identification. Typically, accounts are numbered in the order in which they appear on the financial statements. Balance sheet accounts come first, followed by income statement accounts.

8 Define the accounting terms new to this chapter.

CHAPTER 3: Review and Applications

Glossary

Account balance (p. 62) The difference between the amounts recorded on the two sides of an account

Accounts (p. 56) Written records of the assets, liabilities, and owner's equity of a business

Chart of accounts (p. 75) A list of the accounts used by a business to record its financial transactions

Classification (p. 56) A means of identifying each account as an asset, liability, or owner's equity

Credit (p. 71) An entry on the right side of an account

Debit (p. 71) An entry on the left side of an account

Double-entry system (p. 71) An accounting system that involves recording the effects of each transaction as debits and credits

Drawing account (p. 69) A special type of owner's equity account set up to record the owner's withdrawal of cash from the business

Footing (p. 62) A small pencil figure written at the base of an amount column showing the sum of the entries in the column

Normal balance (p. 63) The increase side of an account

Permanent account (p. 75) An account that is kept open from one accounting period to the next

Slide (p. 74) An accounting error involving a misplaced decimal point

T account (p. 56) A type of account, resembling a T, used to analyze the effects of a business transaction

Temporary account (p. 75) An account whose balance is transferred to another account at the end of an accounting period

Transposition (p. 73) An accounting error involving misplaced digits in a number

Trial balance (p. 71) A statement to test the accuracy of total debits and credits after transactions have been recorded

Comprehensive **Self Review**

1. Your friend has prepared financial statements for her business. She has asked you to review the statements for accuracy. The trial balance debit column totals $71,000 and the credit column totals $84,000. What steps would you take to find the error?

2. What type of accounts are found on the balance sheet?

3. On which side of asset, liability, and owner's equity accounts are decreases recorded?

4. What are withdrawals and how are they recorded?

5. What is a chart of accounts?

(Answers to Comprehensive Self Review are on page 92.)

Discussion Questions

1. How is the balance of an account determined?
2. What is the purpose of a chart of accounts?
3. In what order do accounts appear in the chart of accounts?
4. When a chart of accounts is created, number gaps are left within groups of accounts. Why are these number gaps necessary?
5. Accounts are classified as permanent or temporary accounts. What do these classifications mean?
6. Are the following accounts permanent or temporary accounts?
    a. Fees Income
    b. Johnny Jones, Drawing
    c. Accounts Payable
    d. Accounts Receivable
    e. Johnny Jones, Capital
    f. Prepaid Rent
    g. Cash
    h. Advertising Expense
    i. Utilities Expense
    j. Equipment
    k. Salaries Expense
    l. Prepaid Insurance
7. What are accounts?
8. Why is *Prepaid Rent* considered an asset account?
9. Why is the modern system of accounting usually called the double-entry system?
10. The terms *debit* and *credit* are often used in describing the effects of transactions on different accounts. What do these terms mean?
11. Indicate whether each of the following types of accounts would normally have a debit balance or a credit balance.
    a. An asset account
    b. A liability account
    c. The owner's capital account
    d. A revenue account
    e. An expense account

CHAPTER 3: Review and Applications

APPLICATIONS

Exercises

CHAPTER 3: Review and Applications

Exercise 3.1
Objective 1

▶ **Setting up T accounts.**

The Tick Tock Watch and Jewelry Repair Service has the following account balances on December 31, 2007. Set up a T account for each account and enter the balance on the proper side of the account.

Cash	$ 8,000	Accounts Payable	$ 6,000
Equipment	16,000	Ned Smith, Capital	18,000

Exercise 3.2
Objective 2

▶ **Using T accounts to analyze transactions.**

Tonya Simpson decided to start a dental practice. The first five transactions for the business follow. For each transaction, (1) determine which two accounts are affected, (2) set up T accounts for the affected accounts, and (3) enter the debit and credit amounts in the T accounts.

1. Tonya invested $20,000 cash in the business.

2. Paid $5,000 in cash for equipment.

3. Performed services for cash amounting to $2,000.

4. Paid $700 in cash for advertising expense.

5. Paid $500 in cash for supplies.

Exercise 3.3
Objective 3

▶ **Identifying debits and credits.**

In each of the following sentences, fill in the blanks with the word *debit* or *credit*.

1. Revenue accounts normally have ____?____ balances. These accounts increase on the ____?____ side and decrease on the ____?____ side.

2. Expense accounts normally have ____?____ balances. These accounts increase on the ____?____ side and decrease on the ____?____ side.

3. Asset accounts normally have ____?____ balances. These accounts increase on the ____?____ side and decrease on the ____?____ side.

4. Liability accounts normally have ____?____ balances. These accounts increase on the ____?____ side and decrease on the ____?____ side.

5. The owner's capital account normally has a ____?____ balance. This account increases on the ____?____ side and decreases on the ____?____ side.

Exercise 3.4
Objective 3

▶ **Determining debit and credit balances.**

Indicate whether each of the following accounts normally has a debit balance or a credit balance.

1. Equipment

2. Accounts Receivable

3. Salaries Expense

4. Supplies

5. Accounts Payable

6. Fees Income

7. Cash

8. Andrew Wells, Capital

Determining account balances.

The following T accounts show transactions that were recorded by Antique Restorations, a firm that specializes in restoring antique furniture. The entries for the first transaction are labeled with the letter (a), the entries for the second transaction with the letter (b), and so on. Determine the balance of each account.

◀ **Exercise 3.5**
Objective 3

Cash			
(a)	80,000	(b)	20,000
(d)	10,000	(e)	300
(g)	1,000	(h)	5,000
		(i)	2,000

Equipment	
(c)	30,000

Accounts Receivable			
(f)	4,000	(g)	1,000

Accounts Payable	
(c)	30,000

Supplies	
(b)	20,000

Cecil Hill, Capital	
(a)	80,000

Fees Income			
		(d)	10,000
		(f)	4,000

Telephone Expense	
(e)	300

Cecil Hill, Drawing	
(i)	2,000

Salaries Expense	
(h)	5,000

Preparing a trial balance and an income statement.

Using the account balances from Exercise 3.5, prepare a trial balance and an income statement for Antique Restorations. The trial balance is for December 31, 2007, and the income statement is for the month ended December 31, 2007.

◀ **Exercise 3.6**
Objectives 5, 6
CONTINUING >>>
Problem

Preparing a statement of owner's equity and a balance sheet.

From the trial balance and the net income or net loss determined in Exercise 3.6, prepare a statement of owner's equity and a balance sheet for Antique Restorations as of December 31, 2007.

◀ **Exercise 3.7**
Objective 6
CONTINUING >>>
Problem

Preparing a chart of accounts.

The accounts that will be used by Hidden Valley Company follow. Prepare a chart of accounts for the firm. Classify the accounts by type, arrange them in an appropriate order, and assign suitable account numbers.

◀ **Exercise 3.8**
Objective 7

James Walker, Capital	Salaries Expense
Office Supplies	Prepaid Rent
Accounts Payable	Fees Income
Cash	Accounts Receivable
Utilities Expense	Telephone Expense
Office Equipment	James Walker, Drawing

CHAPTER 3: Review and Applications

PROBLEMS

Problem Set A

Problem 3.1A
Objectives 1, 2

eXcel

▶ **Using T accounts to record transactions involving assets, liabilities, and owner's equity.**

The following transactions took place at Ware's Oil Field Equipment Service.

INSTRUCTIONS

For each transaction, set up T accounts from the following list: *Cash; Shop Equipment; Store Equipment; Truck; Accounts Payable; Alma Ware, Capital;* and *Alma Ware, Drawing.* Analyze each transaction. Record the effects of the transactions in the T accounts. Use plus and minus signs before the amounts to show the increases and decreases.

TRANSACTIONS

1. Alma Ware invested $10,000 cash in the business.
2. Purchased shop equipment for $900 in cash.
3. Bought store fixtures for $600; payment is due in 30 days.
4. Purchased a used truck for $5,000 in cash.
5. Ware gave the firm her personal tools that have a fair market value of $1,500.
6. Bought a used cash register for $1,250; payment is due in 30 days.
7. Paid $200 in cash to apply to the amount owed for store fixtures.
8. Ware withdrew $800 in cash for personal expenses.

Analyze: Which transactions affect the *Cash* account?

Problem 3.2A
Objectives 1, 2

▶ **Using T accounts to record transactions involving assets, liabilities, and owner's equity.**

The following transactions occurred at several different businesses and are not related.

INSTRUCTIONS

Analyze each of the transactions. For each transaction, set up T accounts. Record the effects of the transaction in the T accounts. Use plus and minus signs to show the increases and decreases.

TRANSACTIONS

1. A firm purchased equipment for $8,000 in cash.
2. The owner Mandy Alvarez withdrew $2,000 cash.
3. A firm sold a piece of surplus equipment for $1,500 in cash.
4. A firm purchased a used delivery truck for $6,000 in cash.
5. A firm paid $1,800 in cash to apply against an account owed.
6. A firm purchased office equipment for $2,500. The amount is to be paid in 60 days.
7. Charles Beatty, owner of the company, made an additional investment of $10,000 in cash.
8. A firm paid $750 by check for office equipment that it had previously purchased on credit.

Analyze: Which transactions affect liability accounts?

Using T accounts to record transactions involving revenue and expenses.

The following transactions took place at At Your Service Cleaning Company.

Problem 3.3A
Objectives 2, 4

INSTRUCTIONS

Analyze each of the transactions. For each transaction, decide what accounts are affected and set up T accounts. Record the effects of the transaction in the T accounts. Use plus and minus signs before the amounts to show the increases and decreases.

TRANSACTIONS

1. Paid $1,600 for the current month's rent.
2. Performed services for $2,000 in cash.
3. Paid salaries of $2,400.
4. Performed additional services for $3,600 on credit.
5. Paid $300 for the monthly telephone bill.
6. Collected $1,000 from accounts receivable.
7. Received a $60 refund for an overcharge on the telephone bill.
8. Performed services for $2,400 on credit.
9. Paid $200 in cash for the monthly electric bill.
10. Paid $440 in cash for gasoline purchased for the firm's van during the month.
11. Received $1,800 from charge account customers.
12. Performed services for $3,600 in cash.

Analyze: What total cash was collected for accounts receivable during the month?

Using T accounts to record all business transactions.

The accounts and transactions of Lisa Morgan, Attorney at Law, follow.

Problem 3.4A
Objectives 1, 2, 4
e**X**cel

INSTRUCTIONS

Analyze the transactions. Record each in the appropriate T accounts. Use plus and minus signs in front of the amounts to show the increases and decreases. Identify each entry in the T accounts by writing the letter of the transaction next to the entry.

ASSETS
Cash
Accounts Receivable
Office Equipment
Automobile
LIABILITIES
Accounts Payable
OWNER'S EQUITY
Lisa Morgan, Capital
Lisa Morgan, Drawing
REVENUE
Fees Income
EXPENSES
Automobile Expense
Rent Expense
Utilities Expense
Salaries Expense
Telephone Expense

TRANSACTIONS

a.   Lisa Morgan invested $60,000 in cash to start the business.

b.   Paid $3,200 for the current month's rent.

c.   Bought a used automobile for the firm for $18,000 in cash.

d.   Performed services for $4,000 in cash.

e.   Paid $800 for automobile repairs.

f.   Performed services for $4,575 on credit.

g.   Purchased office chairs for $2,800 on credit.

h.   Received $2,250 from credit clients.

i.   Paid $1,800 to reduce the amount owed for the office chairs.

j.   Issued a check for $650 to pay the monthly utility bill.

k.   Purchased office equipment for $9,800 and paid half of this amount in cash immediately; the balance is due in 30 days.

l.   Issued a check for $6,850 to pay salaries.

m.   Performed services for $2,375 in cash.

n.   Performed services for $2,750 on credit.

o.   Paid $398 for the monthly telephone bill.

p.   Collected $1,900 on accounts receivable from charge customers.

q.   Purchased additional office equipment and received a bill for $2,720 due in 30 days.

r.   Paid $400 in cash for gasoline purchased for the automobile during the month.

s.   Lisa Morgan withdrew $3,000 in cash for personal expenses.

Analyze: What outstanding amount is owed to the company from its credit customers?

Problem 3.5A
▶   **Preparing financial statements from T accounts.**

Objectives 3, 5, 6

The accountant for the firm owned by Lisa Morgan prepares financial statements at the end of each month.

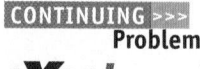

INSTRUCTIONS

Use the figures in the T accounts for Problem 3.4A to prepare a trial balance, an income statement, a statement of owner's equity, and a balance sheet. (The first line of the statement headings should read "Lisa Morgan, Attorney at Law.") Assume that the transactions took place during the month ended April 30, 2007. Determine the account balances before you start work on the financial statements.

Analyze: What net change in owner's equity occurred during the month of April?

Problem Set B

Using T accounts to record transactions involving assets, liabilities, and owner's equity.

◀ **Problem 3.1B**
Objectives 1, 2

The following transactions took place at the profession counseling services business established by Clifford Marshall.

INSTRUCTIONS

For each transaction, set up T accounts from this list: *Cash; Office Furniture; Office Equipment; Automobile; Accounts Payable; Clifford Marshall, Capital;* and *Clifford Marshall, Drawing.* Analyze each transaction. Record the amounts in the T accounts affected by that transaction. Use plus and minus signs to show increases and decreases in each account.

TRANSACTIONS

1. Clifford Marshall invested $30,000 cash in the business.
2. Purchased office furniture for $8,000 in cash.
3. Bought a fax machine for $475; payment is due in 30 days.
4. Purchased a used car for the firm for $8,000 in cash.
5. Marshall invested an additional $5,000 cash in the business.
6. Bought a new computer for $1,500; payment is due in 60 days.
7. Paid $475 to settle the amount owed on the fax machine.
8. Marshall withdrew $2,000 in cash for personal expenses.

Analyze: Which transactions affected asset accounts?

Using T accounts to record transactions involving assets, liabilities, and owner's equity.

◀ **Problem 3.2B**
Objective 1

The following transactions occurred at several different businesses and are not related.

INSTRUCTIONS

Analyze each of the transactions. For each, decide what accounts are affected and set up T accounts. Record the effects of the transaction in the T accounts. Use plus and minus signs before the amounts to show the increases and decreases.

TRANSACTIONS

1. Albert James, an owner, made an additional investment of $4,000 in cash.
2. A firm purchased equipment for $3,500 in cash.
3. A firm sold some surplus office furniture for $300 in cash.
4. A firm purchased a computer for $675, to be paid in 60 days.
5. A firm purchased office equipment for $2,550 on credit. The amount is due in 60 days.
6. Brenda Davis, owner of Davis Travel Agency, withdrew $1,000 of her original cash investment.
7. A firm bought a delivery truck for $9,000 on credit; payment is due in 90 days.
8. A firm issued a check for $550 to a supplier in partial payment of an open account balance.

Analyze: List the transactions that directly affected an owner's equity account.

CHAPTER 3: Review and Applications

Problem 3.3B ▶
Objectives 2, 4

Using T accounts to record transactions involving revenues and expenses.

The following occurred during June at Sampson's Professional Counseling.

INSTRUCTIONS

Analyze each transaction. Use T accounts to record these transactions and be sure to put the name of the account on the top of each account. Record the effects of the transaction in the T accounts. Use plus and minus signs before the amounts to show the increases and decreases.

TRANSACTIONS

1. Purchased office supplies for $1,000.
2. Delivered monthly statements, collected fee income of $10,500.
3. Paid the current month's office rent of $2,000.
4. Completed professional counseling, billed client for $1,500.
5. Client paid fee of $500 for weekly counseling, previously billed.
6. Paid office salary of $1,800.
7. Paid telephone bill of $240.
8. Billed client for $1,000 fee for preparing a counseling memorandum.
9. Purchased office supplies of $500 on account.
10. Paid office salary of $1,800.
11. Collected $1,000 from client who was billed.
12. Clients paid a total of $4,050 cash in fees.

Analyze: How much cash did the business spend during the month of June?

Problem 3.4B ▶
Objectives 1, 2, 4

Using T accounts to record all business transactions.

The following accounts and transactions are for Jeraldine Wells, Landscape Consultant.

INSTRUCTIONS

Analyze the transactions. Record each in the appropriate T accounts. Use plus and minus signs in front of the amounts to show the increases and decreases. Identify each entry in the T accounts by writing the letter of the transaction next to the entry.

ASSETS
Cash
Accounts Receivable
Office Furniture
Office Equipment
LIABILITIES
Accounts Payable
OWNER'S EQUITY
Jeraldine Wells, Capital
Jeraldine Wells, Drawing
REVENUE
Fees Income
EXPENSES
Rent Expense
Utilities Expense
Salaries Expense
Telephone Expense
Miscellaneous Expense

TRANSACTIONS

a. Wells invested $75,000 in cash to start the business.

b. Paid $2,500 for the current month's rent.

c. Bought office furniture for $7,860 in cash.

d. Performed services for $3,600 in cash.

e. Paid $575 for the monthly telephone bill.

f. Performed services for $6,500 on credit.

g. Purchased a computer and copier for $18,000, paid $6,000 in cash immediately with the balance due in 30 days.

h. Received $3,250 from credit clients.

i. Paid $1,500 in cash for office cleaning services for the month.

j. Purchased additional office chairs for $2,400; received credit terms of 30 days.

k. Purchased office equipment for $15,000 and paid half of this amount in cash immediately; the balance is due in 30 days.

l. Issued a check for $4,200 to pay salaries.

m. Performed services for $6,750 in cash.

n. Performed services for $7,500 on credit.

o. Collected $3,500 on accounts receivable from charge customers.

p. Issued a check for $1,200 in partial payment of the amount owed for office chairs.

q. Paid $300 to a duplicating company for photocopy work performed during the month.

r. Paid $560 for the monthly electric bill.

s. Wells withdrew $4,000 in cash for personal expenses.

Analyze: What liabilities does the business have after all transactions have been recorded?

Preparing financial statements from T accounts.

◀ **Problem 3.5B**
Objectives 3, 5, 6

CONTINUING >>>
Problem

The accountant for the firm owned by Jeraldine Wells prepares financial statements at the end of each month.

INSTRUCTIONS

Use the figures in the T accounts for Problem 3.4B to prepare a trial balance, an income statement, a statement of owner's equity, and a balance sheet. (The first line of the statement headings should read "Jeraldine Wells, Landscape Consultant.") Assume that the transactions took place during the month ended June 30, 2007. Determine the account balances before you start work on the financial statements.

Analyze: What is the change in owner's equity for the month of June?

Challenge Problem

Sole Proprietorship

Adele Applegate is an architect who operates her own business. The accounts and transactions for the business follow.

INSTRUCTIONS

(1) Analyze the transactions for January 2007. Record each in the appropriate T accounts. Use plus and minus signs in front of the amounts to show the increases and decreases. Identify each entry in the T account by writing the letter of the transaction next to the entry.

(2) Determine the account balances. Prepare a trial balance, an income statement, a statement of owner's equity, and a balance sheet.

     ASSETS
     Cash
     Accounts Receivable
     Office Furniture
     Office Equipment
     LIABILITIES
     Accounts Payable
     OWNER'S EQUITY
     Adele Applegate, Capital
     Adele Applegate, Drawing
     REVENUE
     Fees Income
     EXPENSES
     Advertising Expense
     Utilities Expense
     Salaries Expense
     Telephone Expense
     Miscellaneous Expense

TRANSACTIONS

a. Adele Applegate invested $30,000 in cash to start the business.

b. Paid $2,000 for advertisements in a design magazine.

c. Purchased office furniture for $4,000 in cash.

d. Performed services for $4,200 in cash.

e. Paid $375 for the monthly telephone bill.

f. Performed services for $2,610 on credit.

g. Purchased a fax machine for $575; paid $175 in cash with the balance due in 30 days.

h. Paid a bill for $650 from the office cleaning service.

i. Received $2,160 from clients on account.

j. Purchased additional office chairs for $1,080; received credit terms of 30 days.

k. Paid $4,000 for salaries.

l. Issued a check for $540 in partial payment of the amount owed for office chairs.

m. Received $2,800 in cash for services performed.

n. Issued a check for $560 for utilities expense.

o. Performed services for $4,200 on credit.

p. Collected $1,200 from clients on account.

q. Adele Applegate withdrew $3,500 in cash for personal expenses.

r. Paid $600 to Vision's Photocopy Service for photocopy work performed during the month.

Analyze: Using the basic accounting equation, what is the financial condition of Adele Applegate's business at month-end?

Critical Thinking Problem

Financial Condition

At the beginning of the summer, Oscar Wilson was looking for a way to earn money to pay for his college tuition in the fall. He decided to start a lawn service business in his neighborhood. To get the business started, Oscar used $1,500 from his savings account to open a checking account for his new business, Specialty Lawn Care. He purchased two used power mowers and various lawn care tools for $500, and paid $900 for a second-hand truck to transport the mowers.

Several of his neighbors hired him to cut their grass on a weekly basis. He sent these customers monthly bills. By the end of the summer, they had paid him $300 in cash and owed him another $575. Oscar also cut grass on an as-needed basis for other neighbors who paid him $250.

During the summer, Oscar spent $100 for gasoline for the truck and mowers. He paid $250 to a friend who helped him on several occasions. An advertisement in the local paper cost $50. Now, at the end of the summer, Oscar is concerned because he has only $250 left in his checking account. He says, "I worked hard all summer and have only $250 to show for it. It would have been better to leave the money in the bank."

Prepare an income statement, a statement of owner's equity, and a balance sheet for Specialty Lawn Care. Explain to Oscar whether or not he is "better off" than he was at the beginning of the summer. (Hint: T accounts might be helpful in organizing the data.)

CHAPTER 3: Review and Applications

CHAPTER 3: Review and Applications

BUSINESS CONNECTIONS

Managerial **FOCUS**

Informed Decisions

1. How do the income statement and the balance sheet help management make sound decisions?

2. How can management find out, at any time, whether a firm can pay its bills as they become due?

3. If a firm's expenses equal or exceed its revenue, what actions might management take?

4. In discussing a firm's latest financial statements, a manager says that it is the "results on the bottom line" that really count. What does the manager mean?

Ethical **DILEMMA**

To Open or Not to Open

As the Full Charge Bookkeeper, you are responsible for keeping the Chart of Accounts up to date. At the end of each year, you analyze the accounts to verify that each account should be active for accumulation of costs, revenues, and expenses. In July, the Accounts Payable clerk has asked you to open an account named New Expenses. You know that an account name should be specific and well defined. You feel that the A/P Clerk might want to charge some expenses to that account that would not be appropriate. Why do you think the A/P clerk needs this New Expense account? Who needs to know this information and what action should you consider?

STREETWISE:
Questions from the
REAL WORLD

Account Categories

Refer to the *2004 Annual Report* for The Home Depot, Inc. in Appendix A.

1. To prepare financial statements, The Home Depot, Inc. summarizes general ledger account balances into summary categories for presentation on statements. List five "permanent" summarized account categories reflected in these statements. List five "temporary" summarized account categories found in the statements.

2. Locate the consolidated balance sheets for The Home Depot, Inc. If The Home Depot, Inc. purchased new store fixtures on account for $25,000, describe the effect on the company's balance sheet categories.

Financial Statement
ANALYSIS

Management Letter

Annual reports released by publicly held companies include a letter to the stockholders written by the chief executive officer, chairman of the board, or president. Excerpts from the Adobe Systems Incorporated *Annual Report* "2004 Letter To Stockholders" are presented below. The appearance of an ellipsis (...) indicates that some of the text of the letter has been deleted to save space.

> Surpasing our record performance in 2003, Adobe Systems Incorporated met or exceeded Wall Street expectations in every quarter of fiscal 2004, delivering double digit growth for the second year in a row. Annual revenue grew to a record of $1.667 billion, a 29 percent increase from fiscal 2003 revenue. . . . Reported net income reached $450.4 million, a 69 percent increase from fiscal 2003. Adobe's Creative Professional revenue was $613.1 million, a 66 percent increase from the prior year. Revenue from our Intelligent Documents business unit grew to $541.8 million, a 22 percent increase year over year. . . . Adobe once again executed on its strategy with remarkable operational efficiency. We have a . . . cash position of approximately $1.3 billion, and no long-term debt. . . .

Analyze:

1. Based on the excerpts above, what types of information can a company's management deliver using the letter to stockholders?

2. What net income did Adobe Systems Incorporated report for fiscal 2004?

3. Which of Adobe's revenue lines showed the highest percentage growth from fiscal 2003 to 2004?

Analyze Online: Locate the Adobe Systems Incorporated Web site (**www.adobe.com**). Within *Investor Relations* in the *About Adobe* link, find the annual report for the current year. Read the letter to the stockholders within the annual report.

4. Are the financial results presented in the current year more or less favorable than those presented for fiscal 2004?

5. What new products were introduced in the current year and mentioned in the stockholders' letter?

Systems

A company's chart of accounts is an organization system. Discuss similar organization systems in subject areas other than accounting.

Memo

The junior accountant in your department does not agree that a trial balance should be prepared before the financial statements are completed. As the senior accountant, write a memo to your co-worker explaining your position on the topic. Express possible ramifications that you foresee if the trial balance is not prepared.

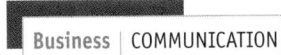

Specific Chart of Accounts

A Chart of Accounts varies with each type of business as well as each company. In a group, compare and contrast the accounts that would appear in Jones Real Estate Office, Christy's Clothing Emporium, Lee's Grocery store, and Sarkis' Plumbing Service. What accounts would appear in all companies? What accounts would be specific to each business?

10K Reports

Financial Statements can reveal a great deal about a company. Corporations are required to produce a 10K report that includes the Income Statement and Balance Sheet. Go to the below listed companies' Web sites, select investor relations, annual report, and 10K report. From the Income Statement, decide the most profitable company. From the Balance Sheet, decide the company with the largest amount of cash available and the one with the most assets.

(www.federated-fds.com) (www.jcpenny.com) (www.honeywell.com)

CHAPTER 3: Review and Applications

Answers to **Self Reviews**

Answers to Section 1 Self Review

1. The increase side of an account. The normal balance of an asset account is on the left side. The normal balance of liability and owner's equity accounts is on the right side.

2. Increases in asset accounts are recorded on the left side. Increases in liability and owner's equity accounts are recorded on the right side.

3. The sum of several entries on either side of an account that is entered in small pencil figures.

4. **b.** $13,075

5. **c.** *Equipment* is increased by $5,400. *Accounts Payable* is increased by $5,400.

6.
Cash	+	Equipment	+	Supplies	=	Accounts Payable	+	Euline Hawkins, Capital
7,700	+	10,000	+	2,300	=	5,000	+	15,000
				20,000	=	20,000		

Answers to Section 2 Self Review

1. A transposition is an error in which the digits of a number are switched, for example, when 517 is recorded as 571.

   A slide is an error in which the decimal point is misplaced, for example, when 317 is written as 3.17.

2. The increase side of *Cash* is the left, or debit, side. The increase side of *Accounts Payable* is the right, or credit, side. The increase side of *Jason Taylor, Capital* is the right, or credit, side.

3. The trial balance is a list of all the accounts and their balances. Its purpose is to prove the equality of the total debits and credits.

4. **b.** *M. J., Drawing*

5. **c.** *Gloria Bahamon, Drawing* would be debited and *Cash* would be credited.

6. *M. Davis, Drawing*—10,000 should be in the Debit column.

   Fees Income—14,000 should be in the Credit column.

   The new column totals will be 51,000.

Answers to Comprehensive Self Review

1. ■ Check the math by adding the columns again.

   ■ Determine whether the account balances are in the correct columns.

   ■ Check the accounts to see whether the balances in the accounts were computed correctly.

   ■ Check the accuracy of transactions recorded during the period.

2. The asset, liability, and owner's equity accounts.

3. Decreases in asset accounts are recorded on the credit side. Decreases in liability and owner's equity accounts are recorded on the debit side.

4. Cash taken from the business by the owner to obtain funds for personal living expenses. Withdrawals are recorded in a special type of owner's equity account called a drawing account.

5. A list of the numbers and names of the accounts of a business. It provides a system by which the accounts of the business can be easily identified and located.

LEARNING OBJECTIVES

1. Record transactions in the general journal.

2. Prepare compound journal entries.

3. Post journal entries to general ledger accounts.

4. Correct errors made in the journal or ledger.

5. Define the accounting terms new to this chapter.

NEW TERMS

accounting cycle	general journal
audit trail	general ledger
balance ledger form	journal
chronological order	journalizing
compound entry	ledger
correcting entry	posting

Chapter 4
The General Journal and the General Ledger

Caterpillar www.caterpillar.com

For more than 80 years, Caterpillar Inc. has been building the world's foundation. Caterpillar is the world's leading manufacturer of construction and mining equipment, diesel and natural gas engines, and industrial gas turbines. The company is a technology leader in construction, transportation, mining, forestry, energy, logistics, electronics, financing, and electric power generation.

Founded in 1925 with roots dating back to the 1870s, Caterpillar focused on tractors. Benjamin Holt, Daniel Best, and C. L. Best first developed steam-driven tractors which they evolved into gas-powered tractors and finally, in 1931, the Diesel Sixty Tractor rolled off the assembly line in East Peoria, Illinois, with a new efficient source of power for track-type tractors. From this single machine, Caterpillar has built its business and now offers over 300 machines—from backhoe loaders to pipelayers, each machine is designed with a specific use in mind. In 2004, sales and revenues were reported at $30.25 billion and the company posted a record profit of $2.03 billion, up 85 percent from 2003.

thinking critically | Why would Caterpillar expand its product offerings beyond its Diesel Sixty Tractor?

Section 1

The General Journal

SECTION OBJECTIVES

▶ **1. Record transactions in the general journal.**

WHY IT'S IMPORTANT

Written records for all business transactions are necessary. The general journal acts as the "diary" of the business.

▶ **2. Prepare compound journal entries.**

WHY IT'S IMPORTANT

Compound entries contain several debits or credits for a single business transaction, creating efficiencies in journalizing.

TERMS TO LEARN

accounting cycle
audit trail
chronological order
compound entry
general journal
journal
journalizing

The **accounting cycle** is a series of steps performed during each accounting period to classify, record, and summarize data for a business and to produce needed financial information. The first step in the accounting cycle is to analyze business transactions. You learned this skill in Chapter 3. The second step in the accounting cycle is to prepare a record of business transactions.

Journals

Business transactions are recorded in a **journal**, which is a diary of business activities. The journal lists transactions in **chronological order**, that is, in the order in which they occur. The journal is sometimes called the *record of original entry* because it is where transactions are first entered in the accounting records. There are different types of journals. This chapter will examine the general journal. You will become familiar with other journals in later chapters.

> Most corporations use accounting software to record business transactions. Texaco International uses Solomon IV accounting software.

▶ **1. OBJECTIVE**

Record transactions in the general journal.

important!

The Diary of a Business

The general journal is similar to a diary. The general journal details, in chronological order, the economic events of the business.

The General Journal

The **general journal** is a financial record for entering all types of business transactions. **Journalizing** is the process of recording transactions in the general journal.

Figure 4.1 shows the general journal for JT's Consulting Services. Notice that the general journal has a page number. To record a transaction, enter the year at the top of the Date column. In the Date column, write the month and day on the first line of the first entry. After the first entry, enter the year and month only when a new page is started or when the year or the month changes. In the Date column, write the day of each transaction on the first line of each transaction.

In the Description column, enter the account to be debited. Write the account name close to the left margin of the Description column, and enter the amount on the same line in the Debit column.

Enter the account to be credited on the line beneath the debit. Indent the account name about one-half inch from the left margin. Enter the amount on the same line in the Credit column.

Then enter a complete but concise description of the transaction in the Description column. Begin the description on the line following the credit. The description is indented about one inch from the left margin.

Write account names exactly as they appear in the chart of accounts. This will minimize errors when amounts are transferred from the general journal to the accounts.

FIGURE 4.1

General Journal Entry

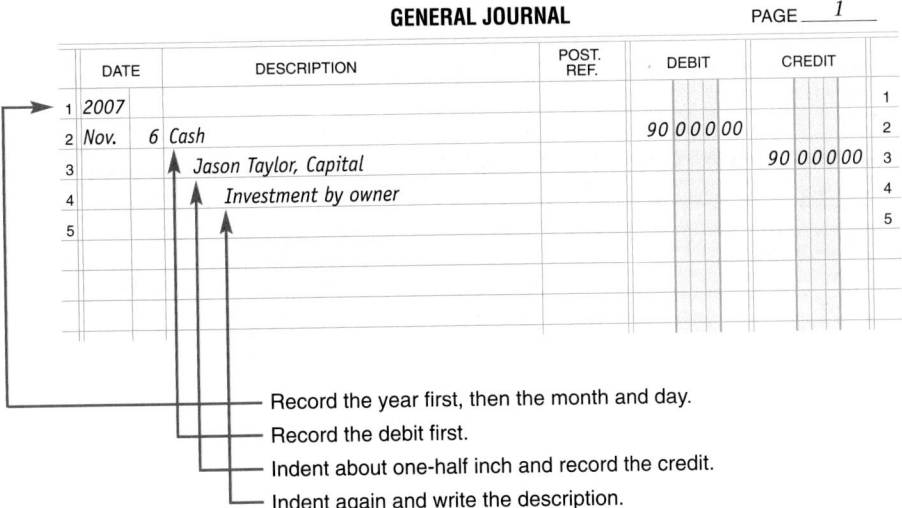

Record the year first, then the month and day.
Record the debit first.
Indent about one-half inch and record the credit.
Indent again and write the description.

Leave a blank line between general journal entries. Some accountants use this blank line to number each general journal entry.

When possible, the journal entry description should refer to the source of the information. For example, the journal entry to record a payment should include the check number in the description. Document numbers are part of the audit trail. The **audit trail** is a chain of references that makes it possible to trace information, locate errors, and prevent fraud. The audit trail provides a means of checking the journal entry against the original data on the documents.

RECORDING NOVEMBER TRANSACTIONS IN THE GENERAL JOURNAL

In Chapters 2 and 3, you learned a step-by-step method for analyzing business transactions. In this chapter you will learn how to complete the journal entry for a business transaction in the same manner. Review the following steps before you continue.

1. Analyze the financial event.
   - Identify the accounts affected.
   - Classify the accounts affected.
   - Determine the amount of increase or decrease for each account affected.

2. Apply the rules of debit and credit.
   a. Which account is debited? For what amount?
   b. Which account is credited? For what amount?

3. Make the entry in T-account form.

4. Record the complete entry in general journal form.

> **important!**
>
> **Audit Trail**
> To maintain the audit trail, descriptions should refer to document numbers whenever possible.

BUSINESS TRANSACTION

On November 6 Jason Taylor withdrew $90,000 from personal savings and deposited it in a new business checking account for JT's Consulting Services.

MEMORANDUM 01

JT'S CONSULTING SERVICES

TO: Tennille Brisbane
FROM: Jason Taylor
DATE: November 6, 2007
SUBJECT: Contributed personal funds to the business

I contributed $90,000 from my personal savings to JT's Consulting Services.

ANALYSIS

a. The asset account, *Cash,* is increased by $90,000.
b. The owner's equity account, *Jason Taylor, Capital,* is increased by $90,000.

DEBIT-CREDIT RULES

DEBIT   Increases to asset accounts are recorded as debits. Debit *Cash* for $90,000.

CREDIT Increases to the owner's equity account are recorded as credits. Credit *Jason Taylor, Capital* for $90,000.

T-ACCOUNT PRESENTATION

Cash			Jason Taylor, Capital	
+	−		−	+
(a) 90,000				(b) 90,000

GENERAL JOURNAL ENTRY

	DATE		DESCRIPTION	POST. REF.	DEBIT	CREDIT	
1	2007						1
2	Nov.	6	Cash		90 0 0 0 00		2
3			Jason Taylor, Capital			90 0 0 0 00	3
4			Investment by owner,				4
5			Memo 01				5

GENERAL JOURNAL   PAGE 1

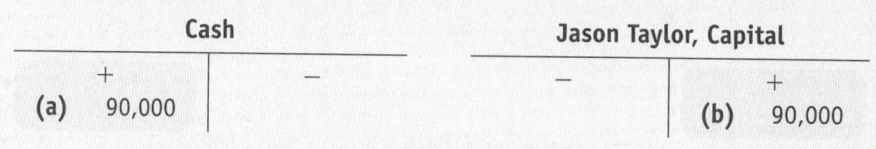

BUSINESS TRANSACTION

On November 7 JT's Consulting Services issued Check 1001 for $10,000 to purchase a computer and other equipment.

ANALYSIS

c. The asset account, *Equipment,* is increased by $10,000.

d. The asset account, *Cash,* is decreased by $10,000.

$	10,000.00		**No. 1001**
Date	November 7,	20	07
To	The Information Technology Store		
For	Office Equipment		

	Dollars	Cents
Balance brought forward	90,000	00
Add deposits		
Total	90,000	00
Less this check	10,000	00
Balance carried forward	80,000	00

DEBIT-CREDIT RULES

DEBIT   Increases to asset accounts are recorded as debits. Debit *Equipment* for $10,000.

CREDIT Decreases to asset accounts are recorded as credits. Credit *Cash* for $10,000.

T-ACCOUNT PRESENTATION

Equipment			Cash	
+	−		+	−
(c) 10,000				(d) 10,000

GENERAL JOURNAL ENTRY

GENERAL JOURNAL PAGE ___1___

	DATE		DESCRIPTION	POST. REF.	DEBIT	CREDIT	
6	Nov.	7	Equipment		10 0 0 0 00		6
7			Cash			10 0 0 0 00	7
8			Purchased equip., Check 1001				8

The check number appears in the description and forms part of the audit trail for the transaction.

BUSINESS TRANSACTION

On November 10 JT's Consulting Services purchased office equipment on account for $12,000.

OFFICE *plus*   **INVOICE NO. 2223**

DATE: Nov. 10, 2007
ORDER NO.: P38
SHIPPED BY: n/a
TERMS: 60 days

TO   JT's Consulting Services

QTY.	ITEM	UNIT PRICE	TOTAL
1	Copier	1,000	1,000
1	Fax Machine	600	600
4	Computers	2,050	8,200
3	Printers	500	1,500
2	Scanners	250	500
2	Calculators	100	200
		Total	12,000

ANALYSIS

e. The asset account, *Equipment,* is increased by $12,000.

f. The liability account, *Accounts Payable,* is increased by $12,000.

DEBIT-CREDIT RULES

DEBIT Increases to asset accounts are recorded as debits. Debit *Equipment* for $12,000.

CREDIT Increases to liability accounts are recorded as credits. Credit *Accounts Payable* for $12,000.

T-ACCOUNT PRESENTATION

Equipment		Accounts Payable	
+	−	−	+
(e) 12,000			(f) 12,000

GENERAL JOURNAL ENTRY

GENERAL JOURNAL PAGE ___1___

	DATE		DESCRIPTION	POST. REF.	DEBIT	CREDIT	
10	Nov.	10	Equipment		12 0 0 0 00		10
11			Accounts Payable			12 0 0 0 00	11
12			Purchased equipment on				12
13			account from Office Plus,				13
14			Inv. 2223, due in 60 days				14

The supplier's name (Office Plus) and invoice number (2223) appear in the journal entry description and form part of the audit trail for the transaction. The journal entry can be checked against the data on the original document, Invoice 2223.

BUSINESS TRANSACTION

On November 28 JT's Consulting Services purchased supplies for $3,000, Check 1002.

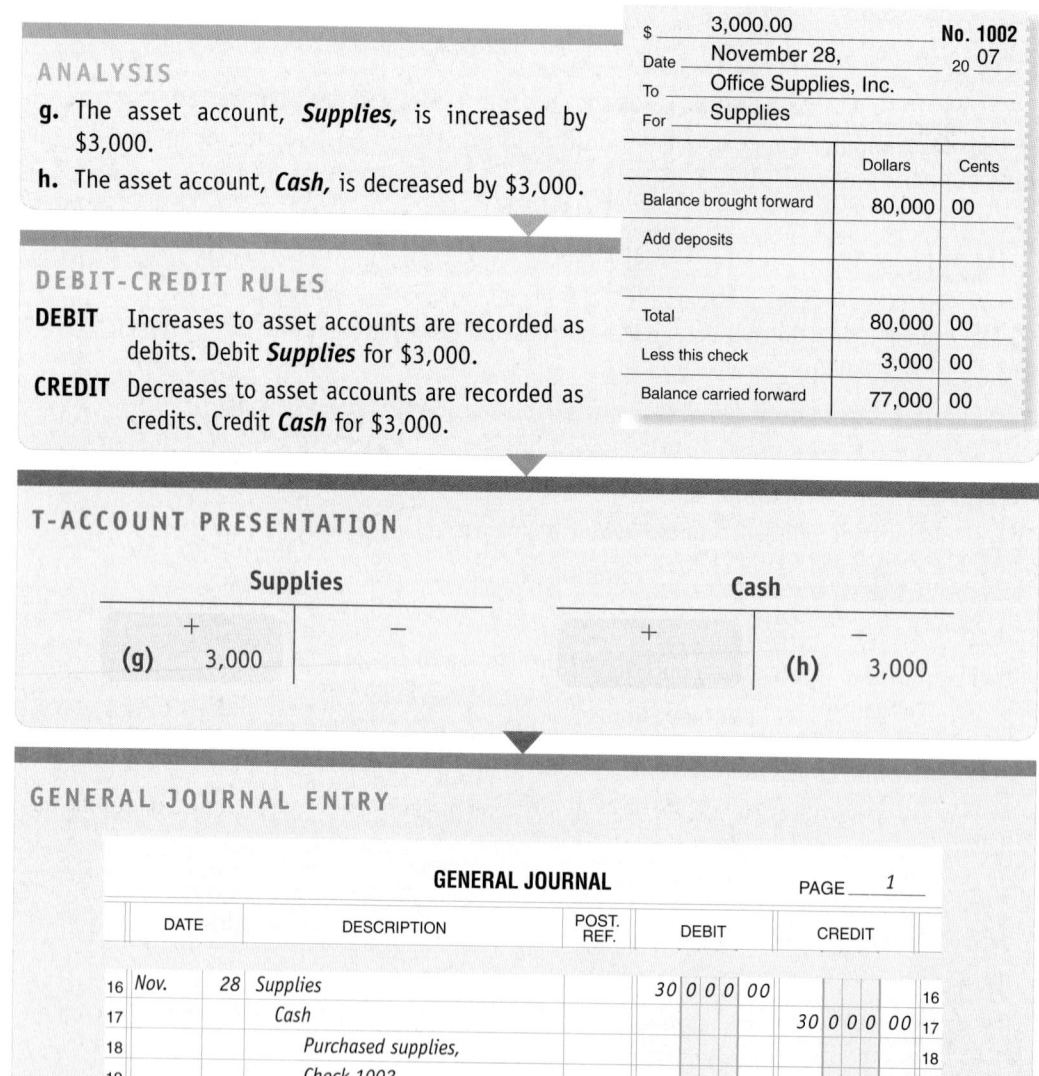

ANALYSIS

g. The asset account, **Supplies,** is increased by $3,000.

h. The asset account, **Cash,** is decreased by $3,000.

DEBIT-CREDIT RULES

DEBIT Increases to asset accounts are recorded as debits. Debit **Supplies** for $3,000.

CREDIT Decreases to asset accounts are recorded as credits. Credit **Cash** for $3,000.

		$ 3,000.00	No. 1002
Date	November 28,		20 07
To	Office Supplies, Inc.		
For	Supplies		

	Dollars	Cents
Balance brought forward	80,000	00
Add deposits		
Total	80,000	00
Less this check	3,000	00
Balance carried forward	77,000	00

T-ACCOUNT PRESENTATION

Supplies			Cash	
+	−		+	−
(g) 3,000				(h) 3,000

GENERAL JOURNAL ENTRY

GENERAL JOURNAL　　PAGE 1

	DATE	DESCRIPTION	POST. REF.	DEBIT	CREDIT	
16	Nov. 28	Supplies		30 0 0 0 00		16
17		Cash			30 0 0 0 00	17
18		Purchased supplies,				18
19		Check 1002				19
20						20

Tennille Brisbane decided to reduce the firm's debt to Office Plus. Recall that the firm had purchased equipment on account in the amount of $12,000. On November 30 JT's Consulting Services issued a check to Office Plus. Tennille Brisbane analyzed the transaction and recorded the journal entry as follows.

BUSINESS TRANSACTION

On November 30 JT's Consulting Services paid Office Plus $5,000 in partial payment of Invoice 2223, Check 1003.

ANALYSIS

i. The asset account, **Cash,** is decreased by $5,000.

j. The liability account, **Accounts Payable,** is decreased by $5,000.

		No. **1003**
$ 5,000.00		
Date November 30,		20 **07**
To Office Plus		
For Payment on Account		

	Dollars	Cents
Balance brought forward	77,000	00
Add deposits		
Total	77,000	00
Less this check	5,000	00
Balance carried forward	72,000	00

DEBIT-CREDIT RULES

DEBIT Decreases to liability accounts are recorded as debits. Debit **Accounts Payable** for $5,000.

CREDIT Decreases to asset accounts are recorded as credits. Credit **Cash** for $5,000.

T-ACCOUNT PRESENTATION

Accounts Payable		Cash	
+	−	+	−
(j) 5,000			(i) 5,000

GENERAL JOURNAL ENTRY

		GENERAL JOURNAL			PAGE _1_	
	DATE	DESCRIPTION	POST. REF.	DEBIT	CREDIT	
21	Nov. 30	Accounts Payable		5 0 0 0 00		21
22		Cash			5 0 0 0 00	22
23		Paid on account, Office Plus,				23
24		Invoice 2223, Check 1003				24

Notice that the general journal Description column includes three important items for the audit trail:

- the supplier name,
- the invoice number,
- the check number.

In the general journal, always enter debits before credits. This is the case even if the credit item is considered first when mentally analyzing the transaction.

JT's Consulting Services issued a check in November to pay December and January rent in advance. Recall that the right to occupy facilities is considered a form of property. Tennille Brisbane analyzed the transaction and recorded the journal entry as follows.

BUSINESS TRANSACTION

On November 30 JT's Consulting Services wrote Check 1004 for $7,000 to prepay rent for December and January.

ANALYSIS

k. The asset account, **Prepaid Rent,** is increased by $7,000.

l. The asset account, **Cash,** is decreased by $7,000.

DEBIT-CREDIT RULES

DEBIT   Increases to asset accounts are recorded as debits. Debit **Prepaid Rent** for $7,000.

CREDIT   Decreases to asset accounts are recorded as credits. Credit **Cash** for $7,000.

$ _____ 7,000.00 _____   **No. 1004**

Date _____ November 30, _____ 20 _07_

To _____ Davidson Properties

For _____ Prepaid Rent

	Dollars	Cents
Balance brought forward	72,000	00
Add deposits		
Total	72,000	00
Less this check	7,000	00
Balance carried forward	65,000	00

T-ACCOUNT PRESENTATION

Prepaid Rent				Cash	
+		−		+	−
(k) 7,000					(l) 7,000

GENERAL JOURNAL ENTRY

GENERAL JOURNAL   PAGE ___1___

	DATE		DESCRIPTION	POST. REF.	DEBIT	CREDIT	
26	Nov.	30	Prepaid Rent		7 0 0 0 00		26
27			Cash			7 0 0 0 00	27
28			Paid Dec. and Jan. rent				28
29			in advance; Check 1004				29

RECORDING DECEMBER TRANSACTIONS IN THE GENERAL JOURNAL

JT's Consulting Services opened for business on December 1. Let's review the transactions that occurred in December. Refer to items **m** through **x** in Chapter 3 for the analysis of each transaction.

1. Performed services for $26,000 in cash.
2. Performed services for $9,000 on credit.
3. Received $4,000 in cash from credit clients on their accounts.
4. Paid $7,000 for salaries.
5. Paid $500 for a utility bill.
6. The owner withdrew $4,000 for personal expenses.

Figure 4.2 shows the entries in the general journal. In an actual business, transactions involving fees income and accounts receivable occur throughout the month and are recorded when they take place. For the sake of simplicity, these transactions are summarized and recorded as of December 31 for JT's Consulting Services.

▶ 2. OBJECTIVE

Prepare compound journal entries.

PREPARING COMPOUND ENTRIES

So far, each journal entry consists of one debit and one credit. Some transactions require a **compound entry** —a journal entry that contains more than one debit or credit. In a compound entry, record all debits first followed by the credits.

GENERAL JOURNAL   PAGE ____2____

	DATE		DESCRIPTION	POST. REF.	DEBIT	CREDIT	
1	2007						1
2	Dec.	31	Cash		26 000 00		2
3			Fees Income			26 000 00	3
4			Performed services for cash				4
5							5
6		31	Accounts Receivable		9 000 00		6
7			Fees Income			9 000 00	7
8			Performed services on credit				8
9							9
10		31	Cash		4 000 00		10
11			Accounts Receivable			4 000 00	11
12			Received cash from credit				12
13			clients on account				13
14							14
15		31	Salaries Expense		7 000 00		15
16			Cash			7 000 00	16
17			Paid monthly salaries to				17
18			employees, Checks				18
19			1005–1006				19
20							20
21		31	Utilities Expense		500 00		21
22			Cash			500 00	22
23			Paid monthly bill for utilities,				23
24			Check 1007				24
25							25
26		31	Jason Taylor, Drawing		4 000 00		26
27			Cash			4 000 00	27
28			Owner withdrew cash for				28
29			personal expenses,				29
30			Check 1008				30
31							31
32							32
33							33
34							34
35							35

FIGURE 4.2

General Journal Entries for December

International INSIGHTS

Trade Agreements

The General Agreement on Tariffs and Trade (GATT) is both an organization and a set of agreements. The organization began in 1947 with 223 member nations. Its purpose is to end quotas and lower tariffs. GATT has had a beneficial effect on world trade.

In 1999 Allstate purchased an insurance division of CNA Financial Corporation. Allstate paid cash and issued a 10-year note payable (a promise to pay). Detailed accounting records are not available to the public, but a compound journal entry was probably used to record this transaction.

Suppose that on November 7, when JT's Consulting Services purchased the equipment for $10,000, Jason Taylor paid $5,000 in cash and agreed to pay the balance in 30 days. This transaction is analyzed below and on page 104.

BUSINESS TRANSACTION

On November 7 the firm purchased equipment for $10,000, issued Check 1001 for $5,000, and agreed to pay the balance in 30 days.

ANALYSIS

The asset account, *Equipment,* is increased by $10,000. The asset account, *Cash,* is decreased by $5,000.
The liability account, *Accounts Payable,* is increased by $5,000.

▼

DEBIT-CREDIT RULES

DEBIT   Increases to assets are recorded as debits. Debit *Equipment* for $10,000.

CREDIT   Decreases to assets are credits. Credit *Cash* for $5,000. Increases to liabilities are credits. Credit *Accounts Payable* for $5,000.

▼

T-ACCOUNT PRESENTATION

Equipment		Cash		Accounts Payable	
+	−	+	−	−	+
10,000			5,000		5,000

▼

recall

Debits = Credits
No matter how many accounts are affected by a transaction, total debits must equal total credits.

GENERAL JOURNAL ENTRY

GENERAL JOURNAL   PAGE ___1___

	DATE		DESCRIPTION	POST. REF.	DEBIT	CREDIT	
6	Nov.	7	Equipment		10 0 0 0 00		6
7			Cash			5 0 0 0 00	7
8			Accounts Payable			5 0 0 0 00	8
9			Bought equip. from The				9
10			Information Technology Store,				10
11			Inv. 11, issued Ck. 1001 for				11
12			$5,000, bal. due in 30 days				12

Section 1: **Self Review**

EXERCISES

1. The part of the journal entry to be recorded first is the
   a. asset.
   b. credit.
   c. debit.
   d. liability.

2. A general journal is like a(n)
   a. address book.
   b. appointment calendar.
   c. diary.
   d. to-do list.

QUESTIONS

3. Why are check and invoice numbers included in the journal entry description?

4. In a compound journal entry, if two accounts are debited, must two accounts be credited?

5. Why is the journal referred to as the "record of original entry"?

ANALYSIS

6. The accountant for Quality Lawncare never includes descriptions when making journal entries. What effect will this have on the accounting system?

(Answers to Section 1 Self Review are on page 128.)

The General Ledger

You learned that a journal contains a chronological (day-by-day) record of a firm's transactions. Each journal entry shows the accounts and the amounts involved. Using the journal as a guide, you can enter transaction data in the accounts.

Ledgers

T accounts are used to analyze transactions quickly but are not used to maintain financial records. Instead, businesses keep account records on a special form that makes it possible to record all data efficiently. There is a separate form for each account. The account forms are kept in a book or binder called a **ledger** . The ledger is called the *record of final entry* because the ledger is the last place that accounting transactions are recorded.

The process of transferring data from the journal to the ledger is known as **posting** . Posting takes place after transactions are journalized. Posting is the third step of the accounting cycle.

THE GENERAL LEDGER

Every business has a general ledger. The **general ledger** is the master reference file for the accounting system. It provides a permanent, classified record of all accounts used in a firm's operations.

LEDGER ACCOUNT FORMS

There are different types of general ledger account forms. Tennille Brisbane decided to use a balance ledger form. A **balance ledger form** shows the balance of the account after each entry is posted. Look at Figure 4.3 on page 106. It shows the first general journal entry, the investment by the owner. It also shows the general ledger forms for *Cash* and *Jason Taylor, Capital.* On the ledger form, notice the

- account name and number;
- columns for date, description, and posting reference (post. ref.);
- columns for debit, credit, balance debit, and balance credit.

POSTING TO THE GENERAL LEDGER

Examine Figure 4.4 on page 107. On November 7 Tennille Brisbane made a general journal entry to record the purchase of equipment. To post the data from the journal to the general ledger, Brisbane entered the debit amount in the Debit column in the *Equipment* account and the credit amount in the Credit column in the *Cash* account.

In the general journal, identify the first account listed. In Figure 4.4, *Equipment* is the first account. In the general ledger, find the ledger form for the first account listed. In Figure 4.4 this is the *Equipment* ledger form.

The steps to post from the general journal to the general ledger follow.

SECTION OBJECTIVES

▶ **3. Post journal entries to general ledger accounts.**

WHY IT'S IMPORTANT
The general ledger provides a permanent, classified record for a company's accounts.

▶ **4. Correct errors made in the journal or ledger.**

WHY IT'S IMPORTANT
Errors must be corrected to ensure a proper audit trail and to provide good information.

TERMS TO LEARN

balance ledger form
correcting entry
general ledger
ledger
posting

important!

General Journal and General Ledger
The general journal is the record of *original* entry. The general ledger is the record of *final* entry.

▶ **3. OBJECTIVE**
Post journal entries to general ledger accounts.

Topic Tackler

PLUS

105

FIGURE 4.3

Posting from the General Journal to the General Ledger

GENERAL JOURNAL   PAGE ___1___

	DATE		DESCRIPTION	POST. REF.	DEBIT	CREDIT	
1	2007						1
2	Nov.	6	Cash	101	90 0 0 0 00		2
3			Jason Taylor, Capital	301		90 0 0 0 00	3
4			Investment by owner				4
5							5
6							
7							

ACCOUNT _Cash_   ACCOUNT NO. __101__

DATE		DESCRIPTION	POST. REF.	DEBIT	CREDIT	BALANCE DEBIT	BALANCE CREDIT
2007							
Nov.	6		J1	90 0 0 0 00		90 0 0 0 00	

ACCOUNT _Jason Taylor, Capital_   ACCOUNT NO. __301__

DATE		DESCRIPTION	POST. REF.	DEBIT	CREDIT	BALANCE DEBIT	BALANCE CREDIT
2007							
Nov.	6		J1		90 0 0 0 00		90 0 0 0 00

ABOUT **ACCOUNTING**

Careers

How do you get to be the president of a large corporation in the United States? Probably by beginning your career as an accountant. More accountants have advanced to be presidents of large corporations than people with any other background.

recall

Normal Balance

The normal balance of an account is its increase side.

1. On the ledger form, enter the date of the transaction. Enter a description of the entry, if necessary. Usually routine entries do not require descriptions.

2. On the ledger form, enter the general journal page in the Posting Reference column. On the *Equipment* ledger form, the **J1** in the Posting Reference column indicates that the journal entry is recorded on page 1 of the general journal. The letter **J** refers to the general journal.

3. On the ledger form, enter the debit amount in the Debit column or the credit amount in the Credit column. In Figure 4.4 on the *Equipment* ledger form, $10,000 is entered in the Debit column.

4. On the ledger form, compute the balance and enter it in the Debit Balance column or the Credit Balance column. In Figure 4.4 the balance in the *Equipment* account is a $10,000 debit.

5. On the general journal, enter the ledger account number in the Posting Reference column. In Figure 4.4 the account number 141 is entered in the Posting Reference column next to "Equipment."

Repeat the process for the next account in the general journal. In Figure 4.4 Brisbane posted the credit amount from the general journal to the *Cash* ledger account. Notice on the *Cash* ledger form that she entered the credit of $10,000 and then computed the account balance. After the transaction is posted, the balance of the *Cash* account is $80,000.

Be sure to enter the numbers in the Posting Reference columns. This indicates that the entry was posted and ensures against posting the same entry twice. Posting references are part of the audit trail. They allow a transaction to be traced from the ledger to the journal entry, and then to the source document.

Figure 4.5 on pages 108–109 shows the general ledger after all the entries for November and December are posted.

Each ledger account provides a complete record of the increases and decreases to that account. The balance ledger form also shows the current balance for the account.

In the general ledger accounts, the balance sheet accounts appear first and are followed by the income statement accounts. The order is:

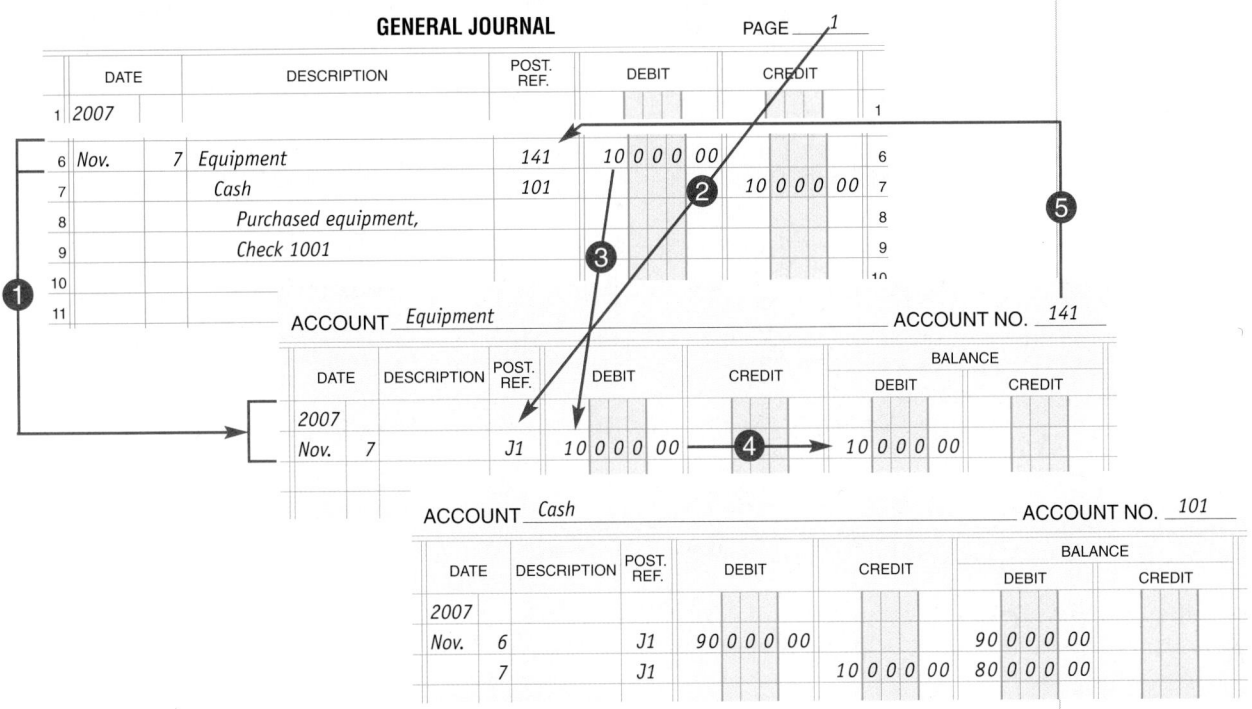

FIGURE 4.4 | **Posting to the General Ledger**

ACCOUNTING ON THE JOB <<

LEGAL & PROTECTIVE SERVICES

Industry Overview

U.S. legal and protective services workers include lawyers, judicial workers, and persons trained in specialized community services like fire protection and law enforcement. The U.S. Department of Justice is the largest employer of law enforcement professionals.

Career Opportunities

- Tax Attorney
- Criminal Investigator
- Corrections Administrator
- Director of Emergency Services
- FBI Agent

Preparing for a Legal or Protective Services Career

- For a career in law:
  - Complete a four-year college degree, three years in law school, and the bar exam.
  - Develop skills in writing, speaking, researching, analyzing, and thinking logically.
  - Gain extensive accounting knowledge to specialize in tax law or corporate law.
  - Apply for a court clerkship.
- For a career in protective services:
  - Obtain a four-year degree, professional certification, or master's degree for specialized protective service careers.
  - For an entry level emergency services job, pass the Medical First Responder (MFR) certification test.

THINKING CRITICALLY

If you were a corporate attorney for an airline, what issues do you think you might be required to handle? Hint: Review news releases on companies' Web sites.

INTERNET APPLICATION

Use the Internet to research job responsibilities, education requirements, and recommended skills for one of the following: Paralegal, Fire Department Chief, Correctional Officer.

ACCOUNT __Cash__　　　　　　　　　　　　　　　　　　　ACCOUNT NO. __101__

DATE		DESCRIPTION	POST. REF.	DEBIT	CREDIT	BALANCE DEBIT	BALANCE CREDIT
2007							
Nov.	6		J1	90 000 00		90 000 00	
	7		J1		10 000 00	80 000 00	
	28		J1		3 000 00	77 000 00	
	30		J1		5 000 00	72 000 00	
	30		J1		7 000 00	65 000 00	
Dec.	31		J2	26 000 00		91 000 00	
	31		J2	4 000 00		95 000 00	
	31		J2		7 000 00	88 000 00	
	31		J2		500 00	87 500 00	
	31		J2		4 000 00	83 500 00	

ACCOUNT __Accounts Receivable__　　　　　　　　　　　　ACCOUNT NO. __111__

DATE		DESCRIPTION	POST. REF.	DEBIT	CREDIT	BALANCE DEBIT	BALANCE CREDIT
2007							
Dec.	31		J2	9 000 00		9 000 00	
	31		J2		4 000 00	5 000 00	

ACCOUNT __Supplies__　　　　　　　　　　　　　　　　　　ACCOUNT NO. __121__

DATE		DESCRIPTION	POST. REF.	DEBIT	CREDIT	BALANCE DEBIT	BALANCE CREDIT
2007							
Nov.	28		J1	3 000 00		3 000 00	

ACCOUNT __Prepaid Rent__　　　　　　　　　　　　　　　ACCOUNT NO. __137__

DATE		DESCRIPTION	POST. REF.	DEBIT	CREDIT	BALANCE DEBIT	BALANCE CREDIT
2007							
Nov.	30		J1	7 000 00		7 000 00	

ACCOUNT __Equipment__　　　　　　　　　　　　　　　　ACCOUNT NO. __141__

DATE		DESCRIPTION	POST. REF.	DEBIT	CREDIT	BALANCE DEBIT	BALANCE CREDIT
2007							
Nov.	7		J1	10 000 00		10 000 00	
	10		J1	12 000 00		22 000 00	

ACCOUNT __Accounts Payable__　　　　　　　　　　　　ACCOUNT NO. __202__

DATE		DESCRIPTION	POST. REF.	DEBIT	CREDIT	BALANCE DEBIT	BALANCE CREDIT
2007							
Nov.	10		J1		12 000 00		12 000 00
	30		J1	5 000 00			7 000 00

FIGURE 4.5 | **Posted General Ledger Accounts**

ACCOUNT _Jason Taylor, Capital_   ACCOUNT NO. _301_

DATE	DESCRIPTION	POST. REF.	DEBIT	CREDIT	BALANCE DEBIT	BALANCE CREDIT
2007						
Nov. 6		J1		90 000 00		90 000 00

ACCOUNT _Jason Taylor, Drawing_   ACCOUNT NO. _302_

DATE	DESCRIPTION	POST. REF.	DEBIT	CREDIT	BALANCE DEBIT	BALANCE CREDIT
2007						
Dec. 31		J2	4 000 00		4 000 00	

ACCOUNT _Fees Income_   ACCOUNT NO. _401_

DATE	DESCRIPTION	POST. REF.	DEBIT	CREDIT	BALANCE DEBIT	BALANCE CREDIT
2007						
Dec. 31		J2		26 000 00		26 000 00
31		J2		9 000 00		35 000 00

ACCOUNT _Salaries Expense_   ACCOUNT NO. _511_

DATE	DESCRIPTION	POST. REF.	DEBIT	CREDIT	BALANCE DEBIT	BALANCE CREDIT
2007						
Dec. 31		J2	7 000 00		7 000 00	

ACCOUNT _Utilities Expense_   ACCOUNT NO. _514_

DATE	DESCRIPTION	POST. REF.	DEBIT	CREDIT	BALANCE DEBIT	BALANCE CREDIT
2007						
Dec. 31		J2	5 00 00		5 00 00	

- assets
- liabilities
- owner's equity
- revenue
- expenses

This arrangement speeds the preparation of the trial balance and the financial statements.

Correcting Journal and Ledger Errors

Sometimes errors are made when recording transactions in the journal. For example, a journal entry may show the wrong account name or amount. The method used to correct an error depends on whether or not the journal entry has been posted to the ledger:

recall

Order of Accounts
The general ledger lists accounts in the same order as they appear on the trial balance: assets, liabilities, owner's equity, revenue, and expenses.

▶ 4. OBJECTIVE
Correct errors made in the journal or ledger.

MANAGERIAL IMPLICATIONS

ACCOUNTING SYSTEMS

- Business managers should be sure that their firms have efficient procedures for recording transactions.
- A well-designed accounting system allows timely and accurate posting of data to the ledger accounts.
- The information that appears in the financial statements is taken from the general ledger.
- Since management uses financial information for decision making, it is essential that the financial statements be prepared quickly at the end of each period and that they contain the correct amounts.
- The promptness and accuracy of the statements depend on the efficiency of the recording process.
- A well-designed accounting system has a strong audit trail.
- Every business should be able to trace amounts through the accounting records and back to the documents where the transactions were first recorded.

THINKING CRITICALLY

What are three situations you might encounter in which you need to "follow" the audit trail?

- If the error is discovered *before* the entry is posted, neatly cross out the incorrect item and write the correct data above it. Do not erase the error. To ensure honesty and provide a clear audit trail, erasures are not made in the journal.
- If the error is discovered *after* posting, a **correcting entry** —a journal entry made to correct the erroneous entry—is journalized and posted. Do not erase or change the journal entry or the postings in the ledger accounts.

Note that erasures are never permitted in the journal or ledger.

Let's look at an example. On September 1 an automobile repair shop purchased some shop equipment for $9,000 in cash. By mistake the journal entry debited the *Office Equipment* account rather than the *Shop Equipment* account, as follows.

GENERAL JOURNAL   PAGE ___16___

	DATE	DESCRIPTION	POST. REF.	DEBIT	CREDIT	
1	2007					1
2	Sept.	1 Office Equipment	141	9 0 0 0 00		2
3		Cash	101		9 0 0 0 00	3
4		Purchased equipment,				4
5		Check 1104				5
6						6
7						7

The error was discovered after the entry was posted to the ledger. To correct the error, a correcting journal entry was prepared and posted. The correcting entry debits *Shop Equipment* and credits *Office Equipment* for $9,000. This entry transfers $9,000 out of the *Office Equipment* account and into the *Shop Equipment* account.

GENERAL JOURNAL PAGE ___28___

	DATE		DESCRIPTION	POST. REF.	DEBIT	CREDIT	
1	2007						1
2	Oct.	1	Shop Equipment	151	9 0 0 0 00		2
3			Office Equipment	141		9 0 0 0 00	3
4			To correct error made on				4
5			Sept. 1 when a purchase				5
6			of shop equipment was				6
7			recorded as office				7
8			equipment				8
9							9
10							10

Suppose that the error was discovered before the journal entry was posted to the ledger. In that case the accountant would neatly cross out "Office Equipment" and write "Shop Equipment" above it. The correct account (**Shop Equipment**) would be posted to the ledger in the usual manner.

Section 2: **Self Review**

QUESTIONS

1. Are the following statements true or false? Why?

   a. "If a journal entry that contains an error has been posted, erase the entry and change the posting in the ledger accounts."

   b. "Once an incorrect journal entry has been posted, the incorrect amounts remain in the general ledger accounts."

2. What is entered in the Posting Reference column of the general journal?

3. Why are posting references made in ledger accounts and in the journal?

EXERCISES

4. The general ledger organizes accounting information in
   a. account order.
   b. alphabetical order.
   c. date order.

5. The general journal organizes accounting information in
   a. account order.
   b. alphabetical order.
   c. date order.

ANALYSIS

6. Draw a diagram of the first three steps of the accounting cycle.

(Answers to Section 2 Self Review are on page 128.)

CHAPTER 4: Review and Applications

REVIEW

Chapter Summary

In this chapter, you have studied the method for journalizing business transactions in the records of a company. The details of each transaction are then posted to the general ledger. A well-designed accounting system provides for prompt and accurate journalizing and posting of all transactions.

Learning Objectives

1 Record transactions in the general journal.

- Recording transactions in a journal is called journalizing, the second step in the accounting cycle.
  - A journal is a daily record of transactions.
  - A written analysis of each transaction is contained in a journal.
- The general journal is widely used in business. It can accommodate all kinds of business transactions. Use the following steps to record a transaction in the general journal:
  - Number each page in the general journal. The page number will be used as a posting reference.
  - Enter the year at the top of the Date column. After that, enter the year only when a new page is started or when the year changes.
  - Enter the month and day in the Date column of the first line of the first entry. After that, enter the month only when a new page is started or when the month changes. Always enter the day on the first line of a new entry.
  - Enter the name of the account to be debited in the Description column.
  - Enter the amount to be debited in the Debit column.
  - Enter the name of the account to be credited on the next line. Indent the account name about one-half inch.
  - Enter the amount to be credited in the Credit column.
  - Enter a complete but concise description on the next line. Indent the description about one inch.
- Note that the debit portion is always recorded first.
- If possible, include source document numbers in descriptions in order to create an audit trail.

2 Prepare compound journal entries.

A transaction might require a journal entry that contains several debits or credits. All debits are recorded first, followed by the credits.

3 Post journal entries to general ledger accounts.

- Posting to the general ledger is the third step in the accounting cycle. Posting is the transfer of data from journal entries to ledger accounts.
- The individual accounts together form a ledger. All the accounts needed to prepare financial statements are found in the general ledger.
- Use the following steps to post a transaction.
  - On the ledger form:
    1. Enter the date of the transaction. Enter the description, if necessary.
    2. Enter the posting reference in the Posting Reference column. When posting from the general journal, use the letter **J** followed by the general journal page number.
    3. Enter the amount in either the Debit column or the Credit column.
    4. Compute the new balance and enter it in either the Debit Balance column or the Credit Balance column.
  - On the general journal:
    5. Enter the ledger account number in the Posting Reference column.
- To summarize the steps of the accounting cycle discussed so far:
  1. Analyze transactions.
  2. Journalize transactions.
  3. Post transactions.

4 Correct errors made in the journal or ledger.

To ensure honesty and to provide a clear audit trail, erasures are not permitted in a journal. A correcting entry is journalized and posted to correct a previous mistake. Posting references in the journal and the ledger accounts cross reference the entries and form another part of the audit trail. They make it possible to trace or recheck any transaction.

5 Define the accounting terms new to this chapter.

Glossary

Accounting cycle (p. 96) A series of steps performed during each accounting period to classify, record, and summarize data for a business and to produce needed financial information

Audit trail (p. 97) A chain of references that makes it possible to trace information, locate errors, and prevent fraud

Balance ledger form (p. 105) A ledger account form that shows the balance of the account after each entry is posted

Chronological order (p. 96) Organized in the order in which the events occur

Compound entry (p. 102) A journal entry with more than one debit or credit

Correcting entry (p. 110) A journal entry made to correct an erroneous entry

General journal (p. 96) A financial record for entering all types of business transactions; a record of original entry

General ledger (p. 105) A permanent, classified record of all accounts used in a firm's operation; a record of final entry

Journal (p. 96) The record of original entry

Journalizing (p. 96) Recording transactions in a journal

Ledger (p. 105) The record of final entry

Posting (p. 105) Transferring data from a journal to a ledger

Comprehensive **Self Review**

1. How do you correct a journal entry that has not been posted?
2. What is recorded in the Posting Reference column of a general journal?
3. Why is the ledger called the "record of final entry"?
4. Which of the following shows both the debits and credits of the entire transaction?
    a. An entry in the general journal
    b. A posting to a general ledger account
5. Give examples of items that might appear in an audit trail.

(Answers to Comprehensive Self Review are on page 128.)

Discussion Questions

1. What is a ledger?
2. What is a compound journal entry?
3. What is the value of having a description for each general journal entry?
4. What procedure is used to record an entry in the general journal?
5. What is the purpose of a journal?
6. What is the accounting cycle?
7. How should corrections be made in the general journal?
8. What is an audit trail? Why is it desirable to have an audit trail?
9. What are posting references? Why are they used?
10. In what order are accounts arranged in the general ledger? Why?
11. What is posting?

APPLICATIONS

Exercises

Exercise 4.1
Objective 1

▶ **Analyzing transactions.**

Selected accounts from the general ledger of the Special Delivery Courier Service follow. Analyze the following transactions and indicate by number what accounts should be debited and credited for each transaction.

101 Cash
111 Accounts Receivable
121 Supplies
131 Equipment
202 Accounts Payable
301 Calvin Jefferson, Capital
401 Fees Income
511 Rent Expense
514 Salaries Expense
517 Utilities Expense

TRANSACTIONS

1. Gave a cash refund of $360 to a customer because of a lost package. (The customer had previously paid in cash.)
2. Sent a check for $750 to the utility company to pay the monthly bill.
3. Provided services for $6,500 on credit.
4. Purchased new equipment for $4,200 and paid for it immediately by check.
5. Issued a check for $3,000 to pay a creditor on account.
6. Performed services for $4,650 in cash.
7. Collected $5,600 from credit customers.
8. The owner made an additional investment of $20,000 in cash.
9. Purchased supplies for $2,000 on credit.
10. Issued a check for $1,850 to pay the monthly rent.

Exercise 4.2
Objective 1

▶ **Recording transactions in the general journal.**

Selected accounts from the general ledger of Classy Creations Company follow. Record the general journal entries that would be made to record the following transactions. Be sure to include dates and descriptions in these entries.

101 Cash
111 Accounts Receivable
121 Supplies
131 Equipment
141 Automobile
202 Accounts Payable
301 Marilyn James, Capital
302 Marilyn James, Drawing
401 Fees Income
511 Rent Expense
514 Salaries Expense
517 Telephone Expense

DATE	TRANSACTIONS
Sept. 1	Marilyn James invested $62,000 in cash to start the firm.
4	Purchased office equipment for $8,500 on credit from Den, Inc.; received Invoice 9823, payable in 30 days.
16	Purchased an automobile that will be used to visit clients; issued Check 1001 for $22,500 in full payment.
20	Purchased supplies for $420; paid immediately with Check 1002.
23	Returned damaged supplies for a cash refund of $120.
30	Issued Check 1003 for $5,600 to Den, Inc., as payment on account for Invoice 9823.
30	Withdrew $2,000 in cash for personal expenses.
30	Issued Check 1004 for $1,200 to pay the rent for October.
30	Performed services for $1,700 in cash.
30	Paid $207 for monthly telephone bill, Check 1005.

Posting to the general ledger.

Post the journal entries that you prepared for Exercise 4.2 to the general ledger. Use the account names shown in Exercise 4.2.

◀ Exercise 4.3
Objectives 1, 3

CONTINUING >>>
Problem

Compound journal entries.

The following transactions took place at the Bahamon's Leading Ladies during November 2007. Give the general journal entries that would be made to record these transactions. Use a compound entry for each transaction.

◀ Exercise 4.4
Objective 2

DATE	TRANSACTIONS
Nov. 5	Performed services for Talent Search, Inc., for $32,000; received $16,000 in cash and the client promised to pay the balance in 60 days.
18	Purchased a graphing calculator for $300 and some supplies for $500 from Office Supply; issued Check 1008 for the total.
23	Received Invoice 1602 for $1,080 from Automotive Technicians Repair for repairs to the firm's automobile; issued Check 1009 for half the amount and arranged to pay the other half in 30 days.

Recording a correcting entry.

On July 9, 2007, an employee of Melbourne Corporation mistakenly debited *Utilities Expense* rather than *Telephone Expense* when recording a bill of $375 for the May telephone service. The error was discovered on July 30. Prepare a general journal entry to correct the error.

◀ Exercise 4.5
Objective 4

Recording a correcting entry.

On September 16, 2007, an employee of Zion Company mistakenly debited the *Truck* account rather than the *Repair Expense* account when recording a bill of $450 for repairs. The error was discovered on October 1. Prepare a general journal entry to correct the error.

◀ Exercise 4.6
Objective 4

CHAPTER 4: Review and Applications

PROBLEMS

 Problem Set A

Problem 4.1A   ▶   **Recording transactions in the general journal.**

Objective 1

The transactions that follow took place at the City Place Recreation Center during September 2007. This firm has indoor courts where customers can play tennis for a fee. It also rents equipment and offers tennis lessons.

INSTRUCTIONS

Record each transaction in the general journal, using the following chart of accounts. Be sure to number the journal page 1 and to write the year at the top of the Date column. Include a description for each entry.

ASSETS
101 Cash
111 Accounts Receivable
121 Supplies
141 Equipment

LIABILITIES
202 Accounts Payable

OWNER'S EQUITY
301 Raul Hinojosa, Capital
302 Raul Hinojosa, Drawing

REVENUE
401 Fees Income

EXPENSES
511 Equipment Repair Expense
512 Rent Expense
513 Salaries Expense
514 Telephone Expense
517 Utilities Expense

DATE	TRANSACTIONS
Sept. 1	Issued Check 1169 for $1,400 to pay the September rent.
5	Performed services for $2,500 in cash.
6	Performed services for $2,175 on credit.
10	Paid $150 for monthly telephone bill; issued Check 1170.
11	Paid for equipment repairs of $210 with Check 1171.
12	Received $800 on account from credit clients.
15	Issued Checks 1172–1177 for $4,200 for salaries.
18	Issued Check 1178 for $500 to purchase supplies.
19	Purchased new tennis rackets for $2,250 on credit from The Tennis Supply Shop; received Invoice 3108, payable in 30 days.
20	Issued Check 1179 for $690 to purchase new nets. (Equip.)
21	Received $850 on account from credit clients.
21	Returned a damaged net and received a cash refund of $212.
22	Performed services for $3,260 in cash.
23	Performed services for $4,810 on credit.
26	Issued Check 1180 for $460 to purchase supplies.
28	Paid the monthly electric bill of $575 with Check 1181.
30	Issued Checks 1182–1187 for $4,200 for salaries.
30	Issued Check 1188 for $1,000 cash to Raul Hinojosa for personal expenses.

Analyze: If the company paid a bill for supplies on October 1, what check number would be included in the journal entry description?

Journalizing and posting transactions.

On October 1, 2007, Linda Carter opened an advertising agency. She plans to use the chart of accounts listed below.

◀ **Problem 4.2A**
Objectives 1, 2, 3

e**X**cel

INSTRUCTIONS

1. Journalize the transactions. Number the journal page 1, write the year at the top of the Date column, and include a description for each entry.

2. Post to the ledger accounts. Before you start the posting process, open accounts by entering account names and numbers in the headings. Follow the order of the accounts in the chart of accounts.

ASSETS
101 Cash
111 Accounts Receivable
121 Supplies
141 Office Equipment
151 Art Equipment

LIABILITIES
202 Accounts Payable

OWNER'S EQUITY
301 Linda Carter, Capital
302 Linda Carter, Drawing

REVENUE
401 Fees Income

EXPENSES
511 Office Cleaning Expense
514 Rent Expense
517 Salaries Expense
520 Telephone Expense
523 Utilities Expense

Credit

DATE	TRANSACTIONS
Oct. 1	Linda Carter invested $70,000 cash in the business.
2	Paid October office rent of $2,250; issued Check 1001.
5	Purchased desks and other office furniture for $14,000 from Office Furniture Mart, Inc.; received Invoice 6704 payable in 60 days.
6	Issued Check 1002 for $4,350 to purchase art equipment.
7	Purchased supplies for $1,070; paid with Check 1003.
10	Issued Check 1004 for $425 for office cleaning service.
12	Performed services for $3,200 in cash and $2,800 on credit. (Use a compound entry.)
15	Returned damaged supplies for a cash refund of $300.
18	Purchased a computer for $2,050 from Office Furniture Mart, Inc., Invoice 7108; issued Check 1005 for a $1,025 down payment, with the balance payable in 30 days. (Use one compound entry.)
20	Issued Check 1006 for $7,000 to Office Furniture Mart, Inc., as payment on account for Invoice 6704.
26	Performed services for $3,875 on credit.
27	Paid $250 for monthly telephone bill; issued Check 1007.
30	Received $3,200 in cash from credit customers.
30	Mailed Check 1008 to pay the monthly utility bill of $592.
30	Issued Checks 1009–1011 for $7,550 for salaries.

Analyze: What is the balance of account 202 in the general ledger?

CHAPTER 4: Review and Applications

CHAPTER 4: Review and Applications

Problem 4.3A ▶ **Recording correcting entries.**

Objective 4

The following journal entries were prepared by an employee of Dexter Company who does not have an adequate knowledge of accounting.

INSTRUCTIONS

Examine the journal entries carefully to locate the errors. Provide a brief written description of each error. Assume that **Office Equipment** and **Office Supplies** were recorded at the correct values.

GENERAL JOURNAL   PAGE ___3___

	DATE		DESCRIPTION	POST. REF.	DEBIT	CREDIT	
1	2007						1
2	April	1	Accounts Payable		6 2 0 0 00		2
3			Fees Income			6 2 0 0 00	3
4			Performed services on credit				4
5							5
6		2	Cash		2 5 0 00		6
7			Telephone Expense			2 5 0 00	7
8			Paid for March telephone				8
9			service, Check 1917				9
10							10
11		3	Office Equipment		3 6 0 0 00		11
12			Office Supplies		4 0 0 00		12
13			Cash			4 2 0 0 00	13
14			Purchased file cabinet and				14
15			office supplies, Check 1918				15
16							16
17							17
18							18
19							19
20							20

Analyze: After the correcting journal entries have been posted, what effect do the corrections have on the company's reported assets?

Journalizing and posting transactions.

Four transactions for Tractor Supply & Repair that took place in November 2007 appear below, along with the general ledger accounts used by the company.

INSTRUCTIONS

Record the transactions in the general journal and post them to the appropriate ledger accounts. Be sure to number the journal page 1 and to write the year at the top of the Date column.

Cash	101	Accounts Payable	202
Accounts Receivable	111	Sandra Altman, Capital	301
Office Supplies	121	Fees Income	401
Tools	131		
Machinery	141		
Equipment	151		

DATE	TRANSACTIONS
Nov. 1	Sandra Altman invested $22,500 in cash plus tools with a fair market value of $500 to start the business.
2	Purchased equipment for $975 and supplies for $225 from Office Depot, Invoice 501; issued Check 100 for $300 as a down payment with the balance due in 30 days.
10	Performed services for Marshall Sanders for $950, who paid $250 in cash with the balance due in 30 days.
20	Purchased machinery for $1,500 from Carson Machinery, Inc., Invoice 709; issued Check 101 for $500 in cash as a down payment with the balance due in 30 days.

Analyze: What liabilities does the business owe as of November 30?

Problem Set B

Problem 4.1B ▶ **Recording transactions in the general journal.**

Objective 1

The transactions listed below took place at Wu Building Cleaning Service during September 2007. This firm cleans commercial buildings for a fee.

INSTRUCTIONS

Analyze and record each transaction in the general journal. Choose the account names from the chart of accounts shown below. Be sure to number the journal page 1 and to write the year at the top of the Date column.

ASSETS
101 Cash
111 Accounts Receivable
141 Equipment

LIABILITIES
202 Accounts Payable

OWNER'S EQUITY
301 Fred Wu, Capital
302 Fred Wu, Drawing

REVENUE
401 Fees Income

EXPENSES
501 Cleaning Supplies Expense
502 Equipment Repair Expense
503 Office Supplies Expense
511 Rent Expense
514 Salaries Expense
521 Telephone Expense
524 Utilities Expense

DATE		TRANSACTIONS
Sept.	1	Fred Wu invested $25,000 in cash to start the business.
	5	Performed services for $2,800 in cash.
	6	Issued Check 1000 for $1,800 to pay the September rent.
	7	Performed services for $3,600 on credit.
	9	Paid $400 for monthly telephone bill; issued Check 1001.
	10	Issued Check 1002 for $230 for equipment repairs.
	12	Received $975 from credit clients.
	14	Issued Checks 1003–1004 for $9,000 to pay salaries.
	18	Issued Check 1005 for $700 for cleaning supplies.
	19	Issued Check 1006 for $600 for office supplies.
	20	Purchased equipment for $6,000 from Ramon's Equipment, Inc., Invoice 1012; issued Check 1007 for $2,000 with the balance due in 30 days.
	22	Performed services for $4,950 in cash.
	24	Issued Check 1008 for $425 for the monthly electric bill.
	26	Performed services for $3,600 on account.
	30	Issued Checks 1009–1010 for $9,000 to pay salaries.
	30	Issued Check 1011 for $3,000 to Fred Wu to pay for personal expenses.

Analyze: How many transactions affected expense accounts?

Journalizing and posting transactions.

In June 2007 Richard Harris opened a photography studio that provides services to public and private schools. His firm's financial activities for the first month of operations and the chart of accounts appear below.

INSTRUCTIONS

1. Journalize the transactions. Number the journal page 1 and write the year at the top of the Date column. Describe each entry.

2. Post to the ledger accounts. Before you start the posting process, open the accounts by entering the names and numbers in the headings. Follow the order of the accounts in the chart of accounts.

ASSETS
101 Cash
111 Accounts Receivable
121 Supplies
141 Office Equipment
151 Photographic Equipment

LIABILITIES
202 Accounts Payable

OWNER'S EQUITY
301 Richard Harris, Capital
302 Richard Harris, Drawing

REVENUE
401 Fees Income

EXPENSES
511 Office Cleaning Expense
514 Rent Expense
517 Salaries Expense
520 Telephone Expense
523 Utilities Expense

DATE		TRANSACTIONS
June	1	Richard Harris invested $32,000 cash in the business.
	2	Issued Check 1001 for $1,800 to pay the June rent.
	5	Purchased desks and other office furniture for $7,500 from Brown, Inc.; received Invoice 5312, payable in 60 days.
	6	Issued Check 1002 for $1,900 to purchase photographic equipment.
	7	Purchased supplies for $475; paid with Check 1003.
	10	Issued Check 1004 for $400 for office cleaning service.
	12	Performed services for $1,200 in cash and $1,300 on credit. (Use one compound entry.)
	15	Returned damaged supplies; received a $100 cash refund.
	18	Purchased a computer for $2,050 from Craft Office Supply, Invoice 304; issued Check 1005 for a $1,000 down payment. The balance is payable in 30 days. (Use one compound entry.)
	20	Issued Check 1006 for $4,200 to Brown, Inc., as payment on account for office furniture, Invoice 5312.
	26	Performed services for $2,000 on credit.
	27	Paid $145 for monthly telephone bill; issued Check 1007.
	30	Received $2,100 in cash from credit clients on account.
	30	Issued Check 1008 to pay the monthly utility bill of $550.
	30	Issued Checks 1009–1011 for $5,600 for salaries.

Analyze: What was the *Cash* account balance after the transaction of June 20 was recorded?

Problem 4.3B   ▶   **Recording correcting entries.**

Objective 4

All the journal entries shown below contain errors. The entries were prepared by an employee of Wilson Corporation who does not have an adequate knowledge of accounting.

INSTRUCTIONS

Examine the journal entries carefully to locate the errors. Provide a brief written description of each error. Assume that *Office Equipment* and *Office Supplies* were recorded at the correct values.

GENERAL JOURNAL

PAGE ___1___

	DATE		DESCRIPTION	POST. REF.	DEBIT	CREDIT	
1	2007						1
2	Jan.	1	Accounts Payable		9 0 0 00		2
3			Fees Income			9 0 0 00	3
4			Performed services on credit				4
5							5
6		2	Cash		1 2 5 00		6
7			Telephone Expense			1 2 5 00	7
8			Paid for January telephone				8
9			service, Check 1601				9
10							10
11		3	Office Equipment		7 5 0 00		11
12			Office Supplies		1 9 0 00		12
13			Cash			9 0 0 00	13
14			Purchased file cabinet and				14
15			office supplies, Check 1602				15
16							16

Analyze: After the correcting journal entries have been posted, what effect do the corrections have on the reported assets of the company?

Journalizing and posting transactions.

Several transactions that occurred during December 2007, the first month of operation for Richey's Accounting Services, follow. The company uses the general ledger accounts listed below.

◀ **Problem 4.4B**
Objectives 1, 2, 3

INSTRUCTIONS

Record the transactions in the general journal (page 1) and post to the appropriate accounts.

Cash	101	Accounts Payable	202
Accounts Receivable	111	Virginia Richey, Capital	301
Office Supplies	121	Fees Income	401
Computers	131		
Office Equipment	141		
Furniture & Fixtures	151		

DATE		TRANSACTIONS
Dec.	3	Virginia Richey began business by depositing $30,000 cash into a business checking account.
	4	Purchased a computer for $2,400 cash.
	5	Purchased furniture and fixtures on account for $8,000.
	6	Purchased office equipment for $2,190 cash.
	10	Rendered services to client and sent bill for $2,575.
	11	Purchased office supplies for $900.
	15	Received invoice for furniture purchased on December 5 and paid it.

Analyze: Describe the activity for account 202 during the month.

CHAPTER 4: Review and Applications

Challenge Problem

Start-Up Business

On June 1, 2007, Nelson Sullivan opened the Moves and Sounds Talent Agency. He plans to use the chart of accounts given below.

INSTRUCTIONS

1. Journalize the transactions. Be sure to number the journal pages and write the year at the top of the Date column. Include a description for each entry.
2. Post to the ledger accounts. Before you start the posting process, open the accounts by entering the account names and numbers in the headings. Using the list of accounts below, assign appropriate account numbers and place them in the correct order in the ledger.
3. Prepare a trial balance.
4. Prepare the income statement.
5. Prepare a statement of owner's equity.
6. Prepare the balance sheet.

ACCOUNTS

Accounts Payable	Nelson Sullivan, Drawing
Office Furniture	Recording Equipment
Accounts Receivable	Rent Expense
Advertising Expense	Salaries Expense
Cash	Supplies
Fees Income	Telephone Expense
Nelson Sullivan, Capital	Utilities Expense

DATE		TRANSACTIONS
June	1	Nelson Sullivan invested $30,000 cash to start the business.
	2	Issued Check 201 for $1,800 to pay the June rent for the office.
	3	Purchased desk and other office furniture for $12,000 from Davis Office Supply, Invoice 5103; issued Check 202 for a $4,000 down payment with the balance due in 30 days.
	4	Issued Check 203 for $1,600 for supplies.
	6	Performed services for $6,000 in cash.
	7	Issued Check 204 for $2,000 to pay for advertising expense.
	8	Purchased recording equipment for $15,000 from Rhythms & Moves, Inc., Invoice 2122; issued Check 205 for a down payment of $5,000 with the balance due in 30 days.
	10	Performed services for $4,900 on account.
	11	Issued Check 206 for $3,000 to Davis Office Supply as payment on account.
	12	Performed services for $9,000 in cash.
	15	Issued Check 207 for $5,000 to pay an employee's salary.
	18	Received payments of $4,000 from credit clients on account.
	20	Issued Check 208 for $6,000 to Rhythms & Moves, Inc. as payment on account.
	25	Issued Check 209 in the amount of $350 for the monthly telephone bill.
	27	Issued Check 210 in the amount of $800 for the monthly electric bill.
	28	Issued Check 211 to Nelson Sullivan for $4,000 for personal living expenses.
	30	Issued Check 212 for $5,000 to pay salary of an employee.

Analyze: How many postings were made to the **Cash** account?

Critical Thinking Problem

Financial Statements

Jan McBee is a new staff accountant for Kirven Chemical Supply. She has asked you to review the financial statements prepared for April to find and correct any errors. Review the income statement and balance sheet that follow and identify the errors McBee made (she did not prepare a statement of owner's equity). Prepare a corrected income statement and balance sheet as well as a statement of owner's equity, for Kirven Chemical Supply.

Kirven Chemical Supply
Income Statement
April 30, 2007

Revenue		
Fees Income		18 3 0 0 00
Expenses		
Salaries Expense	4 5 0 0 00	
Rent Expense	9 0 0 00	
Repair Expense	1 5 0 00	
Utilities Expense	8 5 0 00	
Drawing	2 0 0 0 00	
Total Expenses		8 8 5 0 00
Net Income		10 6 2 5 00

Kirven Chemical Supply
Balance Sheet
Month Ended April 30, 2007

Assets		Liabilities	
Land	6 0 0 0 00	Accounts Receivable	3 5 0 0 00
Building	20 0 0 0 00		
Cash	7 5 0 0 00	*Owner's Equity*	
Accounts Payable	2 5 0 0 00	Joe Kirven, Capital, April 1, 2007	24 6 0 0 00
Total Assets	36 0 0 0 00	Total Liabilities and Owner's Equity	28 1 0 0 00

BUSINESS CONNECTIONS

Business Records

1. The owner of a new business recently questioned the accountant about the value of having both a journal and a ledger. The owner believes that it is a waste of effort to enter data about transactions in two different records. How would you explain the value of having both records?

2. Why should management insist that a firm's accounting system have a strong audit trail?

3. Why should management be concerned about the efficiency of a firm's procedures for journalizing and posting transactions?

4. How might a poor set of recording procedures affect the flow of information to management?

Correcting Entries

As the Full Charge Bookkeeper, your job is to make any corrections to the General Ledger Accounts. Each correction needs the reason for the change and the effect on each account, whether it is an increase or decrease. Louisa has come to you for help. For the third time this month, she has recorded a cash receipt twice. She wants you to record a correcting entry that will reverse her mistakes. The correcting entry she wants you to make will record a credit to the Cash account and a debit to Sales. What should you investigate before making a decision about the correcting entry? What is happening to the cash account? Is this a continual problem for Louisa? Would you accept a dinner offer from Louisa if you fix her mistake?

General Ledger Accounts

Refer to The Home Depot, Inc. *2004 Annual Report* in Appendix A.

1. Review the report called *Executive Summary and Selected Consolidated Statements of Earnings Data.* How many sales transactions were reported for 2004? For sales on account transactions, which accounts would be affected when the transactions are recorded?

2. Based on the financial statements, which account categories would be affected by the following transactions?

   a. Paid $5,000 cash for store rent.

   b. Paid $2,000 cash for store utility bill.

   c. Received $1,000 from a customer in payment of their account.

Balance Sheet

Review the following excerpt taken from the Wal-Mart Stores, Inc. consolidated balance sheet as of January 31, 2004.

(Amounts in millions) January 31, 2004	
Property, Plant and Equipment at cost:	
Land	$12,699
Building and improvements	38,966
Fixtures and equipment	17,861
Transportation equipment	1,269

Analyze:

1. When the accountant for Wal-Mart Stores, Inc. records a purchase of transportation equipment, what type of account is debited? If Wal-Mart purchases transportation equipment on credit, what account might be credited?

2. What type of source document might be reflected in the journal entry to record the purchase of equipment?

3. If the accounting manager reviewed the **Transportation Equipment** account in the general ledger, what types of information might be listed there? What ending balance would be reflected at January 31, 2004?

Analyze Online: Locate the Web site for the Wal-Mart Stores, Inc. (**www.walmartstores.com**), which provides an online store for consumers as well as corporation information. Within the Web site, locate the consolidated balance sheet for the current year.

4. What kinds of property, plant, and equipment are listed on the balance sheet?

5. What is the balance reported for transportation equipment?

Getting Organized

Business transactions are recorded in a financial record called a journal. List and discuss other organizational records and devices used in everyday life. Why are these records and devices used? What similarities do these records share with the journal used in accounting?

Training Manual

You have been asked to teach a new accounting clerk how to journalize business transactions. Create a written step-by-step guide to give to the new accounting clerk on his first day at work. Use a sample business transaction of your choice to illustrate the process.

Audit Trail

An audit trail allows an individual to track a transaction from the journal entry to the General Ledger through to the Financial Statements. The audit trail can also find all the transactions that comprise the dollar amount for each account listed on the Income Statement and Balance Sheet. Your team has been assigned the duty to diagram the audit trail for your company. In your diagram, show several transactions and how they would be tracked from the journal entry to the financial statement and back to the journal entry.

Accounting Careers

Enter "Accounting Careers" in a search tool like Google. Select a site that will provide the skills and talents required for an accountant. Also find the salaries for accountants in your local area. Note the amount of experience and education needed to receive the salary you want to be earning in the next five years.

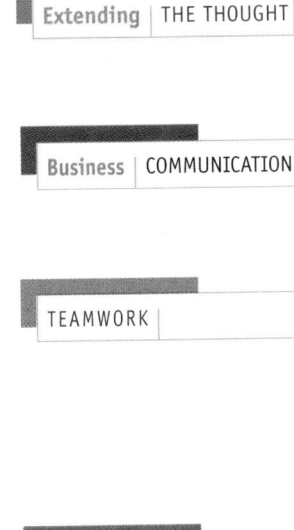

Extending | THE THOUGHT

Business | COMMUNICATION

TEAMWORK

Internet | CONNECTION

Answers to Self Reviews

Answers to Section 1 Self Review

1. **c.** debit.
2. **c.** diary.
3. To provide an audit trail to trace information through the accounting system.
4. No. The only requirement is that the total debits must equal the total credits.
5. It is the first accounting record where transactions are entered.
6. The audit trail will be very difficult to follow.

Answers to Section 2 Self Review

1. Both statements are false. If an incorrect journal entry was posted, a correcting entry should be journalized and posted. To ensure honesty and provide a clear audit trail, erasures are not permitted in the journal.
2. The ledger account number.
3. They indicate that the entry has been posted and ensure against posting the same entry twice.
4. **a.** account order.
5. **c.** date order.
6.

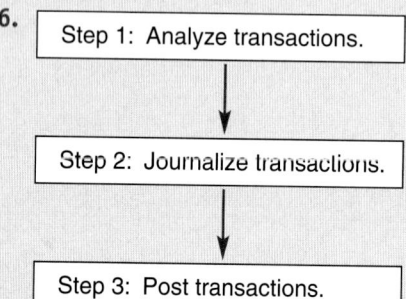

Step 1: Analyze transactions.

Step 2: Journalize transactions.

Step 3: Post transactions.

Answers to Comprehensive Self Review

1. Neatly cross out the incorrect item and write the correct data above it.
2. The general ledger account number.
3. It is the last accounting record in which a transaction is recorded.
4. **a.** An entry in the general journal
5. Check number

   Invoice number for goods purchased on credit from a vendor

   Invoice number for services billed to a charge account customer

   Memorandum number

LEARNING OBJECTIVES

1 Complete a trial balance on a worksheet.

2 Prepare adjustments for unrecorded business transactions.

3 Complete the worksheet.

4 Prepare an income statement, statement of owner's equity, and balance sheet from the completed worksheet.

5 Journalize and post the adjusting entries.

6 Define the accounting terms new to this chapter.

NEW TERMS

account form balance sheet

adjusting entries

adjustments

book value

contra account

contra asset account

depreciation

prepaid expenses

report form balance sheet

salvage value

straight-line depreciation

worksheet

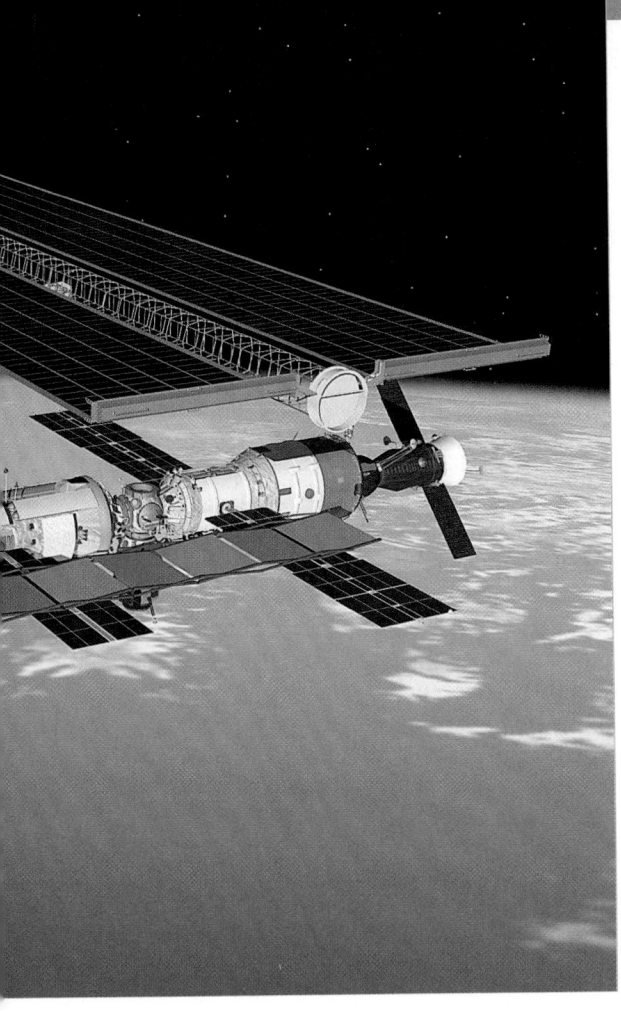

Chapter 5
Adjustments and the Worksheet

BOEING www.boeing.com

The International Space Station (ISS) is a truly global project, involving the scientific and technological resources of 16 countries and the efforts of more than 100,000 people throughout the world. As the prime contractor, Boeing is responsible for design, development, construction, and integration of the ISS and assisting NASA in operating the orbital outpost. About 2,100 Boeing people across the country support the space station with the Boeing program office located in Houston, Texas. The first ISS module was launched in 1998, and the station has been staffed continuously since November 2, 2000. The ISS should be completed about 2010. More than 40 space flights will be required to assemble the 100 major components of the space station. Approximately 28 shuttle flights are remaining to complete the ISS.

Boeing's impressive and important work on the ISS has paid off. Boeing's ISS Program is one of many programs that contributed to the company's Integrated Defense Systems (IDS) 2004 revenue growth.

thinking critically | How do you think Boeing accounts for the wear and tear of its equipment?

Section 1

SECTION OBJECTIVES

▶ 1. **Complete a trial balance on a worksheet.**

WHY IT'S IMPORTANT

Time and effort can be saved when the trial balance is prepared directly on the worksheet. Amounts can be easily transferred to other sections of the worksheet.

▶ 2. **Prepare adjustments for unrecorded business transactions.**

WHY IT'S IMPORTANT

Not all business transactions occur between separate business entities. Some financial events occur within a business and need to be recorded.

TERMS TO LEARN

adjusting entries
adjustments
book value
contra account
contra asset account
depreciation
prepaid expenses
salvage value
straight-line depreciation
worksheet

The Worksheet

Financial statements are completed as soon as possible in order to be useful. One way to speed the preparation of financial statements is to use a worksheet. A **worksheet** is a form used to gather all data needed at the end of an accounting period to prepare the financial statements. Preparation of the worksheet is the fourth step in the accounting cycle.

Figure 5.1 shows a common type of worksheet. The heading shows the company name, report title, and period covered. In addition to the Account Name column, this worksheet contains five sections: Trial Balance, Adjustments, Adjusted Trial Balance, Income Statement, and Balance Sheet. Each section includes a Debit column and a Credit column. The worksheet has 10 columns in which to enter dollar amounts.

The Trial Balance Section

Refer to Figure 5.2 on page 134 as you read about how to prepare the Trial Balance section of the worksheet.

1. Enter the general ledger account names.
2. Transfer the general ledger account balances to the Debit and Credit columns of the Trial Balance section.
3. Total the Debit and Credit columns to prove that the trial balance is in balance.
4. Place a double rule under each Trial Balance column to show that the work in that column is complete.

Notice that the trial balance has four new accounts: *Accumulated Depreciation—Equipment, Supplies Expense, Rent Expense,* and *Depreciation Expense—Equipment.* These accounts have zero balances now, but they will be needed later as the worksheet is completed.

▶ 1. OBJECTIVE

Complete a trial balance on a worksheet.

recall

Trial Balance

If total debits do not equal total credits, there is an error in the financial records. The error must be found and corrected.

FIGURE 5.1 | **Ten-column Worksheet**

JT's Consulting Services
Worksheet
Month Ended December 31, 2007

ACCOUNT NAME	TRIAL BALANCE		ADJUSTMENTS	
	DEBIT	CREDIT	DEBIT	CREDIT
1				
2				
3				
4				
5				

The Adjustments Section

Usually account balances change because of transactions with other businesses or individuals. For JT's Consulting Services, the account changes recorded in Chapter 4 were caused by transactions with the firm's suppliers, customers, the landlord, and employees. It is easy to recognize, journalize, and post these transactions as they occur.

Some changes are not caused by transactions with other businesses or individuals. They arise from the internal operations of the firm during the accounting period. Journal entries made to update accounts for previously unrecorded items are called **adjustments** or **adjusting entries**. These changes are first entered on the worksheet at the end of each accounting period. The worksheet provides a convenient form for gathering the information and determining the effects of the changes. Let's look at the adjustments made by JT's Consulting Services on December 31, 2007.

ADJUSTING FOR SUPPLIES USED

On November 28, 2007, JT's Consulting Services purchased $3,000 of supplies. On December 31 the trial balance shows a $3,000 balance in the **Supplies** account. This amount is too high because some of the supplies were used during December.

An adjustment must be made for the supplies used. Otherwise, the asset account, **Supplies,** is overstated because fewer supplies are actually on hand. The expense account, **Supplies Expense,** is understated. The cost of the supplies used represents an operating expense that has not been recorded.

On December 31 Tennille Brisbane counted the supplies. Remaining supplies totaled $2,000. This meant that supplies amounting to $1,000 were used during December ($3,000 − $2,000 = $1,000). At the end of December, an adjustment must be made to reflect the supplies used. The adjustment reduces the **Supplies** account to $2,000, the amount of supplies remaining. It increases the **Supplies Expense** account by $1,000 for the amount of supplies used. Notice that the adjustment for supplies is based on actual usage.

Refer to Figure 5.2 on page 134 to review the adjustment on the worksheet: a debit of $1,000 to **Supplies Expense** and a credit of $1,000 to **Supplies.** Both the debit and credit are labeled **(a)** to identify the two parts of the adjustment.

Supplies is a type of prepaid expense. **Prepaid expenses** are items that are acquired and paid for in advance of their use. Other common prepaid expenses are prepaid rent, prepaid insurance, and prepaid advertising. When cash is paid for these items, amounts are debited to **Prepaid Rent, Prepaid Insurance,** and **Prepaid Advertising;** all are asset accounts. As prepaid expenses are used, an adjustment is made to reduce the asset accounts and to increase the related expense accounts.

► 2. **OBJECTIVE**
Prepare adjustments for unrecorded business transactions.

Topic Tackler
PLUS

recall

Trial Balance
On the trial balance, accounts are listed in this order: assets, liabilities, owner's equity, revenue, and expenses.

ADJUSTED TRIAL BALANCE		INCOME STATEMENT		BALANCE SHEET		
DEBIT	CREDIT	DEBIT	CREDIT	DEBIT	CREDIT	
						1
						2
						3
						4
						5

JT's Consulting Services
Worksheet
Month Ended December 31, 2007

	ACCOUNT NAME	TRIAL BALANCE DEBIT	TRIAL BALANCE CREDIT	ADJUSTMENTS DEBIT	ADJUSTMENTS CREDIT
1	Cash	83 500 00			
2	Accounts Receivable	5 000 00			
3	Supplies	3 000 00			(a) 1 000 00
4	Prepaid Rent	7 000 00			(b) 3 500 00
5	Equipment	22 000 00			
6	Accumulated Depreciation—Equipment				(c) 3 67 00
7	Accounts Payable		7 000 00		
8	Jason Taylor, Capital		90 000 00		
9	Jason Tyalor, Drawing	4 000 00			
10	Fees Income		35 000 00		
11	Salaries Expense	7 000 00			
12	Utilities Expense	5 00 00			
13	Supplies Expense			(a) 1 000 00	
14	Rent Expense			(b) 3 500 00	
15	Depreciation Expense—Equipment			(c) 3 67 00	
16	Totals	132 000 00	132 000 00	4 867 00	4 867 00
17					

FIGURE 5.2 A Partial Worksheet

ABOUT ACCOUNTING

E-business

E-commerce and e-business are not the same thing. *E-commerce* is only a small piece of e-business. *E-business* relates to automating an entire company and all its business processes, including electronic transaction workflows, online storefronts, self-service data access, and the reengineering of business processes.

ADJUSTMENT

Record the adjustment for supplies.

ANALYSIS

The expense account, **Supplies Expense,** is increased by $1,000. The asset account, **Supplies,** is decreased by $1,000.

DEBIT-CREDIT RULES

DEBIT   Increases to expense accounts are recorded as debits. Debit **Supplies Expense** for $1,000.

CREDIT   Decreases to asset accounts are recorded as credits. Credit **Supplies** for $1,000.

T-ACCOUNT PRESENTATION

Supplies Expense		Supplies	
+	–	+	–
1,000			1,000

Let's review the effect of the adjustment on the asset account, **Supplies.** Recall that the **Supplies** account already had a balance of $3,000. If no adjustment is made, the balance would remain at $3,000, even though only $2,000 of supplies are left.

	Supplies		
	+		–
Bal.	3,000		
		Adj.	1,000
Bal.	2,000		

ADJUSTING FOR EXPIRED RENT

On November 30, 2007, JT's Consulting Services paid $7,000 rent for December and January. The right to occupy facilities for the specified period is an asset. The $7,000 was debited to **Prepaid Rent,** an asset account. On December 31, 2007, the **Prepaid Rent** balance is $7,000. This is too high because one month of rent has been used. The expired rent is $3,500 ($7,000 ÷ 2 months). At the end of December, an adjustment is made to reflect the expired rent.

ADJUSTMENT

Record the adjustment for expired rent.

ANALYSIS
The expense account, **Rent Expense,** is increased by $3,500. The asset account, **Prepaid Rent,** is decreased by $3,500.

DEBIT-CREDIT RULES
DEBIT   Increases to expense accounts are recorded as debits. Debit **Rent Expense** for $3,500.
CREDIT Decreases to asset accounts are recorded as credits. Credit **Prepaid Rent** for $3,500.

T-ACCOUNT PRESENTATION

Rent Expense				Prepaid Rent		
+		–		+		–
3,500						3,500

Let's review the effect of the adjustment on the asset account, **Prepaid Rent.** The beginning balance of $7,000 represents prepaid rent for the months of December and January. By December 31, the prepaid rent for the month of December is "used up." The adjustment reducing **Prepaid Rent** recognizes the expense of occupying the facilities in December. The $3,500 ending balance represents prepaid rent for the month of January.

	Prepaid Rent		
	+		–
Bal.	7,000		
		Adj.	3,500
Bal.	3,500		

important!

Prepaid Expense
Prepaid rent is recorded as an asset at the time it is paid. As time elapses, the asset is used up. An adjustment is made to reduce the asset and to recognize rent expense.

COMPUTERS IN ACCOUNTING

COMPUTERIZED ACCOUNTING SYSTEMS

Computerized systems are widely used by companies to record, summarize, and analyze large volumes of financial data. From the Disney corporate offices in Burbank, California, to the Southwest Airlines headquarters in Dallas, Texas, accountants prepare paychecks, track bank accounts, and generate financial statements using computerized applications. Accounting systems can be standard commercial packages or customized to fit the unique needs of a company. Six common types of accounting applications are available: general ledger, accounts receivable, accounts payable, sales/order processing, inventory control, and payroll.

General ledger programs are basic to any computerized accounting system and are used to record general journal entries. Posting is completed automatically by the computer. The accountant can easily generate reports such as the trial balance, income statement, balance sheet, or statement of owner's equity. At the end of the accounting period, the general ledger program will complete the closing process, preparing the records for the next accounting period.

Other programs provide tools to the accountant for managing accounts receivable, accounts payable, payroll, and inventory.

Companies may use one or more of these accounting applications, or they may build or purchase a completely integrated package of applications. An "integrated" accounting system means that each module, or application, communicates and transfers data to other modules, keeping the accounting records in balance across all programs.

THINKING CRITICALLY

What benefits can you identify to using an integrated computerized accounting system?

INTERNET APPLICATION

Using an Internet search engine, locate information on the general ledger module for AccuBooks accounting software. Create a summary report describing the features of the general ledger module.

Refer to Figure 5.2 to review the adjustment on the worksheet: a debit of $3,500 to *Rent Expense* and a credit of $3,500 to *Prepaid Rent.* Both parts of the adjustment are labeled **(b).**

ADJUSTING FOR DEPRECIATION

There is one more adjustment to make at the end of December. It involves the equipment purchased in November. The cost of long-term assets such as equipment is not recorded as an expense when purchased. Instead the cost is recorded as an asset and spread over the time the assets are used for the business. **Depreciation** is the process of allocating the cost of long-term assets over their expected useful lives. There are many ways to calculate depreciation. JT's Consulting Services uses the **straight-line depreciation** method. This method results in an equal amount of depreciation being charged to each accounting period during the asset's useful life. The formula for straight-line depreciation is

$$\text{Depreciation} = \frac{\text{Cost} - \text{Salvage value}}{\text{Estimated useful life}}$$

Salvage value is an estimate of the amount that may be received by selling or disposing of an asset at the end of its useful life.

JT's Consulting Services purchased $22,000 worth of equipment. The equipment has an estimated useful life of five years and no salvage value. The depreciation for December, the first month of operations, is $367 (rounded).

$$\frac{\$22,000 - \$0}{60 \text{ months}} = \$367 \text{ (rounded)}$$

1. Convert the asset's useful life from years to months: 5 years × 12 months = 60 months.
2. Divide the total depreciation to be taken by the total number of months: $22,000 ÷ 60 = $367 (rounded).
3. Record depreciation expense of $367 each month for the next 60 months.

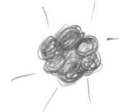

> Conoco Inc. depreciates property such as refinery equipment, pipelines, and deepwater drill ships on a straight-line basis over the estimated life of each asset, ranging from 15 to 25 years.

As the cost of the equipment is gradually transferred to expense, its recorded value as an asset must be reduced. This procedure cannot be carried out by directly decreasing the balance in the asset account. Generally accepted accounting principles require that the original cost of a long-term asset continue to appear in the asset account until the firm has used up or disposed of the asset.

The adjustment for depreciation is recorded in a contra account named ***Accumulated Depreciation—Equipment.*** A **contra account** has a normal balance that is opposite that of a related account. For example, the ***Equipment*** account is an asset and has a normal debit balance. ***Accumulated Depreciation—Equipment*** is a **contra asset account** with a normal credit balance, which is opposite the normal balance of an asset account. The adjustment to reflect depreciation for December is a $367 debit to ***Depreciation Expense—Equipment*** and a $367 credit to ***Accumulated Depreciation—Equipment.***

The ***Accumulated Depreciation—Equipment*** account is a record of all depreciation taken on the equipment. The financial records show the original cost of the equipment (***Equipment,*** $22,000) and all depreciation taken (***Accumulated Depreciation—Equipment,*** $367). The difference between the two accounts is called book value. **Book value** is that portion of an asset's original cost that has not yet been depreciated. Three amounts are reported on the financial statements for equipment:

Equipment	$22,000
Less accumulated depreciation	− 367
Equipment at book value	$21,633

important!

Contra Accounts
The normal balance for a contra account is the opposite of the related account. ***Accumulated Depreciation*** is a contra asset account. The normal balance of an asset account is a *debit*. The normal balance of a contra asset account is a *credit*.

ADJUSTMENT

Record the adjustment for depreciation.

ANALYSIS
The expense account, ***Depreciation Expense—Equipment,*** is increased by $367. The contra asset account, ***Accumulated Depreciation—Equipment,*** is increased by $367.

DEBIT-CREDIT RULES
DEBIT   Increases to expense accounts are recorded as debits. Debit ***Depreciation Expense—Equipment*** for $367.

CREDIT   Increases to contra asset accounts are recorded as credits. Credit ***Accumulated Depreciation—Equipment*** for $367.

T-ACCOUNT PRESENTATION

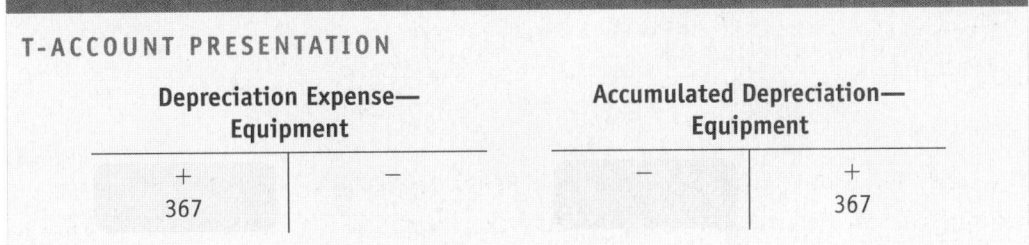

Depreciation Expense—Equipment		Accumulated Depreciation—Equipment	
+	−	−	+
367			367

Refer to Figure 5.2 on page 134 to review the depreciation adjustment on the worksheet. The two parts of the adjustment are labeled **(c).**

If JT's Consulting Services had other kinds of long-term assets, an adjustment for depreciation would be made for each one. Long-term assets include land, buildings, equipment, trucks, automobiles, furniture, and fixtures. Depreciation is calculated on all long-term assets except land. Land is not depreciated.

Notice that each adjustment involved a balance sheet account (an asset or a contra asset) and an income statement account (an expense). When all adjustments have been entered, total and rule the Adjustments columns. Be sure that the totals of the Debit and Credit columns are equal. If they are not, locate and correct the error or errors before continuing. Figure 5.2 shows the completed Adjustments section.

Section 1: **Self Review**

QUESTIONS

1. What are adjustments?
2. Why is the worksheet prepared?
3. Why are prepaid expenses adjusted at the end of an accounting period?

EXERCISES

4. On January 1 a firm paid $10,800 for six months' rent, January through June. What is the adjustment for rent expense at the end of January?

   a. **Rent Expense** is debited for $10,800 and **Prepaid Rent** is credited for $10,800.

   b. **Rent Expense** is debited for $1,800 and **Prepaid Rent** is credited for $1,800.

   c. **Prepaid Rent** is debited for $1,800 and **Rent Expense** is credited for $1,800.

   d. No adjustment is made until the end of June.

5. A firm paid $600 for supplies during the accounting period. At the end of the accounting period, the firm had $150 of supplies on hand. What adjustment is entered on the worksheet?

   a. **Supplies Expense** is debited for $450 and **Supplies** is credited for $450.

   b. **Supplies** is debited for $150 and **Supplies Expense** is credited for $150.

   c. **Supplies Expense** is debited for $150 and **Supplies** is credited for $150.

   d. **Supplies** is debited for $450 and **Supplies Expense** is credited for $450.

ANALYSIS

6. Three years ago C.J. Systems bought a delivery truck for $35,000. The truck has no salvage value and a five-year useful life. What is the book value of the truck at the end of three years?

(Answers to Section 1 Self Review are on page 161.)

Financial Statements

The worksheet is used to prepare the financial statements. Preparing financial statements is the fifth step in the accounting cycle.

The Adjusted Trial Balance Section

The next task is to prepare the Adjusted Trial Balance section.

1. Combine the figures from the Trial Balance section and the Adjustments section of the worksheet. Record the computed results in the Adjusted Trial Balance columns.

2. Total the Debit and Credit columns in the Adjusted Trial Balance section. Confirm that debits equal credits.

Figure 5.3 on pages 140–141 shows the completed Adjusted Trial Balance section of the worksheet. The accounts that do not have adjustments are simply extended from the Trial Balance section to the Adjusted Trial Balance section. For example, the **Cash** account balance of $83,500 is recorded in the Debit column of the Adjusted Trial Balance section without change.

The balances of accounts that are affected by adjustments are recomputed. Look at the **Supplies** account. It has a $3,000 debit balance in the Trial Balance section and shows a $1,000 credit in the Adjustments section. The new balance is $2,000 ($3,000 − $1,000). It is recorded in the Debit column of the Adjusted Trial Balance section.

Use the following guidelines to compute the amounts for the Adjusted Trial Balance section.

- If the account has a debit balance in the Trial Balance section and a debit entry in the Adjustments section, add the two amounts.

- If the account has a debit balance in the Trial Balance section and a credit entry in the Adjustments section, subtract the credit amount.

If the Trial Balance section has a:	AND if the entry in the Adjustments section is a:	Then:
Debit balance	Debit	Add the amounts.
Debit balance	Credit	Subtract the credit amount.
Credit balance	Credit	Add the amounts.
Credit balance	Debit	Subtract the debit amount.

SECTION OBJECTIVES

▶ **3. Complete the worksheet.**

WHY IT'S IMPORTANT
The worksheet summarizes both internal and external financial events of a period.

▶ **4. Prepare an income statement, statement of owner's equity, and balance sheet from the completed worksheet.**

WHY IT'S IMPORTANT
Using a worksheet saves time in preparing the financial statements.

▶ **5. Journalize and post the adjusting entries.**

WHY IT'S IMPORTANT
Adjusting entries update the financial records of the business.

TERMS TO LEARN

account form balance sheet
report form balance sheet

▶ **3. OBJECTIVE**
Complete the worksheet.

JT's Consulting Services
Worksheet
Month Ended December 31, 2007

	ACCOUNT NAME	TRIAL BALANCE		ADJUSTMENTS	
		DEBIT	CREDIT	DEBIT	CREDIT
1	Cash	83 5 0 0 00			
2	Accounts Receivable	5 0 0 0 00			
3	Supplies	3 0 0 0 00			(a) 1 0 0 0 00
4	Prepaid Rent	7 0 0 0 00			(b) 3 5 0 0 00
5	Equipment	22 0 0 0 00			
6	Accumulated Depreciation—Equipment				(c) 3 6 7 00
7	Accounts Payable		7 0 0 0 00		
8	Jason Taylor, Capital		90 0 0 0 00		
9	Jason Taylor, Drawing	4 0 0 0 00			
10	Fees Income		35 0 0 0 00		
11	Salaries Expense	7 0 0 0 00			
12	Utilities Expense	5 0 0 00			
13	Supplies Expense			(a) 1 0 0 0 00	
14	Rent Expense			(b) 3 5 0 0 00	
15	Depreciation Expense—Equipment			(c) 3 6 7 00	
16	Totals	132 0 0 0 00	132 0 0 0 00	4 8 6 7 00	4 8 6 7 00
17	Net Income				

FIGURE 5.3   A Partial Worksheet

- If the account has a credit balance in the Trial Balance section and a credit entry in the Adjustments section, add the two amounts.
- If the account has a credit balance in the Trial Balance section and a debit entry in the Adjustments section, subtract the debit amount.

Prepaid Rent has a Trial Balance debit of $7,000 and an Adjustments credit of $3,500. Enter $3,500 ($7,000 − $3,500) in the Adjusted Trial Balance Debit column.

Four accounts that started with zero balances in the Trial Balance section are affected by adjustments. They are **Accumulated Depreciation—Equipment, Supplies Expense, Rent Expense,** and **Depreciation Expense—Equipment.** The figures in the Adjustments section are simply extended to the Adjusted Trial Balance section. For example, **Accumulated Depreciation—Equipment** has a zero balance in the Trial Balance section and a $367 credit in the Adjustments section. Extend the $367 to the Adjusted Trial Balance Credit column.

Once all account balances are recorded in the Adjusted Trial Balance section, total and rule the Debit and Credit columns. Be sure that total debits equal total credits. If they are not equal, find and correct the error or errors.

The Income Statement and Balance Sheet Sections

The Income Statement and Balance Sheet sections of the worksheet are used to separate the amounts needed for the balance sheet and the income statement. For example, to prepare an income statement, all revenue and expense account balances must be in one place.

Starting at the top of the Adjusted Trial Balance section, examine each general ledger account. For accounts that appear on the balance sheet, enter the amount in the appropriate column of the Balance Sheet section. For accounts that appear on the income statement, enter the amount in the appropriate column of the Income Statement section. Take care to enter debit amounts in the Debit column and credit amounts in the Credit column.

ADJUSTED TRIAL BALANCE		INCOME STATEMENT		BALANCE SHEET		
DEBIT	CREDIT	DEBIT	CREDIT	DEBIT	CREDIT	
83 5 0 0 00						1
5 0 0 0 00						2
2 0 0 0 00						3
3 5 0 0 00						4
22 0 0 0 00						5
	3 6 7 00					6
	7 0 0 0 00					7
	90 0 0 0 00					8
4 0 0 0 00						9
	35 0 0 0 00					10
7 0 0 0 00						11
5 0 0 00						12
1 0 0 0 00						13
3 5 0 0 00						14
3 6 7 00						15
132 3 6 7 00	132 3 6 7 00					16
						17

PREPARING THE BALANCE SHEET SECTION

Refer to Figure 5.4 on pages 142–143 as you learn how to complete the worksheet. Asset, liability, and owner's equity accounts appear on the balance sheet. The first five accounts that appear on the worksheet are assets. Extend the asset accounts to the Debit column of the Balance Sheet section. The next account, *Accumulated Depreciation—Equipment,* is a contra asset account. Extend it to the Credit column of the Balance Sheet section. Extend *Accounts Payable* and *Jason Taylor, Capital* to the Credit column of the Balance Sheet section. Extend *Jason Taylor, Drawing* to the Debit column of the Balance Sheet section.

PREPARING THE INCOME STATEMENT SECTION

Revenue and expense accounts appear on the income statement. Extend the *Fees Income* account to the Credit column of the Income Statement section. The last five accounts on the worksheet are expense accounts. Extend these accounts to the Debit column of the Income Statement section.

After all account balances are transferred from the Adjusted Trial Balance section of the worksheet to the financial statement sections, total the Debit and Credit columns in the Income Statement section. For JT's Consulting Services, the debits (expenses) total $12,367 and the credits (revenue) total $35,000.

Next total the columns in the Balance Sheet section. For JT's Consulting Services the debits (assets and drawing account) total $120,000 and the credits (contra asset, liabilities, and owner's equity) total $97,367.

Return to the Income Statement section. The totals of these columns are used to determine the net income or net loss. Subtract the smaller column total from the larger one. Enter the difference on the line below the smaller total. In the Account Name column, enter "Net Income" or "Net Loss."

In this case the total of the Credit column, $35,000, exceeds the total of the Debit column, $12,367. The Credit column total represents revenue. The Debit column total represents expenses. The difference between the two amounts is a net income of $22,633. Enter $22,633 in the Debit column of the Income Statement section.

recall

Locating Errors
If total debits do not equal total credits, find the difference between total debits and total credits. If the difference is divisible by 9, there could be a transposition error. If the difference is divisible by 2, an amount could be entered in the wrong (Debit or Credit) column.

International INSIGHTS

Proper Names
When conducting business in the international marketplace, it is important to address individuals in the proper manner. Some countries do not use the "first name-last name" style as used in the United States. For example, in Spanish-speaking Latin America, the surname is a combination of the mother's and father's last names. The father's name comes first and is the only one used in conversations.

JT's Consulting Services
Worksheet
Month Ended December 31, 2007

| ACCOUNT NAME | TRIAL BALANCE | | ADJUSTMENTS | |
	DEBIT	CREDIT	DEBIT	CREDIT
1 Cash	83 5 0 0 00			
2 Accounts Receivable	5 0 0 0 00			
3 Supplies	3 0 0 0 00			(a) 1 0 0 0 00
4 Prepaid Rent	7 0 0 0 00			(b) 3 5 0 0 00
5 Equipment	22 0 0 0 00			
6 Accumulated Depreciation—Equipment				(c) 3 6 7 00
7 Accounts Payable		7 0 0 0 00		
8 Jason Taylor, Capital		90 0 0 0 00		
9 Jason Taylor, Drawing	4 0 0 0 00			
10 Fees Income		35 0 0 0 00		
11 Salaries Expense	7 0 0 0 00			
12 Utilities Expense	5 0 0 00			
13 Supplies Expense			(a) 1 0 0 0 00	
14 Rent Expense			(b) 3 5 0 0 00	
15 Depreciation Expense—Equipment			(c) 3 6 7 00	
16 Totals	132 0 0 0 00	132 0 0 0 00	4 8 6 7 00	4 8 6 7 00
17 Net Income				
18				

FIGURE 5.4 | **A Completed Worksheet**

important!

Net Income

The difference between the Debit and Credit columns of the Income Statement section represents net income. The difference between the Debit and Credit columns of the Balance Sheet section should equal the net income amount.

Net income causes a net increase in owner's equity. As a check on accuracy, the amount in the Balance Sheet Debit column is subtracted from the amount in the Credit column and compared to net income. In the Balance Sheet section, subtract the smaller column total from the larger one. The difference should equal the net income or net loss computed in the Income Statement section. Enter the difference on the line below the smaller total. For JT's Consulting Services, enter $22,633 in the Credit column of the Balance Sheet section.

Total the Income Statement and Balance Sheet columns. Make sure that total debits equal total credits for each section.

JT's Consulting Services had a net income. If it had a loss, the loss would be entered in the Credit column of the Income Statement section and the Debit column of the Balance Sheet section. "Net Loss" would be entered in the Account Name column on the worksheet.

Preparing Financial Statements

When the worksheet is complete, the next step is to prepare the financial statements, starting with the income statement. Preparation of the financial statements is the fifth step in the accounting cycle.

▶ **4. OBJECTIVE**

Prepare an income statement, statement of owner's equity, and balance sheet from the completed worksheet.

PREPARING THE INCOME STATEMENT

Use the Income Statement section of the worksheet to prepare the income statement. Figure 5.5 on page 144 shows the income statement for JT's Consulting Services. Compare it to the worksheet in Figure 5.4.

If the firm had incurred a net loss, the final amount on the income statement would be labeled "Net Loss for the Month."

| ADJUSTED TRIAL BALANCE | | INCOME STATEMENT | | BALANCE SHEET | | |
DEBIT	CREDIT	DEBIT	CREDIT	DEBIT	CREDIT	
83 5 0 0 00				83 5 0 0 00		1
5 0 0 0 00				5 0 0 0 00		2
2 0 0 0 00				2 0 0 0 00		3
3 5 0 0 00				3 5 0 0 00		4
22 0 0 0 00				22 0 0 0 00		5
	3 6 7 00				3 6 7 00	6
	7 0 0 0 00				7 0 0 0 00	7
	90 0 0 0 00				90 0 0 0 00	8
4 0 0 0 00				4 0 0 0 00		9
	35 0 0 0 00		35 0 0 0 00			10
7 0 0 0 00		7 0 0 0 00				11
5 0 0 00		5 0 0 00				12
1 0 0 0 00		1 0 0 0 00				13
3 5 0 0 00		3 5 0 0 00				14
3 6 7 00		3 6 7 00				15
132 3 6 7 00	132 3 6 7 00	12 3 6 7 00	35 0 0 0 00	120 0 0 0 00	97 3 6 7 00	16
		22 6 3 3 00			22 6 3 3 00	17
		35 0 0 0 00	35 0 0 0 00	120 0 0 0 00	120 0 0 0 00	18

PREPARING THE STATEMENT OF OWNER'S EQUITY

The statement of owner's equity reports the changes that have occurred in the owner's financial interest during the reporting period. Use the data in the Balance Sheet section of the worksheet, as well as the net income or net loss figure, to prepare the statement of owner's equity.

■ From the Balance Sheet section of the worksheet, use the amounts for owner's capital; owner's withdrawals, if any; and owner's investments, if any.

■ From the Income Statement section of the worksheet, use the amount calculated for net income or net loss.

The statement of owner's equity is prepared before the balance sheet because the ending capital balance is needed to prepare the balance sheet. The statement of owner's equity reports the change in owner's capital during the period ($18,633) as well as the ending capital ($108,633). Figure 5.6 on page 144 shows the statement of owner's equity for JT's Consulting Services.

PREPARING THE BALANCE SHEET

The accounts listed on the balance sheet are taken directly from the Balance Sheet section of the worksheet. Figure 5.7 on page 144 shows the balance sheet for JT's Consulting Services.

Note that the equipment's book value is reported on the balance sheet ($21,633). Do not confuse book value with market value. Book value is the portion of the original cost that has not been depreciated. *Market value* is what a willing buyer will pay a willing seller for the asset. Market value may be higher or lower than book value.

Notice that the amount for ***Jason Taylor, Capital,*** $108,633, comes from the statement of owner's equity.

The balance sheet in Figure 5.7 is prepared using the report form. The **report form balance sheet** lists the asset accounts first, followed by liabilities and owner's equity. Chapters 2 and 3 illustrated the **account form balance sheet** , with assets on the left and liabilities and

(continued on page 145)

FIGURE 5.5

Income Statement

JT's Consulting Services
Income Statement
Month Ended December 31, 2007

Revenue			
Fees Income			3 5 0 0 0 00
Expenses			
Salaries Expense	7 0 0 0 00		
Utilities Expense	5 0 0 00		
Supplies Expense	1 0 0 0 00		
Rent Expense	3 5 0 0 00		
Depreciation Expense—Equipment	3 6 7 00		
Total Expenses		1 2 3 6 7 00	
Net Income for the Month		2 2 6 3 3 00	

FIGURE 5.6

Statement of Owner's Equity

JT's Consulting Services
Statement of Owner's Equity
Month Ended December 31, 2007

Jason Taylor, Capital, December 1, 2007			90 0 0 0 00
Net Income for December	22 6 3 3 00		
Less Withdrawals for December	4 0 0 0 00		
Increase in Capital		18 6 3 3 00	
Jason Taylor, Capital, December 31, 2007		108 6 3 3 00	

FIGURE 5.7

Balance Sheet

JT's Consulting Services
Balance Sheet
December 31, 2007

Assets			
Cash			83 5 0 0 00
Accounts Receivable			5 0 0 0 00
Supplies			2 0 0 0 00
Prepaid Rent			3 5 0 0 00
Equipment	22 0 0 0 00		
Less Accumulated Depreciation	3 6 7 00	21 6 3 3 00	
Total Assets		115 6 3 3 00	
Liabilities and Owner's Equity			
Liabilities			
Accounts Payable			7 0 0 0 00
Owner's Equity			
Jason Taylor, Capital			108 6 3 3 00
Total Liabilities and Owner's Equity			115 6 3 3 00

FIGURE 5.8A Worksheet Summary

The worksheet is used to gather all the data needed at the end of an accounting period to prepare the financial statements. The worksheet heading contains the name of the company (WHO), the title of the statement being prepared (WHAT), and the period covered (WHEN). The worksheet contains ten money columns that are arranged in five sections labeled Trial Balance, Adjustments, Adjusted Trial Balance, Income Statement, and Balance Sheet. Each section includes a Debit column and a Credit column.

The information reflected in the worksheet below is for JT's Consulting Services for the period ending December 31, 2007. The illustrations that follow will highlight the preparation of each part of the worksheet.

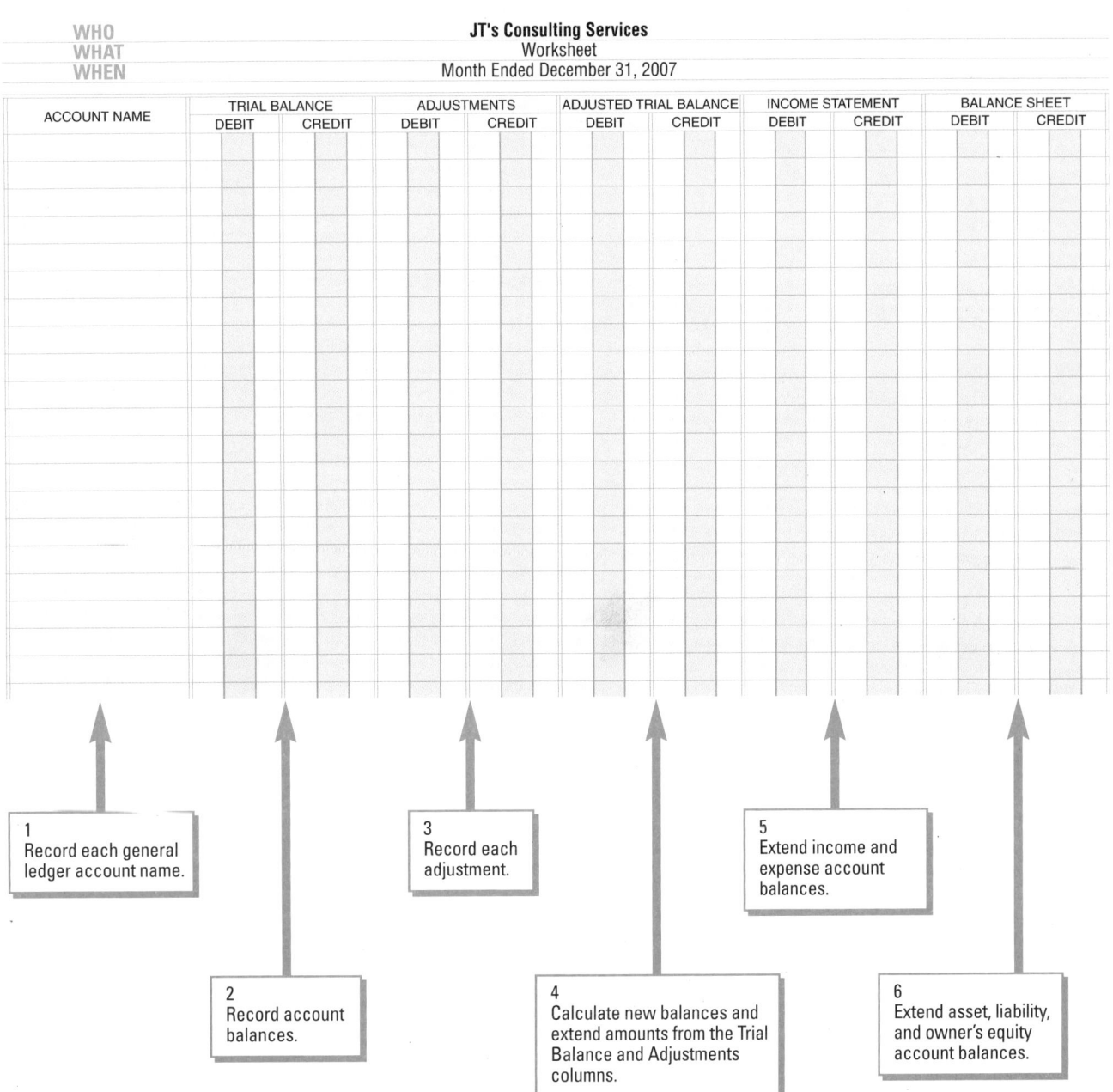

FIGURE 5.8B   The Trial Balance Columns

The first step in preparing the worksheet for JT's Consulting Services is to list the general ledger accounts and their balances in the Account Name and Trial Balance sections of the worksheet. The equality of total debits and credits is proved by totaling the Debit and Credit columns.

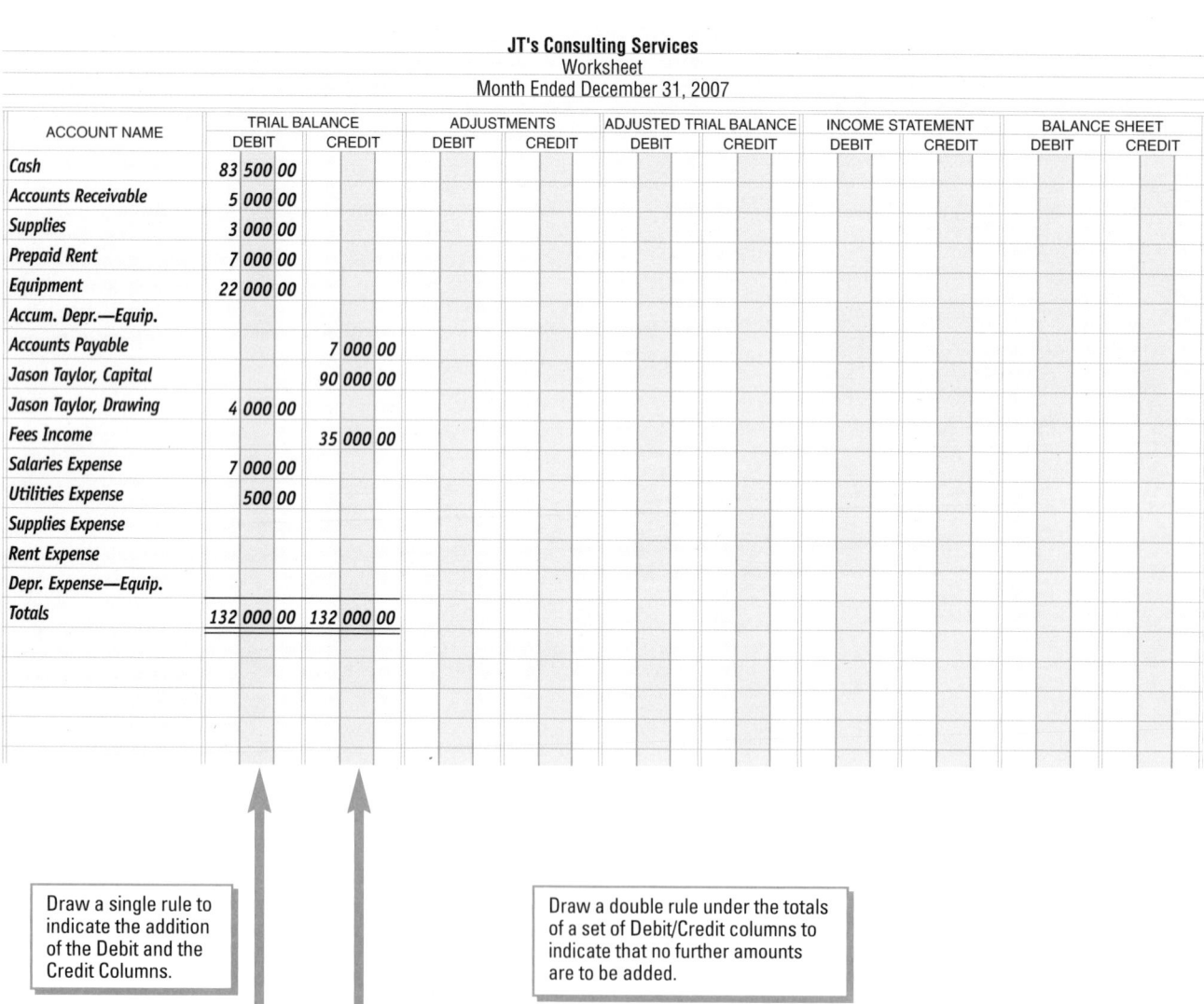

JT's Consulting Services
Worksheet
Month Ended December 31, 2007

ACCOUNT NAME	TRIAL BALANCE DEBIT	TRIAL BALANCE CREDIT	ADJUSTMENTS DEBIT	ADJUSTMENTS CREDIT	ADJUSTED TRIAL BALANCE DEBIT	ADJUSTED TRIAL BALANCE CREDIT	INCOME STATEMENT DEBIT	INCOME STATEMENT CREDIT	BALANCE SHEET DEBIT	BALANCE SHEET CREDIT
Cash	83 500 00									
Accounts Receivable	5 000 00									
Supplies	3 000 00									
Prepaid Rent	7 000 00									
Equipment	22 000 00									
Accum. Depr.—Equip.										
Accounts Payable		7 000 00								
Jason Taylor, Capital		90 000 00								
Jason Taylor, Drawing	4 000 00									
Fees Income		35 000 00								
Salaries Expense	7 000 00									
Utilities Expense	500 00									
Supplies Expense										
Rent Expense										
Depr. Expense—Equip.										
Totals	132 000 00	132 000 00								

Draw a single rule to indicate the addition of the Debit and the Credit Columns.

Draw a double rule under the totals of a set of Debit/Credit columns to indicate that no further amounts are to be added.

Trial Balance totals must be equal.

FIGURE 5.8G Preparing the Financial Statements

The information needed to prepare the financial statements is obtained from the worksheet.

JT's Consulting Services
Income Statement
Month Ended December 31, 2007

Revenue			
Fees Income		35 0 0 0 00	
Expenses			
Salaries Expense	7 0 0 0 00		
Utilities Expense	5 0 0 00		
Supplies Expense	1 0 0 0 00		
Rent Expense	3 5 0 0 00		
Depreciation Expense—Equipment	3 6 7 00		
Total Expenses		12 3 6 7 00	
Net Income for the Month		22 6 3 3 00	

> When expenses for the period are less than revenue, a net income results. The net income is transferred to the statement of owner's equity.

JT's Consulting Services
Statement of Owner's Equity
Month Ended December 31, 2007

Jason Taylor, Capital, December 1, 2005		90 0 0 0 00	
Net Income for December	22 6 3 3 00		
Less Withdrawals for December	4 0 0 0 00		
Increase in Capital		18 6 3 3 00	
Jason Taylor, Capital, December 31, 2007		108 6 3 3 00	

> The withdrawals are subtracted from the net income for the period to determine the change in owner's equity.

JT's Consulting Services
Balance Sheet
December 31, 2007

Assets			
Cash		83 5 0 0 00	
Accounts Receivable		5 0 0 0 00	
Supplies		2 0 0 0 00	
Prepaid Rent		3 5 0 0 00	
Equipment	22 0 0 0 00		
Less Accumulated Depreciation	3 6 7 00	21 6 3 3 00	
Total Assets		115 6 3 3 00	
Liabilities and Owner's Equity			
Liabilities			
Accounts Payable		7 0 0 0 00	
Owner's Equity			
Jason Taylor, Capital		108 6 3 3 00	
Total Liabilities and Owner's Equity		115 6 3 3 00	

> The ending capital balance is transferred from the statement of owner's equity to the balance sheet.

SUMMARY OF FINANCIAL STATEMENTS

THE INCOME STATEMENT

The income statement is prepared directly from the data in the Income Statement section of the worksheet. The heading of the income statement contains the name of the firm (WHO), the name of the statement (WHAT), the period covered by the statement (WHEN). The revenue section of the statement is prepared first. The revenue account name is obtained from the Account Name column of the worksheet. The balance of the revenue account is obtained from the Credit column of the Income Statement section of the worksheet. The expenses section of the income statement is prepared next. The expense account titles are obtained from the Account Name column of the worksheet. The balance of each expense account is obtained from the Debit column of the Income Statement section of the worksheet.

Determining the net income or net loss for the period is the last step in preparing the income statement. If the firm has more revenue than expenses, a net income is reported for the period. If the firm has more expenses than revenue, a net loss is reported. The net income or net loss reported must agree with the amount calculated on the worksheet.

THE STATEMENT OF OWNER'S EQUITY

The statement of owner's equity is prepared from the data in the Balance Sheet section of the worksheet and the general ledger capital account. The statement of owner's equity is prepared before the balance sheet so that the amount of the ending capital balance is available for presentation on the balance sheet. The heading of the statement contains the name of the firm (WHO), the name of the statement (WHAT), and the date of the statement (WHEN).

The statement begins with the capital account balance at the beginning of the period. Next, the increase or decrease in the owner's capital account is determined. The increase or decrease is computed by adding the net income (or net loss) for the period to any additional investments made by the owner during the period and subtracting withdrawals for the period. The increase or decrease is added to the beginning capital balance to obtain the ending capital balance.

THE BALANCE SHEET

The balance sheet is prepared from the data in the Balance Sheet section of the worksheet and the statement of owner's equity. The balance sheet reflects the assets, liabilities, and owner's equity of the firm on the balance sheet date. The heading of the statement contains the name of the firm (WHO), the name of the statement (WHAT), and the date of the statement (WHEN).

The assets section of the statement is prepared first. The asset account titles are obtained from the Account Name column of the worksheet. The balance of each asset account is obtained from the Debit column of the Balance Sheet section of the worksheet. The liability and owner's equity section is prepared next. The liability and owner's equity account titles are obtained from the Account Name column of the worksheet. The balance of each liability account is obtained from the Credit column of the Balance Sheet section of the worksheet. The ending balance for the owner's capital account is obtained from the statement of owner's equity. Total liabilities and owner's equity must equal total assets.

(continued from page 143)

owner's equity on the right. The report form is widely used because it provides more space for entering account names and its format is easier to prepare.

> Some companies show long-term assets at a net amount. "Net" means that accumulated depreciation has been subtracted from the original cost. For example, The Boeing Company's consolidated statement of financial position as of December 31, 2003, states:
>   Property, plant, and equipment, net: $8,432 million
> The accumulated depreciation amount does not appear on the balance sheet.

Figure 5.8A through 5.8G on the preceding pages provides a step-by-step demonstration of how to complete the worksheet and financial statements for JT's Consulting Services.

Journalizing and Posting Adjusting Entries

The worksheet is a tool. It is used to determine the effects of adjustments on account balances. It is also used to prepare the financial statements. However, the worksheet is not part of the permanent accounting record.

After the financial statements are prepared, the adjustments shown on the worksheet must become part of the permanent accounting record. Each adjustment is journalized and posted to the general ledger accounts. Journalizing and posting adjusting entries is the sixth step in the accounting cycle.

For JT's Consulting Services, three adjustments are needed to provide a complete picture of the firm's operating results and its financial position. Adjustments are needed for supplies expense, rent expense, and depreciation expense.

Refer to Figure 5.4 on pages 142–143 for data needed to record the adjustments. Enter the words "Adjusting Entries" in the Description column of the general journal. Some accountants prefer to start a new page when they record the adjusting entries. Then journalize the adjustments in the order in which they appear on the worksheet.

After journalizing the adjusting entries, post them to the general ledger accounts. Figure 5.9 on page 146 shows how the adjusting entries for JT's Consulting Services on December 31, 2007 were journalized and posted. Account numbers appear in the general journal Posting Reference column because all entries have been posted. In each general ledger account, the word "Adjusting" appears in the Description column.

Remember that the worksheet is not part of the accounting records. Adjustments that are on the worksheet must be recorded in the general journal and posted to the general ledger in order to become part of the permanent accounting records.

> ▶ 5. OBJECTIVE
> Journalize and post the adjusting entries.

FIGURE 5.9

Journalized and Posted Adjusting Entries

GENERAL JOURNAL   PAGE 3

	DATE		DESCRIPTION	POST. REF.	DEBIT	CREDIT	
1	2007		*Adjusting Entries*				1
2	Dec.	31	Supplies Expense	517	1 0 0 0 00		2
3			Supplies	121		1 0 0 0 00	3
4							4
5		31	Rent Expense	520	3 5 0 0 00		5
6			Prepaid Rent	137		3 5 0 0 00	6
7							7
8		31	Depr. Expense—Equipment	523	3 6 7 00		8
9			Accum. Depr.—Equipment	142		3 6 7 00	9
10							10
11							

ACCOUNT Supplies   **ACCOUNT NO.** 121

DATE		DESCRIPTION	POST. REF.	DEBIT	CREDIT	BALANCE DEBIT	BALANCE CREDIT
2007							
Nov.	28		J1	3 0 0 0 00		3 0 0 0 00	
Dec.	31	Adjusting	J3		1 0 0 0 00	2 0 0 0 00	

ACCOUNT Prepaid Rent   **ACCOUNT NO.** 137

DATE		DESCRIPTION	POST. REF.	DEBIT	CREDIT	BALANCE DEBIT	BALANCE CREDIT
2007							
Nov.	31		J2	7 0 0 0 00		7 0 0 0 00	
Dec.	31	Adjusting	J3		3 5 0 0 00	3 5 0 0 00	

ACCOUNT Accumulated Depreciation—Equipment   **ACCOUNT NO.** 142

DATE		DESCRIPTION	POST. REF.	DEBIT	CREDIT	BALANCE DEBIT	BALANCE CREDIT
2007							
Dec.	31	Adjusting	J3		3 6 7 00		3 6 7 00

ACCOUNT Supplies Expense   **ACCOUNT NO.** 517

DATE		DESCRIPTION	POST. REF.	DEBIT	CREDIT	BALANCE DEBIT	BALANCE CREDIT
2007							
Dec.	31	Adjusting	J3	1 0 0 0 00		1 0 0 0 00	

ACCOUNT Rent Expense   **ACCOUNT NO.** 520

DATE		DESCRIPTION	POST. REF.	DEBIT	CREDIT	BALANCE DEBIT	BALANCE CREDIT
2007							
Dec.	31	Adjusting	J3	3 5 0 0 00		3 5 0 0 00	

ACCOUNT Depreciation Expense—Equipment   **ACCOUNT NO.** 523

DATE		DESCRIPTION	POST. REF.	DEBIT	CREDIT	BALANCE DEBIT	BALANCE CREDIT
2007							
Dec.	31	Adjusting	J3	3 6 7 00		3 6 7 00	

MANAGERIAL IMPLICATIONS

WORKSHEETS

- The worksheet permits quick preparation of the financial statements. Quick preparation of financial statements allows management to obtain timely information.
- Timely information allows management to
  - evaluate the results of operations,
  - evaluate the financial position of the business,
  - make decisions.
- The worksheet provides a convenient form for gathering information and determining the effects of internal changes such as
  - recording an expense for the use of a long-term asset like equipment,
  - recording the actual use of prepaid items.
- The more accounts that a firm has in its general ledger, the more useful the worksheet is in speeding the preparation of the financial statements.
- It is important to management that the appropriate adjustments are recorded in order to present a complete and accurate picture of the firm's financial affairs.

THINKING CRITICALLY

If you skip the adjustment process, how will this affect the financial statements?

Section 2: **Self Review**

QUESTIONS

1. Why is it necessary to journalize and post adjusting entries even though the data is already recorded on the worksheet?

2. What amounts appear on the statement of owner's equity?

3. What is the difference between a report form balance sheet and an account form balance sheet?

EXERCISES

4. **Accumulated Depreciation— Equipment** is a(n)
   a. asset account.
   b. contra asset account.
   c. liability account.
   d. contra liability account.

5. On a worksheet, the adjusted balance of the **Supplies** account is extended to the
   a. Income Statement Debit column.
   b. Balance Sheet Debit column.
   c. Income Statement Credit column.
   d. Balance Sheet Credit column.

ANALYSIS

6. EZ Repair Shop purchased equipment for $14,000. **Depreciation Expense** for the month is $250. What is the balance of the **Equipment** account after posting the depreciation entry? Why?

(Answers to Section 2 Self Review are on page 162.)

CHAPTER 5: Review and Applications

REVIEW | Chapter Summary

At the end of the operating period, adjustments for internal events are recorded to update the accounting records. In this chapter, you have learned how the accountant uses the worksheet and adjusting entries to accomplish this task.

Learning Objectives

1 Complete a trial balance on a worksheet.

A worksheet is normally used to save time in preparing the financial statements. Preparation of the worksheet is the fourth step in the accounting cycle. The trial balance is the first section of the worksheet to be prepared.

2 Prepare adjustments for unrecorded business transactions.

Some changes arise from the internal operations of the firm itself. Adjusting entries are made to record these changes. Any adjustments to account balances should be entered in the Adjustments section of the worksheet.

■ Prepaid expenses are expense items that are acquired and paid for in advance of their use. At the time of their acquisition, these items represent assets and are recorded in asset accounts. As they are used, their cost is transferred to expense by means of adjusting entries at the end of each accounting period.

   Examples of general ledger asset accounts and the related expense accounts follow:

Asset Accounts	Expense Accounts
Supplies	Supplies Expense
Prepaid Rent	Rent Expense
Prepaid Insurance	Insurance Expense

■ Depreciation is the process of allocating the cost of a long-term asset to operations over its expected useful life. Part of the asset's cost is charged off as an expense at the end of each accounting period during the asset's useful life. The straight-line method of depreciation is widely used. The formula for straight-line depreciation is:

$$\text{Depreciation} = \frac{\text{Cost} - \text{Salvage value}}{\text{Estimated useful life}}$$

3 Complete the worksheet.

An adjusted trial balance is prepared to prove the equality of the debits and credits after adjustments have been entered on the worksheet. Once the Debit and Credit columns have been totaled and ruled, the Income Statement and Balance Sheet columns of the worksheet are completed. The net income or net loss for the period is determined, and the worksheet is completed.

4 Prepare an income statement, statement of owner's equity, and balance sheet from the completed worksheet.

All figures needed to prepare the financial statements are properly reflected on the completed worksheet. The accounts are arranged in the order in which they must appear on the income statement and balance sheet. Preparation of the financial statements is the fifth step of the accounting cycle.

5 Journalize and post the adjusting entries.

After the financial statements have been prepared, the accountant must make permanent entries in the accounting records for the adjustments shown on the worksheet. The adjusting entries are then posted to the general ledger. Journalizing and posting the adjusting entries is the sixth step in the accounting cycle.

To summarize the steps of the accounting cycle discussed so far:

1. Analyze transactions.
2. Journalize transactions.
3. Post the journal entries.
4. Prepare a worksheet.
5. Prepare financial statements.
6. Record adjusting entries.

6 Define the accounting terms new to this chapter.

Glossary

Account form balance sheet (p. 143) A balance sheet that lists assets on the left and liabilities and owner's equity on the right (see Report form balance sheet)

Adjusting entries (p. 133) Journal entries made to update accounts for items that were not recorded during the accounting period

Adjustments (p. 133) See Adjusting entries

Book value (p. 137) That portion of an asset's original cost that has not yet been depreciated

Contra account (p. 137) An account with a normal balance that is opposite that of a related account

Contra asset account (p. 137) An asset account with a credit balance, which is contrary to the normal balance of an asset account

Depreciation (p. 136) Allocation of the cost of a long-term asset to operations during its expected useful life

Prepaid expenses (p. 133) Expense items acquired, recorded, and paid for in advance of their use

Report form balance sheet (p. 143) A balance sheet that lists the asset accounts first, followed by liabilities and owner's equity

Salvage value (p. 136) An estimate of the amount that could be received by selling or disposing of an asset at the end of its useful life

Straight-line depreciation (p. 136) Allocation of an asset's cost in equal amounts to each accounting period of the asset's useful life

Worksheet (p. 132) A form used to gather all data needed at the end of an accounting period to prepare financial statements

Comprehensive **Self Review**

1. The *Drawing* account is extended to which column of the worksheet?

2. The *Supplies* account has a debit balance of $6,000 in the Trial Balance column. The Credit column in the Adjustments section is $1,750. What is the new balance? The new balance will be extended to which column of the worksheet?

3. Is the normal balance for *Accumulated Depreciation* a debit or credit balance?

4. Why is the net income for a period recorded in the Balance Sheet section of the worksheet as well as the Income Statement section?

5. Why are assets depreciated?

(Answers to Comprehensive Self Review are on page 162.)

Discussion Questions

1. A firm purchases machinery, which has an estimated useful life of 10 years and no salvage value, for $15,000 at the beginning of the accounting period. What is the adjusting entry for depreciation at the end of one month if the firm uses the straight-line method of depreciation?

2. What adjustment would be recorded for expired insurance?

3. What are prepaid expenses? Give four examples.

4. Why is it necessary to make an adjustment for supplies used?

5. Are the following assets depreciated? Why or why not?

a. Prepaid Insurance

b. Delivery Truck

c. Land

d. Manufacturing Equipment

e. Prepaid Rent

f. Furniture

g. Store Equipment

h. Prepaid Advertising

i. Computers

6. What effect does each of the following items have on net income?

a. The owner withdrew cash from the business.

b. Credit customers paid $1,000 on outstanding balances that were past due.

c. The business bought equipment on account that cost $10,000.

d. The business journalized and posted an adjustment for depreciation of equipment.

7. What effect does each item in Question 6 have on owner's equity?

8. Why is it necessary to journalize and post adjusting entries?

9. What three amounts are reported on the balance sheet for a long-term asset such as equipment?

10. How does a contra asset account differ from a regular asset account?

11. What is book value?

12. Why is an accumulated depreciation account used in making the adjustment for depreciation?

13. How does the straight-line method of depreciation work?

14. Give three examples of assets that are subject to depreciation.

APPLICATIONS

Exercises

Exercise 5.1
Objective 2

▶ **Calculating adjustments.**

Determine the necessary end-of-June adjustments for Carlson Company.

1. On June 1, 2007, Carlson Company, a new firm, paid $9,000 rent in advance for a six-month period. The $9,000 was debited to the *Prepaid Rent* account.

2. On June 1, 2007, the firm bought supplies for $2,375. The $2,375 was debited to the *Supplies* account. An inventory of supplies at the end of June showed that items costing $900 were on hand.

3. On June 1, 2007, the firm bought equipment costing $27,000. The equipment has an expected useful life of 10 years and no salvage value. The firm will use the straight-line method of depreciation.

Exercise 5.2
Objective 2

▶ **Calculating adjustments.**

For each of the following situations, determine the necessary adjustments.

1. A firm purchased a two-year insurance policy for $6,000 on July 1, 2007. The $6,000 was debited to the *Prepaid Insurance* account. What adjustment should be made to record expired insurance on the firm's July 31, 2007, worksheet?

2. On December 1, 2007, a firm signed a contract with a local radio station for advertising that will extend over a one-year period. The firm paid $5,400 in advance and debited the amount to **Prepaid Advertising.** What adjustment should be made to record expired advertising on the firm's December 31, 2007, worksheet?

Worksheet through Adjusted Trial Balance.

◀   **Exercise 5.3**
Objectives 1, 2

On January 31, 2007, the general ledger of Mason Company showed the following account balances. Prepare the worksheet through the Adjusted Trial Balance section. Assume that every account has the normal debit or credit balance. The worksheet covers the month of January.

ACCOUNTS	
Cash	$62,000
Accounts Receivable	21,500
Supplies	8,000
Prepaid Insurance	7,200
Equipment	90,500
Accum. Depr.—Equip.	0
Accounts Payable	15,700
Jerry Mason, Capital	80,950
Fees Income	112,000
Depreciation Exp.—Equip.	0
Insurance Expense	0
Rent Expense	9,600
Salaries Expense	9,850
Supplies Expense	0

Additional information:

a. Supplies used during January totaled $5,200.

b. Expired insurance totaled $1,800.

c. Depreciation expense for the month was $1,575.

Correcting net income.

◀   **Exercise 5.4**
Objectives 2, 3

Assume that a firm reports net income of $40,000 prior to making adjusting entries for the following items: expired rent, $3,000; depreciation expense, $3,600; and supplies used, $1,300.

Assume that the required adjusting entries have not been made. What effect do these errors have on the reported net income?

Journalizing and posting adjustments.

◀   **Exercise 5.5**
Objective 5

Dakota Company must make three adjusting entries on December 31, 2007.

a. Supplies used, $2,500; (supplies totaling $4,000 were purchased on December 1, 2007, and debited to the **Supplies** account).

b. Expired insurance, $1,800 on December 1, 2007; the firm paid $10,800 for six months' insurance coverage in advance and debited **Prepaid Insurance** for this amount.

c. Depreciation expense for equipment, $1,200.

Make the journal entries for these adjustments and post the entries to the general ledger accounts. Use page 3 of the general journal for the adjusting entries. Use the following accounts and numbers.

Supplies	121
Prepaid Insurance	131
Accum. Depr.—Equip.	142
Depreciation Exp.—Equip.	517
Insurance Expense	521
Supplies Expense	523

PROBLEMS

Problem Set A

Problem 5.1A ▶ **Completing the worksheet.**

Objectives 1, 2, 3

e**X**cel

The trial balance of Denton Company as of January 31, 2007, after the company completed the first month of operations, is shown in the partial worksheet below.

INSTRUCTIONS

1. Record the trial balance in the Trial Balance section of the worksheet.

2. Complete the worksheet by making the following adjustments: supplies on hand at the end of the month, $1,600; expired insurance, $2,500; depreciation expense for the period, $550.

Analyze: How does the insurance adjustment affect **Prepaid Insurance?**

Problem 5.2A ▶ **Reconstructing a partial worksheet.**

Objectives 1, 2, 3

e**X**cel

The adjusted trial balance of Campus Book Store as of November 30, 2007, after the firm's first month of operations, appears on page 153.

Appropriate adjustments have been made for the following items.

a. Supplies used during the month, $2,400.

b. Expired rent for the month, $3,000.

c. Depreciation expense for the month, $700.

INSTRUCTIONS

1. Record the Adjusted Trial Balance in the Adjusted Trial Balance columns of the worksheet.

2. Prepare the adjusting entries in the Adjustments columns.

3. Complete the Trial Balance columns of the worksheet prior to making the adjusting entries.

Analyze: What was the balance of **Prepaid Rent** prior to the adjusting entry for expired rent?

Denton Company

Worksheet (Partial)

Month Ended January 31, 2007

	ACCOUNT NAME	TRIAL BALANCE		ADJUSTMENTS	
		DEBIT	CREDIT	DEBIT	CREDIT
1	Cash	26 0 0 0 00			
2	Accounts Receivable	5 2 0 0 00			
3	Supplies	9 6 0 0 00			
4	Prepaid Insurance	15 0 0 0 00			
5	Equipment	27 0 0 0 00			
6	Accumulated Depreciation—Equipment				
7	Accounts Payable		6 2 0 0 00		
8	Julie Denton, Capital		63 0 0 0 00		
9	Julie Denton, Drawing	3 6 0 0 00			
10	Fees Income		25 8 0 0 00		
11	Depreciation Expense—Equipment				
12	Insurance Expense				
13	Salaries Expense	7 8 0 0 00			
14	Supplies Expense				
15	Utilities Expense	8 0 0 00			
16	Totals	95 0 0 0 00	95 0 0 0 00		

CHAPTER 5: Review and Applications

	Campus Book Store Adjusted Trial Balance November 30, 2007	
Account Name	**Debit**	**Credit**
Cash	22,575	
Accounts Receivable	3,312	
Supplies	3,600	
Prepaid Rent	18,000	
Equipment	27,000	
Accumulated Depreciation—Equipment		700
Accounts Payable		8,000
Chuck Keen, Capital		40,837
Chuck Keen, Drawing	3,000	
Fees Income		42,000
Depreciation Expense—Equipment	700	
Rent Expense	3,000	
Salaries Expense	7,500	
Supplies Expense	2,400	
Utilities Expense	450	
Totals	91,537	91,537

Preparing financial statements from the worksheet.

The completed worksheet for Oxnard Corporation as of December 31, 2007, after the company had completed the first month of operation, appears across the tops of pages 154–155.

◀ **Problem 5.3A**
Objective 4

INSTRUCTIONS

1. Prepare an income statement.
2. Prepare a statement of owner's equity. The owner made no additional investments during the month.
3. Prepare a balance sheet (use the report form).

Analyze: If the adjustment to *Prepaid Advertising* had been $2,400 instead of $1,200, what net income would have resulted?

Preparing a worksheet and financial statements, journalizing adjusting entries, and posting to ledger accounts.

Carlos Ramon owns Ramon Creative Designs. The trial balance of the firm for January 31, 2007, the first month of operations, is shown on the bottom of page 154.

◀ **Problem 5.4A**
Objectives
1, 2, 3, 4, 5
e**X**cel

INSTRUCTIONS

1. Complete the worksheet for the month.
2. Prepare an income statement, statement of owner's equity, and balance sheet. No additional investments were made by the owner during the month.
3. Journalize and post the adjusting entries. Use 3 for the journal page number.

End-of-the-month adjustments must account for the following items:

a. Supplies were purchased on January 1, 2007; inventory of supplies on January 31, 2007, is $550.
b. The prepaid advertising contract was signed on January 1, 2007, and covers a four-month period.

CHAPTER 5: Review and Applications

Oxnard Corporation
Worksheet
Month Ended December 31, 2007

	ACCOUNT NAME	TRIAL BALANCE		ADJUSTMENTS	
		DEBIT	CREDIT	DEBIT	CREDIT
1	Cash	38 6 0 0 00			
2	Accounts Receivable	6 0 0 0 00			
3	Supplies	5 0 5 0 00			(a) 3 0 0 0 00
4	Prepaid Advertising	7 2 0 0 00			(b) 1 2 0 0 00
5	Equipment	30 0 0 0 00			
6	Accumulated Depreciation—Equipment				(c) 6 0 0 00
7	Accounts Payable		6 0 0 0 00		
8	Derrick Wells, Capital		54 0 0 0 00		
9	Derrick Wells, Drawing	3 6 0 0 00			
10	Fees Income		39 7 5 0 00		
11	Advertising Expense			(b) 1 2 0 0 00	
12	Depreciation Expense—Equipment			(c) 6 0 0 00	
13	Salaries Expense	8 4 0 0 00			
14	Supplies Expense			(a) 3 0 0 0 00	
15	Utilities Expense	9 0 0 00			
16	Totals	99 7 5 0 00	99 7 5 0 00	4 8 0 0 00	4 8 0 0 00
17	Net Income				
18					
19					

c. Rent of $800 expired during the month.

d. Depreciation is computed using the straight-line method. The equipment has an estimated useful life of 10 years with no salvage value.

Analyze: If the adjusting entries had not been made for the month, would net income be overstated or understated?

Ramon Creative Designs
Worksheet (Partial)
Month Ended January 31, 2007

	ACCOUNT NAME	TRIAL BALANCE	
		DEBIT	CREDIT
1	Cash	17 7 5 0 00	
2	Accounts Receivable	6 3 0 0 00	
3	Supplies	3 8 7 5 00	
4	Prepaid Advertising	4 2 0 0 00	
5	Prepaid Rent	9 6 0 0 00	
6	Equipment	10 8 0 0 00	
7	Accumulated Depreciation—Equipment		
8	Accounts Payable		7 7 7 5 00
9	Carlos Ramon, Capital		30 0 0 0 00
10	Carlos Ramon, Drawing	3 5 0 0 00	
11	Fees Income		23 8 0 0 00
12	Advertising Expense		
13	Depreciation Expense—Equipment		
14	Rent Expense		
15	Salaries Expense	4 8 5 0 00	
16	Supplies Expense		
17	Utilities Expense	7 0 0 00	
18	Totals	61 5 7 5 00	61 5 7 5 00
19			

	ADJUSTED TRIAL BALANCE		INCOME STATEMENT		BALANCE SHEET		
	DEBIT	CREDIT	DEBIT	CREDIT	DEBIT	CREDIT	
	38 600 00				38 600 00		1
	6 000 00				6 000 00		2
	2 050 00				2 050 00		3
	6 000 00				6 000 00		4
	30 000 00				30 000 00		5
		600 00				600 00	6
		6 000 00				6 000 00	7
		54 000 00				54 000 00	8
	3 600 00				3 600 00		9
		39 750 00		39 750 00			10
	1 200 00		1 200 00				11
	600 00		600 00				12
	8 400 00		8 400 00				13
	3 000 00		3 000 00				14
	900 00		900 00				15
	100 350 00	100 350 00	14 100 00	39 750 00	86 250 00	60 600 00	16
			25 650 00			25 650 00	17
			39 750 00	39 750 00	86 250 00	86 250 00	18
							19

Problem Set B

Completing the worksheet.

The trial balance of Argo Company as of February 28, 2007, appears below.

◀ **Problem 5.1B**
Objectives 1, 2, 3

Argo Company
Worksheet (Partial)
Month Ended February 28, 2007

	ACCOUNT NAME	TRIAL BALANCE		ADJUSTMENTS	
		DEBIT	CREDIT	DEBIT	CREDIT
1	Cash	73 000 00			
2	Accounts Receivable	6 400 00			
3	Supplies	4 200 00			
4	Prepaid Rent	24 000 00			
5	Equipment	46 000 00			
6	Accumulated Depreciation—Equipment				
7	Accounts Payable		12 000 00		
8	Deloros Argo, Capital		98 500 00		
9	Deloros Argo, Drawing	3 000 00			
10	Fees Income		54 000 00		
11	Depreciation Expense—Equipment				
12	Rent Expense				
13	Salaries Expense	6 300 00			
14	Supplies Expense				
15	Utilities Expense	1 600 00			
16	Totals	164 500 00	164 500 00		
17					

INSTRUCTIONS

1. Record the trial balance in the Trial Balance section of the worksheet.

2. Complete the worksheet by making the following adjustments: supplies on hand at the end of the month, $2,200; expired rent, $2,000; depreciation expense for the period, $1,000.

Analyze: Why do you think the account *Accumulated Depreciation—Equipment* has a zero balance on the trial balance shown?

Problem 5.2B
Objectives 1, 2, 3   ▶   **Reconstructing a partial worksheet.**

The adjusted trial balance of Denise De La Rosa, Attorney-at-Law, as of November 30, 2007, after the company had completed the first month of operations, appears below.
   Appropriate adjustments have been made for the following items.

a. Supplies used during the month, $1,800.

b. Expired rent for the month, $1,700.

c. Depreciation expense for the month, $275.

Denise De La Rosa, Attorney-at-Law Adjusted Trial Balance November 30, 2007		
Account Name	**Debit**	**Credit**
Cash	17,525	
Accounts Receivable	4,250	
Supplies	3,400	
Prepaid Rent	20,400	
Equipment	33,000	
Accumulated Depreciation—Equipment		275
Accounts Payable		8,500
Denise De La Rosa, Capital		40,000
Denise De La Rosa, Drawing	3,000	
Fees Income		42,850
Depreciation Expense—Equipment	275	
Rent Expense	1,700	
Salaries Expense	5,400	
Supplies Expense	1,800	
Utilities Expense	875	
Totals	91,625	91,625

INSTRUCTIONS

1. Record the adjusted trial balance in the Adjusted Trial Balance columns of the worksheet.

2. Prepare the adjusting entries in the Adjustments columns.

3. Complete the Trial Balance columns of the worksheet prior to making the adjusting entries.

Analyze: Which contra asset account is on the adjusted trial balance?

Problem 5.3B
Objective 4   ▶   **Preparing financial statements from the worksheet.**

The completed worksheet for Arrow Accounting Services for the month ended December 31, 2007, appears on pages 158–159.

INSTRUCTIONS

1. Prepare an income statement.

2. Prepare a statement of owner's equity. The owner made no additional investments during the month.

3. Prepare a balance sheet.

Analyze: By what total amount did the value of assets reported on the balance sheet decrease due to the adjusting entries?

Preparing a worksheet and financial statements, journalizing adjusting entries, and posting to ledger accounts.

◀ **Problem 5.4B**
Objectives
1, 2, 3, 4, 5

Paul Torres owns Torres Estate Planning and Investments. The trial balance of the firm for June 30, 2007, the first month of operations, is shown below.

Torres Estate Planning and Investments
Worksheet (Partial)
Month Ended June 30, 2007

	ACCOUNT NAME	TRIAL BALANCE DEBIT	TRIAL BALANCE CREDIT	ADJUSTMENTS DEBIT	ADJUSTMENTS CREDIT
1	Cash	9 8 5 0 00			
2	Accounts Receivable	3 0 5 0 00			
3	Supplies	3 8 0 0 00			
4	Prepaid Advertising	7 2 0 0 00			
5	Prepaid Rent	18 0 0 0 00			
6	Equipment	24 0 0 0 00			
7	Accumulated Depreciation—Equipment				
8	Accounts Payable		5 4 0 0 00		
9	Paul Torres, Capital		30 0 5 0 00		
10	Paul Torres, Drawing	2 0 0 0 00			
11	Fees Income		36 9 0 0 00		
12	Advertising Expense				
13	Depreciation Expense—Equipment				
14	Rent Expense				
15	Salaries Expense	3 8 0 0 00			
16	Supplies Expense				
17	Utilities Expense	6 5 0 00			
18	Totals	72 3 5 0 00	72 3 5 0 00		
19					

INSTRUCTIONS

1. Complete the worksheet for the month.

2. Prepare an income statement, statement of owner's equity, and balance sheet. No additional investments were made by the owner during the month.

3. Journalize and post the adjusting entries. Use 3 for the journal page number.

End-of-month adjustments must account for the following.

a. The supplies were purchased on June 1, 2007; inventory of supplies on June 30, 2007, showed a value of $1,500.

b. The prepaid advertising contract was signed on June 1, 2007, and covers a four-month period.

c. Rent of $1,500 expired during the month.

d. Depreciation is computed using the straight-line method. The equipment has an estimated useful life of five years with no salvage value.

Analyze: Why are the costs that reduce the value of equipment not directly posted to the asset account Equipment?

Arrow Accounting Services
Worksheet
Month Ended December 31, 2007

	ACCOUNT NAME	TRIAL BALANCE DEBIT	TRIAL BALANCE CREDIT	ADJUSTMENTS DEBIT	ADJUSTMENTS CREDIT
1	Cash	16 9 5 0 00			
2	Accounts Receivable	2 2 0 0 00			
3	Supplies	1 5 0 0 00			(a) 6 0 0 00
4	Prepaid Advertising	4 0 0 0 00			(b) 8 0 0 00
5	Fixtures	18 0 0 0 00			
6	Accumulated Depreciation—Fixtures				(c) 3 0 0 00
7	Accounts Payable		7 5 0 0 00		
8	John Arrow, Capital		30 0 0 0 00		
9	John Arrow, Drawing	3 0 0 0 00			
10	Fees Income		31 3 3 0 00		
11	Advertising Expense			(b) 8 0 0 00	
12	Depreciation Expense—Fixtures			(c) 3 0 0 00	
13	Rent Expense	3 5 0 0 00			
14	Salaries Expense	18 6 0 0 00			
15	Supplies Expense			(a) 6 0 0 00	
16	Utilities Expense	1 0 8 0 00			
17	Totals	68 8 3 0 00	68 8 3 0 00	1 7 0 0 00	1 7 0 0 00
18	Net Income				
19					
20					

Challenge Problem

Worksheet and Financial Statements

The account balances for the Mandela International Company on January 31, 2007, follow. The balances shown are after the first month of operations.

101	Cash	$18,475	401	Fees Income	$30,925
111	Accounts Receivable	3,400	511	Advertising Expense	1,500
121	Supplies	2,150	514	Depr. Expense—Equip.	0
131	Prepaid Insurance	15,000	517	Insurance Expense	0
141	Equipment	24,000	518	Rent Expense	2,500
142	Accum. Depr.—Equip.	0	519	Salaries Expense	6,700
202	Accounts Payable	6,000	520	Supplies Expense	0
301	Wilson Mandela, Capital	40,000	523	Telephone Expense	350
302	Wilson Mandela, Drawing	2,000	524	Utilities Expense	850

INSTRUCTIONS

1. Prepare the Trial Balance section of the worksheet.
2. Record the following adjustments in the Adjustments section of the worksheet.
   a. Supplies used during the month amounted to $1,050.
   b. The amount in the **Prepaid Insurance** account represents a payment made on January 1, 2007, for six months of insurance coverage.
   c. The equipment, purchased on January 1, 2007, has an estimated useful life of 10 years with no salvage value. The firm uses the straight-line method of depreciation.
3. Complete the worksheet.

CHAPTER 5: Review and Applications

ADJUSTED TRIAL BALANCE		INCOME STATEMENT		BALANCE SHEET		
DEBIT	CREDIT	DEBIT	CREDIT	DEBIT	CREDIT	
16 950 00				16 950 00		1
2 200 00				2 200 00		2
900 00				900 00		3
3 200 00				3 200 00		4
18 000 00				18 000 00		5
	300 00				300 00	6
	7 500 00				7 500 00	7
	30 000 00				30 000 00	8
3 000 00				3 000 00		9
	31 330 00		31 330 00			10
800 00		800 00				11
300 00		300 00				12
3 500 00		3 500 00				13
18 600 00		18 600 00				14
600 00		600 00				15
1 080 00		1 080 00				16
69 130 00	69 130 00	24 880 00	31 330 00	44 250 00	37 800 00	17
		6 450 00			6 450 00	18
		31 330 00	31 330 00	44 250 00	44 250 00	19
						20

4. Prepare an income statement, statement of owner's equity, and balance sheet (use the report form).

5. Record the balances in the general ledger accounts, then journalize and post the adjusting entries. Use 3 for the journal page number.

Analyze: If the useful life of the equipment had been 12 years instead of 10 years, how would net income have been affected?

Critical Thinking Problem

The Effect of Adjustments

Assume you are the accountant for Coppell Industries. Ellis Coppell, the owner of the company, is in a hurry to receive the financial statements for the year ended December 31, 2007, and asks you how soon they will be ready. You tell him you have just completed the trial balance and are getting ready to prepare the adjusting entries. Mr. Coppell tells you not to waste time preparing adjusting entries but to complete the worksheet without them and prepare the financial statements based on the data in the trial balance. According to him, the adjusting entries will not make that much difference. The trial balance shows the following account balances:

Prepaid Rent	$ 42,000
Supplies	18,000
Building	420,000
Accumulated Depreciation—Building	33,600

If the income statement were prepared using trial balance amounts, the net income would be $165,000.

A review of the company's records reveals the following information:

1. Rent of $42,000 was paid on July 1, 2007, for 12 months.

2. Purchases of supplies during the year totaled $18,000. An inventory of supplies taken at year-end showed supplies on hand of $3,500.

3. The building was purchased three years ago and has an estimated life of 25 years.

4. No adjustments have been made to any of the accounts during the year.

Write a memo to Mr. Coppell explaining the effect on the financial statements of omitting the adjustments. Indicate the change to net income that results from the adjusting entries.

BUSINESS CONNECTIONS

Managerial | FOCUS

Understanding Adjustments

1. A building owned by Amos Company was recently valued at $425,000 by a real estate expert. The president of the company is questioning the accuracy of the firm's latest balance sheet because it shows a book value of $275,000 for the building. How would you explain this situation to the president?

2. At the beginning of the year, Wilson Company purchased a new building and some expensive new machinery. An officer of the firm has asked you whether this purchase will affect the firm's year-end income statement. What answer would you give?

3. Suppose the president of a company where you work as an accountant questions whether it is worthwhile for you to spend time making adjustments at the end of each accounting period. How would you explain the value of the adjustments?

4. How does the worksheet help provide vital information to management?

Ethical | DILEMMA

Adjustments

The supplies adjustment records the supplies used for the month from a cupboard that is filled at various times of the month. Sally asks you to record a larger supplies adjustment than is indicated from the ending balance in the supplies cupboard. Sally wants to use these supplies at the non-profit organization she attends. Would you record a higher supplies expense so Sally could take these extra supplies to her charitable organization?

STREETWISE:
Questions from the
REAL WORLD

Internal Changes

Refer to The Home Depot, Inc. *2004 Annual Report* in Appendix A.

1. Based on the account categories listed on the consolidated statements of earnings and the consolidated balance sheets, what types of adjustments do you think the company makes each fiscal year? List three types of adjustments you believe would be necessary for this company. Describe your reasons for the adjustments you have listed.

2. By what amount has the account category "accumulated depreciation and amortization" increased from fiscal year 2003 to fiscal year 2004? Explain why you think this account has increased from 2003 to 2004.

Financial Statement
ANALYSIS

Depreciation

DuPont reported depreciation expense of $1,124 million on its consolidated financial statements for the period ended December 31, 2004. The following excerpt is taken from the company's consolidated balance sheet for the same year.

Analyze:

1. What percentage of the original cost of property, plant, and equipment was depreciated *during* 2004?

2. What percentage of property, plant, and equipment cost was depreciated *as of* December 31, 2004?

Consolidated Balance Sheet	
(Dollars in millions, except per share) December 31, 2004	
Property, Plant and Equipment (Note 15)	23,978
Less: Accumulated Depreciation	13,754
Net Property, Plant and Equipment	10,224

3. If the company continued to record depreciation expense at this level each year, how many years remain until all assets would be fully depreciated? (Assume no salvage values.)

Analyze Online: Connect to the DuPont Web site **(www.dupont.com).** Click on the *Investor Center* link to find information on quarterly earnings.

4. What is the most recent quarterly earnings statement presented? What period does the statement cover?

5. For the most recent quarter, what depreciation expense was reported?

Adjusting Entries

Adjusting entries update accounts at the end of an accounting period. Items that belong to the period and were not previously recorded are recorded using an adjusting entry. Suppose that a customer owes money to your business, but you are informed that the customer plans to file bankruptcy. You believe that the customer will never pay the amount owed. Do you think that an entry should be made for this event? Why or why not?

Prepare for a Telephone Meeting

The owner of a sparkling water bottling business believes that it is sufficient to record depreciation only at year-end, yet financial statements are prepared at the end of every month. As the accountant for the business, you believe adjusting entries should be made to update equipment depreciation expense on a monthly basis. You plan to call the owner to discuss the issue. How will you begin the conversation? How would you suggest that the situation be handled? Prepare notes on what you plan to say before you make the call to the owner.

Matching Expenses with Revenue

Mike Mincks is a building contractor. He and his customer have agreed that he will submit a bill to them when he is 25% complete, 50% complete, 75% complete, and 100% complete. For example, he has a $100,000 room addition. When he has completed 25%, he will bill his customer $25,000. The problem occurs when he is 40% complete, has incurred expenses but cannot yet bill his customer. How can his revenue and expenses match? Discuss in a group several ways that Mike's accountant could solve this problem. What accounts would be used?

Prepaid Insurance

Prepaid Insurance is the most common adjusting entry for a company. Use **google.com** to do a search of the various insurance companies that provide a variety of insurances to business. Try business insurance companies. Which type of insurances do they offer a business?

Answers to **Self Reviews**

Answers to Section 1 Self Review

1. Entries made to update accounts at the end of an accounting period to include previously unrecorded items that belong to the period.

2. So that the financial statements can be prepared more efficiently.

3. To properly reflect the remaining cost to be used by the business (asset) and the amount already used by the business (expense).

4. **b.** *Rent Expense* is debited for $1,800. *Prepaid Rent* is credited for $1,800.

5. **a.** *Supplies Expense* is debited for $450. *Supplies* is credited for $450.

6. $14,000

Answers to Section 2 Self Review

1. The worksheet is only a tool that aids in the preparation of financial statements. Any changes in account balances recorded on the worksheet are not shown in the general journal and the general ledger until the adjusting entries have been journalized and posted.

2. **(a)** Beginning owner's equity

   (b) Net income or net loss for the period

   (c) Additional investments by the owner for the period

   (d) Withdrawals by the owner for the period

   (e) Ending balance of owner's equity

3. On a report form balance sheet, the liabilities and owner's equity are listed under the assets. On the account form, they are listed to the right of the assets.

4. **b.** contra asset account.

5. **b.** Balance Sheet Debit column.

6. $14,000. The adjustment for equipment depreciation is a debit to **Depreciation Expense** and a credit to **Accumulated Depreciation—Equipment**. The **Equipment** account is not changed.

Answers to Comprehensive Self Review

1. Debit column of the Balance Sheet section.

2. $4,250. Debit column of the Balance Sheet section.

3. Credit balance.

4. Net income causes a net increase in owner's equity.

5. To allocate the cost of the asset to operations during its expected useful life.

1. Journalize and post closing entries.
2. Prepare a postclosing trial balance.
3. Interpret financial statements.
4. Review the steps in the accounting cycle.
5. Define the accounting terms new to this chapter.

NEW TERMS

closing entries   interpret

income summary account   postclosing trial balance

Chapter 6
Closing Entries and the Postclosing Trial Balance

)| **Carnival.**
The Fun Ships.   www.carnival.com

For over thirty years, Carnival Cruise Lines has made cruise vacations—vacations once reserved for the very rich—accessible to the average person. Carnival charges $599 for a seven-day Caribbean cruise—the same price it charged 25 years ago. But passengers today are getting a lot more for their money than passengers 25 years ago. Today's cruise ships are a far cry from the cramped ocean-liners of 25 years ago. The new ships are more like floating resorts stocked with expansive spa and children's facilities, soaring atriums, and double-width promenades lined with myriad entertainment venues. In 1972, Carnival's first ship, the *TSS Mardi Gras,* made its maiden voyage. From this humble beginning, Carnival has grown to the largest and most successful cruise line in the world, carrying more passengers than any other. With 20 cruise ships, Carnival serves 3 million passengers annually. The company generated $6.7 billion in revenues in 2003 and realized a total net income of $1.2 billion.

thinking critically   How do Carnival Cruise Lines' executives and managers use financial statements to evaluate financial performance? How might these evaluations affect business policies or strategies?

Section 1

SECTION OBJECTIVE

▶ 1. **Journalize and post closing entries.**

WHY IT'S IMPORTANT

A business ends its accounting cycle at a given point in time. The closing process prepares the accounting records for the beginning of a new accounting cycle.

TERMS TO LEARN

closing entries
Income Summary account

Closing Entries

In Chapter 5 we discussed the worksheet and the adjusting entries. In this chapter you will learn about closing entries.

The Closing Process

The seventh step in the accounting cycle is to journalize and post closing entries. **Closing entries** are journal entries that

- transfer the results of operations (net income or net loss) to owner's equity,
- reduce revenue, expense, and drawing account balances to zero.

THE INCOME SUMMARY ACCOUNT

The **Income Summary account** is a special owner's equity account that is used only in the closing process to summarize results of operations. *Income Summary* has a zero balance after the closing process, and it remains with a zero balance until after the closing procedure for the next period.

FIGURE 6.1 | Worksheet for JT's Consulting Services

JT's Consulting Services
Worksheet
Month Ended December 31, 2007

| | ACCOUNT NAME | TRIAL BALANCE | | ADJUSTMENTS | |
		DEBIT	CREDIT	DEBIT	CREDIT
1	Cash	83 500 00			
2	Accounts Receivable	5 000 00			
3	Supplies	3 000 00			(a) 1 000 00
4	Prepaid Rent	7 000 00			(b) 3 500 00
5	Equipment	22 000 00			
6	Accumulated Depreciation—Equipment				(c) 367 00
7	Accounts Payable		7 000 00		
8	Jason Taylor, Capital		90 000 00		
9	Jason Taylor, Drawing	4 000 00			
10	Fees Income		35 000 00		
11	Salaries Expense	7 000 00			
12	Utilities Expense	500 00			
13	Supplies Expense			(a) 1 000 00	
14	Rent Expense			(b) 3 500 00	
15	Expense—Equipment			(c) 367 00	
16	Totals	132 000 00	132 000 00	4 867 00	4 867 00
17	Net Income				
18					
19					
20					

Income Summary is classified as a temporary owner's equity account. Other names for this account are *Revenue and Expense Summary* and *Income and Expense Summary*.

Topic Tackler PLUS

STEPS IN THE CLOSING PROCESS

There are four steps in the closing process:

▶ **1. OBJECTIVE**
Journalize and post closing entries.

1. Transfer the balance of the revenue account to the ***Income Summary*** account.
2. Transfer the expense account balances to the ***Income Summary*** account.
3. Transfer the balance of the ***Income Summary*** account to the owner's capital account.
4. Transfer the balance of the drawing account to the owner's capital account.

The worksheet contains the data necessary to make the closing entries. Refer to Figure 6.1 as you study each closing entry.

STEP 1: TRANSFER REVENUE ACCOUNT BALANCES

On December 31 the worksheet for JT's Consulting Services shows one revenue account, ***Fees Income***. It has a credit balance of $35,000. To *close* an account means to reduce its balance to zero. In the general journal, enter a debit of $35,000 to close the ***Fees Income*** account. To balance the journal entry, enter a credit of $35,000 to the ***Income Summary*** account. This closing entry transfers the total revenue for the period to the ***Income Summary*** account and reduces the balance of the revenue account to zero.

The analysis of this closing entry is shown on page 168. In this chapter the visual analyses will show the beginning balances in all T accounts in order to illustrate closing entries.

ADJUSTED TRIAL BALANCE		INCOME STATEMENT		BALANCE SHEET		
DEBIT	CREDIT	DEBIT	CREDIT	DEBIT	CREDIT	
83 5 0 0 00				83 5 0 0 00		1
5 0 0 0 00				5 0 0 0 00		2
2 0 0 0 00				2 0 0 0 00		3
3 5 0 0 00				3 5 0 0 00		4
22 0 0 0 00				22 0 0 0 00		5
	3 6 7 00				3 6 7 00	6
	1 0 0 0 00				7 0 0 0 00	7
	90 0 0 0 00				90 0 0 0 00	8
4 0 0 0 00				4 0 0 0 00		9
	35 0 0 0 00		35 0 0 0 00			10
7 0 0 0 00		7 0 0 0 00				11
5 0 0 00		5 0 0 00				12
1 0 0 0 00		1 0 0 0 00				13
3 5 0 0 00		3 5 0 0 00				14
3 6 7 00		3 6 7 00				15
132 3 6 7 00	132 3 6 7 00	12 3 6 7 00	35 0 0 0 00	120 0 0 0 00	97 3 6 7 00	16
		22 6 3 3 00			22 6 3 3 00	17
		35 0 0 0 00	35 0 0 0 00	120 0 0 0 00	120 0 0 0 00	18
						19

CLOSING ENTRY

important!

Income Summary Account

The *Income Summary* account does not have an increase or decrease side and no normal balance side.

First Closing Entry—Close Revenue to Income Summary

ANALYSIS

The revenue account, **Fees Income,** is decreased by $35,000 to zero. The $35,000 is transferred to the temporary owner's equity account, **Income Summary.**

DEBIT-CREDIT RULES

DEBIT   Decreases in revenue accounts are recorded as debits. Debit **Fees Income** for $35,000.

CREDIT   To transfer the revenue to the **Income Summary** account, credit **Income Summary** for $35,000.

T-ACCOUNT PRESENTATION

Fees Income		Income Summary

−	+
Closing 35,000	Balance 35,000

Income Summary
Closing   35,000

GENERAL JOURNAL ENTRY

GENERAL JOURNAL   PAGE ___4___

	DATE		DESCRIPTION	POST. REF.	DEBIT	CREDIT	
1	2007		*Closing Entries*				1
2	Dec.	31	Fees Income		35 0 0 0 00		2
3			Income Summary			35 0 0 0 00	3
4							4

    Write "Closing Entries" in the Description column of the general journal on the line above the first closing entry.

> Safeway Inc. reported sales of $35.5 billion for the fiscal year ended December 31, 2003. To close the revenue, the company would debit the **Sales** account and credit the **Income Summary** account.

STEP 2: TRANSFER EXPENSE ACCOUNT BALANCES

The Income Statement section of the worksheet for JT's Consulting Services lists five expense accounts. Since expense accounts have debit balances, enter a credit in each account to reduce its balance to zero. Debit the total of the expenses, $12,367, to the **Income Summary** account. This closing entry transfers total expenses to the **Income Summary** account and reduces the balances of the expense accounts to zero. This is a compound journal entry; it has more than one credit.

CLOSING ENTRY

Second Closing Entry—Close Expenses to Income Summary

recall

Revenue
Revenue increases owner's equity.

recall

Expenses
Expenses decrease owner's equity.

ANALYSIS
The five expense account balances are reduced to zero. The total, $12,367, is transferred to the temporary owner's equity account, *Income Summary.*

DEBIT-CREDIT RULES
DEBIT   To transfer the expenses to the *Income Summary* account, debit *Income Summary* for $12,367.

CREDIT   Decreases to expense accounts are recorded as credits. Credit *Salaries Expense* for $7,000, *Utilities Expense* for $500, *Supplies Expense* for $1,000, *Rent Expense* for $3,500, and *Depreciation Expense—Equipment* for $367.

T-ACCOUNT PRESENTATION

Income Summary		Salaries Expense	
		+	−
Closing 12,367	Balance 35,000	Balance 7,000	Closing 7,000

Utilities Expense		Supplies Expense	
+	−	+	−
Balance 500	Closing 500	Balance 1,000	Closing 1,000

Rent Expense		Depreciation Expense—Equip.	
+	−	+	−
Balance 3,500	Closing 3,500	Balance 367	Closing 367

GENERAL JOURNAL ENTRY

GENERAL JOURNAL   PAGE ___4___

	DATE		DESCRIPTION	POST. REF.	DEBIT	CREDIT	
4							4
5	Dec.	31	Income Summary		12 3 6 7 00		5
6			Salaries Expense			7 0 0 0 00	6
7			Utilities Expense			5 0 0 00	7
8			Supplies Expense			1 0 0 0 00	8
9			Rent Expense			3 5 0 0 00	9
10			Depreciation Expense—Equip.			3 6 7 00	10

After the second closing entry, the *Income Summary* account reflects all of the entries in the Income Statement columns of the worksheet.

Income Summary

Dr.		Cr.	
Closing	12,367	Closing	35,000
		Balance	22,633

> For the year ended December 31, 2003, operating expenses for Amazon.com totaled $969.2 million. At the end of the year, accountants for Amazon.com transferred the balances of all expense accounts to the **Income Summary** account.

STEP 3: TRANSFER NET INCOME OR NET LOSS TO OWNER'S EQUITY

The next step in the closing process is to transfer the balance of **Income Summary** to the owner's capital account. After the revenue and expense accounts are closed, the **Income Summary** account has a credit balance of $22,633, which is net income for the month. The journal entry to transfer net income to owner's equity is a debit to **Income Summary** and a credit to **Jason Taylor, Capital** for $22,633. When this entry is posted, the balance of the **Income Summary** account is reduced to zero and the owner's capital account is increased by the amount of net income.

CLOSING ENTRY

Third Closing Entry—Close Income Summary to Capital

ANALYSIS

The **Income Summary** account is reduced to zero. The net income amount, $22,633, is transferred to the owner's equity account. **Jason Taylor, Capital** is increased by $22,633.

DEBIT-CREDIT RULES

DEBIT   To reduce **Income Summary** to zero, debit **Income Summary** for $22,633.

CREDIT   Net income increases owner's equity. Increases in owner's equity accounts are recorded as credits. Credit **Jason Taylor, Capital** for $22,633.

T-ACCOUNT PRESENTATION

Income Summary

Closing	22,633	Balance	22,633

Jason Taylor, Capital

−		+	
		Balance	90,000
		Closing	22,633

GENERAL JOURNAL ENTRY

GENERAL JOURNAL   PAGE ___4___

	DATE		DESCRIPTION	POST. REF.	DEBIT	CREDIT	
12	Dec.	31	Income Summary		22 6 3 3 00		12
13			Jason Taylor, Capital			22 6 3 3 00	13

After the third closing entry, the ***Income Summary*** account has a zero balance. The summarized expenses ($12,367) and revenue ($35,000) have been transferred to the owner's equity account ($22,633 net income).

Income Summary	
Dr.	**Cr.**
Expenses 12,367	Revenue 35,000
Closing 22,633	
Balance 0	

Jason Taylor, Capital	
Dr.	**Cr.**
−	+
	Balance 90,000
	Net Inc. 22,633
	Balance 112,633

STEP 4: TRANSFER THE DRAWING ACCOUNT BALANCE TO CAPITAL

You will recall that withdrawals are funds taken from the business by the owner for personal use. Withdrawals are recorded in the drawing account. Withdrawals are not expenses of the business. They do not affect net income or net loss.

Withdrawals appear in the statement of owner's equity as a deduction from capital. Therefore, the drawing account is closed directly to the capital account.

When this entry is posted, the balance of the drawing account is reduced to zero and the owner's capital account is decreased by the amount of the withdrawals.

recall

Withdrawals
Withdrawals decrease owner's equity.

CLOSING ENTRY

Fourth Closing Entry—Close Withdrawals to Capital

ANALYSIS
The drawing account balance is reduced to zero. The balance of the drawing account, $4,000, is transferred to the owner's equity account.

DEBIT-CREDIT RULES
DEBIT Decreases in owner's equity accounts are recorded as debits. Debit ***Jason Taylor, Capital*** for $4,000.

CREDIT Decreases in the drawing account are recorded as credits. Credit ***Jason Taylor, Drawing*** for $4,000.

T-ACCOUNT PRESENTATION

Jason Taylor, Capital	
−	+
Closing 4,000	Balance 112,633

Jason Taylor, Drawing	
+	−
Balance 4,000	Closing 4,000

GENERAL JOURNAL ENTRY

GENERAL JOURNAL   PAGE 4

	DATE	DESCRIPTION	POST. REF.	DEBIT	CREDIT	
15	Dec. 31	Jason Taylor, Capital		4 0 0 0 00		15
16		Jason Taylor, Drawing			4 0 0 0 00	16

The new balance of the **Jason Taylor, Capital** account agrees with the amount listed in the Owner's Equity section of the balance sheet.

Jason Taylor, Drawing				Jason Taylor, Capital			
Dr.		**Cr.**		**Dr.**		**Cr.**	
+		–		–		+	
						Balance	90,000
Balance	4,000	Closing	4,000	Drawing	4,000	Net Inc.	22,633
Balance	0					Balance	108,633

Figure 6.2 shows the general journal and general ledger for JT's Consulting Services after the closing entries are recorded and posted. Note that

■ "Closing" is entered in the Description column of the ledger accounts;

■ the balance of **Jason Taylor, Capital** agrees with the amount shown on the balance sheet for December 31;

■ the ending balances of the drawing, revenue, and expense accounts are zero.

This example shows the closing process at the end of one month. Usually businesses make closing entries at the end of the fiscal year only.

FIGURE 6.2

Closing Process Completed: General Journal and General Ledger

Step 1
Close revenue.

Step 2
Close expense accounts.

Step 3
Close Income Summary.

Step 4
Close Drawing account.

GENERAL JOURNAL   PAGE ___4___

	DATE		DESCRIPTION	POST. REF.	DEBIT	CREDIT	
1	2007		*Closing Entries*				1
2	Dec.	31	Fees Income	401	35 000 00		2
3			Income Summary	309		35 000 00	3
4							4
5		31	Income Summary	309	12 367 00		5
6			Salaries Expense	511		7 000 00	6
7			Utilities Expense	514		500 00	7
8			Supplies Expense	517		1 000 00	8
9			Rent Expense	520		3 500 00	9
10			Depreciation Expense—Equip.	523		367 00	10
11							11
12		31	Income Summary	309	22 633 00		12
13			Jason Taylor, Capital	301		22 633 00	13
14							14
15		31	Jason Taylor, Capital	301	4 000 00		15
16			Jason Taylor, Drawing	302		4 000 00	16
17							17

ACCOUNT _Jason Taylor, Capital_ _____ ACCOUNT NO. _301_

DATE		DESCRIPTION	POST. REF.	DEBIT	CREDIT	BALANCE	
						DEBIT	CREDIT
2007							
Nov.	6		J1		90 000 00		90 000 00
Dec.	31	Closing	J4		22 633 00		112 633 00
	31	Closing	J4	4 000 00			108 633 00

ACCOUNT _Jason Taylor, Drawing_   ACCOUNT NO. _302_

DATE		DESCRIPTION	POST. REF.	DEBIT	CREDIT	BALANCE DEBIT	BALANCE CREDIT
2007							
Dec.	31		J2	4 0 0 0 00		4 0 0 0 00	
	31	Closing	J4		4 0 0 0 00	— 0 —	

ACCOUNT _Income Summary_   ACCOUNT NO. _309_

DATE		DESCRIPTION	POST. REF.	DEBIT	CREDIT	BALANCE DEBIT	BALANCE CREDIT
2007							
Dec.	31	Closing	J4		35 0 0 0 00		35 0 0 0 00
	31	Closing	J4	12 3 6 7 00			22 6 3 3 00
	31	Closing	J4	22 6 3 3 00			— 0 —

ACCOUNT _Fees Income_   ACCOUNT NO. _401_

DATE		DESCRIPTION	POST. REF.	DEBIT	CREDIT	BALANCE DEBIT	BALANCE CREDIT
2007							
Dec.	31		J2		26 0 0 0 00		26 0 0 0 00
	31		J2		9 0 0 0 00		35 0 0 0 00
	31	Closing	J4	35 0 0 0 00			— 0 —

ACCOUNT _Salaries Expense_   ACCOUNT NO. _511_

DATE		DESCRIPTION	POST. REF.	DEBIT	CREDIT	BALANCE DEBIT	BALANCE CREDIT
2007							
Dec.	31		J2	7 0 0 0 00		7 0 0 0 00	
	31	Closing	J4		7 0 0 0 00	— 0 —	

ACCOUNT _Utilities Expense_   ACCOUNT NO. _514_

DATE		DESCRIPTION	POST. REF.	DEBIT	CREDIT	BALANCE DEBIT	BALANCE CREDIT
2007							
Dec.	31		J2	5 0 0 00		5 0 0 00	
	31	Closing	J4		5 0 0 00	— 0 —	

ACCOUNT _Supplies Expense_   ACCOUNT NO. _517_

DATE		DESCRIPTION	POST. REF.	DEBIT	CREDIT	BALANCE DEBIT	BALANCE CREDIT
2007							
Dec.	31	Adjusting	J3	1 0 0 0 00		1 0 0 0 00	
	31	Closing	J4		1 0 0 0 00	— 0 —	

ACCOUNT _Rent Expense_   ACCOUNT NO. _520_

DATE		DESCRIPTION	POST. REF.	DEBIT	CREDIT	BALANCE DEBIT	BALANCE CREDIT
2007							
Dec.	31	Adjusting	J3	3 5 0 0 00		3 5 0 0 00	
	31	Closing	J4		3 5 0 0 00	– 0 –	

ACCOUNT _Depreciation Expense—Equipment_   ACCOUNT NO. _523_

DATE		DESCRIPTION	POST. REF.	DEBIT	CREDIT	BALANCE DEBIT	BALANCE CREDIT
2007							
Dec.	31	Adjusting	J3	3 6 7 00		3 6 7 00	
	31	Closing	J4		3 6 7 00	– 0 –	

You have now seen seven steps of the accounting cycle. The steps we have discussed are (1) analyze transactions, (2) journalize the transactions, (3) post the transactions, (4) prepare a worksheet, (5) prepare financial statements, (6) record adjusting entries, and (7) record closing entries. Two steps remain. They are (8) prepare a postclosing trial balance, and (9) interpret the financial information.

Section 1: **Self Review**

QUESTIONS

1. What is the journal entry to close the drawing account?

2. How is the **Income Summary** account classified?

3. What are the four steps in the closing process?

EXERCISES

4. After the closing entries are posted, which account normally has a balance other than zero?

   a. **Capital**

   b. **Fees Income**

   c. **Income Summary**

   d. **Rent Expense**

5. After closing, which accounts have zero balances?

   a. asset and liability accounts

   b. liability and capital accounts

   c. liability, drawing, and expense accounts

   d. revenue, drawing, and expense accounts

ANALYSIS

6. The business owner removes supplies that are worth $900 from the company stockroom. She intends to take them home for personal use. What effect will this have on the company's net income?

(Answers to Section 1 Self Review are on page 195.)

Using Accounting Information

In this section we will complete the accounting cycle for JT's Consulting Services.

Preparing the Postclosing Trial Balance

The eighth step in the accounting cycle is to prepare the postclosing trial balance, or *after-closing trial balance*. The **postclosing trial balance** is a statement that is prepared to prove the equality of total debits and credits. It is the last step in the end-of-period routine. The postclosing trial balance verifies that

- total debits equal total credits;
- revenue, expense, and drawing accounts have zero balances.

On the postclosing trial balance, the only accounts with balances are the permanent accounts:

- assets
- liabilities
- owner's equity

Figure 6.3 shows the postclosing trial balance for JT's Consulting Services.

SECTION OBJECTIVES

▶ **2. Prepare a postclosing trial balance.**

WHY IT'S IMPORTANT

The postclosing trial balance helps the accountant identify any errors in the closing process.

▶ **3. Interpret financial statements.**

WHY IT'S IMPORTANT

Financial statements contain information that can impact and drive operating decisions and plans for the future of the company.

▶ **4. Review the steps in the accounting cycle.**

WHY IT'S IMPORTANT

Proper treatment of data as it flows through the accounting system ensures reliable financial reports.

TERMS TO LEARN

interpret
postclosing trial balance

JT's Consulting Services
Postclosing Trial Balance
December 31, 2007

ACCOUNT NAME	DEBIT			CREDIT		
Cash	83	5 0 0	00			
Accounts Receivable	5	0 0 0	00			
Supplies	2	0 0 0	00			
Prepaid Rent	3	5 0 0	00			
Equipment	22	0 0 0	00			
Accumulated Depreciation—Equipment					3 6 7	00
Accounts Payable				7	0 0 0	00
Jason Taylor, Capital				108	6 3 3	00
Totals	116	0 0 0	00	116	0 0 0	00

FIGURE 6.3

Postclosing Trial Balance

ACCOUNTING ON THE JOB　<<

INFORMATION TECHNOLOGY SERVICES

Industry Overview

The information technology industry is projected to grow 117 percent between 1998 and 2008, making it the fastest growing industry in the United States. Products include software applications, data processing and retrieval systems, network systems, and Internet technologies.

Career Opportunities

- Financial Systems Analyst
- Database Marketing Programmer
- Data Services Manager
- Instructional Design Manager
- Accounting Technologist
- Director of Accounting Applications Development
- E-Commerce Director

Preparing for an Information Technology Services Career

- For a career as an accounting technologist or financial systems analyst, learn installation and implementation procedures for a variety of accounting applications.

- For general programming careers, obtain a bachelor's degree in computer or information science, mathematics, engineering, or the physical sciences.
- Learn current programming languages such as Java, VRML, or Visual C++.
- Gain extensive knowledge of systems and applications software packages.
- Obtain certification in database systems such as DB2, Oracle, or Sybase.
- Develop analytical and communication skills.
- Apply for a summer or co-op internship with a leading technology company like Intel.

THINKING CRITICALLY

Peachtree Software, Inc., the developer of Windows-based accounting software, frequently employs senior software engineers. What skills, experience, or education do you think would be desirable for this position?

INTERNET APPLICATION

Use Web sites to research information technology job opportunities in Great Plains, Peachtree, and Microsoft programs. Describe one job opportunity of interest to you. Include job title, position responsibilities, and education and skills requirements.

▶ **2. OBJECTIVE**

Prepare a postclosing trial balance.

FINDING AND CORRECTING ERRORS

If the postclosing trial balance does not balance, there are errors in the accounting records. Find and correct the errors before continuing. Refer to Chapter 3 for tips on how to find common errors. Also use the audit trail to trace data through the accounting records to find errors.

▶ **3. OBJECTIVE**

Interpret financial statements.

Interpreting the Financial Statements

The ninth and last step in the accounting cycle is interpreting the financial statements. Management needs timely and accurate financial information to operate the business successfully. To **interpret** the financial statements means to understand and explain the meaning and importance of information in accounting reports. Information in the financial statements provides answers to many questions:

- What is the cash balance?
- How much do customers owe the business?
- How much does the business owe suppliers?
- What is the profit or loss?

> Managers of The Home Depot, Inc. use the corporation's financial statements to answer questions about the business. How much cash does our business have? What net earnings did our company report this year? For the fiscal year ended February 1, 2004, The Home Depot, Inc. reported an ending cash balance of $2.83 billion and net earnings of $4.3 billion.

Figure 6.4 shows the financial statements for JT's Consulting Services at the end of its first accounting period. By interpreting these statements, management learns that

- the cash balance is $83,500,
- customers owe $5,000 to the business,
- the business owes $7,000 to its suppliers,
- the profit was $22,633.

JT's Consulting Services
Income Statement
Month Ended December 31, 2007

Revenue		
Fees Income		35 0 0 0 00
Expenses		
Salaries Expense	7 0 0 0 00	
Utilities Expense	5 0 0 00	
Supplies Expense	1 0 0 0 00	
Rent Expense	3 5 0 0 00	
Depreciation Expense—Equipment	3 6 7 00	
Total Expenses		12 3 6 7 00
Net Income for the Month		22 6 3 3 00

JT's Consulting Services
Statement of Owner's Equity
Month Ended December 31, 2007

Jason Taylor, Capital, December 1, 2007		90 0 0 0 00
Net Income for December	22 6 3 3 00	
Less Withdrawals for December	4 0 0 0 00	
Increase in Capital		18 6 3 3 00
Jason Taylor, Capital, December 31, 2007		108 6 3 3 00

JT's Consulting Services
Balance Sheet
December 31, 2007

Assets		
Cash		83 5 0 0 00
Accounts Receivable		5 0 0 0 00
Supplies		2 0 0 0 00
Prepaid Rent		3 5 0 0 00
Equipment	22 0 0 0 00	
Less Accumulated Depreciation	3 6 7 00	21 6 3 3 00
Total Assets		115 6 3 3 00
Liabilities and Owner's Equity		
Liabilities		
Accounts Payable		7 0 0 0 00
Owner's Equity		
Jason Taylor, Capital		108 6 3 3 00
Total Liabilities and Owner's Equity		115 6 3 3 00

FIGURE 6.4

End-of-Month Financial Statements

ABOUT ACCOUNTING

Medical Accounting
Professionals in the health field, such as doctors and dentists, need to understand accounting so they can bill for services performed. Because patients have different insurance and payment plans, specialized software is used to manage the paperwork and keep track of the payments.

▶ **4. OBJECTIVE**
Review the steps in the accounting cycle.

The Accounting Cycle

You have learned about the entire accounting cycle as you studied the financial affairs of JT's Consulting Services during its first month of operations. Figure 6.5 summarizes the steps in the accounting cycle.

Step 1. **Analyze transactions.** Analyze source documents to determine their effects on the basic accounting equation. The data about transactions appears on a variety of source documents such as:

- sales slips,
- purchase invoices,
- credit memorandums,
- check stubs.

Step 2. **Journalize the transactions.** Record the effects of the transactions in a journal.

Step 3. **Post the journal entries.** Transfer data from the journal to the general ledger accounts.

Step 4. **Prepare a worksheet.** At the end of each period, prepare a worksheet.

- Use the Trial Balance section to prove the equality of debits and credits in the general ledger.
- Use the Adjustments section to enter changes in account balances that are needed to present an accurate and complete picture of the financial affairs of the business.
- Use the Adjusted Trial Balance section to verify the equality of debits and credits after the adjustments. Extend the amounts from the Adjusted Trial Balance section to the Income Statement and Balance Sheet sections.
- Use the Income Statement and Balance Sheet sections to prepare the financial statements.

Step 5. **Prepare financial statements.** Prepare financial statements to report information to owners, managers, and other interested parties.

- The income statement shows the results of operations for the period.
- The statement of owner's equity reports the changes in the owner's financial interest during the period.
- The balance sheet shows the financial position of the business at the end of the period.

recall

The Accounting Cycle
The accounting cycle is a series of steps performed during each period to classify, record, and summarize data to produce needed financial information.

FIGURE 6.5

The Accounting Cycle

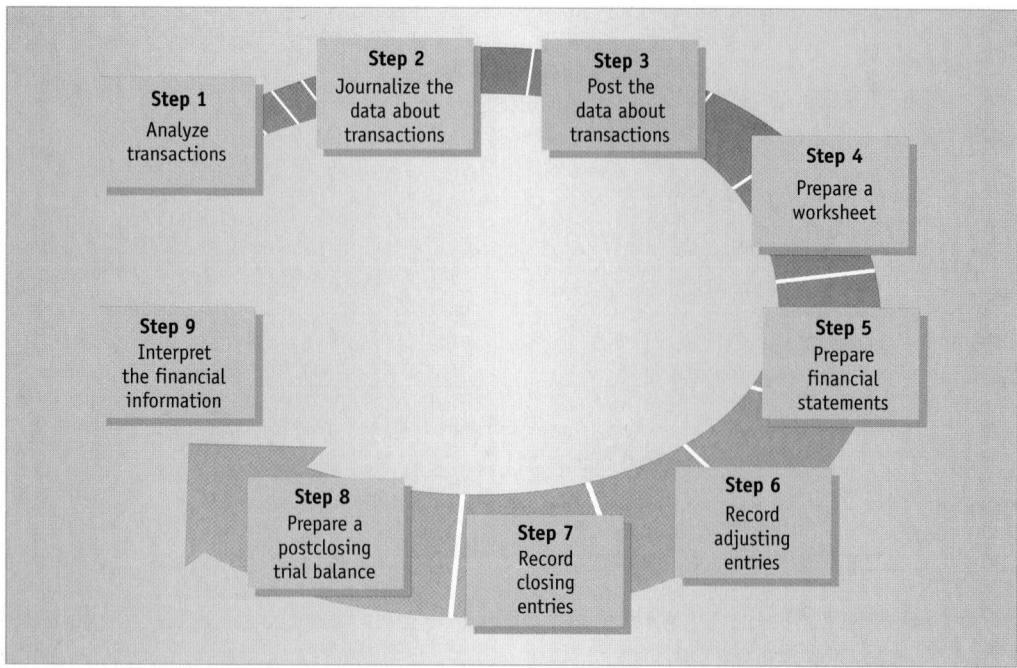

Step 1 Analyze transactions

Step 2 Journalize the data about transactions

Step 3 Post the data about transactions

Step 4 Prepare a worksheet

Step 5 Prepare financial statements

Step 6 Record adjusting entries

Step 7 Record closing entries

Step 8 Prepare a postclosing trial balance

Step 9 Interpret the financial information

MANAGERIAL IMPLICATIONS   <<

FINANCIAL INFORMATION

- Management needs timely and accurate financial information to control operations and make decisions.
- A well-designed and well-run accounting system provides reliable financial statements to management.
- Although management is not involved in day-to-day accounting procedures and end-of-period processes, the efficiency of the procedures affects the quality and promptness of the financial information that management receives.

THINKING CRITICALLY

If you owned or managed a business, how often would you want financial statements prepared? Why?

Step 6. Record adjusting entries. Use the worksheet to journalize and post adjusting entries. The adjusting entries are a permanent record of the changes in account balances shown on the worksheet.

Step 7. Record closing entries. Journalize and post the closing entries to
- transfer net income or net loss to owner's equity;
- reduce the balances of the revenue, expense, and drawing accounts to zero.

Step 8. Prepare a postclosing trial balance. The postclosing trial balance shows that the general ledger is in balance after the closing entries are posted. It is also used to verify that there are zero balances in revenue, expense, and drawing accounts.

Step 9. Interpret the financial information. Use financial statements to understand and communicate financial information and to make decisions. Accountants, owners, managers, and other interested parties interpret financial statements by comparing such things as profit, revenue, and expenses from one accounting period to the next.

> In addition to financial statements, Adobe Systems Incorporated prepares a Financial Highlights report. This report lists total assets, revenue, net income, and number of worldwide employees for the past five years.

After studying the accounting cycle of JT's Consulting Services, you have an understanding of how data flows through a simple accounting system for a small business:
- Source documents are analyzed.
- Transactions are recorded in the general journal.
- Transactions are posted from the general journal to the general ledger.
- Financial information is proved, adjusted, and summarized on the worksheet.
- Financial information is reported on financial statements.

Figure 6.6 illustrates this data flow.

As you will learn in later chapters, some accounting systems have more complex records, procedures, and financial statements. However, the steps of the accounting cycle and the underlying accounting principles remain the same.

International INSIGHTS

European Union

The European Economic Community was formed in 1958 to allow goods, services, workers, and money to move freely among its member countries. Now known as the European Union, the organization has developed a single currency, the *euro*. The euro is divided into one hundred cents.

FIGURE 6.6

Flow of Data through a Simple Accounting System

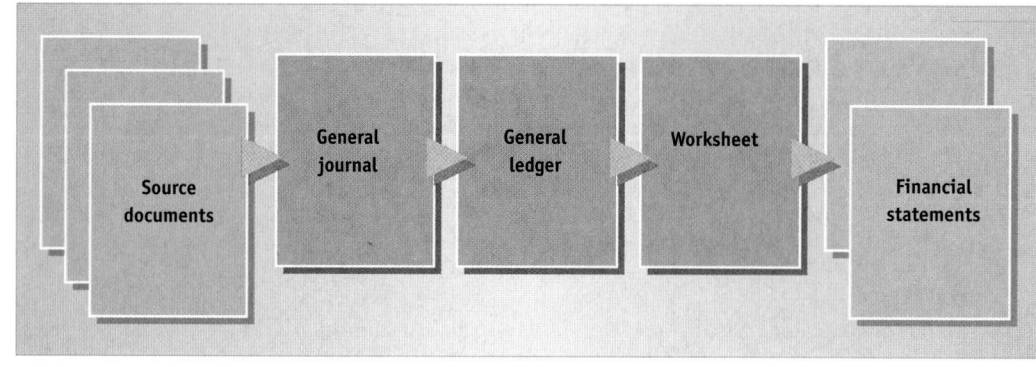

Section 2: **Self Review**

QUESTIONS

1. What are the last three steps in the accounting cycle?

2. Why is a postclosing trial balance prepared?

3. What accounts appear on the postclosing trial balance?

EXERCISES

4. After the revenue and expense accounts are closed, *Income Summary* has a debit balance of $25,000. What does this figure represent?

a. net profit of $25,000

b. net loss of $25,000

c. owner's withdrawals of $25,000

d. increase in owner's equity of $25,000

5. Which of the following accounts will not appear on the postclosing trial balance?

a. *C. J. Thomas, Drawing*

b. *Cash*

c. *C. J. Thomas, Capital*

d. *Accounts Payable*

ANALYSIS

6. On which financial statement would you find the answer to each question?

• What were the total fees earned this month?

• How much money is owed to suppliers?

• Did the business make a profit?

• Is there enough cash to purchase new equipment?

• What were the expenses?

• Do customers owe money to the business?

(Answers to Section 2 Self Review are on page 195.)

REVIEW | Chapter Summary

After the worksheet and financial statements have been completed and adjusting entries have been journalized and posted, the closing entries are recorded and a postclosing trial balance is prepared.

Learning Objectives

1 Journalize and post closing entries.

Journalizing and posting the closing entries is the seventh step in the accounting cycle. Closing entries transfer the results of operations to owner's equity and reduce the balances of the revenue and expense accounts to zero. The worksheet provides the data necessary for the closing entries. A temporary owner's equity account, *Income Summary,* is used. There are four steps in the closing process:

1. The balance of the revenue account is transferred to the *Income Summary* account.

   Debit *Revenue*

   Credit *Income Summary*

2. The balances of the expense accounts are transferred to the *Income Summary* account.

   Debit *Income Summary*

   Credit *Expenses*

3. The balance of the *Income Summary* account—net income or net loss—is transferred to the owner's capital account.

   If *Income Summary* has a credit balance:

   Debit *Income Summary*

   Credit *Owner's Capital*

   If *Income Summary* has a debit balance:

   Debit *Owner's Capital*

   Credit *Income Summary*

4. The drawing account is closed to the owner's capital account.

   Debit *Owner's Capital*

   Credit *Drawing*

After the closing entries have been posted, the capital account reflects the results of operations for the period. The revenue and expense accounts, with zero balances, are ready to accumulate data for the next period.

2 Prepare a postclosing trial balance.

Preparing the postclosing trial balance is the eighth step in the accounting cycle. A postclosing trial balance is prepared to test the equality of total debit and credit balances in the general ledger after the adjusting and closing entries have been recorded. This report lists only permanent accounts open at the end of the period—asset, liability, and the owner's capital accounts. The temporary accounts—revenue, expenses, drawing, and *Income Summary*—apply only to one accounting period and do not appear on the postclosing trial balance.

3 Interpret financial statements.

The ninth step in the accounting cycle is interpreting the financial statements. Business decisions must be based on accurate and timely financial data.

4 Review the steps in the accounting cycle.

The accounting cycle consists of a series of steps that are repeated in each fiscal period. These steps are designed to classify, record, and summarize the data needed to produce financial information.

The steps of the accounting cycle are:

1. Analyze transactions.
2. Journalize the transactions.
3. Post the journal entries.
4. Prepare a worksheet.
5. Prepare financial statements.
6. Record adjusting entries.
7. Record closing entries.
8. Prepare a postclosing trial balance.
9. Interpret the financial information.

5 Define the accounting terms new to this chapter.

Glossary

Closing entries (p. 166) Journal entries that transfer the results of operations (net income or net loss) to owner's equity and reduce the revenue, expense, and drawing account balances to zero

Income Summary account (p. 166) A special owner's equity account that is used only in the closing process to summarize the results of operations

Interpret (p. 176) To understand and explain the meaning and importance of something (such as financial statements)

Postclosing trial balance (p. 175) A statement that is prepared to prove the equality of total debits and credits after the closing process is completed

Comprehensive **Self Review**

1. Is the following statement true or false? Why? "All owner's equity accounts appear on the postclosing trial balance."
2. What is the last step in the accounting cycle?
3. A firm has $35,000 in revenue for the period. Give the entry to close the **Fees Income** account.
4. What three financial statements are prepared during the accounting cycle?
5. A firm has the following expenses: **Rent Expense,** $1,800; **Salaries Expense,** $3,850; **Supplies Expense,** $875. Give the entry to close the expense accounts.

(Answers to Comprehensive Self Review are on page 195.)

Discussion Questions

1. Where does the accountant obtain the data needed for the closing entries?
2. How is the **Income Summary** account used in the closing procedure?
3. Why does the accountant record closing entries at the end of a period?
4. Where does the accountant obtain the data needed for the adjusting entries?
5. What three procedures are performed at the end of each accounting period before the financial information is interpreted?
6. Briefly describe the flow of data through a simple accounting system.
7. Name the steps of the accounting cycle.
8. What is the accounting cycle?
9. What accounts appear on a postclosing trial balance?
10. Why is a postclosing trial balance prepared?

APPLICATIONS

Exercises

Exercise 6.1
Objective 1

▶ **Journalize closing entries.**

On December 31 the ledger of Henderson Company contained the following account balances:

Cash	$36,000	Eugene Henderson, Drawing	$24,000
Accounts Receivable	2,400	Fees Income	85,000
Supplies	1,600	Depreciation Expense	3,000
Equipment	30,000	Salaries Expense	28,000

Accumulated Depreciation	3,000	Supplies Expense	4,000
Accounts Payable	4,000	Telephone Expense	3,600
Eugene Henderson, Capital	46,200	Utilities Expense	7,200

All the accounts have normal balances. Journalize the closing entries. Use 4 as the general journal page number.

Accounting cycle.

◀ **Exercise 6.2**
Objective 4

Following are the steps in the accounting cycle. Arrange the steps in the proper sequence.

1. Post the journal entries. 3
2. Journalize the transactions. 2
3. Analyze transactions. 1
4. Prepare a worksheet. 4
5. Record adjusting entries. 6
6. Prepare financial statements. 5
7. Prepare a postclosing trial balance. 8
8. Interpret the financial information. 9
9. Record closing entries. 7

Postclosing trial balance.

◀ **Exercise 6.3**
Objective 2

From the following list identify the accounts that will appear on the postclosing trial balance.

ACCOUNTS

1. Cash ✓
2. Accounts Receivable ✓
3. Supplies ✓
4. Equipment ✓
5. Accumulated Depreciation ✓
6. Accounts Payable ✓
7. Jane Nelson, Capital ✓
8. Jane Nelson, Drawing
9. Fees Income
10. Depreciation Expense
11. Salaries Expense
12. Supplies Expense
13. Utilities Expense

Financial statements.

◀ **Exercise 6.4**
Objective 3

Managers often consult financial statements for specific types of information. Indicate whether each of the following items would appear on the income statement, statement of owner's equity, or the balance sheet. Use *I* for the income statement, *E* for the statement of owner's equity, and *B* for the balance sheet. If an item appears on more than one statement, use all letters that apply to that item.

1. Owner's withdrawals for the period
2. Accounts payable of the business
3. Total expenses for the period
4. Book value of the firm's equipment
5. Original cost of the firm's equipment
6. Amount of depreciation charged off on the firm's equipment during the period
7. Accumulated depreciation on the firm's equipment

CHAPTER 6: Review and Applications

8. Accounts receivable of the business

9. Cost of supplies used during the period

10. Supplies on hand

11. Owner's capital at the end of the period

12. Net income for the period

13. Total assets of the business

14. Revenue earned during the period

15. Cash on hand

Exercise 6.5
Objective 1

▶ **Closing entries.**

The *Income Summary* and *Kim Zang, Capital* accounts for Zang Production Company at the end of its accounting period follow.

ACCOUNT Income Summary   ACCOUNT NO. 399

DATE		DESCRIPTION	POST. REF.	DEBIT	CREDIT	BALANCE DEBIT	BALANCE CREDIT
2007							
Dec.	31	Closing	J4		23 2 5 0 00		23 2 5 0 00
	31	Closing	J4	15 1 5 0 00			8 1 0 0 00
	31	Closing	J4	8 1 0 0 00			– 0 –

ACCOUNT Kim Zang, Capital   ACCOUNT NO. 301

DATE		DESCRIPTION	POST. REF.	DEBIT	CREDIT	BALANCE DEBIT	BALANCE CREDIT
2007							
Dec.	1		J1		75 0 0 0 00		75 0 0 0 00
	31	Closing	J4		8 1 0 0 00		83 1 0 0 00
	31	Closing	J4	3 0 0 0 00			80 1 0 0 00

Complete the following statements.

1. Total revenue for the period is _____ .

2. Total expenses for the period are _____ .

3. Net income for the period is _____ .

4. Owner's withdrawals for the period are _____ .

Exercise 6.6
Objective 1

▶ **Closing entries.**

The ledger accounts of Easy Access Internet Company appear as follows on March 31, 2007.

ACCOUNT NO.	ACCOUNT	BALANCE
101	Cash	$34,500
111	Accounts Receivable	6,600
121	Supplies	4,050
131	Prepaid Insurance	10,440
141	Equipment	50,400
142	Accumulated Depreciation—Equipment	10,080
202	Accounts Payable	5,400
301	Dennis Ortiz, Capital	58,800
302	Dennis Ortiz, Drawing	3,000
401	Fees Income	138,000
510	Depreciation Expense—Equipment	5,040

511	Insurance Expense	4,800
514	Rent Expense	14,400
517	Salaries Expense	70,800
518	Supplies Expense	1,950
519	Telephone Expense	2,700
523	Utilities Expense	3,600

All accounts have normal balances. Journalize and post the closing entries. Use 4 as the page number for the general journal in journalizing the closing entries.

Closing entries.

◀ **Exercise 6.7**
Objective 1

On December 31 the *Income Summary* account of Victoria Company has a debit balance of $27,000 after revenue of $42,000 and expenses of $69,000 were closed to the account. *Herman Victoria, Drawing* has a debit balance of $3,000 and *Herman Victoria, Capital* has a credit balance of $84,000. Record the journal entries necessary to complete closing the accounts. What is the new balance of *Herman Victoria, Capital?*

Accounting cycle.

◀ **Exercise 6.8**
Objective 4

Complete a chart of the accounting cycle by writing the steps of the cycle in their proper sequence.

PROBLEMS

Problem Set A

Adjusting and closing entries.

◀ **Problem 6.1A**
Objective 1

The Pelton Marketing Research Company, owned by Lou Pelton, is employed by large companies to test consumer reaction to new products. On January 31 the firm's worksheet showed the following adjustments data: (a) supplies used, $560; (b) expired rent, $3,000; and (c) depreciation on office equipment, $1,120. The balances of the revenue and expense accounts listed in the Income Statement section of the worksheet and the drawing account listed in the Balance Sheet section of the worksheet are given below.

REVENUE AND EXPENSE ACCOUNTS

401 Fees Income	$77,000 Cr.
511 Depr. Expense—Office Equipment	1,120 Dr.
514 Rent Expense	3,000 Dr.
517 Salaries Expense	41,200 Dr.
520 Supplies Expense	560 Dr.
523 Telephone Expense	940 Dr.
526 Travel Expense	8,920 Dr.
529 Utilities Expense	460 Dr.

DRAWING ACCOUNT

| 302 Lou Pelton, Drawing | 4,800 Dr. |

INSTRUCTIONS

1. Record the adjusting entries in the general journal, page 3.
2. Record the closing entries in the general journal, page 4.

Analyze: What closing entry is required to close a drawing account?

Problem 6.2A

Objectives 1, 2

▶ **Journalizing and posting adjusting and closing entries and preparing a postclosing trial balance.**

A completed worksheet for Youngblood Enterprises is shown on pages 186–187.

INSTRUCTIONS eXcel

1. Record balances as of December 31, 2007, in the ledger accounts.

2. Journalize (use 3 as the page number) and post the adjusting entries. Use account number 131 for Prepaid Advertising and the same account numbers for all other accounts shown on page 196 for JT's Consulting Services chart of accounts.

3. Journalize (use 4 as the page number) and post the closing entries.

4. Prepare a postclosing trial balance.

Analyze: How many accounts are listed in the Adjusted Trial Balance section? How many accounts are listed on the postclosing trial balance?

Problem 6.3A

Objective 1

eXcel

▶ **Journalizing and posting closing entries.**

On December 31, after adjustments, Vinzant Company's ledger contains the following account balances.

101	Cash	$18,600 Dr.
111	Accounts Receivable	8,400 Dr.
121	Supplies	1,500 Dr.
131	Prepaid Rent	19,800 Dr.
141	Equipment	27,000 Dr.
142	Accumulated Depreciation—Equip.	750 Cr.
202	Accounts Payable	3,750 Cr.
301	Melissa Vinzant, Capital (12/1/2007)	27,810 Cr.
302	Melissa Vinzant, Drawing	3,600 Dr.

Youngblood Enterprises
Worksheet
Month Ended December 31, 2007

	ACCOUNT NAME	TRIAL BALANCE DEBIT	TRIAL BALANCE CREDIT	ADJUSTMENTS DEBIT	ADJUSTMENTS CREDIT
1	Cash	23 1 0 0 00			
2	Accounts Receivable	3 0 0 0 00			
3	Supplies	1 5 0 0 00			(a) 6 0 0 00
4	Prepaid Advertising	6 0 0 0 00			(b) 7 5 0 00
5	Equipment	15 0 0 0 00			
6	Accumulated Depreciation—Equipment				(c) 6 0 0 00
7	Accounts Payable		3 0 0 0 00		
8	Connie Youngblood, Capital		33 0 0 0 00		
9	Connie Youngblood, Drawing	2 1 0 0 00			
10	Fees Income		18 7 5 0 00		
11	Supplies Expense			(a) 6 0 0 00	
12	Advertising Expense			(b) 7 5 0 00	
13	Depreciation Expense—Equipment			(c) 6 0 0 00	
14	Salaries Expense	3 6 0 0 00			
15	Utilities Expense	4 5 0 00			
16	Totals	54 7 5 0 00	54 7 5 0 00	1 9 5 0 00	1 9 5 0 00
17	Net Income				
18					
19					

401 Fees Income	69,000 Cr.
511 Advertising Expense	2,400 Dr.
514 Depreciation Expense—Equip.	450 Dr.
517 Rent Expense	1,800 Dr.
519 Salaries Expense	14,400 Dr.
523 Utilities Expense	3,360 Dr.

INSTRUCTIONS

1. Record the balances in the ledger accounts as of December 31.
2. Journalize the closing entries in the general journal, page 4.
3. Post the closing entries to the general ledger accounts.

Analyze: What is the balance of the **Salaries Expense** account after closing entries are posted?

Worksheet, journalizing and posting adjusting and closing entries, and the postclosing trial balance.

◀   Problem 6.4A
Objectives 1, 2, 4
e**X**cel

A partially completed worksheet for Clifton Auto Detailing Service, a firm that details cars and vans, follows.

INSTRUCTIONS

1. Record balances as of December 31 in the ledger accounts.
2. Prepare the worksheet.
3. Journalize (use 3 as the journal page number) and post the adjusting entries. Use account number 131 for Prepaid Advertising and the same account numbers for all other accounts shown on page 196 for JT's Consulting Services chart of accounts.
4. Journalize (use 4 as the journal page number) and post the closing entries.
5. Prepare a postclosing trial balance.

ADJUSTED TRIAL BALANCE		INCOME STATEMENT		BALANCE SHEET		
DEBIT	CREDIT	DEBIT	CREDIT	DEBIT	CREDIT	
23 1 0 0 00				23 1 0 0 00		1
3 0 0 0 00				3 0 0 0 00		2
9 0 0 00				9 0 0 00		3
5 2 5 0 00				5 2 5 0 00		4
15 0 0 0 00				15 0 0 0 00		5
	6 0 0 00				6 0 0 00	6
	3 0 0 0 00				3 0 0 0 00	7
	33 0 0 0 00				33 0 0 0 00	8
2 1 0 0 00				2 1 0 0 00		9
	18 7 5 0 00		18 7 5 0 00			10
6 0 0 00		6 0 0 00				11
7 5 0 00		7 5 0 00				12
6 0 0 00		6 0 0 00				13
3 6 0 0 00		3 6 0 0 00				14
4 5 0 00		4 5 0 00				15
55 3 5 0 00	55 3 5 0 00	6 0 0 0 00	18 7 5 0 00	49 3 5 0 00	36 6 0 0 00	16
		12 7 5 0 00			12 7 5 0 00	17
		18 7 5 0 00	18 7 5 0 00	49 3 5 0 00	49 3 5 0 00	18
						19

Clifton Auto Detailing Service
Worksheet
Month Ended December 31, 2007

ACCOUNT NAME	TRIAL BALANCE DEBIT	TRIAL BALANCE CREDIT	ADJUSTMENTS DEBIT	ADJUSTMENTS CREDIT
1 Cash	62 1 0 0 00			
2 Accounts Receivable	9 9 0 0 00			
3 Supplies	8 0 0 0 00			(a) 3 2 0 0 00
4 Prepaid Advertising	6 0 0 0 00			(b) 2 8 0 0 00
5 Equipment	40 0 0 0 00			
6 Accumulated Depreciation—Equipment				(c) 9 6 0 00
7 Accounts Payable		10 0 0 0 00		
8 Clifton Davis, Capital		71 0 0 0 00		
9 Clifton Davis, Drawing	4 0 0 0 00			
10 Fees Income		60 0 0 0 00		
11 Salaries Expense	9 6 0 0 00		(a) 3 200 00	(a) 3 2 0 0 00
12 Utilities Expense	1 4 0 0 00			
13 Supplies Expense				
14 Advertising Expense			(b) 2 8 0 0 00	
15 Depreciation Expense—Equipment			(c) 9 6 0 00	
16 Totals	141 0 0 0 00	141 0 0 0 00	6 9 6 0 00	6 9 6 0 00
17				
18				
19				
20				

Analyze: What total debits were posted to the general ledger to complete all closing entries for the month of December?

Problem Set B

Problem 6.1B
Objective 1

▶ **Adjusting and closing entries.**

Zimwalt's Cleaning and Maintenance, owned by Marvel Zimwalt, provides cleaning services to hotels, motels, and hospitals. On January 31 the firm's worksheet showed the following adjustment data. The balances of the revenue and expense accounts listed in the Income Statement section of the worksheet and the drawing account listed in the Balance Sheet section of the worksheet are also given.

ADJUSTMENTS
a. Supplies used, $5,720
b. Expired insurance, $740
c. Depreciation on machinery, $2,240

REVENUE AND EXPENSE ACCOUNTS

401 Fees Income	$65,600 Cr.
511 Depreciation Expense—Machinery	2,240 Dr.
514 Insurance Expense	740 Dr.
517 Rent Expense	6,000 Dr.
520 Salaries Expense	32,000 Dr.
523 Supplies Expense	5,720 Dr.
526 Telephone Expense	420 Dr.

529 Utilities Expense	1,280 Dr.
DRAWING ACCOUNT	
302 Marvel Zimwalt, Drawing	4,800 Dr.

INSTRUCTIONS

1. Record the adjusting entries in the general journal, page 3.
2. Record the closing entries in the general journal, page 4.

Analyze: What effect did the adjusting entry for expired insurance have on the *Insurance Expense* account?

Journalizing and posting adjusting and closing entries and preparing a postclosing trial balance.

◀ **Problem 6.2B**
Objectives 1, 2

A completed worksheet for Cedar Canyon Nursery and Lawn is shown on pages 190–191.

INSTRUCTIONS

1. Record the balances as of December 31 in the ledger accounts.
2. Journalize (use 3 as the page number) and post the adjusting entries. Use account number 131 for Prepaid Advertising and the same account numbers for all other accounts as shown on page 196 for JT's Consulting Services chart of accounts.
3. Journalize (use 4 as the page number) and post the closing entries.
4. Prepare a postclosing trial balance.

Analyze: What total credits were posted to the general ledger to complete the closing entries?

Journalizing and posting closing entries.

◀ **Problem 6.3B**
Objective 1

On December 31, after adjustments, The Chestnut Tree Farm's ledger contains the following account balances.

101 Cash	$28,500 Dr.
111 Accounts Receivable	7,200 Dr.
121 Supplies	3,000 Dr.
131 Prepaid Rent	23,100 Dr.
141 Equipment	36,000 Dr.
142 Accumulated Depreciation—Equip.	900 Cr.
202 Accounts Payable	9,750 Cr.
301 Shawn McGowan, Capital (12/1/2007)	57,450 Cr.
302 Shawn McGowan, Drawing	3,600 Dr.
401 Fees Income	54,000 Cr.
511 Advertising Expense	3,300 Dr.
514 Depreciation Expense—Equip.	900 Dr.
517 Rent Expense	2,100 Dr.
519 Salaries Expense	10,800 Dr.
523 Utilities Expense	3,600 Dr.

INSTRUCTIONS

1. Record the balances in the ledger accounts as of December 31.
2. Journalize the closing entries in the general journal, page 4.
3. Post the closing entries to the general ledger accounts.

Analyze: List the accounts affected by closing entries for the month of December.

Cedar Canyon Nursery and Lawn
Worksheet
Month Ended December 31, 2007

	ACCOUNT NAME	TRIAL BALANCE DEBIT	TRIAL BALANCE CREDIT	ADJUSTMENTS DEBIT	ADJUSTMENTS CREDIT
1	Cash	10 8 0 0 00			
2	Accounts Receivable	2 0 0 0 00			
3	Supplies	2 0 0 0 00			(a) 1 0 0 0 00
4	Prepaid Advertising	3 0 0 0 00			(b) 4 0 0 00
5	Equipment	20 0 0 0 00			
6	Accumulated Depreciation—Equipment				(c) 5 0 0 00
7	Accounts Payable		3 0 0 0 00		
8	Randall Marshall, Capital		27 4 0 0 00		
9	Randall Marshall, Drawing	2 8 0 0 00			
10	Fees Income		15 6 0 0 00		
11	Supplies Expense			(a) 1 0 0 0 00	
12	Advertising Expense			(b) 4 0 0 00	
13	Depreciation Expense—Equipment			(c) 5 0 0 00	
14	Salaries Expense	4 8 0 0 00			
15	Utilities Expense	6 0 0 00			
16	Totals	46 0 0 0 00	46 0 0 0 00	1 9 0 0 00	1 9 0 0 00
17	Net Income				
18					
19					
20					

Problem 6.4B
Objectives 1, 2, 4

▶ **Worksheet, journalizing and posting adjusting and closing entries, and the postclosing trial balance.**

A partially completed worksheet for Finley Graves, CPA, for the month ending June 30, 2007, is shown below.

Finley Graves, CPA
Worksheet
Month Ended June 30, 2007

	ACCOUNT NAME	TRIAL BALANCE DEBIT	TRIAL BALANCE CREDIT	ADJUSTMENTS DEBIT	ADJUSTMENTS CREDIT
1	Cash	10 6 5 0 00			
2	Accounts Receivable	3 7 8 0 00			
3	Supplies	5 2 5 0 00			(a) 9 0 0 00
4	Computers	9 6 0 0 00			
5	Accumulated Depreciation—Computers		9 6 0 00		(b) 8 0 00
6	Accounts Payable		4 2 0 0 00		
7	Finley Graves, Capital		20 7 4 5 00		
8	Finley Graves, Drawing	4 0 0 0 00			
9	Fees Income		22 6 5 0 00		
10	Salaries Expense	12 5 7 5 00			
11	Supplies Expense			(a) 9 0 0 00	
12	Depreciation Expense—Computers			(b) 8 0 00	
13	Travel Expense	1 8 0 0 00			
14	Utilities Expense	9 0 0 00			
15	Totals	48 5 5 5 00	48 5 5 5 00	9 8 0 00	9 8 0 00
16					
17					

ADJUSTED TRIAL BALANCE		INCOME STATEMENT		BALANCE SHEET		
DEBIT	CREDIT	DEBIT	CREDIT	DEBIT	CREDIT	
10 8 0 0 00				10 8 0 0 00		1
2 0 0 0 00				2 0 0 0 00		2
1 0 0 0 00				1 0 0 0 00		3
2 6 0 0 00				2 6 0 0 00		4
20 0 0 0 00				20 0 0 0 00		5
	5 0 0 00				5 0 0 00	6
	3 0 0 0 00				3 0 0 0 00	7
	27 4 0 0 00				27 4 0 0 00	8
2 8 0 0 00				2 8 0 0 00		9
	15 6 0 0 00		15 6 0 0 00			10
1 0 0 0 00		1 0 0 0 00				11
4 0 0 00		4 0 0 00				12
5 0 0 00		5 0 0 00				13
4 8 0 0 00		4 8 0 0 00				14
6 0 0 00		6 0 0 00				15
46 5 0 0 00	46 5 0 0 00	7 3 0 0 00	15 6 0 0 00	39 2 0 0 00	30 9 0 0 00	16
		8 3 0 0 00			8 3 0 0 00	17
		15 6 0 0 00	15 6 0 0 00	39 2 0 0 00	39 2 0 0 00	18
						19
						20

INSTRUCTIONS

1. Record the balances as of June 30 in the ledger accounts.

2. Prepare the worksheet.

3. Journalize (use 3 as the journal page number) and post the adjusting entries. Use account number 519 for Travel and the same account numbers for all other accounts as shown on page 196 for JT's Consulting Services chart of accounts.

4. Journalize (use 4 as the journal page number) and post the closing entries.

5. Prepare a postclosing trial balance.

Analyze: What is the reported net income for the month of June for Finley Graves, CPA?

Challenge Problem

The Closing Process

The Trial Balance section of the worksheet for The Barber Shop for the period ended December 31, 2007, appears below. Adjustments data is also given.

>   ADJUSTMENTS
>   a. Supplies used, $3,600
>   b. Expired insurance, $2,400
>   c. Depreciation expense for machinery, $1,200

INSTRUCTIONS

1. Complete the worksheet.

2. Prepare an income statement.

3. Prepare a statement of owner's equity.

The Barber Shop
Worksheet
Month Ended December 31, 2007

	ACCOUNT NAME	TRIAL BALANCE DEBIT	TRIAL BALANCE CREDIT	ADJUSTMENTS DEBIT	ADJUSTMENTS CREDIT
1	Cash	40 8 0 0 00			
2	Accounts Receivable	9 0 0 0 00			
3	Supplies	7 2 0 0 00			(a) 3 6 0 0 00
4	Prepaid Insurance	10 8 0 0 00			(b) 2 4 0 0 00
5	Machinery	84 0 0 0 00			
6	Accumulated Depreciation—Machinery				(c) 1 2 0 0 00
7	Accounts Payable		13 5 0 0 00		
8	Tommy Brooks, Capital		74 5 8 0 00		
9	Tommy Brooks, Drawing	6 0 0 0 00			
10	Fees Income		82 5 0 0 00		
11	Supplies Expense			(a) 3 6 0 0 00	
12	Insurance Expense			(b) 2 4 0 0 00	
13	Salaries Expense	11 1 0 0 00			
14	Depreciation Expense—Machinery			(c) 1 2 0 0 00	
15	Utilities Expense	1 6 8 0 00			
16	Totals	170 5 8 0 00	170 5 8 0 00	7 2 0 0 00	7 2 0 0 00
17					
18					
19					

4. Prepare a balance sheet.

5. Journalize the adjusting entries in the general journal, page 3.

6. Journalize the closing entries in the general journal, page 4.

7. Prepare a postclosing trial balance.

Analyze: If the adjusting entry for expired insurance had been recorded in error as a credit to *Insurance Expense* and a debit to *Prepaid Insurance* for $2,400, what reported net income would have resulted?

Critical Thinking Problem

Owner's Equity

James Strutton, the bookkeeper for Interior Home Improvements Company, has just finished posting the closing entries for the year to the ledger. He is concerned about the following balances:

Capital account balance in the general ledger: $97,100
Ending capital balance on the statement of owner's equity: 55,600

James knows that these amounts should agree and asks for your assistance in reviewing his work.
     Your review of the general ledger of Interior Home Improvements Company reveals a beginning capital balance of $50,000. You also review the general journal for the accounting period and find the following closing entries.

1. What errors did Mr. Strutton make in preparing the closing entries for the period?

2. Prepare a general journal entry to correct the errors made.

3. Explain why the balance of the capital account in the ledger after closing entries have been posted will be the same as the ending capital balance on the statement of owner's equity.

GENERAL JOURNAL   PAGE ___15___

	DATE		DESCRIPTION	POST. REF.	DEBIT	CREDIT	
1	2007		Closing Entries				1
2	Dec.	31	Fees Income		98 0 0 0 00		2
3			Accumulated Depreciation		8 5 0 0 00		3
4			Accounts Payable		33 0 0 0 00		4
5			Income Summary			139 5 0 0 00	5
6							6
7		31	Income Summary		92 4 0 0 00		7
8			Salaries Expense			78 0 0 0 00	8
9			Supplies Expense			5 0 0 0 00	9
10			Depreciation Expense			2 4 0 0 00	10
11			Brenda Powell, Drawing			7 0 0 0 00	11
12							12
13							13
14							14

BUSINESS CONNECTIONS

Interpreting Financial Statements

1. An officer of Carson Company recently commented that when he receives the firm's financial statements, he looks at just the bottom line of the income statement—the line that shows the net income or net loss for the period. He said that he does not bother with the rest of the income statement because "it's only the bottom line that counts." He also does not read the balance sheet. Do you think this manager is correct in the way he uses the financial statements? Why or why not?

2. The president of Henderson Corporation is concerned about the firm's ability to pay its debts on time. What items on the balance sheet would help her to assess the firm's debt-paying ability?

3. Why is it important that a firm's financial records be kept up to date and that management receive the financial statements promptly after the end of each accounting period?

4. What kinds of operating and general policy decisions might be influenced by data on the financial statements?

Timing of a Check

On the last day of the fiscal year, Gevok Means comes to you for a favor. He asks that you enter a check for $1000 to GM Company for Miscellaneous Expense. You notice the invoice looks a little different from other invoices that are processed. Gevok needs the check immediately to get supplies today to complete the project for a favorite customer. You know that by preparing the closing entries tomorrow, Miscellaneous Expense will be set to zero for the beginning of the new year. Should you write this check and record the expense or find an excuse to write the check tomorrow? What would be the effect if the invoice to GM Company was erroneous and you had written the check?

Closing Process

Refer to The Home Depot, Inc. *2004 Annual Report* in Appendix A.

1. Locate the consolidated balance sheets and consolidated statements of earnings. List ten permanent account categories and five temporary account categories found within these statements.

2. Based on the consolidated statements of earnings, what is the closing entry that should be made to zero out all operating expense categories?

CHAPTER 6: Review and Applications

Income Statement

In 2003 CSX Corporation reported operating expenses of $7,167 million. A partial list of the company's operating expenses follows. CSX Corporation reported revenues from external customers to be $7,793 million for the year. These revenues are divided among three operations: surface transportation, international terminals, and other.

Revenues from External Customers
(Dollars in millions)

Surface Transportation	$7,439
International Terminals	226
Other	128

Operating Expenses (partial list)
(Dollars in millions)

Labor and Fringe Benefits	$2,740
Materials, Supplies, and Other	1,627
Conrail Fees, Rents, and Services	342
Building and Equipment Rent	566
Inland Transportation	320
Depreciation	629
Fuel	581

Analyze:

1. If the given categories represent the related general ledger accounts, what journal entry would be made to close the expense accounts at year-end?

2. What journal entry would be made to close the revenue accounts?

Analyze Online: Locate the Web site for CSX Corporation **(www.csx.com).** Click on *CSX Corporation* and then click on *Investor Relations.* Within the *Financial Information* link, find the most recent annual report.

3. On the consolidated statement of earnings, what was the amount reported for operating expenses?

4. What percentage increase or decrease does this figure represent from the operating expenses reported in 2003 of $7,167 million?

Worksheets

Suppose that an accountant with many years' experience suggests that you skip preparation of the worksheet. The accountant claims that the financial statements can be prepared using only the general ledger account balances. What risks can you identify if the accountant uses this procedure? Do you agree or disagree with this approach? Why?

Training

As the general ledger accountant for a music supply store, you have just completed the trial balance, closing entries, and postclosing trial balance for the month. Next month, you will be on vacation during the closing process. Your boss has hired a temporary employee to perform these duties while you are away. Prepare a descriptive report for your replacement explaining the differences between a postclosing trial balance and a trial balance.

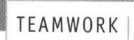

Accounting Cycle

Understanding the steps in the accounting cycle is important to get accurate information about the condition of your company. In teams, make strips of paper with the 9 steps of the accounting cycle. Give two or three strips to each member of the group. Each team member needs to put their strips in the proper order of the 9 steps.

Certified Bookkeeper

Certification in your field indicates you have a certain level of education and training. Go to the American Institute of Professional Bookkeepers Web site at **www.aipb.com**. From the certification program icon, determine the requirements to become a Certified Bookkeeper.

 Internet | **CONNECTION**

Answers to **Self Reviews**

Answers to Section 1 Self Review

1. Debit *Capital* and credit *Drawing.*
2. A temporary owner's equity account.
3. Close the revenue account to *Income Summary.*
   Close the expense accounts to *Income Summary.*
   Close the *Income Summary* account to the capital account.
   Close the drawing account to the capital account.
4. a. *Capital*
5. d. revenue, drawing, and expense accounts
6. No effect on net income.

Answers to Section 2 Self Review

1. (7) Record closing entries, (8) prepare a postclosing trial balance, (9) interpret the financial statements.
2. To make sure the general ledger is in balance after the adjusting and closing entries are posted.
3. Asset, liability, and the owner's capital accounts.
4. b. net loss of $25,000
5. a. *C. J. Thomas, Drawing*
6. The income statement will answer questions about fees earned, expenses incurred, and profit. The balance sheet will answer questions about the cash balance, the amount owed by customers, and the amount owed to suppliers.

Answers to Comprehensive Self Review

1. False. The *temporary* owner's equity accounts do not appear on the postclosing trial balance. The temporary owner's equity accounts are the drawing account and *Income Summary.*
2. Interpret the financial statements.
3. Fees Income   35,000
      Income Summary   35,000
4. Income statement, statement of owner's equity, and balance sheet.
5. Income Summary   6,525
      Rent Expense   1,800
      Salaries Expense   3,850
      Supplies Expense   875

CHAPTER 6: Review and Applications

Mini-Practice Set 1

Service Business Accounting Cycle

JT's Consulting Services

This project will give you an opportunity to apply your knowledge of accounting principles and proce-dures by handling all the accounting work of JT's Consulting Services for the month of January 2008.

INTRODUCTION

Assume that you are the chief accountant for JT's Consulting Services. During January the business will use the same types of records and procedures that you learned about in Chapters 1 through 6. The chart of accounts for JT's Consulting Services has been expanded to include a few new ac-counts. Follow the instructions to complete the accounting records for the month of January.

JT's Consulting Services Chart of Accounts	
Assets	**Revenue**
101 Cash	401 Fees Income
111 Accounts Receivable	
121 Supplies	**Expenses**
134 Prepaid Insurance	511 Salaries Expense
137 Prepaid Rent	514 Utilities Expense
141 Equipment	517 Supplies Expense
142 Accumulated Depreciation—Equipment	520 Rent Expense
	523 Depreciation Expense—Equipment
Liabilities	526 Advertising Expense
202 Accounts Payable	529 Maintenance Expense
	532 Telephone Expense
Owner's Equity	535 Insurance Expense
301 Jason Taylor, Capital	
302 Jason Taylor, Drawing	
309 Income Summary	

INSTRUCTIONS

1. Open the general ledger accounts and enter the balances for January 1, 2008. Obtain the necessary figures from the postclosing trial balance prepared on December 31, 2007, which appears on page 175.

2. Analyze each transaction and record it in the general journal. Use page 3 to begin January's transactions.

3. Post the transactions to the general ledger accounts.

4. Prepare the Trial Balance section of the worksheet.

5. Prepare the Adjustments section of the worksheet.

   a. Compute and record the adjustment for supplies used during the month. An inventory taken on January 31 showed supplies of $1,850 on hand.

   b. Compute and record the adjustment for expired insurance for the month.

   c. Record the adjustment for one month of expired rent of $3,500.

   d. Record the adjustment for depreciation of $367 on the old equipment for the month. The first adjustment for depreciation for the new equipment will be recorded in February.

6. Complete the worksheet.

7. Prepare an income statement for the month.

8. Prepare a statement of owner's equity.

9. Prepare a balance sheet using the report form.

10. Journalize and post the adjusting entries.

11. Journalize and post the closing entries.

12. Prepare a postclosing trial balance.

Analyze: Compare the January 31 balance sheet you prepared with the December 31 balance sheet shown in Chapter 6 on page 177.
a. What changes occurred in total assets, liabilities, and the owner's ending capital?
b. What changes occurred in *Cash* and *Accounts Receivable* accounts?
c. Has there been an improvement in the firm's financial position? Why or why not?

DATE	TRANSACTIONS
Jan. 2	Purchased supplies for $2,500; issued Check 1015.
2	Purchased a one-year insurance policy for $3,600; issued Check 1016.
7	Sold services for $12,800 in cash and $1,575 on credit during the first week of January.
12	Collected a total of $950 on account from credit customers during the first week of January.
12	Issued Check 1017 for $1,850 to pay for special promotional advertising to new businesses on the local radio station during the month.
13	Collected a total of $2,000 on account from credit customers during the second week of January.
14	Returned supplies that were damaged for a cash refund of $178.
15	Sold services for $16,050 in cash and $1,590 on credit during the second week of January.
20	Purchased supplies for $1,700 from Palmer's, Inc.; received Invoice 2384 payable in 30 days.
20	Sold services for $8,950 in cash and $4,670 on credit during the third week of January.
20	Collected a total of $1,450 on account from credit customers during the third week of January.
21	Issued Check 1018 for $3,275 to pay for maintenance work on the office equipment.
22	Issued Check 1019 for $1,568 to pay for special promotional advertising to new businesses in the local newspaper.
23	Received the monthly telephone bill for $390 and paid it with Check 1020.
26	Collected a total of $3,690 on account from credit customers during the fourth week of January.
27	Issued Check 1021 for $6,000 to Office Plus, as payment on account for Invoice 2223.
28	Sent Check 1022 for $560 in payment of the monthly bill for utilities.
29	Sold services for $13,870 in cash and $1,530 on credit during the fourth week of January.
31	Issued Checks 1023–1027 for $12,500 to pay the monthly salaries of the regular employees and three part-time workers.
31	Issued Check 1028 for $3,000 for personal use.
31	Issued Check 1029 for $980 to pay for maintenance services for the month.
31	Purchased additional equipment for $15,000 from Comfort Equipment Company; issued Check 1030 for $3,500 and bought the rest on credit. The equipment has a five-year life and no salvage value.
31	Sold services for $2,350 in cash and $1,300 on credit on January 31.

MINI PRACTICE SET 1

LEARNING OBJECTIVES

1. Record credit sales in a sales journal.

2. Post from the sales journal to the general ledger accounts.

3. Post from the sales journal to the customers' accounts in the accounts receivable subsidiary ledger.

4. Record sales returns and allowances in the general journal.

5. Post sales returns and allowances.

6. Prepare a schedule of accounts receivable.

7. Compute trade discounts.

8. Record credit card sales in appropriate journals.

9. Prepare the state sales tax return.

10. Define the accounting terms new to this chapter.

NEW TERMS

accounts receivable ledger

charge-account sales

contra revenue account

control account

credit memorandum

invoice

list price

manufacturing business

merchandise inventory

merchandising business

net price

net sales

open-account credit

retail business

sales allowance

sales journal

sales return

schedule of accounts receivable

service business

special journal

subsidiary ledger

trade discount

wholesale business

Chapter 7
Accounting for Sales and Accounts Receivable

Wal-Mart www.walmartstores.com

Wal-Mart Stores, Inc., is the world's largest retailer, with $256.3 billion in sales in the fiscal year ending January 31, 2004. The company earned almost $9.1 billion in net income and grew earnings per share by more than 15 percent.

By the turn of the century Wal-Mart had been named "Retailer of the Century" by Discount Store News; made *FORTUNE* magazine's list of the "100 Best Companies To Work For;" and was ranked on *Financial Times'* "Most Respected in the World" list. Like most successful businesses, Wal-Mart had its champion in its founder Sam Walton.

Sam built Wal-Mart on three basic beliefs:

1. Respect for the Individual

2. Service to Our Customers

3. Strive for Excellence

The company has remained true to these beliefs and has grown from a small chain of 15 variety stores in the 1960s to the multibillion dollar retailer it is today with plans to open 50 new discount stores, 180–185 new Supercenters, and 50–55 new SAM'S CLUBS in U.S. in 2005.

| **thinking critically** | What other factors besides customer service are important to the success of a retail company like Wal-Mart? |

Section 1

SECTION OBJECTIVES

▶ **1. Record credit sales in a sales journal.**

WHY IT'S IMPORTANT

Credit sales are a major source of revenue for many businesses. The sales journal is an efficient option for recording large volumes of credit sales transactions.

▶ **2. Post from the sales journal to the general ledger accounts.**

WHY IT'S IMPORTANT

A well-designed accounting system prevents repetitive tasks.

TERMS TO LEARN

manufacturing business
merchandise inventory
merchandising business
retail business
sales journal
service business
special journal
subsidiary ledger

Merchandise Sales

When an accounting system is developed for a firm, one important consideration is the nature of the firm's operations. The three basic types of businesses are a **service business**, which sells services; a **merchandising business**, which sells goods that it purchases for resale; and a **manufacturing business**, which sells goods that it produces.

JT's Consulting Services, the firm that was described in Chapters 2 through 6, is a service business. The firm that we will examine next, The Style Shop, is a merchandising business that sells the latest fashion clothing for men, women, and children. It is a **retail business**, which sells goods and services directly to individual consumers. The Style Shop is a sole proprietorship owned and operated by Mary Amos, who was formerly a sales manager for a major retail clothing store.

The Style Shop must account for purchases and sales of goods, and for **merchandise inventory**—the stock of goods that is kept on hand. Refer to the chart of accounts for The Style Shop on page 201. You will learn about the accounts in this and following chapters.

To allow for efficient recording of financial data, the accounting systems of most merchandising businesses include special journals and subsidiary ledgers.

Special Journals and Subsidiary Ledgers

A **special journal** is a journal that is used to record only one type of transaction. A **subsidiary ledger** is a ledger that contains accounts of a single type. Table 7.1 lists the journals and ledgers that merchandising businesses generally use in their accounting systems. In this chapter we will discuss the sales journal and the accounts receivable subsidiary ledger.

The Sales Journal

The **sales journal** is used to record only sales of merchandise on credit. To understand the need for a sales journal, consider how credit sales made at The Style Shop would be entered and posted using a general journal and general ledger. Refer to Figure 7.1 on pages 202–203.

Note the word "Balance" in the ledger accounts. To record beginning balances, enter the date in the Date column, the word "Balance" in the Description column, a check mark in the Posting Reference column, and the amount in the Debit or Credit Balance column.

Most state and many local governments impose a sales tax on retail sales of certain goods and services. Businesses are required to collect this tax from their customers and send it to the proper tax agency at regular intervals. When goods or services are sold on credit, the sales tax

important!

Business Classifications
The term *merchandising* refers to the type of business operation, not the type of legal entity. The Style Shop could have been a partnership or a corporation instead of a sole proprietorship.

is usually recorded at the time of the sale even though it will not be collected immediately. A liability account called *Sales Tax Payable* is credited for the sales tax charged.

JOURNALS	
Type of Journal	**Purpose**
Sales	To record sales of merchandise on credit
Purchases	To record purchases of merchandise on credit
Cash receipts	To record cash received from all sources
Cash payments	To record all disbursements of cash
General	To record all transactions that are not recorded in another special journal and all adjusting and closing entries

LEDGERS	
Type of Ledger	**Content**
General	Assets, liabilities, owner's equity, revenue, and expense accounts
Accounts receivable	Accounts for credit customers
Accounts payable	Accounts for creditors

TABLE 7.1

Journals and Ledgers Used by Merchandising Businesses

THE STYLE SHOP
Chart of Accounts

Assets

101	Cash
105	Petty Cash Fund
109	Notes Receivable
111	Accounts Receivable
112	Allowance for Doubtful Accounts
116	Interest Receivable
121	Merchandise Inventory
126	Prepaid Insurance
127	Prepaid Interest
129	Supplies
131	Store Equipment
132	Accumulated Depreciation—Store Equipment
141	Office Equipment
142	Accumulated Depreciation—Office Equipment

Liabilities

201	Notes Payable—Trade
202	Notes Payable—Bank
205	Accounts Payable
216	Interest Payable
221	Social Security Tax Payable
222	Medicare Tax Payable
223	Employee Income Tax Payable
225	Federal Unemployment Tax Payable
227	State Unemployment Tax Payable
229	Salaries Payable
231	Sales Tax Payable

Owner's Equity

301	Mary Amos, Capital
302	Mary Amos, Drawing
399	Income Summary

Revenue

401	Sales
451	Sales Returns and Allowances
491	Interest Income
493	Miscellaneous Income

Cost of Goods Sold

501	Purchases
502	Freight In
503	Purchases Returns and Allowances
504	Purchases Discounts

Expenses

611	Salaries Expense—Sales
612	Supplies Expense
614	Advertising Expense
617	Cash Short or Over
626	Depreciation Expense—Store Equipment
634	Rent Expense
637	Salaries Expense—Office
639	Insurance Expense
641	Payroll Taxes Expense
643	Utilities Expense
649	Telephone Expense
651	Uncollectible Accounts Expense
657	Bank Fees Expense
658	Delivery Expense
659	Depreciation Expense—Office Equipment
691	Interest Expense
693	Miscellaneous Expense

FIGURE 7.1

Journalizing and Posting Credit Sales

GENERAL JOURNAL   PAGE ___2___

	DATE		DESCRIPTION	POST. REF.	DEBIT	CREDIT	
1	2007						1
2	Jan.	3	Accounts Receivable	111	4 3 2 00		2
3			Sales Tax Payable	231		3 2 00	3
4			Sales	401		4 0 0 00	4
5			Sold merchandise on				5
6			credit to Roy Anderson,				6
7			Sales Slip 1101				7
8							8
9		8	Accounts Receivable	111	6 4 8 00		9
10			Sales Tax Payable	231		4 8 00	10
11			Sales	401		6 0 0 00	11
12			Sold merchandise on				12
13			credit to Cathy Ball,				13
14			Sales Slip 1102				14
15							15
16		11	Accounts Receivable	111	7 5 6 00		16
17			Sales Tax Payable	231		5 6 00	17
18			Sales	401		7 0 0 00	18
19			Sold merchandise on				19
20			credit to Barbara Coe, Sales				20
21			Slip 1103				21
22							22
23		15	Accounts Receivable	111	3 2 4 00		23
24			Sales Tax Payable	231		2 4 00	24
25			Sales	401		3 0 0 00	25
26			Sold merchandise on				26
27			credit to Amalia Rodriguez,				27
28			Sales Slip 1104				28
29							29
30							30
31							31
32							32

ACCOUNT ___Accounts Receivable___   ACCOUNT NO. ___111___

DATE		DESCRIPTION	POST. REF.	DEBIT	CREDIT	BALANCE DEBIT	BALANCE CREDIT
2007							
Jan.	1	Balance	✓			3 2 4 0 00	
	3		J2	4 3 2 00		3 6 7 2 00	
	8		J2	6 4 8 00		4 3 2 0 00	
	11		J2	7 5 6 00		5 0 7 6 00	
	15		J2	3 2 4 00		5 4 0 0 00	

As you can see, a great amount of repetition is involved in both journalizing and posting these sales. The four credit sales made on January 3, 8, 11, and 15 required four separate entries in the general journal and involved four debits to *Accounts Receivable,* four credits to *Sales Tax Payable,* four credits to *Sales* (the firm's revenue account), and four descriptions. The posting of twelve items to the three general ledger accounts represents still further duplication of effort. This recording procedure is not efficient for a business that has a substantial number of credit sales each month.

ACCOUNT _Sales Tax Payable_   ACCOUNT NO. _231_

DATE		DESCRIPTION	POST. REF.	DEBIT	CREDIT	BALANCE	
						DEBIT	CREDIT
2007							
Jan.	1	Balance	✓				7 5 6 00
	3		J2		3 2 00		7 8 8 00
	8		J2		4 8 00		8 3 6 00
	11		J2		5 6 00		8 9 2 00
	15		J2		2 4 00		9 1 6 00

ACCOUNT _Sales_   ACCOUNT NO. _401_

DATE		DESCRIPTION	POST. REF.	DEBIT	CREDIT	BALANCE	
						DEBIT	CREDIT
2007							
Jan.	3		J2		4 0 0 00		4 0 0 00
	8		J2		6 0 0 00		1 0 0 0 00
	11		J2		7 0 0 00		1 7 0 0 00
	15		J2		3 0 0 00		2 0 0 0 00

RECORDING TRANSACTIONS IN A SALES JOURNAL

A special journal intended only for credit sales provides a more efficient method of recording these transactions. Figure 7.2 shows the January credit sales of The Style Shop recorded in a sales journal. Since The Style Shop is located in a state that has an 8 percent sales tax on retail transactions, its sales journal includes a Sales Tax Payable Credit column. For the sake of simplicity, the sales journal shown here includes a limited number of transactions. The firm actually has many more credit sales each month.

Notice that the headings and columns in the sales journal speed up the recording process. No general ledger account names are entered. Only one line is needed to record all information for each transaction—date, sales slip number, customer's name, debit to **_Accounts Receivable,_** credit to **_Sales Tax Payable,_** and credit to **_Sales._** Since the sales journal is used for a single purpose, there is no need to enter any descriptions. Thus a great deal of repetition is avoided.

Entries in the sales journal are usually made daily. In a retail business such as The Style Shop, the data needed for each entry is taken from a copy of the customer's sales slip, as shown in Figure 7.3.

▶ **1. OBJECTIVE**
Record credit sales in a sales journal.

recall

Journals
A journal is a day-to-day record of a firm's transactions.

		SALES JOURNAL			PAGE ___1___		

	DATE		SALES SLIP NO.	CUSTOMER'S ACCOUNT DEBITED	POST. REF.	ACCOUNTS RECEIVABLE DEBIT	SALES TAX PAYABLE CREDIT	SALES CREDIT	
1	2007								1
2	Jan.	3	1101	Roy Anderson		4 3 2 00	3 2 00	4 0 0 00	2
3		8	1102	Cathy Ball		6 4 8 00	4 8 00	6 0 0 00	3
4		11	1103	Barbara Coe		7 5 6 00	5 6 00	7 0 0 00	4
5		15	1104	Amalia Rodriguez		3 2 4 00	2 4 00	3 0 0 00	5
6		18	1105	Fred Wu		8 1 0 00	6 0 00	7 5 0 00	6
7		21	1106	Linda Carter		4 8 6 00	3 6 00	4 5 0 00	7
8		28	1107	Kim Ramirez		1 0 8 00	8 00	1 0 0 00	8
9		29	1108	Mesia Davis		1 0 8 0 00	8 0 00	1 0 0 0 00	9
10		31	1109	Alma Sanchez		9 7 2 00	7 2 00	9 0 0 00	10
11		31	1110	Roy Anderson		2 7 0 00	2 0 00	2 5 0 00	11
12									12

FIGURE 7.2

A Sales Journal

FIGURE 7.3

Customer's Sales Slip

The Style Shop

2007 Trendsetter Lane
Dallas, Texas 75268-0967

DATE	SALESPERSON	AUTH.
1/3/07	S.Harris	

Goods Taken [X]   To Be Delivered [ ]

Send to

Special Instructions:

I authorize this purchase to be charged
on my account.

Roy Anderson
Signature

SALES SLIP 1101

Qty.	Description	Unit Price	Amount
1	Sports Coat	400 00	400 00
		Sales Tax	32 00
		Amount	432 00

NAME: Roy Anderson
ADDRESS: 8913 South Hampton Road
Dallas, TX 75232-6002

▶ **2. OBJECTIVE**

Post from the sales journal to the general ledger accounts.

Topic Tackler

PLUS

Many small retail firms use a sales journal similar to the one shown in Figure 7.2. However, keep in mind that special journals vary in format according to the needs of individual businesses.

POSTING FROM A SALES JOURNAL

A sales journal not only simplifies the initial recording of credit sales, it also eliminates a great deal of repetition in posting these transactions. With a sales journal, it is not necessary to post each credit sale individually to general ledger accounts. Instead, summary postings are made at the end of the month after the amount columns of the sales journal are totaled. See Figure 7.4 on page 205 for an illustration of posting from the sales journal to the general ledger.

In actual practice, before any posting takes place, the equality of the debits and credits recorded in the sales journal is proved by comparing the column totals. The proof for the sales journal in Figure 7.4 is given below. All multicolumn special journals should be proved in a similar manner before their totals are posted.

Proof of Sales Journal	
	Debits
Accounts Receivable Debit column	$5,886.00
	Credits
Sales Tax Payable Credit column	$436.00
Sales Credit column	5,450.00
	$5,886.00

After the equality of the debits and credits has been verified, the sales journal is ruled and the column totals are posted to the general ledger accounts involved. To indicate that the postings have been made, the general ledger account numbers are entered in parentheses under the column totals in the sales journal. The abbreviation S1 is written in the Posting Reference column of the accounts, showing that the data was posted from page 1 of the sales journal.

The check marks in the sales journal in Figure 7.4 indicate that the amounts have been posted to the individual customer accounts. Posting from the sales journal to the customer accounts in the subsidiary ledger is illustrated later in this chapter.

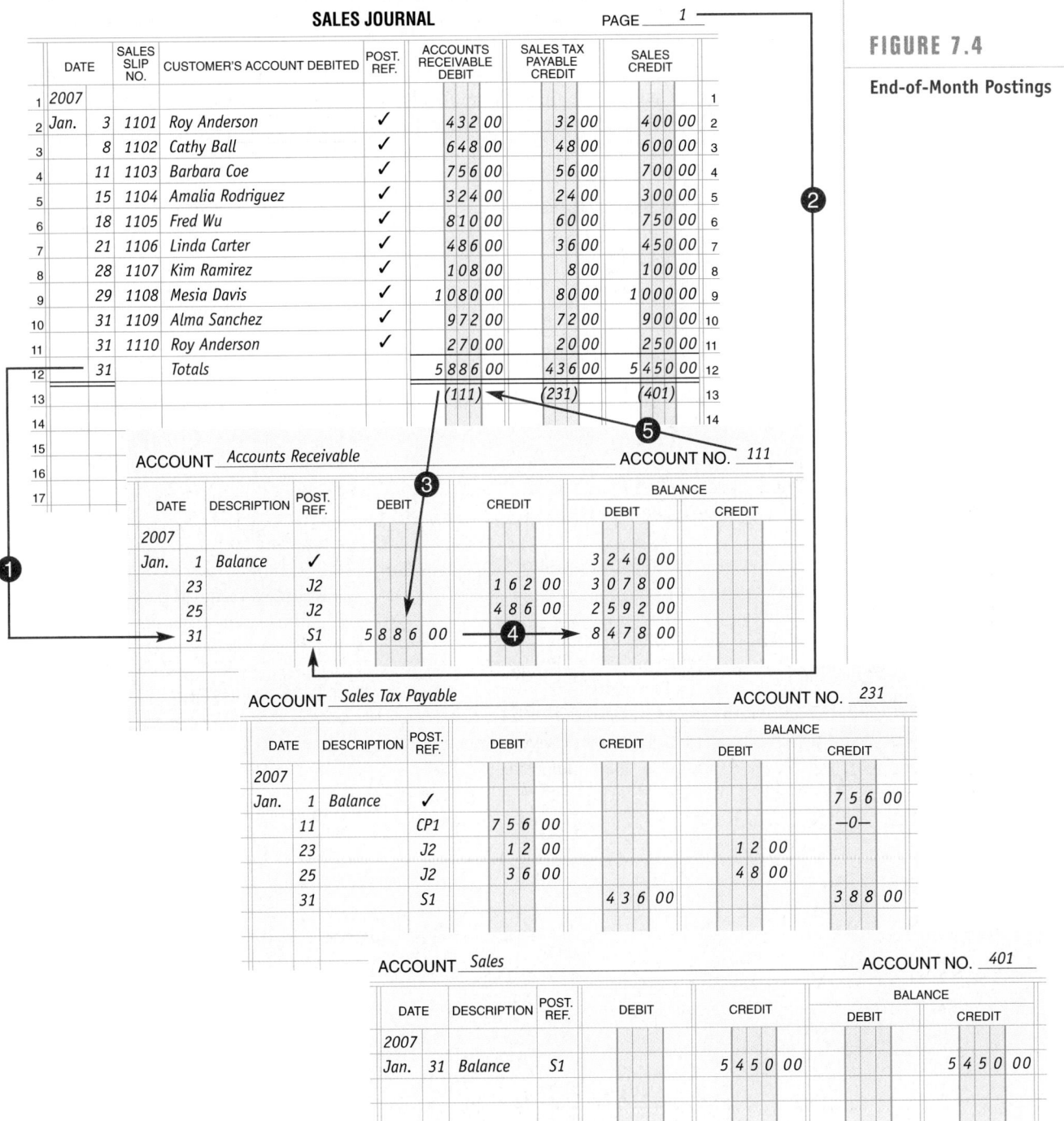

FIGURE 7.4

End-of-Month Postings

ADVANTAGES OF A SALES JOURNAL

Using a special journal for credit sales saves time, effort, and recording space. Both the journalizing process and the posting process become more efficient, but the advantage in the posting process is especially significant. If a business used the general journal to record 300 credit sales a month, the firm would have to make 900 postings to the general ledger—300 to **Accounts Receivable,** 300 to **Sales Tax Payable,** and 300 to **Sales.** With a sales journal, the firm makes only three summary postings to the general ledger at the end of each month no matter how many credit sales were entered.

important!

Posting

When posting from the sales journal, post information moving from left to right across the ledger form.

The use of a sales journal and other special journals also allows division of work. In a business with a fairly large volume of transactions, it is essential that several employees be able to record transactions at the same time.

Finally, the sales journal improves the audit trail by bringing together all entries for credit sales in one place and listing them by source document number as well as by date. This procedure makes it easier to trace the details of such transactions.

Section 1: **Self Review**

QUESTIONS

1. What is a special journal? Give four examples of special journals.

2. What type of transaction is recorded in the sales journal?

3. What is a subsidiary ledger? Give two examples of subsidiary ledgers.

EXERCISES

4. Which of the following is not a reason to use a sales journal?
   a. increases efficiency
   b. allows division of work
   c. increases credit sales
   d. improves audit trail

5. Types of business operations are
   a. service, merchandising, corporation.
   b. sole proprietorship, merchandising, manufacturing.
   c. service, merchandising, manufacturing.

SALES JOURNAL   PAGE 1

	DATE	SALES SLIP NO.	CUSTOMER'S ACCOUNT DEBITED	POST. REF.	ACCOUNTS RECEIVABLE DEBIT	SALES TAX PAYABLE CREDIT	SALES CREDIT	
12	Apr. 25	4100	Carolyn Harris		642 00	42 00	600 00	12
13	25	4101	Teresa Wells		872 00	72 00	900 00	13
14								14

ANALYSIS

6. All sales recorded in this sales journal were made on account and are taxable at a rate of 8 percent. What errors have been made in the entries? Assume the Sales Credit column is correct.

(Answers to Section 1 Self Review are on page 244.)

Accounts Receivable

A business that extends credit to customers must manage its accounts receivable carefully. Accounts receivable represents a substantial asset for many businesses, and this asset must be converted into cash in a timely manner. Otherwise, a firm may not be able to pay its bills even though it has a large volume of sales and earns a satisfactory profit.

The Accounts Receivable Ledger

The accountant needs detailed information about the transactions with credit customers and the balances owed by such customers at all times. This information is provided by an **accounts receivable ledger** with individual accounts for all credit customers. The accounts receivable ledger is referred to as a subsidiary ledger because it is separate from and subordinate to the general ledger.

Using an accounts receivable ledger makes it possible to verify that customers are paying their balances on time and that they are within their credit limits. The accounts receivable ledger also provides a convenient way to answer questions from credit customers. Customers may ask about their current balances or about a possible billing error.

The accounts for credit customers are maintained in a balance ledger form with three money columns, as shown in Figure 7.5 on page 208. Notice that this form does not contain a column for indicating the type of account balance. The balances in the customer accounts are presumed to be debit balances since asset accounts normally have debit balances. However, occasionally there is a credit balance because a customer has overpaid an amount owed or has returned goods that were already paid for. One common procedure for dealing with this situation is to circle the balance in order to show that it is a credit amount.

For a small business such as The Style Shop, customer accounts are alphabetized in the accounts receivable ledger. Larger firms and firms that use computers assign an account number to each credit customer and arrange the customer accounts in numeric order. Postings to the accounts receivable ledger are usually made daily so that the customer accounts can be kept up to date at all times.

POSTING A CREDIT SALE

Each credit sale recorded in the sales journal is posted to the appropriate customer's account in the accounts receivable ledger, as shown in Figure 7.5. The date, the sales slip number, and the

SECTION OBJECTIVES

▶ **3. Post from the sales journal to the customers' accounts in the accounts receivable subsidiary ledger.**

WHY IT'S IMPORTANT

This ledger contains individual records that reflect all transactions of each customer.

▶ **4. Record sales returns and allowances in the general journal.**

WHY IT'S IMPORTANT

Companies can see how much revenue is lost due to merchandise problems.

▶ **5. Post sales returns and allowances.**

WHY IT'S IMPORTANT

Accurate, up-to-date customer records contribute to overall customer satisfaction.

▶ **6. Prepare a schedule of accounts receivable.**

WHY IT'S IMPORTANT

This schedule provides a snapshot of amounts due from customers.

TERMS TO LEARN

accounts receivable ledger
contra revenue account
control account
credit memorandum
net sales
sales allowance
sales return
schedule of accounts receivable

▶ **3. OBJECTIVE**

Post from the sales journal to the customers' accounts in the accounts receivable subsidiary ledger.

FIGURE 7.5

Posting from the Sales Journal
to the Accounts Receivable
Ledger

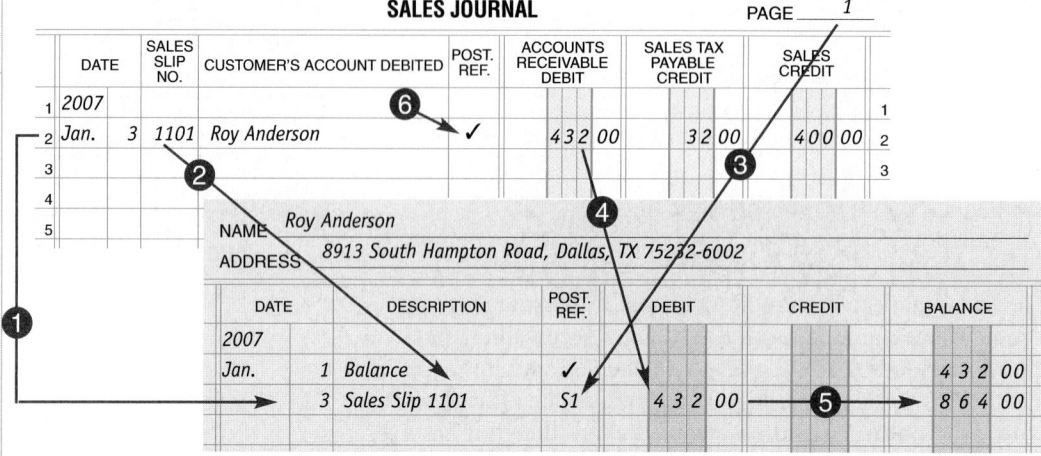

FIGURE 7.6

Posting for Cash Received on
Account

amount that the customer owes as a result of the sale are transferred from the sales journal to the customer's account. The amount is taken from the Accounts Receivable Debit column of the journal and is entered in the Debit column of the account. Next, the new balance is determined and recorded.

To show that the posting has been completed, a check mark (√) is entered in the sales journal and the abbreviation S1 is entered in the Posting Reference column of the customer's account. As noted before, this abbreviation identifies page 1 of the sales journal.

POSTING CASH RECEIVED ON ACCOUNT

When the transaction involves cash received on account from a credit customer, the cash collected is first recorded in a cash receipts journal. (The necessary entry in the cash receipts journal is discussed in Chapter 9.) The cash is then posted to the individual customer account in the accounts receivable ledger. Figure 7.6 shows a posting for cash received on January 7 from John Allen, a credit customer of The Style Shop.

► 4. OBJECTIVE

Record sales returns and allowances in the general journal.

Sales Returns and Allowances

A sale is entered in the accounting records when the goods are sold or the service is provided. If something is wrong with the goods or service, the firm may take back the goods, resulting in a **sales return**, or give the customer a reduction in price, resulting in a **sales allowance**.

When a return or allowance is related to a credit sale, the normal practice is to issue a document called a **credit memorandum** to the customer rather than giving a cash refund. The credit memorandum states that the customer's account is being reduced by the amount of the return or allowance plus any sales tax. A copy of the credit memorandum provides the data needed to enter the transaction in the firm's accounting records.

A debit to the *Sales Returns and Allowances* account is preferred to making a direct debit to *Sales.* This procedure gives a complete record of sales returns and allowances for each accounting period. Business managers use this record as a measure of operating efficiency. The *Sales Returns and Allowances* account is a **contra revenue account** because it has a debit balance, which is contrary, or opposite, to the normal balance for a revenue account.

BUSINESS TRANSACTION

On January 23 The Style Shop issued Credit Memorandum 101 for a sales allowance to Fred Wu for merchandise purchased on account. The merchandise was damaged but still usable.

Wu Style Shop
2007 Trendsetter Lane, Dallas TX 75268-0967

CREDIT MEMORANDUM			NO. 101	
ORIGINAL SALES DATE	ORIGINAL SALES SLIP	APPROVAL	X	MDSE RET
Dec. 29, 2006	No. 1105	S.H.		

DATE: *January 23, 2007*

NAME: *Fred Wu.*
ADDRESS: *4640 Walnut Hill Lane*
Dallas, TX 75267-6205

Fred Wu
CUSTOMER SIGNATURE

QTY	DESCRIPTION	AMOUNT
1	Athletic Suit	
		$150:00
REASON FOR RETURN *damaged*	SUB TOTAL	$150:00
THE TOTAL SHOWN AT THE RIGHT WILL BE CREDITED TO YOUR ACCOUNT.	SALES TAX	12:00
	TOTAL	$162:00

ANALYSIS

The contra revenue account, *Sales Returns and Allowances,* is increased by $150. The liability account, *Sales Tax Payable,* is decreased by $12. The asset account, *Accounts Receivable,* is decreased by $162.

DEBIT-CREDIT RULES

DEBIT Increases to a contra revenue account are recorded as debits. Debit *Sales Returns and Allowances* for $150. Decreases to liability accounts are recorded as debits. Debit *Sales Tax Payable* for $12.

CREDIT Decreases to an asset account are recorded as credits. Credit *Accounts Receivable* for $162.

T-ACCOUNT PRESENTATION

Sales Returns and Allowances		Sales Tax Payable		Accounts Receivable	
+	−	−	+	+	−
150		12			162

GENERAL JOURNAL ENTRY

GENERAL JOURNAL PAGE 1

	DATE	DESCRIPTION	POST. REF.	DEBIT	CREDIT	
1	2007					1
2	Jan. 23	Sales Returns and Allowances		1 5 0 00		2
3		Sales Tax Payable		1 2 00		3
4		Accts. Rec.—Fred Wu			1 6 2 00	4

THE BOTTOM LINE
Allowance for Damaged Merchandise

Income Statement

Contra Revenue	↑ 150
Net Income	↓ 150

Balance Sheet

Assets	↓ 162
Liabilities	↓ 12
Equity	↓ 150

What is the ultimate effect of this transaction on the financial statements? An increase in contra revenue causes a decrease in net income. Note that the $150 decrease in net income causes a $150 decrease in owner's equity. The asset *Accounts Receivable* is decreased, and the liability *Sales Tax Payable* is also decreased. The eventual effect of this transaction on the income statement and the balance sheet is summarized in the box titled *The Bottom Line.*

RECORDING SALES RETURNS AND ALLOWANCES

Depending on the volume of sales returns and allowances, a business may use a general journal to record these transactions, or it may use a special sales returns and allowances journal.

Using the General Journal for Sales Returns and Allowances A small firm that has a limited number of sales returns and allowances each month has no need to establish a special journal for such transactions. Instead, the required entries are made in the general journal.

Using a Sales Returns and Allowances Journal In a business having many sales returns and allowances, it is efficient to use a special journal for these transactions. An example of a *sales returns and allowances journal* is shown in Figure 7.7.

POSTING A SALES RETURN OR ALLOWANCE

▶ **5. OBJECTIVE**

Post sales returns and allowances.

Whether sales returns and allowances are recorded in the general journal or in a special sales returns and allowances journal, each of these transactions must be posted from the general ledger to the appropriate customer's account in the accounts receivable ledger. Figure 7.8 below shows how a return of merchandise was posted from the general journal to the account of Linda Carter.

FIGURE 7.7

Sales Returns and Allowances Journal

SALES RETURNS AND ALLOWANCES JOURNAL   PAGE ___8___

	DATE	SALES SLIP NO.	CUSTOMER'S ACCOUNT CREDITED	POST. REF.	ACCOUNTS RECEIVABLE CREDIT	SALES TAX PAYABLE DEBIT	SALES RET. & ALLOW. DEBIT	
1	2007							1
2	Jan. 23	1105	Fred Wu	✓	162 00	12 00	150 00	2
3	25	1106	Linda Carter	✓	486 00	36 00	450 00	3
4								4
17	31		Totals		3 240 00	240 00	3 000 00	17
18					(111)	(231)	(451)	18
19								19

FIGURE 7.8

Posting a Sales Return to the Customer's Account

GENERAL JOURNAL   PAGE ___1___

	DATE	DESCRIPTION	POST. REF.	DEBIT	CREDIT	
1	2007					1
6	Jan. 25	Sales Returns and Allowances	451	4 50 00		6
7		Sales Tax Payable	231	3 6 00		7
8		Accounts Rec./Linda Carter	111 ✓		4 86 00	8
9		Accepted a return of				9
10		defective merchandise,				10
11		Credit Memorandum 102;				11
12		original sale made on Sales				12
13		Slip 1106 of January 21.				13
14						14
15						15

NAME Linda Carter
ADDRESS 1819 Belt Line Road, Dallas, Texas 75267-6318

DATE	DESCRIPTION	POST. REF.	DEBIT	CREDIT	BALANCE
2007					
Jan. 1	Balance	✓			5 4 00
21	Sales Slip 1106	S1	4 86 00		5 40 00
25	CM 102	J1		4 86 00	5 4 00

Because the credit amount in the general journal entry for this transaction requires two postings, the account number 111 and a check mark are entered in the Posting Reference column of the journal. The 111 indicates that the amount was posted to the *Accounts Receivable* account in the general ledger, and the check mark indicates that the amount was posted to the customer's account in the accounts receivable ledger. Notice that a diagonal line was used to separate the two posting references.

Refer to Figure 7.7, which shows a special sales returns and allowances journal instead of a general journal. The account numbers at the bottom of each column are the posting references for the three general ledger accounts: *Accounts Receivable, Sales Tax Payable,* and *Sales Returns and Allowances.* The check marks in the Posting Reference column show that the credits were posted to individual customer accounts in the accounts receivable subsidiary ledger.

Remember that a business can use the general journal or special journals for transactions related to credit sales. A special journal is an efficient option for recording and posting large numbers of transactions.

Figure 7.9 on pages 212–213 shows the accounts receivable ledger after posting is completed.

REPORTING NET SALES

At the end of each accounting period, the balance of the *Sales Returns and Allowances* account is subtracted from the balance of the *Sales* account in the Revenue section of the income statement. The resulting figure is the **net sales** for the period.

For example, the *Sales Returns and Allowances* account contains a balance of $600 at the end of January. The *Sales* account has a balance of $25,700 at the end of January. The Revenue section of the firm's income statement will appear as follows.

THE STYLE SHOP Income Statement (Partial) Month Ended January 31, 2007	
Revenue	
Sales	$25,700
Less Sales Returns and Allowances	600
Net Sales	$25,100

ABOUT
ACCOUNTING

Investing in Ethics
Are ethical companies—those with a strong internal enforcement policy—really more profitable? Yes, such companies are listed among the top 100 financial performers twice as often as those without an ethics focus, according to a study by Curtis Verschoor at DePaul University.

COMPUTERS IN ACCOUNTING <<

SALES AND FULFILLMENT SYSTEMS

One definition of "fulfill" is "to meet the requirements of a business order."* Department stores like Macy's and Bloomingdale's have developed sophisticated order processing systems for physical store locations and Web site operations.

When a customer places an order online using a credit card, data such as the customer's account number, the product identification number, product attributes like color and size, and the quantity ordered are transmitted to the company fulfillment and credit processing systems. These computerized systems review the data to verify item availability and to secure credit approval. Seconds later, the customer receives an on-screen confirmation, containing order total, sales tax, and shipping details. Behind the scenes, packing slips are generated at the company's fulfillment centers and the customer's order is packed and shipped per the customer's instructions.

Advanced sales and order systems can also identify sales trends by product and by geographic region, and they can pinpoint the most popular purchasing times of the day.

THINKING CRITICALLY
How might management use these reporting features to its benefit?

INTERNET APPLICATION
Visit the Federal Trade Commission Web site to learn more about electronic commerce. Choose an article about e-commerce under *Consumer Protection*. Write a summary of the article.

Merriam-Webster's Collegiate Dictionary, Tenth Edition

FIGURE 7.9

Accounts Receivable Ledger

NAME _Roy Anderson_
ADDRESS _8913 South Hampton Road, Dallas, Texas 75232-6002_

DATE		DESCRIPTION	POST. REF.	DEBIT	CREDIT	BALANCE
2007						
Jan.	1	Balance	✓			4 3 2 00
	3	Sales Slip 1101	S1	4 3 2 00		8 6 4 00
	7		CR1		4 3 2 00	4 3 2 00
	31	Sales Slip 1110	S1	2 7 0 00		7 0 2 00

NAME _Cathy Ball_
ADDRESS _7517 Woodrow Wilson Lane, Dallas, Texas 75267-6205_

DATE		DESCRIPTION	POST. REF.	DEBIT	CREDIT	BALANCE
2007						
Jan.	8	Sales Slip 1102	S1	6 4 8 00		6 4 8 00

NAME _Vickie Bowman_
ADDRESS _1712 Red Bird Lane, Dallas, Texas 75267-6502_

DATE		DESCRIPTION	POST. REF.	DEBIT	CREDIT	BALANCE
2007						
Jan.	1	Balance	✓			2 7 0 00
	11		CR1		2 7 0 00	—0—

NAME _Linda Carter_
ADDRESS _1819 Belt Line Road, Dallas, Texas 75267-6318_

DATE		DESCRIPTION	POST. REF.	DEBIT	CREDIT	BALANCE
2007						
Jan.	1	Balance	✓			5 4 00
	21	Sales Slip 1104	S1	4 8 6 00		5 4 0 00
	25	CM 102	J1		4 8 6 00	5 4 00

NAME _Barbara Coe_
ADDRESS _1864 Elm Street, Dallas, Texas 75267-6205_

DATE		DESCRIPTION	POST. REF.	DEBIT	CREDIT	BALANCE
2007						
Jan.	1	Balance	✓			1 0 8 0 00
	11	Sales Slip 1103	S1	7 5 6 00		1 8 3 6 00
	13		CR1		5 4 0 00	1 2 9 6 00

NAME _Mesia Davis_

ADDRESS _1008 University Boulevard, Dallas, Texas 75267-6318_

DATE		DESCRIPTION	POST. REF.	DEBIT	CREDIT	BALANCE
2007						
Jan.	1	Balance	✓			2 1 6 00
	29	Sales Slip 1108	S1	1 0 8 0 00		1 2 9 6 00
	31		CR1		2 7 5 00	1 0 2 1 00

NAME _Kim Ramirez_

ADDRESS _5787 Valley View Lane, Dallas, Texas 75267-6318_

DATE		DESCRIPTION	POST. REF.	DEBIT	CREDIT	BALANCE
2007						
Jan.	1	Balance	✓			2 1 6 00
	28	Sales Slip 1107	S1	1 0 8 00		3 2 4 00
	31		CR1		1 0 8 00	2 1 6 00

NAME _Amalia Rodriguez_

ADDRESS _8108 Sherman Drive, Dallas, Texas 75267-6205_

DATE		DESCRIPTION	POST. REF.	DEBIT	CREDIT	BALANCE
2007						
Jan.	1	Balance	✓			6 4 8 00
	15	Sales Slip 1106	S1	3 2 4 00		9 7 2 00

NAME _Alma Sanchez_

ADDRESS _1382 Clark Road, Dallas, Texas 75267-6205_

DATE		DESCRIPTION	POST. REF.	DEBIT	CREDIT	BALANCE
2007						
Jan.	1	Balance	✓			1 0 8 00
	16		CR1		1 0 8 00	—0—
	31	Sales Slip 1109	S1	9 7 2 00		9 7 2 00

NAME _Fred Wu_

ADDRESS _4640 Walnut Hill Lane, Dallas, Texas 75267-6205_

DATE		DESCRIPTION	POST. REF.	DEBIT	CREDIT	BALANCE
2007						
Jan.	1	Balance	✓			2 1 6 00
	18	Sales Slip 1105	S1	8 1 0 00		1 0 2 6 00
	22		CR1		4 0 0 00	6 2 6 00
	23	CM 101	J1		1 6 2 00	4 6 4 00

► 6. OBJECTIVE

Prepare a schedule of
accounts receivable.

Schedule of Accounts Receivable

The use of an accounts receivable ledger does not eliminate the need for the **Accounts Receivable** account in the general ledger. This account remains in the general ledger and continues to appear on the balance sheet at the end of each fiscal period. However, the **Accounts Receivable** account is now considered a control account. A **control account** serves as a link between a subsidiary ledger and the general ledger. Its balance summarizes the balances of its related accounts in the subsidiary ledger.

At the end of each month, after all the postings have been made from the sales journal, the cash receipts journal, and the general journal to the accounts receivable ledger, the balances in the accounts receivable ledger must be proved against the balance of the **Accounts Receivable** general ledger account. First a **schedule of accounts receivable**, which lists the subsidiary ledger account balances, is prepared. The total of the schedule is compared with the balance of the **Accounts Receivable** account. If the two figures are not equal, errors must be located and corrected.

On January 31 the accounts receivable ledger at The Style Shop contains the accounts shown in Figure 7.9. To prepare a schedule of accounts receivable, the names of all customers with account balances are listed with the amount of their unpaid balances. Next the figures are added to find the total owed to the business by its credit customers.

> Federated Department Stores, Inc. reported accounts receivable of $3.21 billion or 22.1 percent of the corporation's total assets at January 30, 2004.

A comparison of the total of the schedule of accounts receivable prepared at The Style Shop on January 31 and the balance of the **Accounts Receivable** account in the general ledger shows that the two figures are the same, as shown in Figure 7.10. The posting reference CR1 refers to the cash receipts journal, which is discussed in Chapter 9.

FIGURE 7.10

Schedule of Accounts
Receivable and Accounts
Receivable Account

The Style Shop
Schedule of Accounts Receivable
January 31, 2007

Roy Anderson	7 0 2 00
Cathy Ball	6 4 8 00
Linda Carter	5 4 00
Barbara Coe	1 2 9 6 00
Mesia Davis	1 0 2 1 00
Kim Ramirez	2 1 6 00
Amalia Rodriguez	9 7 2 00
Alma Sanchez	9 7 2 00
Fred Wu	4 6 4 00
Total	6 3 4 5 00

ACCOUNT _Accounts Receivable_   ACCOUNT NO. _111_

DATE		DESCRIPTION	POST. REF.	DEBIT	CREDIT	BALANCE DEBIT	BALANCE CREDIT
2007							
Jan.	1	Balance	✓			3 2 4 0 00	
	23		J1		1 6 2 00	3 0 7 8 00	
	25		J1		4 8 6 00	2 5 9 2 00	
	31		S1	5 8 8 6 00		8 4 7 8 00	
	31		CR1		2 1 3 3 00	6 3 4 5 00	

In addition to providing a proof of the subsidiary ledger, the schedule of accounts receivable serves another function. It reports information about the firm's accounts receivable at the end of the month. Management can review the schedule to see exactly how much each customer owes.

Section 2: **Self Review**

QUESTIONS

1. What are net sales?
2. What is a sales return?
   What is a sales allowance?
3. Which accounts are kept in the accounts receivable ledger?

EXERCISES

4. Which of the following general ledger accounts would appear in a sales returns and allowances journal?

   a. *Sales Returns and Allowances, Sales Tax Payable, Accounts Receivable*
   b. *Sales Returns and Allowances, Sales, Accounts Receivable*
   c. *Sales Returns, Sales Allowances, Sales*

5. Where would you report net sales?

   a. sales general ledger account
   b. general journal
   c. income statement
   d. sales journal

ANALYSIS

6. Draw a diagram showing the relationship between the accounts receivable ledger, the schedule of accounts receivable, and the general ledger.

(Answers to Section 2 Self Review are on page 244.)

Section 3

SECTION OBJECTIVES

▶ **7. Compute trade discounts.**

WHY IT'S IMPORTANT

Trade discounts allow for flexible pricing structures.

▶ **8. Record credit card sales in appropriate journals.**

WHY IT'S IMPORTANT

Credit cards are widely used in merchandising transactions.

▶ **9. Prepare the state sales tax return.**

WHY IT'S IMPORTANT

Businesses are legally responsible for accurately reporting and remitting sales taxes.

TERMS TO LEARN

charge-account sales
invoice
list price
net price
open-account credit
trade discount
wholesale business

Merchandisers have many accounting concerns. These include pricing, credit, and sales taxes.

Credit Sales for a Wholesale Business

The operations of The Style Shop are typical of those of many retail businesses—businesses that sell goods and services directly to individual consumers. In contrast, a **wholesale business** is a manufacturer or distributor of goods that sells to retailers or large consumers such as hotels and hospitals. The basic procedures used by wholesalers to handle sales and accounts receivable are the same as those used by retailers. However, many wholesalers offer cash discounts and trade discounts, which are not commonly found in retail operations.

The procedures used in connection with cash discounts are examined in Chapter 9. The handling of trade discounts is described here.

COMPUTING TRADE DISCOUNTS

A wholesale business offers goods to trade customers at less than retail prices. This price adjustment is based on the volume purchased by trade customers and takes the form of a **trade discount**, which is a reduction from the **list price**—the established retail price. There may be a single trade discount or a series of discounts for each type of goods. The **net price** (list price less all trade discounts) is the amount the wholesaler records in its sales journal.

The same goods may be offered to different customers at different trade discounts, depending on the size of the order and the costs of selling to the various types of customers.

▶ **7. OBJECTIVE**

Compute trade discounts.

important!

Trade Discounts

The amount of sales revenue recorded is the list price minus the trade discount.

Single Trade Discount Suppose the list price of goods is $1,500 and the trade discount is 40 percent. The amount of the discount is $600, and the net price to be shown on the invoice and recorded in the sales journal is $900.

List price	$1,500
Less 40% discount ($1,500 × 0.40)	600
Invoice price	$ 900

Series of Trade Discounts If the list price of goods is $1,500 and the trade discount is quoted in a series such as 25 and 15 percent, a different net price will result.

List price	$1,500.00
Less first discount ($1,500 × 0.25)	375.00
Difference	$1,125.00
Less second discount ($1,125 × 0.15)	168.75
Invoice price	$ 956.25

important!

Special Journal Format
Special journals such as the sales journal can vary in format from company to company.

USING A SALES JOURNAL FOR A WHOLESALE BUSINESS

Since sales taxes apply only to retail transactions, a wholesale business does not need to account for such taxes. Its sales journal may therefore be as simple as the one illustrated in Figure 7.11. This sales journal has a single amount column. The total of this column is posted to the general ledger at the end of the month as a debit to the **Accounts Receivable** account and a credit to the **Sales** account (Figure 7.12). During the month the individual entries in the sales journal are posted to the customer accounts in the accounts receivable ledger.

Wholesale businesses issue invoices. An **invoice** is a customer billing for merchandise bought on credit. Copies of the invoices are used to enter the transactions in the sales journal.

The next merchandising topic, credit policies, applies to both wholesalers and retailers. The discussion in this textbook focuses on credit policies and accounting for retail firms.

SALES JOURNAL   PAGE ___1___

	DATE	INVOICE NO.	CUSTOMER'S ACCOUNT DEBITED	POST. REF.	ACCOUNTS RECEIVABLE DR. SALES CR.	
1	2007					1
2	Jan. 3	7099	Gabbert's Hardware Company		1 8 6 0 0 00	2
3						3
25	31	7151	Neal's Department Store		1 2 0 0 00	25
26	31		Total		40 8 7 5 00	26
27					(111/401)	27
28						28

FIGURE 7.11

Wholesaler's Sales Journal

ACCOUNT __Accounts Receivable__   ACCOUNT NO. __111__

		POST.			BALANCE	
DATE	DESCRIPTION	REF.	DEBIT	CREDIT	DEBIT	CREDIT
2007						
Jan. 1	Balance	✓			46 7 0 0 00	
31		S1	40 8 7 5 00		87 5 7 5 00	

ACCOUNT __Sales__   ACCOUNT NO. __401__

		POST.			BALANCE	
DATE	DESCRIPTION	REF.	DEBIT	CREDIT	DEBIT	CREDIT
2007						
Jan. 31		S1		40 8 7 5 00		40 8 7 5 00

FIGURE 7.12

General Ledger Accounts

Credit Policies

The use of credit is considered to be one of the most important factors in the rapid growth of modern economic systems. Sales on credit are made by large numbers of wholesalers and retailers of goods and by many professional people and service businesses. The assumption is that the volume of both sales and profits will increase if buyers are given a period of a month or more to pay for the goods or services they purchase.

However, the increase in profits a business expects when it grants credit will be realized only if each customer completes the transaction by paying for the goods or services purchased. If payment is not received, the expected profits become actual losses and the purpose for granting the credit is defeated. Business firms try to protect against the possibility of such losses by investigating a customer's credit record and ability to pay for purchases before allowing any credit to the customer.

Professional people, such as doctors, lawyers, and architects, and owners of small businesses like The Style Shop usually make their own decisions about granting credit. Such decisions may be based on personal judgment or on reports available from credit bureaus, information supplied by other creditors, and credit ratings supplied by national firms such as Dun & Bradstreet.

> Equifax, a leader in providing consumer and commercial credit information, was founded in Atlanta in 1899. For the fiscal year ended December 2003, 100 years later, the company reported revenues of $1.23 billion.

Larger businesses maintain a credit department to determine the amounts and types of credit that should be granted to customers. In addition to using credit data supplied by institutions, the credit department may obtain financial statements and related reports from customers who have applied for credit. This information is analyzed to help determine the maximum amount of credit that may be granted and suitable credit terms for the customer. Financial statements that have been audited by certified public accountants are used extensively by credit departments.

Even though the credit investigation is thorough, some accounts receivable become uncollectible. Unexpected business developments, errors of judgment, incorrect financial data, and many other causes may lead to defaults in payments by customers. Experienced managers know that some uncollectible accounts are to be expected in normal business operations and that limited losses indicate that a firm's credit policies are sound. Provisions for such limited losses from uncollectible accounts are usually made in budgets and other financial projections.

Each business must develop credit policies that achieve maximum sales with minimum losses from uncollectible accounts:

- A credit policy that is too tight results in a low level of losses at the expense of increases in sales volume.

- A credit policy that is too lenient may result in increased sales volume accompanied by a high level of losses.

Good judgment based on knowledge and experience must be used to achieve a well balanced credit policy.

Different types of credit have evolved with the growing economy and changing technology. The different types of credit require different accounting treatments.

ACCOUNTING FOR DIFFERENT TYPES OF CREDIT SALES

The most common types of credit sales are

- open-account credit,
- business credit cards,
- bank credit cards,
- cards issued by credit card companies.

International INSIGHTS

Bank Credit Cards

Using a bank credit card is one of the best ways to acquire money when conducting business in another country because you get the bank's exchange rate.

Open-Account Credit The form of credit most commonly offered by professional people and small businesses permits the sale of services or goods to the customer with the understanding that the amount is to be paid at a later date. This type of arrangement is called **open-account credit** . It is usually granted on the basis of personal acquaintance or knowledge of the customer. However, formal credit checks may also be used. The amount involved in each transaction is usually small, and payment is expected within 30 days or on receipt of a monthly statement. Open-account sales are also referred to as **charge-account sales** .

The Style Shop uses the open-account credit arrangement. Sales transactions are recorded as debits to the *Accounts Receivable* account and credits to the *Sales* account. Collections on account are recorded as debits to the *Cash* account and credits to the *Accounts Receivable* account.

Business Credit Cards Many retail businesses, especially large ones such as department store chains and gasoline companies, provide their own credit cards (sometimes called charge cards) to customers who have established credit. Whenever a sale is completed using a business credit card, a sales slip is prepared in the usual manner. Then the sales slip and the credit card are placed in a mechanical device that prints the customer's name, account number, and other data on all copies of the sales slip. Some companies use computerized card readers and sales registers that print out a sales slip with the customer information and a line for the customer's signature. Many businesses require that the salesclerk contact the credit department by telephone or computer terminal to verify the customer's credit status before completing the transaction.

Business credit card sales are similar to open-account credit sales. A business credit card sale is recorded as

- a debit to *Accounts Receivable,*
- a credit to a revenue account such as *Sales.*

A customer payment is recorded as

- a debit to *Cash,*
- a credit to *Accounts Receivable.*

Bank Credit Cards Retailers can provide credit while minimizing or avoiding the risk of losses from uncollectible accounts by accepting bank credit cards. The most widely accepted bank credit cards are MasterCard and Visa. Many banks participate in one or both of these credit card programs, and other banks have their own credit cards. Bank credit cards are issued to consumers directly by banks.

A business may participate in these credit card programs by meeting the conditions set by the bank. When a sale is made to a cardholder, the business completes a special sales slip such as the one shown in Figure 7.13 below. This form must be imprinted with data from the

FIGURE 7.13 | **Sales Slip for a Bank Credit Card Transaction**

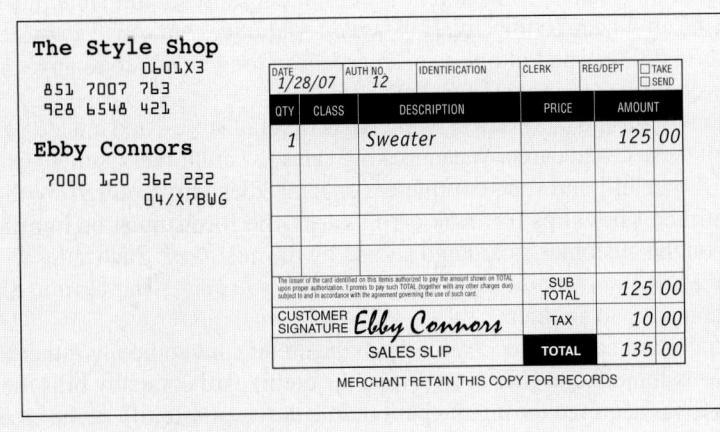
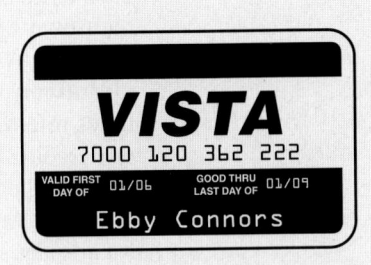

FIGURE 7.14

Deposit Form for Bank Credit
Card Sales

FIGURE 7.14

Deposit Form for Bank Credit Card Sales

The Style Shop

851 7007 763

928 6548 421

Attach calculator tape to Bank Copy when more than one sales slip is enclosed.

X *Mary Amos*

MERCHANT SIGNATURE

DATE _____

ITEM	NO. SLIPS	AMOUNT	
Total Sales	10	2700	00
LESS: Total Credits			
NET SALES		2700	00
LESS: DISCOUNT __3__ %		81	00
NET AMOUNT		2619	00

VISTA MERCHANT
SUMMARY SLIP

customer's bank credit card and then signed by the customer. Many businesses continue to complete their regular sales slips for internal control and other purposes.

When a business makes a sale on a bank credit card, it acquires an asset that can be converted into cash immediately without responsibility for later collection from the customer. Periodically (preferably each day) the completed sales slips from bank credit card sales are totaled. The number of sales slips and the total amount of the sales are recorded on a special deposit form, as shown in Figure 7.14.

The deposit form, along with the completed sales slips, is presented to the firm's bank in much the same manner as a cash deposit. Depending on the arrangements that have been made, either the bank will deduct a fee, called a *discount* (usually between 1 and 8 percent), and immediately credit the depositor's checking account with the net amount of the sales, or it will credit the depositor's checking account for the full amount of the sales and then deduct the discount at the end of the month. If the second procedure is used, the total discount for the month will appear on the bank statement.

The bank is responsible for collecting from the cardholder. If any amounts are uncollectible, the bank sustains the loss. For the retailer, bank credit card sales are like cash sales. The accounting procedures for such sales are therefore quite similar to the accounting procedures for cash sales, which will be discussed in Chapter 9. If the business is billed once each month for the bank's discount, the total amount involved in the daily deposit of the credit card sales slips is debited to **Cash** and credited to **Sales.**

Credit Card Companies Credit cards such as American Express and Diners Club are issued by business firms or subsidiaries of business firms that are operated for the special purpose of handling credit card transactions. The potential cardholder must submit an application and pay an annual fee to the credit card company. If the credit references are satisfactory, the credit card is issued. It is normally reissued at one-year intervals so long as the company's credit experience with the cardholder remains satisfactory.

Hotels, restaurants, airline companies, many types of retail stores, and a wide variety of other businesses accept these credit cards. When making sales to cardholders, sellers usually prepare their own sales slip or bill and then complete a special sales slip required by the credit card company. As with the sales slips for bank credit cards, the forms must be imprinted with the identifying data on the customer's card and signed by the customer. Such sales slips are sometimes referred to as *sales invoices, sales drafts,* or *sales vouchers.* The term used varies from one credit card company to another.

The seller acquires an account receivable from the credit card company rather than from the customer. At approximately one-month intervals, the credit card company bills the cardholders for all sales slips it has acquired during the period. It is the responsibility of the credit card company to collect from the cardholders.

ACCOUNTING FOR CREDIT CARD SALES

The procedure used to account for credit card sales is similar to the procedure for recording open-account credit sales. However, the account receivable is with the credit card company, not with the cardholders who buy the goods or services.

There are two basic methods of recording these sales. Businesses that have few transactions with credit card companies normally debit the amounts of such sales to the usual *Accounts Receivable* account in the general ledger and credit them to the same *Sales* account that is used for cash sales and other types of credit sales. An individual account for each credit card company is set up in the accounts receivable subsidiary ledger. This method of recording sales is shown in Figure 7.15.

Payment from a credit card company is recorded in the cash receipts journal, a procedure discussed in Chapter 9. Fees charged by the credit card companies for processing these sales are debited to an account called *Discount Expense on Credit Card Sales.* For example, assume that American Express charges a 7 percent discount fee on the sale charged by Wilson Davis on January 3 and remits the balance to the firm. This transaction would be recorded in the cash receipts journal by debiting *Cash* for $502.20, debiting *Discount Expense on Credit Card Sales* for $37.80, and crediting *Accounts Receivable* for $540.00.

Firms that do a large volume of business with credit card companies may debit all such sales to a special *Accounts Receivable from Credit Card Companies* account in the general ledger, thus separating this type of receivable from the accounts receivable resulting from open-account credit sales. A special account called *Sales—Credit Card Companies* is credited for the revenue from these transactions. Figure 7.16 shows how the necessary entries are made in the sales journal.

▶ **8. OBJECTIVE**

Record credit card sales in appropriate journals.

FIGURE 7.15

Recording Credit Card Company Sales

SALES JOURNAL   PAGE __17__

	DATE	SALES SLIP NO.	CUSTOMER'S ACCOUNT DEBITED	POST. REF.	ACCOUNTS RECEIVABLE DEBIT	SALES TAX PAYABLE CREDIT	SALES CREDIT	
1	2007							1
2	Jan. 3	533	American Express		540 00	40 00	500 00	2
3			(Wilson Davis)					3
26		11	651	Master Card		216 00	16 00	200 00	26
27			(Teresa Wells)					27
28								28

FIGURE 7.16   Recording Sales for Accounts Receivable from Credit Card Companies

SALES JOURNAL   PAGE __7__

	DATE	SALES SLIP NO.	CUSTOMER'S ACCOUNT DEBITED	POST. REF.	ACCOUNTS RECEIVABLE DEBIT	ACCT. REC.— CREDIT CARD COMPANIES DEBIT	SALES TAX PAYABLE CREDIT	SALES CREDIT	SALES— CREDIT CARD COMPANIES CREDIT	
1	2007									1
2	Jan. 3		Summary of credit card sales/			9 720 00	720 00		9 000 00	2
3			American Express							3
5										5
16		11	Summary of credit card sales/			5 400 00	400 00		5 000 00	16
17			Master Card							17
29		31	Totals			48 600 00	3 600 00		45 000 00	29
30						(114)	(231)		(404)	30
31										31

Sales Taxes

Many cities and states impose a tax on retail sales. Sales taxes imposed by city and state governments vary. However, the procedures used to account for these taxes are similar.

A sales tax may be levied on all retail sales, but often certain items are exempt. In most cases the amount of the sales tax is stated separately and then added to the retail price of the merchandise.

> The California State Board of Equalization collects approximately $22.9 billion dollars annually from sales tax revenues. These revenues foot the bill for state and local programs, including hospitals, social welfare efforts, transportation, schools, and housing.

The retailer is required to collect sales tax from customers, make periodic (usually monthly) reports to the taxing authority, and pay the taxes due when the reports are filed. The government may allow the retailer to retain part of the tax as compensation for collecting it.

▶ 9. OBJECTIVE

Prepare the state sales tax return.

PREPARING THE STATE SALES TAX RETURN

At the end of each month, after the accounts have all been posted, The Style Shop prepares the sales tax return. The information required for the monthly return comes from the accounting data of the current month. Three accounts are involved: **Sales Tax Payable, Sales,** and **Sales Returns and Allowances.** In some states the sales tax return is filed quarterly rather than monthly.

The procedures to file a sales tax return are similar to those used by The Style Shop on February 7 when it filed the monthly sales tax return for January with the state tax commissioner. The firm's sales are subject to an 8 percent state sales tax. To highlight the data needed, the January postings are shown in the ledger accounts in Figure 7.17.

FIGURE 7.17

Ledger Account Postings for Sales Tax

ACCOUNT Sales Tax Payable   ACCOUNT NO. 231

DATE		DESCRIPTION	POST. REF.	DEBIT	CREDIT	BALANCE DEBIT	BALANCE CREDIT
20--							
Jan.	1	Balance	✓				7 5 6 00
	11		CP1	7 5 6 00			—0—
	23		J1	1 2 00		1 2 00	
	25		J1	3 6 00		4 8 00	
	31		S1		4 3 6 00		3 8 8 00
	31		CR1		1 8 0 0 00		2 1 8 8 00

ACCOUNT Sales   ACCOUNT NO. 401

DATE		DESCRIPTION	POST. REF.	DEBIT	CREDIT	BALANCE DEBIT	BALANCE CREDIT
2007							
Jan.	31		S1		5 4 5 0 00		5 4 5 0 00
	31		CR1		22 5 0 0 00		27 9 5 0 00

ACCOUNT Sales Returns and Allowances   ACCOUNT NO. 451

DATE		DESCRIPTION	POST. REF.	DEBIT	CREDIT	BALANCE DEBIT	BALANCE CREDIT
2007							
Jan.	23		J1	1 5 0 00		1 5 0 00	
	25		J1	4 5 0 00		6 0 0 00	

Using these figures as a basis, the amount of the firm's taxable gross sales for January is determined as follows:

Cash Sales	$22,500
Credit Sales	5,450
Total Sales	$27,950
Less Sales Returns and Allowances	600
Taxable Gross Sales for January	$27,350

The 8 percent sales tax on the gross sales of $27,350 amounts to $2,188.00. Note that the firm's increase in assets (**Cash** and **Accounts Receivable**) is equal to sales revenue plus the sales tax liability on that revenue.

In the state where The Style Shop is located, a retailer who files the sales tax return (see Figure 7.18 on page 224) on time and who pays the tax when it is due is entitled to a discount. The discount is intended to compensate the retailer, at least in part, for acting as a collection agent for the government. The discount rate depends on the amount of tax to be paid. For amounts over $1,000, the rate is 1 percent of the total tax due. For The Style Shop, the discount for January is determined as follows:

Taxable Gross Sales for January	$27,350.00
8% Sales Tax Rate	× 0.08
Sales Tax Due	$ 2,188.00
1% Discount Rate	× 0.01
Discount	$21.88
Sales Tax Due	$ 2,188.00
Discount	(21.88)
Net Sales Tax Due	$ 2,166.12

The firm sends a check for the net sales tax due with the sales tax return. The accounting entry made to record this payment includes a debit to **Sales Tax Payable** and a credit to **Cash** (for $2,166.12 in this case). After the amount of the payment is posted, the balance in the **Sales Tax Payable** account should be equal to the discount, as shown in Figure 7.19. Slight differences can arise because the tax collected at the time of the sale is determined by a tax bracket method that can give results slightly more or less than the final computations on the tax return.

THE BOTTOM LINE
Retail Sales

Income Statement

Revenue	↑	27,350.00
Net Income	↑	27,350.00

Balance Sheet

Assets	↑	29,538.00
Liabilities	↑	2,188.00
Equity	↑	27,350.00

ACCOUNT _Sales Tax Payable_   ACCOUNT NO. _231_

DATE		DESCRIPTION	POST. REF.	DEBIT	CREDIT	BALANCE DEBIT	BALANCE CREDIT
2007							
Jan.	1	Balance	✓				7 5 6 00
	11		CP1	7 5 6 00			—0—
	23		J1	1 2 00		1 2 00	
	25		J1	3 6 00		4 8 00	
	31		S1		4 3 6 00		3 8 8 00
	31		CR1		1 8 0 0 00		2 1 8 8 00
Feb.	6		CP1	2 1 6 6 12			2 1 88

Tax payment ⸺⸺⸺   Amount of discount ⸺⸺⸺

FIGURE 7.19

Effect of Paying Sales Tax

SALES TAX RETURN

ALWAYS REFER TO THIS NUMBER WHEN WRITING THE DIVISION →	LICENSE NUMBER 217539

—IMPORTANT—
ANY CHANGE IN OWNERSHIP REQUIRES A NEW LICENSE: NOTIFY THIS DIVISION IMMEDIATELY.

This return DUE on the 1st day of month following period covered by the return, and becomes DELINQUENT on the 21st day.	37-9462315 FED. E.I. NO. OR S.S NO.

STATE TAX COMMISSION
SALES AND USE TAX DIVISION
DRAWER 20
CAPITAL CITY, STATE 78711
RETURN REQUESTED

January 31, 2007

—Sales for period ending—

OWNER'S NAME AND LOCATION

MAKE ALL REMITTANCES PAYABLE TO
STATE TAX COMMISSIOIN
DO NOT SEND CASH
STAMPS NOT ACCEPTED

THE Style Shop
2007 Trendsetter Lane
Dallas, Texas 75268-0967

COMPUTATION OF SALES TAX	For Taxpayer's Use	Do Not Use This Column
1. TOTAL Gross proceeds of sales or Gross Receipts (to include rentals)	27,350.00	
2. Add cost of personal property purchased on a RETAIL LICENSE FOR RESALE but USED BY YOU or YOUR EMPLOYEES, including GIFTS and PREMIUMS	–0–	
3. USE TAX—Add cost of personal property purchased outside of STATE for your use, storage, or consumption	–0–	
4. Total (Lines 1, 2, and 3)	27,350.00	
5. LESS ALLOWABLE DEDUCTIONS (Must be itemized on reverse side)	–0–	
6. Net taxable total (Line 4 minus Line 5)	27,350.00	
7. Sales and Use Tax Due (8% of Line 6)	2,188.00	
8. LESS TAXPAYER'S DISCOUNT—(Deductible only when amount of TAX due is not delinquent at time of payment) →	21.88	
IF LINE 7 IS LESS THAN $100.00 —DEDUCT 3% IF LINE 7 IS $100 BUT LESS THAN $1,000.00 —DEDUCT 2% IF LINE 7 IS $1,000.00 OR MORE —DEDUCT 1%		
9. NET AMOUNT OF TAX PAYABLE (Line 7 minus Line 8)	2,166.12	
Add the following penalty and interest if return or remittance is late. 10. Specific Penalty: 25% of tax _ _ _ _ _ _ _ _ _ _ _ _ _ _ _ _ _ _ $ _ _ _ _ _ _ _ 11. Interest: 1/2 of 1% per month from due date until paid. $ _ _ _ _ _ _ _ TOTAL PENALTY AND INTEREST →		
12. TOTAL TAX, PENALTY AND INTEREST	2,166.12	
13. Subtract credit memo No.		
14. TOTAL AMOUNT DUE (IF NO SALES MADE SO STATE)	2,166.12	

I certify that this return, including the accompanying schedules or statements, has been examined by me and to the best of my knowledge and belief, a true and complete return, made in good faith, for the period stated, pursuant to the provisions of the Code of Laws, 20--, and Acts Amendatory Thereto.

URGENT—SEE THAT LICENSE NUMBER IS ON RETURN

Mary Amos
SIGNATURE

Division Use Only

Owner   February 7, 2007
Owner, partner or title   Date
Return must be signed by owner or if corporation, authorized person.

FIGURE 7.18 | State Sales Tax Return

If there is a balance in the *Sales Tax Payable* account after the sales tax liability is satisfied, the balance is transferred to an account called *Miscellaneous Income* by a general journal entry. This entry consists of a debit to *Sales Tax Payable* and a credit to *Miscellaneous Income.*

RECORDING SALES TAX IN THE SALES ACCOUNT

In some states retailers can credit the entire sales price plus tax to the *Sales* account. At the end of each month or quarter, they must remove from the *Sales* account the amount of tax included and transfer that amount to the *Sales Tax Payable* account. Assume that during January a retailer whose sales are all taxable sells merchandise for a total price of $20,250, which includes an 8 percent tax. The entry to record these sales is summarized in general journal form shown here.

	GENERAL JOURNAL			PAGE 4	
DATE	DESCRIPTION	POST. REF.	DEBIT	CREDIT	
1	2007				1
2	Jan. 31 Accounts Receivable	111	20 250 00		2
3	Sales	401		20 250 00	3
4	To record total sales and				4
5	sales tax collected during				5
6	the month				6
7					7

At the end of the month, the retailer must transfer the sales tax from the *Sales* account to the *Sales Tax Payable* account. The first step in the transfer process is to determine the amount of tax involved. The sales tax payable is computed as follows.

THE BOTTOM LINE
Discount on Sales Tax

Income Statement

Misc. Income	↑	21.88
Net Income	↑	21.88

Balance Sheet

Assets	↓	2,166.12
Liabilities	↓	2,166.12
Equity	↑	21.88

MANAGERIAL IMPLICATIONS <<

CREDIT SALES

- Credit sales are a major source of revenue in many businesses, and accounts receivable represent a major asset.
- Management needs up-to-date and correct information about both sales and accounts receivable in order to monitor the financial health of the firm.
- Special journals save time and effort and reduce the cost of accounting work.
- In a retail firm that must handle sales tax, the sales journal and the cash receipts journal provide a convenient method of recording the amounts owed for sales tax.
  - When the data is posted to the Sales Tax Payable account in the general ledger, the firm has a complete and systematic record that speeds the completion of the periodic sales tax return.
  - The firm has detailed proof of its sales tax figures in the case of a tax audit.

- An accounts receivable subsidiary ledger provides management and the credit department with up-to-date information about the balances owed by all customers.
  - This information is useful in controlling credit and collections.
  - Detailed information helps in evaluating the effectiveness of credit policies.
  - Management must keep a close watch on the promptness of customer payments because much of the cash needed for day-to-day operations usually comes from payments on accounts receivable.
- A well-balanced credit policy helps increase sales volume but also keeps losses from uncollectible accounts at an acceptable level.
- Retailers are liable for any undercollection of sales taxes. This situation can be avoided with an efficient control system.

THINKING CRITICALLY

What are some possible consequences of out-of-date accounts receivable records?

Sales + tax	= $20,250
100% of sales + 8% of sales	= $20,250
108% of sales	= $20,250
Sales	= $20,250/1.08
Sales	= $18,750
Tax	= $18,750 × 0.08 = $1,500

The firm then makes the following entry to transfer the liability from the *Sales* account.

GENERAL JOURNAL   PAGE ___4___

	DATE		DESCRIPTION	POST. REF.	DEBIT	CREDIT	
1	2007						1
8	Jan.	31	Sales	401	1 5 0 0 00		8
9			Sales Tax Payable	231		1 5 0 0 00	9
10			To transfer sales tax				10
11			payable from the Sales				11
12			account to the liability				12
13			account				13
14							14
15							15

The retailer in this example originally recorded the entire sales price plus tax in the *Sales* account. The sales tax was transferred to the *Sales Tax Payable* account at the end of the month.

Section 3: **Self Review**

QUESTIONS

1. What account is used to record sales tax owed by a business to a city or state?

2. What is the difference between list price and net price?

3. What are four types of credit sales?

EXERCISES

4. A company that buys $4,000 of goods from a wholesaler offering trade discounts of 20 and 10 percent will pay what amount for the goods?

   a. $1,760
   b. $2,800
   c. $2,880
   d. $2,780

5. If a wholesale business offers a trade discount of 35 percent on a sale of $3,600, what is the amount of the discount?

   a. $120
   b. $126
   c. $1,200
   d. $1,260

ANALYSIS

6. What factors would you consider in deciding whether or not to extend credit to a customer?

(Answers to Section 3 Self Review are on page 245.)

REVIEW

Chapter Summary

The nature of the operations of a business, the volume of its transactions, and other factors influence the design of an accounting system. In this chapter, you have learned about the use of special journals and subsidiary ledgers suitable for a merchandising business. These additional journals and ledgers increase the efficiency of recording credit transactions and permit the division of labor.

Learning Objectives

1 Record credit sales in a sales journal.

The sales journal is used to record credit sales transactions, usually on a daily basis. For sales transactions that include sales tax, the sales tax liability is recorded at the time of the sale to ensure that company records reflect the appropriate amount of sales tax liability.

2 Post from the sales journal to the general ledger accounts.

At the end of each month, the sales journal is totaled, proved, and ruled. Column totals are then posted to the general ledger. Using a sales journal rather than a general journal to record sales saves the time and effort of posting individual entries to the general ledger during the month.

3 Post from the sales journal to the customers' accounts in the accounts receivable subsidiary ledger.

The accounts of individual credit customers are kept in a subsidiary ledger called the accounts receivable ledger. Daily postings are made to this ledger from the sales journal, the cash receipts journal, and the general journal or the sales returns and allowances journal. The current balance of a customer's account is computed after each posting so that the amount owed is known at all times.

4 Record sales returns and allowances in the general journal.

Sales returns and allowances are usually debited to a contra revenue account. A firm with relatively few sales returns and allowances could use the general journal to record these transactions.

5 Post sales returns and allowances.

Sales returns and allowances transactions must be posted to the general ledger and to the appropriate accounts receivable subsidiary ledgers. The balance of the **Sales Returns and Allowances** account is subtracted from the balance of the **Sales** account to show net sales on the income statement.

6 Prepare a schedule of accounts receivable.

Each month a schedule of accounts receivable is prepared. It is used to prove the subsidiary ledger against the **Accounts Receivable** account. It also reports the amounts due from credit customers.

7 Compute trade discounts.

Wholesale businesses often offer goods to trade customers at less than retail prices. Trade discounts are expressed as a percentage off the list price. Multiply the list price by the percentage trade discount offered to compute the dollar amount.

8 Record credit card sales in appropriate journals.

Credit sales are common, and different credit arrangements are used. Businesses that have few transactions with credit card companies normally record these transactions in the sales journal by debiting the usual **Accounts Receivable** account in the general ledger and crediting the same **Sales** account that is used for cash sales.

9 Prepare the state sales tax return.

In states and cities that have a sales tax, the retailer must prepare a sales tax return and send the total tax collected to the taxing authority.

10 Define the accounting terms new to this chapter.

Glossary

Accounts receivable ledger (p. 207) A subsidiary ledger that contains credit customer accounts

Charge-account sales (p. 219) Sales made through the use of open-account credit or one of various types of credit cards

Contra revenue account (p. 209) An account with a debit balance, which is contrary to the normal balance for a revenue account

Control account (p. 214) An account that links a subsidiary ledger and the general ledger since its balance summarizes the balances of the accounts in the subsidiary ledger

Credit memorandum (p. 208) A note verifying that a customer's account is being reduced by the amount of a sales return or sales allowance plus any sales tax that may have been involved

Invoice (p. 217) A customer billing for merchandise bought on credit

List price (p. 216) An established retail price

Manufacturing business (p. 200) A business that sells goods that it has produced

Merchandise inventory (p. 200) The stock of goods a merchandising business keeps on hand

Merchandising business (p. 200) A business that sells goods purchased for resale

Net price (p. 216) The list price less all trade discounts

Net sales (p. 211) The difference between the balance in the **Sales** account and the balance in the **Sales Returns and Allowances** account

Open-account credit (p. 219) A system that allows the sale of services or goods with the understanding that payment will be made at a later date

Retail business (p. 200) A business that sells directly to individual consumers

Sales allowance (p. 208) A reduction in the price originally charged to customers for goods or services

Sales journal (p. 200) A special journal used to record sales of merchandise on credit

Sales return (p. 208) A firm's acceptance of a return of goods from a customer

Schedule of accounts receivable (p. 214) A listing of all balances of the accounts in the accounts receivable subsidiary ledger

Service business (p. 200) A business that sells services

Special journal (p. 200) A journal used to record only one type of transaction

Subsidiary ledger (p. 200) A ledger dedicated to accounts of a single type and showing details to support a general ledger account

Trade discount (p. 216) A reduction from list price

Wholesale business (p. 216) A business that manufactures or distributes goods to retail businesses or large consumers such as hotels and hospitals

Comprehensive **Self Review**

1. Name the two different time periods usually covered in sales tax returns.
2. What is a control account?
3. Why does a small merchandising business usually need a more complex set of financial records and statements than a small service business?
4. Why is it useful for a firm to have an accounts receivable ledger?
5. Explain how service, merchandising, and manufacturing businesses differ from each other.

(Answers to Comprehensive Self Review are on page 245.)

Discussion Questions

1. How do retail and wholesale businesses differ?
2. What purposes does the schedule of accounts receivable serve?
3. How are the net sales for an accounting period determined?
4. Why is a sales return or allowance usually recorded in a special **Sales Returns and Allowances** account rather than being debited to the **Sales** account?
5. What kind of account is **Sales Returns and Allowances?**
6. How is a multicolumn special journal proved at the end of each month?
7. The sales tax on a credit sale is not collected from the customer immediately. When is this tax usually entered in a firm's accounting records? What account is used to record this tax?
8. In a particular state, the sales tax rate is 5 percent of sales. The retailer is allowed to record both the selling price and the tax in the same account. Explain how to compute the sales tax due when this method is used.
9. What two methods are commonly used to record sales involving credit cards issued by credit card companies?
10. What procedure does a business use to collect amounts owed to it for sales on credit cards issued by credit card companies?
11. When a firm makes a sale involving a credit card issued by a credit card company, does the firm have an account receivable with the cardholder or with the credit card company?
12. What is the discount on credit card sales? What type of account is used to record this item?
13. Why are bank credit card sales similar to cash sales for a business?
14. What is open-account credit?
15. What is a trade discount? Why do some firms offer trade discounts to their customers?

APPLICATIONS

Exercises

Identifying the journal to record transactions.

◄ Exercise 7.1
Objective 1

The accounting system of Dave's Wildlife Resort includes the journals listed below. Indicate the specific journal in which each of the transactions listed below would be recorded.

JOURNALS

Cash receipts journal Sales journal Purchases journal
Cash payments journal General journal

DATE		TRANSACTIONS
May	1	Sold merchandise on credit.
	2	Accepted a return of merchandise from a credit customer.
	3	Sold merchandise for cash.
	4	Purchased merchandise on credit.
	5	Gave a $400 allowance for damaged merchandise.
	6	Collected sums on account from credit customers.
	7	Received an additional cash investment from the owner.
	8	Issued a check to pay a creditor on account.

Exercise 7.2

Objective 1

CONTINUING >>>
Problem

▶ **Identifying the accounts used to record sales and related transactions.**

The transactions below took place at Dave's Wildlife Resort, a retail business that sells outdoor clothing and camping equipment. Indicate the numbers of the general ledger accounts that would be debited and credited to record each transaction.

GENERAL LEDGER ACCOUNTS

101 Cash	401 Sales
111 Accounts Receivable	451 Sales Returns and Allowances
231 Sales Tax Payable	

DATE		TRANSACTIONS
May	1	Sold merchandise on credit; the transaction involved sales tax.
	2	Received checks from credit customers on account.
	3	Accepted a return of merchandise from a credit customer; the original sale involved sales tax.
	4	Sold merchandise for cash; the transaction involved sales tax.
	5	Gave an allowance to a credit customer for damaged merchandise; the original sale involved sales tax.
	6	Provided a cash refund to a customer who returned merchandise; the original sale was made for cash and involved sales tax.

Exercise 7.3

Objective 2

CONTINUING >>>
Problem

▶ **Recording credit sales.**

The following transactions took place at Dave's Wildlife Resort during May. Indicate how these transactions would be entered in a sales journal like the one shown in Figure 7.2.

DATE		TRANSACTIONS
May	1	Sold a tent and other items on credit to Roy Anderson; issued Sales Slip 1101 for $360 plus sales tax of $29.
	2	Sold a backpack, an air mattress, and other items to John Amos; issued Sales Slip 1102 for $240 plus sales tax of $19.
	3	Sold a lantern, cooking utensils, and other items to Teresa Wells; issued Sales Slip 1103 for $200 plus sales tax of $16.

Exercise 7.4

Objective 2

▶ **Recording sales returns and allowances.**

Record the general journal entries for the following transactions of Fashion World that occurred in June 2007.

DATE		TRANSACTIONS
June	7	Accepted a return of some damaged merchandise from Deborah Westgate, a credit customer; issued Credit Memorandum 301 for $648, which includes sales tax of $48; the original sale was made on Sales Slip 1610 of May 31.
	22	Gave an allowance to Brian Barnett, a credit customer, for some merchandise that was slightly damaged but usable; issued Credit Memorandum 121 for $972, which includes sales tax of $72; the original sale was made on Sales Slip 1663 of June 17.

Posting from the sales journal.

The sales journal for Carrington Company is shown below. Describe how the amounts would be posted to the general ledger accounts.

◄ **Exercise 7.5**
Objective 2

	DATE	SALES SLIP NO.	CUSTOMER'S ACCOUNT DEBITED	POST. REF.	ACCOUNTS RECEIVABLE DEBIT	SALES TAX PAYABLE CREDIT	SALES CREDIT	
1	2007							1
2	July 2	1101	Scott Cohen		540 00	40 00	500 00	2
3	7	1102	Julia Hoang		848 00	48 00	800 00	3
11	31	1110	Barbara Baxter		324 00	24 00	300 00	11
12	31		Totals		6 480 00	480 00	6 000 00	12
13					(111)	(231)	(401)	13
14								14

SALES JOURNAL   PAGE ___1___

Computing a trade discount.

Wasserman Wholesale Company made sales using the following list prices and trade discounts. What amount will be recorded for each sale in the sales journal?

1. List price of $475 and trade discount of 40 percent
2. List price of $850 and trade discount of 40 percent
3. List price of $175 and trade discount of 30 percent

◄ **Exercise 7.6**
Objective 7

Computing a series of trade discounts.

Norville Distributing Company, a wholesale firm, made sales using the following list prices and trade discounts. What amount will be recorded for each sale in the sales journal?

1. List price of $3,500 and trade discounts of 25 and 15 percent
2. List price of $4,200 and trade discounts of 25 and 15 percent
3. List price of $2,550 and trade discounts of 20 and 10 percent

◄ **Exercise 7.7**
Objective 7

Computing the sales tax due and recording its payment.

The balances of certain accounts of Carter Corporation on April 30, 2007, were as follows:

Sales	$225,575
Sales Returns and Allowances	2,820

The firm's net sales are subject to an 8 percent sales tax. Give the general journal entry to record payment of the sales tax payable on April 30, 2007.

◄ **Exercise 7.8**
Objective 9

Preparing a schedule of accounts receivable.

The accounts receivable ledger for The Jean Barn follows on page 232.

1. Prepare a schedule of accounts receivable as of January 31, 2007.
2. What should the balance in the **Accounts Receivable** (control) account be?

◄ **Exercise 7.9**
Objective 6

Posting sales returns and allowances.

Post the journal entries below to the appropriate ledger accounts. Assume the following account balances:

Accounts Receivable (control account)	$1,620
Accounts Receivable—Cara Fountain	540
Accounts Receivable—Sadie Palmer	648

◄ **Exercise 7.10**
Objective 5

NAME _Cheryl Amos_
ADDRESS _917 Broadway, New York, NY 10018_

DATE		DESCRIPTION	POST. REF.	DEBIT	CREDIT	BALANCE
2007						
Jan.	1	Balance	✓			1 5 7 5 00
	2	Sales Slip 1801	S1	5 4 0 00		2 1 1 5 00

NAME _Edward Cooke_
ADDRESS _2022 5th Avenue, New York, NY 10018_

DATE		DESCRIPTION	POST. REF.	DEBIT	CREDIT	BALANCE
2007						
Jan.	1	Balance	✓			3 7 8 00
	27	Sales Slip 1824	S1	1 8 9 00		5 6 7 00
	31		CR1		2 8 4 00	2 8 3 00

NAME _Neal Fitzgerald_
ADDRESS _98 Houston Street, New York, NY 10018_

DATE		DESCRIPTION	POST. REF.	DEBIT	CREDIT	BALANCE
2007						
Jan.	1	Balance	✓			3 2 4 00
	15	Sales Slip 1812	CR1		3 2 4 00	—0—
	31		S1	7 5 6 00		7 5 6 00

NAME _David Pifer_
ADDRESS _5063 Park Avenue, New York, NY 10019_

DATE		DESCRIPTION	POST. REF.	DEBIT	CREDIT	BALANCE
2007						
Jan.	1	Balance	✓			6 4 8 00
	20	Sales Slip 1819	S1	2 1 6 00		8 6 4 00
	21		CR1		4 5 0 00	4 1 4 00
	22	Sales Slip 1822	S1	8 1 0 00		1 2 2 4 00

NAME _Lisa Stanton_
ADDRESS _2111 West 32nd Street, New York, NY 10019_

DATE		DESCRIPTION	POST. REF.	DEBIT	CREDIT	BALANCE
2007						
Jan.	1	Balance	✓			4 8 6 00
	31	Sales Slip 1840	S1	2 2 1 4 00		2 7 0 0 00

NAME _Nikki Whitaker_
ADDRESS _721 Lexington Avenue, New York, NY 10027_

DATE		DESCRIPTION	POST. REF.	DEBIT	CREDIT	BALANCE
20--						
Jan.	1	Balance	✓			2 3 7 6 00
	12		CR1		1 1 8 8 00	1 1 8 8 00
	17	Sales Slip 1817	S1	8 6 4 00		2 0 5 2 00

GENERAL JOURNAL   PAGE ___42___

	DATE		DESCRIPTION	POST. REF.	DEBIT	CREDIT	
1	2007						1
2	Mar.	14	Sales Returns and Allowances		3 0 0 00		2
3			Sales Tax Payable		2 4 00		3
4			Accounts Rec.—Cara Fountain			3 2 4 00	4
5			Accepted return on defective				5
6			merchandise, Credit Memo				6
7			101; original sale of Feb. 23,				7
8			Sales Slip 1101				8
9							9
10		22	Sales Returns and Allowances		1 0 0 00		10
11			Sales Tax Payable		8 00		11
12			Accounts Rec.—Sadie Palmer			1 0 8 00	12
13			Gave allowance for damaged				13
14			merchandise, Credit Memo				14
15			102; original sale Mar. 15,				15
16			Sales Slip 1150				16

PROBLEMS

Problem Set A

Recording credit sales and posting from the sales journal.

The Twin Cities Appliance Mart is a retail store that sells household appliances. The firm's credit sales for June are listed below, along with the general ledger accounts used to record these sales. The balance shown for **Accounts Receivable** is for the beginning of the month.

◀ **Problem 7.1A**
Objectives 1, 2

DATE		TRANSACTIONS
July	1	Sold a dishwasher to Bonnie Franklin; issued Sales Slip 501 for $850 plus sales tax of $68.
	6	Sold a washer to Janet Judge; issued Sales Slip 502 for $1,050 plus sales tax of $84.
	11	Sold a high-definition television set to Raymond Clay; issued Sales Slip 503 for $2,600 plus sales tax of $208.
	17	Sold an electric dryer to Melissa Gray; issued Sales Slip 504 for $900 plus sales tax of $72.
	23	Sold a trash compactor to Angela Nguyen; issued Sales Slip 505 for $500 plus sales tax of $40.
	27	Sold a color television set to Clifton Wallace; issued Sales Slip 506 for $950 plus sales tax of $76.
	29	Sold an electric range to Sally Wei; issued Sales Slip 507 for $1,300 plus sales tax of $104.
	31	Sold a microwave oven to Ken Holt; issued Sales Slip 508 for $400 plus sales tax of $32.

INSTRUCTIONS

1. Open the general ledger accounts and enter the balance of **Accounts Receivable** for July 1, 2007.

2. Record the transactions in a sales journal like the one shown in Figure 7.4. Use 8 as the journal page number.

3. Total, prove, and rule the sales journal as of July 31.

4. Post the column totals from the sales journal to the proper general ledger accounts.

GENERAL LEDGER ACCOUNTS

111   Accounts Receivable, $31,400 Dr.

231   Sales Tax Payable

401   Sales

Analyze: What percentage of credit sales were for entertainment items?

Problem 7.2A

Objectives 1, 2, 4

Journalizing, posting, and reporting sales transactions.

Spectra Furniture specializes in modern living room and dining room furniture. Merchandise sales are subject to an 8 percent sales tax. The firm's credit sales and sales returns and allowances for February 2007 are reflected below, along with the general ledger accounts used to record these transactions. The balances shown are for the beginning of the month.

DATE	TRANSACTIONS
Feb. 1	Sold a living room sofa to Julia Cheng; issued Sales Slip 1615 for $3,250 plus sales tax of $260.
5	Sold three recliners to Denise dela Hoya; issued Sales Slip 1616 for $2,100 plus sales tax of $168.
9	Sold a dining room set to Suzanne Tuttle; issued Sales Slip 1617 for $5,500 plus sales tax of $440.
11	Accepted a return of one damaged recliner from Denise dela Hoya that was originally sold on Sales Slip 1616 of February 5; issued Credit Memorandum 702 for $756.00, which includes sales tax of $56.00.
17	Sold living room tables and bookcases to Joan Clay; issued Sales Slip 1618 for $5,400 plus sales tax of $432.
23	Sold eight dining room chairs to Thomas Muir; issued Sales Slip 1619 for $3,400 plus sales tax of $272.
25	Gave Joan Clay an allowance for scratches on her bookcases; issued Credit Memorandum 703 for $432, which includes sales taxes of $32; the bookcases were originally sold on Sales Slip 1618 of February 17.
27	Sold a living room sofa and four chairs to Bernard Slaughter; issued Sales Slip 1620 for $3,975 plus sales tax of $318.
28	Sold a dining room table to Connie Taylor; issued Sales Slip 1621 for $1,800 plus sales tax of $144.
28	Sold a living room modular wall unit to James Walker; issued Sales Slip 1622 for $3,650 plus sales tax of $292.

INSTRUCTIONS

1. Open the general ledger accounts and enter the balances for February 1.

2. Record the transactions in a sales journal and in a general journal. Use 8 as the page number for the sales journal and 24 as the page number for the general journal.

3. Post the entries from the general journal to the general ledger.

4. Total, prove, and rule the sales journal as of February 28.

5. Post the column totals from the sales journal.

6. Prepare the heading and the Revenue section of the firm's income statement for the month ended February 28, 2007.

GENERAL LEDGER ACCOUNTS

111   Accounts Receivable, $15,636 Dr.

231   Sales Tax Payable, $7,170 Cr.

401   Sales

451   Sales Returns and Allowances

Analyze: Based on the beginning balance of the *Sales Tax Payable* account, what was the amount of net sales for January? (Hint: Sales tax returns are filed and paid to the state quarterly.)

Recording sales transactions, posting to the accounts receivable ledger, and preparing a schedule of accounts receivable.

◄ **Problem 7.3A**
Objectives
1, 2, 3, 4, 6

The Dining Elegance China Shop sells china, glassware, and other gift items that are subject to an 8 percent sales tax. The shop uses a general journal and a sales journal similar to those illustrated in this chapter.

DATE	TRANSACTIONS
Nov. 1	Sold china to Pauline Judge; issued Sales Slip 1001 for $1,500 plus $120 sales tax.
5	Sold a brass serving tray to Janet Hutchison; issued Sales Slip 1002 for $2,100 plus $168 sales tax.
6	Sold a vase to Charles Brown; issued Sales Slip 1003 for $700 plus $56 sales tax.
10	Sold a punch bowl and glasses to Lisa Morgan; issued Sales Slip 1004 for $1,700 plus $136 sales tax.
14	Sold a set of serving bowls to Dorothy Watts; issued Sales Slip 1005 for $550 plus $44 sales tax.
17	Gave Lisa Morgan an allowance because of a broken glass discovered when unpacking the punch bowl and glasses sold on November 10, Sales Slip 1004; issued Credit Memorandum 102 for $162.00, which includes sales tax of $12.
21	Sold a coffee table to Winnie Wu; issued Sales Slip 1006 for $3,200 plus $256 sales tax.
24	Sold sterling silver teaspoons to Henry Okafor; issued Sales Slip 1007 for $600 plus $48 sales tax.
25	Gave Winnie Wu an allowance for scratches on his coffee table sold on November 21, Sales Slip 1006; issued Credit Memorandum 103 for $378, which includes $28 in sales tax.
30	Sold a clock to Euline Brock; issued Sales Slip 1008 for $3,800 plus $304 sales tax.

INSTRUCTIONS

1. Record the transactions for November in the proper journal. Use 6 as the page number for the sales journal and 16 as the page number for the general journal.

2. Immediately after recording each transaction, post to the accounts receivable ledger.

3. Post the amounts from the general journal daily. Post the sales journal amount as a total at the end of the month.

4. Prepare a schedule of accounts receivable. Compare the balance of the *Accounts Receivable* control account with the total of the schedule.

Analyze: How many additional postings would be made to the general ledger if the business did not use a sales journal?

Problem 7.4A ▶

Objectives 1, 2, 3, 4, 6

Recording sales transactions, posting to the accounts receivable ledger, and preparing a schedule of accounts receivable.

Special Occasions Flower Shop is a wholesale shop that sells flowers, plants, and plant supplies. The transactions shown below took place during January.

DATE	TRANSACTIONS
Jan. 3	Sold a floral arrangement to Thomas Florist; issued Invoice 1081 for $500.
8	Sold potted plants to Carter Garden Supply; issued Invoice 1082 for $775.
9	Sold floral arrangements to Thomasville Flower Shop; issued Invoice 1083 for $462.
10	Sold corsages to Moore's Flower Shop; issued Invoice 1084 for $530.
15	Gave Thomasville Flower Shop an allowance because of withered blossoms discovered in one of the floral arrangements sold on Invoice 1083 on January 9; issued Credit Memorandum 101 for $50.
20	Sold table arrangements to Cedar Hill Floral Shop; issued Invoice 1085 for $480.
22	Sold plants to Applegate Nursery; issued Invoice 1086 for $680.00.
25	Sold roses to Moore's Flower Shop; issued Invoice 1087 for $427.
27	Sold several floral arrangements to Thomas Florist; issued Invoice 1088 for $925.
31	Gave Thomas Florist an allowance because of withered blossoms discovered in one of the floral arrangements sold on Invoice 1088 on January 27; issued Credit Memorandum 102 for $150.

INSTRUCTIONS

1. Record the transactions in the proper journal. Use 7 as the page number for the sales journal and 11 as the page number for the general journal.
2. Immediately after recording each transaction, post to the accounts receivable ledger.
3. Post the amounts from the general journal daily. Post the sales journal amount as a total at the end of the month.
4. Prepare a schedule of accounts receivable. Compare the balance of the **Accounts Receivable** control account with the total of the schedule.

Analyze: Damaged goods decreased the net sales by what dollar amount? By what percentage amount?

Problem Set B

Problem 7.1B ▶

Objectives 1, 2

Recording credit sales and posting from the sales journal.

Discount Appliance Center is a retail store that sells household appliances. The firm's credit sales for June are listed below, along with the general ledger accounts used to record these sales. The balance shown for Accounts Receivable is for the beginning of the month.

INSTRUCTIONS

1. Open the general ledger accounts and enter the balance of **Accounts Receivable** for June 1.
2. Record the transactions in a sales journal like the one shown in Figure 7.4. Use 8 as the journal page number.

3. Total, prove, and rule the sales journal as of June 30.

4. Post the column totals from the sales journal to the proper general ledger accounts.

DATE		TRANSACTIONS
June	1	Sold a dishwasher to Barbara Merino; issued Sales Slip 201 for $750 plus sales tax of $60.
	6	Sold a washer to David Reed; issued Sales Slip 202 for $1,050 plus sales tax of $84.
	11	Sold a high-definition television set to Brenda Davis; issued Sales Slip 203 for $2,600 plus sales tax of $208.
	17	Sold an electric dryer to Beatrice Wilson; issued Sales Slip 204 for $900 plus sales tax of $72.
	23	Sold a trash compactor to Doris Lazo; issued Sales Slip 205 for $500 plus sales tax of $40.
	27	Sold a portable color television set to Carol West; issued Sales Slip 206 for $1,200 plus sales tax of $96.
	29	Sold an electric range to Rickey Eddie; issued Sales Slip 207 for $1,500 plus sales tax of $120.
	30	Sold a microwave oven to Bridgette Nelson; issued Sales Slip 208 for $600 plus sales tax of $48.

GENERAL LEDGER ACCOUNTS

111 Accounts Receivable, $72,800 Dr.

231 Sales Tax Payable

401 Sales

Analyze: What percentage of credit sales were for entertainment items?

Journalizing, posting, and reporting sales transactions.

Super Furniture Mart is a retail store that specializes in modern living room and dining room furniture. Merchandise sales are subject to an 8 percent sales tax. The firm's credit sales and sales returns and allowances for June are reflected below, along with the general ledger accounts used to record these transactions. The balances shown are for the beginning of the month.

◀ **Problem 7.2B**
Objectives 1, 2, 4

INSTRUCTIONS

1. Open the general ledger accounts and enter the balances for June 1.

2. Record the transactions in a sales journal and a general journal. Use 9 as the page number for the sales journal and 26 as the page number for the general journal.

3. Post the entries from the general journal to the general ledger.

4. Total, prove, and rule the sales journal as of June 30.

5. Post the column totals from the sales journal.

6. Prepare the heading and the Revenue section of the firm's income statement for the month ended June 30, 2007.

GENERAL LEDGER ACCOUNTS

111 Accounts Receivable, $22,576 Dr.

231 Sales Tax Payable, $4,515 Cr.

401 Sales

451 Sales Returns and Allowances

DATE	TRANSACTIONS
June 1	Sold a living room sofa to Christine Berry; issued Sales Slip 1601 for $2,050 plus sales tax of $164.
5	Sold three recliners to Paula Adams; issued Sales Slip 1602 for $1,300 plus sales tax of $104.
9	Sold a dining room set to Patrick Chen; issued Sales Slip 1603 for $7,000 plus sales tax of $560.
11	Accepted a return of a damaged chair from Paula Adams; the chair was originally sold on Sales Slip 1602 of June 5; issued Credit Memorandum 215 for $432, which includes sales tax of $32.
17	Sold living room tables and bookcases to Raul Alvarez; issued Sales Slip 1604 for $4,000 plus sales tax of $320.
23	Sold eight dining room chairs to Kenitra Brown; issued Sales Slip 1605 for $3,800 plus sales tax of $304.
25	Gave Raul Alvarez an allowance for scratches on his bookcases; issued Credit Memorandum 216 for $270, which includes sales taxes of $20; the bookcases were originally sold on Sales Slip 1604 of June 17.
27	Sold a living room sofa and four chairs to Charles Brown; issued Sales Slip 1606 for $3,600 plus sales tax of $288.
29	Sold a dining room table to Rosetta London; issued Sales Slip 1607 for $1,250 plus sales tax of $100.
30	Sold a living room modular wall unit to James Howard; issued Sales Slip 1608 for $3,100 plus sales tax of $248.

Analyze: Based on the beginning balance of the *Sales Tax Payable* account, what was the amount of total net sales for April and May? (Hint: Sales tax returns are filed and paid to the state quarterly.)

Problem 7.3B
Objectives
1, 2, 3, 4, 6

▶ **Recording sales transactions, posting to the accounts receivable ledger, and preparing a schedule of accounts receivable.**

Special Elegance Gift Shop sells cards, supplies, and various holiday gift items. All sales are subject to a sales tax of 8 percent. The shop uses a sales journal and general journal.

DATE	TRANSACTIONS
Feb. 3	Sold Ronald Brown a box of holiday greeting cards for $50 plus sales tax of $4 on Sales Slip 201.
4	Sold to Ken Hamlett a Valentine's Day party pack for $200 plus sales tax of $16 on Sales Slip 202.
5	Vickie Neal bought 10 boxes of Valentine's Day gift packs for her office. Sales Slip 203 was issued for $300 plus sales tax of $24.
8	Sold Amy Peloza a set of crystal glasses for $400 plus sales tax of $32 on Sales Slip 204.
9	Luther Evans purchased two statues for $400 plus $32 sales tax on Sales Slip 205.
9	Gave Vickie Neal an allowance because of incomplete items in two gift packs; issued Credit Memorandum 101 for $54, which includes sales tax of $4.
10	Sold Gordon Edwards a Valentine Birthday package for $150 plus $12 sales tax on Sales Slip 206.

DATE	7.3B (cont.) TRANSACTIONS
Feb. 13	Gave Amy Peloza an allowance of $50 because of two broken glasses in the set she purchased on February 8. Credit Memorandum 102 was issued for the allowance plus sales tax of $4.
14	Sold Ronald Brown 12 boxes of gift candy for $200 plus sales tax of $16 on Sales Slip 207.
15	Sold a punch serving set with glasses for $300 to Kerry Goree. Sales tax of $24 was included on Sales Slip 208.
20	Sold Ned Jones a box of holiday greeting cards for $100 plus sales tax of $8 on Sales Slip 209.
22	Sold Susan Anderson a set of crystal glasses for $500 plus sales tax of $40 on Sales Slip 210.
28	Melissa Thomas purchased three statues for $600 plus $48 sales tax on Sales Slip 211.

INSTRUCTIONS

1. Record the credit sale transactions for February in the proper journal. Use 6 as the page number for the sales journal and 16 as the page number for the general journal.

2. Immediately after recording each transaction, post to the accounts receivable ledger.

3. Post the entries to the appropriate accounts.

4. Prepare a schedule of accounts receivable and compare the balance due with the amount shown in the **Accounts Receivable** control account.

Analyze: How many postings were made to the general ledger? How many additional postings would be needed if the business did not use a sales journal?

Recording sales transactions, posting to the accounts receivable ledger, and preparing a schedule of accounts receivable.

The Vintage Nursery is a wholesale shop that sells flowers, plants, and plant supplies. The transactions shown below took place during February.

◀ **Problem 7.4B**
Objectives
1, 2, 3, 4, 6

DATE	TRANSACTIONS
Feb. 3	Sold a floral arrangement to Thompson Funeral Home; issued Invoice 2201 for $400.
8	Sold potted plants to Meadows Nursery; issued Invoice 2202 for $800.
9	Sold floral arrangements to DeSoto Flower Shop; issued Invoice 2203 for $1,050.
10	Sold corsages to Lovelace Nursery; issued Invoice 2204 for $700.
15	Gave DeSoto Flower Shop an allowance because of withered blossoms discovered in one of the floral arrangements sold on Invoice 2203 on February 9; issued Credit Memorandum 105 for $100.
20	Sold table arrangements to Lovelace Nursery; issued Invoice 2205 for $650.
22	Sold plants to Southwest Nursery; issued Invoice 2206 for $850.
25	Sold roses to Denton Flower Shop; issued Invoice 2207 for $450.
27	Sold several floral arrangements to Thompson Funeral Home; issued Invoice 2208 for $750.
28	Gave Thompson Funeral Home an allowance because of withered blossoms discovered in one of the floral arrangements sold on Invoice 2208 on February 27; issued Credit Memorandum 106 for $75.

CHAPTER 7: Review and Applications

INSTRUCTIONS

1. Record the transactions in the proper journal. Use 5 as the page number for the sales journal and 10 as the page number for the general journal.

2. Immediately after recording each transaction, post to the accounts receivable ledger.

3. Post the amounts from the general journal daily. Post the sales journal amount as a total at the end of the month.

4. Prepare a schedule of accounts receivable. Compare the balance of the **Accounts Receivable** control account with the total of the schedule.

Analyze: Damaged goods decreased the net sales by what dollar amount? By what percentage amount?

Challenge Problem

Wholesaler Transactions

The Toy Shop Company sells toys and games to retail stores. The firm offers a trade discount of 40 percent on toys and 30 percent on games. Its credit sales and sales returns and allowances transactions for August are shown on page 241. The general ledger accounts used to record these transactions are listed below. The balance shown for **Accounts Receivable** is as of the beginning of August.

INSTRUCTIONS

1. Open the general ledger accounts and enter the balance of **Accounts Receivable** for August 1.

2. Set up an accounts receivable subsidiary ledger. Open an account for each of the credit customers listed below and enter the balances as of August 1.

Carter's Department Store	$28,900
Play Therapy Toy Stores	30,500
Delux Bookstores	
Pemberton Toy Center	
Metroplex Game Center	19,010
Hinton Game Store	

3. Record the transactions in a sales journal and in a general journal. Use 9 as the page number for the sales journal and 25 as the page number for the general journal. Be sure to enter each sale at its net price.

4. Post the individual entries from the sales journal and the general journal.

5. Total and rule the sales journal as of August 31.

6. Post the column total from the sales journal to the proper general ledger accounts.

7. Prepare the heading and the Revenue section of the firm's income statement for the month ended August 31.

8. Prepare a schedule of accounts receivable for August 31.

9. Check the total of the schedule of accounts receivable against the balance of the **Accounts Receivable** account in the general ledger. The two amounts should be equal.

GENERAL LEDGER ACCOUNTS

    111 Accounts Receivable, $78,410 Dr.

    401 Sales

    451 Sales Returns and Allowances

DATE	TRANSACTIONS
August 1	Sold toys to Carter's Department Store; issued Invoice 1001, which shows a list price of $18,500 and a trade discount of 40 percent.
5	Sold games to the Delux Bookstores; issued Invoice 1002, which shows a list price of $20,500 and a trade discount of 30 percent.
9	Sold games to the Metroplex Game Center; issued Invoice 1003, which shows a list price of $7,500 and a trade discount of 30 percent.
14	Sold toys to the Play Therapy Toy Stores; issued Invoice 1004, which shows a list price of $25,500 and a trade discount of 40 percent.
18	Accepted a return of all the games shipped to the Metroplex Game Center because they were damaged in transit; issued Credit Memo 151 for the original sale made on Invoice 1003 on August 9.
22	Sold toys to Hinton Game Store; issued Invoice 1005, which shows a list price of $18,400 and a trade discount of 40 percent.
26	Sold games to the Carter's Department Store; issued Invoice 1006, which shows a list price of $21,600 and a trade discount of 30 percent.
30	Sold toys to the Pemberton Toy Center; issued Invoice 1007, which shows a list price of $22,800 and a trade discount of 40 percent.

Analyze: What is the effect on net sales if the company offers a series of trade discounts on toys (25 percent, 15 percent) instead of a single 40 percent discount?

Critical Thinking Problem

Retail Store

Carlos Zayas is the owner of The Home Pantry, a housewares store that sells a wide variety of items for the kitchen, bathroom, and home. The Home Pantry offers a company credit card to customers.

The company has experienced an increase in sales since the credit card was introduced. Carlos is considering replacing his manual system of recording sales with electronic point-of-sale cash registers that are linked to a computer.

Cash sales are now rung up by the salesclerks on a cash register that generates a tape listing total cash sales at the end of the day. For credit sales, salesclerks prepare handwritten sales slips that are forwarded to the accountant for manual entry into the sales journal and accounts receivable ledger.

The electronic register system Carlos is considering would use an optical scanner to read coded labels attached to the merchandise. As the merchandise is passed over the scanner, the code is sent to the computer. The computer is programmed to read the code and identify the item being sold, record the amount of the sale, maintain a record of total sales, update the inventory record, and keep a record of cash received.

If the sale is a credit transaction, the customer's company credit card number is entered into the register. The computer updates the customer's account in the accounts receivable ledger stored in computer memory.

If this system is used, many of the accounting functions are done automatically as sales are entered into the register. At the end of the day, the computer prints a complete sales journal, along with up-to-date balances for the general ledger and the accounts receivable ledger accounts related to sales transactions.

Listed below are four situations that Carlos is eager to eliminate. Would use of an electronic point-of-sale system as described above reduce or prevent these problems? Why or why not?

1. The accountant did not post a sale to the customer's subsidiary ledger account.
2. The salesclerk did not charge a customer for an item.

3. The customer purchased merchandise using a stolen credit card.

4. The salesclerk was not aware that the item purchased was on sale and did not give the customer the sale price.

BUSINESS CONNECTIONS

Managerial | FOCUS

Retail Sales

1. How does the **Sales Returns and Allowances** account provide management with a measure of operating efficiency? What problems might be indicated by a high level of returns and allowances?

2. Suppose you are the accountant for a small chain of clothing stores. Up to now the firm has offered open-account credit to qualified customers but has not allowed the use of bank credit cards. The president of the chain has asked your advice about changing the firm's credit policy. What advantages might there be in eliminating the open-account credit and accepting bank credit cards instead? Do you see any disadvantages?

3. During the past year Cravens Company has had a substantial increase in its losses from uncollectible accounts. Assume that you are the newly hired controller of this firm and that you have been asked to find the reason for the increase. What policies and procedures would you investigate?

4. Suppose a manager in your company has suggested that the firm not hire an accountant to advise it on tax matters and to file tax returns. He states that tax matters are merely procedural in nature and that anyone who can read the tax form instructions can do the necessary work. Comment on this idea.

5. Why is it usually worthwhile for a business to sell on credit even though it will have some losses from uncollectible accounts?

6. How can a firm's credit policy affect its profitability?

7. Why should management insist that all sales on credit and other transactions affecting the firm's accounts receivable be journalized and posted promptly?

8. How can efficient accounting records help management maintain sound credit and collection policies?

Ethical | DILEMMA

Sales Return and Allowances

Credit Memos are created when a product is returned. A debit to Sales Returns and Allowance and a credit to A/R is recorded when a credit memo is created. A credit memo will reduce A/R and write off the invoice. You have noticed Margarita has created an abnormally high number of credit memos. You notice the inventory does not reflect the additional inventory resulting from the Sales Returns and Allowances. What would you do and how would you document this decision?

STREETWISE:
Questions from the
REAL WORLD

Revenue Growth

Refer to the *2004 Annual Report* of The Home Depot, Inc. in Appendix A.

1. Locate Management's Discussion and Analysis of Results of Operations and Financial Condition. By what percentage did net sales increase from fiscal 2003 to fiscal 2004? What factors contributed to this growth?

2. Review the Consolidated Balance Sheets. By what percentage did net accounts receivable change from fiscal 2003 to fiscal 2004? Consider your answer to Question 1 above. Describe the relationship between your answer to Question 1 and the change in net accounts receivable.

Financial Statement
| ANALYSIS

Income Statement

An excerpt from the Consolidated Statements of Income for Wal-Mart Stores, Inc. is presented below. Review the financial data and answer the following analysis questions.

Amounts in millions Fiscal years ended January 31	2004	2003	2002
Revenues:			
Net Sales	$256,329	$229,616	$204,011
Other Income, Net	2,352	1,961	1,812
Total Revenues	$258,681	$231,577	$205,823

Analyze:

1. Based on the financial statement presented above, what is Wal-Mart Stores, Inc.'s fiscal year period?

2. Wal-Mart Stores, Inc.'s statement reports one figure for net sales. Name one account whose balance may have been deducted from the **Sales** account balance to determine a net sales amount.

3. The data presented demonstrates a steady increase in net sales over the three-year period. By what percentage have net sales of 2004 increased over sales of 2002?

Analyze Online: Find the most recent consolidated statements of income on the Wal-Mart Stores, Inc. Web site **(www.walmartstores.com).** Click on *Investor Information* then *Financial Information,* then select the link for the most recent annual report.

4. What dollar amount is reported for net sales for the most recent year?

5. What is the trend in net sales over the last three years?

6. What are some possible reasons for this trend?

e-commerce

Some retailers only operate online and do not have "bricks-and-mortar" physical locations where consumers can shop. What benefits and drawbacks do you see for retailers who operate entirely on-line?

Memo

You and your partner own three children's bookstores. Your partner comments on the separate general ledger accounts used for **Sales, Sales Tax Payable,** and **Sales Returns and Allowances,** saying this seems like unnecessary "busy work." Write a memo to your partner in response to these concerns.

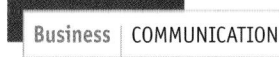

Customer to Vendor

Divide into groups of four individuals. Your company is named Cole's Cooking Supplies. Assign one person as the Cole's Sales Associate, one as the company's A/R clerk, one as the customer, Louisa's Cooking School, and one as Louisa's A/P clerk. Record the transaction each individual would record from a sale of $50,000 for cooking supplies.

Accounting General Ledger Packages

Go to the Quickbooks and Peachtree Web site at **quickbooks.com** and **peachtree.com.** Compare products at each site. What are some activities that each program can accomplish?

CHAPTER 7: Review and Applications

Answers to **Self Reviews**

Answers to Section 1 Self Review

1. A journal that is used to record only one type of transaction. Examples are the sales journal, the purchases journal, the cash receipts journal, and the cash payments journal.

2. Sales of merchandise on credit.

3. A ledger that contains accounts of a single type. Examples are the accounts receivable ledger and the accounts payable ledger.

4. **c.** increases credit sales

5. **c.** service, merchandising, manufacturing.

6. The sale to Harris was recorded at a taxable rate of 7 percent instead of 8 percent. Therefore, the Sales Tax Payable column should have an entry of $48, not $42. The Accounts Receivable Debit column should have an entry of $648, not $642.

   The sale to Wells should have an entry in the Accounts Receivable Debit column of $972, not $872.

Answers to Section 2 Self Review

1. Sales minus sales returns.

2. A sales return results when a customer returns goods and the firm takes them back. A sales allowance results when the firm gives a customer a reduction in the price of the good or service.

3. Individual accounts for all credit customers.

4. **a.** *Sales Returns and Allowances, Sales Tax Payable, Accounts Receivable*

5. **c.** income statement

6.

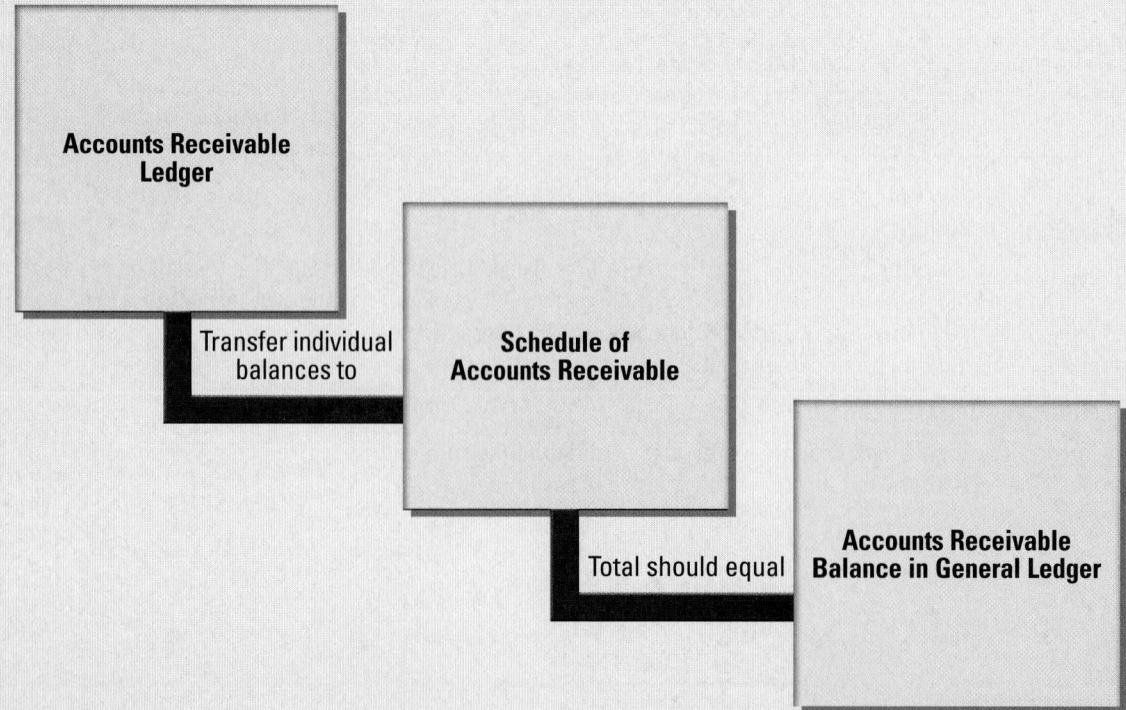

Accounts Receivable Ledger → Transfer individual balances to → **Schedule of Accounts Receivable** → Total should equal → **Accounts Receivable Balance in General Ledger**

Answers to Section 3 Self Review

1. *Sales Tax Payable* is the account used to record the liability for sales taxes to be paid in the future.

2. List price is the established retail price of an item; net price is the amount left after all trade discounts are subtracted from the list price.

3. Four types of credit sales are open-account credit, business credit card sales, bank credit card sales, and credit card company sales.

4. **c.** $2,880

5. **d.** $1,260

6. Possible factors are payment history, amount of current debt, amount of potential debt (available credit cards), employment history, salary, references from other creditors.

Answers to Comprehensive Self Review

1. The month and the quarter.

2. A control account is an account that serves as a link between a subsidiary ledger and the general ledger because its balance summarizes the balances of the accounts in the subsidiary ledger.

3. A merchandising business must account for the purchase and sale of goods and for its merchandise inventory.

4. It contains detailed information about the transactions with credit customers and shows the balances owed by credit customers at all times.

5. A service business sells services; a merchandising business sells goods that it has purchased for resale; and a manufacturing business sells goods that it has produced.

CHAPTER 7: Review and Applications

LEARNING OBJECTIVES

1. Record purchases of merchandise on credit in a three-column purchases journal.

2. Post from the three-column purchases journal to the general ledger accounts.

3. Post credit purchases from the purchases journal to the accounts payable subsidiary ledger.

4. Record purchases returns and allowances in the general journal and post them to the accounts payable subsidiary ledger.

5. Prepare a schedule of accounts payable.

6. Compute the net delivered cost of purchases.

7. Demonstrate a knowledge of the procedures for effective internal control of purchases.

8. Define the accounting terms new to this chapter.

NEW TERMS

accounts payable ledger

cash discount

cost of goods sold

freight in account

purchase allowance

purchase invoice

purchase order

purchase requisition

purchase return

purchases account

purchases discount

purchases journal

receiving report

sales discount

sales invoice

schedule of accounts payable

transportation in account

Chapter 8
Accounting for Purchases and Accounts Payable

www.pier1.com

I n 1962, a small retail store opened in San Mateo, California. Its inventory of love beads, incense, and beanbag chairs was an immediate hit with the burgeoning hippie generation. Pier 1 was born. As the tastes of baby boomers shifted, so did the shelves at Pier 1. From chocolate-covered ants to life-size suits of armor, Pier 1 has prided itself on staying one step ahead of trends and offering unique merchandise to their loyal customers. From initial product development to being displayed on its shelves, Pier 1's merchandise makes a long journey. The process begins with buyers who develop and import merchandise from more than 50 countries. All merchandise is carefully selected in order to offer its customers exclusive, one of a kind merchandise that reflects excellent quality at a great value. The current merchandise assortment ranges from home accessories such as candles, vases, and picture frames to full-sized, upholstered furniture, hand-carved armoires, large-scale vases, and eclectic wall décor. As much as 75 percent of Pier 1's merchandise assortment includes new product introductions each year.

Pier 1 now operates over 1,200 stores in all 50 states, Canada, Mexico, Puerto Rico, and the United Kingdom.

thinking critically | How do you think Pier 1 Imports' buyers determine the types of products that will appeal to its customers?

Section 1

SECTION OBJECTIVES

▶ **1. Record purchases of merchandise on credit in a three-column purchases journal.**

WHY IT'S IMPORTANT

Most merchandisers purchase goods on credit, and the use of a special journal improves efficiency when recording these transactions.

▶ **2. Post from the three-column purchases journal to the general ledger accounts.**

WHY IT'S IMPORTANT

Summary postings from the purchases journal minimize repetitive tasks.

TERMS TO LEARN

cash discount
cost of goods sold
Freight In account
purchase invoice
purchase order
purchase requisition
Purchases account
purchases discount
purchases journal
receiving report
sales discount
sales invoice
Transportation In account

Merchandise Purchases

In this chapter you will learn how The Style Shop manages its purchases of goods for resale and its accounts payable.

Accounting for Purchases

Most merchandising businesses purchase goods on credit under open-account arrangements. A large firm usually has a centralized purchasing department that is responsible for locating suppliers, obtaining price quotations, negotiating credit terms, and placing orders. In small firms purchasing activities are handled by a single individual, usually the owner or manager.

PURCHASING PROCEDURES

When a sales department needs goods, it sends the purchasing department a purchase requisition (Figure 8.1 on page 249). A **purchase requisition** lists the items to be ordered. It is signed by someone with the authority to approve requests for merchandise, usually the manager of the sales department. The purchasing department selects a supplier who can furnish the goods at a competitive price and then issues a purchase order (Figure 8.2 on page 249). The **purchase order** specifies the exact items, quantity, price, and credit terms. It is signed by someone with authority to approve purchases, usually the purchasing agent.

When the goods arrive at the business, they are inspected. A **receiving report** is prepared to show the quantity and condition of the goods received. The purchasing department receives a copy of the receiving report and compares it to the purchase order. If defective goods or the wrong quantity of goods are received, the purchasing department contacts the supplier and settles the problem.

Figure 8.3 on page 249 shows the invoice, or *bill,* for items ordered and shipped. The customer, The Style Shop, calls it a **purchase invoice** . The supplier, International Apparel Shop, calls it a **sales invoice** . The customer's accounting department compares the invoice to copies of the purchase order and receiving report. The accounting department checks the quantities, prices, and math on the invoice and then records the purchase. It is important to record purchases in the accounting records as soon as the invoice is verified. Shortly before the due date of the invoice, the accounting department issues a check to the supplier and records the payment.

> The purchasing department for The Home Depot, Inc., purchases 40,000 to 50,000 different kinds of home improvement supplies, building materials, and lawn and garden products.

The Style Shop
2007 Trendsetter Lane
Dallas, TX 75268-0967

PURCHASE REQUISITION

No. ___325___

DEPARTMENT ___Men's___   DATE OF REQUEST ___January 2, 2007___

ADVISE ON DELIVERY ___John Amos___   DATE REQUIRED ___January 25, 2007___

QUANTITY	DESCRIPTION
10	Assorted colors men's suits

APPROVED BY _____   REQUESTED BY _____

FOR PURCHASING DEPARTMENT USE ONLY

PURCHASE ORDER ___9001___   ISSUED TO: International Apparel Shop
DATE ___January 5, 2007___   1718 Sherry Lane
                                                       Dallas, TX 75267-6205

FIGURE 8.1

Purchase Requisition

The Style Shop
2007 Trendsetter Lane
Dallas, TX 75268-0967

PURCHASE ORDER

To | International Apparel Shop
   | 1718 Sherry Lane
   | Dallas, TX 75267-6205

Date: January 5, 2007
Order No: 9001
Terms: n/30

QUANTITY	ITEM	UNIT PRICE	TOTAL
10	Assorted colors men's suits	476.00	4,760.00

APPROVED BY _____

FIGURE 8.2

Purchase Order

International Apparel Shop
1718 Sherry Lane
Dallas, TX 75267-6205

INVOICE NO. 7985

SOLD TO: The Style Shop
          2007 Trendsetter Lane
          Dallas, TX 75268-0967

DATE: January 23, 2007
ORDER NO.: 9001
SHIPPED BY: Metroplex Express
TERMS: n/30

YOUR ORDER NO.	SALESPERSON	TERMS
9001		n/30

DATE SHIPPED	SHIPPED BY	FOB
January 23, 2007	Metroplex Express	Dallas

QUANTITY	DESCRIPTION	UNIT PRICE	TOTAL
10	Assorted colors men's suits	476 00	4,760 00
	Freight		360 00
	Total		5,120 00

FIGURE 8.3

Invoice

International INSIGHTS

National Preferences

When conducting business, the customer's tastes should be considered. Consumers around the world have different preferences in product packaging. For example, in France and Italy, consumers expect stylish looks, while in Germany many consumers look for recyclable materials. Accountants who work with international clients should consider national preferences when designing letterhead, creating portfolios, or choosing paper quality.

THE PURCHASES ACCOUNT

The purchase of merchandise for resale is a cost of doing business. The purchase of merchandise is debited to the **Purchases account** . *Purchases* is a temporary account classified as a cost of goods sold account. The **cost of goods sold** is the actual cost to the business of the merchandise sold to customers.

Cost of goods sold accounts follow the debit and credit rules of expense accounts. The *Purchases* account is increased by debits and decreased by credits. Its normal balance is a debit. In the chart of accounts, the cost of goods sold accounts appear just before the expense accounts.

> Wal-Mart Stores, Inc. purchases private-label products from suppliers and markets these as Wal-Mart brands. Products such as Ol'Roy™ dog food, Spring Valley® vitamins, and EverStart® automotive batteries are purchased at lower costs than nationally known brands. Thus, Wal-Mart Stores, Inc., can sell these items at a lower price to its customers.

FREIGHT CHARGES FOR PURCHASES

Sometimes the buyer pays the freight charge—the cost of shipping the goods from the seller's warehouse to the buyer's location. There are two ways to handle the freight charges paid by the buyer:

- The buyer is billed directly by the transportation company for the freight charge. The buyer issues a check directly to the freight company.
- The seller pays the freight charge and includes it on the invoice. The invoice includes the price of the goods and the freight charge.

The freight charge is debited to the **Freight In** or **Transportation In account** . This is a cost of goods sold account showing transportation charges for merchandise purchased. The buyer enters three elements in the accounting records:

Price of goods (debit *Purchases*)	$4,760.00
Freight charge (debit *Freight In*)	360.00
Total invoice (credit *Accounts Payable*)	$5,120.00

Purchases		Freight In		Accounts Payable	
Dr.	Cr.	Dr.	Cr.	Dr.	Cr.
+	−	+	−	−	+
4,760		360			5,120

important!

Credit Purchases

The purchases journal is used to record *only credit purchases of merchandise for resale*. Credit purchases of other items used in the business are recorded in the general journal.

THE PURCHASES JOURNAL

For most merchandising businesses, it is not efficient to enter purchases of goods in the general journal. Instead, credit purchases of merchandise are recorded in a special journal called the **purchases journal** .

The following illustrates how credit purchases appear in a general journal. Each entry involves a debit to *Purchases* and *Freight In* and a credit to *Accounts Payable* plus a detailed explanation.

These 4 general journal entries require 12 separate postings to general ledger accounts: 4 to *Purchases,* 4 to *Freight In,* and 4 to *Accounts Payable.* As you can see from the ledger accounts that follow, it takes a great deal of time and effort to post these entries.

GENERAL JOURNAL   PAGE ___1___

	DATE		DESCRIPTION	POST. REF.	DEBIT	CREDIT	
1	2007						1
2	Jan.	3	Purchases	501	2 675 00		2
3			Freight In	502	190 00		3
4			Accounts Payable	205		2 865 00	4
5			Purchased merchandise from				5
6			Fashion Design, Invoice 5879,				6
7			dated December 29, 2006,				7
8			terms 2/10, n/30				8
9							9
10		5	Purchases	501	3 880 00		10
11			Freight In	502	175 00		11
12			Accounts Payable	205		4 055 00	12
13			Purchased merchandise from				13
14			The Trend Center, Invoice 633,				14
15			dated December 30, 2006,				15
16			terms n/30				16
17							17
18		6	Purchases	501	2 900 00		18
19			Freight In	502	240 00		19
20			Accounts Payable	205		3 140 00	20
21			Purchased merchandise from				21
22			The Modern Woman, Invoice 8011,				22
23			dated December 31, 2006,				23
24			terms n/30				24
25							25
26		7	Purchases	501	3 675 00		26
27			Freight In	502	260 00		27
28			Accounts Payable	205		3 935 00	28
29			Purchased merchandise from				29
30			World of Fashions, Invoice 4321,				30
31			dated December 31, 2006,				31
			terms 2/10, n/30				

ACCOUNT _Accounts Payable_   ACCOUNT NO. _205_

DATE		DESCRIPTION	POST. REF.	DEBIT	CREDIT	BALANCE DEBIT	BALANCE CREDIT
2007							
Jan.	1	Balance	✓				10 800 00
	3		J1		2 865 00		13 665 00
	5		J1		4 055 00		17 720 00
	6		J1		3 140 00		20 860 00
	7		J1		3 935 00		24 795 00

ACCOUNT _Purchases_   ACCOUNT NO. _501_

DATE		DESCRIPTION	POST. REF.	DEBIT	CREDIT	BALANCE DEBIT	BALANCE CREDIT
2007							
Jan.	3		J1	2 675 00		2 675 00	
	5		J1	3 880 00		6 555 00	
	6		J1	2 900 00		9 455 00	
	7		J1	3 675 00		13 130 00	

ACCOUNT _Freight In_   ACCOUNT NO. _502_

DATE		DESCRIPTION	POST. REF.	DEBIT	CREDIT	BALANCE DEBIT	BALANCE CREDIT
2007							
Jan.	3		J1	1 9 0 00		1 9 0 00	
	5		J1	1 7 5 00		3 6 5 00	
	6		J1	2 4 0 00		6 0 5 00	
	7		J1	2 6 0 00		8 6 5 00	

Figure 8.4 shows the purchases journal for The Style Shop. Remember that the purchases journal is only for credit purchases of merchandise for resale to customers. Notice how the columns efficiently organize the data about the credit purchases. The purchases journal makes it possible to record each purchase on a single line. In addition, there is no need to enter account names and descriptions.

▶ 1. OBJECTIVE

Record purchases of merchandise on credit in a three-column purchases journal.

RECORDING TRANSACTIONS IN A PURCHASES JOURNAL

Use the information on the purchase invoice to make the entry in the purchases journal.

1. Enter the date, supplier name, invoice number, invoice date, and credit terms.
2. In the Accounts Payable Credit column, enter the total owed to the supplier.
3. In the Purchases Debit column, enter the price of the goods purchased.
4. In the Freight In Debit column, enter the freight amount.

The total of the Purchases Debit and Freight In Debit columns must equal the amount entered in the Accounts Payable Credit column.

The invoice date and credit terms determine when payment is due. The following credit terms often appear on invoices:

- *Net 30 days* or *n/30* means that payment in full is due 30 days after the date of the invoice.
- *Net 10 days EOM,* or *n/10 EOM,* means that payment in full is due 10 days after the end of the month in which the invoice was issued.
- *2% 10 days, net 30 days,* or *2/10, n/30* means that if payment is made within 10 days of the invoice date, the customer can take a 2 percent discount. Otherwise, payment in full is due in 30 days.

FIGURE 8.4   Purchases Journal

PURCHASES JOURNAL   PAGE _1_

DATE		PURCHASED FROM	INVOICE NUMBER	INVOICE DATE	TERMS	POST. REF.	ACCOUNTS PAYABLE CREDIT	PURCHASES DEBIT	FREIGHT IN DEBIT
2007									
Jan.	3	Fashion Designs	5879	12/29/06	2/10, n/30		2 8 6 5 00	2 6 7 5 00	1 9 0 00
	5	The Trend Center	633	12/30/06	n/30		4 0 5 5 00	3 8 8 0 00	1 7 5 00
	6	Modern Woman	8011	12/31/06	n/30		3 1 4 0 00	2 9 0 0 00	2 4 0 00
	7	World of Fashions	4321	12/31/06	2/10, n/30		3 9 3 5 00	3 6 7 5 00	2 6 0 00
	19	Fashion Warehouse	8997	01/15/07	2/10, n/30		4 2 0 0 00	3 8 6 0 00	3 4 0 00
	23	International Apparel Shop	7985	01/22/07	n/30		5 1 2 0 00	4 7 6 0 00	3 6 0 00
	31						23 3 1 5 00	21 7 5 0 00	1 5 6 5 00

ACCOUNTING ON THE JOB

RETAIL/WHOLESALE SALES & SERVICE

Industry Overview

In the United States today, retailing represents $3 trillion in annual sales. Wholesale markets fuel these sales, supplying products and services for resale in department stores, discount stores, factory outlets, catalogs, and on the Web. The retail industry alone employs more than 20 million workers in the United States.

Career Opportunities

- Store Manager
- Vice President of Acquisitions and Real Estate
- Inventory Specialist
- Manager of Logistics
- Fashion Merchandiser
- Senior Buyer
- Director of E-Commerce Distribution
- Customer Service Manager

Preparing for a Retail/Wholesale Career

- Obtain a business-related degree to open doors to management-level positions.
- Apply to corporate executive training programs for paths to senior buyer, manager of planning and distribution, or regional merchandise manager.
- Complete college courses in marketing, finance, accounting, communications, merchandising, and information systems, as recommended by the National Retail Federation.
- Complete one or two introductory accounting courses, one financial accounting course, and one managerial accounting course for degree programs in fashion merchandising and retail marketing.
- Obtain specialized certifications such as the Buyers Certification or Logistics Certification.

THINKING CRITICALLY

Describe why an understanding of credit policies and credit terms might help a retail store manager direct the operations of the store more effectively.

INTERNET APPLICATION

Locate a recruiting Web site for a company such as Federated Department Stores. Review the job description for store manager or buyer. In a half-page report, list the primary responsibilities for this job. What accounting or financial responsibilities does the position entail?

The 2 percent discount is a **cash discount**; it is a discount offered by suppliers to encourage quick payment by customers. To the customer it is known as a **purchases discount**. To the supplier it is known as a **sales discount**.

POSTING TO THE GENERAL LEDGER

The purchases journal simplifies the posting process. Summary amounts are posted at the end of the month. Refer to Figure 8.5 as you learn how to post from the purchases journal to the general ledger accounts.

---

important!

Cash Discounts
In the purchases journal, record the amount shown on the invoice. The cash discount is recorded when the payment is made.

▶ 2. **OBJECTIVE**
Post from the three-column purchases journal to the general ledger accounts.

PURCHASES JOURNAL   PAGE ___1___

DATE		PURCHASED FROM	INVOICE NUMBER	INVOICE DATE	TERMS	POST. REF.	ACCOUNTS PAYABLE CREDIT	PURCHASES DEBIT	FREIGHT IN DEBIT
2007									
Jan.	3	Fashion Designs	5879	12/29/06	2/10, n/30	✓	2 865 00	2 675 00	190 00
	5	The Trend Center	633	12/30/06	n/30	✓	4 055 00	3 880 00	175 00
	6	Modern WomAn	8011	12/31/06	n/30	✓	3 140 00	2 900 00	240 00
	7	World of Fashions	4321	12/31/06	2/10, n/30	✓	3 935 00	3 675 00	260 00
	19	Fashion Warehouse	8997	01/15/07	2/10, n/30	✓	4 200 00	3 860 00	340 00
	23	International Apparel Shop	7985	01/23/07	n/30	✓	5 120 00	4 760 00	360 00
	31						23 315 00	21 750 00	1 565 00
							(205)	(501)	(502)

ACCOUNT _Accounts Payable_   ACCOUNT NO. _205_

DATE		DESCRIPTION	POST. REF.	DEBIT	CREDIT	BALANCE DEBIT	BALANCE CREDIT
2007							
Jan.	1	Balance	✓				10 800 00
	31		P1		23 3 1 5 00		34 1 1 5 00

ACCOUNT _Purchases_   ACCOUNT NO. _501_

DATE	DESCRIPTION	POST. REF.	DEBIT	CREDIT	BALANCE DEBIT	BALANCE CREDIT
2007						
Jan. 31		P1	21 7 5 0 00		21 7 5 0 00	

ACCOUNT _Freight In_   ACCOUNT NO. _502_

DATE	DESCRIPTION	POST. REF.	DEBIT	CREDIT	BALANCE DEBIT	BALANCE CREDIT
2007						
Jan. 31		P1	1 5 6 5 00		1 5 6 5 00	

FIGURE 8.5   Posting to the General Ledger

Total the Accounts Payable Credit, the Purchases Debit, and the Freight In Debit columns. Before posting, prove the equality of the debits and credits recorded in the purchases journal.

Proof of Purchases Journal	
	Debits
Purchases Debit column	$21,750.00
Freight In Debit column	1,565.00
	$23,315.00
	Credits
Accounts Payable Credit column	$23,315.00

After the equality of debits and credits is verified, rule the purchases journal. The steps to post the column totals to the general ledger follow.

1. Locate the **Accounts Payable** ledger account.

2. Enter the date.

3. Enter the posting reference, P1. The **P** is for purchases journal. The **1** is the purchases journal page number.

4. Enter the amount from the Accounts Payable Credit column in the purchases journal in the Credit column of the **Accounts Payable** ledger account.

5. Compute the new balance and enter it in the Balance Credit column.

6. In the purchases journal, enter the **Accounts Payable** ledger account number (205) under the column total.

7. Repeat the steps for the **Purchases** Debit and **Freight In** Debit columns.

During the month the individual entries in the purchases journal are posted to the creditor accounts in the accounts payable ledger. The check marks in the purchases journal in Figure 8.5 indicate that these postings have been completed. This procedure is discussed later in this chapter.

ADVANTAGES OF A PURCHASES JOURNAL

Every business has certain types of transactions that occur over and over again. A well-designed accounting system includes journals that permit efficient recording of such transactions. In most merchandising firms, purchases of goods on credit take place often enough to make it worthwhile to use a purchases journal.

A special journal for credit purchases of merchandise saves time and effort when recording and posting purchases. The use of a purchases journal and other special journals allows for the division of accounting work among different employees. The purchases journal strengthens the audit trail. All credit purchases are recorded in one place, and each entry refers to the number and date of the invoice.

Section 1: Self Review

QUESTIONS

1. What activities does a purchasing department perform?

2. What type of transaction is recorded in the purchases journal?

3. What are the advantages of using a purchases journal?

EXERCISES

4. What form is sent to the supplier to order goods?

a. Purchase invoice
b. Purchase order
c. Purchase requisition
d. Sales invoice

5. When the sales department needs goods, what document is sent to the purchasing department?

a. Purchase invoice
b. Purchase order
c. Purchase requisition
d. Sales requisition

ANALYSIS

6. An invoice dated January 15 for $2,000 shows credit terms 2/10, n/30. What do the credit terms mean?

(Answers to Section 1 Self Review are on page 280.)

Section 2

SECTION OBJECTIVES

▶ **3. Post credit purchases from the purchases journal to the accounts payable subsidiary ledger.**

WHY IT'S IMPORTANT

Up-to-date records allow prompt payment of invoices.

▶ **4. Record purchases returns and allowances in the general journal and post them to the accounts payable subsidiary ledger.**

WHY IT'S IMPORTANT

For unsatisfactory goods received, an allowance or return is reflected in the accounting records.

▶ **5. Prepare a schedule of accounts payable.**

WHY IT'S IMPORTANT

This schedule provides a snapshot of amounts owed to suppliers.

▶ **6. Compute the net delivered cost of purchases.**

WHY IT'S IMPORTANT

This is an important component in measuring operational results.

▶ **7. Demonstrate a knowledge of the procedures for effective internal control of purchases.**

WHY IT'S IMPORTANT

Businesses try to prevent fraud, errors, and holding excess inventory.

TERMS TO LEARN

accounts payable ledger
purchase allowance
purchase return
schedule of accounts payable

Accounts Payable

Businesses that buy merchandise on credit can conduct more extensive operations and use financial resources more effectively than if they paid cash for all purchases. It is important to pay invoices on time so that the business maintains a good credit reputation with its suppliers.

The Accounts Payable Ledger

Businesses need detailed records in order to pay invoices promptly. The **accounts payable ledger** provides information about the individual accounts for all creditors. The accounts payable ledger is a subsidiary ledger; it is separate from and subordinate to the general ledger. The accounts payable ledger contains a separate account for each creditor. Each account shows purchases, payments, and returns and allowances. The balance of the account shows the amount owed to the creditor.

Figure 8.6 on page 257 shows the accounts payable ledger account for International Apparel Shop. Notice that the Balance column does not indicate whether the balance is a debit or a credit. The form assumes that the balance will be a credit because the normal balance of liability accounts is a credit. A debit balance may exist if more than the amount owed was paid to the creditor or if returned goods were already paid for. If the balance is a debit, circle the amount to show that the account does not have the normal balance.

Small businesses like The Style Shop arrange the accounts payable ledger in alphabetical order. Large businesses and businesses that use computerized accounting systems assign an account number to each creditor and arrange the accounts payable ledger in numeric order.

POSTING A CREDIT PURCHASE

To keep the accounting records up to date, invoices are posted to the accounts payable subsidiary ledger every day. Refer to Figure 8.6 as you learn how to post to the accounts payable ledger.

1. Locate the accounts payable ledger account for the creditor International Apparel Shop.
2. Enter the date.
3. In the Description column, enter the invoice number and date.
4. In the Posting Reference column, enter the purchases journal page number.
5. Enter the amount from the *Accounts Payable* Credit column in the purchases journal in the Credit column of the accounts payable subsidiary ledger.

6. Compute and enter the new balance in the Balance column.

7. In the purchases journal (Figure 8.5 on page 254), enter a check mark (✓) in the Posting Reference column. This indicates that the transaction is posted in the accounts payable subsidiary ledger.

POSTING CASH PAID ON ACCOUNT

When the transaction involves cash paid on account to a supplier, the payment is first recorded in a cash payments journal. (The cash payments journal is discussed in Chapter 9.) The cash payment is then posted to the individual creditor's account in the accounts payable ledger. Figure 8.7 shows a posting for cash paid to a creditor on January 27.

Purchases Returns and Allowances

When merchandise arrives, it is examined to confirm that it is satisfactory. Occasionally, the wrong goods are shipped, or items are damaged or defective. A **purchase return** is when the business returns the goods. A **purchase allowance** is when the purchaser keeps the goods but receives a reduction in the price of the goods. The supplier issues a credit memorandum for the return or allowance. The credit memorandum reduces the amount that the purchaser owes.

Purchases returns and allowances are entered in the *Purchases Returns and Allowances* account, not in the *Purchases* account. The *Purchases Returns and Allowances* account is a complete record of returns and allowances. Business managers analyze this account to identify problem suppliers.

Purchases Returns and Allowances is a contra cost of goods sold account. The normal balance of cost of goods sold accounts is a debit. The normal balance of *Purchases Returns and Allowances,* a contra cost of goods sold account, is a credit.

RECORDING PURCHASES RETURNS AND ALLOWANCES

The Style Shop received merchandise from International Apparel Shop on January 23. Some goods were damaged, and the supplier granted a $476 purchase allowance. The Style Shop recorded the full amount of the invoice, $5,120, in the purchases journal. The purchase allowance was recorded separately in the general journal.

▶ 3. OBJECTIVE

Post credit purchases from the purchases journal to the accounts payable subsidiary ledger.

▶ 4. OBJECTIVE

Record purchases returns and allowances in the general journal and post them to the accounts payable subsidiary ledger.

Topic Tackler

PLUS

recall

Subsidiary Ledger
The total of the accounts in the subsidiary ledger must equal the control account balance.

NAME __International Apparel Shop__   TERMS _n/30_
ADDRESS __1718 Sherry Lane, Dallas, Texas 75267-6205__

DATE		DESCRIPTION	POST. REF.	DEBIT	CREDIT	BALANCE
2007						
Jan.	1	Balance	✓			1 6 0 0 00
	23	Invoice 7985, 01/23/07	P1		5 1 2 0 00	6 7 2 0 00

FIGURE 8.6

Accounts Payable Ledger Account

NAME __International Apparel Shop__   TERMS _n/30_
ADDRESS __1718 Sherry Lane, Dallas, Texas 75267-6205__

DATE		DESCRIPTION	POST. REF.	DEBIT	CREDIT	BALANCE
2007						
Jan.	1	Balance	✓			1 6 0 0 00
	23	Invoice 7985, 01/23/07	P1		5 1 2 0 00	6 7 2 0 00
	27		CP1	2 4 0 0 00		4 3 2 0 00

FIGURE 8.7

Posting a Payment Made on Account

BUSINESS TRANSACTION

On January 30 The Style Shop received a credit memorandum for $476 from International Apparel Shop as an allowance for damaged merchandise.

International Apparel Shop
1718 Sherry Lane
Dallas, TX 75267-6205

CREDIT MEMORANDUM
NUMBER: 103
DATE: January 30, 2007

TO: The Style Shop
2007 Trendsetter Lane
Dallas, TX 75268-0967

ORIGINAL INVOICE: 7985
INVOICE DATE: January 23, 2007
DESCRIPTION: Credit for damaged suit: $476.00

ANALYSIS

The liability account, **Accounts Payable,** is decreased by $476. The contra cost of goods sold account, **Purchases Returns and Allowances**, is increased by $476.

DEBIT-CREDIT RULES

DEBIT   Decreases to liabilities are debits. Debit **Accounts Payable** for $476.

CREDIT   Increases to contra cost of goods sold accounts are recorded as credits. Credit **Purchases Returns and Allowances** for $476.

T-ACCOUNT PRESENTATION

Accounts Payable		Purchases Returns and Allowances	
−	+	−	+
476			476

THE BOTTOM LINE
Purchase Allowance

Income Statement

Contra Cost of Goods Sold	↑ 476
Net Income	↑ 476

Balance Sheet

Liabilities	↓ 476
Equity	↑ 476

GENERAL JOURNAL ENTRY

GENERAL JOURNAL   PAGE _2_

	DATE		DESCRIPTION	POST. REF.	DEBIT	CREDIT	
15	Jan.	30	Accounts Payable/International Apparel Shop		476 00		15
16			Purchases Returns and Allowances			476 00	16
17			Received Credit Memo 103 for				17
18			an allowance for damaged				18
19			merchandise; original Invoice				19
20			7985, January 23, 2007				20

Notice that this entry includes a debit to **Accounts Payable** and a credit to **Purchases Returns and Allowances.** In addition, there is a debit to the creditor's account in the accounts payable subsidiary ledger. Businesses that have few returns and allowances use the general journal to record these transactions. Businesses with many returns and allowances use a special journal for purchases returns and allowances.

POSTING A PURCHASES RETURN OR ALLOWANCE

Whether recorded in the general journal or in a special journal, it is important to promptly post returns and allowances to the creditor's account in the accounts payable ledger. Refer to Figure 8.8 to learn how to post purchases returns and allowances to the supplier's account.

GENERAL JOURNAL   PAGE ___1___

	DATE	DESCRIPTION	POST. REF.	DEBIT	CREDIT	
1	2007					1
15	Jan. 30	Accounts Payable/Int'l Apparel Shop	205 ✓	4 7 6 00		15
16		Purchases Returns and Allowances	503		4 7 6 00	16
17		Received Credit Memo 103 for				17
18		damaged merchandise that was				18
19		returned; original purchase was made				19
20		on Invoice 7985, January 23, 2007				20
21						21
22						

NAME ___International Apparel Shop___   TERMS ___n/30___

ADDRESS ___1718 Sherry Lane, Dallas, Texas 75267-6205___

DATE	DESCRIPTION	POST. REF.	DEBIT	CREDIT	BALANCE
2007					
Jan. 1	Balance	✓			1 6 0 0 00
23	Invoice 7985, 01/23/07	P1		5 1 2 0 00	6 7 2 0 00
27		CP1	2 4 0 0 00		4 3 2 0 00
30	CM 103	J1	4 7 6 00		3 8 4 4 00

FIGURE 8.8

Posting to a Creditor's Account

recall

Contra Accounts
The *Purchases Returns and Allowances* account is a contra account. Contra accounts have normal balances that are the opposite of related accounts.

1. Enter the date.
2. In the Description column, enter the credit memorandum number.
3. In the Posting Reference column, enter the general journal page number.
4. Enter the amount of the return or allowance in the Debit column.
5. Compute the new balance and enter it in the Balance column.
6. In the general journal, enter a check mark (✓) to show that the transaction was posted to the creditor's account in the accounts payable subsidiary ledger.

After the transaction is posted to the general ledger, enter the *Purchases Returns and Allowances* ledger account number in the Posting Reference column.

Schedule of Accounts Payable

The total of the individual creditor accounts in the subsidiary ledger must equal the balance of the *Accounts Payable* control account. To prove that the control account and the subsidiary ledger are equal, businesses prepare a **schedule of accounts payable** —a list of all balances owed to creditors. Figure 8.9 on page 260 shows the accounts payable subsidiary ledger for The Style Shop on January 31.

Figure 8.10 on page 261 shows the schedule of accounts payable for The Style Shop. Notice that the accounts payable control account balance is $22,989. This equals the total on the schedule of accounts payable. If the amounts are not equal, it is essential to locate and correct the errors.

▶ **5. OBJECTIVE**
Prepare a schedule of accounts payable.

Determining the Cost of Purchases

The *Purchases* account accumulates the cost of merchandise bought for resale. The income statement of a merchandising business contains a section showing the total cost of purchases. This section combines information about the cost of the purchases, freight in, and purchases returns and allowances for the period. The Style Shop has the following general ledger account balances at January 31:

▶ **6. OBJECTIVE**
Compute the net delivered cost of purchases.

FIGURE 8.9

The Accounts Payable Ledger

NAME _Fashion Designs_ TERMS _2/10, n/30_
ADDRESS _2313 Belt Line Road, Dallas, Texas 75267-6205_

DATE		DESCRIPTION	POST. REF.	DEBIT	CREDIT	BALANCE
2007						
Jan.	1	Balance	✓			2 2 0 0 00
	3	Invoice 5879, 12/29/06	P1		2 8 6 5 00	5 0 6 5 00
	13		CP1	3 2 0 0 00		1 8 6 5 00
	30		CP1	8 0 0 00		1 0 6 5 00

NAME _Fashion Warehouse_ TERMS _2/10, n/30_
ADDRESS _1027 St James Avenue, Dallas, Texas 75267-6205_

DATE		DESCRIPTION	POST. REF.	DEBIT	CREDIT	BALANCE
2007						
Jan.	19	Invoice 8997, 01/15/07	P1		4 2 0 0 00	4 2 0 0 00

NAME _International Apparel Shop_ TERMS _n/30_
ADDRESS _1718 Sherry Lane, Dallas, Texas 75267-6205_

DATE		DESCRIPTION	POST. REF.	DEBIT	CREDIT	BALANCE
2007						
Jan.	1	Balance	✓			1 6 0 0 00
	23	Invoice 7985, 01/23/07	P1		5 1 2 0 00	6 7 2 0 00
	27		CP1	2 4 0 0 00		4 3 2 0 00
	30	CM 103	J1	4 7 6 00		3 8 4 4 00

NAME _Modern Woman_ TERMS _n/30_
ADDRESS _2860 Jackson Drive, Dallas, Texas 75267-6205_

DATE		DESCRIPTION	POST. REF.	DEBIT	CREDIT	BALANCE
2007						
Jan.	1	Balance	✓			1 6 0 0 00
	6	Invoice 8011, 12/31/06	P1		3 1 4 0 00	4 7 4 0 00

NAME _The Trend Center_ TERMS _n/30_
ADDRESS _1313 Sunset Drive, Dallas, Texas 75267-6205_

DATE		DESCRIPTION	POST. REF.	DEBIT	CREDIT	BALANCE
2007						
Jan.	1	Balance	✓			2 4 0 0 00
	5	Invoice 633, 12/30/06	P1		4 0 5 5 00	6 4 5 5 00
	17		CP1	4 2 5 0 00		2 2 0 5 00

NAME _World of Fashions_ TERMS _2/10, n/30_
ADDRESS _1729 Parker Road, Dallas, Texas 75267-6205_

DATE		DESCRIPTION	POST. REF.	DEBIT	CREDIT	BALANCE
2007						
Jan.	1	Balance	✓			3 0 0 0 00
	7	Invoice 4321, 12/31/06	P1		3 9 3 5 00	6 9 3 5 00

The Style Shop
Schedule of Accounts Payable
January 31, 2007

Fashion Designs	1 0 6 5 00
Fashion Warehouse	4 2 0 0 00
International Apparel Shop	3 8 4 4 00
Modern Woman	4 7 4 0 00
The Trend Center	2 2 0 5 00
World of Fashions	6 9 3 5 00
Total	2 2 9 8 9 00

ACCOUNT Accounts Payable _____ ACCOUNT NO. 205

DATE		DESCRIPTION	POST. REF.	DEBIT	CREDIT	BALANCE	
						DEBIT	CREDIT
2007							
Jan.	1	Balance					10 8 0 0 00
	30		J1	4 7 6 00			10 3 2 4 00
	31		P1		23 3 1 5 00		33 6 3 9 00
	31		CP1	10 6 5 0 00			22 9 8 9 00

FIGURE 8.10

Schedule of Accounts Payable
and the Accounts Payable
Account

Purchases	$23,315
Freight In	1,565
Purchases Returns and Allowances	476

The net delivered cost of purchases for The Style Shop for January is calculated as follows.

Purchases	$23,315
Freight In	1,565
Delivered Cost of Purchases	$24,880
Less Purchases Returns and Allowances	476
Net Delivered Cost of Purchases	$24,404

For firms that do not have freight charges, the amount of net purchases is calculated as follows.

Purchases	$23,315
Less Purchases Returns and Allowances	476
Net Purchases	$22,839

In Chapter 13 you will see how the complete income statement for a merchandising business is prepared. You will learn about the Cost of Goods Sold section and how the net delivered cost of purchases is used in calculating the results of operations.

Internal Control of Purchases

Because of the large amount of money spent to buy goods, most businesses develop careful procedures for the control of purchases and payments. Some firms have a *voucher system,* a special system used to achieve internal control. Whether the voucher system is used or not, a business should be sure that its control process includes sufficient safeguards. The objectives of the controls are to

▶ 7. **OBJECTIVE**

Demonstrate a
knowledge of the
procedures for effective
internal control of
purchases.

- create written proof that purchases and payments are authorized;
- ensure that different people are involved in the process of buying goods, receiving goods, and making payments.

Separating duties among employees provides a system of checks and balances. In a small business with just a few employees, it might be difficult or impossible to separate duties. However, the business should design as effective a set of control procedures as the company's resources will allow. Effective systems have the following controls in place.

1. All purchases should be made only after proper authorization has been given in writing.
2. Goods should be carefully checked when they are received. They should then be compared with the purchase order and with the invoice received from the supplier.
3. The purchase order, receiving report, and invoice should be checked to confirm that the information on the documents is in agreement.
4. The computations on the invoice should be checked for accuracy.
5. Authorization for payment should be made by someone other than the person who ordered the goods, and this authorization should be given only after all the verifications have been made.
6. Another person should write the check for payment.
7. Prenumbered forms should be used for purchase requisitions, purchase orders, and checks. The numbers of the documents issued should be verified periodically to make sure that all forms can be accounted for.

ABOUT ACCOUNTING

Employee Fraud

According to the U.S. Chamber of Commerce, businesses lose $20 to $40 billion each year to employee fraud. The best defense against fraud is to use good internal controls: Have multiple employees in contact with suppliers and screen employees and vendors to reduce fraud opportunities.

MANAGERIAL IMPLICATIONS   <<

ACCOUNTING FOR PURCHASES

- Management and the accounting staff need to work together to make sure that there are good internal controls over purchasing.
- A carefully designed system of checks and balances protects the business against fraud, errors, and excessive investment in merchandise.
- The accounting staff needs to record transactions efficiently so that up-to-date information about creditors is available.
- Using the purchases journal and the accounts payable subsidiary ledger improves efficiency.
- To maintain a good credit reputation with suppliers, it is important to have an accounting system that ensures prompt payment of invoices.
- A well-run accounting system provides management with information about cash: cash required to pay suppliers, short-term loans needed to cover temporary cash shortages, and cash available for short-term investments.
- Separate accounts for recording purchases, freight charges, and purchases returns and allowances make it easy to analyze the elements in the cost of purchases.

THINKING CRITICALLY

As a manager, what internal controls would you put in your accounting system?

Section 2: **Self Review**

QUESTIONS

1. What is the purpose of the schedule of accounts payable?

2. A firm has a debit balance of $60,550 in its **Purchases** account and a credit balance of $2,875 in its **Purchases Returns and Allowances** account. Calculate net purchases for the period.

3. A firm receives an invoice that reflects the price of goods as $1,275 and the freight charge as $82. How is this transaction recorded?

EXERCISES

4. In the accounts payable ledger, a supplier's account has a beginning balance of $4,800. A transaction of $1,600 is posted from the purchases journal. What is the balance of the supplier's account?

   a. $3,200 debit

   b. $3,200 credit

   c. $6,400 credit

   d. $6,400 debit

5. The net delivered cost of purchases for the period appears on the

   a. balance sheet.

   b. income statement.

   c. schedule of accounts payable.

   d. statement of owner's equity.

ANALYSIS

6. In the general ledger, the **Accounts Payable** account has a balance of $15,500. The schedule of accounts payable lists accounts totaling $20,500. What could cause this error?

(Answers to Section 2 Self Review are on page 280.)

REVIEW   Chapter Summary

In this chapter, you have learned about the accounting journals and ledgers required for the efficient processing of purchases for a business. Businesses with strong internal controls establish and follow procedures for approving requests for new merchandise, choosing suppliers, placing orders with suppliers, checking goods after they arrive, identifying invoices, and approving payments.

Learning Objectives

1 Record purchases of merchandise on credit in a three-column purchases journal.

Purchases and payments on account must be entered in the firm's accounting records promptly and accurately. Most merchandising businesses normally purchase goods on credit. The most efficient system for recording purchases on credit is the use of a special purchases journal. With this type of journal, only one line is needed to enter all the data.

The purchases journal is used only to record the credit purchase of goods for resale. General business expenses are not recorded in the purchases journal.

2 Post from the three-column purchases journal to the general ledger accounts.

The use of the three-column purchases journal simplifies the posting process because nothing is posted to the general ledger until the month's end. Then, summary postings are made to the *Purchases, Freight In,* and *Accounts Payable* accounts.

3 Post credit purchases from the purchases journal to the accounts payable subsidiary ledger.

An accounts payable subsidiary ledger helps a firm keep track of the amounts it owes to creditors. Postings are made to this ledger on a daily basis.

- Each credit purchase is posted from the purchases journal to the accounts payable subsidiary ledger.
- Each payment on account is posted from the cash payments journal to the accounts payable subsidiary ledger.

4 Record purchases returns and allowances in the general journal and post them to the accounts payable subsidiary ledger.

Returns and allowances on purchases of goods are credited to an account called *Purchases Returns and Allowances.* These transactions may be recorded in the general journal or in a special purchases returns and allowances journal. Each return or allowance on a credit purchase is posted to the accounts payable subsidiary ledger.

5 Prepare a schedule of accounts payable.

At the month's end, a schedule of accounts payable is prepared. The schedule lists the balances owed to the firm's creditors and proves the accuracy of the subsidiary ledger. The total of the schedule of accounts payable is compared with the balance of the *Accounts Payable* account in the general ledger, which acts as a control account. The two amounts should be equal.

6 Compute the net delivered cost of purchases.

The net delivered cost of purchases is computed by adding the cost of purchases and freight in, then subtracting any purchases returns and allowances. Net delivered cost of purchases is reported in the Cost of Goods Sold section of the income statement.

7 Demonstrate a knowledge of the procedures for effective internal control of purchases.

Purchases and payments should be properly authorized and processed with appropriate documentation to provide a system of checks and balances. A division of responsibilities within the purchases process ensures strong internal controls.

8 Define the accounting terms new to this chapter.

Glossary

Accounts payable ledger (p. 256) A subsidiary ledger that contains a separate account for each creditor

Cash discount (p. 253) A discount offered by suppliers for payment received within a specified period of time

Cost of goods sold (p. 250) The actual cost to the business of the merchandise sold to customers

Freight In account (p. 250) An account showing transportation charges for items purchased

Purchase allowance (p. 257) A price reduction from the amount originally billed

Purchase invoice (p. 248) A bill received for goods purchased

Purchase order (p. 248) An order to the supplier of goods specifying items needed, quantity, price, and credit terms

Purchase requisition (p. 248) A list sent to the purchasing department showing the items to be ordered

Purchase return (p. 257) Return of unsatisfactory goods

Purchases account (p. 250) An account used to record cost of goods bought for resale during a period

Purchases discount (p. 253) A cash discount offered to the customer for payment within a specified period

Purchases journal (p. 250) A special journal used to record the purchase of goods on credit

Receiving report (p. 248) A form showing quantity and condition of goods received

Sales discount (p. 253) A cash discount offered by the supplier for payment within a specified period

Sales invoice (p. 248) A supplier's billing document

Schedule of accounts payable (p. 259) A list of all balances owed to creditors

Transportation In account (p. 250) See Freight In account

Comprehensive **Self Review**

1. What type of account is *Purchases Returns and Allowances?*
2. What is a cash discount and why is it offered?
3. What is the purpose of the *Freight In* account?
4. What is the purpose of a purchase requisition? A purchase order?
5. What is the difference between a receiving report and an invoice?

(Answers to Comprehensive Self Review are on page 280.)

Discussion Questions

1. Why are the invoice date and terms recorded in the purchases journal?
2. What major safeguards should be built into a system of internal control for purchases of goods?
3. What is the purpose of a credit memorandum?
4. What is a purchase allowance?
5. What is a purchase return?
6. What is a schedule of accounts payable? Why is it prepared?
7. What is the relationship of the *Accounts Payable* account in the general ledger to the accounts payable subsidiary ledger?
8. What type of accounts are kept in the accounts payable ledger?
9. Why is it useful for a business to have an accounts payable ledger?
10. How is the net delivered cost of purchases computed?

11. What journals can be used to enter various merchandise purchase transactions?

12. What is the difference between a purchase invoice and a sales invoice?

13. What is the normal balance of the **Purchases** account?

14. On what financial statement do the accounts related to purchases of merchandise appear? In which section of this statement are they reported?

15. Why is the use of a **Purchases Returns and Allowances** account preferred to crediting these transactions to **Purchases?**

16. What do the following credit terms mean?

   a. n/30

   b. 2/10, n/30

   c. n/10 EOM

   d. n/20

   e. 1/10, n/20

   f. 3/5, n/30

   g. n/15 EOM

17. A business has purchased some new equipment for use in its operations, not for resale to customers. The terms of the invoice are n/30. Should this transaction be entered in the purchases journal? If not, where should it be recorded?

APPLICATIONS

 Exercises

Exercise 8.1
Objective 1

▶ **Identifying the journals used to record purchases and related transactions.**

The accounting system of Shoe City includes the following journals. Indicate which journal is used to record each transaction.

JOURNALS

Cash receipts journal
Cash payments journal
Purchases journal
Sales journal
General journal

TRANSACTIONS

1. Purchased merchandise for $3,000; the terms are 2/10, n/30.

2. Returned damaged merchandise to a supplier and received a credit memorandum for $800.

3. Issued a check for $3,600 to a supplier as a payment on account.

4. Purchased merchandise for $2,000 plus a freight charge of $140; the supplier's invoice is payable in 30 days.

5. Received an allowance for merchandise that was damaged but can be sold at a reduced price; the supplier's credit memorandum is for $475.

6. Purchased merchandise for $3,500 in cash.

Exercise 8.2
Objective 1

▶ **Identifying journals used to record purchases and related transactions.**

The following transactions took place at Serene Trails Hike and Bike Shop. Indicate the general ledger account numbers that would be debited and credited to record each transaction.

CHAPTER 8: Review and Applications

GENERAL LEDGER ACCOUNTS

101 Cash

205 Accounts Payable

501 Purchases

502 Freight In

503 Purchases Returns and Allowances

TRANSACTIONS

1. Purchased merchandise for $1,500; the terms are 2/10, n/30.

2. Returned damaged merchandise to a supplier and received a credit memorandum for $300.

3. Issued a check for $800 to a supplier as a payment on account.

4. Purchased merchandise for $2,400 plus a freight charge of $260; the supplier's invoice is payable in 30 days.

5. Received an allowance for merchandise that was damaged but can be sold at a reduced price; the supplier's credit memorandum is for $400.

6. Purchased merchandise for $4,200 in cash.

◀ **Exercise 8.3**
Objective 1

Recording credit purchases.

The following transactions took place at Dallas Auto Parts and Custom Shop during the first week of July. Indicate how these transactions would be entered in a purchases journal like the one shown in this chapter.

DATE	TRANSACTIONS
July 1	Purchased batteries for $1,950 plus a freight charge of $128 from Auto Parts Corporation; received Invoice 6812, dated June 27, which has terms of n/30.
3	Purchased mufflers for $3,120 plus a freight charge of $80 from Aplex Company; received Invoice 441, dated June 30, which has terms of 1/10, n/60.
5	Purchased car radios for $2,450 plus freight of $100 from The Custom Sounds Shop, Inc.; received Invoice 5601, dated July 1, which has terms of 2/10, n/30.
10	Purchased truck tires for $4,250 from Specialty Tire Company; received Invoice 1102, dated July 8, which has terms of 2/10, n/30.

◀ **Exercise 8.4**
Objective 4

Recording a purchase return.

On February 9, 2007, Kitchen Appliance Center, a retail store, received Credit Memorandum 244 for $3,920 from Discount Appliance Corporation. The credit memorandum covered a return of damaged trash compactors originally purchased on Invoice 4101 dated January 3. Prepare the general journal entry that Kitchen Appliance Center would make for this transaction.

◀ **Exercise 8.5**
Objective 4

Recording a purchase allowance.

On March 17, 2007, The Wholesale Appliance Company was given an allowance of $1,000 by Town Appliance Mart, which issued Credit Memorandum 112. The allowance was for scratches on stoves that were originally purchased on Invoice 911 dated February 20. Prepare the general journal entry that The Wholesale Appliance Company would make for this transaction.

◀ **Exercise 8.6**
Objective 4

Determining the cost of purchases.

On June 30 the general ledger of Trendsetters, a clothing store, showed a balance of $42,840 in the *Purchases* account, a balance of $2,076 in the *Freight In* account, and a balance of $4,890 in the *Purchases Returns and Allowances* account. What was the delivered cost of the purchases made during June? What was the net delivered cost of these purchases?

Exercise 8.7
Objectives 1, 4

▶ **Errors in recording purchase transactions.**

The following errors were made in recording transactions in posting from the purchases journal. How will these errors be detected?

a. A credit of $2,000 to Brock Furniture Company account in the accounts payable ledger was posted as $200.

b. The Accounts Payable column total of the purchases journal was understated by $200.

c. An invoice of $1,680 for merchandise from Jackson Company was recorded as having been received from Baxton Company, another supplier.

d. A $500 payment to Baxton Company was debited to Jackson Company.

Exercise 8.8
Objective 4

▶ **Determining the cost of purchases.**

Complete the following schedule by supplying the missing information.

Net Delivered Cost of Purchases	Case A	Case B
Purchases	(a)	96,970
Freight In	4,670	(c)
Delivered Cost of Purchases	98,090	(d)
Less Purchases Returns and Allowances	(b)	3,880
Net Delivered Cost of Purchases	94,840	96,770

PROBLEMS

Problem Set A

Problem 8.1A
Objectives 1, 2, 3

▶ **Journalizing credit purchases and purchases returns and allowances and posting to the general ledger.**

Photo Mart is a retail store that sells cameras and photography supplies. The firm's credit purchases and purchases returns and allowances transactions for June 2007 appear on page 269, along with the general ledger accounts used to record these transactions. The balance shown in **Accounts Payable** is for the beginning of June.

INSTRUCTIONS

1. Open the general ledger accounts and enter the balance of **Accounts Payable** for June 1, 2007.
2. Record the transactions in a three-column purchases journal and in a general journal. Use 14 as the page number for the purchases journal and 38 as the page number for the general journal.
3. Post entries from the general journal to the general ledger accounts.
4. Total and rule the purchases journal as of June 30.
5. Post the column totals from the purchases journal to the proper general ledger accounts.
6. Compute the net purchases of the firm for the month of June.

GENERAL LEDGER ACCOUNTS

205 Accounts Payable, $13,904 Cr.
501 Purchases
502 Freight In
503 Purchases Returns and Allowances

DATE	TRANSACTIONS
June 1	Purchased instant cameras for $1,995 plus a freight charge of $180 from Jones Company, Invoice 4241, dated May 27; the terms are 60 days net.
8	Purchased film for $1,390 from Camera & Films Products, Invoice 1102, dated June 3, net payable in 45 days.
12	Purchased lenses for $906 from The Optical Supply Store, Invoice 7282, dated June 9; the terms are 1/10, n/60.
18	Received Credit Memorandum 110 for $375 from Jones Company for defective cameras that were returned; they were originally purchased on Invoice 4241, dated May 27.
20	Purchased color film for $1,050 plus freight of $75 from Camera & Films Products, Invoice 1148, dated June 15, net payable in 45 days.
23	Purchased camera cases for $1,940 from Chicago Case Company, Invoice 3108, dated June 18, net due and payable in 45 days.
28	Purchased disk cameras for $2,470 plus freight of $120 from Zant Corporation, Invoice 5027, dated June 24; the terms are 2/10, n/30.
30	Received Credit Memorandum 1108 for $240 from Chicago Case Company; the amount is an allowance for damaged but usable goods purchased on Invoice 3108, dated June 18.

(**Note:** Save your working papers for use in Problem 8.2A.)

Analyze: What total purchases were posted to the *Purchases* general ledger account for June?

Posting to the accounts payable ledger and preparing a schedule of accounts payable.

This problem is a continuation of Problem 8.1A.

◀ **Problem 8.2A**
Objectives 4, 6
CONTINUING >>>
Problem

INSTRUCTIONS

1. Set up an accounts payable subsidiary ledger for Photo Mart. Open an account for each of the creditors listed below and enter the balances as of June 1, 2007.

2. Post the individual entries from the purchases journal and the general journal prepared in Problem 8.1A.

3. Prepare a schedule of accounts payable for June 30.

4. Check the total of the schedule of accounts payable against the balance of the *Accounts Payable* account in the general ledger. The two amounts should be equal.

Creditors		
Name	**Terms**	**Balance**
Camera & Films Products	n/45	$10,480
Chicago Case Company	n/45	1,200
Jones Company	n/60	
The Optical Supply Store	1/10, n/60	2,224
Zant Corporation	2/10, n/30	

Analyze: What amount is owed to The Optical Supply Store on June 30?

Journalizing credit purchases and purchases returns and allowances, computing the net delivered cost of goods, posting to the general ledger, posting to the accounts payable ledger, and preparing a schedule of accounts payable.

◀ **Problem 8.3A**
Objectives
1, 2, 3, 4, 5, 6

CHAPTER 8: Review and Applications

The Patio Shop is a retail store that sells garden equipment, furniture, and supplies. Its credit purchases and purchases returns and allowances for July are listed below. The general ledger accounts used to record these transactions are also provided. The balance shown is for the beginning of July 2007.

INSTRUCTIONS

PART I

1. Open the general ledger accounts and enter the balance of *Accounts Payable* for July 1.
2. Record the transactions in a three-column purchases journal and in a general journal. Use 8 as the page number for the purchases journal and 20 as the page number for the general journal.
3. Post the entries from the general journal to the proper general ledger accounts.
4. Total, prove, and rule the purchases journal as of July 31.
5. Post the column totals from the purchases journal to the proper general ledger accounts.
6. Compute the net delivered cost of the firm's purchases for the month of July.

GENERAL LEDGER ACCOUNTS

205   Accounts Payable, $35,880 Cr.   502   Freight In

501   Purchases   503   Purchases Returns and Allowances

DATE	TRANSACTIONS
July 1	Purchased lawn mowers for $4,700 plus a freight charge of $520 from Brown Corporation, Invoice 1011, dated June 26, net due and payable in 60 days.
5	Purchased outdoor chairs and tables for $4,370 plus a freight charge of $552 from Brooks Garden Furniture Company, Invoice 639, dated July 2, net due and payable in 45 days.
9	Purchased grass seed for $950 from Lawn and Gardens Supply, Invoice 8164, dated July 5; the terms are 30 days net.
16	Received Credit Memorandum 110 for $600 from Brooks Garden Furniture Company; the amount is an allowance for scratches on some of the chairs and tables originally purchased on Invoice 639, dated July 2.
19	Purchased fertilizer for $1,200 plus a freight charge of $256 from Lawn and Gardens Supply, Invoice 9050, dated July 15; the terms are 30 days net.
21	Purchased hoses from Cameron Rubber Company for $3,680 plus a freight charge of $224, Invoice 1785, dated July 17; terms are 1/15, n/60.
28	Received Credit Memorandum 223 for $800 from Cameron Rubber Company for damaged hoses that were returned; the goods were purchased on Invoice 1785, dated June 17.
31	Purchased lawn sprinkler systems for $22,800 plus a freight charge of $640 from Wilson Industrial Products, Invoice 8985, dated July 26; the terms are 2/10, n/30.

INSTRUCTIONS

PART II

1. Set up an accounts payable subsidiary ledger for The Patio Shop. Open an account for each of the creditors listed below and enter the balances as of July 1.
2. Post the individual entries from the purchases journal and the general journal prepared in Part I.

3. Prepare a schedule of accounts payable for July 31, 2007.

4. Check the total of the schedule of accounts payable against the balance of the **Accounts Payable** account in the general ledger. The two amounts should be equal.

Creditors		
Name	Terms	Balance
Brooks Garden Furniture Company	n/45	$11,120
Brown Corporation	n/60	18,120
Cameron Rubber Company	1/15, n/60	
Lawn and Gardens Supply	n/30	6,640
Wilson Industrial Products	2/10, n/30	

Analyze: What total freight charges were posted to the general ledger for the month of July?

Journalizing credit purchases and purchases returns and allowances, posting to the general ledger, posting to the accounts payable ledger, and preparing a schedule of accounts payable.

◀ **Problem 8.4A**
Objectives
1, 2, 3, 4, 5, 6

Professional Office Products Center is a retail business that sells office equipment, furniture, and supplies. Its credit purchases and purchases returns and allowances for September are shown on page 272. The general ledger accounts and the creditors' accounts in the accounts payable subsidiary ledger used to record these transactions are also provided. All balances shown are for the beginning of September.

INSTRUCTIONS

1. Open the general ledger accounts and enter the balance of **Accounts Payable** for September 1, 2007.

2. Open the creditors' accounts in the accounts payable subsidiary ledger and enter the balances for September 1.

3. Record the transactions in a three-column purchases journal and in a general journal. Use 5 as the page number for the purchases journal and 14 as the page number for the general journal.

4. Post to the accounts payable subsidiary ledger daily.

5. Post the entries from the general journal to the proper general ledger accounts at the end of the month.

6. Total and rule the purchases journal as of September 30.

7. Post the column totals from the purchases journal to the proper general ledger accounts.

8. Prepare a schedule of accounts payable and compare the balance of the **Accounts Payable** control account with the schedule of accounts payable.

GENERAL LEDGER ACCOUNTS

205 Accounts Payable, $28,256 Cr.   502 Freight In
501 Purchases   503 Purchases Returns and Allowances

Creditors		
Name	Terms	Balance
Apex Office Machines, Inc.	n/60	$10,960
Brown Paper Company	1/10, n/30	2,120
Dalton Office Furniture Company	n/30	9,576
Davis Corporation	n/30	
Zenn Furniture, Inc.	2/10, n/30	5,600

DATE	TRANSACTIONS
Sept. 3	Purchased desks for $7,920 plus a freight charge of $212 from Dalton Office Furniture Company, Invoice 4213, dated August 29; the terms are 30 days net.
7	Purchased computers for $11,300 from Apex Office Machines, Inc., Invoice 9217, dated September 2, net due and payable in 60 days.
10	Received Credit Memorandum 511 for $600 from Dalton Office Furniture Company; the amount is an allowance for damaged but usable desks purchased on Invoice 4213, dated August 29.
16	Purchased file cabinets for $2,556 plus a freight charge of $124 from Davis Corporation, Invoice 8066, dated September 11; the terms are 30 days net.
20	Purchased electronic desk calculators for $1,000 from Apex Office Machines, Inc., Invoice 11011, dated September 15, net due and payable in 60 days.
23	Purchased bond paper and copy machine paper for $7,500 plus a freight charge of $100 from Brown Paper Company, Invoice 6498, dated September 18; the terms are 1/10, n/30.
28	Received Credit Memorandum 312 for $880 from Apex Office Machines, Inc., for defective calculators that were returned; the calculators were originally purchased on Invoice 11011, dated September 15.
30	Purchased office chairs for $3,840 plus a freight charge of $160 from Zenn Furniture, Inc., Invoice 696, dated September 25, the terms are 2/10, n/30.

Analyze: What total amount was recorded for purchases returns and allowances in the month of September? What percentage of total purchases does this represent?

Problem Set B

Problem 8.1B
Objectives 1, 2, 3

▶ **Journalizing credit purchases and purchases returns and allowances and posting to the general ledger.**

Denver Ski Shop is a retail store that sells ski equipment and clothing. The firm's credit purchases and purchases returns and allowances during May 2007 follow, along with the general ledger accounts used to record these transactions. The balance shown in **Accounts Payable** is for the beginning of May.

INSTRUCTIONS

1. Open the general ledger accounts and enter the balance of **Accounts Payable** for May 1, 2007.
2. Record the transactions in a three-column purchases journal and in a general journal. Use 15 as the page number for the purchases journal and 38 as the page number for the general journal.
3. Post the entries from the general journal to the proper general ledger accounts.
4. Total and rule the purchases journal as of May 30.
5. Post the column totals from the purchases journal to the proper general ledger accounts.
6. Compute the net purchases of the firm for the month of May.

GENERAL LEDGER ACCOUNTS

205 Accounts Payable, $21,608 Cr.
501 Purchases
502 Freight In
503 Purchases Returns and Allowances

DATE		TRANSACTIONS
May	1	Purchased ski boots for $6,600 plus a freight charge of $220 from Colorado Shop for Skiers, Invoice 6572, dated April 28; the terms are 45 days net.
	8	Purchased skis for $11,100 from Alaska Supply Company, Invoice 4916, dated May 2; the terms are net payable in 30 days.
	9	Received Credit Memorandum 155 for $1,600 from Colorado Shop for Skiers for damaged ski boots that were returned; the boots were originally purchased on Invoice 6572, dated April 28.
	12	Purchased ski jackets for $5,000 from Barrons Winter Fashions, Inc., Invoice 986, dated May 11, net due and payable in 60 days.
	16	Purchased ski poles for $3,160 from Alaska Supply Company, Invoice 5011, dated May 15; the terms are n/30.
	22	Purchased ski pants for $2,240 from Cold Mountain Clothing Company, Invoice 4019, dated May 16; the terms are 1/10, n/60.
	28	Received Credit Memorandum 38 for $420 from Alaska Supply Company for defective ski poles that were returned; the items were originally purchased on Invoice 5011, dated May 15.
	31	Purchased sweaters for $3,300 plus a freight charge of $100 from Taylor Ski Goods, Invoice 8354, dated May 27; the terms are 2/10, n/30.

(**Note:** Save your working papers for use in Problem 8.2B.)

Analyze: What total accounts payable were posted from the purchases journal to the general ledger for the month?

Posting to the accounts payable ledger and preparing a schedule of accounts payable.

This problem is a continuation of Problem 8.1B.

◀ Problem 8.2B
Objectives 4, 6
CONTINUING >>>
Problem

INSTRUCTIONS

1. Set up an accounts payable subsidiary ledger for Denver Ski Shop. Open an account for each of the creditors listed and enter the balances as of May 1, 2007.

2. Post the individual entries from the purchases journal and the general journal prepared in Problem 8.1B.

3. Prepare a schedule of accounts payable for May 31.

4. Check the total of the schedule of accounts payable against the balance of the *Accounts Payable* account in the general ledger. The two amounts should be equal.

Creditors		
Name	**Terms**	**Balance**
Alaska Supply Company	n/30	$1,700
Barrons Winter Fashions, Inc.	n/60	8,720
Cold Mountain Clothing Company	1/10, n/60	5,000
Colorado Shop for Skiers	n/45	6,188
Taylor Ski Goods	2/10, n/30	

Analyze: What amount did Denver Ski Shop owe to its supplier, Colorado Shop for Skiers, on May 31?

Problem 8.3B
Objectives
1, 2, 3, 4, 5, 6

▶ **Journalizing credit purchases and purchases returns and allowances, computing the net delivered cost of goods, posting to the general ledger, posting to the accounts payable ledger, and preparing a schedule of accounts payable.**

The Landscape Supply Center is a retail store that sells garden equipment, furniture, and supplies. Its credit purchases and purchases returns and allowances for December are shown below. The general ledger accounts used to record these transactions are also provided. The balance shown is for the beginning of December 2007.

INSTRUCTIONS

PART I

1. Open the general ledger accounts and enter the balance of **Accounts Payable** for December 1.
2. Record the transactions in a three-column purchases journal and in a general journal. Use 8 as the page number for the purchases journal and 20 as the page number for the general journal.
3. Post the entries from the general journal to the proper general ledger accounts.
4. Total, prove, and rule the purchases journal as of December 31.
5. Post the column totals from the purchases journal to the proper general ledger accounts.
6. Compute the net delivered cost of the firm's purchases for the month of December.

GENERAL LEDGER ACCOUNTS

205   Accounts Payable, $13,490 Cr.
501   Purchases
502   Freight In
503   Purchases Returns and Allowances

DATE	TRANSACTIONS
Dec. 1	Purchased lawn mowers for $5,780 plus a freight charge of $156 from Selby Corporation, Invoice 2110, dated November 26, net due and payable in 45 days.
5	Purchased outdoor chairs and tables for $5,700 plus a freight charge of $100 from Patio Furniture Shop, Invoice 633, dated December 2; the terms are 1/15, n/60.
9	Purchased grass seed for $1,148 from Spring Lawn Center, Invoice 1127, dated December 4; the terms are 30 days net.
16	Received Credit Memorandum 101 for $400 from Patio Furniture Shop; the amount is an allowance for scratches on some of the chairs and tables originally purchased on Invoice 633, dated December 2.
19	Purchased fertilizer for $1,600 plus a freight charge of $156 from Spring Lawn Center, Invoice 5731, dated December 15; the terms are 30 days net.
21	Purchased garden hoses for $760 plus a freight charge of $76 from Delta Rubber Company, Invoice 8517, dated December 17; the terms are n/60.
28	Received Credit Memorandum 210 for $150 from Delta Rubber Company for damaged hoses that were returned; the goods were purchased on Invoice 8517, dated December 17.
31	Purchased lawn sprinkler systems for $3,700 plus a freight charge of $80 from Cason Industries, Invoice 8819, dated December 26; the terms are 2/10, n/30.

INSTRUCTIONS

PART II

1. Set up an accounts payable subsidiary ledger for The Landscape Supply Center. Open an account for each of the following creditors and enter the balances as of December 1.

2. Post the individual entries from the purchases journal and the general journal prepared in Part I.

3. Prepare a schedule of accounts payable for December 31.

4. Check the total of the schedule of accounts payable against the balance of the **Accounts Payable** account in the general ledger. The two amounts should be equal.

Creditors		
Name	Terms	Balance
Cason Industries	2/10, n/30	$2,150
Delta Rubber Company	n/60	3,850
Patio Furniture Shop	1/15, n/60	
Selby Corporation	n/45	4,842
Spring Lawn Center	n/30	2,648

Analyze: By what amount did **Accounts Payable** increase during the month of December?

Journalizing credit purchases and purchases returns and allowances, posting to the general ledger, posting to the accounts payable ledger, and preparing a schedule of accounts payable.

◄ **Problem 8.4B**
Objectives
1, 2, 3, 4, 5, 6

Simpson's Card and Novelty Shop is a retail card, novelty, and business supply store. Its credit purchases and purchases returns and allowances for February 2007 appear on page 276. The general ledger accounts and the creditors' accounts in the accounts payable subsidiary ledger used to record these transactions are also provided. The balance shown is for the beginning of February.

INSTRUCTIONS

1. Open the general ledger accounts and enter the balance of **Accounts Payable** for February.

2. Open the creditors' accounts in the accounts payable subsidiary ledger and enter the balances for February 1, 2007.

3. Record each transaction in the appropriate journal, purchases or general. Use page 4 in the purchases journal and page 12 in the general journal.

4. Post entries to the accounts payable subsidiary ledger daily.

5. Post entries in the general journal to the proper general ledger accounts at the end of the month.

6. Total and rule the purchases journal as of February 28.

7. Post the totals to the appropriate general ledger accounts.

8. Calculate the net delivered cost of purchases.

9. Prepare a schedule of accounts payable and compare the balance of the **Accounts Payable** control account with the schedule of accounts payable.

GENERAL LEDGER ACCOUNTS

203 Accounts Payable, $15,200 credit balance
501 Purchases
502 Freight In
503 Purchases Returns and Allowances

CHAPTER 8: Review and Applications

Creditors		
Name	**Terms**	**Balance**
Business Forms, Inc.	n/30	$8,000
Gifts and Holiday Cards	2/10, n/30	4,000
Packing and Mailing Supply Center	2/10, n/30	3,200
Specialty Business Cards	1/10, n/45	

DATE		TRANSACTIONS
Feb.	5	Purchased copy paper from Packing and Mailing Supply Center for $2,000 plus $100 shipping charges on Invoice 502, dated February 2.
	8	Purchased assorted holiday cards from Gifts and Holiday Cards on Invoice 2808, $1,900, dated February 5.
	12	Purchased five boxes of novelty items from Gifts and Holiday Cards for a total cost of $1,200, Invoice 2904, dated February 8.
	13	Purchased tray of cards from Specialty Business Cards on Invoice 2013 for $1,100, dated February 9.
	19	Purchased supply of forms from Business Forms, Inc., for $1,980 plus shipping charges of $60 on Invoice 2019, dated February 16.
	20	One box of cards purchased on February 8 from Gifts and Holiday Cards was water damaged. Received Credit Memorandum 102 for $200.
	21	Toner supplies are purchased from Specialty Business Cards for $3,600 plus shipping charges of $110, Invoice 1376, dated February 19.
	27	Received Credit Memorandum 118 for $240 from Gifts and Holiday Cards as an allowance for damaged novelty items purchased on February 12.

Analyze: What total amount did Simpson's Card and Novelty Shop pay in freight charges during the month of February? What percentage of delivered cost of purchases does this represent?

Challenge Problem

Merchandising: Sales and Purchases

World of Fashions is a retail clothing store. Sales of merchandise and purchases of goods on account for January 2007, the first month of operations, appear on page 277.

INSTRUCTIONS

1. Record the purchases of goods on account on page 6 of a three-column purchases journal.
2. Record the sales of merchandise on account on page 1 of a sales journal.
3. Post the entries from the purchases journal and the sales journal to the individual accounts in the accounts payable and accounts receivable subsidiary ledgers.
4. Total, prove, and rule the journals as of January 31.
5. Post the column totals from the special journals to the proper general ledger accounts.
6. Prepare a schedule of accounts payable for January 31.
7. Prepare a schedule of accounts receivable for January 31.

		PURCHASES OF GOODS ON ACCOUNT
Jan.	3	Purchased dresses for $5,000 plus a freight charge of $112 from Fashion Center, Invoice 101, dated December 26; the terms are net 30 days.
	5	Purchased handbags for $3,480 plus a freight charge of $89 from Handbag Depot, Invoice 223, dated December 28; the terms are 2/10, n/30.
	7	Purchased blouses for $3,900 plus a freight charge of $68 from House of Styles, Invoice 556, dated January 3; the terms are 2/10, n/30.
	9	Purchased casual pants for $2,360 from Modern Woman Pants and Suits Company, Invoice 110, dated January 5; terms are n/30.
	12	Purchased business suits for $5,400 plus a freight charge of $129 from International Executive, Invoice 104, dated January 9; the terms are 2/10, n/30.
	18	Purchased shoes for $3,120 plus freight of $80 from Mr. John's Shoes, Invoice 118, dated January 14; the terms are n/60.
	25	Purchased hosiery for $900 from Hosiery Warehouse, Invoice 1012, dated January 20; the terms are 2/10, n/30.
	29	Purchased scarves and gloves for $1,600 from Modern Woman Pants and Suits Company, Invoice 315, dated January 26; the terms are n/30.
	31	Purchased party dresses for $5,250 plus a freight charge of $225 from Special Occasion Wholesale Dress Shop, Invoice 1044, dated January 27; the terms are 2/10, n/30.

		SALES OF MERCHANDISE ON ACCOUNT
Jan.	4	Sold two dresses to Sarah Valdez; issued Sales Slip 101 for $800 plus $64 sales tax.
	5	Sold a handbag to Linda Carter; issued Sales Slip 102 for $400 plus $32 sales tax.
	6	Sold four blouses to Teresa Collins; issued Sales Slip 103 for $400 plus $32 sales tax.
	10	Sold casual pants and a blouse to Demetria Davis; issued Sales Slip 104 for $600 plus $48 sales tax.
	14	Sold a business suit to Jeraldine Wells; issued Sales Slip 105 for $500 plus $40 sales tax.
	17	Sold hosiery, shoes, and gloves to Amalia Rodriguez; issued Sales Slip 106 for $800 plus $64 sales tax.
	21	Sold dresses and scarves to Rosabla Vasquez; issued Sales Slip 107 for $2,000 plus $160 sales tax.
	24	Sold a business suit to Sherrye Samuels; issued Sales Slip 108 for $400 plus $32 sales tax.
	25	Sold shoes to Cecila Lin; issued Sales Slip 109 for $300 plus $24 sales tax.
	29	Sold a casual pants set to Tonya Ennis; issued Sales Slip 110 for $600 plus $48 sales tax.
	31	Sold a dress and handbag to Isabel James; issued Sales Slip 111 for $750 plus $60 sales tax.

Analyze: What is the net delivered cost of purchases for the month of January?

Critical Thinking Problem

Internal Control

Dora Alexander, owner of Passions Linen Shop, was preparing checks for payment of the current month's purchase invoices when she realized that there were two invoices from Sensuous Linen Company, each for the purchase of 100 red, heart-imprinted king size linen sets. Alexander thinks that Sensuous Linen Company must have billed Passions Linen Shop twice for the same shipment because she knows the shop would not have needed two orders for 100 red linen sets within a month.

1. How can Alexander determine whether Sensuous Linen Company billed Passions Linen Shop in error or whether Passions Linen Shop placed two identical orders for red, heart-imprinted linen sets?

2. If two orders were placed, how can Alexander prevent duplicate purchases from happening in the future?

BUSINESS CONNECTIONS

Cash Management

Managerial | FOCUS

1. Why should management be concerned about the timely payment of invoices?

2. Why is it important for a firm to maintain a satisfactory credit rating?

3. Suppose you are the new controller of a small but growing company and you find that the firm has a policy of paying cash for all purchases of goods even though it could obtain credit. The president of the company does not like the idea of having debts, but the vice president thinks this is a poor business policy that will hurt the firm in the future. The president has asked your opinion. Would you agree with the president or the vice president? Why?

4. Why should management be concerned about the internal control of purchases?

5. How can good internal control of purchases protect a firm from fraud and errors and from excessive investment in merchandise?

6. In what ways would excessive investment in merchandise harm a business?

Adding New Vendors

Ethical | DILEMMA

Anait Artununian is the Accounts Payable Clerk in Jiffy Delivery Service. This company runs ten branches in the San Diego area. The company pays for a variety of expenses. Anait writes the checks for each of the vendors and the controller signs the checks. Anait has decided she needs a raise and the controller has told her to wait for six months. Anait has devised a plan to get a raise on her own. She creates a new vendor for her friend's business with the name Gevok Car Detailing. She also creates two purchase orders for car detailing service from Gevok's for $75 and $70. She writes checks to Gevok Car Detailing to pay these invoices. She knows the controller will sign all checks only looking at the checks over $100. She delivers the check to Gevok who will deposit the checks in his bank account. Gevok then writes a check to her for $145. Is this a good way for Anait to obtain a raise? Is it an ethical practice? Eventually what will be the effect of Anait's actions? What can the company do to prevent this type of behavior?

Accounts Payable and Cost of Merchandise

STREETWISE:
Questions from the REAL WORLD

Refer to the *2004 Annual Report* for The Home Depot, Inc. in Appendix A.

1. Locate the consolidated balance sheets. What is the reported amount of accounts payable at January 30, 2005? Has this balance increased or decreased since the prior fiscal year-end? By what amount?

2. Review Management's Discussion and Analysis of Results of Operations and Financial Condition for The Home Depot, Inc. What factors contributed to the lower cost of merchandise for the operating period?

Income Statement

Financial Statement | **ANALYSIS**

The following financial statement excerpt is taken from the *2004 Annual Report* for Amazon.com, Inc.

Consolidated Statements of Operations		
December 31,	*For the year ended December 31,*	
	2004	*2003*
(In thousands)		
Net Sales	*$ 6,921,124*	*$ 5,263,699*
Cost of Sales	*5,319,127*	*4,006,531*
Gross Profit	*$ 1,601,997*	*$ 1,257,168*

1. The Cost of Sales amount on Amazon.com, Inc. consolidated statements of operations represents the net cost of the goods that were sold for the period. For 2004, what percentage of net sales was the cost of sales? For fiscal 2003?

2. What factors might affect a merchandising company's cost of sales from one period to another?

Analyze Online: On the Amazon.com, Inc. Web site **(www.amazon.com)**, locate the investor relations section.

3. Review the consolidated statements of operations found in the current year's annual report.

4. What amount is reported for cost of sales?

5. What amount is reported for net sales?

Timing

Extending | THE THOUGHT

A purchase order expresses an authorized intent to buy a particular item at a specific price from a supplier. Some companies record a debit to **Purchases** and a credit to **Accounts Payable** at the time the purchase order is issued. Other companies wait until the invoice for the merchandise arrives and then record the purchase. Which method do you think is better? Why?

Memo

Business | COMMUNICATION

You own a retail gourmet cooking supply store. As the owner of the business, you have noticed that your manager, bookkeeper, and sales clerk all place orders with suppliers, sometimes resulting in duplicate orders and confusion in processing invoices. You need to strengthen your internal controls in regard to the purchase of goods for resale. Prepare a memo to your staff that outlines proper procedures for placement of merchandise orders, receipt of goods, and payment of invoices.

Payment Terms

TEAMWORK

A company needs to develop an objective for paying their bills. Do they want to stretch their cash flow as far as they can? Do they want to have a good reputation of always paying bills on time? Do they want to be sure to get paid by their customers before they pay their vendors? In a group, discuss what would be the best payment terms to use for each objective and its impact on the company.

Computer Check Format

Internet | CONNECTION

Go to the Quickbooks and Peachtree Web sites at **quickbooks.com** and **peachtree.com**. Select product overview and more information. You want to be sure to see a copy of a check and purchase order. Compare and contrast the information contained on each check and purchase order. How many copies can you get of the check and purchase order? How is the form different? How is it the same? What information should be included on a company's check and purchase invoice?

Answers to Self Reviews

Answers to Section 1 Self Review

1. Locating suitable suppliers, obtaining price quotations and credit terms, and placing orders.
2. Merchandise purchased on credit for resale.
3. It saves time and effort, and it strengthens the audit trail.
4. **b.** Purchase order
5. **c.** Purchase requisition
6. The business will receive a 2 percent discount if the invoice is paid within 10 days. If the invoice is not paid within 10 days, the total amount is due within 30 days.

Answers to Section 2 Self Review

1. It lists all of the creditors to whom money is owed.
2. $57,675 ($60,550 − 2,875)
3.

Purchases	1,275.00	
Freight In	82.00	
Accounts Payable		1,357.00

4. **c.** $6,400 credit ($4,800 + $1,600)
5. **b.** income statement.
6. A payment was made and recorded in the general ledger account, but was not recorded in the creditor's subsidiary ledger account.

Answers to Comprehensive Self Review

1. A contra cost of goods sold account.
2. A price reduction offered to encourage quick payment of invoices by customers.
3. To accumulate freight charges paid for purchases.
4. The purchase requisition is used by a sales department to notify the purchasing department of the items wanted. The purchase order is prepared by the purchasing department to order the necessary goods at an appropriate price from the selected supplier.
5. The receiving report shows the quantity of goods received and the condition of the goods. The invoice shows quantities and prices; it is the document from which checks are prepared in payment of purchases.

LEARNING OBJECTIVES

1. Record cash receipts in a cash receipts journal.

2. Account for cash short or over.

3. Post from the cash receipts journal to subsidiary and general ledgers.

4. Record cash payments in a cash payments journal.

5. Post from the cash payments journal to subsidiary and general ledgers.

6. Demonstrate a knowledge of procedures for a petty cash fund.

7. Demonstrate a knowledge of internal control routines for cash.

8. Write a check, endorse checks, prepare a bank deposit slip, and maintain a checkbook balance.

9. Reconcile the monthly bank statement.

10. Record any adjusting entries required from the bank reconciliation.

11. Define the accounting terms new to this chapter.

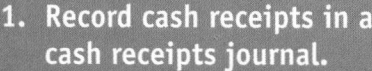

NEW TERMS

bank reconciliation statement

blank endorsement

bonding

canceled check

cash

cash payments journal

cash receipts journal

cash register proof

cash short or over account

check

credit memorandum

debit memorandum

deposit in transit

deposit slip

dishonored (NSF) check

drawee

drawer

endorsement

full endorsement

negotiable

outstanding checks

payee

petty cash analysis sheet

petty cash fund

petty cash voucher

postdated check

promissory note

restrictive endorsement

service charge

statement of account

Chapter 9
Cash Receipts, Cash Payments, and Banking Procedures

H&R BLOCK®   www.hrblock.com

Fresh from Wharton and Harvard, Henry and Richard Bloch were eager to start a business in their home town of Kansas City. They decided on an accounting services company and so, with a $5,000 loan from a relative, United Business Company was founded.

By 1954, United Business Company had 12 employees keeping books for various small local businesses. One of their clients, a newspaper reporter, convinced the Bloch brothers to run an ad for their tax preparation service. The day the ad ran, the Bloch's office was flooded with customers. Their timing had been perfect. Up until the mid 1950s, anyone having trouble preparing their taxes could go into a local IRS office and have the IRS prepare the taxes—for free. The IRS was phasing out this service just as the Bloch brothers were phasing it in.

United Business Company was renamed H&R Block and had a new focus—tax preparation. Within a year, business tripled and has kept growing ever since. Over the years, H&R Block has evolved and now offers its clients comprehensive financial services, including brokerage services, annuities, mutual funds, and IRAs. They prepare over 18 million tax returns annually and service 22 million clients. Over 15% of all tax returns are filed with the help of H&R Block.

thinking critically | What types of daily receipts and payments occur in a local H&R Block office?

Section 1

Cash Receipts

SECTION OBJECTIVES

▶ **1. Record cash receipts in a cash receipts journal.**

WHY IT'S IMPORTANT

The cash receipts journal is an efficient option for recording incoming cash.

▶ **2. Account for cash short or over.**

WHY IT'S IMPORTANT

Discrepancies in cash are a possible indication that cash is mismanaged.

▶ **3. Post from the cash receipts journal to subsidiary and general ledgers.**

WHY IT'S IMPORTANT

The subsidiary and general ledgers must hold accurate, up-to-date information about cash transactions.

TERMS TO LEARN

cash
cash receipts journal
cash register proof
Cash Short or Over account
petty cash fund
promissory note
statement of account

Cash is the business asset that is most easily lost, mishandled, or even stolen. A well-managed business has careful procedures for controlling cash and recording cash transactions.

Cash Transactions

In accounting, the term **cash** is used for currency, coins, checks, money orders, and funds on deposit in a bank. Most cash transactions involve checks.

CASH RECEIPTS

The type of cash receipts depends on the nature of the business. Supermarkets receive checks as well as currency and coins. Department stores receive checks in the mail from charge account customers. Cash received by wholesalers is usually in the form of checks.

CASH PAYMENTS

For safety and convenience, most businesses make payments by check. Sometimes a limited number of transactions are paid with currency and coins. The **petty cash fund** is used to handle payments involving small amounts of money, such as postage stamps, delivery charges, and minor purchases of office supplies. Some businesses maintain a fund to provide cash for business-related travel and entertainment expenses.

The Cash Receipts Journal

To improve the recordkeeping of cash receipts, many businesses use a special **cash receipts journal**. The cash receipts journal simplifies the recording of transactions and eliminates repetition in posting.

▶ **1. OBJECTIVE**

Record cash receipts in a cash receipts journal.

RECORDING TRANSACTIONS IN THE CASH RECEIPTS JOURNAL

The format of the cash receipts journal varies according to the needs of each business. Figure 9.1 on page 285 shows the cash receipts journal for The Style Shop. The Style Shop has two major sources of cash receipts: checks from credit customers who are making payments on account, and currency and coins from cash sales.

The cash receipts journal has separate columns for the accounts frequently used when recording cash receipts. There are columns for

- debits to *Cash,*
- credits to *Accounts Receivable* for payments received on account,
- credits to *Sales* and *Sales Tax Payable* for cash sales.

CASH RECEIPTS JOURNAL   PAGE __1__

DATE		DESCRIPTION	POST. REF.	ACCOUNTS RECEIVABLE CREDIT	SALES TAX PAYABLE CREDIT	SALES CREDIT	OTHER ACCOUNTS CREDIT			CASH DEBIT
							ACCOUNT NAME	POST. REF.	AMOUNT	
2007										
Jan.	7	Roy Anderson		432 00						432 00
	8	Cash Sales			360 00	4500 00				4860 00
	11	Vickie Bowman		270 00						270 00
	12	Investment					M. Amos, Capital		15000 00	15000 00
	13	Barbara Coe		540 00						540 00
	15	Cash Sales			384 00	4800 00	Cash Short/Over		18 00	5166 00
	16	Alma Sanchez		108 00						108 00
	17	Cash Refund					Supplies		75 00	75 00
	22	Fred Wu		400 00						400 00
	22	Cash Sales			400 00	5000 00				5400 00
	29	Cash Sales			216 00	2700 00	Cash Short/Over		16 00	2932 00
	31	Kim Ramirez		108 00						108 00
	31	Mesia Davis		275 00						275 00
	31	Cash Sales			440 00	5500 00				5940 00
	31	Note Collection/					Notes Receivable		800 00	
		Stacee Fairley					Interest Income		36 00	836 00

FIGURE 9.1   Cash Receipts Journal

At the end of the month, the totals of these columns are posted to the general ledger.

Notice the Other Accounts Credit section, which is for entries that do not fit into one of the special columns. Entries in the Other Accounts Credit section are individually posted to the general ledger.

Cash Sales and Sales Taxes The Style Shop uses a cash register to record cash sales and to store currency and coins. As each transaction is entered, the cash register prints a receipt for the customer. It also records the sale and the sales tax on an audit tape locked inside the machine. At the end of the day, when the machine is cleared, the cash register prints the transaction totals on the audit tape. The manager of the store removes the audit tape, and a cash register proof is prepared. The **cash register proof** is a verification that the amount in the cash register agrees with the amount shown on the audit tape. The cash register proof is used to record cash sales and sales tax in the cash receipts journal. The currency and coins are deposited in the firm's bank.

Refer to Figure 9.1, the cash receipts journal for The Style Shop. To keep it simple, it shows weekly, rather than daily, cash sales entries. Look at the January 8 entry. The steps to record the January 8 sales follow.

1. Enter the sales tax collected, $360.00, in the Sales Tax Payable Credit column.
2. Enter the sales, $4,500.00, in the Sales Credit column.
3. Enter the cash received, $4,860.00, in the Cash Debit column.
4. Confirm that total credits equal total debits ($360.00 + $4,500.00 = $4,860.00).

Cash Short or Over Occasionally errors occur when making change. When errors happen, the cash in the cash register is either more than or less than the cash listed on the audit tape. When cash in the register is more than the audit tape, cash is over. When cash in the register is less than the audit tape, cash is *short*. Cash tends to be short more often than over because customers are more likely to notice and complain if they receive too little change.

Record short or over amounts in the **Cash Short or Over account**. If the account has a credit balance, there is an overage, which is treated as revenue. If the account has a debit balance, there is a shortage, which is treated as an expense.

ABOUT
ACCOUNTING

Automated Teller Machines
The banking industry paved the way for the Internet's self-service applications (such as ordering products online) with ATMs.

▶ 2. **OBJECTIVE**
Account for cash short or over.

important!

Cash Short or Over
Expect errors when employees make change, but investigate large and frequent errors. They may indicate dishonesty or incompetence.

Figure 9.1 shows how cash overages and shortages appear in the cash receipts journal. Look at the January 29 entry. Cash sales were $2,700. Sales tax collected was $216. The cash drawer was over $16. Overages are recorded as credits. Notice that the account name and the overage are entered in the Other Accounts Credit section.

Now look at the January 15 entry. This time the cash register was short. Shortages are recorded as debits. Debits are not the normal balance of the Other Accounts Credit column, so the debit entry is circled.

Businesses that have frequent entries for cash shortages and overages add a Cash Short or Over column to the cash receipts journal.

Cash Received on Account The Style Shop makes sales on account and bills customers once a month. It sends a **statement of account** that shows the transactions during the month and the balance owed. Customers are asked to pay within 30 days of receiving the statement. Checks from credit customers are entered in the cash receipts journal, and then the checks are deposited in the bank.

Figure 9.1 shows how cash received on account is recorded. Look at the January 7 entry for Roy Anderson. The check amount is entered in the Accounts Receivable Credit and the Cash Debit columns.

Cash Discounts on Sales The Style Shop, like most retail businesses, does not offer cash discounts. However, many wholesale businesses offer cash discounts to customers who pay within a certain time period. For example, a wholesaler may offer a 1 percent discount if the customer pays within 10 days. To the wholesaler this is a *sales discount*. Sales discounts are recorded when the payment is received. Sales discounts are recorded in a contra revenue account, **Sales Discounts.** Businesses with many sales discounts add a Sales Discounts Debit column to the cash receipts journal.

Additional Investment by the Owner Figure 9.1 shows that on January 12, the owner Mary Amos invested an additional $15,000 in The Style Shop. She intends to use the money to expand the product line. The account name and amount are entered in the Other Accounts Credit section. The debit is entered in the Cash Debit column.

Receipt of a Cash Refund Sometimes a business receives a cash refund for supplies, equipment, or other assets that are returned to the supplier. Figure 9.1 shows that on January 17, The Style Shop received a $75 cash refund for supplies that were returned to the seller. The account name and amount are entered in the Other Accounts Credit section. The debit is entered in the Cash Debit column.

Collection of a Promissory Note and Interest A **promissory note** is a written promise to pay a specified amount of money on a certain date. Most notes require that interest is paid at a specified rate. Businesses use promissory notes to extend credit for some sales transactions.

Sometimes promissory notes are used to replace an accounts receivable balance when the account is overdue. For example, on July 31 The Style Shop accepted a six-month promissory note from Stacee Fairley, who owed $800 on account (see Figure 9.2). Fairley had asked for

FIGURE 9.2

A Promissory Note

$ 800.00 _____   July 31, 2006 _____

___Six Months_____ AFTER DATE _I_ PROMISE TO PAY

TO THE ORDER OF ___Style Shop_____

___Eight Hundred and no/100_____ DOLLARS

PAYABLE AT _First Texas Bank_____

VALUE RECEIVED _with interest at 9%_

NO. _30___ DUE _January 31, 2007_   *Stacee Fairley*

more time to pay his balance. The Style Shop agreed to grant more time if Fairley signed a promissory note with 9 percent annual interest. The note provides more legal protection than an account receivable. The interest is compensation for the delay in receiving payment.

On the date of the transaction, July 31, The Style Shop recorded a general journal entry to increase notes receivable and to decrease accounts receivable for $800. The asset account, **Notes Receivable,** was debited and **Accounts Receivable** was credited.

GENERAL JOURNAL   PAGE _16_

	DATE		DESCRIPTION	POST. REF.	DEBIT	CREDIT	
1	2006						1
2	July	31	Notes Receivable	109	800 00		2
3			Accounts Receivable/Stacee Fairley	111 ✓		800 00	3
4			Received a 6-month, 9% note from				4
5			Stacee Fairley to replace open account				5

On January 31, the due date of the note, The Style Shop received a check for $836 from Fairley. This sum covered the amount of the note ($800) and the interest owed for the six-month period ($36). Figure 9.1 shows the entry in the cash receipts journal. The account names, **Notes Receivable** and **Interest Income,** and the amounts are entered on two lines in the Other Accounts Credit section. The debit is in the Cash Debit column.

POSTING FROM THE CASH RECEIPTS JOURNAL

During the month the amounts recorded in the Accounts Receivable Credit column are posted to individual accounts in the accounts receivable subsidiary ledger. Similarly, the amounts that appear in the Other Accounts Credit column are posted individually to the general ledger accounts during the month. The "CR1" posting references in the **Cash Short or Over** general ledger account below show that the entries appear on the first page of the cash receipts journal.

▶ **3. OBJECTIVE**
Post from the cash receipts journal to subsidiary and general ledgers.

ACCOUNT _Cash Short or Over_   ACCOUNT NO. _617_

					BALANCE	
DATE	DESCRIPTION	POST. REF.	DEBIT	CREDIT	DEBIT	CREDIT
2007						
Jan. 15		CR1	18 00		18 00	
29		CR1		16 00	2 00	

Posting the Column Totals At the end of the month, the cash receipts journal is totaled and the equality of debits and credits is proved.

Proof of Purchases Journal	
	Debits
Cash Debit column	$42,342.00
	Credits
Accounts Receivable Credit column	$2,133.00
Sales Tax Payable Credit column	1,800.00
Sales Credit column	22,500.00
Other Accounts Credit column	15,909.00
Total Credits	$42,342.00

CASH RECEIPTS JOURNAL   PAGE ___1___

DATE		DESCRIPTION	POST. REF.	ACCOUNTS RECEIVABLE CREDIT	SALES TAX PAYABLE CREDIT	SALES CREDIT	OTHER ACCOUNTS CREDIT			CASH DEBIT
							ACCOUNT NAME	POST. REF.	AMOUNT	
2007										
Jan.	7	Roy Anderson	✓	432 00						432 00
	8	Cash Sales			360 00	4500 00				4860 00
	11	Vickie Bowman	✓	270 00						270 00
	12	Investment					M. Amos, Capital	301	15000 00	15000 00
	13	Barbara Coe	✓	540 00						540 00
	15	Cash Sales			384 00	4800 00	Cash Short/Over	617	⟨18 00⟩	5166 00
	16	Alma Sanchez	✓	108 00						108 00
	17	Cash Refund					Supplies	129	75 00	75 00
	22	Fred Wu	✓	400 00						400 00
	22	Cash Sales			400 00	5000 00				5400 00
	29	Cash Sales			216 00	2700 00	Cash Short/Over	617	16 00	2932 00
	31	Kim Ramirez	✓	108 00						108 00
	31	Mesia Davis	✓	275 00						275 00
	31	Cash Sales			440 00	5500 00				5940 00
	31	Note Collection/					Notes Receivable	109	800 00	
		Stacee Fairley					Interest Income	491	36 00	836 00
		Totals		2133 00	1800 00	22500 00			15909 00	42342 00
				(111)	(231)	(401)			(X)	(101)

FIGURE 9.3   **Posted Cash Receipts Journal**

Figure 9.3 shows The Style Shop's cash receipts journal after all posting is completed.

When the cash receipts journal has been proved, rule the columns and post the totals to the general ledger. Figure 9.4 on page 289 shows how to post from the cash receipts journal to the general ledger accounts.

To post a column total to a general ledger account, enter "CR1" in the Posting Reference column to show that the entry is from the first page of the cash receipts journal. Enter the column total in the general ledger account Debit or Credit column. Figure 9.4 shows the entries to *Accounts Receivable* (1), *Sales Tax Payable* (2), *Sales* (3), and *Cash* (4). Compute the new balance for each account and enter it in the Balance Debit or Balance Credit column.

Enter the general ledger account numbers under the column totals on the cash receipts journal. The (X) in the Other Accounts Credit Amount column indicates that the individual amounts were posted, not the total.

Posting to the Accounts Receivable Ledger   To keep customer balances current, accountants post entries from the Accounts Receivable Credit column to the customers' accounts in the accounts receivable subsidiary ledger daily. For example, on January 7, $432 was posted to Roy Anderson's account in the subsidiary ledger. The "CR1" in the Posting Reference column indicates that the transaction appears on page 1 of the cash receipts journal. The check mark (✓) in the Posting Reference column in the cash receipts journal (Figure 9.4 on page 289) shows that the amount was posted to Roy Anderson's account in the accounts receivable subsidiary ledger.

NAME   Roy Anderson

ADDRESS   8913 South Hampton Road, Dallas, Texas 75232-6002

DATE		DESCRIPTION	POST. REF.	DEBIT	CREDIT	BALANCE
2007						
Jan.	1	Balance	✓			432 00
	3	Sales Slip 1101	S1	432 00		864 00
	7		CR1		432 00	432 00
	31	Sales Slip 1110	S1	267 50		699 50

FIGURE 9.4   Posting from the Cash Receipts Journal

CASH RECEIPTS JOURNAL   PAGE 1

DATE	DESCRIPTION	POST. REF.	ACCOUNTS RECEIVABLE CREDIT	SALES TAX PAYABLE CREDIT	SALES CREDIT	OTHER ACCOUNTS CREDIT ACCOUNT NAME	POST. REF.	AMOUNT	CASH DEBIT
2007									
Jan. 7	Roy Anderson	✓	432 00						432 00
	Totals		2 133 00	1 800 00	22 500 00			15 909 00	42 342 00
			(111)	(231)	(401)			(X)	(101)

ACCOUNT **Cash**   ACCOUNT NO. **101**

DATE	DESCRIPTION	POST. REF.	DEBIT	CREDIT	BALANCE DEBIT	BALANCE CREDIT
2007						
Jan. 1	Balance	✓			12 025 50	
31		CR1	42 342 00		54 367 50	

ACCOUNT **Accounts Receivable**   ACCOUNT NO. **111**

DATE	DESCRIPTION	POST. REF.	DEBIT	CREDIT	BALANCE DEBIT	BALANCE CREDIT
2007						
Jan. 1	Balance	✓			3 240 00	
23		J1		162 00	3 078 00	
25		J1		486 00	2 592 00	
31		S1	5 886 00		8 478 00	
31		CR1		2 133 00	6 345 00	

ACCOUNT **Sales Tax Payable**   ACCOUNT NO. **231**

DATE	DESCRIPTION	POST. REF.	DEBIT	CREDIT	BALANCE DEBIT	BALANCE CREDIT
2007						
Jan. 1	Balance	✓				756 00
11		CP1	756 00			- 0 -
23		J1	8 00		8 00	
25		J1	36 00		44 00	
31		S1		436 00		392 00
31		CR1		1 800 00		2 192 00

ACCOUNT **Sales**   ACCOUNT NO. **401**

DATE	DESCRIPTION	POST. REF.	DEBIT	CREDIT	BALANCE DEBIT	BALANCE CREDIT
2007						
Jan. 31		S1		5 450 00		5 450 00
31		CR1		22 500 00		27 950 00

ADVANTAGES OF THE CASH RECEIPTS JOURNAL

The cash receipts journal

- saves time and effort when recording and posting cash receipts,
- allows for the division of work among the accounting staff,
- strengthens the audit trail by recording all cash receipts transactions in one place.

Section 1: **Self Review**

QUESTIONS

1. How and when are the amounts in the Accounts Receivable Credit column posted?

2. What is a promissory note? In what situation would a business accept a promissory note?

3. What is a cash shortage? A cash overage? How are they recorded?

EXERCISES

4. Collection of a note receivable is recorded in the

   a. accounts receivable journal.
   b. cash receipts journal.
   c. general journal.
   d. promissory note journal.

5. Which items are considered cash?

   a. Currency
   b. Funds on deposit in the bank
   c. Money orders
   d. All of the above

ANALYSIS

6. You notice that the **Cash Short or Over** account has 15 entries during the month. The ending balance is a $10 shortage for the month. Is this a problem? Why or why not?

(Answers to Section 1 Self Review are on page 335.)

Cash Payments

A good system of internal control requires that payments be made by check. In a good internal control system one employee approves payments, another employee prepares the checks, and another employee records the transactions.

The Cash Payments Journal

Unless a business has just a few cash payments each month, the process of recording these transactions in the general journal is time consuming. The **cash payments journal** is a special journal used to record transactions involving the payment of cash.

RECORDING TRANSACTIONS IN THE CASH PAYMENTS JOURNAL

Refer to Figure 9.5 on page 293 for The Style Shop's cash payments journal. Notice that there are separate columns for the accounts frequently used when recording cash payments—*Cash, Accounts Payable,* and *Purchases Discounts.* At the end of the month, the totals of these columns are posted to the general ledger.

The Other Accounts Debit section is for entries that do not fit into one of the special columns. Entries in the Other Accounts Debit section are individually posted to the general ledger.

Payments for Expenses Businesses write checks for a variety of expenses each month. In January The Style Shop issued checks for rent, electricity, telephone service, advertising, and salaries. Refer to the January 3 entry for rent expense in Figure 9.5. Notice that the account name and amount are entered in the Other Accounts Debit section. The credit is in the Cash Credit column.

Refer to Figure 9.5 on page 293

Section 2

SECTION OBJECTIVES

▶ **4. Record cash payments in a cash payments journal.**

WHY IT'S IMPORTANT
The cash payments journal is an efficient option for recording payments by check.

▶ **5. Post from the cash payments journal to subsidiary and general ledgers.**

WHY IT'S IMPORTANT
The subsidiary and general ledgers must hold accurate, up-to-date information about cash transactions.

▶ **6. Demonstrate a knowledge of procedures for a petty cash fund.**

WHY IT'S IMPORTANT
Businesses use the petty cash fund to pay for small operating expenditures.

▶ **7. Demonstrate a knowledge of internal control routines for cash.**

WHY IT'S IMPORTANT
Internal controls safeguard business assets.

TERMS TO LEARN

bonding
cash payments journal
petty cash analysis sheet
petty cash voucher

Most banks currently offer online banking (also called home and electronic banking) that allows a customer to access account information 24 hours a day, seven days a week. Online banking allows account viewing, bill payment for recurring and future transactions, the ability to export account information to Quicken and other accounting software, and performs a variety of other transactions. To participate in online banking, bank customers must complete and sign an enrollment form, be accepted by the bank for the service, have a computer with Adobe Acrobat software, and have their own Internet access.

▶ **4. OBJECTIVE**
Record cash payments in a cash payments journal.

Payments on Account Merchandising businesses usually make numerous payments on account for goods that were purchased on credit. If there is no cash discount, the entry in the cash

recall

Discount Terms

The terms 2/10, n/30 mean that if payment is made within 10 days, the customer can take a 2 percent discount. Otherwise, payment in full is due in 30 days.

payments journal is a debit to **Accounts Payable** and a credit to **Cash.** For an example of a payment without a discount, refer to the January 27 entry for International Apparel Shop in Figure 9.5.

Purchases Discounts is a contra cost of goods sold account that appears in the Cost of Goods Sold section of the income statement. Purchases discounts are subtracted from purchases to obtain net purchases.

For an example of a payment with a discount, refer to the January 13 entry for Fashion Designs in Figure 9.5. The Style Shop takes a 2 percent discount for paying within the discount period ($2,865 \times 0.02 = \$57.30$). When there is a cash discount, three elements must be recorded.

- Debit **Accounts Payable** for the invoice amount, $2,865.
- Credit **Purchases Discounts** for the amount of the discount, $57.30.
- Credit **Cash** for the amount of cash paid, $2,807.70.

> Debit cards (also called check cards) look like credit cards or ATM (automated teller machine) cards, but operate like cash or a personal check. In this context, debit means "subtract" so when you use your debit card, you are subtracting your money from your bank account. Funds on deposit with a bank represent a liability to the bank. By debiting accounts when depositors use their debit cards, the bank reduces the depositors' account balances thus reducing the bank's liabilities to depositors. Debit cards are accepted almost everywhere including grocery stores, retail stores, gasoline stations, and restaurants. Debit cards are popular because they offer an alternative to carrying checks or cash. Transactions that are completed with the debit card will appear on your bank statement.

Cash Purchases of Equipment and Supplies Businesses use cash to purchase equipment, supplies, and other assets. These transactions are recorded in the cash payments journal. In January The Style Shop issued checks for store fixtures and store supplies. Refer to the entries on January 10 and 14 in Figure 9.5. Notice that the account names and amounts appear in the Other Accounts Debit section. The credits are recorded in the Cash Credit column.

Payment of Taxes Retail businesses collect sales tax from their customers. Periodically the sales tax is remitted to the taxing authority. Refer to the entry on January 11 in Figure 9.5. The Style Shop issued a check for $756 to pay the December sales tax. Notice that the account name and amount appear in the Other Accounts Debit section. The credit is in the Cash Credit column.

Cash Purchases of Merchandise Most merchandising businesses buy their goods on credit. Occasionally purchases are made for cash. These purchases are recorded in the cash payments journal. Refer to the January 31 entry for the purchase of goods in Figure 9.5.

Payment of Freight Charges Freight charges on purchases of goods are handled in two ways. In some cases, the seller pays the freight charge and then includes it on the invoice. This method was covered in Chapter 8. The other method is for the buyer to pay the transportation company when the goods arrive. The buyer issues a check for the freight charge and records it in the cash payments journal. Refer to the entry on January 31 in Figure 9.5. The account name and amount appear in the Other Accounts Debit section. The credit is in the Cash Credit column.

Payment of a Cash Refund When a customer purchases goods for cash and later returns them or receives an allowance, the customer is usually given a cash refund. Refer to the January 31 entry in Figure 9.5. The Style Shop issued a check for $172.80 to a customer who returned a defective item. When there is a cash refund, three elements are recorded.

International INSIGHTS

Currency

If an American business buys a product from a French company and promises to pay in 90 days, does the business pay in euros or dollars? The accountant reads the terms of the invoice before making payment. If the invoice is in euros, the accountant uses the exchange rate to calculate the amount of the payment.

CASH PAYMENTS JOURNAL   PAGE ___1___

DATE	CK. NO.	DESCRIPTION	POST. REF.	ACCOUNTS PAYABLE DEBIT	OTHER ACCOUNTS DEBIT			PURCHASES DISCOUNTS CREDIT	CASH CREDIT
					ACCOUNT TITLE	POST. REF.	AMOUNT		
2007									
Jan. 3	111	January rent			Rent Expense		1 500 00		1 500 00
10	112	Store fixtures			Store Equipment		2 400 00		2 400 00
11	113	Tax remittance			Sales Tax Payable		756 00		756 00
11	114	World of Fashions		3 935 00				78 70	3 856 30
13	115	Fashion Designs		2 865 00				57 30	2 807 70
14	116	Store Supplies			Supplies		900 00		900 00
15	117	Withdrawal			M. Amos, Drawing		3 000 00		3 000 00
17	118	Electric bill			Utilities Expense		318 00		318 00
17	119	The Trend Center		4 250 00					4 250 00
21	120	Telephone bill			Telephone Expense		276 00		276 00
25	121	Newspaper ad			Advertising Expense		840 00		840 00
27	122	International Apparel Shop		2 400 00					2 400 00
30	123	Fashion Designs		1 135 00					1 135 00
31	124	World of Fashions		565 00					565 00
31	125	January payroll			Salaries Expense		4 950 00		4 950 00
31	126	Purchase of goods			Purchases		3 200 00		3 200 00
31	127	Freight charge			Freight In		175 00		175 00
31	128	Cash refund			Sales Returns & Allow.		160 00		
					Sales Tax Payable		12 80		172 80
31	129	Note Paid to			Notes Payable		6 000 00		
		Metroplex Equip. Co.			Interest Expense		300 00		6 300 00
31	130	Establish Petty Cash fund			Petty Cash Fund		175 00		175 00
		TOTALS		15 150 00			24 962 80	136 00	39 976 80

FIGURE 9.5 | Cash Payments Journal

- Debit *Sales Returns and Allowances* for the amount of the purchase, $160.00.
- Debit *Sales Tax Payable* for the sales tax, $12.80.
- Credit *Cash* for the amount of cash paid, $172.80.

Notice that the debits in the Other Accounts Debit section appear on two lines because two general ledger accounts are debited.

Payment of a Promissory Note and Interest A promissory note can be issued to settle an overdue account or to obtain goods, equipment, or other property. For example, on August 2 The Style Shop issued a six-month promissory note for $6,000 to purchase store fixtures from Metroplex Equipment Company. The note had an interest rate of 10 percent. The Style Shop recorded this transaction in the general journal by debiting *Store Equipment* and crediting *Notes Payable,* a liability account.

GENERAL JOURNAL   PAGE ___16___

	DATE	DESCRIPTION	POST. REF.	DEBIT	CREDIT	
1	2006					1
2	Aug. 2	Store Equipment	131	6 000 00		2
3		Notes Payable	201		6 000 00	3
4		Issued a 6-month, 10% note to				4
5		Metroplex Equipment Company for				5
6		purchase of new store fixtures				6
7						7

On January 31 The Style Shop issued a check for $6,300 in payment of the note, $6,000, and the interest, $300. This transaction was recorded in the cash payments journal in Figure 9.5.

- Debit *Notes Payable,* $6,000.
- Debit *Interest Expense,* $300.
- Credit *Cash,* $6,300.

Notice that the debits in the Other Accounts Debit section appear on two lines.

▶ 5. **OBJECTIVE**

Post from the cash payments journal to subsidiary and general ledgers.

POSTING FROM THE CASH PAYMENTS JOURNAL

During the month the amounts recorded in the Accounts Payable Debit column are posted to individual accounts in the accounts payable subsidiary ledger. The amounts in the Other Accounts Debit column are also posted individually to the general ledger accounts during the month. For example, the January 3 entry in the cash payments journal was posted to the **Rent Expense** account. The "CP1" indicates that the entry is recorded on page 1 of the cash payments journal.

ACCOUNT	Rent Expense				ACCOUNT NO.	634	
		POST.				BALANCE	
DATE	DESCRIPTION	REF.	DEBIT	CREDIT	DEBIT		CREDIT
2007							
Jan. 3		CP1	1 5 0 0 00		1 5 0 0 00		

Posting the Column Totals At the end of the month, the cash payments journal is totaled and proved. The total debits must equal total credits.

Proof of Cash Payments Journal	
	Debits
Accounts Payable Debit column	$15,150.00
Other Accounts Debit column	24,962.80
Total Debits	$40,112.80
	Credits
Purchases Discount Credit column	$ 136.00
Cash Credit column	39,976.80
Total Credits	$40,112.80

Figure 9.6 on page 295 shows the January cash payments journal after posting for The Style Shop. Notice that the account numbers appear in the Posting Reference column of the Other Accounts Debit section to show that the amounts were posted.

When the cash payments journal has been proved, rule the columns and post the totals to the general ledger. Figure 9.7 on page 296 shows how to post from the cash payments journal to the general ledger accounts.

To post a column total to a general ledger account, enter "CP1" in the Posting Reference column to show that the entry is from page 1 of the cash payments journal.

Enter the column total in the general ledger account Debit or Credit column. Figure 9.7 shows the entries to **Accounts Payable** (1), **Purchases Discounts** (2), and **Cash** (3). Compute the new balance and enter it in the Balance Debit or Balance Credit column.

Enter the general ledger account numbers under the column totals on the cash payments journal. The (X) in the Other Accounts Debit column indicates that the individual accounts were posted, not the total.

CASH PAYMENTS JOURNAL

PAGE 1

DATE	CK. NO.	DESCRIPTION	POST. REF.	ACCOUNTS PAYABLE DEBIT	OTHER ACCOUNTS DEBIT ACCOUNT TITLE	POST. REF.	AMOUNT	PURCHASES DISCOUNTS CREDIT	CASH CREDIT
2007									
Jan. 3	111	January rent			Rent Expense	634	1500 00		1500 00
10	112	Store fixtures			Store Equipment	131	2400 00		2400 00
11	113	Tax remittance			Sales Tax Payable	231	756 00		756 00
11	114	World of Fashions	✓	3935 00				78 70	3856 30
13	115	Fashion Designs	✓	2865 00				57 30	2807 70
14	116	Store Supplies			Supplies	129	900 00		900 00
15	117	Withdrawal			M. Amos, Drawing	302	3000 00		3000 00
17	118	Electric bill			Utilities Expense	643	318 00		318 00
17	119	The Trend Center	✓	4250 00					4250 00
21	120	Telephone bill			Telephone Expense	649	276 00		276 00
25	121	Newspaper ad			Advertising Expense	614	840 00		840 00
27	122	International Apparel Shop	✓	2400 00					2400 00
30	123	Fashion Designs	✓	1135 00					1135 00
31	124	World of Fashion	✓	565 00					565 00
31	125	January payroll			Salaries Expense	637	4950 00		4950 00
31	126	Purchase of goods			Purchases	501	3200 00		3200 00
31	127	Freight charge			Freight In	502	175 00		175 00
31	128	Cash refund			Sales Returns & Allow.	451	160 00		
					Sales Tax Payable	231	12 80		172 80
31	129	Note Paid to Metroplex			Notes Payable	201	6000 00		
		Equipment Company			Interest Expense	691	300 00		6300 00
31	130	Establish Petty Cash fund			Petty Cash Fund	105	175 00		175 00
31		Totals		15150 00			24962 80	136 00	39976 80
				(205)			(X)	(504)	(101)

FIGURE 9.6 | Posted Cash Payments Journal

Posting to the Accounts Payable Ledger To keep balances current, accountants post entries from the Accounts Payable Debit column of the cash payments journal to the vendor accounts in the accounts payable subsidiary ledger daily. For example, on January 13, $2,865 was posted to Fashion Designs account in the subsidiary ledger. The "CP1" in the Posting Reference column indicates that the entry is recorded on page 1 of the cash payments journal. The check mark (✓) in the Posting Reference column of the cash payments journal (Figure 9.7 on page 296) shows that the amount was posted to the supplier's account in the accounts payable subsidiary ledger.

NAME Fashion Design   TERMS 2/10, n/30
ADDRESS 2313 Belt Line Road, Dallas, Texas 75267-6205

DATE	DESCRIPTION	POST. REF.	DEBIT	CREDIT	BALANCE
2007					
Jan. 1	Balance	✓			2200 00
3	Invoice 5879, 12/29/06	P1		2865 00	5065 00
13		CP1	2865 00		2200 00
30		CP1	1135 00		1065 00

FIGURE 9.7   **Posted General Ledger Accounts**

CASH PAYMENTS JOURNAL   PAGE __1__

DATE	CK. NO.	DESCRIPTION	POST. REF.	ACCOUNTS PAYABLE DEBIT	OTHER ACCOUNTS DEBIT			PURCHASES DISCOUNTS CREDIT	CASH CREDIT
					ACCOUNT TITLE	POST. REF.	AMOUNT		
2007									
Jan. 3	111	January rent			Rent Expense	535	1 500 00		1 500 00
10	112	Store fixtures			Store Equipment	131	2 400 00		2 400 00
11	113	Tax remittance			Sales Tax Payable	231	756 00		756 00
11	114	World of Fashions	✓	3 935 00				78 70	3 856 30
13	115	Fashion Designs	✓	2 865 00				57 30	2 807 70
		Totals		15 150 00			24 962 80	136 00	39 976 80
				(205)			(X)	(504)	(101)

ACCOUNT _Cash_   ACCOUNT NO. __101__ ❹

DATE	DESCRIPTION	POST. REF.	DEBIT	CREDIT	BALANCE	
					DEBIT ❸	CREDIT
2007						
Jan. 1	Balance	✓			12 025 50	
31		CR1	42 342 00		54 367 50	
31		CP1		39 976 80	14 390 70	

ACCOUNT _Accounts Payable_   ACCOUNT NO. __205__

DATE	DESCRIPTION	POST. REF.	DEBIT	CREDIT	BALANCE	
					DEBIT	CREDIT
2007						
Jan. 1	Balance	✓				10 800 00
18		J1	476 00			10 324 00
31		P1		23 315 00		33 639 00
31		CP1	15 150 00			18 489 00

ACCOUNT _Purchases Discounts_   ACCOUNT NO. __504__

DATE	DESCRIPTION	POST. REF.	DEBIT	CREDIT	BALANCE	
					DEBIT	CREDIT
2007						
Jan. 31		CP1		136 00		136 00

ADVANTAGES OF THE CASH PAYMENTS JOURNAL

The cash payments journal

- saves time and effort when recording and posting cash payments,
- allows for a division of labor among the accounting staff,
- improves the audit trail because all cash payments are recorded in one place and listed by check number.

▶ **6. OBJECTIVE**

Demonstrate a knowledge of procedures for a petty cash fund.

The Petty Cash Fund

In a well-managed business, most bills are paid by check. However, there are times when small expenditures are made with currency and coins. Most businesses use a petty cash fund to pay for small expenditures. Suppose that in the next two hours the office manager needs a $4 folder for a customer. It is not practical to obtain an approval and write a check for $4 in the time available. Instead, the office manager takes $4 from the petty cash fund to purchase the folder.

ESTABLISHING THE FUND

The amount of the petty cash fund depends on the needs of the business. Usually the office manager, cashier, or assistant is in charge of the petty cash fund. The Style Shop's cashier is responsible for petty cash. To set up the petty cash fund, The Style Shop wrote a $175 check to the cashier. She cashed the check and put the currency in a locked cash box.

The establishment of the petty cash fund should be recorded in the cash payments journal. Debit *Petty Cash Fund* in the Other Accounts Debit section of the journal, and enter the credit in the Cash Credit column.

MAKING PAYMENTS FROM THE FUND

Petty cash fund payments are limited to small amounts. A **petty cash voucher** is used to record the payments made from the petty cash fund. The petty cash voucher shows the voucher number, amount, purpose of the expenditure, and account to debit. The person receiving the funds signs the voucher, and the person who controls the petty cash fund initials the voucher. Figure 9.8 shows a petty cash voucher for $16.25 for office supplies.

THE PETTY CASH ANALYSIS SHEET

Most businesses use a **petty cash analysis sheet** to record transactions involving petty cash. The Receipts column shows cash put in the fund, and the Payments column shows the cash paid out. There are special columns for accounts that are used frequently, such as *Supplies, Freight In,* and *Miscellaneous Expense.* There is an Other Accounts Debit column for entries that do not fit in a special column. Figure 9.9 on page 298 shows the petty cash analysis sheet for The Style Shop for February.

Replenishing the Fund   The total vouchers plus the cash on hand should always equal the amount of the fund—$175 for The Style Shop. Replenish the petty cash fund at the end of each month or sooner if the fund is low. Refer to Figures 9.9 and 9.10 on page 298 as you learn how to replenish the petty cash fund.

1. Total the columns on the petty cash analysis sheet.
2. Prove the petty cash fund by adding cash on hand and total payments. This should equal the petty cash fund balance ($15.25 + $159.75 = $175.00).
3. Write a check to restore the petty cash fund to its original balance.
4. Record the check in the cash payments journal. Refer to the petty cash analysis sheet for the accounts and amounts to debit. Notice that the debits appear on four lines of the Other Accounts Debit section. The credit appears in the Cash Credit column.

INTERNAL CONTROL OF THE PETTY CASH FUND

Whenever there is valuable property or cash to protect, appropriate safeguards must be established. Petty cash is no exception. The following internal control procedures apply to petty cash.

PETTY CASH VOUCHER 1

NOTE: This form must be computer processed or filled out in black ink.

DESCRIPTION OF EXPENDITURE	ACCOUNTS TO BE CHARGED	AMOUNT	
Office supplies	Supplies 129	16	25
	Total	16	25

RECEIVED
THE SUM OF Sixteen -- DOLLARS AND 25/100 CENTS
SIGNED L.T. Green DATE 2/3/07   APPROVED BY M.A.   DATE 2/3/07
Metroplex Office Supply Co.

important!

Petty Cash

Only one person controls the petty cash fund. That person keeps receipts for all expenditures.

FIGURE 9.8

Petty Cash Voucher

PETTY CASH ANALYSIS   PAGE ___1___

DATE	VOU. NO.	DESCRIPTION	RECEIPTS	PAYMENTS	SUPPLIES DEBIT	DELIVERY EXPENSE DEBIT	MISC. EXPENSE DEBIT	OTHER ACCOUNTS DEBIT	
								ACCOUNT TITLE	AMOUNT
2007									
Feb. 1		Establish fund	175 00						
3	1	Office supplies		16 25	16 25				
6	2	Delivery service		24 00		24 00			
11	3	Withdrawal		25 00				M. Amos, Drawing	25 00
15	4	Postage stamps		3 70			3 70		
20	5	Delivery service		17 50		17 50			
26	6	Window washing		26 00			26 00		
28	7	Store supplies		14 00	14 00				
28		Totals	175 00	159 75	30 25	41 50	63 00		25 00
28		Balance on hand		15 25					
			175 00	175 00					
28		Balance on hand	15 25						
28		Replenish fund	159 75						
28		Carried forward	175 00						

FIGURE 9.9 | Petty Cash Analysis Sheet

CASH PAYMENTS JOURNAL   PAGE ___1___

DATE	CK. NO.	DESCRIPTION	POST. REF.	ACCOUNTS PAYABLE DEBIT	OTHER ACCOUNTS DEBIT			PURCHASES DISCOUNTS CREDIT	CASH CREDIT
					ACCOUNT TITLE	POST. REF.	AMOUNT		
2007									
Feb. 28	191	Replenish Petty Cash fund			Supplies	129	30 25		
					M. Amos, Drawing	302	25 00		
					Delivery Expense	523	41 50		
					Miscellaneous Expense	593	63 00		159 75

FIGURE 9.10 | Reimbursing the Petty Cash Fund

1. Use the petty cash fund only for small payments that cannot conveniently be made by check.
2. Limit the amount set aside for petty cash to the approximate amount needed to cover one month's payments from the fund.
3. Write petty cash fund checks to the person in charge of the fund, not to the order of "Cash."
4. Assign one person to control the petty cash fund. This person has sole control of the money and is the only one authorized to make payments from the fund.
5. Keep petty cash in a safe, a locked cash box, or a locked drawer.
6. Obtain a petty cash voucher for each payment. The voucher should be signed by the person who receives the money and should show the payment details. This provides an audit trail for the fund.

▶ **7. OBJECTIVE**

Demonstrate a knowledge of internal control routines for cash.

Internal Control over Cash

In a well-managed business, there are internal control procedures for handling and recording cash receipts and cash payments. The internal control over cash should be tailored to the needs of the business. Accountants play a vital role in designing, establishing, and monitoring the cash control system. In developing internal control procedures for cash, certain basic principles must be followed.

CONTROL OF CASH RECEIPTS

As noted already, cash is the asset that is most easily stolen, lost, or mishandled. Yet cash is essential to carrying on business operations. It is important to protect all cash receipts to make sure that funds are available to pay expenses and take care of other business obligations. The following are essential cash receipt controls.

1. Have only designated employees receive and handle cash whether it consists of checks and money orders, or currency and coins. These employees should be carefully chosen for reliability and accuracy and should be carefully trained. In some businesses employees who handle cash are bonded. **Bonding** is the process by which employees are investigated by an insurance company. Employees who pass the background check can be bonded; that is, the employer can purchase insurance on the employees. If the bonded employees steal or mishandle cash, the business is insured against the loss.

2. Keep cash receipts in a cash register, a locked cash drawer, or a safe while they are on the premises.

3. Make a record of all cash receipts as the funds come into the business. For currency and coins, this record is the audit tape in a cash register or duplicate copies of numbered sales slips. The use of a cash register provides an especially effective means of control because the machine automatically produces a tape showing the amounts entered. This tape is locked inside the cash register until it is removed by a supervisor.

4. Before a bank deposit is made, check the funds to be deposited against the record made when the cash was received. The employee who checks the deposit is someone other than the one who receives or records the cash.

5. Deposit cash receipts in the bank promptly—every day or several times a day. Deposit the funds intact—do not make payments directly from the cash receipts. The person who makes the bank deposit is someone other than the one who receives and records the funds.

6. Enter cash receipts transactions in the accounting records promptly. The person who records cash receipts is not the one who receives or deposits the funds.

7. Have the monthly bank statement sent to and reconciled by someone other than the employees who handle, record, and deposit the funds.

One of the advantages of efficient procedures for handling and recording cash receipts is that the funds reach the bank sooner. Cash receipts are not kept on the premises for more than a short time, which means that the funds are safer and are readily available for paying bills owed by the firm.

CONTROL OF CASH PAYMENTS

It is important to control cash payments so that the payments are made only for authorized business purposes. The following are essential cash payment controls.

1. Make all payments by check except for payments from special-purpose cash funds such as a petty cash fund or a travel and entertainment fund.

2. Issue checks only with an approved bill, invoice, or other document that describes the reason for the payment.

3. Have only designated personnel, who are experienced and reliable, approve bills and invoices.

4. Have checks prepared and recorded in the checkbook or check register by someone other than the person who approves the payments.

5. Have still another person sign and mail the checks to creditors.

6. Use prenumbered check forms. Periodically the numbers of the checks that were issued and the numbers of the blank check forms remaining should be verified to make sure that all check numbers are accounted for.

7. During the bank reconciliation process, compare the canceled checks to the checkbook or check register. The person who does the bank reconciliation should be someone other than the person who prepares or records the checks.

8. Enter promptly in the accounting records all cash payment transactions. The person who records cash payments should not be the one who approves payments or the one who writes the checks.

Small businesses usually cannot achieve the division of responsibility recommended for cash receipts and cash payments. However, no matter what size the firm, efforts should be made to set up effective control procedures for cash.

Section 2: **Self Review**

QUESTIONS

1. How and when are amounts in the Other Accounts Debit column of the cash payments journal posted?

2. Why does a business use a petty cash fund?

3. What cash payments journal entry records a cash withdrawal by the owner of a sole proprietorship?

EXERCISES

4. To take the discount, what is the payment date for an invoice dated January 20 with terms 3/15, n/30?
   a. February 3
   b. February 4
   c. February 5
   d. February 6

5. Cash purchases of merchandise are recorded in the
   a. cash payments journal.
   b. general journal.
   c. merchandise journal.
   d. purchases journal.

ANALYSIS

6. Your employer keeps a $75 petty cash fund. She asked you to replenish the fund. She is missing a receipt for $7.40, which she says she spent on postage. How should you handle this?

(Answers to Section 2 Self Review are on page 335.)

Banking Procedures

Businesses with good internal control systems safeguard cash. Many businesses make a daily bank deposit, and some make two or three deposits a day. Keeping excess cash is a dangerous practice. Also, frequent bank deposits provide a steady flow of funds for the payment of expenses.

Writing Checks

A **check** is a written order signed by an authorized person, the **drawer**, instructing a bank, the **drawee**, to pay a specific sum of money to a designated person or business, the **payee**. The checks in Figure 9.11 on page 302 are **negotiable**, which means that ownership of the checks can be transferred to another person or business.

Before writing the check, complete the check stub. In Figure 9.11, the check stub for Check 111 shows

- Balance brought forward: $12,025.50
- Check amount: $1,500.00
- Balance: $10,525.50
- Date: January 3, 2007
- Payee: Carter Real Estate Group
- Purpose: January rent

Once the stub has been completed, fill in the check. Carefully enter the date, the payee, and the amount in figures and words. Draw a line to fill any empty space after the payee's name and after the amount in words. To be valid, checks need an authorized signature. For The Style Shop only Mary Amos, the owner, is authorized to sign checks.

Figure 9.11 shows the check stub for Check 112, a cash purchase from The Retail Equipment Center for $2,400. After Check 112, the account balance is $8,125.50 ($10,525.50 − $2,400.00).

Endorsing Checks

Each check needs an endorsement to be deposited. The **endorsement** is a written authorization that transfers ownership of a check. After the payee transfers ownership to the bank by an endorsement, the bank has a legal right to collect payment from the drawer, the person or business that issued the check. If the check cannot be collected, the payee guarantees payment to all subsequent holders.

Section 3

SECTION OBJECTIVES

▶ **8. Write a check, endorse checks, prepare a bank deposit slip, and maintain a checkbook balance.**

WHY IT'S IMPORTANT

Banking tasks are basic practices in every business.

▶ **9. Reconcile the monthly bank statement.**

WHY IT'S IMPORTANT

Reconciliation of the bank statement provides a good control of cash.

▶ **10. Record any adjusting entries required from the bank reconciliation.**

WHY IT'S IMPORTANT

Certain items are not recorded in the accounting records during the month.

TERMS TO LEARN

bank reconciliation statement
blank endorsement
canceled check
check
credit memorandum
debit memorandum
deposit in transit
deposit slip
dishonored (NSF) check
drawee
drawer
endorsement
full endorsement
negotiable
outstanding checks
payee
postdated check
restrictive endorsement
service charge

	BAL BRO'T FOR'D	12,025	50
No. 111			
January 3 20 07			
Carter Real Estate Group			
TO ORDER OF			
January rent			
FOR			
TOTAL	12,025	50
AMOUNT THIS CHECK	1,500	00
BALANCE	10,525	50

The Style Shop
2007 Trendsetter Lane
Dallas, TX 75268-0967

No. 111

11-8640 / 1210

DATE   January 3   20 07

PAY TO THE ORDER OF   Carter Real Estate Group _____ $ 1,500.00

One thousand five hundred 00/100 _____ DOLLARS

FIRST TEXAS NATIONAL BANK
Dallas, TX 75267-6205

MEMO   Rent for January   Mary Amos

⑈1210⸺8640⑈ ⑇38⑇ 149886 7⑇

	BAL BRO'T FOR'D	10,525	50
No. 112			
January 10 20 07			
The Retail Equip. Ctr.			
TO ORDER OF			
store fixtures			
FOR			
TOTAL	10,525	50
AMOUNT THIS CHECK	2,400	00
BALANCE	8,125	50

The Style Shop
2007 Trendsetter Lane
Dallas, TX 75268-0967

No. 112

11-8640 / 1210

DATE   January 10   20 07

PAY TO THE ORDER OF   The Retail Equipment Center _____ $ 2,400.00

Two thousand four hundred 00/100 _____ DOLLARS

FIRST TEXAS NATIONAL BANK
Dallas, TX 75267-6205

MEMO   store fixtures   Mary Amos

⑈1210⸺8640⑈ ⑇38⑇ 149886 7⑇

FIGURE 9.11 | Checks and Check Stubs

FIGURE 9.12

Types of Check Endorsement

Full Endorsement

PAY TO THE ORDER OF
FIRST TEXAS NATIONAL BANK
THE STYLE SHOP
38-14-98867

Blank Endorsement

Mary Amos
38-14-98867

Restrictive Endorsement

PAY TO THE ORDER OF
FIRST TEXAS NATIONAL BANK
FOR DEPOSIT ONLY
THE STYLE SHOP
38-14-98867

Several forms of endorsement are shown in Figure 9.12 above. Endorsements are placed on the back of the check, on the left, near the perforated edge where the check was separated from the stub.

A **blank endorsement** is the signature of the payee that transfers ownership of the check without specifying to whom or for what purpose. Checks with a blank endorsement can be further endorsed by anyone who has the check, even if the check is lost or stolen.

A **full endorsement** is a signature transferring a check to a specific person, business, or bank. Only the person, business, or bank named in the full endorsement can transfer it to someone else.

The safest endorsement is the **restrictive endorsement**. A restrictive endorsement is a signature that transfers the check to a specific party for a specific purpose, usually for deposit to a bank account. Most businesses restrictively endorse the checks they receive using a rubber stamp.

FIGURE 9.13

Deposit Slip

CHECKING ACCOUNT DEPOSIT

DATE *January 8, 2007*

THE STYLE SHOP
2007 Trendsetter Lane
Dallas, TX 75268-0967

FIRST TEXAS NATIONAL BANK
Dallas, TX 75267-6205

ENTER ADDITIONAL CHECKS ON OTHER SIDE

CURRENCY	DOLLARS	CENTS
	1810	*00*
COIN	*219*	*80*
1 *11-2818*	*260*	*75*
2 *11-2818*	*290*	*18*
3 *11-1652*	*180*	*65*
4 *11-1652*	*598*	*32*
5 *11-5074*	*800*	*30*
6 *11-5074*	*700*	*00*
7		
8		
9		
10		
11		
12		
TOTAL FROM OTHER SIDE OR ATTACHED LIST		
TOTAL	*4,860.00*	

Checks and other items are received for deposit subject to the terms and conditions of this bank's collection agreement.

⑆1210⑈8640⑆ ⑈38⑈1498867⑈

Preparing the Deposit Slip

▶ 8. OBJECTIVE
Write a check, endorse checks, prepare a bank deposit slip, and maintain a checkbook balance.

Businesses prepare a **deposit slip** to record each deposit of cash or checks to a bank account. Usually the bank provides deposit slips preprinted with the account name and number. Figure 9.13 above shows the deposit slip for the January 8 deposit for The Style Shop.

Notice the printed numbers on the lower edge of the deposit slip. These are the same numbers on the bottom of the checks, Figure 9.11. The numbers are printed using a special *magnetic ink character recognition (MICR)* type that can be "read" by machine. Deposit slips and checks encoded with MICR are rapidly and efficiently processed by machine.

- The 12 indicates that the bank is in the 12th Federal Reserve District.
- The 10 is the routing number used in processing the document.
- The 8640 identifies First Texas National Bank.
- The 38 14 98867 is The Style Shop account number.

The deposit slip for The Style Shop shows the date, January 8. *Currency* is the paper money, $1,810.00. *Coin* is the amount in coins, $219.80. The checks and money orders are individually listed. Some banks ask that the *American Bankers Association (ABA) transit number* for each check be entered on the deposit slip. The transit number appears on the top part of the fraction that appears in the upper right corner of the check. In Figure 9.11, the transit number is 11-8640.

Handling Postdated Checks

Occasionally a business will receive a postdated check. A **postdated check** is dated some time in the future. If the business receives a postdated check, it should not deposit it before the date on the check. Otherwise, the check could be refused by the drawer's bank. Postdated checks are written by drawers who do not have sufficient funds to cover the check. The drawer expects to have adequate funds in the bank by the date on the check. Issuing or accepting postdated checks is not a proper business practice.

Topic Tackler PLUS

Reconciling the Bank Statement

▶ 9. OBJECTIVE
Reconcile the monthly bank statement.

Once a month the bank sends a statement of the deposits received and the checks paid for each account. Figure 9.14 on page 304 shows the bank statement for The Style Shop. It shows a day-

FIGURE 9.14

Bank Statement

FIRST TEXAS NATIONAL BANK

THE STYLE SHOP
2007 Trendsetter Lane
Dallas, TX 75268-0967

Account Number: 38-14-98867

Period Ending   January, 31, 2007

CHECKS		DEPOSITS	DATE	BALANCE
Beginning Balance			December 31, 2006	$12,025.50
1,500.00-		432.00+	January 7	10,957.50
2,400.00-		4,860.00+	January 8	13,417.50
756.00-		270.00+	January 11	12,931.50
3,856.30-		15,000.00+	January 12	24,075.20
2,807.70-		540.00+	January 13	21,807.50
900.00-		5,166.00+	January 15	26,073.50
3,000.00-	318.00-	108.00+	January 17	22,863.50
276.00-	4,250.00-	75.00+	January 18	18,412.50
840.00-	2,400.00-	400.00+	January 22	15,572.50
1,600.00-		5,400.00+	January 22	19,372.50
525.00- DM		2,932.00+	January 29	21,779.50
25.00- SC		108.00+	January 31	21,862.50
1,135.00-		275.00+	January 31	21,002.50
		836.00+	January 31	21,838.50

LAST AMOUNT IN THIS
COLUMN IS YOUR BALANCE

Codes:	CC	Certified Check		EC	Error Correction
	CM	Credit Memorandum		OD	Overdrawn
	DM	Debit Memorandum		SC	Service Charge

PLEASE EXAMINE THIS STATEMENT UPON RECEIPT AND REPORT ANY ERRORS WITHIN TEN DAYS.

to-day listing of all transactions during the month. A code, explained at the bottom, identifies transactions that do not involve checks or deposits. For example, SC indicates a service charge. The last column of the bank statement shows the account balance at the beginning of the period, after each day's transactions, and at the end of the period.

Often the bank encloses canceled checks with the bank statement. **Canceled checks** are checks paid by the bank during the month. The bank stamps the word *PAID* across the face of each check. Canceled checks are proof of payment. They are filed after the bank reconciliation is complete.

Usually there is a difference between the ending balance shown on the bank statement and the balance shown in the checkbook. A bank reconciliation determines why the difference exists and brings the records into agreement.

CHANGES IN THE CHECKING ACCOUNT BALANCE

A **credit memorandum** explains any addition, other than a deposit, to the checking account. For example, when a note receivable is due, the bank may collect the note from the maker and place the proceeds in the checking account. The amount collected appears on the bank statement, and the credit memorandum showing the details of the transaction is enclosed with the bank statement.

A **debit memorandum** explains any deduction, other than a check, to the checking account. Service charges and dishonored checks appear as debit memorandums.

Bank **service charges** are fees charged by banks to cover the costs of maintaining accounts and providing services, such as the use of the night deposit box and the collection of promissory notes. The debit memorandum shows the type and amount of each service charge.

BANK FRAUD AND IDENTITY THEFT

The banking industry has long been a major user of technology to process and maintain accurate records for internal operations and customer accounts. ATMs, direct deposit, online banking, electronic funds transfer, and bill payment are all technological changes that are now part of our daily existence. These changes have made banking safer and more convenient than ever. However, as technology progresses are more readily available, bank management must accept the changing environment and implement the technology and security safeguards that customers have come to expect in order to be competitive.

Bank fraud and identity theft have become two of the most organized and costly crimes of our time. The Department of Justice prosecutes cases of identity theft and fraud under a variety of federal statutes. In October 1998, Congress enacted the *Identity Theft and Assumption Deterrence Act.* This Act makes it a crime if anyone "knowingly transfers or uses, without lawful authority, a means of identification of another person with the intent to commit, or to aid or abet, any unlawful activity that constitutes a violation of federal law, or that constitutes a felony under any applicable state or local law." Credit, ATM, and debit cards as well as social security numbers, drivers licenses, cellular telephones, and many other items are considered a means of identification. Schemes to commit identity theft or fraud may also involve violations of other statutes, such as credit card fraud, computer fraud, mail fraud, wire fraud, financial institution fraud, or social security fraud. Each of these offenses is a felony and carries substantial penalties, in some cases as high as 30 years.

Another new federal law called *Check 21,* or *The Check Clearing for the 21st Century Act* is designed to increase the security and efficiency of the national check payment system (and thus decrease bank fraud and identity theft) through the use of electronic image technology. The provisions of this new law are also designed to help detect fraud faster, decrease the amount of paper to process and store checks, allow faster clearing of payments by checks, and reduce vulnerability of the national check processing system to disruption due to weather or other events such as a terrorist attack. Two major changes resulting from this Act will impact you when you make a payment or pay a bill by check. The first change involves the payor shredding your check and processing your payment electronically. This is called accounts receivable conversion or "ARC." The second change involves payments to merchants to pay for purchases. The merchant may scan your check and convert it to an electronic payment on the spot. You will be asked to sign an authorization and you will receive your original check back, along with your receipt. This is referred to as point-of-purchase conversion or "POP."

THINKING CRITICALLY

As a banking customer, what concerns do you have about online banking? What benefits and disadvantages can you identify? What can you do to prevent identity theft?

INTERNET APPLICATION

Locate the Web site for your banking institution. What online banking services are offered? What costs are associated with these services?

Figure 9.15 on page 306 shows a debit memorandum for a $525.00 dishonored check. A **dishonored check** is one that is returned to the depositor unpaid. Normally, checks are dishonored because there are insufficient funds in the drawer's account to cover the check. The bank usually stamps the letters *NSF* for *Not Sufficient Funds* on the check. The business records a journal entry to create an account receivable from the drawer for the amount of the dishonored check.

When a check is dishonored, the business contacts the drawer to arrange for collection. The drawer can ask the business to redeposit the check because the funds are now in the account. If so, the business records the check deposit again. Sometimes, the business requests a cash payment.

THE BANK RECONCILIATION PROCESS: AN ILLUSTRATION

When the bank statement is received, it is reconciled with the financial records of the business. On February 5 The Style Shop received the bank statement shown in Figure 9.14. The ending cash balance according to the bank is $21,838.50. On January 31 the *Cash* account, called the *book balance of cash,* is $14,390.70. The same amount appears on the check stub at the end of January.

FIGURE 9.15

Debit Memorandum

DEBIT: **THE STYLE SHOP**   **FIRST TEXAS NATIONAL BANK**
2007 Trendsetter Lane
Dallas, TX 75268-0967

38-14-98867   DATE: _January 31, 2007_

NSF Check - David Newhouse	525	00

APPROVED: _____

Sometimes the difference between the bank balance and the book balance is due to errors. The bank might make an arithmetic error, give credit to the wrong depositor, or charge a check against the wrong account. Many banks require that errors in the bank statement be reported within a short period of time, usually 10 days. The errors made by businesses include not recording a check or deposit, or recording a check or deposit for the wrong amount.

Other than errors, there are four reasons why the book balance of cash may not agree with the balance on the bank statement.

1. **Outstanding checks** are checks that are recorded in the cash payments journal but have not been paid by the bank.

2. **Deposit in transit** is a deposit that is recorded in the cash receipts journal but that reaches the bank too late to be shown on the monthly bank statement.

3. Service charges and other deductions are not recorded in the business records.

4. Deposits, such as the collection of promissory notes, are not recorded in the business records.

Figure 9.16 on page 307 shows a **bank reconciliation statement** that accounts for the differences between the balance on the bank statement and the book balance of cash. The bank reconciliation statement format is:

First Section	**Second Section**
Bank statement balance	Book balance
+ deposits in transit	+ deposits not recorded
− outstanding checks	− deductions
+ **or** − bank errors	+ **or** − errors in the books
Adjusted bank balance	Adjusted book balance

When the bank reconciliation statement is complete, the adjusted bank balance must equal the adjusted book balance.

Use the following steps to prepare the bank reconciliation statement:

First Section

1. Enter the balance on the bank statement, $21,838.50.

2. Compare the deposits in the checkbook with the deposits on the bank statement. The Style Shop had one deposit in transit. On January 31 receipts of $5,940.00 were placed in the bank's night deposit box. The bank recorded the deposit on February 1. The deposit will appear on the February bank statement.

3. List the outstanding checks.
   - Put the canceled checks in numeric order.
   - Compare the canceled checks to the check stubs, verifying the check numbers and amounts.
   - Examine the endorsements to make sure that they agree with the names of the payees.

FIGURE 9.16

Bank Reconciliation Statement

The Style Shop
Bank Reconciliation Statement
January 31, 2007

Balance on Bank Statement			21 838 50
Additions:			
Deposits of January 31 in transit	5 940 00		
Check incorrectly charged to account	1 600 00	7 540 00	
		29 378 50	
Deductions for outstanding checks:			
Check 124 of January 31	565 00		
Check 125 of January 31	4 950 00		
Check 126 of January 31	3 200 00		
Check 127 of January 31	175 00		
Check 128 of January 31	172 80		
Check 129 of January 31	6 300 00		
Check 130 of January 31	175 00		
Total Checks Outstanding		15 537 80	
Adjusted Bank Balance		13 840 70	
Balance in Books		14 390 70	
Deductions:			
NSF Check	525 00		
Bank Service Charge	25 00	550 00	
Adjusted Book Balance		13 840 70	

- List the checks that have not cleared the bank.
- The Style Shop has seven outstanding checks totaling $15,537.80.

4. While reviewing the canceled checks for The Style Shop, Mary Amos found a $1,600 check issued by The Dress Barn. The $1,600 was deducted from The Style Shop's account; it should have been deducted from the account for The Dress Barn. This is a bank error. Mary Amos contacted the bank about the error. The correction will appear on the next bank statement. The bank error amount is added to the bank statement balance on the bank reconciliation statement.

5. The adjusted bank balance is $13,840.70.

Second Section

1. Enter the balance in books from the *Cash* account, $14,390.70.

2. Record any deposits made by the bank that have not been recorded in the accounting records. The Style Shop did not have any.

3. Record deductions made by the bank. There are two items:
   - the NSF check for $525,
   - the bank service charge for $25.

4. Record any errors in the accounting records that were discovered during the reconciliation process. The Style Shop did not have any errors in January.

5. The adjusted book balance is $13,840.70.

Notice that the adjusted bank balance and the adjusted book balance agree.

Adjusting the Financial Records

Items in the second section of the bank reconciliation statement include additions and deductions made by the bank that do not appear in the accounting records. Businesses prepare journal entries to record these items in the books.

important!

Adjusted Book Balance
Make journal entries to record additions and deductions that appear on the bank statement but that have not been recorded in the general ledger.

▶ 10. OBJECTIVE
Record any adjusting entries required from the bank reconciliation.

MANAGERIAL IMPLICATIONS

CASH

- It is important to safeguard cash against loss and theft.
- Management and the accountant need to work together
  - to make sure that there are effective controls for cash receipts and cash payments,
  - to monitor the internal control system to make sure that it functions properly,
  - to develop procedures that ensure the quick and efficient recording of cash transactions.
- To make decisions, management needs up-to-date information about the cash position so that it can anticipate cash shortages and arrange loans or arrange for the temporary investment of excess funds.
- Management and the accountant need to establish controls over the banking activities—depositing funds, issuing checks, recording checking account transactions, and reconciling the monthly bank statement.

THINKING CRITICALLY

How would you determine how much cash to keep in the business checking account, as opposed to in a short-term investment?

For The Style Shop, two entries must be made. The first entry is for the NSF check from David Newhouse, a credit customer. The second entry is for the bank service charge. The effect of the two items is a decrease in the **Cash** account balance.

BUSINESS TRANSACTION

The January bank reconciliation statement (Figure 9.16 on page 307) shows an NSF check of $525 and a bank service charge of $25.

ANALYSIS

The asset account, **Accounts Receivable**, is increased by $525 for the returned check. The expense account, **Bank Fees Expense**, is increased by $25 for the service charge. The asset account, **Cash**, is decreased by $550 ($525 + $25).

DEBIT-CREDIT RULES

DEBIT   Increases to assets are debits. Debit **Accounts Receivable** for $525. Increases to expenses are debits. Debit **Bank Fees Expense** for $25.

CREDIT   Decreases to assets are credits. Credit **Cash** for $550.

T-ACCOUNT PRESENTATION

Accounts Receivable		Bank Fees Expense		Cash	
+	−	+	−	+	−
525		25			550

GENERAL JOURNAL ENTRY

GENERAL JOURNAL   PAGE _17_

	DATE	DESCRIPTION	POST. REF.	DEBIT	CREDIT	
29	Feb. 1	Accounts Receivable/ David Newhouse	111/✓	5 2 5 00		29
30		Bank Fees Expense	593	2 5 00		30
31		Cash	101		5 5 0 00	31
32		To record NSF check and bank				32
33		service charge				33

THE BOTTOM LINE
Adjusting Entries

Income Statement

Expenses	↑	25
Net Income	↓	25

Balance Sheet

Assets	↓	25
Equity	↓	25

After these entries are posted, the *Cash* account appears as follows.

ACCOUNT _Cash_   ACCOUNT NO. _101_

DATE	DESCRIPTION	POST. REF.	DEBIT	CREDIT	BALANCE DEBIT	BALANCE CREDIT
2007						
Jan. 1	Balance	✓			12 0 2 5 50	
31		CR1	42 3 4 2 00		54 3 6 7 50	
31		CP1		39 9 7 6 80	14 3 9 0 70	
Feb. 1		J17		5 5 0 00	13 8 4 0 70	

Notice that $13,840.70 is the adjusted bank balance, the adjusted book balance, and the general ledger *Cash* balance. A notation is made on the latest check stub to deduct the amounts ($525 and $25). The notation includes the reasons for the deductions.

Sometimes the bank reconciliation reveals an error in the firm's financial records. For example, the February bank reconciliation for The Style Shop found that Check 151 was written for $465. The amount on the bank statement is $465. However, the check was recorded in the accounting records as $445. The business made a $20 error when recording the check. The Style Shop prepared the following journal entry to correct the error. The $20 is also deducted on the check stub.

GENERAL JOURNAL   PAGE _18_

	DATE	DESCRIPTION	POST. REF.	DEBIT	CREDIT	
1	2007					1
2						2
29	Mar. 3	Advertising Expense	514	2 0 00		29
30		Cash	101		2 0 00	30
31		To correct error for check				31
32		151 of February 22				32

Internal Control of Banking Activities

Well-run businesses put the following internal controls in place.

1. Limit access to the checkbook to designated employees. When the checkbook is not in use, keep it in a locked drawer or cabinet.

2. Use prenumbered check forms. Periodically, verify and account for all checks. Examine checks before signing them. Match each check to an approved invoice or other payment authorization.

3. Separate duties.
   - The person who writes the check should not sign or mail the check.
   - The person who performs the bank reconciliation should not handle or deposit cash receipts or write, record, sign, or mail checks.

4. File all deposit receipts, canceled checks, voided checks, and bank statements for future reference. These documents provide a strong audit trail for the checking account.

Section 3: **Self Review**

QUESTIONS

1. Which bank reconciliation items require journal entries?

2. Why does a payee endorse a check before depositing it?

3. What is a postdated check? When should postdated checks be deposited?

EXERCISES

4. Which of the following does not require an adjustment to the financial records?
   a. NSF check
   b. Bank service charge
   c. Check that was incorrectly recorded at $85, but was written and paid by the bank as $58
   d. Deposits in transit

5. On the bank reconciliation statement, you would not find a list of
   a. canceled checks.
   b. deposits in transit.
   c. outstanding checks.
   d. NSF checks.

ANALYSIS

6. James is one of several accounting clerks at Uptown Beverage Company. His job duties include recording invoices as they are received, filing the invoices, and writing the checks for accounts payable. He is a fast and efficient clerk and usually has some time available each day to help other clerks. It has been suggested that reconciling the bank statement should be added to his job duties. Do you agree or disagree? Why or why not?

(Answers to Section 3 Self Review are on page 336.)

REVIEW   Chapter Summary

In this chapter, you have learned the basic principles of accounting for cash payments and cash receipts.

Learning Objectives

1 Record cash receipts in a cash receipts journal.

Use of special journals leads to an efficient recording process for cash transactions. The cash receipts journal has separate columns for the accounts used most often for cash receipt transactions.

2 Account for cash short or over.

Errors can occur when making change. Cash register discrepancies should be recorded using the expense account **Cash Short or Over.**

3 Post from the cash receipts journal to subsidiary and general ledgers.

Individual accounts receivable amounts are posted to the subsidiary ledger daily. Figures in the Other Accounts Credit column are posted individually to the general ledger during the month. All other postings are done on a summary basis at month-end.

4 Record cash payments in a cash payments journal.

The cash payments journal has separate columns for the accounts used most often, eliminating the need to record the same account names repeatedly.

5 Post from the cash payments journal to subsidiary and general ledgers.

Individual accounts payable amounts are posted daily to the accounts payable subsidiary ledger. Amounts listed in the Other Accounts Debit column are posted individually to the general ledger during the month. All other postings are completed on a summary basis at the end of the month.

6 Demonstrate a knowledge of procedures for a petty cash fund.

Although most payments are made by check, small payments are often made through a petty cash fund. A petty cash voucher is prepared for each payment and signed by the person receiving the money. The person in charge of the fund records expenditures on a petty cash analysis sheet. The fund is replenished with a check for the sum spent. An entry is made in the cash payments journal to debit the accounts involved.

7 Demonstrate a knowledge of internal control routines for cash.

All businesses need a system of internal controls to protect cash from theft and mishandling and to ensure accurate records of cash transactions. A checking account is essential to store cash safely and to make cash payments efficiently. For maximum control over outgoing cash, all payments should be made by check except those from carefully controlled special-purpose cash funds such as a petty cash fund.

8 Write a check, endorse checks, prepare a bank deposit slip, and maintain a checkbook balance.

Check writing requires careful attention to details. If a standard checkbook is used, the stub should be completed before the check so that it will not be forgotten. The stub gives the data needed to journalize the payment.

9 Reconcile the monthly bank statement.

A bank statement should be immediately reconciled with the cash balance in the firm's financial records. Usually, differences are due to deposits in transit, outstanding checks, and bank service charges, but many factors can cause lack of agreement between the bank balance and the book balance.

10 Record any adjusting entries required from the bank reconciliation.

Some differences between the bank balance and the book balance may require that the firm's records be adjusted after the bank statement is reconciled. Journal entries are recorded and then posted to correct the *Cash* account balance and the checkbook balance.

11 Define the accounting terms new to this chapter.

Glossary

Bank reconciliation statement (p. 306) A statement that accounts for all differences between the balance on the bank statement and the book balance of cash

Blank endorsement (p. 302) A signature of the payee written on the back of the check that transfers ownership of the check without specifying to whom or for what purpose

Bonding (p. 299) The process by which employees are investigated by an insurance company that will insure the business against losses through employee theft or mishandling of funds

Canceled check (p. 304) A check paid by the bank on which it was drawn

Cash (p. 284) In accounting, currency, coins, checks, money orders, and funds on deposit in a bank

Cash payments journal (p. 291) A special journal used to record transactions involving the payment of cash

Cash receipts journal (p. 284) A special journal used to record and post transactions involving the receipt of cash

Cash register proof (p. 285) A verification that the amount of currency and coins in a cash register agrees with the amount shown on the cash register audit tape

Cash Short or Over account (p. 285) An account used to record any discrepancies between the amount of currency and coins in the cash register and the amount shown on the audit tape

Check (p. 301) A written order signed by an authorized person instructing a bank to pay a specific sum of money to a designated person or business

Credit memorandum (p. 304) A form that explains any addition, other than a deposit, to a checking account

Debit memorandum (p. 304) A form that explains any deduction, other than a check, from a checking account

Deposit in transit (p. 306) A deposit that is recorded in the cash receipts journal but that reaches the bank too late to be shown on the monthly bank statement

Deposit slip (p. 303) A form prepared to record the deposit of cash or checks to a bank account

Dishonored check (p. 305) A check returned to the depositor unpaid because of insufficient funds in the drawer's account; also called an NSF check

Drawee (p. 301) The bank on which a check is written

Drawer (p. 301) The person or firm issuing a check

Endorsement (p. 301) A written authorization that transfers ownership of a check

Full endorsement (p. 302) A signature transferring a check to a specific person, firm, or bank

Negotiable (p. 301) A financial instrument whose ownership can be transferred to another person or business

Outstanding checks (p. 306) Checks that have been recorded in the cash payments journal but have not yet been paid by the bank

Payee (p. 301) The person or firm to whom a check is payable

Petty cash analysis sheet (p. 297) A form used to record transactions involving petty cash

Petty cash fund (p. 284) A special-purpose fund used to handle payments involving small amounts of money

Petty cash voucher (p. 297) A form used to record the payments made from a petty cash fund

Postdated check (p. 303) A check dated some time in the future

Promissory note (p. 286) A written promise to pay a specified amount of money on a specific date

Restrictive endorsement (p. 302) A signature that transfers a check to a specific party for a stated purpose

Service charge (p. 304) A fee charged by a bank to cover the costs of maintaining accounts and providing services

Statement of account (p. 286) A form sent to a firm's customers showing transactions during the month and the balance owed

Comprehensive **Self Review**

1. Describe a full endorsement.
2. What is a petty cash voucher?
3. When is the petty cash fund replenished?
4. What are the advantages of using special journals for cash receipts and cash payments?
5. What does the term *cash* mean in business?

(Answers to Comprehensive Self Review are on page 336.)

Discussion Questions

1. What procedures are used to achieve internal control over banking activities?
2. Why are journal entries sometimes needed after the bank reconciliation statement is prepared?
3. Give some reasons why the bank balance and the book balance of cash might differ.
4. What is the book balance of cash?
5. Why is a bank reconciliation prepared?
6. What information is shown on the bank statement?
7. What type of information is entered on a check stub? Why should a check stub be prepared before the check is written?
8. What is a check?
9. Why are MICR numbers printed on deposit slips and checks?
10. Which type of endorsement is most appropriate for a business to use?
11. How are cash shortages and overages recorded?
12. Describe the major controls for petty cash.
13. When are petty cash expenditures entered in a firm's accounting records?
14. What type of account is **Purchases Discounts?** How is this account presented on the income statement?
15. How does a firm record a payment on account to a creditor when a cash discount is involved? Which journal is used?
16. How does a wholesale business record a check received on account from a customer when a cash discount is involved? Which journal is used?
17. Why do some wholesale businesses offer cash discounts to their customers?
18. What is a promissory note? What entry is made to record the collection of a promissory note and interest? Which journal is used?
19. Describe the major controls for cash payments.
20. Explain what *bonding* means. How does bonding relate to safeguarding cash?
21. Describe the major controls for cash receipts.

22. Explain the meaning of the following terms.

   a. Canceled check

   b. Outstanding check

   c. Deposit in transit

   d. Debit memorandum

   e. Credit memorandum

   f. Dishonored check

   g. Blank endorsement

   h. Deposit slip

   i. Drawee

   j. Restrictive endorsement

   k. Payee

   l. Drawer

   m. Service charge

APPLICATIONS

 Exercises

Exercise 9.1

Objective 1

▶ **Recording cash receipts.**

The following transactions took place at Sneaky Pete's Shoe Store during the first week of September 2007. Indicate how these transactions would be entered in a cash receipts journal.

DATE	TRANSACTIONS
Sept. 1	Had cash sales of $5,600 plus sales tax of $448; there was a cash overage of $16.
2	Collected $720 on account from James Floyd, a credit customer.
3	Had cash sales of $5,250 plus sales tax of $420.
4	Susan Anderson, the owner, made an additional cash investment of $17,000.
5	Had cash sales of $6,400 plus sales tax of $512; there was a cash shortage of $30.

Exercise 9.2

Objective 4

CONTINUING >>>
    Problem

▶ **Recording cash payments.**

The following transactions took place at Sneaky Pete's Shoe Store during the first week of September 2007. Indicate how these transactions would be entered in a cash payments journal.

DATE		TRANSACTIONS
Sept.	1	Issued Check 3850 for $2,400 to pay the monthly rent.
	1	Issued Check 3851 for $2,950 to Carter Company, a creditor, on account.
	2	Issued Check 3852 for $10,250 to purchase new equipment.
	2	Issued Check 3853 for $1,380 to remit sales tax to the state sales tax authority.
	3	Issued Check 3854 for $1,470 to Waller Company, a creditor, on account for invoice of $1,500 less cash discount of $30.
	4	Issued Check 3855 for $2,675 to purchase merchandise.
	5	Issued Check 3856 for $1,800 as a cash withdrawal for personal use by Susan Anderson, the owner.

Recording the establishment of a petty cash fund.

◀ **Exercise 9.3**
Objective 6

On January 2 Goree Insurance Company issued Check 2108 for $175 to establish a petty cash fund. Indicate how this transaction would be recorded in a cash payments journal.

Recording the replenishment of a petty cash fund.

◀ **Exercise 9.4**
Objective 6

On January 31 Zoe Inc. issued Check 3144 to replenish its petty cash fund. An analysis of payments from the fund showed these totals: *Supplies,* $42; *Delivery Expense,* $36; and *Miscellaneous Expense,* $30. Indicate how this transaction would be recorded in a cash payments journal.

Determining an adjusted bank balance.

◀ **Exercise 9.5**
Objectives 9, 10

Cheng Corporation received a bank statement showing a balance of $14,920 as of October 31, 2007. The firm's records showed a book balance of $14,362 on October 31. The difference between the two balances was caused by the following items. Prepare the adjusted bank balance section and the adjusted book balance section of the bank reconciliation statement. Also prepare the necessary journal entry.

1. A debit memorandum for an NSF check from James Dear for $300.
2. Three outstanding checks: Check 7017 for $129, Check 7098 for $65 and Check 7107 for $1,533.
3. A bank service charge of $12.
4. A deposit in transit of $857.

Analyzing bank reconciliation items.

◀ **Exercise 9.6**
Objective 9

At Thompson Delivery and Courier Service the following items were found to cause a difference between the bank statement and the firm's records. Indicate whether each item will affect the bank balance or the book balance when the bank reconciliation statement is prepared. Also indicate which items will require an accounting entry after the bank reconciliation is completed.

1. A deposit in transit.
2. A debit memorandum for a dishonored check.
3. A credit memorandum for a promissory note that the bank collected for Thompson.
4. An error found in Thompson's records, which involves the amount of a check. The firm's checkbook and cash payments journal indicate $808 as the amount, but the canceled check itself and the listing on the bank statement show that $880 was the actual sum.
5. An outstanding check.
6. A bank service charge.
7. A check issued by another firm that was charged to Thompson's account by mistake.

Exercise 9.7

Objective 9

▶ **Preparing a bank reconciliation statement.**

Cantu Office Supply Company received a bank statement showing a balance of $67,905 as of March 31, 2007. The firm's records showed a book balance of $69,387 on March 31. The difference between the two balances was caused by the following items. Prepare a bank reconciliation statement for the firm as of March 31 and the necessary journal entries from the statement.

1. A debit memorandum for $21, which covers the bank's collection fee for the note.

2. A deposit in transit of $3,720.

3. A check for $267 issued by another firm that was mistakenly charged to Cantu's account.

4. A debit memorandum for an NSF check of $5,775 issued by Wilson Construction Company, a credit customer.

5. Outstanding checks: Check 3782 for $2,130; Check 3840 for $171.

6. A credit memorandum for a $6,000 noninterest-bearing note receivable that the bank collected for the firm.

PROBLEMS

Problem Set A

Problem 9.1A

Objectives 1, 2, 3

▶ **Journalizing cash receipts and posting to the general ledger.**

Movie Courier Service is a retail store that rents movies and sells music CDs over the Internet. The firm's cash receipts for February are listed below and on page 317. The general ledger accounts used to record these transactions appear below.

INSTRUCTIONS

1. Open the general ledger accounts and enter the balances as of February 1, 2007.

2. Record the transactions in a cash receipts journal. Use 4 as the page number.

3. Post the individual entries from the Other Accounts Credit section of the cash receipts journal to the proper general ledger accounts.

4. Total, prove, and rule the cash receipts journal as of February 28, 2007.

5. Post the column totals from the cash receipts journal to the proper general ledger accounts.

GENERAL LEDGER ACCOUNTS

101	Cash	$ 4,960 Dr.	401	Sales
109	Notes Receivable	800 Dr.	491	Interest Income
111	Accounts Receivable	4,075 Dr.	620	Cash Short or Over
129	Supplies	610 Dr.		
231	Sales Tax Payable	295 Cr.		
301	Jason Wilson, Capital	34,000 Cr.		

DATE	TRANSACTIONS
Feb. 3	Received $500 from Danielle Pelzel, a credit customer, on account.
5	Received a cash refund of $120 for damaged supplies.
7	Had cash sales of $4,800 plus sales tax of $384 during the first week of February; there was a cash shortage of $60.
9	Jason Wilson, the owner, invested an additional $15,000 cash in the business.

Continued

DATE		9.1A (cont.) TRANSACTIONS
Feb.	12	Received $380 from Kyela Jones, a credit customer, in payment of her account.
	14	Had cash sales of $4,050 plus sales tax of $324 during the second week of February; there was an overage of $28.
	16	Received $450 from Sadie Nelson, a credit customer, to apply toward her account.
	19	Received a check from Ketura Pittman to pay her $800 promissory note plus interest of $32.
	21	Had cash sales of $4,550 plus sales tax of $364 during the third week of February.
	25	Alfred Herron, a credit customer, sent a check for $580 to pay the balance he owes.
	28	Had cash sales of $4,100 plus sales tax of $328 during the fourth week of February; there was a cash shortage of $36.

Analyze: What total accounts receivable were collected in February?

Journalizing cash payments, recording petty cash, and posting to the general ledger.

◀   **Problem 9.2A**
     Objectives 4, 5, 6

The cash payments of Royalty Jewelry Store, a retail business, for June are listed on page 318. The general ledger accounts used to record these transactions appear below.

INSTRUCTIONS

1. Open the general ledger accounts and enter the balances as of June 1.
2. Record all payments by check in a cash payments journal; use 8 as the page number.
3. Record all payments from the petty cash fund on a petty cash analysis sheet; use 8 as the sheet number.
4. Post the individual entries from the Other Accounts Debit section of the cash payments journal to the proper general ledger accounts.
5. Total, prove, and rule the petty cash analysis sheet as of June 30. Record the replenishment of the fund and the final balance on the sheet.
6. Total, prove, and rule the cash payments journal as of June 30.
7. Post the column totals from the cash payments journal to the proper general ledger accounts.

GENERAL LEDGER ACCOUNTS

101	Cash	$42,840 Dr.
105	Petty Cash Fund	
129	Supplies	1,060 Dr.
201	Notes Payable	3,200 Cr.
205	Accounts Payable	18,880 Cr.
231	Sales Tax Payable	4,200 Cr.
302	Larry Jennings, Drawing	
451	Sales Returns and Allowances	
504	Purchases Discounts	
611	Delivery Expense	
620	Rent Expense	
623	Salaries Expense	
626	Telephone Expense	
634	Interest Expense	
635	Miscellaneous Expense	

DATE	TRANSACTIONS
June 1	Issued Check 4121 for $2,500 to pay the monthly rent.
2	Issued Check 4122 for $4,200 to remit the state sales tax.
3	Issued Check 4123 for $2,780 to Perfect Timing Watch Company, a creditor, in payment of Invoice 6808, dated May 5.
4	Issued Check 4124 for $200 to establish a petty cash fund. (After journalizing this transaction, be sure to enter it on the first line of the petty cash analysis sheet.)
5	Paid $30 from the petty cash fund for office supplies, Petty Cash Voucher 1.
7	Issued Check 4125 for $3,328 to Perry Corporation in payment of a $3,200 promissory note and interest of $128.
8	Paid $20 from the petty cash fund for postage stamps, Petty Cash Voucher 2.
10	Issued Check 4126 for $594 to a customer as a cash refund for a defective watch that was returned; the original sale was made for cash.
12	Issued Check 4127 for $276 to pay the telephone bill.
14	Issued Check 4128 for $5,880 to International Jewelry Company, a creditor, in payment of Invoice 8629, dated May 6 ($6,000), less a cash discount ($120).
15	Paid $18 from the petty cash fund for delivery service, Petty Cash Voucher 3.
17	Issued Check 4129 for $860 to purchase store supplies.
20	Issued Check 4130 for $3,430 to Nelson's Jewelry and Accessories, a creditor, in payment of Invoice 1513, dated June 12 ($3,500), less a cash discount ($70).
22	Paid $24 from the petty cash fund for a personal withdrawal by Larry Jennings, the owner, Petty Cash Voucher 4.
25	Paid $30 from the petty cash fund to have the store windows washed and repaired, Petty Cash Voucher 5.
27	Issued Check 4131 for $3,650 to Classy Creations, a creditor, in payment of Invoice 667, dated May 30.
30	Paid $24 from the petty cash fund for delivery service, Petty Cash Voucher 6.
30	Issued Check 4132 for $7,675 to pay the monthly salaries.
30	Issued Check 4133 for $5,000 to Larry Jennings, the owner, as a withdrawal for personal use.
30	Issued Check 4134 for $146 to replenish the petty cash fund. (Foot the columns of the petty cash analysis sheet in order to determine the accounts that should be debited and the amounts involved.)

Analyze: What total payments were made from the petty cash fund for the month?

Problem 9.3A ▶   **Journalizing sales and cash receipts and posting to the general ledger.**

Objectives 1, 2, 3

Unlimited Sounds is a wholesale business that sells musical instruments. Transactions involving sales and cash receipts for the firm during April 2007 follow, along with the general ledger accounts used to record these transactions.

INSTRUCTIONS

1. Open the general ledger accounts and enter the balances as of April 1, 2007.
2. Record the transactions in a sales journal, a cash receipts journal, and a general journal. Use 7 as the page number for each of the special journals and 17 as the page number for the general journal.
3. Post the entries from the general journal to the general ledger.

4. Total, prove, and rule the special journals as of April 30, 2007.

5. Post the column totals from the special journals to the proper general ledger accounts.

6. Prepare the heading and the Revenue section of the firm's income statement for the month ended April 30.

GENERAL LEDGER ACCOUNTS

101	Cash	$16,400 Dr.
109	Notes Receivable	
111	Accounts Receivable	21,000 Dr.
401	Sales	
451	Sales Returns and Allowances	
452	Sales Discounts	

DATE	TRANSACTIONS
April 1	Sold merchandise for $3,900 to Soprano Music Center; issued Invoice 9312 with terms of 2/10, n/30.
3	Received a check for $1,470 from Music Supply Store in payment of Invoice 6718 of March 25 ($1,500), less a cash discount ($30.00).
5	Sold merchandise for $1,575 in cash to a new customer who has not yet established credit.
8	Sold merchandise for $4,500 to Music Warehouse, issued Invoice 9313 with terms of 2/10, n/30.
10	Soprano Music Center sent a check for $3,822 in payment of Invoice 9312 of April 1 ($3,900), less a cash discount ($78).
15	Accepted a return of damaged merchandise from Music Warehouse; issued Credit Memorandum 105 for $800; the original sale was made on Invoice 9313 of April 8.
19	Sold merchandise for $10,500 to Eagleton Music Center; issued Invoice 9314 with terms of 2/10, n/30.
23	Collected $2,975 from Sounds From Yesterday for Invoice 6725 of March 25.
26	Accepted a two-month promissory note for $5,500 from Country Music Store in settlement of its overdue account; the note has an interest rate of 12 percent.
28	Received a check for $10,290 from Eagleton Music Center in payment of Invoice 9314, dated April 19 ($10,500), less a cash discount ($210).
30	Sold merchandise for $9,800 to Contemporary Sounds, Inc.; issued Invoice 9315 with terms of 2/10, n/30.

Analyze: What total sales on account were made in the month of April prior to any returns or allowances?

Journalizing purchases, cash payments, and purchases discounts; posting to the general ledger.

◀ **Problem 9.4A**
Objectives 4, 5

The Hiker and Biker Outlet Center is a retail store. Transactions involving purchases and cash payments for the firm during June 2007 are listed on page 320. The general ledger accounts used to record these transactions appear below.

INSTRUCTIONS

1. Open the general ledger accounts and enter the balances as of June 1, 2007.

2. Record the transactions in a purchases journal, a cash payments journal, and a general journal. Use 8 as the page number for each of the special journals and 20 as the page number for the general journal.

3. Post the entries from the general journal and from the Other Accounts Debit section of the cash payments journal to the proper general ledger accounts.

4. Total, prove, and rule the special journals as of June 30.

5. Post the column totals from the special journals to the general ledger.

6. Show how the firm's net cost of purchases would be reported on its income statement for the month ended June 30.

GENERAL LEDGER ACCOUNTS

101	Cash	$18,500 Dr.
131	Equipment	56,000 Dr.
201	Notes Payable	
205	Accounts Payable	4,880 Cr.
501	Purchases	
503	Purchases Ret. and Allow.	
504	Purchases Discounts	
611	Rent Expense	
614	Salaries Expense	
617	Telephone Expense	

DATE	TRANSACTIONS
June 1	Issued Check 1101 for $2,400 to pay the monthly rent.
3	Purchased merchandise for $2,600 from Perfect Fit Shoe Shop, Invoice 746, dated May 30; the terms are 2/10, n/30.
5	Purchased new store equipment for $4,500 from Middleton Company, Invoice 9067 dated June 4, net payable in 30 days.
7	Issued Check 1102 for $1,470 to Leisure Wear Clothing Company, a creditor, in payment of Invoice 3342 of May 9.
8	Issued Check 1103 for $2,548 to Perfect Fit Shoe Shop, a creditor, in payment of Invoice 746 dated May 30 ($2,600), less a cash discount ($52).
12	Purchased merchandise for $2,050 from Juanda's Coat Shop, Invoice 9922, dated June 9, net due and payable in 30 days.
15	Issued Check 1104 for $228 to pay the monthly telephone bill.
18	Received Credit Memorandum 203 for $550 from Juanda's Coat Shop for defective goods that were returned; the original purchase was made on Invoice 9922 dated June 9.
21	Purchased new store equipment for $9,500 from Warren Company; issued a three-month promissory note with interest at 12 percent.
23	Purchased merchandise for $5,400 from The Motor Speedway, Invoice 1927, dated June 20; terms of 2/10, n/30.
25	Issued Check 1105 for $1,250 to Juanda's Coat Shop, a creditor, in payment of Invoice 7416 dated May 28.
28	Issued Check 1106 for $5,292 to The Motor Speedway, a creditor, in payment of Invoice 1927 of June 20 ($5,400), less a cash discount ($108).
30	Purchased merchandise for $1,980 from Jogging Shoes Store, Invoice 4713, dated June 26; the terms are 1/10, n/30.
30	Issued Check 1107 for $4,800 to pay the monthly salaries of the employees.

Analyze: Assuming that all relevant information is included in this problem, what total liabilities does the company have at month-end?

Preparing a bank reconciliation statement and journalizing entries to adjust the cash balance.

◀ **Problem 9.5A**
Objectives 9, 10
e**X**cel

On May 2, 2007, Vacation Paradise received its April bank statement from First City Bank and Trust. Enclosed with the bank statement, which appears below, was a debit memorandum for $160 that covered an NSF check issued by Doris Fisher, a credit customer. The firm's checkbook contained the following information about deposits made and checks issued during April. The balance of the *Cash* account and the checkbook on April 30, 2007, was $3,972.

DATE		TRANSACTIONS	
April	1	Balance	$6,089
	1	Check 1207	100
	3	Check 1208	300
	5	Deposit	350
	5	Check 1209	275
	10	Check 1210	2,000
	17	Check 1211	50
	19	Deposit	150
	22	Check 1212	9
	23	Deposit	150
	26	Check 1213	200
	28	Check 1214	18
	30	Check 1215	15
	30	Deposit	200

FIRST CITY BANK AND TRUST

Vacation Paradise
1718 Jade Lane
Dallas, TX 75232-6002

Account Number: 23-11070-08

Period Ending April 30, 2007

CHECKS		DEPOSITS	DATE	BALANCE
			Beginning Balance	
			March 31	6,089.00
100.00-		350.00+	April 6	6,339.00
275.00-	300.00-		April 10	5,764.00
2,000.00-			April 13	3,764.00
6.00- SC			April 14	3,758.00
		150.00+	April 20	3,908.00
50.00-			April 22	3,858.00
		150.00+	April 25	4,008.00
			April 26	3,999.00
9.00-			April 29	3,639.00
200.00-	160.00- DM			

INSTRUCTIONS

1. Prepare a bank reconciliation statement for the firm as of April 30, 2007.

2. Record general journal entries for any items on the bank reconciliation statement that must be journalized. Date the entries May 2, 2007.

Analyze: What checks remain outstanding after the bank statement has been reconciled?

Problem 9.6A ▶   **Preparing a bank reconciliation statement and journalizing entries to adjust the cash balance.**

Objectives 9, 10

e**X**cel

On August 31, 2007, the balance in the checkbook and the *Cash* account of the Hampton Inn was $11,549. The balance shown on the bank statement on the same date was $13,097.

Notes

a. The firm's records indicate that a $880.00 deposit dated August 30 and a $477.00 deposit dated August 31 do not appear on the bank statement.

b. A service charge of $8 and a debit memorandum of $320 covering an NSF check have not yet been entered in the firm's records. (The check was issued by Neal Woodson, a credit customer.)

c. The following checks were issued but have not yet been paid by the bank.

   Check 712, $110.00

   Check 713, $25.00

   Check 716, $238.00

   Check 736, $577.00

   Check 739, $78.00

   Check 741, $145.00

d. A credit memorandum shows that the bank collected a $2,000 note receivable and interest of $60 for the firm. These amounts have not yet been entered in the firm's records.

INSTRUCTIONS

1. Prepare a bank reconciliation statement for the firm as of August 31.

2. Record general journal entries for items on the bank reconciliation statement that must be journalized. Date the entries September 4, 2007.

Analyze: What effect did the journal entries recorded as a result of the bank reconciliation have on the fundamental accounting equation?

Problem 9.7A ▶   **Correcting errors revealed by a bank reconciliation.**

Objectives 9, 10

e**X**cel

During the bank reconciliation process at Baxter Company on May 2, 2007, the following two errors were discovered in the firm's records.

a. The checkbook and the cash payments journal indicated that Check 2104 dated April 15 was issued for $800 to make a cash purchase of supplies. However, examination of the canceled check and the listing on the bank statement showed that the actual amount of the check was $80.

b. The checkbook and the cash payments journal indicated that Check 2147 dated April 20 was issued for $308 to pay a utility bill. However, examination of the canceled check and the listing on the bank statement showed that the actual amount of the check was $388.

INSTRUCTIONS

1. Prepare the adjusted book balance section of the firm's bank reconciliation statement. The book balance as of April 30 was $20,275. The errors listed above are the only two items that affect the book balance.

2. Prepare general journal entries to correct the errors. Use page 11 and date the entries May 2, 2007. Check 2104 was correctly debited to *Supplies Expense* on April 15, and Check 2147 was debited to *Utilities Expense* on April 20.

Analyze: If the errors described had not been corrected, would net income for the period be overstated or understated? By what amount?

Problem Set B

Journalizing cash receipts and posting to the general ledger.

◀ **Problem 9.1B**
Objectives 1, 2, 3

The Avid Reader is a retail store that sells books, cards, business supplies, and novelties. The firm's cash receipts during June 2007 are shown below. The general ledger accounts used to record these transactions appear below.

INSTRUCTIONS

1. Open the general ledger accounts and enter the balances as of June 1.
2. Record the transactions in a cash receipts journal. (Use page 14.)
3. Post the individual entries from the Other Accounts Credit section of the cash receipts journal to the proper general ledger accounts.
4. Total, prove, and rule the cash receipts journal as of June 30.
5. From the cash receipts journal, post the totals to the general ledger.

GENERAL LEDGER ACCOUNTS

102 Cash	$1,200	231 Sales Tax Payable	$ 400
111 Accounts Receivable	8,400	302 Sergio Guzman, Capital	7,600
115 Notes Receivable	1,600	401 Sales	
129 Office Supplies	1,000	791 Interest Income	

DATE	TRANSACTIONS
June 3	Received $400 from Clear Images Copy Center, a credit customer.
4	Received a check for $1,702 from Amanda Guttirez to pay her note receivable; the total included $102 of interest.
5	Received a $360 refund for damaged supplies purchased from Books-R-Us.
7	Recorded cash sales of $1,700 plus sales tax payable of $136.
10	Received $1,400 from Linda James, a credit customer.
13	Sergio Guzman, the owner, contributed additional capital of $10,000 to the business.
14	Recorded cash sales of $1,600 plus sales tax of $128.
18	Received $1,060 from Karen Carter, a credit customer.
19	Received $1,200 from Nelsy Marroquin, a credit customer.
21	Recorded cash sales of $1,800 plus sales tax of $144.
27	Received $800 from Alexander Neal, a credit customer.

Analyze: Assuming that all relevant information is included in this problem, what are total assets for The Avid Reader at June 30, 2007?

Journalizing cash payments and recording petty cash; posting to the general ledger.

◀ **Problem 9.2B**
Objectives 4, 5, 6

The cash payments of European Gift Shop, a retail business, for September are listed on page 324. The general ledger accounts used to record these transactions appear below and on page 324.

INSTRUCTIONS

1. Open the general ledger accounts and enter the balances as of September 1, 2007.
2. Record all payments by check in a cash payments journal. Use 12 as the page number.
3. Record all payments from the petty cash fund on a petty cash analysis sheet with special columns for **Delivery Expense** and **Miscellaneous Expense.** Use 12 as the sheet number.

CHAPTER 9: Review and Applications

4. Post the individual entries from the Other Accounts Debit section of the cash payments journal to the proper general ledger accounts.

5. Total, prove, and rule the petty cash analysis sheet as of September 30, then record the replenishment of the fund and the final balance on the sheet.

6. Total, prove, and rule the cash payments journal as of September 30.

7. Post the column totals from the cash payments journal to the proper general ledger accounts.

GENERAL LEDGER ACCOUNTS

101	Cash	$21,530 Dr.	504	Purchases Discounts
105	Petty Cash Fund		511	Delivery Expense
141	Equipment	43,000 Dr.	611	Interest Expense
201	Notes Payable	1,000 Cr.	614	Miscellaneous Expense
205	Accounts Payable	9,800 Cr.	620	Rent Expense
231	Sales Tax Payable	1,344 Cr.	623	Salaries Expense
302	Fred Lin, Drawing		626	Telephone Expense
451	Sales Ret. and Allow.			

DATE		TRANSACTIONS
Sept.	1	Issued Check 401 for $1,344 to remit sales tax to the state tax commission.
	2	Issued Check 402 for $1,700 to pay the monthly rent.
	4	Issued Check 403 for $100 to establish a petty cash fund. (After journalizing this transaction, be sure to enter it on the first line of the petty cash analysis sheet.)
	5	Issued Check 404 for $1,470 to Elegant Glassware, a creditor, in payment of Invoice 6793, dated August 28 ($1,500), less a cash discount ($30).
	6	Paid $12.00 from the petty cash fund for delivery service, Petty Cash Voucher 1.
	9	Purchased store equipment for $1,000; issued Check 405.
	11	Paid $16 from the petty cash fund for office supplies, Petty Cash Voucher 2 (charge to *Miscellaneous Expense*).
	13	Issued Check 406 for $970 to Taylor Company, a creditor, in payment of Invoice 7925, dated August 15.
	14	Issued Check 407 for $425 to a customer as a cash refund for a defective watch that was returned; the original sale was made for cash.
	16	Paid $10 from the petty cash fund for a personal withdrawal by Fred Lin, the owner, Petty Cash Voucher 3.
	18	Issued Check 408 for $187 to pay the monthly telephone bill.
	21	Issued Check 409 for $833 to African Imports, a creditor, in payment of Invoice 1822, dated September 13 ($850), less a cash discount ($17).
	23	Paid $13 from the petty cash fund for postage stamps, Petty Cash Voucher 4.
	24	Issued Check 410 for $1,040 to Zachary Corporation in payment of a $1,000 promissory note and interest of $40.
	26	Issued Check 411 for $1,240 to Atlantic Ceramics, a creditor, in payment of Invoice 3510, dated August 29.
	27	Paid $10 from the petty cash fund for delivery service, Petty Cash Voucher 5.
	28	Issued Check 412 for $1,500 to Fred Lin, the owner, as a withdrawal for personal use.
	30	Issued Check 413 for $2,500 to pay the monthly salaries of the employees.
	30	Issued Check 414 for $61 to replenish the petty cash fund. (Foot the columns of the petty cash analysis sheet in order to determine the accounts that should be debited and the amounts involved.)

Analyze: What was the amount of total debits to general ledger liability accounts during the month of September?

Journalizing sales and cash receipts and posting to the general ledger.

Royal Construction Company is a wholesale business. The transactions involving sales and cash receipts for the firm during August 2007 are listed below. The general ledger accounts used to record these transactions are listed below.

◄   **Problem 9.3B**
Objectives 1, 2, 3

INSTRUCTIONS

1. Open the general ledger accounts and enter the balances as of August 1, 2007.
2. Record the transactions in a sales journal, a cash receipts journal, and a general journal. Use 10 as the page number for each of the special journals and 24 as the page number for the general journal.
3. Post the entries from the general journal to the proper general ledger accounts.
4. Total, prove, and rule the special journals as of August 31, 2007.
5. Post the column totals from the special journals to the proper general ledger accounts.
6. Prepare the heading and the Revenue section of the firm's income statement for the month ended August 31, 2007.

GENERAL LEDGER ACCOUNTS

101 Cash	$15,070 Dr.	401 Sales	
109 Notes Receivable		451 Sales Returns and Allowances	
111 Accounts Receivable	22,507 Dr.	452 Sales Discounts	

DATE		TRANSACTIONS
Aug.	1	Received a check for $6,468 from Construction Supply Company in payment of Invoice 8277 dated July 21 ($6,600), less a cash discount ($132).
	2	Sold merchandise for $19,450 to Jamison Builders; issued Invoice 2978 with terms of 2/10, n/30.
	4	Accepted a three-month promissory note for $12,000 from Davis Custom Homes to settle its overdue account; the note has an interest rate of 12 percent.
	7	Sold merchandise for $18,550 to Branch Construction Company; issued Invoice 2979 with terms of 2/10, n/30.
	11	Collected $19,061 from Jamison Builders for Invoice 2978 dated August 2 ($19,450), less a cash discount ($389.00).
	14	Sold merchandise for $7,050 in cash to a new customer who has not yet established credit.
	16	Branch Construction Company sent a check for $18,179 in payment of Invoice 2979 dated August 7 ($18,550), less a cash discount ($371.00).
	22	Sold merchandise for $6,850 to Contemporary Homes; issued Invoice 2980 with terms of 2/10, n/30.
	24	Received a check for $6,000 from Garcia Homes Center to pay Invoice 2877, dated July 23.
	26	Accepted a return of damaged merchandise from Contemporary Homes; issued Credit Memorandum 101 for $550; the original sale was made on Invoice 2980, dated August 22.
	31	Sold merchandise for $17,440 to Denton County Builders; issued Invoice 2981 with terms of 2/10, n/30.

Analyze: What total sales on account were made in August? Include sales returns and allowances in your computation.

Problem 9.4B

Objectives 4, 5

▶ **Journalizing purchases, cash payments, and purchase discounts; posting to the general ledger.**

Contemporary Appliance Center is a retail store that sells a variety of household appliances. Transactions involving purchases and cash payments for the firm during December 2007 are listed below and on page 327. The general ledger accounts used to record these transactions appear below.

INSTRUCTIONS

1. Open the general ledger accounts and enter the balances in these accounts as of December 1, 2007.

2. Record the transactions in a purchases journal, a cash payments journal, and a general journal. Use 12 as the page number for each of the special journals and 30 as the page number for the general journal.

3. Post the entries from the general journal and from the Other Accounts Debit section of the cash payments journal to the proper accounts in the general ledger.

4. Total, prove, and rule the special journals as of December 31, 2007.

5. Post the column totals from the special journals to the general ledger accounts.

6. Show how the firm's cost of purchases would be reported on its income statement for the month ended December 31, 2007.

GENERAL LEDGER ACCOUNTS

101	Cash	$60,700 Dr.
131	Equipment	68,000 Dr.
201	Notes Payable	
205	Accounts Payable	7,600 Cr.
501	Purchases	
503	Purchases Returns and Allowances	
504	Purchases Discounts	
611	Rent Expense	
614	Salaries Expense	
617	Telephone Expense	

DATE	TRANSACTIONS
Dec. 1	Purchased merchandise for $6,600 from Alexis Products for Homes, Invoice 6559, dated November 28; the terms are 2/10, n/30.
2	Issued Check 1801 for $3,000 to pay the monthly rent.
4	Purchased new store equipment for $14,000 from Kesterson Company; issued a two-month promissory note with interest at 10 percent.
6	Issued Check 1802 for $6,468 to Alexis Products for Homes, a creditor, in payment of Invoice 6559, dated November 28 ($6,600), less a cash discount ($132).
10	Purchased merchandise for $9,200 from the Baxter Corporation, Invoice 5119, dated December 7; terms of 2/10, n/30.
13	Issued Check 1803 for $265 to pay the monthly telephone bill.
15	Issued Check 1804 for $9,016 to Baxter Corporation, a creditor, in payment of Invoice 5119, dated December 7 ($9,200), less a cash discount ($184).
18	Purchased merchandise for $12,400 from Household Appliance Center, Invoice 7238, dated December 16; terms of 3/10, n/30.

Continued

DATE	9.4B (cont.) TRANSACTIONS
Dec. 20	Purchased new store equipment for $6,000 from Safety Security Systems Inc., Invoice 536, dated December 17, net payable in 45 days.
21	Issued Check 1805 for $4,200 to Chain Lighting and Appliances, a creditor, in payment of Invoice 7813, dated November 23.
22	Purchased merchandise for $5,800 from Zale Corporation, Invoice 3161, dated December 19, net due in 30 days.
24	Issued Check 1806 for $12,028 to Household Appliance Center, a creditor, in payment of Invoice 7238, dated December 16 ($12,400), less a cash discount ($372).
28	Received Credit Memorandum 201 for $1,050 from Zale Corporation for damaged goods that were returned; the original purchase was made on Invoice 3161, dated December 19.
31	Issued Check 1807 for $6,500 to pay the monthly salaries of the employees.

Analyze: List the dates for transactions in December that would be categorized as expenses of the business.

Preparing a bank reconciliation statement and journalizing entries to adjust the cash balance.

◀ **Problem 9.5B**
Objectives 9, 10

On October 7, 2007, Peter Chen, Attorney-at-Law, received his September bank statement from First Texas National Bank. Enclosed with the bank statement, which appears on page 328, was a debit memorandum for $118 that covered an NSF check issued by Annette Cole, a credit customer. The firm's checkbook contained the following information about deposits made and checks issued during September. The balance of the *Cash* account and the checkbook on September 30 was $8,134.

INSTRUCTIONS

1. Prepare a bank reconciliation statement for the firm as of September 30, 2007.

2. Record general journal entries for any items on the bank reconciliation statement that must be journalized. Date the entries October 5, 2007.

DATE	TRANSACTIONS	
Sept. 1	Balance	$6,500
1	Check 104	100
3	Check 105	10
3	Deposit	500
6	Check 106	225
10	Deposit	410
11	Check 107	200
15	Check 108	75
21	Check 109	60
22	Deposit	730
25	Check 110	16
25	Check 111	80
27	Check 112	140
28	Deposit	900

FIRST TEXAS NATIONAL BANK

Peter Chen, Attorney-at-Law
3510 North Central Expressway
Dallas, TX 75232-2709

Account Number: 22-8654-30

Period Ending September 30, 2007

CHECKS		DEPOSITS	DATE	BALANCE
Beginning Balance			August 31	6,500.00
		500.00+	September 3	7,000.00
100.00-			September 6	6,900.00
200.00-	10.00-	410.00+	September 11	7,100.00
225.00-			September 15	6,875.00
60.00-			September 19	6,815.00
		730.00+	September 23	7,545.00
80.00-	16.00-		September 25	7,449.00
7.50- SC	118.00- DM		September 28	7,323.50

Analyze: How many checks were paid (cleared the bank) according to the September 30 bank statement?

Problem 9.6B
Objectives 9, 10

▶ **Preparing a bank reconciliation statement and journalizing entries to adjust the cash balance.**

On June 30, 2007, the balance in Wells Builder's checkbook and **Cash** account was $6,418.59. The balance shown on the bank statement on the same date was $7,542.03.

Notes

a. The following checks were issued but have not yet been paid by the bank: Check 533 for $148.95, Check 535 for $97.50, and Check 537 for $425.40.

b. A credit memorandum shows that the bank has collected a $1,500 note receivable and interest of $30 for the firm. These amounts have not yet been entered in the firm's records.

c. The firm's records indicate that a deposit of $944.07 made on June 30 does not appear on the bank statement.

d. A service charge of $14.34 and a debit memorandum of $120 covering an NSF check have not yet been entered in the firm's records. (The check was issued by Robert Boley, a credit customer.)

INSTRUCTIONS

1. Prepare a bank reconciliation statement for the firm as of June 30, 2007.

2. Record general journal entries for any items on the bank reconciliation statement that must be journalized. Date the entries July 3, 2007.

Analyze: After all journal entries have been recorded and posted, what is the balance in the **Cash** account?

Problem 9.7B
Objectives 9, 10

▶ **Correcting errors revealed by a bank reconciliation.**

During the bank reconciliation process at Little Guy Movers Corporation on March 3, 2007, the following errors were discovered in the firm's records.

a. The checkbook and the cash payments journal indicated that Check 1201 dated February 8 was issued for $316 to pay for hauling expenses. However, examination of the canceled check and the listing on the bank statement showed that the actual amount of the check was $308.

b. The checkbook and the cash payments journal indicated that Check 1222 dated February 24 was issued for $404 to pay a telephone bill. However, examination of the canceled check and the listing on the bank statement showed that the actual amount of the check was $440.

INSTRUCTIONS

1. Prepare the adjusted book balance section of the firm's bank reconciliation statement. The book balance as of February 28, 2007, was $19,451. The errors listed are the only two items that affect the book balance.

2. Prepare general journal entries to correct the errors. Date the entries March 3, 2007. Check 1201 was debited to *Hauling Expense* on February 8, and Check 1222 was debited to *Telephone Expense* on February 24.

Analyze: What net change to the *Cash* account occurred as a result of the correcting journal entries?

Challenge Problem

Special Journals

During September 2007 Interior Designs Specialty Shop, a retail store, had the transactions listed on pages 330–331. The general ledger accounts used to record these transactions are provided on page 330.

INSTRUCTIONS

1. Open the general ledger accounts and enter the balances as of September 1, 2007.

2. Record the transactions in a sales journal, a cash receipts journal, a purchases journal, a cash payments journal, and a general journal. Use page 12 as the page number for each of the special journals and page 32 as the page number for the general journal.

3. Post the entries from the general journal to the proper general ledger accounts.

4. Post the entries from the Other Accounts Credit section of the cash receipts journal to the proper general ledger accounts.

5. Post the entries from the Other Accounts Debit section of the cash payments journal to the proper general ledger accounts.

6. Total, prove, and rule the special journals as of September 30.

7. Post the column totals from the special journals to the proper general ledger accounts.

8. Set up an accounts receivable ledger for Interior Designs Specialty Shop. Open an account for each of the customers listed below, and enter the balances as of September 1. All of these customers have terms of n/30.

Credit Customers	
Name	**Balance 9/01/07**
Rachel Carter	
Mesia Davis	$1,260.00
Robert Kent	1,730.00
Pam Lawrence	
David Prater	1,050.00
Henry Tolliver	
Jason Williams	2,100.00

9. Post the individual entries from the sales journal, cash receipts journal, and the general journal to the accounts receivable subsidiary ledger.

10. Prepare a schedule of accounts receivable for September 30, 2007.

11. Check the total of the schedule of accounts receivable against the balance of the *Accounts Receivable* account in the general ledger. The two amounts should be the same.

Creditors		
Name	Balance 9/01/07	Terms
Booker, Inc.		n/45
McKnight Corporation	$5,500	1/10, n/30
Nelson Craft Products		2/10, n/30
Rocker Company		n/30
Reed Millings Company		2/10, n/30
Sadler Floor Coverings	1,940	n/30
Wells Products	2,120	n/30

12. Set up an accounts payable subsidiary ledger for Interior Designs Specialty Shop. Open an account for each of the creditors listed above, and enter the balances as of September 1, 2007.

13. Post the individual entries from the purchases journal, the cash payments journal, and the general journal to the accounts payable subsidiary ledger.

14. Prepare a schedule of accounts payable for September 1, 2007.

15. Check the total of the schedule of accounts payable against the balance of the **Accounts Payable** account in the general ledger. The two amounts should be the same.

GENERAL LEDGER ACCOUNTS

101	Cash	$18,945 Dr.	451	Sales Returns and Allowances	
109	Notes Receivable		501	Purchases	
111	Accounts Receivable	6,140 Dr.	502	Freight In	
121	Supplies	710 Dr.	503	Purchases Returns and Allowances	
131	Inventory	29,365 Dr.	504	Purchases Discounts	
201	Notes Payable		611	Cash Short or Over	
205	Accounts Payable	9,560 Cr.	614	Rent Expense	
231	Sales Tax Payable		617	Salaries Expense	
301	Sergio Cortez, Capital	45,600 Cr.	619	Utilities Expense	
401	Sales				

DATE		TRANSACTIONS
Sept.	1	Received a check for $1,050 from David Prater to pay his account.
	1	Issued Check 1401 for $1,940 to Sadler Floor Coverings, a creditor, in payment of Invoice 6325 dated August 3.
	2	Issued Check 1402 for $2,500 to pay the monthly rent.
	3	Sold a table on credit for $650 plus sales tax of $52.00 to Pam Lawrence, Sales Slip 1850.
	5	Sergio Cortez, the owner, invested an additional $15,000 cash in the business in order to expand operations.
	6	Had cash sales of $3,900 plus sales tax of $312 during the period September 1–6; there was a cash shortage of $20.
	6	Purchased carpeting for $4,450 from Reed Millings Company, Invoice 827, dated September 3; terms of 2/10, n/30.
	6	Issued Check 1403 for $158 to Tri-City Trucking Company to pay the freight charge on goods received from Reed Millings Company.

Continued

should include questions that will help you verify that the department is enforcing the appropriate controls over cash payments and cash receipts.

Internal Controls for Cash

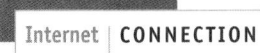

You and four friends have decided to create a new service company called Unpacking for You. Your company unpacks for families once they have moved into a new house. Your business is primarily a cash business. Each family will pay you $100 for each room that is unpacked on the same day you finish the service. How will your business make sure that the payment from the customer is valid? How will you insure that you will receive the cash when the customer pays the employee in cash?

Bank Charges

Many times a negative cash flow is a potential problem in a business. Go to the Web site for the local banks in your community. Check the requirements for a line of credit or mortgage in case your company needs cash quickly to buy a product you know you will sell for a large profit. Some banks Web sites could be: **www.bankofamerica.com**   **www.wellsfargo.com**   **www.chasebank.com**

CHAPTER 9: Review and Applications

Answers to Self Reviews

Answers to Section 1 Self Review

1. Amounts from the Accounts Receivable Credit column are posted as credits to the individual customers' accounts in the accounts receivable subsidiary ledger daily. The total of the Accounts Receivable Credit column is posted as a credit to the **Accounts Receivable** control account in the general ledger at the end of the accounting period.

2. A written promise to pay a specified amount of money on a specified date. To grant credit in certain sales transactions or to replace open-account credit when a customer has an overdue balance.

3. A cash shortage occurs when cash in the register is less than the audit tape; an overage occurs when cash is more than the audit tape. Debit shortages and credit overages in the **Cash Short or Over** account.

4. **b.** cash receipts journal

5. **d.** all of the above

6. The frequency of cash discrepancies indicates that a problem may exist in the handling of the cash (depending on the size of the business and the number of registers, 15 entries may not be unusual).

Answers to Section 2 Self Review

1. Amounts in the Other Accounts Debit section are posted individually to the general ledger accounts daily. The total of the Other Accounts Debit column is not posted because the individual amounts were previously posted to the general ledger.

2. To make small expenditures that require currency and coins.

3. Record the name of the owner's drawing account and the amount in the Other Accounts Debit section of the cash payments journal, and record the amount in the Cash Credit column.

4. **b.** February 4

5. **a.** cash payments journal

6. You should explain to your employer that she must keep all receipts regardless of the amount. Ask your employer to complete a voucher for that amount, then record the entry in the proper account.

Answers to Section 3 Self Review

1. Items in the second section of the bank reconciliation statement require entries in the firm's financial records to correct the *Cash* account balance and make it equal to the checkbook balance. These may include bank fees, debit memorandums, NSF checks, and interest income.

2. Endorsement is the legal process by which the payee transfers ownership of the check to the bank.

3. A check that is dated in the future. It should not be deposited before its date because the drawer of the check may not have sufficient funds in the bank to cover the check at the current time.

4. **d.** Deposits in transit

5. **a.** canceled checks

6. Disagree. Good internal control requires separation of duties.

Answers to Comprehensive Self Review

1. A full endorsement contains the name of the payee plus the name of the firm or bank to whom the check is payable.

2. A record of when a payment is made from petty cash, the amount and purpose of the expenditure, and the account to be charged.

3. Petty cash can be replenished at any time if the fund runs low, but it should be replenished at the end of each month so that all expenses for the month are recorded.

4. They eliminate repetition in postings; the initial recording of transactions is faster.

5. Checks, money orders, and funds on deposit in a bank as well as currency and coins.

LEARNING OBJECTIVES

1. Explain the major federal laws relating to employee earnings and withholding.

2. Compute gross earnings of employees.

3. Determine employee deductions for social security tax.

4. Determine employee deductions for Medicare tax.

5. Determine employee deductions for income tax.

6. Enter gross earnings, deductions, and net pay in the payroll register.

7. Journalize payroll transactions in the general journal.

8. Maintain an earnings record for each employee.

9. Define the accounting terms new to this chapter.

NEW TERMS

commission basis

compensation record

employee

Employee's Withholding Allowance Certificate (Form W-4)

exempt employees

federal unemployment taxes

hourly rate basis

independent contractor

individual earnings record

medicare tax

payroll register

piece-rate basis

salary basis

Social Security Act

Social Security (FICA) tax

state unemployment taxes

tax-exempt wages

time and a half

wage-bracket table method

workers' compensation insurance

Chapter 10
Payroll Computations, Records, and Payment

Adobe   www.adobe.com

Adobe Systems Incorporated has been at the forefront of the software industry since the company began. With its Adobe Portable Document Format (PDF) technology and the Adobe Reader®, Adobe Systems Incorporated has made sharing information across a variety of platforms a seamless operation. Founded in 1982, Adobe is now one of the world's largest software companies, generating annual revenues exceeding $1.2 billion. The company is not only a financial success story but is also a company to follow for the environment it has established for its employees. In 2005, Adobe made the Fortune "Top 100 Companies to Work For" for the sixth year in a row. Fortune also named Adobe the best software company to work for in America.

The company's headquarters—which include private offices for nearly every employee, a fitness center, basketball and bocce courts, and a seasonal farmers' market—is just one of the things that makes Adobe an attractive place to work.

thinking critically   What types of benefits would be important to you if you worked for a software company like Adobe?

Section 1

Payroll Laws and Taxes

SECTION OBJECTIVE

▶ 1. **Explain the major federal laws relating to employee earnings and withholding.**

WHY IT'S IMPORTANT

Tax and labor laws protect the rights of both the employee and the employer. Income tax withholding laws ensure continued funding of certain federal and state programs.

TERMS TO LEARN

employee
federal unemployment taxes
independent contractor
Medicare tax
Social Security Act
social security (FICA) tax
state unemployment taxes
time and a half
workers' compensation insurance

A large component of the activity of any business is concerned with payroll work. Payroll accounting is so important that it requires special consideration.

Who Is an Employee?

Payroll accounting relates only to earnings of those individuals classified as employees. An **employee** is hired by and works under the control and direction of the employer. Usually the employer provides the tools or equipment used by the employee, sets the employee's working hours, and determines how the employee completes the job. Examples of employees are the company president, the bookkeeper, the sales clerk, and the warehouse worker.

In contrast to an employee, an **independent contractor** is paid by the company to carry out a specific task or job, but is not under the direct supervision or control of the company. The independent contractor is told what needs to be done, but the means of doing the job is left to the independent contractor. Examples of independent contractors are the accountant who performs the independent audit, the outside attorney who renders legal advice, and the consultant who installs a new accounting system.

This text addresses issues related to employees but not to independent contractors. When dealing with independent contractors, businesses do not have to follow federal labor laws regulating minimum rates of pay and maximum hours of employment. The business is not required to withhold or match payroll taxes on amounts paid to independent contractors.

▶ 1. **OBJECTIVE**

Explain the major federal laws relating to employee earnings and withholding.

Topic Tackler

PLUS

Federal Employee Earnings and Withholding Laws

Since the 1930s many federal and state laws have affected the relationship between employers and employees. Some of these laws deal with working conditions, including hours and earnings. Others relate to income tax withholding. Some concern taxes that are levied against the employer to provide specific employee benefits.

THE FAIR LABOR STANDARDS ACT

The *Fair Labor Standards Act* of 1938, often referred to as the Wage and Hour Law, applies only to firms engaged directly or indirectly in interstate commerce. It sets a minimum hourly rate of pay and maximum hours of work per week to be performed at the regular rate of pay. When this book was printed, the minimum hourly rate of pay was $5.15, and the maximum number of hours at the regular pay rate was 40 hours per week. When an employee works more

340

than 40 hours in a week, the employee earns at least one and one-half times the regular hourly rate of pay for the extra hours. This overtime rate is called **time and a half**. Even if the federal law does not apply to them, many employers pay time and a half for overtime because of union contracts or simply as good business practice.

SOCIAL SECURITY TAX

The *Federal Insurance Contributions Act (FICA)* is commonly referred to as the **Social Security Act**. The act, first passed in the 1930s, has been amended frequently. The Social Security Act provides the following benefits:

■ Retirement benefits, or pension, when a worker reaches age 62.

■ Benefits for the dependents of the retired worker.

■ Benefits for the worker and the worker's dependents when the worker is disabled.

These retirement and disability benefits are paid by the **social security tax**, sometimes called the **FICA tax**. Both the employer and the employee pay an equal amount of social security tax. The employer is required to withhold social security tax from the employee's pay. Periodically the employer sends the social security tax withheld to the federal government.

The rate of the social security tax and the calendar year earnings base to which it applies are frequently changed by Congress. In recent years, the social security tax rate has remained constant at 6.2 percent. The earnings base to which the tax applies has increased yearly. In 2005 the social security tax rate was 6.2 percent of the first $90,000 of salary or wages paid to each employee. In examples and problems, this text uses a social security tax rate of 6.2 percent of the first $90,000 of salary or wages.

MEDICARE TAX

The Medicare tax is closely related to the social security tax. Prior to 1992 it was a part of the social security tax. The **Medicare tax** is a tax levied equally on employees and employers to provide medical care for the employee and the employee's spouse after each has reached age 65.

In recent years, the Medicare tax rate has remained constant at 1.45 percent. The Medicare tax applies to all salaries and wages paid during the year. The employer is required to withhold the Medicare tax from the employee's pay and periodically send it to the federal government.

Note that the social security tax has an earnings base limit. The Medicare tax does not have an earnings base limit. The Medicare tax applies to *all* earnings paid during the year.

FEDERAL INCOME TAX

Employers are required to withhold from employees' earnings an estimated amount of income tax that will be payable by the employee on the earnings. The amount depends on several factors. Later in this chapter you will learn how to determine the amount to withhold from an employee's paycheck.

State and Local Taxes

Most states, and many local governments, require employers to withhold income taxes from employees' earnings to prepay the employees' state and local income taxes. These rules are generally almost identical to those governing federal income tax withholding, but they require separate general ledger accounts in the firm's accounting system.

Employer's Payroll Taxes and Insurance Costs

Remember that employers withhold social security and Medicare taxes from employees' earnings. In addition, employers pay social security and Medicare taxes on their employees' earnings. Employers are also required to pay federal and state taxes for unemployment benefits and to carry workers' compensation insurance.

important!

Wage Base Limit
The social security tax has a wage base limit. There is no wage base limit for the Medicare tax. All salaries and wages are subject to the Medicare tax.

SOCIAL SECURITY TAX

The employer's share of the social security tax is 6.2 percent up to the earnings base. (In this text, the social security tax is 6.2 percent of the first $90,000 of earnings.) Periodically the employer pays to the federal government the social security tax withheld plus the employer's share of the social security tax.

	FICA
Employee (withheld)	6.2%
Employer (match)	6.2
Total	12.4%

MEDICARE TAX

The employer's share of Medicare tax is 1.45 percent of earnings. Periodically the employer pays to the federal government the Medicare tax withheld plus the employer's share of the Medicare tax.

The Medicare taxes the employer remits to the federal government are shown below.

	Medicare
Employee (withheld)	1.45%
Employer (match)	1.45
Total	2.90%

FEDERAL UNEMPLOYMENT TAX

The *Federal Unemployment Tax Act (FUTA)* provides benefits for employees who become unemployed. Taxes levied by the federal government against employers to benefit unemployed workers are called **federal unemployment taxes (FUTA)**. Employers pay the entire amount of these taxes. In this text we assume that the taxable earnings base is $7,000. That is, the tax applies to the first $7,000 of each employee's earnings for the year. The FUTA tax rate is 6.2 percent.

STATE UNEMPLOYMENT TAX

The federal and state unemployment programs work together to provide benefits for employees who become unemployed. Employers pay all of the **state unemployment taxes (SUTA)**. Usually the earnings base for the federal and state unemployment taxes are the same, the first $7,000 of each employee's earnings for the year. For many states the SUTA tax rate is 5.4 percent.

The federal tax rate (6.2 percent) can be reduced by the rate charged by the state (5.4 percent in this example), so the FUTA rate can be as low as 0.8 percent (6.2% − 5.4%).

SUTA tax		5.4%
FUTA tax rate	6.2%	
Less SUTA tax	(5.4)	
Net FUTA tax		0.8
Total federal and state unemployment tax		6.2%

WORKERS' COMPENSATION INSURANCE

Workers' compensation insurance protects employees against losses from job-related injuries or illnesses, or compensates their families if death occurs in the course of the employment. Workers' compensation requirements are defined by each state. Most states mandate workers' compensation insurance.

HUMAN SERVICES

Industry Overview

The human services field provides essential services to those who are not fully equipped to help themselves. Social disabilities, economic disadvantage, employment difficulties, food and housing hardships, and alcohol and drug dependencies are issues addressed by professionals in this field.

Career Opportunities

- Child Support Payment Specialist
- Social Worker
- Senior Accounting Supervisor—Human Services
- Income Maintenance Program Advisor
- Social Services Grant Administrator
- Budget Analyst—U.S. Administration on Aging

Preparing for a Human Services Career

- Demonstrate an understanding of and sensitivity to individual, ethnic, and cultural differences among individuals and families.
- Complete governmental accounting courses to prepare for administration of human service department budgets and funds.
- Develop proficiencies in electronic spreadsheets and database applications to manage client files, administer benefits, and track human services programs.

- Obtain certification or an associate's degree in social work or human services for middle management or entry-level positions.
- Secure a bachelor's degree for supervisory or managerial positions with an emphasis in human services management, social work, behavioral science, math, science, child development, world languages, computer science, or consumer science.
- Apply to participate in a Presidential Management Internship Program with the U.S. Department of Health and Human Services.

THINKING CRITICALLY

Social worker planners and policymakers develop programs to address issues such as homelessness, poverty, and violence. What skills or proficiencies do you think might be beneficial to these professionals as they identify specific problems, create plans of action, and suggest solutions?

INTERNET APPLICATION

Locate the Web site for the U.S. Department of Health and Human Services. Describe the purpose of this human services agency. What is the department's budget for the current year? How many individuals does this agency employ?

Employee Records Required by Law

> Some companies outsource payroll duties to professional payroll companies. ADP, Inc., is the world's largest provider of payroll services and employee information systems.

Federal laws require that certain payroll records be maintained. For each employee the employer must keep a record of

- the employee's name, address, social security number, and date of birth;
- hours worked each day and week, and wages paid at the regular and overtime rates (certain exceptions exist for employees who earn salaries);
- cumulative wages paid throughout the year;
- amount of income tax, social security tax, and Medicare tax withheld for each pay period;
- proof that the employee is a United States citizen or has a valid work permit.

Section 1: **Self Review**

QUESTIONS

1. How are social security benefits financed?

2. How are unemployment insurance benefits financed?

3. What is "time and a half"?

EXERCISES

4. The purpose of FUTA is to provide benefits for

   a. employees who become unemployed.

   b. employees who become injured while on the job.

   c. retired workers.

   d. disabled employees.

5. The earnings base limit for Medicare

   a. is the same as the earnings base limit for social security.

   b. is lower than the earnings base limit for social security.

   c. is higher than the earnings base limit for social security.

   d. does not exist.

ANALYSIS

6. Susan Kennedy was hired by Harvey Architects to create three oil paintings for the president's office. Is Kennedy an employee? Why or why not?

(Answers to Section 1 Self Review are on page 374.)

Calculating Earnings and Taxes

Kent Furniture and Novelty Company is a sole proprietorship owned and managed by Sarah Kent. Kent Furniture and Novelty Company imports furniture and novelty items to sell over the Internet. It has five employees. The three shipping clerks and the shipping supervisor are paid on an hourly basis. The office clerk is paid a weekly salary. Payday is each Monday; it covers the wages and salaries earned the previous week. The employees are subject to withholding of social security, Medicare, and federal income taxes. The business pays social security and Medicare taxes, and federal and state unemployment insurance taxes. The business is required by state law to carry workers' compensation insurance. Since it is involved in interstate commerce, Kent Furniture and Novelty Company is subject to the Fair Labor Standards Act.

From time to time, Sarah Kent, the owner, makes cash withdrawals to cover her personal expenses. The withdrawals of the owner of a sole proprietorship are not treated as salaries or wages.

Computing Total Earnings of Employees

The first step in preparing payroll is to compute the gross wages or salary for each employee. There are several ways to compute earnings.

Hourly rate basis workers earn a stated rate per hour. Gross pay depends on the number of hours worked.

Salary basis workers earn an agreed-upon amount for each week, month, or other period.

Commission basis workers, usually salespeople, earn a percentage of net sales.

Piece-rate basis manufacturing workers are paid based on the number of units produced.

Section 2

SECTION OBJECTIVE

▶ **2. Compute gross earnings of employees.**

WHY IT'S IMPORTANT

Payroll is a large part of business activity.

▶ **3. Determine employee deductions for social security tax.**

WHY IT'S IMPORTANT

Employers are legally responsible for collecting and remitting this tax.

▶ **4. Determine employee deductions for Medicare tax.**

WHY IT'S IMPORTANT

Employers have legal responsibility.

▶ **5. Determine employee deductions for income tax.**

WHY IT'S IMPORTANT

Employers are legally responsible.

▶ **6. Enter gross earnings, deductions, and net pay in the payroll register.**

WHY IT'S IMPORTANT

The payroll register provides information needed to prepare paychecks.

TERMS TO LEARN

commission basis
Employee's Withholding Allowance Certificate (Form W-4)
exempt employees
hourly rate basis
payroll register
piece-rate basis
salary basis
tax-exempt wages
wage-bracket table method

Wal-Mart Stores, Inc., has approximately 1,500,000 employees in its worldwide operations, which include Wal-Mart Discount Stores, SAM's Clubs, the distribution centers, and the home office. Nearly 75 percent of its stores are in the United States, but Wal-Mart is expanding internationally. It is the number 1 retailer in Canada and Mexico. It also has operations in Asia, Europe, and South America. The company reports that 65 percent of Wal-Mart managers, who are compensated on a salary basis, first entered the company as hourly employees.

▶ 2. OBJECTIVE
Compute gross earnings of employees.

recall

Owner Withdrawals

Withdrawals by the owner of a sole proprietorship are debited to a temporary owner's equity account (in this case, **Sarah Kent, Drawing**). Withdrawals are not treated as salary or wages.

Determining Pay for Hourly Employees

Two pieces of data are needed to compute gross pay for hourly rate basis employees: the number of hours worked during the payroll period, and the rate of pay.

HOURS WORKED

At Kent Furniture and Novelty Company, the shipping supervisor keeps a weekly time sheet. Each day she enters the hours worked by each shipping clerk. At the end of the week, the office clerk uses the time sheet to compute the total hours worked and to prepare the payroll.

Many businesses use time clocks for hourly employees. Each employee has a time card and inserts it in the time clock to record the times of arrival and departure. The payroll clerk collects the cards at the end of the week, determines the hours worked by each employee, and multiplies the number of hours by the pay rate to compute the *gross pay*. Some time cards are machine readable. A computer determines the hours worked and makes the earnings calculations.

GROSS PAY

Alicia Martinez, Jorge Rodriguez, and George Dunlap are shipping clerks at Kent Furniture and Novelty Company. They are hourly employees. Their gross pay for the week ended January 6 is determined as follows:

- Martinez worked 40 hours. She earns $10 an hour. Her gross pay is $400 (40 hours × $10).
- Rodriguez worked 40 hours. He earns $9.50 an hour. His gross pay is $380 (40 × $9.50).
- Dunlap earns $9 per hour. He worked 45 hours. He is paid 40 hours at regular pay and 5 hours at time and a half. There are two ways to compute Dunlap's gross pay:

  1. The Wage and Hour Law method identifies the *overtime premium*, the amount the firm could have saved if all the hours were paid at the regular rate. The overtime premium rate is $4.50, one-half of the regular rate ($9 × 1/2 = $4.50).

Total hours × regular rate:	
45 hours × $9	$405.00
Overtime premium:	
5 hours × $4.50	22.50
Gross pay	$427.50

  2. The second method identifies how much the employee earned by working overtime.

Regular earnings:	
40 hours × $9	$360.00
Overtime earnings:	
5 hours × $13.50 ($9 × 1 1/2)	67.50
Gross pay	$427.50

Cecilia Wu is the shipping supervisor at Kent Furniture and Novelty Company. She is an hourly employee. She earns $14 an hour, and she worked 40 hours. Her gross pay is $560 (40 × $14).

International INSIGHTS

Salaries

More than three million Americans live and work overseas. One of the reasons may be the salary. Americans working abroad can earn up to 300 percent more than the same job pays in the United States.

WITHHOLDINGS FOR HOURLY EMPLOYEES REQUIRED BY LAW

Recall that three deductions from employees' gross pay are required by federal law. They are FICA (social security) tax, Medicare tax, and federal income tax withholding.

Social Security Tax The social security tax is levied on both the employer and the employee. This text calculates social security tax using a 6.2 percent tax rate on the first $90,000 of wages paid during the calendar year. **Tax-exempt wages** are earnings in excess of the base amount set by the Social Security Act ($90,000). Tax-exempt wages are not subject to FICA withholding.

> **3. OBJECTIVE**
> Determine employee deductions for social security tax.

If an employee works for more than one employer during the year, the FICA tax is deducted and matched by each employer. When the employee files a federal income tax return, any excess FICA tax withheld from the employee's earnings is refunded by the government or applied to payment of the employee's federal income taxes.

To determine the amount of social security tax to withhold from an employee's pay, multiply the taxable wages by the social security tax rate. Round the result to the nearest cent.

The following shows the social security tax deductions for Kent Furniture and Novelty Company's hourly employees.

Employee	Gross Pay	Tax Rate	Tax
Alicia Martinez	$400.00	6.2%	$ 24.80
Jorge Rodriguez	380.00	6.2	23.56
George Dunlap	427.50	6.2	26.51
Cecilia Wu	560.00	6.2	34.72
Total social security tax			$109.59

Medicare Tax The Medicare tax is levied on both the employee and the employer. To compute the Medicare tax to withhold from the employee's paycheck, multiply the wages by the Medicare tax rate, 1.45 percent. The following shows the Medicare tax deduction for hourly employees.

> **4. OBJECTIVE**
> Determine employee deductions for Medicare tax.

Employee	Gross Pay	Tax Rate	Tax
Alicia Martinez	$400.00	1.45%	$ 5.80
Jorge Rodriguez	380.00	1.45	5.51
George Dunlap	427.50	1.45	6.20
Cecilia Wu	560.00	1.45	8.12
Total Medicare tax			$25.63

Federal Income Tax A substantial portion of the federal government's revenue comes from the income tax on individuals. Employers are required to withhold federal income tax from employees' pay. Periodically the employer pays the federal income tax withheld to the federal government. After the end of the year, the employee files an income tax return. If the amount of federal income tax withheld does not cover the amount of income tax due, the employee pays the balance. If too much federal income tax has been withheld, the employee receives a refund.

> **5. OBJECTIVE**
> Determine employee deductions for income tax.

> The federal income tax is a pay-as-you-go tax. There are two ways to pay. If you are an employee, your employer will withhold income tax from your pay based on your instructions in Form W-4. If you do not pay tax through withholdings, or do not pay enough taxes through withholdings because of income

from other sources, you might have to pay estimated taxes. Individuals who are in business for themselves generally have to pay taxes through the estimated tax system. The Electronic Federal Tax Payment System (EFTPS) is a free service from the IRS through which taxpayers can use the Internet or telephone to pay their federal taxes, especially 1040 estimated taxes.

important!

Pay-As-You-Go
Employee income tax withholding is designed to place employees on a pay-as-you-go basis in paying their federal income tax.

Withholding Allowances The amount of federal income tax to withhold from an employee's earnings depends on the

- earnings during the pay period,
- length of the pay period,
- marital status,
- number of withholding allowances.

Determining the number of withholding allowances for some taxpayers is complex. In the simplest circumstances, a taxpayer claims a withholding allowance for

- the taxpayer,
- a spouse who does not also claim an allowance,
- each dependent for whom the taxpayer provides more than half the support during the year.

As the number of withholding allowances increases, the amount of federal income tax withheld decreases. The goal is to claim the number of withholding allowances so that the federal income tax withheld is about the same as the employee's tax liability.

To claim withholding allowances, employees complete **Employee's Withholding Allowance Certificate, Form W-4**. The employee gives the completed Form W-4 to the employer. If the number of exemption allowances decreases, the employee must file a new Form W-4 within 10 days. If the number of exemption allowances increases, the employee may, but is not required to, file another Form W-4. If an employee does not file a Form W-4, the employer withholds federal income tax based on zero withholding allowances.

Figure 10.1 shows Form W-4 for Alicia Martinez. Notice that on Line 5, Martinez claims one withholding allowance.

Computing Federal Income Tax Withholding Although there are several ways to compute the federal income tax to withhold from an employee's earnings, the **wage-bracket table method** is almost universally used. The wage-bracket tables are in *Publication 15, Circular E.* This publication contains withholding tables for weekly, biweekly, semimonthly, monthly, and daily or miscellaneous payroll periods for single and married persons. Figure 10.2 on pages 350–351 shows partial tables for single and married persons who are paid weekly.

Use the following steps to determine the amount to withhold:

1. Choose the table for the pay period and the employee's marital status.
2. Find the row in the table that matches the wages earned. Find the column that matches the number of withholding allowances claimed on Form W-4. The income tax to withhold is the intersection of the row and the column.

important!

Get It in Writing
Employers need a signed Form W-4 in order to change the employee's federal income tax withholding.

Employee	Gross Pay	Marital Status	Withholding Allowances	Income Tax Withholding
Alicia Martinez	$400.00	Married	1	$ 19.00
Jorge Rodriguez	380.00	Single	1	34.00
George Dunlap	427.50	Single	3	23.00
Cecilia Wu	560.00	Married	2	30.00
				$106.00

Form **W-4**	**Employee's Withholding Allowance Certificate**	OMB No. 1545-0010

Cut here and give Form W-4 to your employer. Keep the top part for your records.

Form W-4

Department of the Treasury
Internal Revenue Service

Employee's Withholding Allowance Certificate

► Whether you are entitled to claim a certain number of allowances or exemption from withholding is subject to review by the IRS. Your employer may be required to send a copy of this form to the IRS.

OMB No. 1545-0010

2007

1 Type or print your first name and middle initial	Last name	2 Your social security number
Alicia	Martinez	123 45 6789

Home address (number and street or rural route)	3 ☐ Single ☑ Married ☐ Married, but withhold at higher Single rate.
1712 Windmill Hill Lane	**Note.** If married, but legally separated, or spouse is a nonresident alien, check the "Single" box.
City or town, state, and ZIP code	4 If your last name differs from that shown on your social security card, check here. You must call 1-800-772-1213 for a new card. ► ☐
Dallas, TX 75232-6002	

5 Total number of allowances you are claiming (from line **H** above **or** from the applicable worksheet on page 2) . **5** | 1

6 Additional amount, if any, you want withheld from each paycheck . . . . **6** $

7 I claim exemption from withholding for 2005, and I certify that I meet **both** of the following conditions for exemption.
 ● Last year I had a right to a refund of **all** federal income tax withheld because I had **no** tax liability **and**
 ● This year I expect a refund of **all** federal income tax withheld because I expect to have **no** tax liability.
 If you meet both conditions, write "Exempt" here . . . . ► **7**

Under penalties of perjury, I declare that I have examined this certificate and to the best of my knowledge and belief, it is true, correct, and complete.

Employee's signature
(Form is not valid unless you sign it.) ► *Alicia Martinez*   Date ► *December 1, 2006*

8 Employer's name and address (Employer: Complete lines 8 and 10 only if sending to the IRS.)	9 Office code (optional)	10 Employer identification number (EIN)
Kent Furniture and Novelty Co. 5910 Lake June Road, Dallas, TX 75232-6017		75 1234567

For Privacy Act and Paperwork Reduction Act Notice, see page 2.   Cat. No. 10220Q   Form **W-4** (2005)

FIGURE 10.1 | Form W-4 (Partial)

As an example, let's determine the amount to withhold from Cecilia Wu's gross pay. Wu is married, claims two withholding allowances, and earned $560 for the week.

1. Go to the table for married persons paid weekly, Figure 10.2b.
2. Find the line covering wages between $560 and $570. Find the column for two withholding allowances. The tax to withhold is $30; this is where the row and the column intersect.

Using the wage-bracket tables, can you find the federal income tax amounts to withhold for Martinez, Rodriguez, and Dunlap?

Other Deductions Required by Law Most states and some local governments require employers to withhold state and local income taxes from earnings. In some states employers are also required to withhold unemployment tax or disability tax. The procedures are similar to those for federal income tax withholding. Apply the tax rate to the earnings, or use withholding tables.

WITHHOLDINGS NOT REQUIRED BY LAW

There are many payroll deductions not required by law but made by agreement between the employee and the employer. Some examples are

- group life insurance,
- group medical insurance,
- company retirement plans,
- bank or credit union savings plans or loan repayments,
- United States saving bonds purchase plans,
- stocks and other investment purchase plans,
- employer loan repayments,
- union dues.

FIGURE 10.2A

Federal Withholding Tax Tables (Partial) Single Persons— Weekly Payroll Period

SINGLE Persons—WEEKLY Payroll Period   (For Wages Paid Through December 2007)

If the wages are —		And the number of withholding allowances claimed is —										
At least	But less than	0	1	2	3	4	5	6	7	8	9	10
		The amount of income tax to be withheld is —										
$0	$55	$0	$0	$0	$0	$0	$0	$0	$0	$0	$0	$0
55	60	1	0	0	0	0	0	0	0	0	0	0
60	65	1	0	0	0	0	0	0	0	0	0	0
65	70	2	0	0	0	0	0	0	0	0	0	0
70	75	2	0	0	0	0	0	0	0	0	0	0
75	80	3	0	0	0	0	0	0	0	0	0	0
80	85	3	0	0	0	0	0	0	0	0	0	0
85	90	4	0	0	0	0	0	0	0	0	0	0
90	95	4	0	0	0	0	0	0	0	0	0	0
95	100	5	0	0	0	0	0	0	0	0	0	0
100	105	5	0	0	0	0	0	0	0	0	0	0
105	110	6	0	0	0	0	0	0	0	0	0	0
110	115	6	0	0	0	0	0	0	0	0	0	0
115	120	7	1	0	0	0	0	0	0	0	0	0
120	125	7	1	0	0	0	0	0	0	0	0	0
125	130	8	2	0	0	0	0	0	0	0	0	0
130	135	8	2	0	0	0	0	0	0	0	0	0
135	140	9	3	0	0	0	0	0	0	0	0	0
140	145	9	3	0	0	0	0	0	0	0	0	0
145	150	10	4	0	0	0	0	0	0	0	0	0
150	155	10	4	0	0	0	0	0	0	0	0	0
155	160	11	5	0	0	0	0	0	0	0	0	0
160	165	11	5	0	0	0	0	0	0	0	0	0
165	170	12	6	0	0	0	0	0	0	0	0	0
170	175	12	6	0	0	0	0	0	0	0	0	0
175	180	13	7	1	0	0	0	0	0	0	0	0
180	185	13	7	1	0	0	0	0	0	0	0	0
185	190	14	8	2	0	0	0	0	0	0	0	0
190	195	14	8	2	0	0	0	0	0	0	0	0
195	200	15	9	3	0	0	0	0	0	0	0	0
200	210	16	9	3	0	0	0	0	0	0	0	0
210	220	18	10	4	0	0	0	0	0	0	0	0
220	230	19	11	5	0	0	0	0	0	0	0	0
230	240	21	12	6	1	0	0	0	0	0	0	0
240	250	22	13	7	2	0	0	0	0	0	0	0
250	260	24	15	8	3	0	0	0	0	0	0	0
260	270	25	16	9	4	0	0	0	0	0	0	0
270	280	27	18	10	5	0	0	0	0	0	0	0
280	290	28	19	11	6	0	0	0	0	0	0	0
290	300	30	21	12	7	1	0	0	0	0	0	0
300	310	31	22	13	8	2	0	0	0	0	0	0
310	320	33	24	15	9	3	0	0	0	0	0	0
320	330	34	25	16	10	4	0	0	0	0	0	0
330	340	36	27	18	11	5	0	0	0	0	0	0
340	350	37	28	19	12	6	0	0	0	0	0	0
350	360	39	30	21	13	7	1	0	0	0	0	0
360	370	40	31	22	14	8	2	0	0	0	0	0
370	380	42	33	24	15	9	3	0	0	0	0	0
380	390	43	34	25	17	10	4	0	0	0	0	0
390	400	45	36	27	18	11	5	0	0	0	0	0
400	410	46	37	28	20	12	6	0	0	0	0	0
410	420	48	39	30	21	13	7	1	0	0	0	0
420	430	49	40	31	23	14	8	2	0	0	0	0
430	440	51	42	33	24	15	9	3	0	0	0	0
440	450	52	43	34	26	17	10	4	0	0	0	0
450	460	54	45	36	27	18	11	5	0	0	0	0
460	470	55	46	37	29	20	12	6	0	0	0	0
470	480	57	48	39	30	21	13	7	1	0	0	0
480	490	58	49	40	32	23	14	8	2	0	0	0
490	500	60	51	42	33	24	15	9	3	0	0	0
500	510	61	52	43	35	26	17	10	4	0	0	0
510	520	63	54	45	36	27	18	11	5	0	0	0
520	530	64	55	46	38	29	20	12	6	0	0	0
530	540	66	57	48	39	30	21	13	7	1	0	0
540	550	67	58	49	41	32	23	14	8	2	0	0
550	560	69	60	51	42	33	24	15	9	3	0	0
560	570	70	61	52	44	35	26	17	10	4	0	0
570	580	72	63	54	45	36	27	18	11	5	0	0
580	590	73	64	55	47	38	29	20	12	6	0	0
590	600	75	66	57	48	39	30	21	13	7	1	0

MARRIED Persons—WEEKLY Payroll Period (For Wages Paid Through December 2007)

| If the wages are — | | And the number of withholding allowances claimed is — | | | | | | | | | | |
At least	But less than	0	1	2	3	4	5	6	7	8	9	10
		The amount of income tax to be withheld is —										
$0	$125	$0	$0	$0	$0	$0	$0	$0	$0	$0	$0	$0
125	130	0	0	0	0	0	0	0	0	0	0	0
130	135	0	0	0	0	0	0	0	0	0	0	0
135	140	0	0	0	0	0	0	0	0	0	0	0
140	145	0	0	0	0	0	0	0	0	0	0	0
145	150	0	0	0	0	0	0	0	0	0	0	0
150	155	0	0	0	0	0	0	0	0	0	0	0
155	160	0	0	0	0	0	0	0	0	0	0	0
160	165	1	0	0	0	0	0	0	0	0	0	0
165	170	1	0	0	0	0	0	0	0	0	0	0
170	175	2	0	0	0	0	0	0	0	0	0	0
175	180	2	0	0	0	0	0	0	0	0	0	0
180	185	3	0	0	0	0	0	0	0	0	0	0
185	190	3	0	0	0	0	0	0	0	0	0	0
190	195	4	0	0	0	0	0	0	0	0	0	0
195	200	4	0	0	0	0	0	0	0	0	0	0
200	210	5	0	0	0	0	0	0	0	0	0	0
210	220	6	0	0	0	0	0	0	0	0	0	0
220	230	7	1	0	0	0	0	0	0	0	0	0
230	240	8	2	0	0	0	0	0	0	0	0	0
240	250	9	3	0	0	0	0	0	0	0	0	0
250	260	10	4	0	0	0	0	0	0	0	0	0
260	270	11	5	0	0	0	0	0	0	0	0	0
270	280	12	6	0	0	0	0	0	0	0	0	0
280	290	13	7	1	0	0	0	0	0	0	0	0
290	300	14	8	2	0	0	0	0	0	0	0	0
300	310	15	9	3	0	0	0	0	0	0	0	0
310	320	16	10	4	0	0	0	0	0	0	0	0
320	330	17	11	5	0	0	0	0	0	0	0	0
330	340	18	12	6	0	0	0	0	0	0	0	0
340	350	19	13	7	1	0	0	0	0	0	0	0
350	360	20	14	8	2	0	0	0	0	0	0	0
360	370	21	15	9	3	0	0	0	0	0	0	0
370	380	22	16	10	4	0	0	0	0	0	0	0
380	390	23	17	11	5	0	0	0	0	0	0	0
390	400	24	18	12	6	0	0	0	0	0	0	0
400	410	25	19	13	7	1	0	0	0	0	0	0
410	420	26	20	14	8	2	0	0	0	0	0	0
420	430	27	21	15	9	3	0	0	0	0	0	0
430	440	28	22	16	10	4	0	0	0	0	0	0
440	450	30	23	17	11	5	0	0	0	0	0	0
450	460	31	24	18	12	6	0	0	0	0	0	0
460	470	33	25	19	13	7	1	0	0	0	0	0
470	480	34	26	20	14	8	2	0	0	0	0	0
480	490	36	27	21	15	9	3	0	0	0	0	0
490	500	37	28	22	16	10	4	0	0	0	0	0
500	510	39	30	23	17	11	5	0	0	0	0	0
510	520	40	31	24	18	12	6	0	0	0	0	0
520	530	42	33	25	19	13	7	1	0	0	0	0
530	540	43	34	26	20	14	8	2	0	0	0	0
540	550	45	36	27	21	15	9	3	0	0	0	0
550	560	46	37	29	22	16	10	4	0	0	0	0
560	570	48	39	30	23	17	11	5	0	0	0	0
570	580	49	40	32	24	18	12	6	0	0	0	0
580	590	51	42	33	25	19	13	7	1	0	0	0
590	600	52	43	35	26	20	14	8	2	0	0	0
600	610	54	45	36	27	21	15	9	3	0	0	0
610	620	55	46	38	29	22	16	10	4	0	0	0
620	630	57	48	39	30	23	17	11	5	0	0	0
630	640	58	49	41	32	24	18	12	6	0	0	0
640	650	60	51	42	33	25	19	13	7	1	0	0
650	660	61	52	44	35	26	20	14	8	2	0	0
660	670	63	54	45	36	27	21	15	9	3	0	0
670	680	64	55	47	38	29	22	16	10	4	0	0
680	690	66	57	48	39	30	23	17	11	5	0	0
690	700	67	58	50	41	32	24	18	12	6	0	0
700	710	69	60	51	42	33	25	19	13	7	1	0
710	720	70	61	53	44	35	26	20	14	8	2	0
720	730	72	63	54	45	36	27	21	15	9	3	0
730	740	73	64	56	47	38	29	22	16	10	4	0

FIGURE 10.2B

Federal Withholding Tax Tables (Partial) Married Persons—Weekly Payroll Period

These and other payroll deductions increase the payroll recordkeeping work but do not involve any new principles or procedures. They are handled in the same way as the deductions for social security, Medicare, and federal income taxes.

Kent Furniture and Novelty Company pays all medical insurance premiums for each employee. If the employee chooses to have medical coverage for a spouse or dependent, Kent Furniture and Novelty Company deducts $40 per week for coverage for the spouse and each dependent. Dunlap and Wu each have $40 per week deducted to obtain the medical coverage.

Determining Pay for Salaried Employees

A salaried employee earns a specific sum of money for each payroll period. The office clerk at Kent Furniture and Novelty Company earns a weekly salary.

HOURS WORKED

Salaried workers who do not hold supervisory jobs are covered by the provisions of the Wage and Hour Law that deal with maximum hours and overtime premium pay. Employers keep time records for all nonsupervisory salaried workers to make sure that their hourly earnings meet the legal requirements.

Salaried employees who hold supervisory or managerial positions are called **exempt employees**. They are not subject to the maximum hour and overtime premium pay provisions of the Wage and Hour Law.

GROSS EARNINGS

Cynthia Booker is the office clerk at Kent Furniture and Novelty Company. During the first week of January, she worked 40 hours, her regular schedule. There are no overtime earnings because she did not work more than 40 hours during the week. Her salary of $480 is her gross pay for the week.

WITHHOLDINGS FOR SALARIED EMPLOYEES REQUIRED BY LAW

The procedures for withholding taxes for salaried employees is the same as withholding for hourly rate employees. Apply the tax rate to the earnings, or use withholding tables.

Recording Payroll Information for Employees

A payroll register is prepared for each pay period. The **payroll register** shows all the payroll information for the pay period.

FIGURE 10.3 | Payroll Register

PAYROLL REGISTER   **WEEK BEGINNING** _January 1, 2007_

NAME	NO. OF ALLOW.	MARITAL STATUS	CUMULATIVE EARNINGS	NO. OF HRS.	RATE/ SALARY	EARNINGS			CUMULATIVE EARNINGS
						REGULAR	OVERTIME	GROSS AMOUNT	
Martinez, Alicia	1	M		40	10.00	400 00		400 00	400 00
Rodriguez, Jorge	1	S		40	9.50	380 00		380 00	380 00
Dunlap, George	3	S		45	9.00	360 00	67 50	427 50	427 50
Wu, Cecil	2	M		40	14.00	560 00		560 00	560 00
Booker, Cynthia	1	S		40	480.00	480 00		480 00	480 00
			0 00			2 180 00	67 50	2 247 50	2 247 50
(A)	(B)		(C)	(D)	(E)	(F)	(G)	(H)	(I)

THE PAYROLL REGISTER

Figure 10.3 on pages 352–353 shows the payroll register for Kent Furniture and Novelty Company for the week ended January 7. Note that all employees were paid for eight hours on January 1, a holiday. To learn how to complete the payroll register, refer to Figure 10.3 and follow these steps.

1. *Columns A, B, and E.* Enter the employee's name (Column A), number of withholding allowances and marital status (Column B), and rate of pay (Column E). In a computerized payroll system, this information is entered once and is automatically retrieved each time payroll is prepared.

2. *Column C.* The Cumulative Earnings column (Column C) shows the total earnings for the calendar year before the current pay period. This figure is needed to determine whether the employee has exceeded the earnings limit for the FICA and FUTA taxes. Since this is the first payroll period of the year, there are no cumulative earnings prior to the current pay period.

3. *Column D.* In Column D enter the total number of hours worked in the current period. This data comes from the weekly time sheet.

4. *Columns F, G, and H.* Using the hours worked and the pay rate, calculate regular pay (Column F), the overtime earnings (Column G), and gross pay (Column H).

5. *Column I.* Calculate the cumulative earnings after this pay period (Column I) by adding the beginning cumulative earnings (Column C) and the current period's gross pay (Column H).

6. *Columns J, K, and L.* The Taxable Wages columns show the earnings subject to taxes for social security (Column J), Medicare (Column K), and FUTA (Column L). Only the earnings at or under the earnings limit are included in these columns.

7. *Columns M, N, O, and P.* The Deductions columns show the withholding for social security tax (Column M), Medicare tax (Column N), federal income tax (Column O), and medical insurance (Column P).

8. *Column Q.* Subtract the deductions (Columns M, N, O, and P) from the gross earnings (Column H). Enter the results in the Net Amount column (Column Q). This is the amount paid to each employee.

9. *Column R.* Enter the check number in Column R.

10. *Columns S and T.* The payroll register's last two columns classify employee earnings as office salaries (Column S) or shipping wages (Column T).

When the payroll data for all employees has been entered in the payroll register, total the columns. Check the balances of the following columns:

■ Total regular earnings plus total overtime earnings must equal the gross amount (Columns F + G = Column H).

AND ENDING _January 6, 2007_   **PAID** _January 8, 2007_

TAXABLE WAGES			DEDUCTIONS				DISTRIBUTION			
SOCIAL SECURITY	MEDICARE	FUTA	SOCIAL SECURITY	MEDICARE	INCOME TAX	HEALTH INSURANCE	NET AMOUNT	CHECK NO.	OFFICE SALARIES	SHIPPING WAGES
400 00	400 00	400 00	24 80	5 80	19 00		350 40	1601		400 00
380 00	380 00	380 00	23 56	5 51	34 00		316 93	1602		380 00
427 50	427 50	427 50	26 51	6 20	23 00	40 00	331 79	1603		427 50
560 00	560 00	560 00	34 72	8 12	30 00	40 00	447 16	1604		560 00
480 00	480 00	480 00	29 76	6 96	49 00		394 28	1605	480 00	
2 247 50	2 247 50	2 247 50	139 35	32 59	155 00	80 00	1 840 56		480 00	1 767 50
(J)	(K)	(L)	(M)	(N)	(O)	(P)	(Q)	(R)	(S)	(T)

■ The total gross amount less total deductions must equal the total net amount.

Gross amount		$2,247.50
Less deductions:		
Social security tax	$139.35	
Medicare tax	32.59	
Income tax	155.00	
Health insurance	80.00	
Total deductions		406.94
Net amount		$1,840.56

■ The office salaries and the shipping wages must equal gross earnings (Columns S + T = Column H).

The payroll register supplies all the information to make the journal entry to record the payroll. Journalizing the payroll is discussed in Section 3.

Section 2: **Self Review**

QUESTIONS

1. List four payroll deductions that are not required by law but can be made by agreement between the employee and the employer.

2. What factors determine the amount of federal income tax to be withheld from an employee's earnings?

3. What three payroll deductions does federal law require?

EXERCISES

4. Which of the following affects the amount of Medicare tax to be withheld from an hourly rate employee's pay?
   a. medical insurance premium
   b. marital status
   c. withholding allowances claimed on Form W-4
   d. hours worked

5. Stacy Amos worked 48 hours during the week ending November 17. Her regular rate is $9 per hour. Calculate her gross earnings for the week.
   a. $432
   b. $492
   c. $468
   d. $444

ANALYSIS

6. Rosie Perez left a voice mail asking you to withhold an additional $40 of federal income tax from her wages each pay period, starting June 1. When should you begin withholding the extra amount?

(Answers to Section 2 Self Review are on page 375.)

Recording Payroll Information

In this section you will learn how to prepare paychecks and journalize and post payroll transactions by following the January payroll activity for Kent Furniture and Novelty Company.

Recording Payroll

Recording payroll involves two separate entries: one to record the payroll expense and another to pay the employees. The general journal entry to record the payroll expense is based on the payroll register. The gross pay is debited to **Shipping Wages Expense** for the shipping clerks and supervisor and to **Office Salaries Expense** for the office clerk. Each type of deduction is credited to a separate liability account *(Social Security Tax Payable, Medicare Tax Payable, Employee Income Tax Payable, Health Insurance Premiums Payable)*. Net pay is credited to the liability account, **Salaries and Wages Payable.**

Refer to Figure 10.3 on pages 352–353 to see how the data on the payroll register is used to prepare the January 8 payroll journal entry for Kent Furniture and Novelty Company. Following is an analysis of the entry.

SECTION OBJECTIVE

▶ **7. Journalize payroll transactions in the general journal.**

WHY IT'S IMPORTANT
Payroll cost is an operating expense.

▶ **8. Maintain an earnings record for each employee.**

WHY IT'S IMPORTANT
Federal law requires that employers maintain records.

TERMS TO LEARN

compensation record
individual earnings record

▶ **7. OBJECTIVE**
Journalize payroll transactions in the general journal.

BUSINESS TRANSACTION

The information in the payroll register (Figure 10.3) is used to record the payroll expense.

ANALYSIS
The expense account, **Office Salaries Expense,** is increased by $480.00. The expense account, **Shipping Wages Expense,** is increased by $1,767.50. The liability account for each deduction is increased: **Social Security Tax Payable,** $139.35; **Medicare Tax Payable,** $32.59; **Employee Income Tax Payable,** $155.00; **Health Insurance Premiums Payable,** $80.00. The liability account, **Salaries and Wages Payable,** is increased by the net amount of the payroll, $1,840.56.

DEBIT-CREDIT RULES
DEBIT Increases in expenses are recorded as debits. Debit **Office Salaries Expense** for $480.00. Debit **Shipping Wages Expense** for $1,767.50.

CREDIT Increases in liability accounts are recorded as credits. Credit **Social Security Tax Payable** for $139.35. Credit **Medicare Tax Payable** for $32.59. Credit **Employee Income Tax Payable** for $155.00. Credit **Health Insurance Premiums Payable** for $80.00. Credit **Salaries and Wages Payable** for $1,840.56

T-ACCOUNT PRESENTATION

Office Salaries Expense	
+	−
480.00	

Social Security Tax Payable	
−	+
	139.35

Medicare Tax Payable	
−	+
	32.59

Shipping Wages Expense	
+	−
1,767.50	

Employee Income Tax Payable	
−	+
	155.00

Health Insurance Premiums Payable	
−	+
	80.00

Salaries and Wages Payable	
−	+
	1,840.56

GENERAL JOURNAL ENTRY

GENERAL JOURNAL   PAGE ___1___

	DATE		DESCRIPTION	POST. REF.	DEBIT	CREDIT	
1	2007						1
2	Jan.	8	Office Salaries Expense		480 00		2
3			Shipping Wages Expense		1 767 50		3
4			Social Security Tax Payable			139 35	4
5			Medicare Tax Payable			32 59	5
6			Employee Income Tax Payable			155 00	6
7			Health Insurance Premiums Payable			80 00	7
8			Salaries and Wages Payable			1 840 56	8
9			Payroll for week ending Jan. 6				9

THE BOTTOM LINE
Record Payroll

Income Statement

Expenses	↑ 2,247.50
Net Income	↓ 2,247.50

Balance Sheet

Liabilities	↑ 2,247.50
Equity	↓ 2,247.50

Southwest Airlines Co. recorded salaries, wages, and benefits of more than $3.10 billion for the year ended December 31, 2003.

Paying Employees

Most businesses pay their employees by check or by direct deposit. By using these methods, the business avoids the inconvenience and risk involved in dealing with currency.

PAYING BY CHECK

Paychecks may be written on the firm's regular checking account or on a payroll bank account. The check stub shows information about the employee's gross earnings, deductions, and net pay. Employees detach the stubs and keep them as a record of their payroll data. The check number is entered in the Check Number column of the payroll register (Figure 10.3, Column

important!

Payroll Liabilities
Deductions from employee paychecks are liabilities for the employer.

R). The canceled check provides a record of the payment, and the employee's endorsement serves as a receipt. Following is an analysis of the transaction to pay Kent Furniture and Novelty Company's employees.

BUSINESS TRANSACTION

On January 8 Kent Furniture and Novelty Company wrote five checks for payroll, Check numbers 1601–1605.

ANALYSIS
The liability account, **Salaries and Wages Payable,** is decreased by $1,840.56. The asset account, **Cash,** is decreased by $1,840.56.

DEBIT-CREDIT RULES
DEBIT   Decreases to liability accounts are recorded as debits. Debit **Salaries and Wages Payable** for $1,840.56.

CREDIT   Decreases to assets are credits. Credit **Cash** for $1,840.56.

T-ACCOUNT PRESENTATION

Salaries and Wages Payable		Cash	
−	+	+	−
1,840.56			1,840.56

GENERAL JOURNAL ENTRY

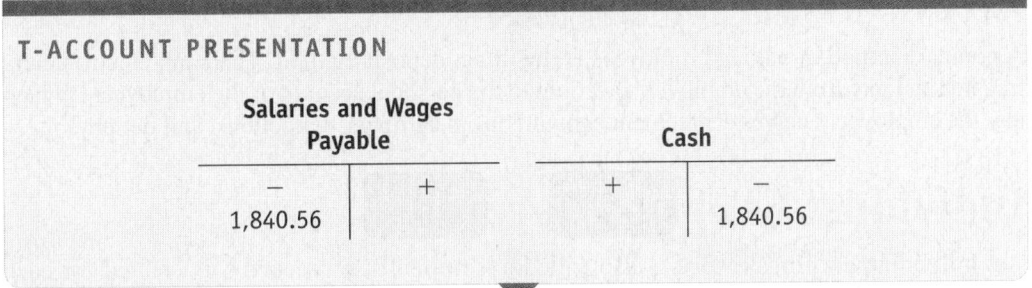

	DATE		DESCRIPTION	POST. REF.	DEBIT	CREDIT	
11	Jan.	8	Salaries and Wages Payable		1 840 56		11
12			Cash			1 840 56	12
13			To record payment of salaries and wages				13
14			for week ended Jan. 6				14

GENERAL JOURNAL   PAGE ___1___

THE BOTTOM LINE
Issue Paychecks

Income Statement

No effect on net income

Balance Sheet

Assets   ↓ 1,840.56
Liabilities   ↓ 1,840.56
No effect on equity

Checks Written on Regular Checking Account The above entry is shown in general journal form for illustration purposes only. When paychecks are written on the regular checking account, the entries are recorded in the cash payments journal. Figure 10.4 on page 358 shows the January 8 entries to pay employees. Notice that there is a separate Salaries and Wages Payable Debit column.

Checks Written on a Separate Payroll Account Many businesses write payroll checks from a separate payroll bank account. This is a two-step process.

1. A check is drawn on the regular bank account for the total amount of net pay and deposited in the payroll bank account.
2. Individual payroll checks are issued from the payroll bank account.

FIGURE 10.4

Cash Payments Journal

important!

Separate Payroll Account
Using a separate payroll account facilitates the bank reconciliation and provides better internal control.

CASH PAYMENTS JOURNAL   PAGE _____1_____

DATE	CK. NO.	DESCRIPTION	POST. REF.	ACCOUNTS PAYABLE DEBIT	SALARIES AND WAGES PAYABLE DEBIT	PURCHASES DISCOUNT CREDIT	CASH CREDIT
Jan. 2	1711	International Furniture Company		1 4 0 0 00		2 8 00	1 3 7 2 00
8	1601	Alicia Martinez			3 5 0 40		3 5 0 40
8	1602	Jorge Rodriguez			3 1 6 93		3 1 6 93
8	1603	Georg Dunlap			3 3 1 79		3 3 1 79
8	1604	Cecil Wu			4 4 7 16		4 4 7 16
8	1605	Cynthia Booker			3 9 4 28		3 9 4 28
31		Totals		XX X X X XX	7 3 6 2 24	XX X X X XX	XX X X X XX

Using a separate payroll account simplifies the bank reconciliation of the regular checking account and makes it easier to identify outstanding payroll checks.

PAYING BY DIRECT DEPOSIT

A popular method of paying employees is the direct deposit method. The bank electronically transfers net pay from the employer's account to the personal account of the employee. On payday the employee receives a statement showing gross earnings, deductions, and net pay.

▶ 8. OBJECTIVE

Maintain an earnings record for each employee.

Individual Earnings Records

An **individual earnings record**, also called a **compensation record**, is created for each employee. This record contains the employee's name, address, social security number, date of birth, number of withholding allowances claimed, rate of pay, and any other information needed to compute earnings and complete tax reports.

The payroll register provides the details that are entered on the employee's individual earnings record for each pay period. Figure 10.5 on page 359 shows the earnings record for Alicia Martinez.

MANAGERIAL IMPLICATIONS <<

LAWS AND CONTROLS

- It is management's responsibility to ensure that the payroll procedures and records comply with federal, state, and local laws.
- For most businesses, wages and salaries are a large part of operating expenses. Payroll records help management to keep track of and control expenses.
- Management should investigate large or frequent overtime expenditures.
- To prevent errors and fraud, management periodically should have the payroll records audited and payroll procedures evaluated.
- Two common payroll frauds are the overstatement of hours worked and the issuance of checks to nonexistent employees.

THINKING CRITICALLY

What controls would you put in place to prevent payroll fraud?

EARNINGS RECORD FOR ___2007___

NAME _Alicia Martinez_ RATE _$10 per hour_ SOCIAL SECURITY NO. _123-45-6789_

ADDRESS _1712 Windmill Hill Lane, Dallas, TX 75232-6002_ DATE OF BIRTH _November 23, 1979_

WITHHOLDING ALLOWANCES ___1___ MARITAL STATUS _M_

PAYROLL NO.	DATE WK. END	DATE PAID	HOURS RG	HOURS OT	EARNINGS REGULAR	EARNINGS OVERTIME	EARNINGS TOTAL	EARNINGS CUMULATIVE	DEDUCTIONS SOCIAL SECURITY	DEDUCTIONS MEDICARE	DEDUCTIONS INCOME TAX	DEDUCTIONS OTHER	NET PAY
1	1/06	1/08	40		4 0 0 00		4 0 0 00	4 0 0 00	2 4 80	5 80	1 9 00		3 5 0 40
2	1/13	1/15	40		4 0 0 00		4 0 0 00	4 0 0 00	2 4 80	5 80	1 9 00		3 5 0 40
3	1/20	1/22	40		4 0 0 00		4 0 0 00	4 0 0 00	2 4 80	5 80	1 9 00		3 5 0 40
4	1/27	1/29	40		4 0 0 00		4 0 0 00	4 0 0 00	2 4 80	5 80	1 9 00		3 5 0 40
	January				1 6 0 0 00		16 0 0 00	1 6 0 0 00	9 9 20	2 3 20	7 6 00		1 4 0 1 60

FIGURE 10.5 | An Individual Earnings Record

The earnings record shows the payroll period, the date paid, the regular and overtime hours, the regular and overtime earnings, the deductions, and the net pay. The cumulative earnings on the earnings record agrees with Column I of the payroll register (Figure 10.3). The earnings records are totaled monthly and at the end of each calendar quarter. This provides information needed to make tax payments and file tax returns.

Completing January Payrolls

Figure 10.6 on pages 359–360 shows the entire cycle of computing, paying, journalizing, and posting payroll data. In order to complete the January payroll for Kent Furniture and Novelty Company, assume that all employees worked the same number of hours each week of the month as they did the first week. Thus they had the same earnings, deductions, and net pay each week.

FIGURE 10.6 | Journalizing and Posting Payroll Data

AND ENDING ___January 6, 2007___   PAID ___January 8, 2007___

TAXABLE WAGES SOCIAL SECURITY	TAXABLE WAGES MEDICARE	TAXABLE WAGES FUTA	DEDUCTIONS SOCIAL SECURITY	DEDUCTIONS MEDICARE	DEDUCTIONS INCOME TAX	DEDUCTIONS HEALTH INSURANCE	DISTRIBUTION NET AMOUNT	CHECK NO.	OFFICE SALARIES	SHIPPING WAGES
4 0 0 00	4 0 0 00	4 0 0 00	2 4 80	5 80	1 9 00		3 5 0 40	1601		4 0 0 00
3 8 0 00	3 8 0 00	3 8 0 00	2 3 56	5 51	3 4 00		3 1 6 93	1602		3 8 0 00
4 2 7 50	4 2 7 50	4 2 7 50	2 6 51	6 20	2 3 00	4 0 00	3 3 1 79	1603		4 2 7 50
5 6 0 00	5 6 0 00	5 6 0 00	3 4 72	8 12	3 0 00	4 0 00	4 4 7 16	1604		5 6 0 00
4 8 0 00	4 8 0 00	4 8 0 00	2 9 76	6 96	4 9 00		3 9 4 28	1605	4 8 0 00	
2 2 4 7 50	2 2 4 7 50	2 2 4 7 50	1 3 9 35	3 2 59	1 5 5 00	8 0 00	1 8 4 0 56		4 8 0 00	1 7 6 7 50
(J)	(K)	(L)	(M)	(N)	(O)	(P)	(Q)	(R)	(S)	(T)

1	2007						1
2	Jan.	8	Office Salaries Expense	541	4 8 0 00		2
3			Shipping Wages Expense	542	1 7 6 7 50		3
4			Social Security Tax Payable	221		1 3 9 35	4
5			Medicare Tax Payable	222		3 2 59	5
6			Employee Income Tax Payable	223		1 5 5 00	6
7			Health Insurance Premiums Payable	224		8 0 00	7
8			Salaries and Wages Payable	229		1 8 4 0 56	8
9			Payroll for week ending Jan. 6				9

FIGURE 10.6 (CONTINUED)   Journalizing and Posting Payroll Data

1	2007						1
2	Jan. 8	Office Salaries Expense	541	480 00			2
3		Shipping Wages Expense	542	1 767 50			3
4		Social Security Tax Payable	221		1 39 35		4
5		Medicare Tax Payable	222		32 59		5
6		Employee Income Tax Payable	223		1 55 00		6
7		Health Insurance Premiums Payable	224		80 00		7
8		Salaries and Wages Payable	229		1 840 56		8
9		Payroll for week ending Jan. 6					9
10							10
11							11

Office Salaries Expense

1/08	480.00
1/15	480.00
1/22	480.00
1/29	480.00

Medicare Tax Payable

1/08	32.59
1/15	32.59
1/22	32.59
1/29	32.59

Shipping Wages Expense

1/08	1,767.50
1/15	1,767.50
1/22	1,767.50
1/29	1,767.50

Employee Income Tax Payable

1/08	155.00
1/15	155.00
1/22	155.00
1/29	155.00

Health Ins. Premiums Payable

1/08	80.00
1/15	80.00
1/22	80.00
1/29	80.00

Social Security Tax Payable

1/08	139.35
1/15	139.35
1/22	139.35
1/29	139.35

Salaries and Wages Payable

1/31	7,362.24	1/08	1,840.56
		1/15	1,840.56
		1/22	1,840.56
		1/29	1,840.56

CASH PAYMENTS JOURNAL   PAGE ___1___

DATE	CK. NO.	DESCRIPTION	POST. REF.	ACCOUNTS PAYABLE DEBIT	SALARIES AND WAGES PAYABLE DEBIT	PURCHASES DISCOUNT CREDIT	CASH CREDIT
Jan. 2	1589	International Furniture Co.		1 400 00		28 00	1 372 00
	31	Totals		XX X XX XX	7 362 24	XX XX XX	XX XX XX

ENTRY TO RECORD PAYROLL

As illustrated earlier in this section, one general journal entry is made to record the weekly payroll for all employees of Kent Furniture and Novelty Company. This general journal entry records the payroll expense and liability, but not the payments to employees. Since we are assuming an identical payroll for each week of the month, each of the four weekly payrolls requires general journal entries identical to the one shown in Figure 10.6. Notice how the payroll register column totals are recorded in the general journal.

ENTRY TO RECORD PAYMENT OF PAYROLL

The weekly entries in the cash payments journal to record payments to employees are the same as the January 8 entries in Figure 10.4 on page 358. At the end of January, the columns in the cash payments journal are totaled, including the Salaries and Wages Payable Debit column.

POSTINGS TO LEDGER ACCOUNTS

The entries to record the weekly payroll expense and liability amounts are posted from the general journal to the accounts in the general ledger. The total of the Salaries and Wages Payable Debit column in the cash payments journal is posted to the *Salaries and Wages Payable* general ledger account.

ABOUT
ACCOUNTING

Tax Returns

Research conducted by the Tax Foundation found that Americans spend 5.4 billion hours each year completing their tax returns.

Section 3: **Self Review**

QUESTIONS

1. What is the purpose of a payroll bank account?

2. What appears on an individual earnings record?

3. What accounts are debited and credited when individual payroll checks are written on the regular checking account?

EXERCISES

4. Details related to all employees' gross earnings, deductions, and net pay for a period are found in the
   a. payroll register.
   b. individual earnings record.
   c. general journal.
   d. cash payments journal.

5. Payroll deductions are recorded in a separate
   a. asset account.
   b. expense account.
   c. liability account.
   d. revenue account.

ANALYSIS

6. This general journal entry was made to record the payroll liability.

Ofc. Salaries Exp.	600.00
Shipping Wages Exp.	2,586.00
Health Ins. Prem. Exp.	40.00
Soc. Sec. Taxes Exp.	197.41
Medicare Taxes Pay.	48.17
Employee Income Tax Payable	266.00
Cash	2,634.42

What corrections should be made to this journal entry?

(Answers to Section 3 Self Review are on page 375.)

CHAPTER 10: Review and Applications

REVIEW

Chapter Summary

The main goal of payroll work is to compute the gross wages or salaries earned by each employee, the amounts to be deducted for various taxes and other purposes, and the net amount payable.

Learning Objectives

1 Explain the major federal laws relating to employee earnings and withholding.

Several federal laws affect payroll.

- The federal Wage and Hour Law limits to 40 the number of hours per week an employee can work at the regular rate of pay. For more than 40 hours of work a week, an employer involved in interstate commerce must pay one and one-half times the regular rate.

- Federal laws require that the employer withhold at least three taxes from the employee's pay: the employee's share of social security tax, the employee's share of Medicare tax, and federal income tax. Instructions for computing these taxes are provided by the government.

- If they are required, state and city income taxes can also be deducted. Some states require the employer to withhold contributions to an unemployment fund from the employee's paycheck.

- Voluntary deductions can also be made.

2 Compute gross earnings of employees.

To compute gross earnings for an employee, it is necessary to know whether the employee is paid using an hourly rate basis, a salary basis, a commission basis, or a piece-rate basis.

3 Determine employee deductions for social security tax.

The social security tax is levied in an equal amount on both the employer and the employee. The tax is a percentage of the employee's gross wages during a calendar year up to a wage base limit.

4 Determine employee deductions for Medicare tax.

The Medicare tax is levied in an equal amount on both the employer and the employee. There is no wage base limit for Medicare taxes.

5 Determine employee deductions for income tax.

Income taxes are deducted from an employee's paycheck by the employer and then are paid to the government periodically. Although several methods can be used to compute the amount of federal income tax to be withheld from employee earnings, the wage-bracket table method is most often used. The wage-bracket tables are in *Publication 15, Circular E, Employer's Tax Guide*. Withholding tables for various pay periods for single and married persons are contained in *Circular E*.

6 Enter gross earnings, deductions, and net pay in the payroll register.

Daily records of the hours worked by each nonsupervisory employee are kept. Using these hourly time sheets, the payroll clerk computes the employees' earnings, deductions, and net pay for each payroll period and records the data in a payroll register.

7 Journalize payroll transactions in the general journal.

The payroll register is used to prepare a general journal entry to record payroll expense and liability amounts. A separate journal entry is made to record payments to employees.

8 Maintain an earnings record for each employee.

At the beginning of each year, the employer sets up an individual earnings record for each employee. The amounts in the payroll register are posted to the individual earnings records throughout the year so that the firm has detailed payroll information for each employee. At the end of the year, employers provide reports that show gross earnings and total deductions to each employee.

9 Define the accounting terms new to this chapter.

Glossary

Commission basis (p. 345) A method of paying employees according to a percentage of net sales

Compensation record (p. 358) See Individual earnings record

Employee (p. 340) A person who is hired by and works under the control and direction of the employer

Employee's Withholding Allowance Certificate, Form W-4 (p. 348) A form used to claim exemption (withholding) allowances

Exempt employees (p. 352) Salaried employees who hold supervisory or managerial positions who are not subject to the maximum hour and overtime pay provisions of the Wage and Hour Law

Federal unemployment taxes (FUTA) (p. 342) Taxes levied by the federal government against employers to benefit unemployed workers

Hourly rate basis (p. 345) A method of paying employees according to a stated rate per hour

Independent contractor (p. 340) One who is paid by a company to carry out a specific task or job but is not under the direct supervision or control of the company

Individual earnings record (p. 358) An employee record that contains information needed to compute earnings and complete tax reports

Medicare tax (p. 341) A tax levied on employees and employers to provide medical care for the employee and the employee's spouse after each has reached age 65

Payroll register (p. 352) A record of payroll information for each employee for the pay period

Piece-rate basis (p. 345) A method of paying employees according to the number of units produced

Salary basis (p. 345) A method of paying employees according to an agreed-upon amount for each week or month

Social Security Act (p. 341) A federal act providing certain benefits for employees and their families; officially the Federal Insurance Contributions Act

Social security (FICA) tax (p. 341) A tax imposed by the Federal Insurance Contributions Act and collected on employee earnings to provide retirement and disability benefits

State unemployment taxes (SUTA) (p. 342) Taxes levied by a state government against employers to benefit unemployed workers

Tax-exempt wages (p. 345) Earnings in excess of the base amount set by the Social Security Act

Time and a half (p. 341) Rate of pay for an employee's work in excess of 40 hours a week

Wage-bracket table method (p. 348) A simple method to determine the amount of federal income tax to be withheld using a table provided by the government

Workers' compensation insurance (p. 342) Insurance that protects employees against losses from job-related injuries or illnesses, or compensates their families if death occurs in the course of the employment

Comprehensive **Self Review**

1. How does an independent contractor differ from an employee?
2. What is the purpose of the payroll register?
3. From an accounting and internal control viewpoint, would it be preferable to pay employees by check or cash? Explain.
4. How is the amount of social security tax to be withheld from an employee's earnings determined?
5. What is the purpose of workers' compensation insurance?

(Answers to Comprehensive Self Review are on page 375.)

Discussion Questions

1. What factors affect how much federal income tax must be withheld from an employee's earnings?

CHAPTER 10: Review and Applications

2. How does the Fair Labor Standards Act affect the wages paid by many firms? What types of firms are regulated by the act?

3. What aspects of employment are regulated by the Fair Labor Standards Act? What is another commonly used name for this act?

4. Give two examples of common payroll fraud.

5. What is an exempt employee?

6. How are the federal and state unemployment taxes related?

7. Does the employee bear any part of the SUTA tax? Explain.

8. How are earnings determined when employees are paid on the hourly rate basis?

9. What is the purpose of the Medicare tax?

10. What is the purpose of the social security tax?

11. How does the direct deposit method of paying employees operate?

12. What are the four bases for determining employee gross earnings?

13. What is the simplest method for finding the amount of federal income tax to be deducted from an employee's gross pay?

14. What publication of the Internal Revenue Service provides information about the current federal income tax rates and the procedures that employers should use to withhold federal income tax from an employee's earnings?

15. How does the salary basis differ from the hourly rate basis of paying employees?

 # APPLICATIONS

Exercises

Exercise 10.1
Objective 2

▶ **Computing gross earnings.**

The hourly rates of four employees of Brown Enterprises follow, along with the hours that these employees worked during one week. Determine the gross earnings of each employee.

Employee No.	Hourly Rate	Hours Worked
1	$9.70	38
2	8.75	40
3	9.50	40
4	8.90	35

Exercise 10.2
Objective 2

▶ **Computing regular earnings, overtime earnings, and gross pay.**

During one week four production employees of Mason Manufacturing Company worked the hours shown below. All these employees receive overtime pay at one and one-half times their regular hourly rate for any hours worked beyond 40 in a week. Determine the regular earnings, overtime earnings, and gross earnings for each employee.

Employee No.	Hourly Rate	Hours Worked
1	$9.75	44
2	9.50	48
3	9.25	33
4	8.90	45

Determining social security withholding.

The monthly salaries for December and the year-to-date earnings of the employees of Carter Consulting Company as of November 30 follow.

◀ Exercise 10.3
Objective 3

Employee No.	December Salary	Year-to-Date Earnings through November 30
1	$9,200	$87,900
2	8,750	83,450
3	8,975	90,100
4	6,650	67,500

Determine the amount of social security tax to be withheld from each employee's gross pay for December. Assume a 6.2 percent social security tax rate and an earnings base of $90,000 for the calendar year.

Determining deduction for Medicare tax.

Using the earnings data given in Exercise 10.3, determine the amount of Medicare tax to be withheld from each employee's gross pay for December. Assume a 1.45 percent Medicare tax rate and that all salaries and wages are subject to the tax.

◀ Exercise 10.4
Objective 4
CONTINUING >>>
Problem

Determining federal income tax withholding.

Data about the marital status, withholding allowances, and weekly salaries of the four office workers at Amos Publishing Company follow. Use the tax tables in Figure 10.2 on pages 350–351 to find the amount of federal income tax to be deducted from each employee's gross pay.

◀ Exercise 10.5
Objective 5

Employee No.	Marital Status	Withholding Allowances	Weekly Salary
1	M	1	$650
2	S	2	595
3	M	3	735
4	S	2	590

Recording payroll transactions in the general journal.

Imperial Corporation has two office employees. A summary of their earnings and the related taxes withheld from their pay for the week ending August 7, 2007, follows.

◀ Exercise 10.6
Objective 7

	Sandra Cox	David Matthews
Gross earnings	$1,245.00	$1,197.00
Social security deduction	(77.19)	(74.21)
Medicare deduction	(18.05)	(17.36)
Income tax withholding	(333.24)	(216.42)
Net pay for week	$ 816.52	$ 889.01

1. Give the general journal entry to record the company's payroll for the week. Use the account names given in this chapter.

2. Give the general journal entry to summarize the checks to pay the weekly payroll.

Journalizing payroll transactions.

On July 31, 2007, the payroll register of Hill Institutional Wholesale Company showed the following totals for the month: gross earnings, $38,400; social security tax, $2,381; Medicare tax, $557;

◀ Exercise 10.7
Objective 7

income tax, $3,040; and net amount due, $32,422. Of the total earnings, $30,400 was for sales salaries and $8,000 was for office salaries. Prepare a general journal entry to record the monthly payroll of the firm on July 31, 2007.

 PROBLEMS

Problem Set A

Problem 10.1A ▶
Objectives
2, 3, 4, 5, 7
e**X**cel

Computing gross earnings, determining deductions, journalizing payroll transactions.

Cindy Taylor works for Trinity Industries. Her pay rate is $12.75 per hour and she receives overtime pay at one and one-half times her regular hourly rate for any hours worked beyond 40 in a week. During the pay period that ended December 31, 2007, Cindy worked 48 hours. Cindy is married and claims three withholding allowances on her W-4 form. Cindy's cumulative earnings prior to this pay period total $27,922.50. Cindy's wages are subject to the following deductions:

1. Social Security tax at 6.2 percent
2. Medicare tax at 1.45 percent
3. Federal income tax (Use the withholding table shown in Figure 10.2b on page 351)
4. Health and disability insurance premiums ($176)
5. United Way contribution, $20
6. United States Savings Bond, $50

INSTRUCTIONS

1. Compute Cindy's regular, overtime, gross, and net pay.
2. Journalize the payment of her wages for the week ended December 31, 2007.

Analyze: Based on Cindy's cumulative earnings to date, how many overtime hours and how much overtime pay has she earned?

Problem 10.2A ▶
Objectives 2, 3, 4, 5
e**X**cel

Computing gross earnings, determining deductions, preparing payroll register, journalizing payroll transactions.

City Place Movie Theaters has four employees and pays them on an hourly basis. During the week beginning June 24 and ending June 30, 2007, these employees worked the hours shown below. Information about hourly rates, marital status, withholding allowances, and cumulative earnings prior to the current pay period also appears below.

Employee	Regular Hours Worked	Hourly Rate	Marital Status	Withholding Allowances	Cumulative Earnings
Nelda Anderson	48	$11.75	M	1	$17,540
Earl Benson	49	10.50	M	4	16,875
Frank Cortez	40	10.25	M	1	15,980
Winnie Wu	52	9.75	S	2	14,560

INSTRUCTIONS

1. Enter the basic payroll information for each employee in a payroll register. Record the employee's name, number of withholding allowances, marital status, total and overtime hours, and regular hourly rate. Consider any hours worked beyond 40 in the week as overtime hours.
2. Compute the regular, overtime, and gross earnings for each employee. Enter the figures in the payroll register.

3. Compute the amount of social security tax to be withheld from each employee's earnings. Assume a 6.2 percent social security rate on the first $90,000 earned by the employee during the year. Enter the figures in the payroll register.

4. Compute the amount of Medicare tax to be withheld from each employee's earnings. Assume a 1.45 percent Medicare tax rate on all salaries and wages earned by the employee during the year. Enter the figures in the payroll register.

5. Determine the amount of federal income tax to be withheld from each employee's total earnings. Use the tax tables in Figure 10.2 on pages 350–351. Enter the figures in the payroll register.

6. Compute the net pay of each employee and enter the figures in the payroll register.

7. Total and prove the payroll register. Wu is an office worker. All other employees work in the theater.

8. Prepare a general journal entry to record the payroll for the week ended June 30, 2007.

9. Record the general journal entry to summarize payment of the payroll on July 3, 2007.

Analyze: What are Nelda Anderson's cumulative earnings on June 30, 2007?

Computing gross earnings, determining deductions, preparing payroll register, journalizing payroll transactions.

◀ **Problem 10.3A**
Objectives 2, 3, 4, 5

Alexander Wilson operates Metroplex Courier and Delivery Service. He has four employees who are paid on an hourly basis. During the work week beginning December 15 and ending December 21, 2007, his employees worked the number of hours shown below. Information about their hourly rates, marital status, and withholding allowances also appears below, along with their cumulative earnings for the year prior to the December 15–21 payroll period.

Employee	Hours Worked	Regular Hourly Rate	Marital Status	Withholding Allowances	Cumulative Earnings
Gloria Bahamon	46	$15.75	M	4	$32,760
Alex Garcia	42	27.50	S	1	57,200
Ron Price	48	25.90	M	3	53,872
Sara Russell	40	12.75	S	0	26,520

INSTRUCTIONS

1. Enter the basic payroll information for each employee in a payroll register. Record the employee's name, number of withholding allowances, marital status, total and overtime hours, and regular hourly rate. Consider any hours worked beyond 40 in the week as overtime hours.

2. Compute the regular, overtime, and gross earnings for each employee. Enter the figures in the payroll register.

3. Compute the amount of social security tax to be withheld from each employee's gross earnings. Assume a 6.2 percent social security rate on the first $90,000 earned by the employee during the year. Enter the figures in the payroll register.

4. Compute the amount of Medicare tax to be withheld from each employee's gross earnings. Assume a 1.45 percent Medicare tax rate on all salaries and wages earned by the employee during the year. Enter the figures in the payroll register.

5. Determine the amount of federal income tax to be withheld from each employee's total earnings. Use the tax tables in Figure 10.2 on pages 350–351 to determine the withholding for Russell. Withholdings for Bahamon is $103.00, $299.00 for Garcia, and $241 for Price. Enter the figures in the payroll register.

6. Compute the net amount due each employee and enter the figures in the payroll register.

7. Total and prove the payroll register. Bahamon and Russell are office workers. Garcia and Price are delivery workers.

8. Prepare a general journal entry to record the payroll for the week ended December 21, 2007.

9. Give the entry in general journal form on December 23 to summarize payment of wages for the week.

Analyze: What percentage of total taxable wages was delivery wages?

Problem 10.4A ▶
Objectives
2, 3, 4, 5, 6, 7

e**X**cel

Computing gross earnings, determining deduction and net amount due, journalizing payroll transactions.

Taylor-Wells Publishing Company pays its employees monthly. Payments made by the company on October 31, 2007, follow. Cumulative amounts paid to the persons named prior to October 31 are also given.

1. James Taylor, president, gross monthly salary of $19,000; gross earnings prior to October 31, $171,000.

2. Carolyn Wells, vice president, gross monthly salary of $17,000; gross earnings paid prior to October 31, $153,000.

3. Kawonza Carter, independent accountant who audits the company's accounts and performs consulting services, $16,500; gross amounts paid prior to October 31, $42,500.

4. Linda Taylor, treasurer, gross monthly salary of $6,000; gross earnings prior to October 31, $54,000.

5. Payment to Editorial Publishing Services for monthly services of Betty Jo Bradley, an editorial expert, $5,500; amount paid to Editorial Publishing Services prior to October 31, 2007, $32,500.

INSTRUCTIONS

1. Use an earnings ceiling of $90,000 for social security taxes and a tax rate of 6.2 percent and a tax rate of 1.45 percent on all earnings for Medicare taxes. Prepare a schedule showing the following information:

   a. Each employee's cumulative earnings prior to October 31.

   b. Each employee's gross earnings for October.

   c. The amounts to be withheld for each payroll tax from each employee's earnings; the employee's income tax withholdings are James Taylor, $5,088; Carolyn Wells, $4,388; Linda Taylor, $1,147.

   d. The net amount due each employee.

   e. The total gross earnings, the total of each payroll tax deduction, and the total net amount payable to employees.

2. Give the general journal entry to record the company's payroll on October 31. Use journal page 22. Omit explanations.

3. Give the general journal entry to record payments to employees on October 31.

Analyze: What distinguishes an employee from an independent contractor?

Problem Set B

Problem 10.1B ▶
Objectives
2, 3, 4, 5, 7

Computing gross earnings, determining deductions, journalizing payroll transactions.

Treschell Seymore works for Oak Cliff Builders, Inc. Her pay rate is $13.75 per hour and she receives overtime pay at one and one-half times her regular hourly rate for any hours worked beyond 40 in a week. During the pay period ended December 31, 2007, Treschell worked 48 hours. Treschell is married and claims four withholding allowances on her W-4 form. Treschell's cumulative earnings prior to this pay period total $54,723. Treschell's wages are subject to the following deductions:

1. Social security tax at 6.2 percent

2. Medicare tax at 1.45 percent

3. Federal income tax (use the withholding table shown in Figure 10.2b on page 351)

4. Health insurance premiums ($197)

5. American Cancer Society contribution, $25

6. Credit Union Savings, $150

INSTRUCTIONS

1. Compute Treschell's regular, overtime, gross, and net pay.

2. Journalize the payment of her wages for the week ended December 31, 2007.

Analyze: Based on Treschell's cumulative earnings to date, how many overtime hours and how much overtime pay has she earned?

Computing earnings, determining deductions and net amount due, preparing payroll register, journalizing payroll transactions.

◄ Problem 10.2B
Objectives 2, 3, 4, 5

The four employees for Cotton Cleaners are paid on an hourly basis. During the week of December 25–31, 2007, these employees worked the hours indicated. Information about their hourly rates, marital status, withholding allowances, and cumulative earnings prior to the current pay period also appears below.

Employee	Hours Worked	Regular Hourly Rate	Marital Status	Withholding Allowances	Cumulative Earnings
Barbara Brooks	47	$12.75	M	3	$ 44,179.00
Cynthia Carter	48	13.25	M	2	53,015.00
Mabel Easley	44	29.50	M	4	82,748.00
James Periot	28	37.25	S	2	104,486.00

INSTRUCTIONS

1. Enter the basic payroll information for each employee in a payroll register. Record the employee's name, number of withholding allowances, marital status, total hours, overtime hours, and regular hourly rate. Consider any hours worked beyond 40 in the week as overtime hours.

2. Compute the regular earnings, overtime premium, and gross earnings for each employee. Enter the figures in the payroll register.

3. Compute the amount of social security tax to be withheld from each employee's gross earnings. Assume a 6.2 percent social security tax rate on the first $90,000 earned by each employee during the year. Enter the figures in the payroll register.

4. Compute the amount of Medicare tax to be withheld from each employee's gross earnings. Assume a 1.45 percent Medicare tax rate on all earnings for each employee during the year. Enter the figure on the payroll register.

5. Determine the amount of federal income tax to be withheld from each employee's gross earnings. Income tax withholdings for Easley is $235 and $238 for Periot. Enter these figures in the payroll register.

6. Compute the net amount due each employee and enter the figures in the payroll register.

7. Complete the payroll register for the store employees.

8. Prepare a general journal entry to record the payroll for the week ended December 31, 2007. Use page 18 for the journal.

9. Record the general journal entry to summarize the payment on December 31, 2007, of the net amount due employees.

CHAPTER 10: Review and Applications

Analyze: What is the difference between the amount credited to the *Cash* account on December 31, 2007, for the payroll week ended December 31 and the amount debited to *Store Wages Expenses* for the same payroll period? What causes the difference between the two figures?

Problem 10.3B ▶

Objectives 2, 3, 4, 5

Computing earnings, determining deductions and net amount due, preparing payroll register, journalizing payroll transactions.

Barbara Merino operates Merino Consulting Services. She has four employees and pays them on an hourly basis. During the week ended November 12, 2007, her employees worked the number of hours shown below. Information about their hourly rates, marital status, withholding allowances, and cumulative earnings for the year prior to the current pay period also appears below.

Employee	Hours Worked	Regular Hourly Rate	Marital Status	Withholding Allowances	Cumulative Earnings
Kathryn Allen	43	$10.50	M	3	$26,565
Calvin Cooke	36	10.25	S	2	25,933
Maria Vasquez	45	29.75	M	4	75,268
Hollie Visage	41	32.75	S	2	82,858

INSTRUCTIONS

1. Enter the basic payroll information for each employee in a payroll register. Record the employee's name, number of withholding allowances, marital status, total hours, overtime hours, and regular hourly rate. Consider any hours worked beyond 40 in the week as overtime hours.

2. Compute the regular earnings, overtime premium, and gross earnings for each employee. Enter the figures in the payroll register.

3. Compute the amount of social security tax to be withheld from each employee's gross earnings. Assume a 6.2 percent social security rate on the first $90,000 earned by the employee during the year. Enter the figures in the payroll register.

4. Compute the amount of Medicare tax to be withheld from each employee's gross earnings. Assume a 1.45 percent Medicare tax rate on all earning paid during the year. Enter the figures in the payroll register.

5. Use the tax tables in Figure 10.2 on pages 350–351 to determine the federal income tax to be withheld. Federal income tax to be withheld from Vasquez's pay is $192 and from Visage's pay is $267 Enter the figures in the payroll register.

6. Compute the net amount due each employee and enter the figures in the payroll register.

7. Complete the payroll register. Allen and Cooke are office workers. Earnings for Vasquez and Visage are charged to consulting wages.

8. Prepare a general journal entry to record the payroll for the week ended November 12, 2007. Use the account titles given in this chapter.

9. Give the general journal entry to summarize payment of amounts due employees.

Analyze: What total deductions were taken from employee paychecks for the pay period ended November 12?

Problem 10.4B ▶

Objectives
2, 3, 4, 5, 6, 7

Computing gross earnings, determining deduction and net amount due, journalizing payroll transactions.

Braxton Media and Public Relations pays its employees monthly. Payments made by the company on November 30, 2007, follow. Cumulative amounts paid to the persons named prior to November 30 are also given.

1. Troy Braxton, president, gross monthly salary of $18,500; gross earnings prior to November 30, $185,000.

2. Sherrye Braxton, vice president, gross monthly salary of $16,000; gross earnings paid prior to November 30, $160,000.

3. Brenda Cates, independent media buyer who purchases media contracts for companies and performs other public relations consulting services, $15,650; gross amounts paid prior to November 30, $52,850.

4. Henry Thomas, treasurer, gross monthly salary of $6,250; gross earnings prior to November 30, $62,500.

5. Payment to the King Marketing Group for monthly services of Johnny King, a marketing and public relations expert, $15,500; amount paid to the King Marketing Group prior to November 30, $46,500.

INSTRUCTIONS

1. Use an earnings ceiling of $90,000 for social security taxes and a tax rate of 6.2 percent and a tax rate of 1.45 percent on all earnings for Medicare taxes. Prepare a schedule showing the following information:

   a. Each employee's cumulative earnings prior to November 30.

   b. Each employee's gross earnings for November.

   c. The amounts to be withheld for each payroll tax from each employee's earnings; the employee's income tax withholdings are Troy Braxton, $5,110; Sherrye Braxton, $3,640; Henry Thomas, $1,190.

   d. The net amount due each employee.

   e. The total gross earnings, the total of each payroll tax deduction, and the total net amount payable to employees.

2. Give the general journal entry to record the company's payroll on November 30. Use journal page 24. Omit explanations.

3. Give the general journal entry to record payments to employees on November 30.

Analyze: What month in 2007 did Troy Braxton reach the withholding limit for social security?

Challenge Problem

Payroll Accounting

Arizona Company pays salaries and wages on the last day of each month. Payments made on December 31, 2007, for amounts incurred during December are shown below. Cumulative amounts paid prior to December 31 to the persons named are also shown.

a. Cynthia Arnold, president, gross monthly salary $15,000; gross earnings paid prior to December 31, $165,000.

b. Richard Chen, vice president, gross monthly salary $13,000; gross earnings paid prior to December 31, $78,000.

c. Jean Keller, independent accountant who audits the company's accounts and performs certain consulting services, $13,000; gross amount paid prior to December 31, $39,000.

d. Vladimir Grebennikov, treasurer, gross monthly salary $6,000; gross earnings paid prior to December 31, $66,000.

e. Payment to Wright Security Services for Eddie Wright, a security guard who is on duty on Saturdays and Sundays, $1,050; amount paid to Wright Security Services prior to December 31, $11,550.

INSTRUCTIONS

1. Using the tax rates and earnings ceilings given in this chapter, prepare a schedule showing the following information:

   a. Each employee's cumulative earnings prior to December 31.

   b. Each employee's gross earnings for December.

   c. The amounts to be withheld for each payroll tax from each employee's earnings (employee income tax withholdings for Arnold are $3,206; for Chen, $2,646; and for Grebennikov, $801).

   d. The net amount due each employee.

   e. The total gross earnings, the total of each payroll tax deduction, and the total net amount payable to employees.

2. Record the general journal entry for the company's payroll on December 31.

3. Record the general journal entry for payments to employees on December 31.

Analyze: What is the balance of the *Salaries Payable* account after all payroll entries have been posted for the month?

Critical Thinking Problem

Payroll Internal Controls

Several years ago, Paul Torres opened Taco Havana, a restaurant specializing in homemade tacos. The restaurant was so successful that Torres was able to expand, and his company now operates eight restaurants in the local area.

Torres tells you that when he first started, he handled all aspects of the business himself. Now that there are eight Taco Havanas, he depends on the managers of each restaurant to make decisions and oversee day-to-day operations. Paul oversees operations at the company's headquarters, which is located at the first Taco Havana.

Each manager interviews and hires new employees for a restaurant. The new employee is required to complete a W-4, which is sent by the manager to the headquarters office. Each restaurant has a time clock and employees are required to clock in as they arrive or depart. Blank time cards are kept in a box under the time clock. At the beginning of each week, employees complete the top of the card they will use during the week. The manager collects the cards at the end of the week and sends them to headquarters.

Paul hired his cousin Mireya to prepare the payroll instead of assigning this task to the accounting staff. Because she is a relative, Paul trusts her and has confidence that confidential payroll information will not be divulged to other employees.

When Mireya receives a W-4 for a new employee, she sets up an individual earnings record for the employee. Each week, using the time cards sent by each restaurant's manager, she computes the gross pay, deductions, and net pay for all the employees. She then posts details to the employees' earnings records and prepares and signs the payroll checks. The checks are sent to the managers, who distribute them to the employees.

As long as Mireya receives a time card for an employee, she prepares a paycheck. If she fails to get a time card for an employee, she checks with the manager to see if the employee was terminated or has quit. At the end of the month, Mireya reconciles the payroll bank account and prepares quarterly and annual payroll tax returns.

1. Identify any weaknesses in Taco Havana's payroll system.

2. Identify one way a manager could defraud Taco Havana under the present payroll system.

3. What internal control procedures would you recommend to Paul to protect against the fraud you identified above?

BUSINESS CONNECTIONS

Cash Management

1. Why should managers check the amount spent for overtime?
2. The new controller for Ellis Company, a manufacturing firm, has suggested to management that the business change from paying the factory employees in cash to paying them by check. What reasons would you offer to support this suggestion?
3. Why should management make sure that a firm has an adequate set of payroll records?
4. How can detailed payroll records help managers to control expenses?

Salary vs. Hourly

Jeremy's Sweater Factory employs two managers for the factory. These managers work 12 hours per day at $15 per hour. After 8 hours, they receive overtime pay. Management is trying to cut costs. They have decided to promote the managers to a salary position. The managers will be offered a daily salary of $200. Since they would be promoted to a salary position they will not receive overtime. The company has required they accept the promotion or find employment elsewhere. Is it ethical for the company to offer the managers a salary position? Is it ethical to require the employee to accept the promotion? Should the managers accept the promotion?

Human Resources

Refer to the *2004 Annual Report* of The Home Depot in Appendix A.

1. Locate the letter written by the president and chief executive officer to the customers, suppliers, shareholders, and associates. Describe the goals and company vision in regard to the employees of The Home Depot. Based on your knowledge of The Home Depot stores and the financial information presented in Appendix A, what types of positions do you think the company hires? Describe whether you think each job position listed is paid on hourly rate, commission, or salary basis.
2. Locate the financial discussion titled "Fiscal 2004 Compared to Fiscal 2003." Describe the financial data regarding payroll expenses. What factors contributed to increases or decreases in payroll expenses?

Income Statement

Southwest Airlines Co. reported the following data on its consolidated statement of income for the years ended December 31, 2004, 2003, and 2002.

Southwest Airlines Co.			
Consolidated Statement of Income			
(in millions except per share amounts)	Years Ended December 31		
	2004	*2003*	*2002*
Operating expenses:			
Salaries, wages, and benefits	2,443	2,224	1,993
Total operating expenses	5,976	5,454	5,105

Analyze:

1. The amounts reported for the line item "Salaries, wages, and benefits" include expenses for company retirement plans and profit-sharing plans. If Southwest Airlines Co. spent approximately $1,905 million on wages and salaries alone, compute the employer's Medicare tax expense for 2004. Use a rate of 1.45 percent.
2. What percentage of total operating expenses was spent on salaries, wages, and benefits in 2004?
3. By what amount did salaries, wages, and benefits increase from 2002 to 2004?

Analyze Online: Go to the company Web site for Southwest Airlines Co. (**www.southwest.com**). Locate the company fact sheet within the *About SWA* section of the site.

4. How many employees does Southwest Airlines Co. employ?

5. How many resumes were submitted to the company for consideration in the current year?

Extending | THE THOUGHT

Exempt Employees

Salaried exempt employees generally work for a predetermined annual rate regardless of the actual number of hours they work. In many cases, supervisors and managers work considerably more than 40 hours per week. What do you think of this practice from the employee's perspective? From the employer's perspective?

Business | COMMUNICATION

Pie Chart

Employees should understand how take-home, or net, pay is computed. As the payroll manager, you have been asked to make a presentation to the employees of Broad Street Bakery on how their gross earnings are allocated to taxes and net pay. You decide that a visual representation of the allocation would be most effective. Create a pie chart for the following information.

Employee: Carol Blakley	
Gross earnings:	$312.00
Social security tax:	20.79
Medicare tax:	4.86
Federal income tax:	$ 35.00
State income tax:	6.71
Medical insurance:	4.10
Net pay:	240.54

TEAMWORK

Cycle to Pay Employee

There are many approvals needed to create a paycheck for an employee. Divide into groups of 5 to identify the jobs necessary to create a paycheck for an employee. Describe the function and, if necessary, the journal entry for each job.

Internet | CONNECTION

Certified Payroll Professional

Log onto the Certified Payroll Professional (CPP) Web site at www.americanpayroll.org. Find the requirements to become a CPP. How many years of experience are required? Describe the testing procedure.

Answers to Self Reviews

Answers to Section 1 Self Review

1. By a tax levied equally on both employers and employees. The tax amount is based on the earnings.

2. By state and federal taxes levied on the employer.

3. The federal requirement that covered employees be paid at a rate equal to one and one-half times their normal hourly rate for each hour worked in excess of 40 hours per week.

4. **a.** employees who become unemployed

5. **d.** does not exist

6. She is not an employee. She is an independent contractor because she has been hired to complete a specific job and is not under the control of the employer.

Answers to Section 2 Self Review

1. Health insurance premiums, life insurance premiums, union dues, retirement plans.
2. Amount of earnings, period covered by the payment, employee's marital status, and the number of withholding allowances.
3. Social security tax, Medicare tax, and federal income tax.
4. **d.** hours worked
5. **c.** $468
6. When you receive a signed Form W-4 for the change in withholding.

Answers to Section 3 Self Review

1. Using a separate payroll account simplifies the bank reconciliation procedure and makes it easier to identify outstanding payroll checks.
2. Employee's name, address, social security number, date of birth, number of withholding allowances claimed, rate of pay, and any other information needed to compute earnings and complete tax reports.
3. Debit *Salaries and Wages Payable* and credit *Cash.*
4. **a.** payroll register
5. **c.** liability account
6. *Health Insurance Premiums Expense* Dr. 40.00 should be *Health Insurance Premiums Payable* Cr. 40.00; *Social Security Taxes Expense* Cr. 197.41 should be *Social Security Tax Payable* Cr. 197.41; *Cash* Cr. 2,634.42 should be *Salaries and Wages Payable* Cr. 2,634.42

Answers to Comprehensive Self Review

1. An employee is one who is hired by the employer and who is under the control and direction of the employer. An independent contractor is paid by the company to carry out a specific task or job and is not under the direct supervision and control of the employer.
2. To record in one place all information about an employee's earnings and withholdings for the period.
3. By check because there is far less possibility of mistake, lost money, or fraud. The check serves as a receipt and permanent record of the transaction.
4. Social security taxes are determined by multiplying the amount of taxable earnings by the social security tax rate.
5. To compensate workers for losses suffered from job-related injuries or to compensate their families if the employee's death occurs in the course of employment.

LEARNING OBJECTIVES

1. Explain how and when payroll taxes are paid to the government.

2. Compute and record the employer's social security and Medicare taxes.

3. Record deposit of social security, Medicare, and employee income taxes.

4. Prepare an Employer's Quarterly Federal Tax Return, Form 941.

5. Prepare Wage and Tax Statement (Form W-2) and Annual Transmittal of Wage and Tax Statements (Form W-3).

6. Compute and record liability for federal and state unemployment taxes and record payment of the taxes.

7. Prepare an Employer's Federal Unemployment Tax Return, Form 940 or 940-EZ.

8. Compute and record workers' compensation insurance premiums.

9. Define the accounting terms new to this chapter.

NEW TERMS

Employer's Annual Federal Unemployment Tax Return, Form 940 or Form 940-EZ

Employer's Quarterly Federal Tax Return, Form 941

Experience rating system

Merit rating system

Transmittal of Wage and Tax Statements, Form W-3

Unemployment insurance program

Wage and Tax Statement, Form W-2

Withholding statement

Chapter 11
Payroll Taxes, Deposits, and Reports

www.Ikea.com

Ingvar Kamprad, the founder of IKEA, was only seventeen when he began his career in retail. In 1943 he opened a store in a small farming village in Sweden. Ingvar sold his neighbors small goods—pens, wallets, picture frames, table runners, watches, and jewelry.

In 1955 a furniture supplier boycott forced Ingvar and his employees to take matters into their own hands. They began to design furniture and to make transportation easier—an employee decided to remove a table's legs so the table would fit into a car. The idea of flat packaging was born. Inventory and shipping costs dropped and so did IKEA's prices to their customers. The concept of low cost, high style design was born.

IKEA's vision is "to create a better everyday life for the many." The vision applies to both customers and employees. The variety of benefits offered and the family-friendly programs have put IKEA on top of Working Mother's 100 Best Companies for two years in a row. Employee satisfaction is also evident in the low staff turnover rates. IKEA has seen a continuous decline in its sales staff turnover from 76% in 2000 to 56% in 2002 and an industry-low of 36% in 2003.

thinking critically | How does a lower sales staff turnover rate affect IKEA's payroll accounting department?

Section 1

SECTION OBJECTIVES

▶ 1. **Explain how and when payroll taxes are paid to the government.**

WHY IT'S IMPORTANT

Employers are required by law to deposit payroll taxes.

▶ 2. **Compute and record the employer's social security and Medicare taxes.**

WHY IT'S IMPORTANT

Accounting records should reflect all liabilities.

▶ 3. **Record deposit of social security, Medicare, and employee income taxes.**

WHY IT'S IMPORTANT

Payments decrease the payroll tax liability.

▶ 4. **Prepare an Employer's Quarterly Federal Tax Return, Form 941.**

WHY IT'S IMPORTANT

Completing a federal tax return is part of the employer's legal obligation.

▶ 5. **Prepare Wage and Tax Statement (Form W-2) and Annual Transmittal of Wage and Tax Statements (Form W-3).**

WHY IT'S IMPORTANT

Employers are legally required to provide end-of-year payroll information.

TERMS TO LEARN

Employer's Quarterly Federal Tax Return, Form 941
Transmittal of Wage and Tax Statements, Form W-3
Wage and Tax Statement, Form W-2
withholding statement

Social Security, Medicare, and Employee Income Tax

In Chapter 10 you learned that the law requires employers to act as collection agents for certain taxes due from employees. In this chapter you will learn how to compute the employer's taxes, make tax payments, and file the required tax returns and reports.

Payment of Payroll Taxes

The payroll register provides information about wages subject to payroll taxes. Figure 11.1 on page 379 shows a portion of the payroll register for Kent Furniture and Novelty Company for the week ending January 6.

Employers make tax deposits for federal income tax withheld from employee earnings, the employees' share of social security and Medicare taxes withheld from earnings, and the employer's share of social security and Medicare taxes. The deposits are made in a Federal Reserve Bank or other authorized financial institution. Businesses usually make payroll tax deposits at their own bank. There are two ways to deposit payroll taxes: by electronic deposit or with a tax deposit coupon.

The *Electronic Federal Tax Payment System (EFTPS)* is a system for electronically depositing employment taxes using a telephone or a computer. Any employer can use EFTPS. An employer *must* use EFTPS if the annual federal tax deposits are more than $200,000. Employers who are required to make electronic deposits and do not do so can be subject to a 10 percent penalty.

Employers who are not required to use EFTPS may deposit payroll taxes using a *Federal Tax Deposit Coupon, Form 8109.* The employer's name, tax identification number, and address are preprinted on Form 8109. The employer enters the deposit amount on the form and makes the payment with a check, money order, or cash.

In some cases an employer may use Form 8109-B. *Form 8109-B* is a coupon that is *not* preprinted. Form 8109-B may be used if a new employer has been assigned an identification number but has not yet received a supply of Forms 8109, or an employer has not received a resupply of Forms 8109. Figure 11.2 on page 379 shows the completed Form 8109-B for Kent Furniture and Novelty Company.

AND ENDING _January 7, 2007_   **PAID** _January 8, 2007_

TAXABLE WAGES			DEDUCTIONS				DISTRIBUTION			
SOCIAL SECURITY	MEDICARE	FUTA	SOCIAL SECURITY	MEDICARE	INCOME TAX	HEALTH INSURANCE	NET AMOUNT	CHECK NO.	OFFICE SALARIES	SHIPPING WAGES
400 00	400 00	400 00	24 80	5 80	19 00		350 40	1601		400 00
380 00	380 00	380 00	23 56	5 51	34 00		316 93	1602		380 00
427 50	427 50	427 50	26 51	6 20	23 00	40 00	331 79	1603		427 50
560 00	560 00	560 00	34 72	8 12	30 00	40 00	447 16	1604		560 00
480 00	480 00	480 00	29 76	6 96	49 00		394 28	1605	480 00	
2 247 50	2 247 50	2 247 50	139 35	32 59	155 00	80 00	1 840 56		480 00	1 767 50

FIGURE 11.1 | **Portion of a Payroll Register**

The frequency of deposits depends on the amount of tax liability. The amount currently owed is compared to the tax liability threshold. For simplicity this textbook uses $2,500 as the tax liability threshold.

The deposit schedules are not related to how often employees are paid. The deposit schedules are based on the amount currently owed and the amount reported in the lookback period. The *lookback period* is a four-quarter period ending on June 30 of the preceding year.

1. If the amount owed is less than $2,500, payment is due quarterly with the payroll tax return (Form 941).

> **Example.** An employer's tax liability is as follows:
>
> | | |
> |---|---|
> | January | $580 |
> | February | 640 |
> | March | 620 |
> | | $1,840 |

▶ 1. **OBJECTIVE**

Explain how and when payroll taxes are paid to the government.

FIGURE 11.2 | **Federal Tax Deposit Coupon, Form 8109-B**

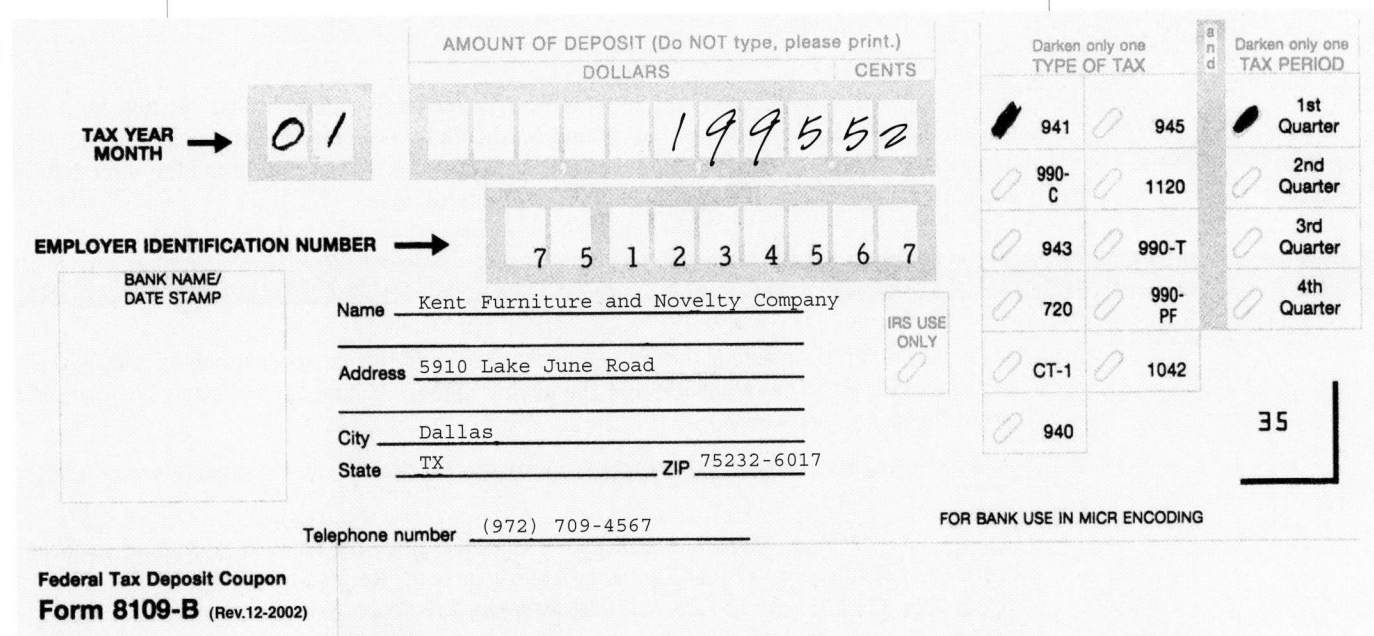

Since at no time during the quarter is the accumulated tax liability $2,500 or more, no deposit is required during the quarter. The employer may pay the amount with the payroll tax returns.

2. If the amount owed is $2,500 or more, the schedule is determined from the total taxes reported on Form 941 during the lookback period.

   a. If the amount reported in the lookback period was $50,000 or less, the employer is subject to the *Monthly Deposit Schedule Rule.* Monthly payments are due on the 15th day of the following month. For example, the January payment is due by February 15.

   b. If the amount reported in the lookback period was more than $50,000, the employer is subject to the *Semiweekly Deposit Schedule Rule.* "Semiweekly" refers to the fact that deposits are due on either Wednesdays or Fridays, depending on the employer's payday.

   - If payday is a Wednesday, Thursday, or Friday, the deposit is due on the following Wednesday.
   - If payday is a Saturday, Sunday, Monday, or Tuesday, the deposit is due on the following Friday.

   c. For new employers with no lookback period, if the amount owed is $2,500 or more, payments are due under the Monthly Deposit Schedule Rule.

3. If the total accumulated tax liability reaches $100,000 or more on any day, a deposit is due on the next banking day. This applies even if the employer is on a monthly or a semiweekly deposit schedule.

EMPLOYER'S SOCIAL SECURITY AND MEDICARE TAX EXPENSES

▶ 2. **OBJECTIVE**

Compute and record the employer's social security and Medicare taxes.

important!

Tax Liability

The employer's tax liability is the amount owed for

- employee withholdings (income tax, social security tax, Medicare tax);
- employer's share of social security and Medicare taxes.

Remember that both employers and employees pay social security and Medicare taxes. Figure 11.1 shows the *employee's* share of these payroll taxes. The *employer* pays the same amount of payroll taxes. At the assumed rate of 6.2 percent for social security and 1.45 percent for Medicare tax, the employer's tax liability is $343.88.

	Employee (Withheld)	Employer (Matched)
Social security	$139.35	$139.35
Medicare	32.59	32.59
	$171.94	$171.94
Total	$343.88	

In Chapter 10 you learned how to record employee payroll deductions. The entry to record the employer's share of social security and Medicare taxes is made at the end of each payroll period. The debit is to the *Payroll Taxes Expense* account. The credits are to the same liability accounts used to record the employee's share of payroll taxes.

BUSINESS TRANSACTION

On January 8 Kent Furniture and Novelty Company recorded the employer's share of social security and Medicare taxes. The information on the payroll register (Figure 11.1 on page 379) is used to record the payroll taxes expense.

ANALYSIS

The expense account, *Payroll Taxes Expense,* is increased by the employer's share of social security and Medicare taxes, $171.94. The liability account, *Social Security Tax Payable,* is increased by $139.35. The liability account, *Medicare Tax Payable,* is increased by $32.59.

DEBIT-CREDIT RULES

DEBIT Increases to expense accounts are recorded as debits. Debit **Payroll Taxes Expense** for $171.94.

CREDIT Increases to liability accounts are recorded as credits. Credit **Social Security Tax Payable** for $139.35. Credit **Medicare Tax Payable** for $32.59.

T-ACCOUNT PRESENTATION

Payroll Taxes Expense		Social Security Tax Payable		Medicare Tax Payable	
+	−	−	+	−	+
171.94			139.35		32.59

GENERAL JOURNAL ENTRY

GENERAL JOURNAL   PAGE __1__

	DATE		DESCRIPTION	POST. REF.	DEBIT	CREDIT	
1	2007						1
2	Jan.	8	Payroll Taxes Expense		171 94		2
3			Social Security Tax Payable			139 35	3
4			Medicare Tax Payable			32 59	4
5			To record social security and				5
6			Medicare taxes for Jan. 8 payroll				6

THE BOTTOM LINE
Employer's Payroll Taxes

Income Statement

Expenses	↑ 171.94
Net Income	↓ 171.94

Balance Sheet

Liabilities	↑ 171.94
Equity	↓ 171.94

According to the American Payroll Association, the Social Security Administration provides benefits to approximately 44 million men, women, and children. It is essential that earnings are correctly reported so that future benefits can be calculated accurately.

RECORDING THE PAYMENT OF TAXES WITHHELD

▶ **3. OBJECTIVE**
Record deposit of social security, Medicare, and employee income taxes.

At the end of January, the accounting records for Kent Furniture and Novelty Company contained the following information.

	Employee (Withheld)	Employer (Matched)	Total
Social security	$ 557.40	$557.40	$1,114.80
Medicare	130.36	130.36	260.72
Federal income tax	620.00	—	620.00
Total	$1,307.76	$687.76	$1,995.52

Kent Furniture and Novelty Company is on a monthly payment schedule. The amount reported in the lookback period is less than $50,000. The payroll tax liability for the quarter ending March 31, 2007, is more than $2,500. (Recall that this textbook uses $2,500 as the tax liability threshold.) A tax payment is due on the 15th day of the following month, February 15.

Figure 11.2 on page 379 shows the Federal Tax Deposit Coupon for Kent Furniture and Novelty Company. Notice that the type of tax (Form 941) and the tax period (first quarter) are indicated on the form. The coupon is accompanied by a check from Kent Furniture and Novelty Company for $1,995.52 written to First State Bank, an authorized financial institution.

The entry to record the tax deposit is shown below. The entry is shown in general journal form for illustration purposes only. (Kent Furniture and Novelty Company actually uses a cash payments journal.)

	DATE		DESCRIPTION	POST. REF.	DEBIT	CREDIT	
1	2007						1
21							21
22	Feb.	15	Social Security Tax Payable		1 1 1 4 80		22
23			Medicare Tax Payable		2 6 0 72		23
24			Employee Income Tax Payable		6 2 0 00		24
25			Cash			1 9 9 5 52	25
26			Deposit of payroll taxes withholding				26
27			at First State Bank				27
28							28

GENERAL JOURNAL   PAGE __2__

FEBRUARY PAYROLL RECORDS

There were four weekly payroll periods in February. Each hourly employee worked the same number of hours each week and had the same gross pay and deductions as in January. The office clerk earned her regular salary and had the same deductions as in January. At the end of the month

- the individual earnings records were updated;
- Form 8109, Federal Tax Deposit Coupon, was prepared, and the taxes were deposited before March 15;
- the tax deposit was recorded in the cash payments journal.

MARCH PAYROLL RECORDS

There were five weekly payroll periods in March. Assume that the payroll period ended on March 31, and the payday was on March 31. Also assume that the earnings and deductions of the employees were the same for each week as in January and February. At the end of the month the individual earnings records were updated, the taxes were deposited, and the tax deposit was recorded in the cash payments journal.

QUARTERLY SUMMARY OF EARNINGS RECORDS

At the end of each quarter, the individual earnings records are totaled. This involves adding the columns in the Earnings, Deductions, and Net Pay sections. Figure 11.3 on page 383 shows the earnings record, posted and summarized, for Alicia Martinez for the first quarter.

Table 11.1 below shows the quarterly totals for each employee of Kent Furniture and Novelty Company. This information is taken from the individual earnings records. Through the end of the first quarter, no employee has exceeded the social security earnings limit ($90,000) and the FUTA/SUTA limit ($7,000) has only been exceeded by Cecilia Wu.

EMPLOYER'S QUARTERLY FEDERAL TAX RETURN

Each quarter an employer files an **Employer's Quarterly Federal Tax Return, Form 941** with the Internal Revenue Service. Form 941 must be filed by all employers subject to federal income tax withholding, social security tax, or Medicare tax, with certain exceptions as specified in *Publication 15, Circular E*. This tax return provides information about employee earnings, the tax liability for each month in the quarter, and the deposits made.

Topic Tackler

PLUS

▶ 4. OBJECTIVE

Prepare an Employer's Quarterly Federal Tax Return, Form 941.

EARNINGS RECORD FOR ___2007___

NAME _Alicia Martinez_   **RATE** _$10 per hour_   **SOCIAL SECURITY NO.** _123-45-6789_

ADDRESS _1712 Windmill Hill Lane, Dallas TX 75232-6002_   **DATE OF BIRTH** _October 31, 1979_

WITHHOLDING ALLOWANCES ___1___   **MARITAL STATUS** _M_

PAYROLL NO.	WK. END.	PAID	RG	OT	REGULAR	OVERTIME	TOTAL	CUMULATIVE	SOCIAL SECURITY	MEDICARE	INCOME TAX	OTHER	NET PAY
1	1/06	1/08	40		400 00		400 00	400 00	24 80	5 80	19 00		350 40
2	1/13	1/15	40		400 00		400 00	400 00	24 80	5 80	19 00		350 40
3	1/20	1/22	40		400 00		400 00	400 00	24 80	5 80	19 00		350 40
4	1/27	1/29	40		400 00		400 00	400 00	24 80	5 80	19 00		350 40
	January				1600 00		1600 00	1600 00	99 20	23 20	76 00		1401 60
1	2/03	2/05	40		400 00		400 00	400 00	24 80	5 80	19 00		350 40
2	2/10	2/12	40		400 00		400 00	400 00	24 80	5 80	19 00		350 40
3	2/17	2/19	40		400 00		400 00	400 00	24 80	5 80	19 00		350 40
4	2/24	2/25	40		400 00		400 00	400 00	24 80	5 80	19 00		350 40
	February				1600 00		1600 00	1600 00	99 20	23 20	76 00		1401 60
1	3/03	3/05	40		400 00		400 00	400 00	24 80	5 80	19 00		350 40
2	3/10	3/12	40		400 00		400 00	400 00	24 80	5 80	19 00		350 40
3	3/17	3/19	40		400 00		400 00	400 00	24 80	5 80	19 00		350 40
4	3/24	3/26	40		400 00		400 00	400 00	24 80	5 80	19 00		350 40
5	3/31	3/31	40		400 00		400 00	400 00	24 80	5 80	19 00		350 40
					2000 00		2000 00	2000 00	124 00	29 00	95 00		1752 00
	March				5200 00		5200 00	5200 00	322 40	75 40	247 00		4555 20
	First Quarter												

FIGURE 11.3 | Individual Earnings Record

The Social Security Administration administers the Old Age and Survivors, Disability Insurance, and Supplemental Security Income Programs. These programs are funded by the social security taxes collected from employees and matched by employers. The system currently takes in more in revenue from the 12.4 percent payroll taxes than it pays out in benefits. The trust fund is expected to begin paying out more in benefits than it collects in 2018.

TABLE 11.1

Summary of Earnings, Quarter Ended March 31, 2007

	Taxable Earnings				Deductions		
Employee	Total Earnings	Social Security	Medicare	SUTA & FUTA	Social Security	Medicare Tax	Income Tax
Alicia Martinez	5,200.00	5,200.00	5,200.00	5,200.00	322.40	75.40	247.00
Jorge Rodriguez	4,940.00	4,940.00	4,940.00	4,940.00	306.28	71.63	442.00
George Dunlap	5,557.50	5,557.50	5,557.50	5,557.50	344.63	80.60	299.00
Cecilia Wu	7,280.00	7,280.00	7,280.00	7,000.00	451.36	105.56	390.00
Cynthia Booker	6,240.00	6,240.00	6,240.00	6,240.00	386.88	90.48	637.00
Totals	29,217.50	29,217.50	29,217.50	28,937.50	1,811.55	423.67	2,015.00

important!

Quarters

A quarter is a three-month period. There are four quarters in a year:

- 1st quarter: January, February, March
- 2nd quarter: April, May, June
- 3rd quarter: July, August, September
- 4th quarter: October, November, December

International INSIGHTS

Working Abroad

The IRS has tax treaties with more than 50 countries including Canada, Germany, and France. These tax treaties spell out exactly how income taxes are handled for U.S. citizens working abroad.

recall

Tax Calculations

Social security and Medicare taxes are calculated by multiplying the taxable wages by the tax rate.

When to File Form 941 The due date for Form 941 is the last day of the month following the end of each calendar quarter. If the taxes for the quarter were deposited when due, the due date is extended by 10 days.

Completing Form 941 Figure 11.4 on pages 385 and 386 shows Form 941 for Kent Furniture and Novelty Company. Form 941 is prepared using the data on the quarterly summary of earnings records, Table 11.1 on page 383. Let's examine Form 941.

- Use the preprinted form if it is available. Otherwise, enter the employer's name, address, and identification number at the top of Form 941. Check the applicable quarter.
- *Line 1* is completed for each quarter. Enter the number of employees for the pay periods indicated.
- *Line 2* shows total wages and tips subject to withholding. For Kent Furniture and Novelty Company the total subject to withholdings is $29,217.50.
- *Line 3* shows the total employee income tax withheld during the quarter, $2,015.00.
- *Line 4* is checked if no wages or tips are subject to social security or Medicare tax.
- *Line 5a* shows the total amount of wages that are subject to social security taxes, $29,217.50. The amount is multiplied by the combined social security rate, 12.4 percent.

Social Security Tax:	
Employee's share	6.2%
Employer's share	6.2
Total	12.4%

The amount of taxes is $3,622.97 ($29,217.50 × 12.4%).

- *Line 5b* is left blank since no employees at Kent Furniture and Novelty Company had taxable social security tips.
- *Line 5c* shows the total amount of wages that are subject to Medicare taxes, $29,217.50. The amount is multiplied by the combined Medicare tax rate, 2.9 percent.

Medicare Tax:	
Employee's share	1.45%
Employer's share	1.45
Total	2.90%

The amount of taxes is $847.31 ($29,217.50 × 2.90%).

- *Line 5d* shows the total social security and Medicare taxes, $4,470.28.
- *Line 6* shows the total tax liability for withheld income taxes, social security, and Medicare Taxes, $6,485.28.
- *Lines 7a* through *7h* are for adjustments. Kent Furniture and Novelty Company had no adjustments this quarter. If there is a difference due to rounding that difference can be adjusted on line 7a.
- *Line 8* shows total taxes after adjustments, $6,485.28.
- *Line 9* is for deducting the amount of any advance earned income credit payments to employees. Kent Furniture and Novelty Company had no advance payments for earned income credit payments to employees.
- *Line 10* shows total taxes after adjustments, $6,485.28.
- *Line 11* shows total deposits made during the quarter including overpayments applied from a prior quarter, $6,485.28.
- Any balance due is entered on *Line 12* or overpayment is entered on *Line 13*.
- The state where deposits were made is entered on *Line 14*.
- *Line 15* shows the monthly deposits made by Kent Furniture and Novelty Company.

FIGURE 11.4 | Employer's Quarterly Federal Tax Return, Form 941

Form **941 for 2007:** **Employer's Quarterly Federal Tax Return**

9901

(Rev. January 2005)

Department of the Treasury — Internal Revenue Service

OMB No. 1545-0029

Employer identification number 7 5 — 1 2 3 4 5 6 7

Name (not your trade name) **Sarah Kent**

Trade name (if any) **Kent Furniture and Novelty Company**

Address **5910 Lake June Road**

Number   Street   Suite or room number

Dallas   **TX**   **75232-6017**

City   State   ZIP code

Report for this Quarter ...
(Check one.)

☑ **1:** January, February, March

☐ **2:** April, May, June

☐ **3:** July, August, September

☐ **4:** October, November, December

Read the separate instructions before you fill out this form. Please type or print within the boxes.

Part 1: Answer these questions for this quarter.

1 Number of employees who received wages, tips, or other compensation for the pay period including: *Mar. 12* (Quarter 1), *June 12* (Quarter 2), *Sept. 12* (Quarter 3), *Dec. 12* (Quarter 4) **1**   5

2 Wages, tips, and other compensation . . . . **2**   29,217 . 50

3 Total income tax withheld from wages, tips, and other compensation . . . . **3**   2,015 . 00

4 If no wages, tips, and other compensation are subject to social security or Medicare tax . . ☐ Check and go to line 6.

5 Taxable social security and Medicare wages and tips:

	Column 1		Column 2
5a Taxable social security wages	29,217 . 50	× .124 =	3,622 . 97
5b Taxable social security tips	.	× .124 =	.
5c Taxable Medicare wages & tips	29,217 . 50	× .029 =	847 . 31

5d Total social security and Medicare taxes (*Column 2*, lines 5a + 5b + 5c = line 5d) . . **5d**   4,470 . 28

6 Total taxes before adjustments (lines 3 + 5d = line 6) . . . . **6**   6,485 . 28

7 Tax adjustments (If your answer is a negative number, write it in brackets.):

7a Current quarter's fractions of cents . . . .

7b Current quarter's sick pay . . . .

7c Current quarter's adjustments for tips and group-term life insurance   .

7d Current year's income tax withholding (Attach Form 941c) . . .   .

7e Prior quarters' social security and Medicare taxes (Attach Form 941c)

7f Special additions to federal income tax (reserved use) . . . . .   .

7g Special additions to social security and Medicare (reserved use)   .

7h Total adjustments (Combine all amounts: lines 7a through 7g.) . . . . **7h**   .

8 Total taxes after adjustments (Combine lines 6 and 7h.) . . . . **8**   6,485 . 28

9 Advance earned income credit (EIC) payments made to employees . . . . **9**   .

10 Total taxes after adjustment for advance EIC (lines 8 – 9 = line 10) . . . . **10**   6,485 . 28

11 Total deposits for this quarter, including overpayment applied from a prior quarter . . . **11**   6,485 . 28

12 Balance due (lines 10 – 11 = line 12) Make checks payable to the *United States Treasury* . . **12**   0 .

13 Overpayment (If line 11 is more than line 10, write the difference here.)   .   Check one ☐ Apply to next return.
☐ Send a refund.

Next ➡

For Privacy Act and Paperwork Reduction Act Notice, see the back of the Payment Voucher.   Cat. No. 17001Z   Form **941**

FIGURE 11.4 | Concluded

9902

Name *(not your trade name)*
Sarah Kent

Employer identification number
75-1234567

Part 2: Tell us about your deposit schedule for this quarter.

If you are unsure about whether you are a monthly schedule depositor or a semiweekly schedule depositor, see *Pub. 15 (Circular E)*, section 11.

14 **T** **X**   Write the state abbreviation for the state where you made your deposits OR write "MU" if you made your deposits in *multiple* states.

15 Check one: ☐ **Line 10 is less than $2,500.** Go to Part 3.

☑ **You were a monthly schedule depositor for the entire quarter. Fill out your tax liability for each month.** Then go to Part 3.

Tax liability:		
Month 1	1,995 . 52	
Month 2	1,995 . 52	
Month 3	2,494 . 24	
Total	6,485 . 28	**Total must equal line 10.**

☐ **You were a semiweekly schedule depositor for any part of this quarter. Fill out** *Schedule B (Form 941): Report of Tax Liability for Semiweekly Schedule Depositors,* and attach it to this form.

Part 3: Tell us about your business. If a question does NOT apply to your business, leave it blank.

16 If your business has closed and you do not have to file returns in the future . . . . ☐ Check here, and

enter the final date you paid wages [/   /] .

17 If you are a seasonal employer and you do not have to file a return for every quarter of the year . . ☐ Check here.

Part 4: May we contact your third-party designee?

Do you want to allow an employee, a paid tax preparer, or another person to discuss this return with the IRS? See the instructions for details.

☐ Yes. Designee's name

Phone (   )   –   Personal Identification Number (PIN) ☐ ☐ ☐ ☐ ☐

☑ No.

Part 5: Sign here

Under penalties of perjury, I declare that I have examined this return, including accompanying schedules and statements, and to the best of my knowledge and belief, it is true, correct, and complete.

X

Sign your name here *Sarah Kent*

Print name and title **Sarah Kent, Owner**

Date 04 / 30 / 07   Phone (972) 709 – 4567

Part 6: For paid preparers only *(optional)*

Preparer's signature

Firm's name

Address

EIN

ZIP code

Date /   /   Phone (   )   –   SSN/PTIN

☐ Check if you are self-employed.

Form **941**

Notice that on Line 15 if the amount of taxes is less than $2,500, the amount may be paid with the return or with a financial depositor. There is no need to complete the record of monthly deposits. Since the amount of taxes due for Kent Furniture and Novelty Company is greater than $2,500, and Kent is a monthly depositor, the record of monthly tax deposits must be completed on Line 15. The total deposits shown on Line 15 must equal the taxes shown on Line 10.

If the employer did not make sufficient deposits, a check for the balance due is mailed to the Internal Revenue Service with Form 941. An employer may instead make a deposit at an authorized financial institution.

If the employer did not deduct enough taxes from an employee's earnings, the business pays the difference. The deficiency is debited to *Payroll Taxes Expense.*

Wage and Tax Statement, Form W-2

Employers provide a **Wage and Tax Statement, Form W-2** , to each employee by January 31 of the following year. Form W-2 is sometimes called a **withholding statement** . Form W-2 contains information about the employee's earnings and tax withholdings for the year. The information for Form W-2 comes from the employee's earnings record.

Employees who stop working for the business during the year may ask that a Form W-2 be issued early. The Form W-2 must be issued within 30 days after the request or after the final wage payment, whichever is later.

Figure 11.5 on page 388 shows Form W-2 for Alicia Martinez. This is the standard form provided by the Internal Revenue Service (IRS). Some employers use a "substitute" Form W-2 that is approved by the IRS. The substitute form permits the employer to list total deductions and to reconcile the gross earnings, the deductions, and the net pay. If the firm issues 250 or more Forms W-2, the returns must be filed electronically.

At least four copies of each of Form W-2 are prepared:

1. One copy for the employer to send to the Social Security Administration, which shares the information with the IRS.
2. One copy for the employee to attach to the federal income tax return.
3. One copy for the employee's records.
4. One copy for the employer's records.

If there is a state income tax, two more copies of Form W-2 are prepared:

5. One copy for the employer to send to the state tax department.
6. One copy for the employee to attach to the state income tax return.

Additional copies are prepared if there is a city or county income tax.

Annual Transmittal of Wage and Tax Statements, Form W-3

The **Transmittal of Wage and Tax Statements, Form W-3** , is submitted with Forms W-2 to the Social Security Administration. Form W-3 reports the total social security wages; total Medicare wages; total social security tax withheld; total Medicare tax withheld; total wages, tips, and other compensation; total federal income tax withheld; and other information.

A copy of Form W-2 for each employee is attached to Form W-3. Form W-3 is due by the last day of February following the end of the calendar year. The Social Security Administration shares the tax information on Forms W-2 with the Internal Revenue Service. Figure 11.6 on page 389 shows the completed Form W-3 for Kent Furniture and Novelty Company.

The amounts on Form W-3 must equal the sums of the amounts on the attached Forms W-2. For example, the amount entered in Box 1 of Form W-3 must equal the sum of the amounts entered in Box 1 of all the Forms W-2.

▶ **5. OBJECTIVE**
Prepare Wage and Tax Statement (Form W-2) and Annual Transmittal of Wage and Tax Statements (Form W-3).

important!

Form W-2
The employer must provide each employee with a Wage and Tax Statement, Form W-2, by January 31 of the following year.

ABOUT
ACCOUNTING

IRS Electronic Filing
More than 19 million taxpayers have filed their tax returns electronically. Returns that are filed electronically are more accurate than paper returns. Electronic filing means refunds in half the time, especially if the taxpayer chooses direct deposit of the refund.

FIGURE 11.5 | Wage and Tax Statement, Form W-2

a Control number 22222	Void ☐	For Official Use Only ▶ ⬦ OMB No. 1545-0008	
b Employer identification number 75-1234567		**1** Wages, tips, other compensation 20,800.00	**2** Federal income tax withheld 988.00
c Employer's name, address, and ZIP code Kent Furniture and Novelty Co. 5910 Lake June Road Dallas, TX 75232-6017		**3** Social security wages 20,800.00	**4** Social security tax withheld 1,289.60
		5 Medicare wages and tips 20,800.00	**6** Medicare tax withheld 301.60
		7 Social security tips	**8** Allocated tips
d Employee's social security number 123-45-6789		**9** Advance EIC payment	**10** Dependent care benefits
e Employee's first name and initial Last name Alicia Martinez 1712 Windmill Hill Lane Dallas, Texas 75232-6002		**11** Nonqualified plans	**12a** See instructions for box 12
		13 Statutory employee ☐ Retirement plan ☐ Third-party sick pay ☐	**12b**
		14 Other	**12c**
			12d
f Employee's address and ZIP code			

15 State Employer's state I.D. no. TX │ 12-9876500	**16** State wages, tips, etc. 20,800.00	**17** State income tax	**18** Local wages, tips, etc.	**19** Local income tax	**20** Locality name

Form W-2 Wage and Tax Statement   **2007**

Department of the Treasury—Internal Revenue Service

Copy A For Social Security Administration—Send this entire page with Form W-3 to the Social Security Administration; photocopies are **not** acceptable.

Cat. No. 10134D

For Privacy Act and Paperwork Reduction Act Notice, see back of Copy D.

Do NOT Cut, Fold, or Staple Forms on This Page—Do NOT Cut, Fold, or Staple Forms on This Page

The amounts on Form W-3 also must equal the sums of the amounts reported on the Forms 941 during the year. For example, the social security wages reported on the Form W-3 must equal the sum of the social security wages reported on the four Forms 941.

The filing of Form W-3 marks the end of the routine procedures needed to account for payrolls and for payroll tax withholdings.

a Control number	33333	For Official Use Only ▶ OMB No. 1545-0008		

b Kind of Payer ▶	941 ☒ Military ☐ 943 ☐ CT-1 ☐ Hshld. emp. ☐ Medicare govt. emp. ☐ Third-party sick pay ☐	1 Wages, tips, other compensation 116,870.00	2 Federal income tax withheld 8,060.00

3 Social security wages 116,870.00	4 Social security tax withheld 7,246.20

c Total number of Forms W-2 5	d Establishment number	5 Medicare wages and tips 116,870.00	6 Medicare tax withheld 1,694.68

e Employer identification number 75-1234567	7 Social security tips	8 Allocated tips

f Employer's name Kent Furniture and Novelty Co.	9 Advance EIC payments	10 Dependent care benefits

11 Nonqualified plans	12 Deferred compensation

5910 Lake June Road
Dallas, TX 75232-6017

13 For third-party sick pay use only

14 Income tax withheld by third-party sick pay

g Employer's address and ZIP code

h Other EIN used this year

15 State TX	Employer's state I.D. no. 12-9876500	16 State wages, tips, etc.	17 State income tax

18 Local wages, tips, etc.	19 Local income tax

Contact person Sarah Kent	Telephone number (972) 709-4567	For Official Use Only

E-mail address Kent@aol.net	Fax number (972) 709-4568	

Under penalties of perjury, I declare that I have examined this return and accompanying documents, and, to the best of my knowledge and belief, they are true, correct, and complete.

Signature ▶ _Sarah Kent_   Title ▶ _Owner_   Date ▶ _February 16, 2008_

Form **W-3** Transmittal of Wage and Tax Statements **2007**   Department of the Treasury Internal Revenue Service

FIGURE 11.6

Transmittal of Wage and Tax Statements, Form W-3

Section 1: **Self Review**

QUESTIONS

1. What is the purpose of Form W-2?

2. Where does a business deposit federal payroll taxes?

3. What is the purpose of Form 941?

EXERCISES

4. Which tax is shared equally by the employee and employer?

   a. Federal income tax

   b. State income tax

   c. Social security tax

   d. Federal unemployment tax

5. Employers usually record social security taxes in the accounting records at the end of

   a. each payroll period.

   b. each month.

   c. each quarter.

   d. the year.

ANALYSIS

6. Your business currently owes $2,910 in payroll taxes. During the lookback period, your business paid $10,000 in payroll taxes. How often does your business need to make payroll tax deposits?

(Answers to Section 1 Self Review are on page 412.)

Section 2

SECTION OBJECTIVES

▶ **6. Compute and record liability for federal and state unemployment taxes and record payment of the taxes.**

WHY IT'S IMPORTANT

Businesses need to record all payroll tax liabilities.

▶ **7. Prepare an Employer's Federal Unemployment Tax Return, Form 940 or 940-EZ.**

WHY IT'S IMPORTANT

The unemployment insurance programs provide support to individuals during temporary periods of unemployment.

▶ **8. Compute and record workers' compensation insurance premiums.**

WHY IT'S IMPORTANT

Businesses need insurance to cover workplace injury claims.

TERMS TO LEARN

Employer's Annual Federal Unemployment Tax Return, Form 940 or Form 940-EZ

experience rating system

merit rating system

unemployment insurance program

Unemployment Tax and Workers' Compensation

In Section 1 we discussed taxes that are withheld from employees' earnings and in some cases matched by the employer. In this section we will discuss payroll related expenses that are paid solely by the employer.

Unemployment Compensation Insurance Taxes

The unemployment compensation tax program, often called the **unemployment insurance program**, provides unemployment compensation through a tax levied on employers.

COORDINATION OF FEDERAL AND STATE UNEMPLOYMENT RATES

The unemployment insurance program is a federal program that encourages states to provide unemployment insurance for employees working in the state. The federal government allows a credit—or reduction—in the federal unemployment tax for amounts charged by the state for unemployment taxes.

This text assumes that the federal unemployment tax rate is 6.2 percent less a state unemployment tax credit of 5.4 percent; thus the federal tax rate is reduced to 0.8 percent (6.2% − 5.4%). The earnings limits for the federal and the state unemployment tax are usually the same, $7,000.

A few states levy an unemployment tax on the employee. The tax is withheld from employee pay and remitted by the employer to the state.

For businesses that provide steady employment, the state unemployment tax rate may be lowered based on an **experience rating system**, or a **merit rating system**. Under the experience rating system, the state tax rate may be reduced to less than 1 percent for businesses that provide steady employment. In contrast, some states levy penalty rates as high as 10 percent for employers with poor records of providing steady employment.

The reduction of state unemployment taxes because of favorable experience ratings does not affect the credit allowable against the federal tax. An employer may take a credit against the federal unemployment tax as though it were paid at the normal state rate even though the employer actually pays the state a lower rate.

Because of its experience rating, Kent Furniture and Novelty Company pays state unemployment tax of 4.0 percent, which is less than the standard rate of 5.4 percent. Note that the business may take the credit for the full amount of the state rate (5.4%) against the federal rate, even though the business actually pays a state rate of 4.0%.

COMPUTING AND RECORDING UNEMPLOYMENT TAXES

▶ **6. OBJECTIVE**

Compute and record liability for federal and state unemployment taxes and record payment of the taxes.

Kent Furniture and Novelty Company records its state and federal unemployment tax expense at the end of each payroll period. The unemployment taxes for the payroll period ending January 6 are as follows.

Federal unemployment tax	($2,247.50 × 0.008)	=	$ 17.98
State unemployment tax	($2,247.50 × 0.040)	=	89.90
Total unemployment taxes		=	$107.88

The entry to record the employer's unemployment payroll taxes follows.

GENERAL JOURNAL   PAGE __1__

	DATE		DESCRIPTION	POST. REF.	DEBIT	CREDIT	
1	2007						1
8	Jan.	8	Payroll Taxes Expense		1 0 7 88		8
9			Federal Unemployment Tax Payable			1 7 98	9
10			State Unemployment Tax Payable			8 9 90	10
11			Unemployment taxes on				11
12			weekly payroll				12

REPORTING AND PAYING STATE UNEMPLOYMENT TAXES

In most states the due date for the unemployment tax return is the last day of the month following the end of the quarter. Generally the tax is paid with the return.

Employer's Quarterly Report Figure 11.7 on page 392 shows the Employer's Quarterly Report for the State of Texas filed by Kent Furniture and Novelty Company in April for the first quarter. The report for Texas is similar to the tax forms of other states. The top of the form contains information about the company.

■ *Block 4* at the top of the form shows the tax rate assigned by the state based on the experience rating. The tax rate for Kent Furniture and Novelty Company is 4.0 percent.

■ *Block 10* (3 boxes) shows the number of employees in the state on the 12th day of each month of the quarter.

■ *Line 13* shows the total wages paid during the quarter to employees in the state, $29,217.50.

■ *Line 14* shows the total *taxable* wages paid during the quarter, $28,937.50. Note that the limit on taxable wages is $7,000. Table 11.1 on page 383 shows that at the end of the first quarter, one employee, Cecilia Wu, earned more than $7,000. All other wages and salaries are taxable for state unemployment. Actually, the base in Texas is $9,000. We use a base of $7,000 for the sake of simplicity.

■ *Line 15* shows the total tax for the quarter. Taxable wages are multiplied by the tax rate ($28,937.50 × 0.04 = $1,157.50).

■ *Lines 16a* and *b* are a breakdown of the amount on Line 15. In Texas, part of the 4 percent tax is set aside for job training and other incentive programs. Box 4a contains the tax rate for the unemployment tax (3.9%). Box 4b contains the tax rate for training incentives or *Smart Jobs Assessment* (0.1%).

■ *Lines 17* and *18* are blank. There are no penalties or interest because no taxes or reports are past due.

■ *Line 19* is blank. There is no balance due from prior periods.

■ *Line 20* shows the tax due.

FIGURE 11.7 | Employer's Quarterly Report Form for State Unemployment Taxes

---

TEXAS WORKFORCE COMMISSION
AUSTIN, TEXAS 78714-9037
(512)-463-2222

EMPLOYER'S QUARTERLY REPORT

11111

1. ACCOUNT NUMBER	2. COUNTY CODE	3. TAX AREA	4. TAX RATE	5. SIC CODE	6. FEDERAL I.D. NUMBER	7. QTR. YR.
12-9876500	121	2	4.0 %	59	75-1234567	1st/2007

8. EMPLOYER NAME AND ADDRESS (SEE ITEM 25 FOR CHANGES TO NAME, ADDRESS, ETC.)

9. TELEPHONE NUMBER
(972) 709-4567

Sarah Kent

Kent Furniture and Novelty Company

5910 Lake June Road

Dallas, TX 75232-6017

4a. UI TAX RATE	4b. SMART JOBS ASSESSMENT
3.9 %	.1 %

ALIGNMENT

9A. QUARTER ENDING

1st Month	2nd Month	3rd Month
5	5	5

10. Enter in the boxes above the number of employees both full-time and part-time, in pay periods that include 12th day of the calendar month. (ENTER NUMERALS ONLY)

9B. PENALTIES WILL BE ASSESSED IF REPORT IS NOT POSTMARKED BY

11. SHOW THE COUNTY CODE (see list on the back of this form) in which you had the greatest number of employees — 121

12. IF you have employees in more than one county in TEXAS, how many are outside the county shown in Item 11?

You must FILE this return even though you had no payroll this quarter. If you had no payroll show '0' in item 13 and sign the declaration (Item 26) on this form.

		DOLLARS	CENTS
13.	Total (Gross) Wages Paid During this Quarter to Texas Employees	29,217	50
14.	Taxable Wages paid this quarter to each employee up to $7000, the annual maximum amount. (If none, enter "0")	28,937	50
15.	Tax Due (Multiply Taxable Wages By Tax Rate, Item 4 Above)	1,157	50
16a. UI TAX	1128 : 56		
b. Smart Jobs Assessment	28 : 94		
17.	Interest, If Tax Is Past Due		
18.	Penalty, If Report Is Past Due		
19.	Balance Due From Prior Periods (Subtract Credit Or Add Debit)		
20.	Total Due - Make Remittance Payable To TEXAS WORKFORCE COMMISSION	1,157	50

14a. Mark box with an 'X' if reporting wages to another state during the year for employees listed in Item 22.

FOR TWC USE ONLY

	MONTH	DAY	YEAR
POSTMARK DATE C3			
POSTMARK DATE S			
EX DATE C3			
EX DATE S			

Est

DOLLARS	CENTS	INITIALS

AMOUNT RECEIVED

	21. SOCIAL SECURITY NUMBER	1ST INIT	2ND INIT	22. EMPLOYEE NAME LAST NAME	23. TOTAL WAGES PAID THIS QUARTER
1	587-XX-XXXX			C. Booker	6,240 : 00
2	427-XX-XXXX			G. Dunlap	5,557 : 50
3	687-XX-XXXX			A. Martinez	5,200 : 00
4	123-XX-XXXX			J. Rodriguez	4,940 : 00
5	587-XX-XXXX			C. Wu	7,280 : 00
6					
7					
8					
9					
10					

26. I DECLARE that the information herein is true and correct to the best of my knowledge and belief.

SIGNATURE _Sarah Kent_

TITLE _Owner_   DATE _4/29/2007_

PREPARERS NAME _Sarah Kent_

PREPARERS PHONE NUMBER _(972) 709-4567_

For assistance in completing form call,

24. PAGE TOTAL   29,217 : 50

MAIL REPORT AND REMITTANCE TO:
CASHIER
TEXAS WORKFORCE COMMISSION
P.O. BOX 149037
AUSTIN, TEXAS 78714-9037
DO NOT STAPLE REPORT
(Write Account No. On Check)

FORM C - 3 (6/99)
SCANC3

25. MAKE CHANGES TO EMPLOYER INFORMATION USING C-3 **INSTRUCTION SHEET.** CHANGES NOTED ON THIS FORM MAY NOT BE CAPTURED DURING PROCESSING.

Kent Furniture and Novelty Company submits the report and issues a check payable to the state tax authority for the amount shown on Line 20. The entry is recorded in the cash payments journal. The transaction is shown here in general journal form for purposes of illustration.

GENERAL JOURNAL   PAGE _____

	DATE		DESCRIPTION	POST. REF.	DEBIT	CREDIT	
1	2007						1
2	Apr.	29	State Unemployment Tax Payable		1 1 5 7 50		2
3			Cash			1 1 5 7 50	3
4			Paid SUTA taxes for quarter				4
5			ending March 31				5
6							6

Earnings in Excess of Base Amount State unemployment tax is paid on the first $7,000 of annual earnings for each employee. Earnings over $7,000 are not subject to state unemployment tax.

For example, Cecilia Wu earns $560 every week of the year. Table 11.1 on page 383 shows that she earned $7,280 at the end of the first quarter. In the four weeks of January, February, and March she earned $2,240 ($560 × 4).

	Earnings	Cumulative Earnings
January	$2,240	$2,240
February	2,240	4,480
March	2,240	6,720
March, week 5	560	7,280

In the fifth week of March, Wu earned $560, but only $280 of it is subject to state unemployment tax ($7,000 earnings limit − $6,720 cumulative earnings = $280). For the rest of the calendar year, Wu's earnings are not subject to state unemployment tax.

REPORTING AND PAYING FEDERAL UNEMPLOYMENT TAXES

The rules for reporting and depositing federal unemployment taxes differ from those used for social security and Medicare taxes.

Depositing Federal Unemployment Taxes There are two ways to make federal unemployment tax deposits: with electronic deposits using EFTPS or with a Federal Tax Deposit Coupon, Form 8109, at an authorized financial institution. Deposits are made quarterly and are due on the last day of the month following the end of the quarter.

The federal unemployment tax is calculated at the end of each quarter. It is computed by multiplying the first $7,000 of each employee's wages by 0.008. A deposit is required when more than $100 of federal unemployment tax is owed. If $100 or less is owed, no deposit is due. The deposit requirement has changed to $500 for tax years after 2004. For simplicity, we use $100 in the text.

For example, suppose that a business calculates its federal unemployment tax to be $90 at the end of the first quarter. Since it is not more than $100, no deposit is due. At the end of the second quarter, it calculates its federal unemployment taxes on second quarter wages to be $70. The total undeposited unemployment tax now is more than $100, so a deposit is required.

First quarter undeposited tax	$ 90
Second quarter undeposited tax	70
Total deposit due	$160

In the case of Kent Furniture and Novelty Company, the company owed $231.50 in federal unemployment tax at the end of March. Since this is more than $100, a deposit of $231.50 is due by April 30.

Month	Taxable Earnings Paid	Rate	Tax Due	Deposit Due Date
January	$ 8,990.00	0.008	$ 71.92	April 30
February	8,990.00	0.008	71.92	April 30
March	10,957.50	0.008	87.66	April 30
Total	$28,937.50		$231.50	

On April 30 Kent Furniture and Novelty Company records the payment of federal unemployment tax in the cash payments journal. The transaction is shown here in general journal form for illustration purposes.

GENERAL JOURNAL   PAGE _____

	DATE		DESCRIPTION	POST. REF.	DEBIT	CREDIT	
1	2007						1
8	Apr.	30	Federal Unemployment Tax Payable		2 3 1 50		8
9			Cash			2 3 1 50	9
10			Deposit FUTA due				10
11							11

▶ **7. OBJECTIVE**

Prepare an Employer's Federal Unemployment Tax Return, Form 940 or 940-EZ.

Reporting Federal Unemployment Tax, Form 940 or 940-EZ Tax returns are not due quarterly for the federal unemployment tax. The employer submits an annual return. The **Employer's Annual Federal Unemployment Tax Return, Form 940 or 940-EZ**, is a preprinted government form used to report unemployment taxes for the calendar year. It is due by January 31 of the following year. The due date is extended to February 10 if all tax deposits were made on time. Instead of using Form 940, businesses can use Form 940-EZ if

- they paid unemployment tax to only one state,
- they paid all federal unemployment taxes by January 31 of the following year,
- all wages that were taxable for federal unemployment were also taxable for state unemployment.

Kent Furniture and Novelty Company prepares Form 940-EZ. The information needed to complete Form 940-EZ comes from the annual summary of individual earnings records and from the state unemployment tax returns filed during the year.

Figure 11.8 on page 395 shows Form 940-EZ prepared for Kent Furniture and Novelty Company. Refer to it as you learn how to complete Form 940-EZ.

- *Line A* shows the total state unemployment tax paid. All five employees of Kent Furniture and Novelty Company reached the earnings limit during the year. Wages subject to state unemployment tax are $35,000 ($7,000 × 5 employees). The state rate is 4 percent. Kent Furniture and Novelty Company paid state unemployment tax of $1,400 ($35,000 × 0.04).

balance due. If the actual premium is less than the estimated premium paid, the employer receives a refund.

Kent Furniture and Novelty Company has two work classifications: office work and shipping work. The workers' compensation premium rates are

Office workers	$0.45 per $100 of labor costs
Shipping workers	1.25 per $100 of labor costs

The insurance premium rates recognize that injuries are more likely to occur to shipping workers than to office workers. Based on employee earnings for the previous year, Kent Furniture and Novelty Company paid an estimated premium of $1,000 for the new year. The payment was made on January 15.

GENERAL JOURNAL   PAGE _____

	DATE		DESCRIPTION	POST. REF.	DEBIT	CREDIT	
1	2007						1
14	Jan.	15	Workers' Compensation Insurance Expense		1 000 00		14
15			Cash			1 000 00	15
16			Estimated workers' compensation				16
17			insurance for 2007				17
18							18

At the end of the year, the actual premium was computed, $1,261.20. The actual premium was computed by applying the proper rates to the payroll data for the year:

- The office wages were $24,960.

$$(\$24,960 \div \$100) \quad \times \quad \$0.45 \quad =$$
$$249.60 \quad \times \quad \$0.45 \quad = \quad \$ \ 112.32$$

- The shipping wages were $91,910.

$$(\$91,910 \div \$100) \quad \times \quad \$1.25 \quad =$$
$$919.1 \quad \times \quad \$1.25 \quad = \quad \$1,148.88$$

Total premium for year   = $1,261.20

Classification	Payroll	Rate	Premium
Office work	$24,960	$0.45 per $100	$ 112.32
Shipping work	91,910	1.25 per $100	1,148.88
Total premium for year			$1,261.20
Less estimated premium paid			1,000.00
Balance of premium due			$ 261.20

On December 31 the balance due to the insurance company is recorded as a liability by an adjusting entry. Kent Furniture and Novelty Company owes $261.20 ($1,261.20 − $1,000.00) for the workers' compensation insurance.

GENERAL JOURNAL   PAGE _____

	DATE		DESCRIPTION	POST. REF.	DEBIT	CREDIT	
1	2007						1
2	Dec.	31	Workers' Compensation Insurance Expense		261 20		2
3			Workers' Compensation Insurance Payable			261 20	3
4							4

MANAGERIAL IMPLICATIONS

PAYROLL TAXES

- Management must ensure that payroll taxes are computed properly and paid on time.
- In order to avoid penalties, it is essential that a business prepares its payroll tax returns accurately and files the returns and required forms promptly.
- The payroll system should ensure that payroll reports are prepared in an efficient manner.
- Managers need to be familiar with all payroll taxes and how they impact operating expenses.

- Managers must be knowledgeable about unemployment tax regulations in their state because favorable experience ratings can reduce unemployment tax expense.
- Management is responsible for developing effective internal control procedures over payroll operations and ensuring that they are followed.

THINKING CRITICALLY

What accounting records are used to prepare Form 941?

Suppose that on January 15 Kent Furniture and Novelty Company had paid an estimated premium of $1,400 instead of $1,000. The actual premium at the end of the year was $1,261.20. Kent Furniture and Novelty Company would be due a refund from the insurance company for the amount overpaid, $138.80 ($1,400.00 − $1,261.20).

GENERAL JOURNAL   PAGE _____

	DATE		DESCRIPTION	POST. REF.	DEBIT	CREDIT	
1	2007						1
2	Dec.	31	Workers' Compensation Refund Receivable		1 3 8 80		2
3			Workers' Compensation Insurance Expense			1 3 8 80	3
4							4

THE BOTTOM LINE

Workers' Compensation Refund Receivable

Income Statement

Expenses	↓ 138.80
Net Income	↑ 138.80

Balance Sheet

Assets	↑ 138.80
Equity	↑ 138.80

Deposit and Monthly Premium Payments Employers with many employees use a different method to handle workers' compensation insurance. At the beginning of the year, they make large deposits, often 25 percent of the estimated annual premium. From January through November, they pay the actual premium due based on an audit of the month's wages. The premium for the last month is deducted from the deposit. Any balance is refunded or applied toward the following year's deposit.

Internal Control over Payroll Operations

Now that we have examined the basic accounting procedures used for payrolls and payroll taxes, let's look at some internal control procedures that are recommended to protect payroll operations.

1. Assign only highly responsible, well-trained employees to work in payroll operations.
2. Keep payroll records in locked files. Train payroll employees to maintain confidentiality about pay rates and other information in the payroll records.
3. Add new employees to the payroll system and make all changes in employee pay rates only with proper written authorization from management.
4. Make changes to an employee's withholding allowances based only on a Form W-4 properly completed and signed by the employee.
5. Make voluntary deductions from employee earnings based only on a signed authorization from the employee.

6. Have the payroll checks examined by someone other than the person who prepares them. Compare each check to the entry for the employee in the payroll register.

7. Have payroll checks distributed to the employees by someone other than the person who prepares them.

8. Have the monthly payroll bank account statement received and reconciled by someone other than the person who prepares the payroll checks.

9. Use prenumbered forms for the payroll checks. Periodically the numbers of the checks issued and the numbers of the unused checks should be verified to make sure that all checks can be accounted for.

10. Maintain files of all authorization forms for adding new employees, changing pay rates, and making voluntary deductions. Also retain all Forms W-4.

Section 2: **Self Review**

QUESTIONS

1. Why is it important for workers' compensation wages to be classified according to the type of work performed?

2. Who pays the federal unemployment tax? The state unemployment tax?

3. How does a favorable experience rating affect the state unemployment tax rate?

EXERCISES

4. The federal unemployment taxes are reported on
   a. Form 941.
   b. Form 8109.
   c. Form W-3.
   d. Form 940.

5. State unemployment taxes are filed
   a. monthly.
   b. quarterly.
   c. yearly.
   d. at the end of each pay period.

ANALYSIS

6. At the end of the year, the business has a balance due for workers' compensation insurance. If no adjusting entry is made, will the amount of net income reported be correct? If not, how will it be wrong?

(Answers to Section 2 Self Review are on page 413.)

REVIEW

Chapter Summary

Employers must pay social security, SUTA, FUTA, and Medicare taxes. They must also collect federal and state taxes from their employees and then remit those taxes to the appropriate taxing authorities. In this chapter, you have learned how to compute the employer's taxes and how to file the required tax returns and reports.

Learning Objectives

1 Explain how and when payroll taxes are paid to the government.

Employers act as collection agents for social security, Medicare, and federal income taxes withheld from employee earnings. Employers must remit these sums, with their own share of social security and Medicare taxes, to the government. The taxes must be deposited in an authorized depository, usually a commercial bank. The methods and schedules for deposits vary according to the sums involved.

2 Compute and record the employer's social security and Medicare taxes.

Employers should multiply the social security and Medicare tax rates by taxable wages to compute the employer's portion of taxes due.

3 Record deposit of social security, Medicare, and employee income taxes.

As taxes are paid to the government, the accounting records should be updated to reflect the payment, thereby reducing tax liability accounts.

4 Prepare an Employer's Quarterly Federal Tax Return, Form 941.

The Form 941 reports wages paid, federal employee income tax withheld, and applicable social security and Medicare taxes.

5 Prepare Wage and Tax Statement (Form W-2) and Annual Transmittal of Wage and Tax Statements (Form W-3).

By the end of January each employee must be given a Wage and Tax Statement, Form W-2, showing the previous year's earnings and withholdings for social security, Medicare, and employee income tax. The employer files a Transmittal of Wage and Tax Statements, Form W-3, with copies of employees' Forms W-2. Form W-3 is due by the last day of February following the end of the calendar year.

6 Compute and record liability for federal and state unemployment taxes and record payment of the taxes.

Unemployment insurance taxes are paid by the employer to both state and federal governments. State unemployment tax returns differ from state to state but usually require a list of employees, their social security numbers, and taxable wages paid. The rate of state unemployment tax depends on the employer's experience rating. The net federal unemployment tax rate can be as low as 0.8 percent.

7 Prepare an Employer's Federal Unemployment Tax Return, Form 940 or 940-EZ.

An Employer's Annual Federal Unemployment Tax Return, Form 940 or 940-EZ, must be filed in January for the preceding calendar year. The form shows the total wages paid, the amount of wages subject to unemployment tax, and the federal unemployment tax owed for the year. A credit is allowed against gross federal tax for unemployment tax charged under state plans, up to 5.4 percent of wages subject to the federal tax.

8 Compute and record workers' compensation insurance premiums.

By state law, employers might be required to carry workers' compensation insurance. For companies with a few employees, an estimated premium is paid at the start of the year. A final settlement is made with the insurance company on the basis of an audit of the payroll after the end of the year. Premiums vary according to the type of work performed by each employee. Other premium payment plans can be used for larger employers.

9 Define the accounting terms new to this chapter.

Glossary

Employer's Annual Federal Unemployment Tax Return, Form 940 (p. 394) Preprinted government form used by the employer to report unemployment taxes for the calendar year

Employer's Annual Federal Unemployment Tax Return, Form 940-EZ (p. 394) See Employer's Annual Federal Unemployment Tax Return, Form 940

Employer's Quarterly Federal Tax Return, Form 941 (p. 382) Preprinted government form used by the employer to report payroll tax information relating to social security, Medicare, and employee income tax withholding to the Internal Revenue Service

Experience rating system (p. 390) A system that rewards an employer for maintaining steady employment conditions by reducing the firm's state unemployment tax rate

Merit rating system (p. 390) See Experience rating system

Transmittal of Wage and Tax Statements, Form W-3 (p. 387) Preprinted government form submitted with Forms W-2 to the Social Security Administration

Unemployment insurance program (p. 390) A program that provides unemployment compensation through a tax levied on employers

Wage and Tax Statement, Form W-2 (p. 387) Preprinted government form that contains information about an employee's earnings and tax withholdings for the year

Withholding statement (p. 387) See Wage and Tax Statement, Form W-2

Comprehensive **Self Review**

1. What is Form W-3?
2. Is the ceiling on earnings subject to unemployment taxes larger than or smaller than the ceiling on earnings subject to the social security tax?
3. How do the FUTA and SUTA taxes relate to each other?
4. Under the monthly deposit schedule rule, when must deposits for employee income tax and other withheld taxes be made?
5. Which of the following factors determine the frequency of deposits of social security, Medicare, and income tax withholdings?
    a. Experience rating.
    b. Amount of taxes reported in the lookback period.
    c. Company's net income.
    d. Amount of taxes currently owed.
    e. How often employees are paid.

(Answers to Comprehensive Self Review are on page 413.)

Discussion Questions

1. Which of the following are withheld from employees' earnings?
    a. FUTA
    b. income tax
    c. Medicare
    d. social security
    e. SUTA
    f. workers' compensation
2. What does "monthly" refer to in the Monthly Deposit Schedule Rule?
3. What does "semiweekly" refer to in the Semiweekly Deposit Schedule Rule?
4. What is EFTPS? When is EFTPS required?
5. When is the use of Form 8109-B permitted?
6. What is a business tax identification number?
7. What are the four taxes levied on employers?

8. What is the lookback period?

9. What is the purpose of Form W-3? When must it be issued? To whom is it sent?

10. When must Form W-2 be issued? To whom is it sent?

11. What happens if the employer fails to deduct enough employee income tax or FICA tax from employee earnings?

12. What government form is prepared to accompany deposits of federal taxes?

13. How can an employer keep informed about changes in the rates and bases for the social security, Medicare, and FUTA taxes?

14. When is the premium for workers' compensation insurance usually paid?

15. Who pays for workers' compensation insurance?

16. What is Form 941? How often is the form filed?

17. Is the employer required to deposit the federal unemployment tax during the year? Explain.

18. A state charges a basic SUTA tax rate of 5.4 percent. Because of an excellent experience rating, an employer in the state has to pay only 1.0 percent of the taxable payroll as state tax. What is the percentage to be used in computing the credit against the federal unemployment tax?

19. What is the purpose of Form 940? How often is it filed?

20. What is the purpose of allowing a credit against the FUTA for state unemployment taxes?

21. Why was the unemployment insurance system established?

APPLICATIONS

Exercises

Exercise 11.1
Objective 1

▶ **Depositing payroll taxes.**

The amounts of employee income tax withheld and social security and Medicare taxes (both employee and employer shares) shown below were owed by different businesses on the specified dates. In each case decide whether the firm is required to deposit the sum in an authorized financial institution. If a deposit is necessary, give the date by which it should be made. The employers are monthly depositors.

1. Total taxes of $550 owed on July 31, 2007.

2. Total taxes of $1,650 owed on April 30, 2007.

3. Total taxes of $1,200 owed on March 31, 2007.

4. Total taxes of $8,750 owed on February 28, 2007.

Exercise 11.2
Objective 3

▶ **Recording deposit of social security, Medicare, and income taxes.**

After Hennessey Corporation paid its employees on July 15, 2007, and recorded the corporation's share of payroll taxes for the payroll paid that date, the firm's general ledger showed a balance of $20,160 in the **Social Security Tax Payable** account, a balance of $4,644 in the **Medicare Tax Payable** account, and a balance of $18,360 in the **Employee Income Tax Payable** account. On July 16 the business issued a check to deposit the taxes owed in the First Texas Bank. Record this transaction in general journal form.

Exercise 11.3
Objectives 2, 6

▶ **Computing employer's payroll taxes.**

At the end of the weekly payroll period on June 30, 2007, the payroll register of Seymore Professional Consultants Company showed employee earnings of $71,200. Determine the firm's payroll taxes for the period. Use a social security rate of 6.2 percent, Medicare rate of 1.45 percent, FUTA rate of 0.8 percent, and SUTA rate of 5.4 percent. Consider all earnings subject to social security tax and Medicare tax and $39,000 subject to FUTA and SUTA taxes.

Depositing federal unemployment tax.

On March 31, 2007, the **Federal Unemployment Tax Payable** account in the general ledger of The Conover Barter Company showed a balance of $1,152. This represents the FUTA tax owed for the first quarter of the year. On April 30, 2007, the firm issued a check to deposit the amount owed in the First Security National Bank. Record this transaction in general journal form.

◀ **Exercise 11.4**
Objective 6

Computing SUTA tax.

On April 30, 2007, Wilson Furniture Company prepared its state unemployment tax return for the first quarter of the year. The firm had taxable wages of $100,050. Because of a favorable experience rating, Wilson pays SUTA tax at a rate of 1.6 percent. How much SUTA tax did the firm owe for the quarter?

◀ **Exercise 11.5**
Objective 6

Paying SUTA tax.

On June 30, 2007, the **State Unemployment Tax Payable** account in the general ledger of Champion Grocery Company showed a balance of $2,736. This represents the SUTA tax owed for the second quarter of the year. On July 31, 2007, the business issued a check to the state unemployment insurance fund for the amount due. Record this payment in general journal form.

◀ **Exercise 11.6**
Objective 6

Computing FUTA tax.

On January 31 Talk of the Town Salon prepared its Employer's Annual Federal Unemployment Tax Return, Form 940. During the previous year, the business paid total wages of $395,600 to its eight employees. Of this amount, $128,400 was subject to FUTA tax. Using a rate of 0.8 percent, determine the FUTA tax owed and the balance due on January 31, 2007, when Form 940 was filed. A deposit of $1,000 was made during the year.

◀ **Exercise 11.7**
Objective 6

Computing workers' compensation insurance premiums.

Clark Computer Services Company estimates that its office employees will earn $180,000 next year and its factory employees will earn $960,000. The firm pays the following rates for workers' compensation insurance: $0.40 per $100 of wages for the office employees and $8.00 per $100 of wages for the factory employees. Determine the estimated premium for each group of employees and the total estimated premium for next year.

◀ **Exercise 11.8**
Objective 8

PROBLEMS

Problem Set A

Computing and recording employer's payroll tax expense.

The payroll register of Quality Lawn Care showed total employee earnings of $2,800 for the payroll period ended June 14, 2007.

◀ **Problem 11.1A**
Objectives 2, 6

INSTRUCTIONS

1. Compute the employer's payroll taxes for the period. Use rates of 6.2 percent for the employer's share of the social security tax, 1.45 percent for Medicare tax, 0.8 percent for FUTA tax, and 5.4 percent for SUTA tax. All earnings are taxable.

2. Prepare a general journal entry to record the employer's payroll taxes for the period.

Analyze: Which of the above taxes are paid by the employee and matched by the employer?

Computing employer's social security tax, Medicare tax, and unemployment taxes.

A payroll summary for Marvel Turner, who owns and operates Turner Broadcasting Company, for the quarter ending June 30, 2007, appears on page 404. The firm prepared the required tax deposit forms and issued checks as follows.

◀ **Problem 11.2A**
Objectives 2, 3

a. Federal Tax Deposit Coupon, Form 8109, check for April taxes, paid on May 15.

b. Federal Tax Deposit Coupon, Form 8109, check for May taxes, paid on June 17.

Date Wages Paid	Total Earnings	Social Security Tax Deducted	Medicare Tax Deducted	Income Tax Withheld
April 8	$ 2,332.00	$ 144.58	$ 33.81	$ 231.00
15	2,420.00	150.04	35.09	238.00
22	2,332.00	144.58	33.81	231.00
29	2,376.00	147.31	34.45	235.00
	$ 9,460.00	$ 586.51	$137.16	$ 935.00
May 5	$ 2,288.00	$ 141.86	$ 33.18	227.00
12	2,332.00	144.58	33.81	231.00
19	2,332.00	144.58	33.81	231.00
26	2,376.00	147.31	34.45	235.00
	$ 9,328.00	$ 578.33	$135.25	$ 924.00
June 2	$ 2,420.00	$ 150.04	$ 35.09	$ 238.00
9	2,332.00	144.58	33.81	231.00
16	2,376.00	147.31	34.45	235.00
23	2,332.00	144.58	33.81	231.00
30	2,288.00	141.86	33.18	227.00
	$11,748.00	$ 728.37	$170.34	$1,162.00
Total	$30,536.00	$1,893.21	$442.75	$3,021.00

INSTRUCTIONS

1. Using the tax rates given below, and assuming that all earnings are taxable, make the general journal entry on April 8, 2007, to record the employer's payroll tax expense on the payroll ending that date.

Social security	6.2 percent
Medicare	1.45
FUTA	0.8
SUTA	5.4

2. Give the entries in general journal form to record deposit of the employee income tax withheld and the social security and Medicare taxes (employee and employer shares) on May 15 for April taxes and on June 17 for May taxes.

Analyze: How were the amounts for *Income Tax Withheld* determined?

Problem 11.3A
Objectives 4, 6

CONTINUING >>>
Problem

This is a continuation of Problem 11.2A for Turner Broadcasting Company; recording payment of taxes and preparing employer's quarterly federal tax return.

1. On July 15, the firm issued a check to deposit the federal income tax withheld and the FICA tax (both employee and employer shares for the third month [June]). Based on your computations in Problem 11.2A, record the issuance of the check in general journal form.

2. Complete Form 941 in accordance with the discussions in this chapter. Use a 12.4 percent social security rate and a 2.9 percent Medicare rate in computations. Use the following address for the company: 3750 Belt Line Parkway, Dallas, TX 76539-6205. Use 75-4444444 as the employer identification number. Date the return July 31, 2007. Mr. Turner's phone number is 972-709-3654.

Analyze: Based on the entries that you have recorded, what is the balance of the *Employee Income Tax Payable* account at July 15?

Computing and recording unemployment taxes; completing Form 940.

◀ **Problem 11.4A**
Objectives 6, 7

Certain transactions and procedures relating to federal and state unemployment taxes follow for The Style Shop, a retail store owned by Mary Amos. The firm's address is 2007 Trendsetter Lane, Dallas, TX 75268-0967. The employer's federal and state identification numbers are 75-9462315 and 37-9462315, respectively. Carry out the procedures as instructed in each of the following steps.

INSTRUCTIONS

1. Compute the state unemployment insurance tax owed on the employees' wages for the quarter ended March 31, 2007. This information will be shown on the employer's quarterly report to the state agency that collects SUTA tax. The employer has recorded the tax on each payroll date. Although the state charges a 5.4 percent unemployment tax rate, The Style Shop's rate is only 1.7 percent because of its experience rating. The employee earnings for the first quarter are shown below. All earnings are subject to SUTA tax.

Name of Employee	Total Earnings
Terri Wells	$ 5,075
Jelencia Guyton	3,775
Gloria Harris	4,098
Stacee Fairley	5,270
Anita Thomas	4,875
Jeraldine Wells	4,460
Total	$27,553

2. On April 30, 2007, the firm issued a check to the state employment commission for the amount computed above. In general journal form, record the issuance of the check.

Analyze: What is the relevance of the business experience rating to the state unemployment tax rate?

This is a continuation of Problem 11.4A for The Style Shop; computing and recording unemployment taxes; completing Form 940.

◀ **Problem 11.5A**
Objectives 6, 7

CONTINUING >>>
Problem

1. Complete Form 940-EZ, the Employer's Annual Federal Unemployment Tax Return. Assume that all wages have been paid and that all quarterly payments have been submitted to the state as required. The payroll information for 2007 appears below. The required federal tax deposit forms and checks were submitted as follows: a deposit of $220.42 on April 21, a deposit of $198.72 on July 22, and a deposit of $74.64 on October 21. Date the unemployment tax return January 28, 2008. A check for the balance due will be sent with Form 940.

Quarter Ended	Total Wages Paid	Wages Paid in Excess of $7,000	State Unemployment Tax Paid
Mar. 31	$ 27,553.00	– 0 –	$ 468.40
June 30	28,915.00	$ 4,075.00	422.28
Sept. 30	29,880.00	20,550.00	158.61
Dec. 31	31,350.00	28,910.00	41.48
Totals	$117,698.00	$53,535.00	$1,090.77

2. In general journal form, record issuance of a check on January 28, 2008, for the balance of FUTA tax due for 2007.

Analyze: What total debits were made to liability accounts for entries you recorded in Problem 11.4A and Problem 11.5A?

Problem 11.6A ▶   **Computing and recording workers' compensation insurance premiums.**

Objective 8

e**X**cel

The following information relates to Pondexter Manufacturing Company's workers' compensation insurance premiums for 2007. On January 15, 2008, the company estimated its premium for workers' compensation insurance for the year on the basis of that data.

Work Classification	Amount of Estimated Wages	Insurance Rates
Office work	$ 68,000	$0.40/$100
Shop work	315,000	$5.00/$100

INSTRUCTIONS

1. Compute the estimated premiums.

2. Record in general journal form payment of the estimated premium on January 15, 2007.

3. On January 4, 2008, an audit of the firm's payroll records showed that it had actually paid wages of $72,000 to its office employees and wages of $319,000 to its shop employees. Compute the actual premium for the year and the balance due the insurance company or the credit due the firm.

4. Give the general journal entry to adjust the *Workers' Compensation Insurance Expense* account as of the end of 2007. Date the entry December 31, 2007.

Analyze: If all wages were attributable to shop employees, what premium estimate would have been calculated and recorded on January 15, 2007?

Problem Set B

Problem 11.1B ▶   **Computing and recording employer's payroll tax expense.**

Objectives 2, 6

The payroll register of Clifton's Automotive and Detail Repair Shop showed total employee earnings of $2,890 for the week ended April 8, 2007.

INSTRUCTIONS

1. Compute the employer's payroll taxes for the period. The tax rates are as follows:

Social security	6.2 percent
Medicare	1.45
FUTA	0.8
SUTA	2.2

2. Prepare a general journal entry to record the employer's payroll taxes for the period.

Analyze: If the FUTA tax rate had been 1.2 percent, what total employer payroll taxes would have been recorded?

Problem 11.2B ▶   **Computing employer's social security tax, Medicare tax, and unemployment taxes.**

Objectives 2, 3

A payroll summary for Carolyn Wells, who owns and operates The Fashion Shop, for the quarter ending September 30, 2007, appears below. The business prepared the tax deposit forms and issued checks as follows during the quarter.

a. Federal Tax Deposit Coupon, Form 8109, check for July taxes, paid on August 15.

b. Federal Tax Deposit Coupon, Form 8109, check for August taxes, paid on September 15.

Date Wages Paid	Total Earnings	Social Security Tax Withheld	Medicare Tax Withheld	Income Tax Withheld
July 7	$ 1,980.00	$ 122.76	$ 28.71	$ 192.50
14	1,980.00	122.76	28.71	192.50
21	2,310.00	143.22	33.50	225.50
28	1,980.00	122.76	28.71	192.50
	$ 8,250.00	$ 511.50	$119.63	$ 803.00
Aug. 4	$ 2,310.00	$ 143.22	$ 33.50	225.50
11	2,970.00	184.14	43.07	291.50
18	2,970.00	184.14	43.07	291.50
25	2,640.00	163.68	38.28	258.50
	$10,890.00	$ 675.18	$157.92	$1,067.00
Sept. 2	$ 1,980.00	$ 122.76	$ 28.71	$ 192.50
9	2,310.00	143.22	33.50	225.50
16	2,310.00	143.22	33.50	225.50
23	2,310.00	143.22	33.50	225.50
30	1,980.00	122.76	28.71	192.50
	$10,890.00	$ 675.18	$157.92	$1,061.50
Total	$30,030.00	$1,861.86	$435.47	$2,931.50

INSTRUCTIONS

1. Prepare the general journal entry on July 7, 2007, to record the employer's payroll tax expense on the payroll ending that date. All earnings are subject to the following taxes:

Social security	6.2 percent
Medicare	1.45
FUTA	0.8
SUTA	2.2

2. Make the entries in general journal form to record deposit of the employee income tax withheld and the social security and Medicare taxes (both employees' withholding and employer's matching portion) on August 15 for July taxes and on September 15 for the August taxes.

Analyze: How much would a SUTA rate of 1.5 reduce the tax for the payroll of July 7?

This is a continuation of Problem 11.2B for The Fashion Shop; recording payment of taxes and preparing employer's quarterly federal tax return.

◀ **Problem 11.3B**
Objectives 4, 6

CONTINUING >>>
Problem

1. On October 15, the firm issued a check to deposit the federal income tax withheld and the FICA tax (both employees' withholding and employer's matching portion). Based on your computations in Problem 11.2B, record the issuance of the check in general journal form.

2. Complete Form 941 in accordance with the discussions in this chapter and the instructions on the form. Use a 12.4 percent social security rate and a 2.9 percent Medicare rate in computations. Use the following address for the company: 2008 Trendsetter Lane, Dallas, TX 75268-0967. Use 75-5555555 as the employer identification number. Date the return October 31, 2007.

Analyze: What total taxes were deposited with the IRS for the quarter ended September 30, 2007?

Problem 11.4B ▶

Objectives 6, 7

Computing and recording unemployment taxes; completing Form 940.

Certain transactions and procedures relating to federal and state unemployment taxes are given below for The Hobby Shop, a retail store owned by Helen Franz. The firm's address is 4560 LBJ Freeway, Dallas, TX 75232-6002. The employer's federal and state identification numbers are 75-9999999 and 37-6789015, respectively. Carry out the procedures as instructed in each step.

INSTRUCTIONS

1. Compute the state unemployment insurance tax owed for the quarter ended March 31, 2007. This information will be shown on the employer's quarterly report to the state agency that collects SUTA tax. The employer has recorded the tax expense and liability on each payroll date. Although the state charges a 5.4 percent unemployment tax rate, The Hobby Shop has received a favorable experience rating and therefore pays only a 2.3 percent state tax rate. The employee earnings for the first quarter are given below. All earnings are subject to SUTA tax.

Name of Employee	Total Earnings
Amy Booker	$ 3,880
Stanley Carpenter	3,650
Alicia Cantu	3,225
Robert Dragon	3,780
Patricia Ellis	2,890
John Williams	2,910
Total	$20,335

2. On April 30, 2007, the firm issued a check for the amount computed above. Record the transaction in general journal form.

Analyze: If all employees made the same amount for the quarter ended June 30, 2007, how much would be subject to the federal unemployment tax?

Problem 11.5B ▶

Objectives 6, 7

CONTINUING >>>
Problem

This is a continuation of Problem 11.4B for The Hobby Shop; computing and recording unemployment taxes; completing Form 940.

1. Complete Form 940-EZ, the Employer's Annual Federal Unemployment Tax Return. Assume that all wages have been paid and that all quarterly payments have been submitted to the state as required. The payroll information for 2007 appears below. The required federal tax deposit forms and checks were submitted as follows: a deposit of $162.68 on April 12, a deposit of $170.00 on July 14, and a deposit of $102.00 on October 12. Date the unemployment tax return January 27, 2008. A check for the balance due will be sent with Form 940.

Quarter Ended	Total Wages Paid	Wages Paid in Excess of $7,000	State Unemployment Tax Paid
Mar. 31	$20,335.00	– 0 –	$ 467.71
June 30	21,250.00	– 0 –	488.75
Sept. 30	22,050.00	$ 9,300.00	293.25
Dec. 31	24,800.00	20,250.00	104.65
Totals	$88,435.00	$29,550.00	$1,354.36

2. On January 27, 2008, the firm issued a check for the amount shown on line 8, Part I of form 940-EZ. In general journal form, record issuance of a check.

Analyze: What is the balance of the *Federal Unemployment Tax Payable* account on January 27, 2008?

Computing and recording premiums on workers' compensation insurance.

◄ **Problem 11.6B**
Objectives 8

The following information is for Uptown Courier and Delivery Service workers' compensation insurance premiums. On January 15, 2007, the company estimated its premium for workers' compensation insurance for the year on the basis of the following data.

Work Classification	Amount of Estimated Wages	Insurance Rates
Office work	$ 96,000	$0.39/$100
Delivery work	290,000	$7.50/$100

INSTRUCTIONS

1. Use the information to compute the estimated premium for the year.

2. A check was issued to pay the estimated premium on January 17, 2007. Record the transaction in general journal form.

3. On January 19, 2008, an audit of the firm's payroll records showed that it had actually paid wages of $99,080 to its office employees and wages of $310,050 to its delivery employees. Compute the actual premium for the year and the balance due the insurance company or the credit due the firm.

4. Give the general journal entry to adjust the *Workers' Compensation Insurance Expense* account. Date the entry December 31, 2007.

Analyze: What is the balance of the *Workers' Compensation Insurance Expense* account at December 31, 2007, after all journal entries have been posted?

Challenge Problem

Determining Employee Status

In each of the following independent situations, decide whether the business organization should treat the person being paid as an employee and should withhold social security, Medicare, and employee income taxes from the payment made.

1. After working several years as an editor for a magazine publisher, Leora quit her job to stay at home with her two small children. Later the publisher asked her to work in her home performing editorial work as needed. Leora is paid an hourly fee for the work she performs. In some cases she goes to the publishing company's offices to pick up or return a manuscript, and in other cases the firm sends a manuscript to her or she returns one by mail. During the current month Leora's hourly earnings totaled $2,250.

2. Ken, a registered nurse, has retired from full-time work. However, because of his experience and special skills, on each Monday, Wednesday, and Thursday afternoon he assists Dr. Wilson Kent, a dermatologist. Ken is paid an hourly fee by Dr. Kent. During the current week, his hourly fees totaled $1,050.

3. Horace Jones owns and operates a crafts shop, using the sole proprietorship form of business. Each week a check for $2,000 is written on the crafts shop's bank account as a salary payment to Jones.

4. Guy Gagliardi is a public stenographer, or court reporter. He has an office at the Metroplex Court Reporting Center but pays no rent. The manager of the center receives requests from attorneys for public stenographers to take depositions at legal hearings. The manager then chooses a stenographer who best meets the needs of the client and contacts the stenographer chosen. The stenographer has the right to refuse to take on the job, and the stenographer

controls his or her working hours and days. Clients make payments to the center, which deducts a 30 percent fee for providing facilities and rendering services to support the stenographer. The balance is paid to the stenographer. During the current month, the center collected fees of $30,000 for Guy, deducted $7,500 for the center's fee, and remitted the proper amount to Guy.

5. Investor Corporation carries on very little business activity. It merely holds land and certain assets. The board of directors has concluded that they need no employees. They have decided instead to pay Sherry Peoples, one of the shareholders, a consulting fee of $15,000 per year to serve as president, secretary, and treasurer and to manage all the affairs of the company. Peoples spends an average of one hour per week on the corporation's business affairs. However, her fee is fixed regardless of how few or how many hours she works.

Analyze: What characteristics do the persons you identified as "employees" have in common?

Critical Thinking Problem

Comparing Employees and Independent Contractors

The *Town Record Chronicle* is a local newspaper that is published Monday through Friday. It sells 90,000 copies daily. The paper is currently in a profit squeeze, and the publisher, Brenda Davis, is looking for ways to reduce expenses.

A review of current distribution procedures reveals that the *Town Record Chronicle* employs 110 truck drivers to drop off bundles of newspapers to 1,300 teenagers who deliver papers to individual homes. The drivers are paid an hourly wage while the teenagers receive 4 cents for each paper they deliver.

Davis is considering an alternative method of distributing the papers, which she says has worked in other cities the size of Flower Mound (where the *Town Record Chronicle* is published). Under the new system, the newspaper would retain 30 truck drivers to transport papers to five distribution centers around the city. The distribution centers are operated by independent contractors who would be responsible for making their own arrangements to deliver papers to subscribers' homes. The 30 drivers retained by the *Town Record Chronicle* would receive the same hourly rate as they currently earn, and the independent contractors would receive 20 cents for each paper delivered.

1. What payroll information does Davis need in order to make a decision about adopting the alternative distribution method?

2. Assume the following information:
   a. The average driver earns $48,000 per year.
   b. Average employee income tax withholding is 18 percent.
   c. The social security tax is 6.2 percent of the first $90,000 of earnings.
   d. The Medicare tax is 1.45 percent of all earnings.
   e. The state unemployment tax is 5 percent, and the federal unemployment tax is 0.8 percent of the first $7,000 of earnings.
   f. Workers' compensation insurance is 70 cents per $100 of wages.
   g. The paper pays $310 per month for health insurance for each driver and contributes $250 per month to each driver's pension plan.
   h. The paper has liability insurance coverage for all teenage carriers that costs $110,000 per year.

   Prepare a schedule showing the costs of distributing the newspapers under the current system and the proposed new system. Based on your analysis, which system would you recommend to Davis?

3. What other factors, monetary and nonmonetary, might influence your decision?

BUSINESS CONNECTIONS

Payroll

Managerial | **FOCUS**

1. Davis Company recently discovered that a payroll clerk had issued checks to nonexistent employees for several years and cashed the checks himself. The firm does not have any internal control procedures for its payroll operations. What specific controls might have led to the discovery of this fraud more quickly or discouraged the payroll clerk from even attempting the fraud?

2. Johnson Company has 20 employees. Some employees work in the office, others in the warehouse, and still others in the retail store. In the company's records, all employees are simply referred to as "general employees." Explain to management why this is not an acceptable practice.

3. Why should management be concerned about the accuracy and promptness of payroll tax deposits and payroll tax returns?

4. What is the significance to management of the experience rating system used to determine the employer's tax under the state unemployment insurance laws?

Ghost Employee

Ethical | **DILEMMA**

Johan Jones owns a dress shop that has been very successful. He employs 3 sales associates who get paid $10 per hour for a 40-hour week. He decides to open up another dress shop on the other side of town. He hires three more sales associates with the same pay arrangements. After three months, Johan notices he is not making the same profit he did. His sales have doubled and his expenses are the same proportion except for wages. He knows that each sales associate should receive $1,720 each month yet his total wages expense for the month is $12,040. He worries that he is not paying close enough attention to the old store. What is his problem? Should he discuss this problem with all the sales associates?

Payroll and Promotions

STREETWISE:
Questions from the
REAL WORLD

Refer to The Home Depot, Inc. *2004 Annual Report* in Appendix A.

1. Locate the consolidated balance sheets. When The Home Depot, Inc. records payroll tax liabilities, which category reflected on the balance sheet most likely contains these obligations?

2. The Home Depot, Inc. employed 325,000 associates at the close of fiscal 2004. According to the company's employment strategies, store managers are rarely recruited externally. Most store managers are promoted from within the organization. Discuss why you think The Home Depot, Inc. employs this strategy. What advantages and disadvantages do you think the company experiences as a result of this procedure?

Income Statement

Financial Statement
| **ANALYSIS**

The following excerpt was taken from H&R Block, Inc.'s consolidated statements of earnings for the year ended April 30, 2004.

H&R BLOCK

H&R Block			
Consolidated Statements of Earnings			
(Amounts in thousands, except per share amounts)			
	Year Ended April 30		
	2004	*2003*	*2002*
Expenses:			
Employee compensation and benefits	1,610,103	1,387,731	1,298,159
Occupancy and equipment	384,622	345,960	305,387
Depreciation and amortization	172,038	161,821	155,386
Marketing and advertising	188,317	150,847	155,729
Interest	84,556	92,644	116,141
Supplies, freight and postage	89,189	88,748	75,710
Impairment of goodwill	–	35,777	–
Other	522,442	502,687	463,761
Total Operating Expenses	3,051,267	2,766,215	2,570,273

Analyze:

1. What percentage of total operating expenses was spent on employee compensation and benefits in the year ended April 30, 2004?

2. Assume that FICA (social security) wages for the first quarter of 2004 were $434,728,000. What deposit did H&R Block send to the federal government for FICA taxes for the quarter? (Assume FICA rate of 6.2%.)

3. By what percentage did employee compensation and benefits increase from the years ended April 30, 2002 to 2003; and 2003 to 2004?

Analyze Online: Find the H&R Block Web site **(www.hrblock.com).** Click Our Company, then Investors. Find the most recent annual report.

4. What percentage of total operating expenses was spent on employee compensation and benefits?

5. Which expense line had the highest percentage increase in the last two years?

Unemployment Insurance

Businesses must pay unemployment insurance taxes required by federal and state agencies. The program provides benefits to unemployed workers. Your business has never fired or laid off an employee, yet you are required to pay the minimum tax rate on gross salaries. Do you agree or disagree with this system? Why?

Memo—Payroll Forms

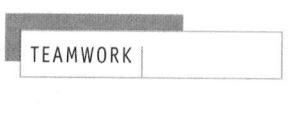

You have opened a new office supply store and plan to hire 10 employees to help with sales, inventory maintenance, and advertising. You would like your payroll clerk to set up his office to prepare for the year's payroll duties. Write a memo to your payroll clerk requesting that he gather all the necessary employee forms, payroll tax return forms, and accounting forms that will be needed for payroll. Include a detailed list of the items that should be gathered.

Determining Information

Wages and payroll tax expense are the largest cost that a company incurs. At times a company has a problem paying wages and cash deposits for payroll taxes. Your company has a cash flow problem. In a group of 4 employees, brainstorm ways to cut the costs of wages and payroll taxes.

Internal Revenue Service

Go to the Internal Revenue Web site at www.irs.gov. Does the Web site contain the necessary federal forms? Can you use these forms to submit your report? What reports must be obtained from the IRS in an original, not downloaded, form?

Answers to **Self Reviews**

Answers to Section 1 Self Review

1. Form W-2 provides information to enable the employees to complete their federal income tax return. Copies are given to the employee and to the federal government (and to other governmental units that levy an income tax).

2. Federal Reserve Bank or a commercial bank that is designated as a federal depository.

3. Form 941 shows income taxes withheld, social security and Medicare taxes due for the quarter, and tax deposits. The form is due on the last day of the month following the end of the quarter.

4. **c.** Social security tax

5. **a.** each payroll period

6. Monthly

Answers to Section 2 Self Review

1. The amount of the premium depends on the type of work the employee performs.
2. The employer pays FUTA. Usually the employer pays SUTA, although a few states also levy SUTA on employees.
3. It reduces the rate of SUTA tax that must actually be paid.
4. **d.** Form 940
5. **b.** quarterly
6. Expenses will be understated. Net income will be overstated.

Answers to Comprehensive Self Review

1. Form W-3 is sent to the Social Security Administration. It reports the total social security wages; total Medicare wages; total social security and Medicare taxes withheld; total wages, tips, and other compensation; total employee income tax withheld; and other information.
2. Smaller
3. A credit, with limits, is allowed against the federal tax for unemployment tax charged by the state.
4. By the 15th day of the following month.
5. **b.** Amount of taxes reported in the lookback period
   d. Amount of taxes currently owed

LEARNING OBJECTIVES

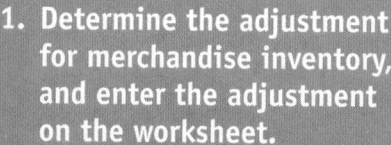

1. Determine the adjustment for merchandise inventory, and enter the adjustment on the worksheet.

2. Compute adjustments for accrued and prepaid expense items, and enter the adjustments on the worksheet.

3. Compute adjustments for accrued and deferred income items, and enter the adjustments on the worksheet.

4. Complete a 10-column worksheet.

5. Define the accounting terms new to this chapter.

NEW TERMS

Accrual basis

Accrued expenses

Accrued income

Deferred expenses

Deferred income

Inventory sheet

Net income line

Prepaid expenses

Property, plant, and equipment

Unearned income

Updated account balances

Chapter 12
Accruals, Deferrals, and the Worksheet

AMERICAN EAGLE OUTFITTERS
ae.com   www.ae.com

Clothing from American Eagle Outfitters is hip, fun, and youthful. American Eagle designs, markets, and sells its own brand of casual, fashion-right clothing for 15- to 25-year-olds, providing high-quality merchandise at affordable prices. AE's collection focuses on wardrobe staples like jeans, khakis, and graphic Ts as well as a stylish assortment of funky accessories, outerwear, footwear, and swimwear.

While overall sales in 2003 reached a record $1.5 billion, store sales declined 7 percent. Managers at American Eagle attributed the decline in store sales to merchandise that was not focused clearly enough on AE's target customer—15- to 25-year-olds. Too sophisticated fashions were blamed for a dip in store sales. AE undertook extensive market research to better understand the expectations of their target customers and made adjustments to their merchandise assortment, boosting sales and profitability.

thinking critically | What types of adjustments do you think the accountants at American Eagle Outfitter recorded as a result of the sales decline the company faced in 2003?

Section 1

SECTION OBJECTIVES

▶ 1. **Determine the adjustment for merchandise inventory, and enter the adjustment on the worksheet.**

   WHY IT'S IMPORTANT

   The change in merchandise inventory affects the financial statements.

▶ 2. **Compute adjustments for accrued and prepaid expense items, and enter the adjustments on the worksheet.**

   WHY IT'S IMPORTANT

   Each expense item needs to be assigned to the accounting period in which it helped to earn revenue.

▶ 3. **Compute adjustments for accrued and deferred income items, and enter the adjustments on the worksheet.**

   WHY IT'S IMPORTANT

   The accrual basis of accounting states that income is recognized in the period it is earned.

TERMS TO LEARN

accrual basis
accrued expenses
accrued income
deferred expenses
deferred income
inventory sheet
prepaid expenses
property, plant, and equipment
unearned income

In Chapter 5 you learned how to make adjustments so that all revenue and expenses that apply to a fiscal period appear on the income statement for that period. In this chapter you will learn more about adjustments and how they affect Simpson Antiques, a retail merchandising business owned by Patricia Simpson.

The Accrual Basis of Accounting

Financial statements usually are prepared using the **accrual basis** of accounting because it most nearly attains the goal of matching expenses and revenue in an accounting period.

- *Revenue is recognized when earned, not necessarily when the cash is received.* Revenue is recognized when the sale is complete. A sale is complete when title to the goods passes to the customer or when the service is provided. For sales on account, revenue is recognized when the sale occurs even though the cash is not collected immediately.

- *Expenses are recognized when incurred or used, not necessarily when cash is paid.* Each expense is assigned to the accounting period in which it helped to earn revenue for the business, even if cash is not paid at that time. This is often referred to as *matching revenues and expenses.*

Sometimes cash changes hands before the revenue or expense is recognized. For example, insurance premiums are normally paid in advance, and the coverage extends over several accounting periods. In other cases cash changes hands after the revenue or expense has been recognized. For example, employees might work during December but be paid in January of the following year. Because of these timing differences, adjustments are made to ensure that revenue and expenses are recognized in the appropriate period.

Using the Worksheet to Record Adjustments

The worksheet is used to assemble data about adjustments and to organize the information for the financial statements. Figure 12.1 on pages 418–419 shows the first two sections of the worksheet for Simpson Antiques. Let's review how to prepare the worksheet.

- Enter the trial balance in the Trial Balance section. Total the columns. Be sure that total debits equal total credits.

- Enter the adjustments in the Adjustments section. Use the same letter to identify the debit part and the credit part of each adjustment. Total the columns. Be sure that total debits equal total credits.

- For each account, combine the amounts in the Trial Balance section and the Adjustments section. Enter the results in the Adjusted Trial Balance section, total the columns, and make sure that total debits equal total credits.

- Extend account balances to the Income Statement and Balance Sheet sections and complete the worksheet.

ADJUSTMENT FOR MERCHANDISE INVENTORY

Merchandise inventory consists of the goods that a business has on hand for sale to customers. An asset account for merchandise inventory is maintained in the general ledger. During the accounting period, all purchases of merchandise are debited to the **Purchases** account. All sales of merchandise are credited to the revenue account **Sales.**

Notice that no entries are made directly to the **Merchandise Inventory** account during the accounting period. Consequently, when the trial balance is prepared at the end of the period, the **Merchandise Inventory** account still shows the *beginning* inventory for the period. At the end of each period a business determines the *ending* balance of the **Merchandise Inventory** account. The first step in determining the ending inventory is to count the number of units of each type of item on hand. As the merchandise is counted, the quantity on hand is entered on an inventory sheet. The **inventory sheet** lists the quantity of each type of goods a firm has in stock. For each item the quantity is multiplied by the unit cost to find the totals per item. The totals for all items are added to compute the total cost of merchandise inventory.

The trial balance for Simpson Antiques shows **Merchandise Inventory** of $52,000. Based on a count taken on December 31, merchandise inventory at the end of the year actually totaled $47,000. Simpson Antiques needs to adjust the **Merchandise Inventory** account to reflect the balance at the end of the year.

The adjustment is made in two steps, using the accounts **Merchandise Inventory** and **Income Summary.**

1. The beginning inventory ($52,000) is taken off the books by transferring the account balance to the **Income Summary** account. This entry is labeled **(a)** on the worksheet in Figure 12.1 and is illustrated in T-account form below.

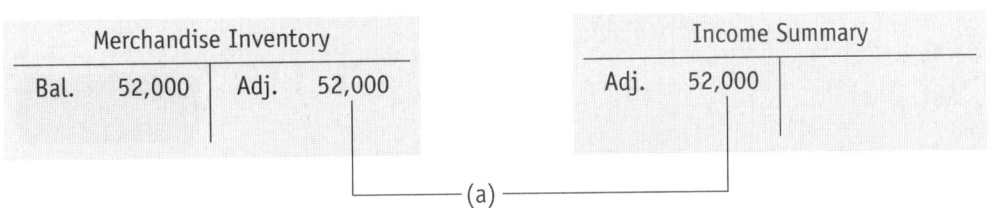

2. The ending inventory ($47,000) is placed on the books by debiting **Merchandise Inventory** and crediting **Income Summary.** This entry is labeled **(b)** on the worksheet in Figure 12.1.

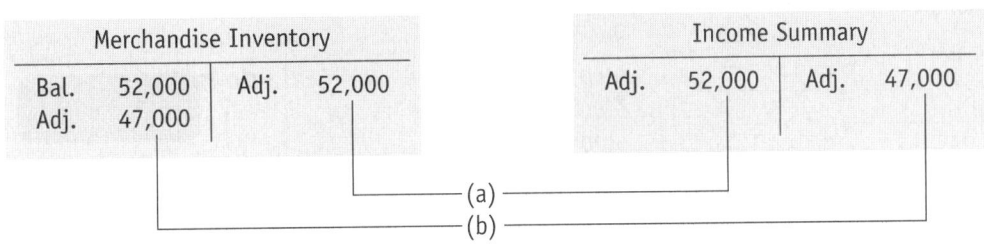

The effect of this adjustment is to remove the beginning merchandise inventory balance and replace it with the ending merchandise inventory balance. Merchandise inventory is adjusted in two steps on the worksheet because both the beginning and the ending inventory figures appear on the income statement, which is prepared directly from the worksheet.

important!

Recognize
The word "recognize" means to record in the accounting records.

▶ 1. **OBJECTIVE**
    Determine the adjustment for merchandise inventory, and enter the adjustment on the worksheet.

Topic Tackler

PLUS

recall

Income Summary
The **Income Summary** account is a temporary owner's equity account used in the closing process.

FIGURE 12.1 | **10-Column Worksheet—Partial**

Simpson Antiques

Worksheet

Year Ended December 31, 2007

	ACCOUNT NAME	TRIAL BALANCE		ADJUSTMENTS	
		DEBIT	CREDIT	DEBIT	CREDIT
1	Cash	13 1 3 6 00			
2	Petty Cash Fund	1 0 0 00			
3	Notes Receivable	1 2 0 0 00			
4	Accounts Receivable	32 0 0 0 00			
5	Allowance for Doubtful Accounts		2 5 0 00		(c) 8 0 0 00
6	Interest Receivable			(m) 3 0 00	
7	Merchandise Inventory	52 0 0 0 00		(b) 47 0 0 0 00	(a) 52 0 0 0 00
8	Prepaid Insurance	7 3 5 0 00			(k) 2 4 5 0 00
9	Prepaid Interest	2 2 5 00			(l) 1 5 0 00
10	Supplies	6 3 0 0 00			(j) 4 9 7 5 00
11	Store Equipment	30 0 0 0 00			
12	Accumulated Depreciation—Store Equipment				(d) 2 4 0 0 00
13	Office Equipment	5 0 0 0 00			
14	Accumulated Depreciation—Office Equipment				(e) 7 0 0 00
15	Notes Payable—Trade		2 0 0 0 00		
16	Notes Payable—Bank		9 0 0 0 00		
17	Accounts Payable		24 1 2 9 00		
18	Interest Payable				(i) 2 0 00
19	Social Security Tax Payable		1 0 8 4 00		(g) 7 4 40
20	Medicare Tax Payable		2 5 0 00		(g) 1 7 40
21	Employee Income Taxes Payable		9 9 0 00		
22	Federal Unemployment Tax Payable				(h) 9 60
23	State Unemployment Tax Payable				(h) 6 4 80
24	Salaries Payable				(f) 1 2 0 0 00
25	Sales Tax Payable		7 2 0 0 00	(n) 2 1 6 00	
26	Patricia Simpson, Capital		61 2 2 1 00		
27	Patricia Simpson, Drawing	27 6 0 0 00			
28	Income Summary			(a) 52 0 0 0 00	(b) 47 0 0 0 00
29	Sales		561 6 5 0 00		
30	Sales Returns and Allowances	12 5 0 0 00			
31	Interest Income		1 3 6 00		(m) 3 0 00
32	Miscellaneous Income		3 6 6 00		(n) 2 1 6 00
33	Purchases	321 5 0 0 00			
34	Freight In	9 8 0 0 00			
35	Purchases Returns and Allowances		3 0 5 0 00		
36	Purchase Discounts		3 1 3 0 00		
37	Salaries Expense—Sales	78 4 9 0 00		(f) 1 2 0 0 00	
38	Advertising Expense	7 4 2 5 00			
39	Cash Short or Over	1 2 5 00			
40	Supplies Expense			(j) 4 9 7 5 00	

FIGURE 12.1 | (concluded) 10-Column Worksheet—Partial

	ACCOUNT NAME	TRIAL BALANCE		ADJUSTMENTS	
		DEBIT	CREDIT	DEBIT	CREDIT
41	Depreciation Expense—Store Equipment			(d) 2 4 0 0 00	
42	Rent Expense	27 6 0 0 00			
43	Salaries Expense—Office	26 5 0 0 00			
44	Insurance Expense			(k) 2 4 5 0 00	
45	Payroll Taxes Expense	7 2 0 5 00		(g) 9 1 80	
46				(h) 7 4 40	
47	Telephone Expense	1 8 7 5 00			
48	Uncollectible Accounts Expense			(c) 8 0 0 00	
49	Utilities Expense	5 9 2 5 00			
50	Depreciation Expense—Office Equipment			(e) 7 0 0 00	
51	Interest Expense	6 0 0 00		(i) 2 0 00	
52				(l) 1 5 0 00	
53	Totals	674 4 5 6 00	674 4 5 6 00	112 1 0 7 20	112 1 0 7 20

ADJUSTMENT FOR LOSS FROM UNCOLLECTIBLE ACCOUNTS

Credit sales are made with the expectation that the customers will pay the amount due later. Sometimes the account receivable is never collected. Losses from uncollectible accounts are classified as operating expenses.

Under accrual accounting, the expense for uncollectible accounts is recorded in the same period as the related sale. The expense is estimated because the actual amount of uncollectible accounts is not known until later periods. To match the expense for uncollectible accounts with the sales revenue for the same period, the estimated expense is debited to an account named **Uncollectible Accounts Expense.**

Several methods exist for estimating the expense for uncollectible accounts. Simpson Antiques uses the *percentage of net credit sales* method. The rate used is based on the company's past experience with uncollectible accounts and management's assessment of current business conditions. Simpson Antiques estimates that four-fifths of 1 percent (0.80 percent) of net credit sales will be uncollectible. Net credit sales for the year were $100,000. The estimated expense for uncollectible accounts is $800 ($100,000 × 0.0080).

The entry to record the expense for uncollectible accounts includes a credit to a contra asset account, **Allowance for Doubtful Accounts.** This account appears on the balance sheet as follows.

Accounts Receivable	$32,000
Allowance for Doubtful Accounts ($800 + $250)	1,050
Net Accounts Receivable	$30,950

Adjustment **(c)** appears on the worksheet in Figure 12-1 for the expense for uncollectible accounts.

Uncollectible Accounts Expense		Allowance for Doubtful Accounts	
Adj. 800			Bal. 250
			Adj. 800

(c)

▶ 2. OBJECTIVE
Compute adjustments for accrued and prepaid expense items, and enter the adjustments on the worksheet.

THE BOTTOM LINE
Uncollectible Accounts Expense

Income Statement
| Expenses | ↑ 800 |
| Net income | ↓ 800 |

Balance Sheet
| Assets | ↓ 800 |
| Equity | ↓ 800 |

When a specific account becomes uncollectible, it is written off.

■ The entry is a debit to *Allowance for Doubtful Accounts* and a credit to *Accounts Receivable.*

■ The customer's account in the accounts receivable subsidiary ledger is also reduced.

Uncollectible Accounts Expense is not affected by the write-off of individual accounts identified as uncollectible. It is used only when the end-of-period adjustment is recorded.

Notice that net income is decreased at the end of the period when the adjustment for *estimated* expense for uncollectible accounts is made. When a specific customer account is written off, net income is *not* affected. The write-off of a specific account affects only the balance sheet accounts *Accounts Receivable* (asset) and *Allowance for Doubtful Accounts* (contra asset).

The balance of *Allowance for Doubtful Accounts* is reduced throughout the year as customer accounts are written off. Notice that *Allowance for Doubtful Accounts* already has a credit balance of $250 in the Trial Balance section of the worksheet. When the estimate of uncollectible accounts expense is based on sales, any remaining balance from previous periods is not considered when recording the adjustment.

ADJUSTMENTS FOR DEPRECIATION

Most businesses have long-term assets that are used in the operation of the business. These are often referred to as **property, plant, and equipment** . Property, plant, and equipment includes buildings, trucks, automobiles, machinery, furniture, fixtures, office equipment, and land.

Property, plant, and equipment costs are not charged to expense accounts when purchased. Instead, the cost of a long-term asset is allocated over the asset's expected useful life by depreciation. This process involves the gradual transfer of acquisition cost to expense. There is one exception. Land is not depreciated.

There are many ways to calculate depreciation. Simpson Antiques uses the straight-line method, so an equal amount of depreciation is taken in each year of the asset's useful life. The formula for straight-line depreciation is

$$\frac{\text{Cost} - \text{Salvage value}}{\text{Estimated useful life}} = \text{Depreciation}$$

Salvage value is an estimate of the amount that could be obtained from the sale or disposition of an asset at the end of its useful life. Cost minus salvage value is called the *depreciable base.*

Depreciation of Store Equipment The trial balance shows that Simpson Antiques has $30,000 of store equipment. Estimated salvage value is $6,000. What is the amount of annual depreciation expense using the straight-line method?

Cost of store equipment	$30,000
Salvage value	(6,000)
Depreciable base	$24,000
Expected useful life	10 years

$$\frac{\$30,000 - \$6,000}{10 \text{ years}} = \$2,400 \text{ per year}$$

The annual depreciation expense is $2,400. Adjustment **(d)** appears on the worksheet in Figure 12.1 for the depreciation expense for store equipment.

important!

Depreciation

To calculate monthly straight-line depreciation, divide the depreciable base by the number of months in the useful life.

Depr. Expense—Store Equipment		Accum. Depr.—Store Equipment	
Adj. 2,400			Adj. 2,400

(d)

Depreciation of Office Equipment Simpson Antiques reports $5,000 of office equipment on the trial balance. What is the amount of annual depreciation expense using the straight-line method if estimated salvage value is $800 and estimated life is 6 years?

Cost of office equipment	$5,000
Salvage value	(800)
Depreciable base	$4,200
Expected useful life	6 years

$$\frac{\$5,000 - \$800}{6 \text{ Years}} = \$700 \text{ per year}$$

Annual depreciation expense is $700. Adjustment **(e)** appears on the worksheet in Figure 12.1 for depreciation expense for office equipment.

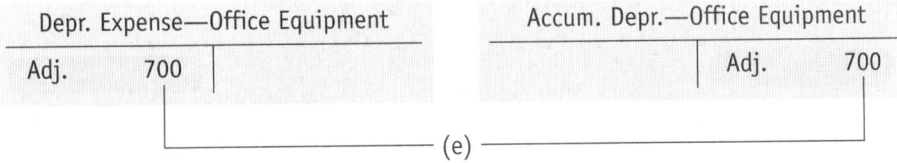

Depr. Expense—Office Equipment		Accum. Depr.—Office Equipment
Adj. 700		Adj. 700

— (e) —

ADJUSTMENTS FOR ACCRUED EXPENSES

Many expense items are paid for, recorded, and used in the same accounting period. However, some expense items are paid for and recorded in one period but used in a later period. Other expense items are used in one period and paid for in a later period. In these situations adjustments are made so that the financial statements show all expenses in the appropriate period.

Accrued expenses are expenses that relate to (are used in) the current period but have not yet been paid and do not yet appear in the accounting records. Simpson Antiques makes adjustments for three types of accrued expenses:

- accrued salaries
- accrued payroll taxes
- accrued interest on notes payable

Because accrued expenses involve amounts that must be paid in the future, the adjustment for each item is a debit to an expense account and a credit to a liability account.

Accrued Salaries At Simpson Antiques all full-time sales and office employees are paid semimonthly—on the 15th and the last day of the month. The trial balance in Figure 12.1 shows the correct salaries expense for the full-time employees for the year. From December 28 to January 3, the firm hired several part-time sales clerks for the year-end sale. Through December 31, 2007, these employees earned $1,200. The part-time salaries expense has not yet been recorded because the employees will not be paid until January 3, 2008. An adjustment is made to record the amount owed, but not yet paid, as of the end of December.

Adjustment **(f)** appears on the worksheet in Figure 12.1 for accrued salaries.

Salaries Expense—Sales		Salaries Payable
Adj. 1,200		Adj. 1,200

— (f) —

Accrued Payroll Taxes Payroll taxes are not legally owed until the salaries are paid. Businesses that want to match revenue and expenses in the appropriate period make adjustments to accrue the employer's payroll taxes even though the taxes are technically not yet due. Simpson Antiques makes adjustments for accrued employer's payroll taxes.

important!

Matching

Adjustments for accrued expenses match the expense to the period in which the expense was used.

The payroll taxes related to the full-time employees of Simpson Antiques have been recorded and appear on the trial balance. However, the payroll taxes for the part-time sales clerks have not been recorded. None of the part-time clerks have reached the social security wage base limit. The entire $1,200 of accrued salaries is subject to the employer's share of social security and Medicare taxes. The accrued employer's payroll taxes are

Social security tax	$1,200	×	0.0620	=	$74.40
Medicare tax	$1,200	×	0.0145	=	17.40
Total accrued payroll taxes					$91.80

Adjustment (g) appears on the worksheet in Figure 12.1 for accrued payroll taxes.

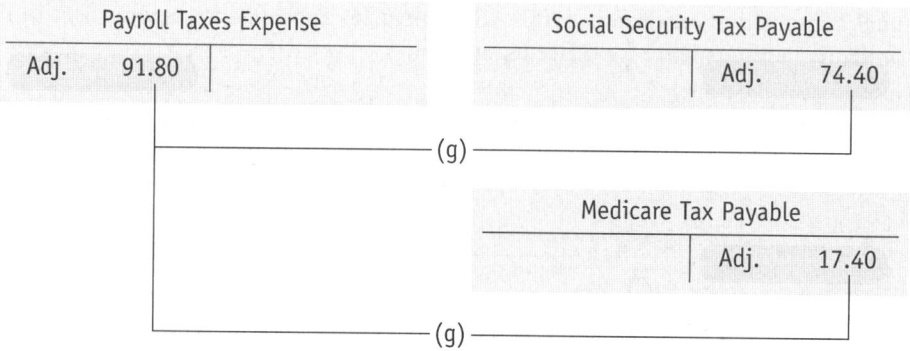

The entire $1,200 of accrued salaries is also subject to unemployment taxes. The unemployment tax rates for Simpson Antiques are 0.8 percent for federal and 5.4 percent for state.

Federal unemployment tax	$1,200	×	0.008	=	$ 9.60
State unemployment tax	$1,200	×	0.054	=	64.80
Total accrued taxes					$74.40

Adjustment (h) appears on the worksheet in Figure 12.1 for accrued unemployment taxes.

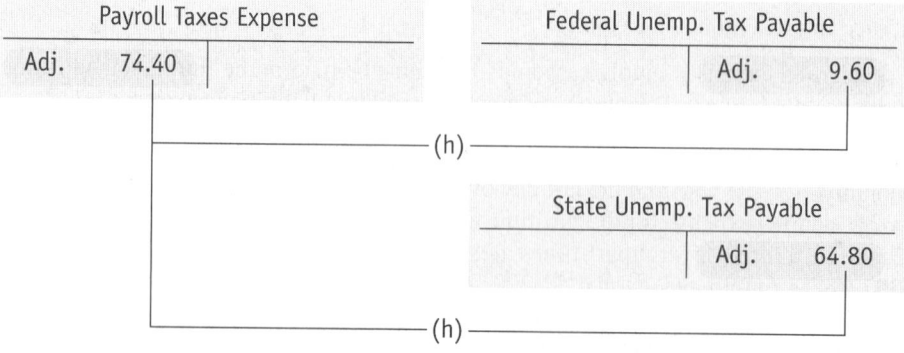

Accrued Interest on Notes Payable On December 1, 2007, Simpson Antiques issued a two-month note for $2,000, with annual interest of 12 percent. The note was recorded in the *Notes Payable—Trade* account. Simpson Antiques will pay the interest when the note matures on February 1, 2008. However, the interest expense is incurred day by day and should be allocated to each fiscal period involved in order to obtain a complete and accurate picture of expenses. The accrued interest amount is determined by using the interest formula *Principal* × *Rate* × *Time*.

| **Principal** | × | **Rate** | × | **Time** | | |
| $2,000 | × | 0.12 | × | 1/12 | = | $20 |

The fraction $\frac{1}{12}$ represents one month, which is 1/12 of a year.

Adjustment **(i)** appears on the worksheet in Figure 12.1 for the accrued interest expense.

Interest Expense			Interest Payable	
Adj.	20		Adj.	20

———————————— (i) ————————————

Other Accrued Expenses Most businesses pay property taxes to state and local governments. They accrue these taxes at the end of the accounting period. Adjustments might also be necessary for commissions, professional services, and many other accrued expenses.

ADJUSTMENTS FOR PREPAID EXPENSES

Prepaid expenses, or **deferred expenses,** are expenses that are paid for and recorded before they are used. Often a portion of a prepaid item remains unused at the end of the period; it is applicable to future periods. When paid for, these items are recorded as assets. At the end of the period, an adjustment is made to recognize as an expense the portion used during the period. Simpson Antiques makes adjustments for three types of prepaid expenses:

- prepaid supplies
- prepaid insurance
- prepaid interest on notes payable

> In its balance sheet for 2003, American Eagle Outfitters reported total current liabilities of $189.035 million. Included in that total were these items (all expressed in millions of dollars): Accounts Payable, $71.33; Current Portion of Note Payable, $4.832; Accrued Compensation and Payroll Taxes, $14.409; Accrued Rent, $30.985; Accrued Income and Other Taxes, $28.669; Unredeemed Stored Value Cards and Gift Certificates, $25.785; Other Liabilities and Accrued Expenses, $13.025.

Supplies Used When supplies are purchased, they are debited to the asset account **Supplies.** On the trial balance in Figure 12.1, **Supplies** has a balance of $6,300. A physical count on December 31 showed $1,325 of supplies on hand. This means that $4,975 ($6,300 − $1,325) of supplies were used during the year. An adjustment is made to charge the cost of supplies used to the current year's operations and to reflect the value of the supplies on hand.

Adjustment **(j)** appears on the worksheet in Figure 12.1 for supplies expense.

Supplies Expense			Supplies			
Adj.	4,975		Bal.	6,300	Adj.	4,975

———————————— (j) ————————————

Expired Insurance On January 2, 2007, Simpson Antiques wrote a check for $7,350 for a three-year insurance policy. The asset account **Prepaid Insurance** was debited for $7,350. On December 31, 2007, one year of insurance had expired. An adjustment for $2,450 ($7,350 × 1/3) was made to charge the cost of the expired insurance to operations and to decrease **Prepaid Insurance** to reflect the prepaid insurance premium that remains.

Adjustment **(k)** appears on the worksheet in Figure 12.1 for the insurance.

Insurance Expense			Prepaid Insurance			
Adj.	2,450		Bal.	7,350	Adj.	2,450

———————————— (k) ————————————

Prepaid Interest on Notes Payable On November 1, 2007, Simpson Antiques borrowed $9,000 from its bank and signed a three-month note at an annual interest rate of 10 percent. The bank deducted the entire amount of interest in advance. The interest for three months is $225.

Principal	×	Rate	×	Time		
$9,000	×	0.10	×	3/12	=	$225

Simpson Antiques received $8,775 ($9,000 − $225). The transaction was recorded as a debit to *Cash* for $8,775, a debit to *Prepaid Interest* for $225, and a credit to *Notes Payable—Bank* for $9,000.

On December 31 two months of prepaid interest ($225 × 2/3 = $150) had been incurred and needed to be recorded as an expense. The adjustment consists of a debit to *Interest Expense* and a credit to *Prepaid Interest.*

Adjustment (**l**) appears on the worksheet in Figure 12.1 for the interest expense.

Interest Expense			Prepaid Interest			
Adj.	150		Bal.	225	Adj.	150

——————————————————— (l) ———————————————————

Other Prepaid Expenses Other common prepaid expenses are prepaid rent, prepaid advertising, and prepaid taxes. When paid, the amounts are debited to the asset accounts *Prepaid Rent, Prepaid Advertising,* and *Prepaid Taxes.* At the end of each period, an adjustment is made to transfer the portion used from the asset account to an expense account. For example, the adjustment for expired rent would be a debit to *Rent Expense* and a credit to *Prepaid Rent.*

Alternative Method Some businesses use a different method for prepaid expenses. At the time cash is paid, they debit an expense account (not an asset account). At the end of each period, they make an adjustment to transfer the portion that is not used from the expense account to an asset account.

Suppose that Simpson used this alternative method when she purchased the two-year insurance policy. On January 1, 2007, the transaction would have been recorded as a debit to *Insurance Expense* for $7,350 and a credit to *Cash* for $7,350. On December 31, 2007, after the insurance coverage for one year had expired, coverage for two years remained. The adjustment would be recorded as a debit to *Prepaid Insurance* for $4,900 ($7,350 × 2/3) and a credit to *Insurance Expense* for $4,900.

Identical amounts appear on the financial statements at the end of each fiscal period no matter which method is used to handle prepaid expenses.

ADJUSTMENTS FOR ACCRUED INCOME

Accrued income is income that has been earned but not yet received and recorded. On December 31, 2007, Simpson Antiques had two types of accrued income: accrued interest on notes receivable and accrued commission on sales tax.

Accrued Interest on Notes Receivable Interest-bearing notes receivable are recorded at face value and are carried in the accounting records at this value until they are collected. The interest income is recorded when it is received, which is normally when the note matures. However, interest income is earned day by day. At the end of the period, an adjustment is made to recognize interest income earned but not yet received or recorded.

On November 1, 2007, Simpson Antiques accepted from a customer a four-month, 15 percent note for $1,200. The note and interest are due on March 1, 2008. As of December 31, 2007, two months (November and December) of interest income was earned but not received. The amount of earned interest income is $30.

Principal	×	Rate	×	Time		
$1,200	×	0.15	×	2/12	=	$30

---

important!

Some assets and liabilities always require adjustments Although prepaid expenses are usually charged to an asset account when they are paid, some businesses charge most prepayments to expense. In either case, at the time financial statements are prepared the accounts must be adjusted to show the correct expense and prepayment.

▶ **3. OBJECTIVE**

Compute adjustments for accrued and deferred income items, and enter the adjustments on the worksheet.

BUSINESS & ADMINISTRATION

Industry Overview

Business and administration services extend into every sector of the economy. The coordination and support of business operations is required in organizations ranging from insurance firms to government offices, steel manufacturers to retail stores.

Career Opportunities

- Account Executive
- Cost Accountant
- Payroll Supervisor
- Human Resources Manager
- Facility Manager
- Contract Administrator
- Chief Financial Officer

Preparing for a Career in Business & Administration

- Develop solid communication and analytical skills. Be flexible, decisive, and capable of coordinating many activities at once. Develop strategies to cope with deadlines.
- Attain certification specific to your area of interest. For example, the Certified Administrative Manager (CAM) is offered by the Institute of Certified Professional Managers.

- Complete a bachelor's degree with a major in accounting, finance, management, management information systems, marketing, or production and operations management.
- Become proficient in database, spreadsheet, and word processing applications.
- Complete a degree in engineering, architecture, business administration, or facility management for a career as a facility manager.
- Become familiar with basic office equipment such as fax machines, telephone systems, and personal computers.
- Gain a solid understanding of standard business forms such as purchase orders, invoices, contracts, and packing slips.
- Be prepared to interpret and analyze financial statements to effectively contribute to business discussions and decisions.

THINKING CRITICALLY

Describe 10 business tasks or responsibilities involved in the operation of Southwest Airlines Co. or a similar company.

INTERNET APPLICATION

The Internet contains a wealth of information provided to help individuals as they launch new businesses. Using an Internet search engine, list five resources that offer entrepreneurs guidance on their new endeavors. Describe the information or resources offered at each Web site.

Adjustment **(m)** appears on the worksheet in Figure 12.1 for the interest income. To record the interest income of $30 earned, but not yet received, an adjustment debiting the asset account **Interest Receivable** and crediting a revenue account called **Interest Income** is made.

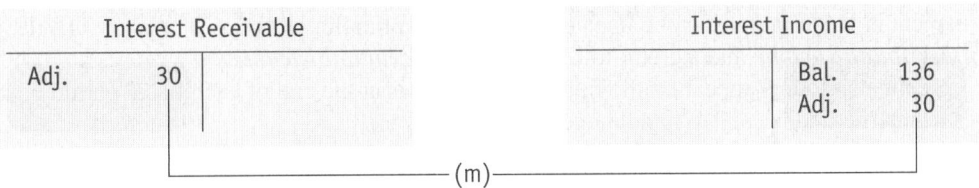

(m)

Accrued Commission on Sales Tax Simpson Antiques collects sales tax on retail sales. It sends the tax to the state agency on a quarterly basis. The state sales tax law allows firms that file the quarterly tax returns and pay the tax promptly to keep 3 percent of the tax. On December 31, 2007, Simpson Antiques owed $7,200 of sales tax. In January the tax will be paid less the permitted commission of $216 ($7,200 \times 0.03$). The commission represents income earned and is recorded in the **Miscellaneous Income** account.

Adjustment **(n)** appears on the worksheet in Figure 12.1. The adjustment decreases the sales tax liability.

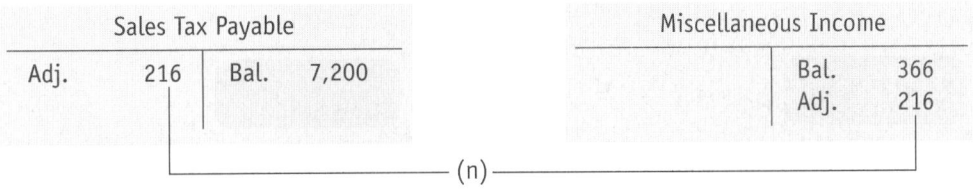

(n)

ADJUSTMENTS FOR UNEARNED INCOME

Unearned income, or **deferred income,** exists when income is received before it is earned. Under the accrual basis of accounting, only income that has been earned appears on the income statement. Simpson Antiques has no unearned income. The following is an example of unearned income for another business.

Unearned Subscription Income for a Publisher Magazine publishers receive cash in advance for subscriptions. When the publisher receives the cash, it is unearned income and is a liability. It is a liability because the publisher has an obligation to provide magazines during the subscription period. As the magazines are sent to the subscribers, income is earned and the liability decreases.

Tech Publishing Corporation publishes *Consumer Technology Today.* When subscriptions are received, **Cash** is debited and **Unearned Subscription Income,** a liability account, is credited. At the end of the year, **Unearned Subscription Income** had a balance of $450,000. During the year $184,000 of magazines were delivered; income was earned in the amount of $184,000. The adjustment to recognize income is a debit to **Unearned Subscription Income** for $184,000 and a credit to **Subscription Income** for $184,000.

After the adjustment the **Unearned Subscription Income** account has a balance of $266,000, which represents subscriptions for future periods.

Unearned Subscription Income			
		12/31 Bal.	450,000
12/31 Adj.	184,000		
		12/31 Bal.	266,000

Other Unearned Income Items Other types of unearned income include management fees, rental income, legal fees, architectural fees, construction fees, and advertising income. The cash received in advance is recorded as unearned income. As the income is earned, the amount is transferred from the liability account to a revenue account.

Alternative Method Some businesses use a different method to handle unearned income. At the time the cash is received, a credit is made to a revenue account (not a liability account). At the end of each period, the adjustment transfers the portion that is not earned to a liability account. For example, suppose Tech Publishing Corporation uses this method. When cash for subscriptions is received, it is credited to **Subscription Income.** At the end of the period, an adjustment is made to transfer the unearned income to a liability account. The entry is a debit to **Subscription Income** and a credit to **Unearned Subscription Income.**

Identical amounts appear on the financial statements at the end of each fiscal period no matter which method is used to handle unearned income.

recall

Two Ways to Record Transactions

Earlier in this chapter you learned that prepaid expenses are usually charged to an asset account when paid, but may be charged to an expense account at that time. Likewise, unearned income is usually credited to a liability account when received, but may be credited to an income account. Be sure to understand how the transaction was originally entered before you begin making the adjusting entry.

Section 1: **Self Review**

QUESTIONS

1. Why is a 10-column worksheet used as part of the procedures for adjusting and closing accounts and preparing financial statements?

2. Why are there two amounts (a debit and a credit) in the adjustments column on the line for Merchandise Inventory in the 10-column worksheet?

3. Why are adjusting entries necessary?

EXERCISES

4. Samek Company adjusts and closes its accounts and prepares financial statements each month. In the December 31 Trial Balance column for debit balances, a balance of $6,000 is found in the Prepaid Rent account. A payment of $12,000 for prepayment of six months' rent was made on September 1.

    a. What is the amount of the adjusting entry for this item?

    b. What account would be debited and what account would be credited in the December 31 adjustments?

5. In Samek's December 31 trial balance, a credit balance of $14,000 appears in Unearned Fee Income. This amount represents a part of $21,000 received from a customer on November 1 covering work to be performed by Samek in November through January. What account will be debited and what account will be credited in the adjusting entry on December 31? What is the amount of the adjustment?

ANALYSIS

6. Your company prepares financial statements each month, using a 10-column worksheet to assemble data. What is the primary difference between the adjustments made on a monthly basis and those made on an annual basis?

(Answers to Section 1 Self Review are on page 451.)

Section 2

SECTION OBJECTIVE

▶ **4. Complete a 10-column worksheet.**

WHY IT'S IMPORTANT

Using the worksheet is a convenient way to gather the information needed for the financial statements.

TERMS TO LEARN

net income line

updated account balances

▶ 4. **OBJECTIVE**

Complete a 10-column worksheet.

Completing the Worksheet

After all adjustments have been entered on the worksheet, total the Adjustments Debit and Credit columns and verify that debits and credits are equal. The next step in the process is to prepare the Adjusted Trial Balance section.

Preparing the Adjusted Trial Balance Section

Figure 12.2 on pages 530–531 shows the completed worksheet for Simpson Antiques. The Adjusted Trial Balance section of the worksheet is completed as follows.

1. Combine the amount in the Trial Balance section and the Adjustments section for each account.

2. Enter the results in the Adjusted Trial Balance section. The accounts that do not have adjustments are simply extended from the Trial Balance section to the Adjusted Trial Balance section. For example, the balance of the *Cash* account is recorded in the Debit column of the Adjusted Trial Balance section without change.

3. The accounts that are affected by adjustments are recomputed. Follow these rules to combine amounts on the worksheet.

Trial Balance Section	Adjustments Section	Action
Debit	Debit	Add
Debit	Credit	Subtract
Credit	Credit	Add
Credit	Debit	Subtract

- If the account has a debit balance in the Trial Balance section and a debit entry in the Adjustments section, add the two amounts. Look at the *Salaries Expense—Sales* account. It has a $78,490 debit balance in the Trial Balance section and a $1,200 debit entry in the Adjustments section. The new balance is $79,690 ($78,490 + $1,200). It is entered in the Debit column of the Adjusted Trial Balance section.

- If the account has a debit balance in the Trial Balance section and a credit entry in the Adjustments section, subtract the credit amount. Look at the *Supplies* account. It has a $6,300 debit balance in the Trial Balance section and a $4,975 credit entry in the Adjustments section. The new balance is $1,325 ($6,300 − $4,975). It is entered in the Debit column of the Adjusted Trial Balance section.

- If the account has a credit balance in the Trial Balance section and a credit entry in the Adjustments section, add the two amounts. Look at *Allowance for Doubtful Accounts.* It has a $250 credit balance in the Trial Balance section and a $800 credit entry in the Adjustments section. The new balance is $1,050 ($250 + $800). It is entered in the Credit column of the Adjusted Trial Balance section.

- If the account has a credit balance in the Trial Balance section and a debit entry in the Adjustments section, subtract the debit amount. Look at the *Sales Tax Payable* account. It has a $7,200 Credit balance in the Trial Balance section and a $216 debit entry in the Adjustments section. The new balance is $6,984 ($7,200 − $216). It is entered in the Credit column of the Adjusted Trial Balance section.

The Adjusted Trial Balance section now contains the **updated account balances** that will be used in preparing the financial statements.

Look at the *Income Summary* account. Recall that the debit entry in this account removed the *beginning* balance from *Merchandise Inventory* and the credit entry added the *ending* balance to *Merchandise Inventory.* (See pages 530–531.) Notice that the debit and credit amounts in *Income Summary* are not combined in the Adjusted Trial Balance section.

Once all the updated account balances have been entered in the Adjusted Trial Balance section, total and rule the columns. Confirm that total debits equal total credits.

Preparing the Balance Sheet and Income Statement Sections

To complete the Income Statement and Balance Sheet sections of the worksheet, identify the accounts that appear on the balance sheet. On Figure 12.2 the accounts from *Cash* through *Patricia Simpson, Drawing* appear on the balance sheet. For each account enter the amount in the appropriate Debit or Credit column of the Balance Sheet section of the worksheet.

For accounts that appear on the income statement, *Sales* through *Interest Expense,* enter the amounts in the appropriate Debit or Credit column of the Income Statement section. The *Income Summary* debit and credit amounts are also entered in the Income Statement section of the worksheet. Notice that the debit and credit amounts in *Income Summary* are not combined in the Income Statement section.

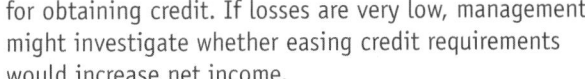

MANAGERIAL IMPLICATIONS

EFFECT OF ADJUSTMENTS ON FINANCIAL STATEMENTS

- If managers are to know the true revenue, expenses, and net income or net loss for a period, the matching process is necessary.
- If accounts are not adjusted, the financial statements will be incomplete, misleading, and of little help in evaluating operations.
- Managers need to be familiar with the procedures and underlying assumptions used by the accountant to make adjustments because adjustments increase or decrease net income.
- Managers need information about uncollectible accounts expense in order to review the firm's credit policy. If losses are too high, management might tighten the requirements

for obtaining credit. If losses are very low, management might investigate whether easing credit requirements would increase net income.

- The worksheet is a useful device for gathering data about adjustments and for preparing the financial statements.
- Managers are keenly interested in receiving timely financial statements, especially the income statement, which shows the results of operations.
- Managers are also interested in the prompt preparation of the balance sheet because it shows the financial position of the business at the end of the period.

THINKING CRITICALLY

What are some possible consequences of not making adjusting entries?

Simpson Antiques

Worksheet

Year Ended December 31, 2007

	ACCOUNT NAME	TRIAL BALANCE DEBIT	TRIAL BALANCE CREDIT	ADJUSTMENTS DEBIT	ADJUSTMENTS CREDIT
1	Cash	13 136 00			
2	Petty Cash Fund	100 00			
3	Notes Receivable	1 200 00			
4	Accounts Receivable	32 000 00			
5	Allowance for Doubtful Accounts		250 00		(c) 800 00
6	Interest Receivable			(m) 30 00	
7	Merchandise Inventory	52 000 00		(b) 47 000 00	(a) 52 000 00
8	Prepaid Insurance	7 350 00			(k) 2 450 00
9	Prepaid Interest	225 00			(l) 150 00
10	Supplies	6 300 00			(j) 4 975 00
11	Store Equipment	30 000 00			
12	Accumulated Depreciation—Store Equipment				(d) 2 400 00
13	Office Equipment	5 000 00			
14	Accumulated Depreciation—Office Equipment				(e) 700 00
15	Notes Payable—Trade		2 000 00		
16	Notes Payable—Bank		9 000 00		
17	Accounts Payable		24 129 00		
18	Interest Payable				(i) 20 00
19	Social Security Tax Payable		1 084 00		(g) 74 40
20	Medicare Tax Payable		250 00		(g) 17 40
21	Employee Income Taxes Payable		990 00		
22	Federal Unemployment Tax Payable				(h) 9 60
23	State Unemployment Tax Payable				(h) 64 80
24	Salaries Payable				(f) 1 200 00
25	Sales Tax Payable		7 200 00	(n) 216 00	
26	Patricia Simpson, Capital		61 221 00		
27	Patricia Simpson, Drawing	27 600 00			
28	Income Summary			(a) 52 000 00	(b) 47 000 00
29	Sales		561 650 00		
30	Sales Returns and Allowances	12 500 00			
31	Interest Income		136 00		(m) 30 00
32	Miscellaneous Income		366 00		(n) 216 00
33	Purchases	321 500 00			
34	Freight In	9 800 00			
35	Purchases Returns and Allowances		3 050 00		
36	Purchase Discounts		3 130 00		
37	Salaries Expense—Sales	78 490 00		(f) 1 200 00	
38	Advertising Expense	7 425 00			
39	Cash Short or Over	125 00			
40	Supplies Expense			(j) 4 975 00	

FIGURE 12.2 Ten-Column Worksheet—Complete

ADJUSTED TRIAL BALANCE		INCOME STATEMENT		BALANCE SHEET		
DEBIT	CREDIT	DEBIT	CREDIT	DEBIT	CREDIT	
13 1 3 6 00				13 1 3 6 00		1
1 0 0 00				1 0 0 00		2
1 2 0 0 00				1 2 0 0 00		3
32 0 0 0 00				32 0 0 0 00		4
	1 0 5 0 00				1 0 5 0 00	5
	3 0 00				3 0 00	6
47 0 0 0 00				47 0 0 0 00		7
4 9 0 0 00				4 9 0 0 00		8
	7 5 00				7 5 00	9
1 3 2 5 00				1 3 2 5 00		10
30 0 0 0 00				30 0 0 0 00		11
	2 4 0 0 00				2 4 0 0 00	12
5 0 0 0 00				5 0 0 0 00		13
	7 0 0 00				7 0 0 00	14
	2 0 0 0 00				2 0 0 0 00	15
	9 0 0 0 00				9 0 0 0 00	16
	24 1 2 9 00				24 1 2 9 00	17
	2 00				2 00	18
	1 1 5 8 40				1 1 5 8 40	19
	2 6 7 40				2 6 7 40	20
	9 9 0 00				9 9 0 00	21
	9 60				9 60	22
	6 4 80				6 4 80	23
	1 2 0 0 00				1 2 0 0 00	24
	6 9 8 4 00				6 9 8 4 00	25
	61 2 2 1 00				61 2 2 1 00	26
27 6 0 0 00				27 6 0 0 00		27
52 0 0 0 00	47 0 0 0 00	52 0 0 0 00	47 0 0 0 00			28
	561 6 5 0 00		561 6 5 0 00			29
12 5 0 0 00		12 5 0 0 00				30
	1 6 6 00		1 6 6 00			31
	5 8 2 00		5 8 2 00			32
321 5 0 0 00		321 5 0 0 00				33
9 8 0 0 00		9 8 0 0 00				34
	3 0 5 0 00		3 0 5 0 00			35
	3 1 3 0 00		3 1 3 0 00			36
79 6 9 0 00		79 6 9 0 00				37
7 4 2 5 00		7 4 2 5 00				38
1 2 5 00		1 2 5 00				39
4 9 7 5 00		4 9 7 5 00				40

FIGURE 12.2 | (continued) Ten-Column Worksheet—Complete

	ACCOUNT NAME	TRIAL BALANCE		ADJUSTMENTS	
		DEBIT	CREDIT	DEBIT	CREDIT
41	Depreciation Expense—Store Equipment			(d) 2 4 0 0 00	
42	Rent Expense	27 6 0 0 00			
43	Salaries Expense—Office	26 5 0 0 00			
44	Insurance Expense			(k) 2 4 5 0 00	
45	Payroll Taxes Expense	7 2 0 5 00		(g) 9 1 80	
46				(h) 7 4 40	
47	Telephone Expense	1 8 7 5 00			
48	Uncollectible Accounts Expense			(c) 8 0 0 00	
49	Utilities Expense	5 9 2 5 00			
50	Depreciation Expense—Office Equipment			(e) 7 0 0 00	
51	Interest Expense	6 0 0 00		(i) 2 0 00	
52				(l) 1 5 0 00	
53	Totals	674 4 5 6 00	674 4 5 6 00	112 1 0 7 20	112 1 0 7 20
54	Net Income				

FIGURE 12.2 (continued) Ten-Column Worksheet—Complete

Calculating Net Income or Net Loss

Once all account balances have been entered in the financial statement sections of the worksheet, the net income or net loss for the period is determined.

1. Total the Debit and Credit columns in the Income Statement section. For Simpson Antiques, the debits total $564,406.20 and the credits total $615,578.00. Since the credits exceed the debits, the difference represents net income of $51,171.80.

2. To balance the Debit and the Credit columns in the Income Statement section, enter $51,171.80 in the Debit column of the Income Statement section. Total each column again and record the final total of each column ($615,578.00) on the worksheet.

3. Total the columns in the Balance Sheet section. Total debits are $162,366.00 and total credits are $111,194.20. The difference must equal the net income for the year, $51,171.80.

4. Enter $51,171.80 in the Credit column of the Balance Sheet section. Total each column again and record the final total in each column ($162,366.00).

5. Rule the Debit and Credit columns in all sections to show that the worksheet is complete.

Notice that the net income is recorded in two places on the **net income line** of the worksheet. It is recorded in the Credit column of the Balance Sheet section because net income *increases* owner's equity. It is recorded in the Debit column of the Income Statement section to balance the two columns in that section.

ADJUSTED TRIAL BALANCE		INCOME STATEMENT		BALANCE SHEET		
DEBIT	CREDIT	DEBIT	CREDIT	DEBIT	CREDIT	
2 400 00		2 400 00				41
27 600 00		27 600 00				42
26 500 00		26 500 00				43
2 450 00		2 450 00				44
7 371 20		7 371 20				45
						46
1 875 00		1 875 00				47
800 00		800 00				48
5 925 00		5 925 00				49
700 00		700 00				50
770 00		770 00				51
						52
726 772 20	726 772 20	564 406 20	615 578 00	162 366 00	111 194 20	53
		51 171 80			51 171 80	54
		615 578 00	615 578 00	162 366 00	162 366 00	55
						56

FIGURE 12.2   (concluded) Ten-Column Worksheet—Complete

Section 2: **Self Review**

QUESTIONS

1. In the adjusting entry for depreciation, is the **Depreciation Expense** account increased or decreased? Is the book value of the asset being depreciated increased or is it decreased?

2. In its December 31, 2007, financial reports, St. Claire Company's accountant made two errors: (1) failed to record interest of $300 accrued on a note payable and (2) failed to record interest of $800 accrued on a note receivable. What is the net effect of these two errors on assets, on liabilities, on expenses, on income, and on owner's equity?

3. The trial balance in the first two columns of the worksheet balances and the adjustments in the next two columns balance. However, the adjusted trial balance does not balance. What is likely the source of the trouble?

EXERCISES

4. The amount of net income appears on the worksheet in the
   a. Credit column of the balance sheet section.
   b. Debit column of the balance sheet section.
   c. Credit column of the income statement section.
   d. Debit column of the income statement section.

5. What account is debited and what account is credited to accrue interest on notes payable?

ANALYZE

6. Explain why an error in the amount of an adjusting entry usually affects at least two accounting periods.

(Answers to Section 2 Self Review are on page 451.)

REVIEW

Chapter Summary

Accrual basis accounting requires that all revenue and expenses for a fiscal period be matched and reported on the income statement to determine net income or net loss for the period. In this chapter, you have learned the techniques used to adjust accounts so that they accurately reflect the operations of the period.

Learning Objectives

1 Determine the adjustment for merchandise inventory, and enter the adjustment on the worksheet.

Merchandise inventory consists of goods that a business has on hand for sale to customers. When the trial balance is prepared at the end of the period, the **Merchandise Inventory** account still reflects the beginning inventory. Before the financial statements can be prepared, **Merchandise Inventory** must be updated to reflect the ending inventory for the period. The actual quantity of the goods on hand at the end of the period must be counted. Then the adjustment is completed in two steps:

1. Remove the beginning inventory balance from the **Merchandise Inventory** account. Debit **Income Summary**; credit **Merchandise Inventory**.

2. Add the ending inventory to the **Merchandise Inventory** account. Debit **Merchandise Inventory**; credit **Income Summary**.

2 Compute adjustments for accrued and prepaid expense items, and enter the adjustments on the worksheet.

Expense accounts are adjusted at the end of the period so that they correctly reflect the current period. Examples of adjustments include provision for uncollectible accounts and depreciation. Other typical adjustments of expense accounts involve accrued expenses and prepaid expenses.

- Accrued expenses are expense items that have been incurred or used but not yet paid or recorded. They include salaries, payroll taxes, interest on notes payable, and property taxes.

- Prepaid expenses are expense items that a business pays for and records before it actually uses

the items. Rent, insurance, and advertising paid in advance are examples.

3 Compute adjustments for accrued and deferred income items, and enter the adjustments on the worksheet.

Revenue accounts are adjusted at the end of the period so that they correctly reflect the current period.

- Adjustments can affect either accrued income or deferred income.

- Accrued income is income that has been earned but not yet received and recorded.

- Deferred, or unearned, income is income that has not yet been earned but has been received.

4 Complete a 10-column worksheet.

When all adjustments have been entered on the worksheet, the worksheet is completed so that the financial statements can be prepared easily.

1. Figures in the Trial Balance section are combined with the adjustments to obtain an adjusted trial balance.

2. Each item in the Adjusted Trial Balance section is extended to the Income Statement and Balance Sheet sections of the worksheet.

3. The Income Statement columns are totaled and the net income or net loss is determined and entered in the net income line.

4. The amount of net income or net loss is entered in the net income line in the Balance Sheet section. After net income or net loss is added, the total debits must equal the total credits in the Balance Sheet section columns.

5 Define the accounting terms new to this chapter.

Glossary

Accrual basis (p. 416) A system of accounting by which all revenues and expenses are matched and reported on financial statements for the applicable period, regardless of when the cash related to the transaction is received or paid

Accrued expenses (p. 421) Expense items that relate to the current period but have not yet been paid and do not yet appear in the accounting records

Accrued income (p. 424) Income that has been earned but not yet received and recorded

Deferred expenses (p. 421) See Prepaid expenses

Deferred income (p. 426) See Unearned income

Inventory sheet (p. 417) A form used to list the volume and type of goods a firm has in stock

Net income line (p. 432) The worksheet line immediately following the column totals on which net income (or net loss) is recorded in two places: the Income Statement section and the Balance Sheet section

Prepaid expenses (p. 423) Expenses that are paid for and recorded before they are used, such as rent or insurance

Property, plant, and equipment (p. 420) Long-term assets that are used in the operation of a business and that are subject to depreciation (except for land, which is not depreciated)

Unearned income (p. 426) Income received before it is earned

Updated account balances (p. 429) The amounts entered in the Adjusted Trial Balance section of the worksheet

Comprehensive **Self Review**

1. Why is the accrual basis of accounting favored?

2. What is meant by the term "accrued income"?

3. How, if at all, does "accrued income" differ from "unearned income"?

4. On July 1, 2007, a landlord received $24,000 cash from a tenant, covering rent from that date through June 30, 2008. The payment was credited to **Rent Income.** Assuming no entry has been made in the income account since receipt of the payment, what would be the adjusting entry on December 31, 2007?

5. A completed worksheet for Holiday Company on December 31, 2007, showed a total of $930,000 in the debit column of the Income Statement section and a total credit of $905,000 in the credit column. Does this represent a profit or a loss for the year? How much?

(Answers to Comprehensive Self Review are on page 452.)

Discussion Questions

1. When a specific account receivable is deemed uncollectible it is written off by debiting ———————— and crediting ————————.

2. Income Summary amounts are extended to which statement columns on the worksheet?

3. What adjustment is made to record the estimated expense for uncollectible accounts?

4. Why is depreciation recorded?

5. What types of assets are subject to depreciation? Give three examples of such assets.

6. Explain the meaning of the following terms that relate to depreciation.

    a. Salvage value

    b. Depreciable base

    c. Useful life

    d. Straight-line method

7. What adjustment is made for depreciation on office equipment?

8. What is an accrued expense? Give three examples of items that often become accrued expenses.

9. What adjustment is made to record accrued salaries?

10. What is a prepaid expense? Give three examples of prepaid expense items.

11. How is the cost of an insurance policy recorded when the policy is purchased?

12. What adjustment is made to record expired insurance?

13. What is the alternative method of handling prepaid expenses?

14. What is accrued income? Give an example of an item that might produce accrued income.

15. What adjustment is made for accrued interest on a note receivable?

16. What is unearned income? Give two examples of items that would be classified as unearned income.

17. How is unearned income recorded when it is received?

18. What adjustment is made to record income earned during a period?

19. What is the alternative method of handling unearned income?

20. How does the worksheet help the accountant to prepare financial statements more efficiently?

21. *Unearned Fees Income* is classified as which type of account?

APPLICATIONS

 Exercises

Exercise 12.1
Objective 1

▶ **Determining the adjustments for inventory.**

The beginning inventory of a merchandising business was $135,000, and the ending inventory is $115,000. What entries are needed at the end of the fiscal period to adjust *Merchandise Inventory*?

Exercise 12.2
Objective 1

▶ **Determining the adjustments for inventory.**

The Income Statement section of the worksheet of Smith Company for the year ended December 31, 2007, has $166,000 recorded in the Debit column and $190,000 in the Credit column on the line for the *Income Summary* account. What were the beginning and ending balances for *Merchandise Inventory?*

Exercise 12.3
Objective 2

▶ **Computing adjustments for accrued and prepaid expense items.**

For each of the following independent situations, indicate the adjusting entry that must be made on the December 31, 2007, worksheet. Omit descriptions.

a. During the year 2007, Sam & Sons Company had net credit sales of $920,000. Past experience shows that 0.9 percent of the firm's net credit sales result in uncollectible accounts.

b. Equipment purchased by One Stop Shops for $28,700 on January 2, 2007, has an estimated useful life of nine years and an estimated salvage value of $1,700. What adjustment for depreciation should be recorded on the firm's worksheet for the year ended December 31, 2007?

c. On December 31, 2007, Parrish Plumbing Supply owed wages of $6,400 to its factory employees, who are paid weekly.

d. On December 31, 2007, Parrish Plumbing Supply owed the employer's social security (6.2%) and Medicare (1.45%) taxes on the entire $6,400 of accrued wages for its factory employees.

e. On December 31, 2007, Parrish Plumbing Supply owed federal (0.8%) and state (5.4%) unemployment taxes on the entire $6,400 of accrued wages for its factory employees.

Computing adjustments for accrued and prepaid expense items.

◄   Exercise 12.4
Objective 2

For each of the following independent situations, indicate the adjusting entry that must be made on the December 31, 2007, worksheet. Omit descriptions.

a. On December 31, 2007, the **Notes Payable** account at King Manufacturing Company had a balance of $12,000. This balance represented a three-month, 12 percent note issued on October 1.

b. On January 2, 2007, Wayland's Word Processing Service purchased floppy disks, paper, and other supplies for $5,100 in cash. On December 31, 2007, an inventory of supplies showed that items costing $1,300 were on hand. The **Supplies** account has a balance of $5,100.

c. On August 1, 2007, North Texas Manufacturing paid a premium of $10,560 in cash for a one-year insurance policy. On December 31, 2007, an examination of the insurance records showed that coverage for a period of five months had expired.

d. On April 1, 2007, Connie Crafts signed a one-year advertising contract with a local radio station and issued a check for $11,100 to pay the total amount owed. On December 31, 2007, the **Prepaid Advertising** account has a balance of $11,100.

Recording adjustments for accrued and prepaid expense items.

◄   Exercise 12.5
Objective 2

On December 1, 2007, Joe's Java Joint borrowed $32,000 from its bank in order to expand its operations. The firm issued a four-month, 15 percent note for $32,000 to the bank and received $30,400 in cash because the bank deducted the interest for the entire period in advance. In general journal form, show the entry that would be made to record this transaction and the adjustment for prepaid interest that should be recorded on the firm's worksheet for the year ended December 31, 2007. Omit descriptions.

Recording adjustments for accrued and prepaid expense items.

◄   Exercise 12.6
Objective 2

On December 31, 2007, the **Notes Payable** account at Beth's Boutique Shop had a balance of $42,000. This amount represented funds borrowed on a four-month, 12 percent note from the firm's bank on December 1. Record the journal entry for interest expense on this note that should be recorded on the firm's worksheet for the year ended December 31, 2007. Omit descriptions.

Recording adjustments for accrued and deferred income items.

◄   Exercise 12.7
Objective 3

For each of the following independent situations, indicate the adjusting entry that must be made on the December 31, 2007, worksheet. Omit descriptions.

a. On December 31, 2007, the **Notes Receivable** account at Montague Materials had a balance of $12,600, which represented a six-month, 10 percent note received from a customer on July 1.

b. On December 31, 2007, the **Sales Tax Payable** account at Hawaiian Clothing Store had a balance of $1,720. This balance represented the sales tax owed for the fourth quarter. The firm is scheduled to send the amount to the state sales tax agency on January 15. At that time the firm will deduct a commission of 2 percent of the tax due, as allowed by state law.

c. During the week ended January 7, 2007, Taylor Magazine Publishing received $32,000 from customers for subscriptions to its magazine *Modern Business*. On December 31, 2007, an analysis of the **Unearned Subscription Revenue** account showed that $16,000 of the subscriptions were earned in 2007.

d. On November 1, 2007, Peacock Realty Company rented a commercial building to a new tenant and received $42,000 in advance to cover the rent for six months. Upon receipt, the $42,000 was recorded in a balance sheet account.

PROBLEMS

Problem Set A

Problem 12.1A ▶

Objectives 2, 3

Recording adjustments for accrued and prepaid expense items and unearned income.

On July 1, 2007, Shawn Smith established his own accounting practice. Selected transactions for the first few days of July follow.

INSTRUCTIONS

1. Record the transactions on page 1 of the general journal. Omit descriptions. Assume that the firm initially records prepaid expenses as assets and unearned income as a liability.

2. Record the adjusting journal entries that must be made on July 31, 2007, on page 2 of the general journal. Omit descriptions.

DATE	TRANSACTIONS
July 1	Signed a lease for an office and issued Check 101 for $15,000 to pay the rent in advance for six months.
1	Borrowed money from First National Bank by issuing a four-month, 12 percent note for $18,000; received $17,280 because the bank deducted the interest in advance.
1	Signed an agreement with Stevens, Stroll & Co. to provide accounting and tax services for one year at $5,050 per month; received the entire fee of $60,600 in advance.
1	Purchased office equipment for $15,600 from Office Outfitters; issued a two-month, 12 percent note in payment. The equipment is estimated to have a useful life of six years and a $1,200 salvage value. The equipment will be depreciated using the straight-line method.
1	Purchased a one-year insurance policy and issued Check 102 for $1,440 to pay the entire premium.
3	Purchased office furniture for $16,800 from Walter's Warehouse; issued Check 103 for $8,400 and agreed to pay the balance in 60 days. The equipment has an estimated useful life of five years and a $1,200 salvage value. The office furniture will be depreciated using the straight-line method.
5	Purchased office supplies for $2,300 with Check 104. Assume $800 of supplies are on hand July 31, 2007.

Analyze: What balance should be reflected in **Unearned Accounting Fees** at July 31, 2007?

Problem 12.2A ▶

Objectives 2, 3

eXcel

Recording adjustments for accrued and prepaid expense items and earned income.

On July 31, 2007, after one month of operation, the general ledger of Sarah Webb, Consultant, contained the accounts and balances given below.

INSTRUCTIONS

1. Prepare a partial worksheet with the following sections: Trial Balance, Adjustments, and Adjusted Trial Balance. Use the data about the firm's accounts and balances to complete the Trial Balance section.

2. Enter the adjustments described below in the Adjustments section. Identify each adjustment with the appropriate letter.

3. Complete the Adjusted Trial Balance section.

ACCOUNTS AND BALANCES

Cash	$22,010	Dr.
Accounts Receivable	1,300	Dr.
Supplies	860	Dr.
Prepaid Rent	9,000	Dr.
Prepaid Insurance	1,620	Dr.
Prepaid Interest	400	Dr.
Furniture	12,050	Dr.
Accumulated Depreciation—Furniture		
Equipment	6,400	Dr.
Accumulated Depreciation—Equipment		
Notes Payable	17,900	Cr.
Accounts Payable	4,500	Cr.
Interest Payable		
Unearned Consulting Fees	3,600	Cr.
Sarah Webb, Capital	25,220	Cr.
Sarah Webb, Drawing	2,000	Dr.
Consulting Fees	8,000	Cr.
Salaries Expense	3,200	Dr.
Utilities Expense	220	Dr.
Telephone Expense	160	Dr.
Supplies Expense		
Rent Expense		
Insurance Expense		
Depreciation Expense—Furniture		
Depreciation Expense—Equipment		
Interest Expense		

ADJUSTMENTS

a. On July 31 an inventory of the supplies showed that items costing $680 were on hand.

b. On July 1 the firm paid $9,000 in advance for six months of rent.

c. On July 1 the firm purchased a one-year insurance policy for $1,620.

d. On July 1 the firm paid $400 interest in advance on a four-month note that it issued to the bank.

e. On July 1 the firm purchased office furniture for $12,050. The furniture is expected to have a useful life of seven years and a salvage value of $1,550.

f. On July 1 the firm purchased office equipment for $6,400. The equipment is expected to have a useful life of five years and a salvage value of $1,600.

g. On July 1 the firm issued a three-month, 12 percent note for $7,250.

h. On July 1 the firm received a consulting fee of $3,600 in advance for a one-year period.

Analyze: By what total amount were the expense accounts of the business adjusted?

Recording adjustments and completing the worksheet.

The Green Thumb Gallery is a retail store that sells plants, soil, and decorative pots. On December 31, 2007, the firm's general ledger contained the accounts and balances that appear on page 440.

◀ **Problem 12.3A**
Objectives 1, 2, 3, 4
e**X**cel

INSTRUCTIONS

1. Prepare the Trial Balance section of a 10-column worksheet. The worksheet covers the year ended December 31, 2007.

2. Enter the adjustments below in the Adjustments section of the worksheet. Identify each adjustment with the appropriate letter.

3. Complete the worksheet.

ACCOUNTS AND BALANCES

Cash	$ 5,700	Dr.
Accounts Receivable	2,600	Dr.
Allowance for Doubtful Accounts	52	Cr.
Merchandise Inventory	11,300	Dr.
Supplies	1,200	Dr.
Prepaid Advertising	960	Dr.
Store Equipment	8,100	Dr.
Accumulated Depreciation—Store Equipment	1,500	Cr.
Office Equipment	1,600	Dr.
Accumulated Depreciation—Office Equipment	280	Cr.
Accounts Payable	2,625	Cr.
Social Security Tax Payable	430	Cr.
Medicare Tax Payable	98	Cr.
Federal Unemployment Tax Payable		
State Unemployment Tax Payable		
Salaries Payable		
Beth Argo, Capital	25,457	Cr.
Beth Argo, Drawing	20,000	Dr.
Sales	90,048	Cr.
Sales Returns and Allowances	1,100	Dr.
Purchases	46,400	Dr.
Purchases Returns and Allowances	430	Cr.
Rent Expense	6,000	Dr.
Telephone Expense	590	Dr.
Salaries Expense	14,100	Dr.
Payroll Taxes Expense	1,270	Dr.
Income Summary		
Supplies Expense		
Advertising Expense		
Depreciation Expense—Store Equipment		
Depreciation Expense—Office Equipment		
Uncollectible Accounts Expense		

ADJUSTMENTS

a.–b. Merchandise inventory on December 31, 2007, is $12,321.

c. During 2007 the firm had net credit sales of $35,000; the firm estimates that 0.6 percent of these sales will result in uncollectible accounts.

d. On December 31, 2007, an inventory of the supplies showed that items costing $275 were on hand.

e. On October 1, 2007, the firm signed a six-month advertising contract for $960 with a local newspaper and paid the full amount in advance.

f. On January 2, 2006, the firm purchased store equipment for $8,100. At that time, the equipment was estimated to have a useful life of five years and a salvage value of $600.

g. On January 2, 2006, the firm purchased office equipment for $1,600. At that time the equipment was estimated to have a useful life of five years and a salvage value of $200.

h. On December 31, 2007, the firm owed salaries of $1,830 that will not be paid until 2008.

i. On December 31, 2007, the firm owed the employer's social security tax (assume 6.2 percent) and Medicare tax (assume 1.45 percent) on the entire $1,830 of accrued wages.

j. On December 31, 2007, the firm owed federal unemployment tax (assume 0.8 percent) and state unemployment tax (assume 5.4 percent) on the entire $1,830 of accrued wages.

Analyze: By what total amount were the net assets of the business affected by adjustments?

Recording adjustments and completing the worksheet.

◀ **Problem 12.4A**
Objectives 1, 2, 3, 4

Healthy Habits Foods Company is a distributor of nutritious snack foods such as granola bars. On December 31, 2007, the firm's general ledger contained the accounts and balances that follow.

INSTRUCTIONS

1. Prepare the Trial Balance section of a 10-column worksheet. The worksheet covers the year ended December 31, 2007.

2. Enter the adjustments in the Adjustments section of the worksheet. Identify each adjustment with the appropriate letter.

3. Complete the worksheet.

Note: This problem will be required to complete Problem 13-3A in Chapter 13.

ACCOUNTS AND BALANCES

Cash	$ 30,100	Dr.
Accounts Receivable	35,200	Dr.
Allowance for Doubtful Accounts	420	Cr.
Merchandise Inventory	86,000	Dr.
Supplies	10,400	Dr.
Prepaid Insurance	5,400	Dr.
Office Equipment	8,300	Dr.
Accum. Depreciation—Office Equipment	2,650	Cr.
Warehouse Equipment	28,000	Dr.
Accum. Depreciation—Warehouse Equipment	9,600	Cr.
Notes Payable—Bank	32,000	Cr.
Accounts Payable	12,200	Cr.
Interest Payable		
Social Security Tax Payable	1,680	Cr.
Medicare Tax Payable	388	Cr.
Federal Unemployment Tax Payable		
State Unemployment Tax Payable		
Salaries Payable		
Phillip Tucker, Capital	108,684	Cr.
Phillip Tucker, Drawing	56,000	Dr.
Sales	653,778	Cr.
Sales Returns and Allowances	10,000	Dr.
Purchases	350,000	Dr.
Purchases Returns and Allowances	9,200	Cr.
Income Summary		
Rent Expense	36,000	Dr.
Telephone Expense	2,200	Dr.
Salaries Expense	160,000	Dr.
Payroll Taxes Expense	13,000	Dr.

ACCOUNTS AND BALANCES (CONT.)

Supplies Expense

Insurance Expense

Depreciation Expense—Office Equip.

Depreciation Expense—Warehouse Equip.

Uncollectible Accounts Expense

Interest Expense

ADJUSTMENTS

a.–b. Merchandise inventory on December 31, 2007, is $78,000.

c. During 2007 the firm had net credit sales of $560,000; past experience indicates that 0.5 percent of these sales should result in uncollectible accounts.

d. On December 31, 2007, an inventory of supplies showed that items costing $1,180 were on hand.

e. On May 1, 2007, the firm purchased a one-year insurance policy for $5,400.

f. On January 2, 2005, the firm purchased office equipment for $8,300. At that time the equipment was estimated to have a useful life of six years and a salvage value of $350.

g. On January 2, 2005, the firm purchased warehouse equipment for $28,000. At that time the equipment was estimated to have a useful life of five years and a salvage value of $4,000.

h. On November 1, 2007, the firm issued a four-month, 12 percent note for $32,000.

i. On December 31, 2007, the firm owed salaries of $5,000 that will not be paid until 2008.

j. On December 31, 2007, the firm owed the employer's social security tax (assume 6.2 percent) and Medicare tax (assume 1.45 percent) on the entire $5,000 of accrued wages.

k. On December 31, 2007, the firm owed the federal unemployment tax (assume 0.8 percent) and the state unemployment tax (assume 5.4 percent) on the entire $5,000 of accrued wages.

Analyze: When the financial statements for Healthy Habits Foods Company are prepared, what net income will be reported for the period ended December 31, 2007?

Problem Set B

Problem 12.1B ▶
Objectives 2, 3

Recording adjustments for accrued and prepaid expense items and unearned income.

On June 1, 2007, Pepe Cruz established her own advertising firm. Selected transactions for the first few days of June follow.

1. Record the transactions on page 1 of the general journal. Omit descriptions. Assume that the firm initially records prepaid expenses as assets and unearned income as a liability.

2. Record the adjusting journal entries that must be made on June 30, 2007, on page 2 of the general journal. Omit descriptions.

DATE	TRANSACTIONS
2007	
June 1	Signed a lease for an office and issued Check 101 for $15,000 to pay the rent in advance for six months.
1	Borrowed money from National Trust Bank by issuing a three-month, 10 percent note for $16,000; received $15,600 because the bank deducted interest in advance.

DATE	TRANSACTIONS
June 1	Signed an agreement with World of Wax Candle Store to provide advertising consulting for one year at $4,600 per month; received the entire fee of $55,200 in advance.
1	Purchased office equipment for $21,600 from The Furniture Depot; issued a three-month, 12 percent note in payment. The equipment is estimated to have a useful life of five years and a $1,200 salvage value and will be depreciated using the straight-line method.
1	Purchased a one-year insurance policy and issued Check 102 for $3,660 to pay the entire premium.
3	Purchased office furniture for $19,200 from Office Gallery; issued Check 103 for $9,600 and agreed to pay the balance in 60 days. The equipment is estimated to have a useful life of five years and a $1,200 salvage value and will be depreciated using the straight-line method.
5	Purchased office supplies for $2,750 with Check 104; assume $1,150 of supplies are on hand June 30, 2007.

Analyze: At the end of the year, 2007, how much of the rent paid on June 1 will have been charged to expense?

Recording adjustments for accrued and prepaid expense items and unearned income.

◀ Problem 12.2B
Objectives 2, 3

On September 30, 2007, after one month of operation, the general ledger of Cross Timbers Company contained the accounts and balances shown below.

INSTRUCTIONS

1. Prepare a partial worksheet with the following sections: Trial Balance, Adjustments, and Adjusted Trial Balance. Use the data about the firm's accounts and balances to complete the Trial Balance section.

2. Enter the adjustments described below in the Adjustments section. Identify each adjustment with the appropriate letter. (Some items may not require adjustments.)

3. Complete the Adjusted Trial Balance section.

ACCOUNTS AND BALANCES

Cash	$26,460	Dr.
Supplies	740	Dr.
Prepaid Rent	4,200	Dr.
Prepaid Advertising	3,750	Dr.
Prepaid Interest	450	Dr.
Furniture	4,840	Dr.
Accumulated Depreciation—Furniture		
Equipment	9,000	Dr.
Accumulated Depreciation—Equipment		
Notes Payable	20,250	Cr.
Accounts Payable	4,400	Cr.
Interest Payable		
Unearned Course Fees	22,000	Cr.
Scott Nelson, Capital	6,730	Cr.
Scott Nelson, Drawing	2,000	Dr.

ACCOUNTS AND BALANCES (CONT.)

Course Fees		
Salaries Expense	1,600	Dr.
Telephone Expense	120	Dr.
Entertainment Expense	220	Dr.
Supplies Expense		
Rent Expense		
Advertising Expense		
Depreciation Expense—Furniture		
Depreciation Expense—Equipment		
Interest Expense		

ADJUSTMENTS

a. On September 30 an inventory of the supplies showed that items costing $705 were on hand.

b. On September 1 the firm paid $4,200 in advance for six months of rent.

c. On September 1 the firm signed a six-month advertising contract for $3,750 and paid the full amount in advance.

d. On September 1 the firm paid $450 interest in advance on a three-month note that it issued to the bank.

e. On September 1 the firm purchased office furniture for $4,840. The furniture is expected to have a useful life of five years and a salvage value of $340.

f. On September 3 the firm purchased equipment for $9,000. The equipment is expected to have a useful life of five years and a salvage value of $1,200.

g. On September 1 the firm issued a two-month, 8 percent note for $5,250.

h. During September the firm received $22,000 fees in advance. An analysis of the firm's records shows that $7,000 applies to services provided in September and the rest pertains to future months.

Analyze: What was the net dollar effect on income of the adjustments to the accounting records of the business?

Problem 12.3B ▶ **Recording adjustments and completing the worksheet.**

Objectives 1, 2, 3, 4

Fun Depot is a retail store that sells toys, games, and bicycles. On December 31, 2007, the firm's general ledger contained the following accounts and balances.

INSTRUCTIONS

1. Prepare the Trial Balance section of a 10-column worksheet. The worksheet covers the year ended December 31, 2007.

2. Enter the adjustments below in the Adjustments section of the worksheet. Identify each adjustment with the appropriate letter.

3. Complete the worksheet.

ACCOUNTS AND BALANCES

Cash	$	26,400	Dr.
Accounts Receivable		22,700	Dr.
Allowance for Doubtful Accounts		320	Cr.
Merchandise Inventory		138,000	Dr.
Supplies		11,600	Dr.
Prepaid Advertising		5,280	Dr.
Store Equipment		32,500	Dr.

ACCOUNTS AND BALANCES (CONT.)

Accumulated Depreciation—Store Equipment	$ 5,760	Cr.
Office Equipment	8,400	Dr.
Accumulated Depreciation—Office Equipment	1,440	Cr.
Accounts Payable	8,600	Cr.
Social Security Tax Payable	5,920	Cr.
Medicare Tax Payable	1,368	Cr.
Federal Unemployment Tax Payable		
State Unemployment Tax Payable		
Salaries Payable		
Janie Fielder, Capital	112,250	Cr.
Janie Fielder, Drawing	100,000	Dr.
Sales	1,043,662	Cr.
Sales Returns and Allowances	17,200	Dr.
Purchases	507,600	Dr.
Purchases Returns and Allowances	5,040	Cr.
Rent Expense	125,000	Dr.
Telephone Expense	4,280	Dr.
Salaries Expense	164,200	Dr.
Payroll Taxes Expense	15,200	Dr.
Income Summary		
Supplies Expense		
Advertising Expense	6,000	Dr.
Depreciation Expense—Store Equipment		
Depreciation Expense—Office Equipment		
Uncollectible Accounts Expense		

ADJUSTMENTS

a.–b. Merchandise inventory on December 31, 2007, is $148,000.

c. During 2007 the firm had net credit sales of $440,000. The firm estimates that 0.7 percent of these sales will result in uncollectible accounts.

d. On December 31, 2007, an inventory of the supplies showed that items costing $2,960 were on hand.

e. On September 1, 2007, the firm signed a six-month advertising contract for $5,280 with a local newspaper and paid the full amount in advance.

f. On January 2, 2006, the firm purchased store equipment for $32,500. At that time the equipment was estimated to have a useful life of five years and a salvage value of $3,700.

g. On January 2, 2006, the firm purchased office equipment for $8,400. At that time the equipment was estimated to have a useful life of five years and a salvage value of $1,200.

h. On December 31, 2007, the firm owed salaries of $8,000 that will not be paid until 2008.

i. On December 31, 2007, the firm owed the employer's social security tax (assume 6.2 percent) and Medicare tax (assume 1.45 percent) on the entire $8,000 of accrued wages.

j. On December 31, 2007, the firm owed federal unemployment tax (assume 0.8 percent) and state unemployment tax (assume 5.4 percent) on the entire $8,000 of accrued wages.

Analyze: If the adjustment for advertising had not been recorded, what would the reported net income have been?

Problem 12.4B ▶

Objectives 1, 2, 3, 4

CONTINUING >>>
Problem

Recording adjustments and completing the worksheet.

Whatnots is a retail seller of cards, novelty items, and business products. On December 31, 2007, the firm's general ledger contained the following accounts and balances.

INSTRUCTIONS

1. Prepare the Trial Balance section of a 10-column worksheet. The worksheet covers the year ended December 31, 2007.

2. Enter the adjustments in the Adjustments section of the worksheet. Identify each adjustment with the appropriate letter.

3. Complete the worksheet.

Note: This problem will be required to complete Problem 13-3B in Chapter 13.

ACCOUNTS AND BALANCES

Cash	$ 3,235	Dr.
Accounts Receivable	6,910	Dr.
Allowance for Doubtful Accounts	600	Cr.
Merchandise Inventory	16,985	Dr.
Supplies	750	Dr.
Prepaid Insurance	2,400	Dr.
Store Equipment	6,000	Dr.
Accumulated Depreciation—Store Equip.	2,000	Cr.
Store Fixtures	15,760	Dr.
Accumulated Depreciation—Store Fixtures	4,100	Cr.
Notes Payable	4,000	Cr.
Accounts Payable	600	Cr.
Interest Payable		
Social Security Tax Payable		
Medicare Tax Payable		
Federal Unemployment Tax Payable		
State Unemployment Tax Payable		
Salaries Payable		
Preston Allen, Capital	39,780	Cr.
Preston Allen, Drawing	8,000	Dr.
Sales	236,560	Cr.
Sales Returns and Allowances	6,000	Dr.
Purchases	160,000	Dr.
Purchases Returns and Allowances	2,000	Cr.
Income Summary		
Rent Expense	18,000	Dr.
Telephone Expense	2,400	Dr.
Salaries Expense	40,000	Dr.
Payroll Tax Expense	3,200	Dr.
Supplies Expense		
Insurance Expense		
Depreciation Expense—Store Equipment		
Depreciation Expense—Store Fixtures		
Uncollectible Accounts Expense		
Interest Expense		

ADJUSTMENTS

a.–b. Merchandise inventory on hand on December 31, 2007, is $15,840.

c. During 2007 the firm had net credit sales of $160,000. Past experience indicates that 0.8 percent of these sales should result in uncollectible accounts.

d. On December 31, 2007, an inventory of supplies showed that items costing $245 were on hand.

e. On July 1, 2007, the firm purchased a one-year insurance policy for $2,400.

f. On January 2, 2005, the firm purchased store equipment for $6,000. The equipment was estimated to have a five-year useful life and a salvage value of $1,000.

g. On January 4, 2005, the firm purchased store fixtures for $15,760. At the time of the purchase, the fixtures were assumed to have a useful life of seven years and a salvage value of $1,410.

h. On October 1, 2007, the firm issued a six-month, $4,000 note payable at 9 percent interest with a local bank.

i. At year-end (December 31, 2007), the firm owed salaries of $1,450 that will not be paid until January 2008.

j. On December 31, 2007, the firm owed the employer's social security tax (assume 6.2 percent) and Medicare tax (assume 1.45 percent) on the entire $1,450 of accrued wages.

k. On December 31, 2007, the firm owed federal unemployment tax (assume 1.0 percent) and state unemployment tax (assume 5.0 percent) on the entire $1,450 of accrued wages.

Analyze: After all adjustments have been recorded, what is the net book value of the company's assets?

Challenge Problem

Completing the Worksheet

The unadjusted trial balance of Jerry's Jewelers on December 31, 2007, the end of its fiscal year, appears on page 448.

INSTRUCTIONS

1. Copy the unadjusted trial balance onto a worksheet and complete the worksheet using the following information.

   a.–b. Ending merchandise inventory, $98,700.

   c. Uncollectible accounts expense, $1,000.

   d. Store supplies on hand December 31, 2007, $625.

   e. Office supplies on hand December 31, 2007, $305.

   f. Depreciation on store equipment, $11,360.

   g. Depreciation on office equipment, $3,300.

   h. Accrued sales salaries, $4,000, and accrued office salaries, $1,000.

   i. Social security tax on accrued salaries, $326; Medicare tax on accrued salaries, $76. (Assumes that tax rates have increased.)

   j. Federal unemployment tax on accrued salaries, $56; state unemployment tax on accrued salaries, $270.

2. Journalize the adjusting entries on page 30 of the general journal. Omit descriptions.

3. Journalize the closing entries on page 32 of the general journal. Omit descriptions.

4. Compute the following:

   a. net sales

   b. net delivered cost of purchases

c. cost of goods sold

d. net income or net loss

e. balance of *Jerry Whatley, Capital* on December 31, 2007.

Analyze: What change(s) to *Jerry Whatley, Capital* will be reported on the statement of owner's equity?

JERRY'S JEWELERS Trial Balance December 31, 2007		
Cash	$ 13,050	Dr
Accounts Receivable	49,900	Dr.
Allowance for Doubtful Accounts	2,000	Cr.
Merchandise Inventory	105,900	Dr.
Store Supplies	4,230	Dr.
Office Supplies	2,950	Dr.
Store Equipment	113,590	Dr.
Accumulated Depreciation—Store Equipment	13,010	Cr.
Office Equipment	27,640	Dr.
Accumulated Depreciation—Office Equipment	4,930	Cr.
Accounts Payable	4,390	Cr.
Salaries Payable		
Social Security Tax Payable		
Medicare Tax Payable		
Federal Unemployment Tax Payable		
State Unemployment Tax Payable		
Jerry Whatley, Capital	166,310	Cr.
Jerry Whatley, Drawing	30,000	Dr.
Income Summary		
Sales	862,230	Cr.
Sales Returns and Allowances	7,580	Dr.
Purchases	504,810	Dr.
Purchases Returns and Allowances	4,240	Cr.
Purchases Discounts	10,770	Cr.
Freight In	7,000	Dr.
Salaries Expense—Sales	75,950	Dr.
Rent Expense	35,500	Dr.
Advertising Expense	12,300	Dr.
Store Supplies Expense		
Depreciation Expense—Store Equipment		
Salaries Expense—Office	77,480	Dr.
Payroll Taxes Expense		
Uncollectible Accounts Expense		
Office Supplies Expense		
Depreciation Expense—Office Equipment		

Critical Thinking Problem

Net Profit

When Waylon Skagg's father died suddenly, Waylon had just completed the semester in college, so he stepped in to run the family business, Skagg's Delivery Service until it could be sold. Under his father's direction, the company was a successful operation and provided ample money to meet the family's needs.

Waylon was majoring in music in college and knew little about business or accounting, but he was eager to do a good job of running the business so it would command a good selling price. Since all of the services performed were paid in cash, Waylon figured that he would do all right as long as the *Cash* account increased. Thus he was delighted to watch the cash balance increase from $24,800 at the beginning of the first month to $63,028 at the end of the second month—an increase of $38,228 during the two months he had been in charge. When he was presented an income statement for the two months by the company's bookkeeper, he could not understand why it did not show that amount as income but instead reported only $21,100 as net income.

Knowing that you are taking an accounting class, Waylon brings the income statement, shown below, to you and asks if you can help him understand the difference.

SKAGG'S DELIVERY SERVICE		
Income Statement		
Months of June and July, 2007		
Operating Revenues		
Delivery Fees		$205,018
Operating Expenses		
Salaries and Related Taxes	$128,224	
Gasoline and Oil	31,000	
Repairs Expense	6,570	
Supplies Expense	2,268	
Insurance Expense	2,856	
Depreciation Expense	13,000	
Total Operating Expense		183,918
Net Income		$ 21,100

In addition, Waylon permits you to examine the accounting records, which show that the balance of *Salaries Payable* was $2,680 at the beginning of the first month but had increased to $4,240 at the end of the second month. Most of the balance in the *Insurance Expense* account reflects monthly insurance payments covering only one month each. However, the *Prepaid Insurance* account had decreased $300 during the two months, and all supplies had been purchased before Waylon took over. The balances of the company's other asset and liability accounts showed no changes.

1. Explain the cause of the difference between the increase in the *Cash* account balance and the net income for the two months.

2. Prepare a schedule that accounts for this difference.

Out of Balance

The president of Murray Stainless Steel Corporation has told you to go out to the factory and count merchandise inventory. He said the stockholders were coming for a meeting and he wanted to put on a good show. He asked you to make the inventory a bit heavy by counting one row twice. The higher ending inventory will show a higher net income. What should you do?

Ethical | DILEMMA

STREETWISE:
Questions from the
REAL WORLD

Balance Sheet Accounts

Refer to the 2004 *Annual Report* for The Home Depot, Inc., found in Appendix A.

1. Review the balance sheet. Based only on the asset account categories shown, list two types of adjusting entries you think are required each fiscal period. Which accounts are affected?

2. Based on the account categories found in the Liabilities section, describe two types of adjusting entries that may be recorded by The Home Depot, Inc., in an effort to match revenues with expenses.

Financial Statement
ANALYSIS

Balance Sheet

The following financial data was reported in the DuPont 2004 *Annual Report*.

Consolidated Balance Sheet As of December 31		
(Dollars in millions, except per share)	*2004*	*2003*
Assets		
Current Assets		
Cash and Cash Equivalents	$ 3,369	$ 3,273
Marketable Securities	167	25
Accounts and Notes Receivable	4,889	4,218
Inventories	4,489	4,107
Prepaid Expenses	209	208
Deferred Income Taxes	1,557	1,141
Assets Held for Sale	531	5,490
Total Current Assets	15,211	18,462
Property, Plant and Equipment	23,978	24,149
Less: Accumulated Depreciation	13,754	14,257
Net Property, Plant and Equipment	10,224	9,892

Analyze:

1. Based on the information presented above, which categories do you think might require adjustments at the end of an operating period?

2. List the potential adjusting entries that would be necessary. Do not worry about the dollar amounts.

3. By what percentage did DuPont's inventories increase from 2003 to 2004?

Analyze Online: Log on to the DuPont Web site (www.dupont.com). Review the current annual report and answer the following questions.

4. What method is used to depreciate property, plant, and equipment at DuPont?

5. What is the company's policy for revenue recognition?

Catalog Sales

Extending | THE THOUGHT

JC Penney Company, Inc., records sales for in-store purchases, catalog, and Internet transactions. For catalog orders, sales are not recorded in the accounting records until customers pick up the merchandise they have ordered. Other retailers record catalog or Internet sales at the point that an order is placed and credit card information has been submitted. Do you agree or disagree with the method that JC Penney, Inc., uses to record catalog sales? Prepare a statement supporting your opinion.

Memo

Business | COMMUNICATION

You are the owner of a raw furniture company that sells products via two channels of distribution: the Internet and catalogs. Your accounting clerk has prepared a ten-column worksheet for the month ended September 30, 2007. As you review the worksheet, you notice the following errors.

1. The balances of the *Depreciation Expense* account and the *Insurance Expense* account were carried over into the Balance Sheet Debit columns in error.

2. There were no adjustments recorded for *Merchandise Inventory.*

Prepare a memo to the accounting clerk outlining the errors you have noticed. Explain the impact of the errors on the financial statements. Be sure to explain the importance of the adjustment to the *Merchandise Inventory* account.

Both Sellers and Servers Adjust

Accruals and deferrals can vary for each company. The adjusting entries for a service company will differ from those of a merchandising company. Brainstorm the adjusting entries similarities and differences for a service company and a merchandising company.

TEAMWORK

There is Help for Preparing a Trial Balance

The trial balance worksheet is an organizational tool to view the accruals and deferrals on one piece of paper. Use your search engine to search for *Trial Balance Worksheet Templates.* Download several different forms of worksheets and notice the number of helpful excel templates available to download.

Internet | **CONNECTION**

Answers to **Self Reviews**

Answers to Section 1 Self Review

1. The worksheet facilitates the end-of-period activities by assembling in one document all data needed. The worksheet provides a place for the trial balance, for entering the necessary adjusting entries, an adjusted trial balance to greatly reduce the chance for mathematical errors, and all the information necessary for closing entries and preparing the income statement and balance sheet.

2. Both the beginning and ending inventory are presented in the income statement, so both should ultimately appear in the Income Statement columns. In the adjusting entries, in effect the beginning balance is closed and transferred to the Income Summary. The ending inventory is entered in the Inventory account by a debit in the Adjustments column and a credit to Income Summary because it reduces the cost of goods sold.

3. Adjusting entries are necessary because the amounts shown for many accounts in the trial balance reflect old data that ignore the fact that assets shown have been partially consumed, that expenses and incomes have not been entered in the accounts even though they have been incurred or earned, and that some liabilities and assets are not reflected in the accounts.

4. **a.** The amount of adjustments is $2,000 ($12,000 ÷ 6).

   b. *Rent Expense* will be debited and *Prepaid Rent* will be credited.

5. *Unearned Fee Income* will be debited for $7,000 and *Fee Income* will be credited for that amount.

6. There is no difference except that the amounts will be different because in one case they reflect only one month's activities and in the other case they reflect 12 months' activities.

Answers to Section 2 Self Review

1. The *Depreciation Expense* account is increased. The book value of the asset is decreased.

2. The net effects are:

   a. Assets are understated by $800.

   b. Liabilities are understated by $300.

   c. Income is understated by $800.

   d. Expenses are understated by $300.

   e. Owner's equity is understated by $500.

3. It appears that there is an error in adding the adjustment amount, or subtracting that amount from, some trial balance amount(s).

4. **a.** "credit" balance sheet column

   b. "debit" income statement column

5. *Interest Expense* is debited and *Interest Payable* is credited.

6. Adjusting entries almost invariably involve the assignment of revenues or expenses to a specific accounting period. If the revenue or expense is not assigned to the correct period, it is assigned to an incorrect period. Thus, both periods are incorrectly stated.

Answers to Comprehensive Self Review

1. The accrual method properly matches expenses with revenues in each accounting period so that statement users can rely on the financial statements prepared for each period.

2. Accrued income is income that has been earned but which has not yet been received in cash or other assets.

3. Accrued income is income earned but not yet received. Unearned income is the reverse of accrued income: It is an amount that has been received, but which has not yet been earned.

4. *Rent Income* will be debited for $12,000 and *Unearned Rent Income* will be credited for that amount.

5. This represents a loss because expenses are greater than income. The loss is $25,000.

LEARNING OBJECTIVES

1. Prepare a classified income statement from the worksheet.

2. Prepare a statement of owner's equity from the worksheet.

3. Prepare a classified balance sheet from the worksheet.

4. Journalize and post the adjusting entries.

5. Journalize and post the closing entries.

6. Prepare a postclosing trial balance.

7. Journalize and post reversing entries.

8. Define the accounting terms new to this chapter.

NEW TERMS

Classified financial statement

Current assets

Current liabilities

Current ratio

Gross profit

Gross profit percentage

Inventory turnover

Liquidity

Long-term liabilities

Multiple-step income statement

Plant and equipment

Reversing entries

Single-step income statement

Chapter 13
Financial Statements and Closing Procedures

SAFEWAY   **www.safeway.com**

I n 1915, M.B. Skaggs purchased a single grocery store from his father. By 1926 he was operating 428 Skaggs stores in 10 states. That same year Skaggs merged his company with 322 Safeway stores. Today there are approximately 1,820 Safeway stores across the U.S. and Canada. These include Vons stores in California and Nevada, Dominick's stores in the Chicago area, Randalls and Tom Thumb stores in Texas, Genuardi's stores in the Philadelphia area, and Carrs stores in Alaska.

Safeway has one of the most extensive private labels programs in North America. Safeway customers choose from more than 2,500 private label products including Safeway, Lucerne, and Mrs. Wright's and 1,250 premium products marketed under the Safeway SELECT label. Approximately 24% of Safeway's private label merchandise is manufactured in company-owned plants. Along with its chain of grocery stores, Safeway owns and operates 9 milk plants, 8 bread baking plants, 4 ice cream plants, 2 cheese and meat packaging plants, 4 soft drink bottling plants, 4 fruit and vegetable processing plants, and a pet food plant.

thinking critically   If you owned stock in Safeway, Inc., what types of financial information would be most important to you?

Section 1

SECTION OBJECTIVES

▶ 1. **Prepare a classified income statement from the worksheet.**

   WHY IT'S IMPORTANT

   To help decision makers, financial information needs to be presented in a meaningful and easy-to-use way.

▶ 2. **Prepare a statement of owner's equity from the worksheet.**

   WHY IT'S IMPORTANT

   The statement of owner's equity reports changes to and balances of the owner's equity account.

▶ 3. **Prepare a classified balance sheet from the worksheet.**

   WHY IT'S IMPORTANT

   Grouping accounts helps financial statement users to identify total assets, equity, and financial obligations of the business.

TERMS TO LEARN

classified financial statement
current assets
current liabilities
gross profit
liquidity
long-term liabilities
multiple-step income statement
plant and equipment
single-step income statement

Preparing the Financial Statements

The information needed to prepare the financial statements is on the worksheet in the Income Statement and Balance Sheet sections. At the end of the period, Simpson Antiques prepares three financial statements: income statement, statement of owner's equity, and balance sheet, based on the Worksheet you studied in Chapter 12. The income statement and the balance sheet are arranged in a classified format. On **classified financial statements**, revenues, expenses, assets, and liabilities are divided into groups of similar accounts and a subtotal is given for each group. This makes the financial statements more useful to the readers.

> The annual report of the Coca-Cola Company includes Consolidated Balance Sheets, Consolidated Statements of Income, and Consolidated Statements of Share-Owners' Equity. The annual report also contains a statement of Selected Financial Data that reports 11 consecutive years of summarized financial information.

The Classified Income Statement

A classified income statement is sometimes called a **multiple-step income statement** because several subtotals are computed before net income is calculated. The simpler income statement you learned about in previous chapters is called a **single-step income statement**. It lists all revenues in one section and all expenses in another section. Only one computation is necessary to determine the net income (Total Revenue − Total Expenses = Net Income).

Figure 13.1 on page 457 shows the classified income statement for Simpson Antiques. Refer to it as you learn how to prepare a multiple-step income statement.

OPERATING REVENUE

The first section of the classified income statement contains the revenue from operations. This is the revenue earned from normal business activities. Other income is presented separately near the bottom of the statement. For Simpson all operating revenue comes from sales of merchandise.

Simpson Antiques
Income Statement
Year Ended December 31, 2007

Operating Revenue					
Sales					561 650 00
Less Sales Returns and Allowances					12 500 00
Net Sales					549 150 00
Cost of Goods Sold					
Merchandise Inventory, Jan. 1, 2007				52 000 00	
Purchases		321 500 00			
Freight In		9 800 00			
Delivered Cost of Purchases		331 300 00			
Less Purchases Returns and Allowances	3 050 00				
Purchases Discounts	3 130 00	6 180 00			
Net Delivered Cost of Purchases			325 120 00		
Total Merchandise Available for Sale			377 120 00		
Less Merchandise Inventory, Dec. 31, 2007			47 000 00		
Cost of Goods Sold				330 120 00	
Gross Profit on Sales				219 030 00	
Operating Expenses					
Selling Expenses					
Salaries Expense—Sales		79 690 00			
Advertising Expense		7 425 00			
Cash Short or Over		125 00			
Supplies Expense		4 975 00			
Depreciation Expense—Store Equipment		2 400 00			
Total Selling Expenses			94 615 00		
General and Administrative Expenses					
Rent Expense		27 600 00			
Salaries Expense—Office		26 500 00			
Insurance Expense		2 450 00			
Payroll Taxes Expense		7 371 20			
Telephone Expense		1 875 00			
Uncollectible Accounts Expense		800 00			
Utilities Expense		5 925 00			
Depreciation Expense—Office Equipment		700 00			
Total General and Administrative Expenses			73 221 20		
Total Operating Expenses				167 836 20	
Net Income from Operations				51 193 80	
Other Income					
Interest Income		166 00			
Miscellaneous Income		582 00			
Total Other Income			748 00		
Other Expenses					
Interest Expense			770 00		
Net Nonoperating Expense				22 00	
Net Income for Year				51 171 80	

FIGURE 13.1 | Classified Income Statement

▶ 1. OBJECTIVE

Prepare a classified income statement from the worksheet.

Topic Tackler

PLUS

Because Simpson Antiques is a retail firm, it does not offer sales discounts to its customers. If it did, the sales discounts would be deducted from total sales in order to compute net sales. The net sales amount is computed as follows.

```
Sales
(Sales Returns and Allowances)
(Sales Discounts)
─────────────────────────────
Net Sales
```

The parentheses indicate that the amount is subtracted. Net sales for Simpson Antiques are $549,150 for 2007.

COST OF GOODS SOLD

The Cost of Goods Sold section contains information about the cost of the merchandise that was sold during the period. Three elements are needed to compute the cost of goods sold: beginning inventory, net delivered cost of purchases, and ending inventory. The format is

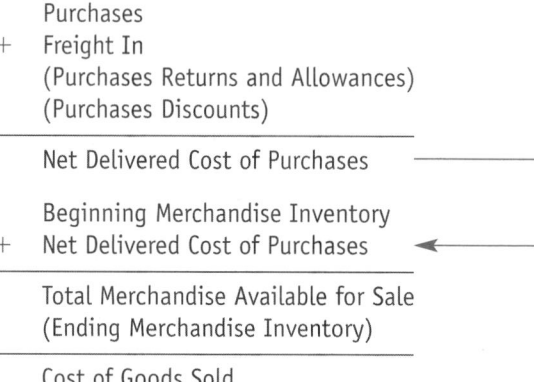

For Simpson Antiques the net delivered cost of purchases is $325,120 and the cost of goods sold is $330,120. **Merchandise Inventory** is the one account that appears on both the income statement and the balance sheet. Beginning and ending merchandise inventory balances appear on the income statement. Ending merchandise inventory also appears on the balance sheet in the Assets section.

GROSS PROFIT ON SALES

The **gross profit** on sales is the difference between the net sales and the cost of goods sold. For Simpson net sales is the revenue earned from selling antique items. Cost of goods sold is what Simpson paid for the antiques that were sold during the fiscal period. Gross profit is what is left to cover operating expenses and provide a profit. The format is

```
Net Sales
(Cost of Goods Sold)
────────────────────
Gross Profit on Sales
```

For Simpson's gross profit on sales is $219,030.

OPERATING EXPENSES

Operating expenses are expenses that arise from normal business activities. Simpson Antiques separates operating expenses into two categories: *Selling Expenses* and *General and Administrative Expenses*. The selling expenses relate directly to the sale and delivery of goods. The general and administrative expenses are necessary for business operations but are not directly connected with the sales function. Rent, utilities, and salaries for office employees are examples of general and administrative expenses.

NET INCOME OR NET LOSS FROM OPERATIONS

Keeping operating and nonoperating income separate helps financial statement users learn about the operating efficiency of the firm. The format for determining net income (or net loss) from operations is

Gross Profit on Sales
(Total Operating Expenses)

Net Income (or Net Loss) from Operations

For Simpson, net income from operations is $51,193.80.

OTHER INCOME AND OTHER EXPENSES

Income that is earned from sources other than normal business activities appears in the Other Income section. For Simpson Antiques other income includes interest on notes receivable and one miscellaneous income item.

Expenses that are not directly connected with business operations appear in the Other Expenses section. The only other expense for Simpson Antiques is interest expense.

NET INCOME OR NET LOSS

Net income is all the revenue minus all the expenses. For Simpson Antiques net income is $51,171.80. If there is a net loss, it appears in parentheses. Net income or net loss is used to prepare the statement of owner's equity.

The Statement of Owner's Equity

The statement of owner's equity reports the changes that occurred in the owner's financial interest during the period. Figure 13.2 shows the statement of owner's equity for Simpson Antiques. The ending capital balance for Patricia Simpson, $84,792.80, is used to prepare the balance sheet.

▶ 2. **OBJECTIVE**
Prepare a statement of owner's equity from the worksheet.

Simpson Antiques				
Statement of Owner's Equity				
Year Ended December 31, 2007				
Patricia Simpson, Capital, January 1, 2007			61 2 2 1 00	
Net Income for Year	51 1 7 1 80			
Less Withdrawals for the Year	27 6 0 0 00			
Increase in Capital			23 5 7 1 80	
Patricia Simpson, Capital, December 31, 2007			84 7 9 2 80	

FIGURE 13.2

Statement of Owner's Equity

The Classified Balance Sheet

The classified balance sheet divides the various assets and liabilities into groups. Figure 13.3 on page 460 shows the balance sheet for Simpson Antiques. Refer to it as you learn how to prepare a classified balance sheet.

▶ 3. **OBJECTIVE**
Prepare a classified balance sheet from the worksheet.

CURRENT ASSETS

Current assets consist of cash, items that will normally be converted into cash within one year, and items that will be used up within one year. Current assets are usually listed in order of

FIGURE 13.3

Classified Balance Sheet

Simpson Antiques
Balance Sheet
December 31, 2007

Assets					
Current Assets					
Cash				13 1 3 6 00	
Petty Cash Fund				1 0 0 00	
Notes Receivable				1 2 0 0 00	
Accounts Receivable		32 0 0 0 00			
Less Allowance for Doubtful Accounts		1 0 5 0 00	30 9 5 0 00		
Interest Receivable				3 0 00	
Merchandise Inventory				47 0 0 0 00	
Prepaid Expenses					
Supplies		1 3 2 5 00			
Prepaid Insurance		4 9 0 0 00			
Prepaid Interest		7 5 00	6 3 0 0 00		
Total Current Assets				98 7 1 6 00	
Plant and Equipment					
Store Equipment	30 0 0 0 00				
Less Accumulated Depreciation	2 4 0 0 00	27 6 0 0 00			
Office Equipment	5 0 0 0 00				
Less Accumulated Depreciation	7 0 0 00	4 3 0 0 00			
Total Plant and Equipment				31 9 0 0 00	
Total Assets				130 6 1 6 00	
Liabilities and Owner's Equity					
Current Liabilities					
Notes Payable—Trade				2 0 0 0 00	
Notes Payable—Bank				9 0 0 0 00	
Accounts Payable				24 1 2 9 00	
Interest Payable				2 0 00	
Social Security Tax Payable				1 1 5 8 40	
Medicare Tax Payable				2 6 7 40	
Employee Income Tax Payable				9 9 0 00	
Federal Unemployment Tax Payable				9 60	
State Unemployment Tax Payable				6 4 80	
Salaries Payable				1 2 0 0 00	
Sales Tax Payable				6 9 8 4 00	
Total Current Liabilities				45 8 2 3 20	
Owner's Equity					
Patricia Simpson, Capital				84 7 9 2 80	
Total Liabilities and Owner's Equity				130 6 1 6 00	

ABOUT ACCOUNTING

Financial Reports

Most large companies present condensed income statements and balance sheets for a period of 5 to 10 years in their annual reports. This provides users information that helps assess the progress in profit and financial strength of the company.

recall

Book Value

Book value is the portion of the original cost that has not been depreciated. Often book value bears no relation to the market value of the asset.

liquidity. **Liquidity** is the ease with which an item can be converted into cash. Current assets are vital to the survival of a business because they provide the funds needed to pay bills and meet expenses. The current assets for Simpson Antiques total $98,716.

PLANT AND EQUIPMENT

Noncurrent assets are called *long-term assets*. An important category of long-term assets is plant and equipment. **Plant and equipment** consists of property that will be used in the business for longer than one year. For many businesses plant and equipment represents a sizable investment. The balance sheet shows three amounts for each category of plant and equipment:

Asset
(Accumulated depreciation)
_____
Book value

For Simpson, total plant and equipment is $31,900.

CURRENT LIABILITIES

Current liabilities are the debts that must be paid within one year. They are usually listed in order of priority of payment. Management must ensure that funds are available to pay current liabilities when they become due in order to maintain the firm's good credit reputation. For Simpson, total current liabilities are $45,823.20.

LONG-TERM LIABILITIES

Long-term liabilities are debts of the business that are due more than one year in the future. Although repayment of long-term liabilities might not be due for several years, management must make sure that periodic interest is paid promptly. Long-term liabilities include mortgages, notes payable, and loans payable. Simpson Antiques had no long-term liabilities on December 31, 2007.

OWNER'S EQUITY

Simpson prepares a separate statement of owner's equity that reports all information about changes that occurred in her financial interest during the period. The ending balance from that statement is transferred to the Owner's Equity section of the balance sheet.

International INSIGHTS

Paying Bills
According to a payment survey conducted by Dun & Bradstreet, businesses in Germany are more likely to pay their bills on time; only 20 percent of invoices were paid more than 15 days after their due date. In contrast, the European average was 35 percent.

Section 1: Self Review

QUESTIONS

1. Why are financial statements prepared in classified form?

2. What is the distinction between current liabilities and long-term liabilities?

3. What is gross profit on sales?

EXERCISES

4. Which of the following is not a current asset?

   a. Merchandise inventory

   b. A note receivable due in 13 months

   c. Prepaid insurance covering the next eight months

   d. A note receivable due in eight months

5. How should purchases returns and allowances be shown on the income statement?

   a. As Other Income

   b. As a deduction from the delivered cost of purchases

   c. As an addition to Sales

   d. As Other Expenses

ANALYSIS

6. Assume that a business listed the *Freight In* account in the Operating Expense section of the income statement. What is the effect on net purchases? On total operating expenses? On net income from operations?

(Answers to Section 1 Self Review are on page 495.)

Section 2

SECTION OBJECTIVES

▶ **4. Journalize and post the adjusting entries.**

WHY IT'S IMPORTANT

Adjusting entries match revenue and expenses to the proper periods.

▶ **5. Journalize and post the closing entries.**

WHY IT'S IMPORTANT

The temporary accounts are closed in order to prepare for the next accounting period.

▶ **6. Prepare a postclosing trial balance.**

WHY IT'S IMPORTANT

The general ledger must remain in balance.

▶ **7. Journalize and post reversing entries.**

WHY IT'S IMPORTANT

Reversing entries are made so that transactions can be recorded in the usual way in the next accounting period.

TERMS TO LEARN

current ratio
gross profit percentage
inventory turnover
reversing entries

Completing the Accounting Cycle

The complete accounting cycle was presented in Chapter 6 (pages 178–179). In this section we will complete the accounting cycle for Simpson Antiques.

Journalizing and Posting the Adjusting Entries

All adjustments are shown on the worksheet. After the financial statements have been prepared, the adjustments are made a permanent part of the accounting records. They are recorded in the general journal as adjusting journal entries and are posted to the general ledger.

JOURNALIZING THE ADJUSTING ENTRIES

Figure 13.4 on pages 463–465 shows the adjusting journal entries for Simpson Antiques. Each adjusting entry shows how the adjustment was calculated. Supervisors and auditors need to understand, without additional explanation, why the adjustment was made.

Let's review the types of adjusting entries made by Simpson Antiques:

Type of Adjustment	Worksheet Reference	Purpose
Inventory	(a–b)	Removes beginning inventory and adds ending inventory to the accounting records.
Expense	(c–e)	Matches expense to revenue for the period; the credit is to a contra asset account.
Accrued Expense	(f–i)	Matches expense to revenue for the period; the credit is to a liability account.
Prepaid Expense	(j–l)	Matches expense to revenue for the period; the credit is to an asset account.
Accrued Income	(m–n)	Recognizes income earned in the period. The debit is to an asset account *(Interest Receivable)* or a liability account *(Sales Tax Payable).*

GENERAL JOURNAL   PAGE ____25____

	DATE		DESCRIPTION	POST. REF.	DEBIT	CREDIT	
1			*Adjusting Entries*				1
2	2007		*(Adjustment a)*				2
3	Dec.	31	Income Summary	399	52 000 00		3
4			Merchandise Inventory	121		52 000 00	4
5			To transfer beginning inventory				5
6			to Income Summary				6
7							7
8			*(Adjustment b)*				8
9		31	Merchandise Inventory	121	47 000 00		9
10			Income Summary	399		47 000 00	10
11			To record ending inventory				11
12							12
13			*(Adjustment c)*				13
14		31	Uncollectible Accounts Expense	685	800 00		14
15			Allowance For Doubtful Accounts	112		800 00	15
16			To record estimated loss				16
17			from uncollectible accounts				17
18			based on 0.80% of net				18
19			credit sales of $100,000				19
20							20
21			*(Adjustment d)*				21
22		31	Depreciation Expense—Store Equip.	620	2 400 00		22
23			Accum. Depreciation—Store Equip.	132		2 400 00	23
24			To record depreciation				24
25			for 2007 as shown by				25
26			schedule on file				26
27							27
28			*(Adjustment e)*				28
29		31	Depreciation Expense—Office Equip.	689	700 00		29
30			Accum. Depreciation—Office Equip.	142		700 00	30
31			To record depreciation				31
32			for 2007 as shown by				32
33			schedule on file				33
34							34
35			*(Adjustment f)*				35
36		31	Salaries Expense—Sales	602	1 200 00		36
37			Salaries Payable	229		1 200 00	37
38			To record accrued salaries				38
39			of part-time sales clerks				39
40			for Dec. 28–31				40

FIGURE 13.4

Adjusting Entries in the General Journal

FIGURE 13.4

(continued) Adjusting Entries
in the General Journal

GENERAL JOURNAL   PAGE _____26_____

	DATE		DESCRIPTION	POST. REF.	DEBIT	CREDIT	
1			*Adjusting Entries*				1
2	*2007*		*(Adjustment g)*				2
3	*Dec.*	*31*	*Payroll Taxes Expense*	*665*	*9 1 80*		3
4			*Social Security Tax Payable*	*221*		*7 4 40*	4
5			*Medicare Tax Payable*	*223*		*1 7 40*	5
6			*To record accrued payroll*				6
7			*taxes on accrued salaries*				7
8			*for Dec. 28–31*				8
9							9
10			*(Adjustment h)*				10
11		*31*	*Payroll Taxes Expense*	*665*	*7 4 40*		11
12			*Fed. Unemployment Tax Payable*	*225*		*9 60*	12
13			*State Unemployment Tax Payable*	*227*		*6 4 80*	13
14			*To record accrued payroll*				14
15			*taxes on accrued salaries*				15
16			*for Dec. 28–31*				16
17							17
18			*(Adjustment i)*				18
19		*31*	*Interest Expense*	*695*	*2 0 00*		19
20			*Interest Payable*	*216*		*2 0 00*	20
21			*To record interest on a*				21
22			*2-month, $2,000, 12%*				22
23			*note payable dated*				23
24			*Dec. 1, 2007*				24
25							25
26			*(Adjustment j)*				26
27		*31*	*Supplies Expense*	*615*	*4 9 7 5 00*		27
28			*Supplies*	*129*		*4 9 7 5 00*	28
29			*To record supplies used*				29
30							30
31			*(Adjustment k)*				31
32		*31*	*Insurance Expense*	*660*	*2 4 5 0 00*		32
33			*Prepaid Insurance*	*126*		*2 4 5 0 00*	33
34			*To record expired*				34
35			*insurance on 3-year*				35
36			*policy purchased for*				36
37			*$7,350 on Jan. 2, 2007*				37
38							38
39							39
40							40

GENERAL JOURNAL   PAGE ___27___

	DATE		DESCRIPTION	POST. REF.	DEBIT	CREDIT	
1	2007		(Adjustment l)				1
2	Dec.	31	Interest Expense	695	1 5 0 00		2
3			Prepaid Interest	127		1 5 0 00	3
4			To record transfer of 2/3				4
5			of prepaid interest of				5
6			$225 for a 3-month,				6
7			10% note payable issued				7
8			to bank on Nov. 1, 2007				8
9							9
10			(Adjustment m)				10
11		31	Interest Receivable	116	3 0 00		11
12			Interest Income	491		3 0 00	12
13			To record accrued interest				13
14			earned on a 4-month,				14
15			15% note receivable				15
16			dated Nov. 1, 2007				16
17			($1,200 x 0.15 x 2/12)				17
18							18
19			(Adjustment n)				19
20		31	Sales Tax Payable	231	2 1 6 00		20
21			Miscellaneous Income	493		2 1 6 00	21
22			To record accrued				22
23			commission earned on				23
24			sales tax owed for fourth				24
25			quarter of 2007:				25
26			Sales Tax Payable $7,200				26
27			Commission rate x 0.03				27
28			Commission due $ 216				28
29							29

FIGURE 13.4

(concluded) Adjusting Entries in the General Journal

POSTING THE ADJUSTING ENTRIES

After the adjustments have been recorded in the general journal, they are promptly posted to the general ledger. The word *Adjusting* is entered in the Description column of the general ledger account. This distinguishes it from entries for transactions that occurred during that period. After the adjusting entries have been posted, the general ledger account balances match the amounts shown in the Adjusted Trial Balance section of the worksheet in Figure 12.2.

▶ **4. OBJECTIVE**
Journalize and post the adjusting entries.

Journalizing and Posting the Closing Entries

At the end of the period, the temporary accounts are closed. The temporary accounts are the revenue, cost of goods sold, expense, and drawing accounts.

Journalize and post the closing entries.

JOURNALIZING THE CLOSING ENTRIES

The Income Statement section of the worksheet in Figure 12.2 on pages 430–432 provides the data needed to prepare closing entries. There are four steps in the closing process.

1. Close revenue accounts and cost of goods sold accounts with credit balances to *Income Summary.*

2. Close expense accounts and cost of goods sold accounts with debit balances to *Income Summary.*

3. Close *Income Summary,* which now reflects the net income or loss for the period, to owner's capital.

4. Close the drawing account to owner's capital.

Step 1: Closing the Revenue Accounts and the Cost of Goods Sold Accounts with Credit Balances. The first entry closes the revenue accounts and other temporary income statement accounts with credit balances. Look at the Income Statement section of the worksheet in Figure 12.2. There are five items listed in the Credit column, not including *Income Summary.* Debit each account, except *Income Summary,* for its balance. Credit *Income Summary* for the total, $568,578.

GENERAL JOURNAL   PAGE __28__

	DATE		DESCRIPTION	POST. REF.	DEBIT	CREDIT	
1	2007		*Closing Entries*				1
2	Dec.	31	Sales	401	561 650 00		2
3			Interest Income	491	166 00		3
4			Miscellaneous Income	493	582 00		4
5			Purchases Returns and Allowances	503	3 050 00		5
6			Purchases Discounts	504	3 130 00		6
7			Income Summary			568 578 00	7

Step 2: Closing the Expense Accounts and the Cost of Goods Sold Accounts with Debit Balances. The Debit column of the Income Statement section of the worksheet in Figure 12.2 shows the expense accounts and the cost of goods sold accounts with debit balances. Credit each account, *except Income Summary,* for its balance. Debit *Income Summary* for the total, $512,406.20.

GENERAL JOURNAL   PAGE __28__

	DATE		DESCRIPTION	POST. REF.	DEBIT	CREDIT	
1	20--						1
9	Dec.	31	Income Summary	399	512 406 20		9
10			Sales Returns and Allowances	451		12 500 00	10
11			Purchases	501		321 500 00	11
12			Freight In	502		9 800 00	12
13			Salaries Expense—Sales	602		79 690 00	13
14			Advertising Expense	605		7 425 00	14
15			Cash Short or Over	610		125 00	15
16			Supplies Expense	615		4 975 00	16
17			Depreciation Expense—Store Equip.	620		2 400 00	17
18			Rent Expense	640		27 600 00	18
19			Salaries Expense—Office	645		26 500 00	19
20			Insurance Expense	660		2 450 00	20
21			Payroll Taxes Expense	665		7 371 20	21
22			Telephone Expense	680		1 875 00	22
23			Uncollectible Accounts Expense	685		800 00	23
24			Utilities Expense	687		5 925 00	24
25			Depreciation Expense—Office Equip.	689		700 00	25
26			Interest Expense	695		770 00	26

Step 3: **Closing the Income Summary Account.** After the first two closing entries have been posted, the balance of the *Income Summary* account is net income or net loss for the period. The third closing entry transfers the *Income Summary* balance to the owner's capital account. *Income Summary* after the second closing entry has a balance of $51,171.80.

	Income Summary			
Adjusting Entries (a–b)	12/31	52,000.00	12/31	47,000.00
Closing Entries	12/31	512,406.20	12/31	568,578.00
		564,406.20		615,578.00
			Bal.	51,171.80

For Simpson Antiques the third closing entry is as follows. This closes the *Income Summary* account, which remains closed until it is used in the end-of-period process for the next year.

GENERAL JOURNAL   PAGE __28__

	DATE		DESCRIPTION	POST. REF.	DEBIT	CREDIT	
28	Dec.	31	Income Summary	399	51 171 80		28
29			Patricia Simpson, Capital	301		51 171 80	29

Step 4: **Closing the Drawing Account.** This entry closes the drawing account and updates the capital account so that its balance agrees with the ending capital reported on the statement of owner's equity and on the balance sheet.

GENERAL JOURNAL   PAGE __28__

	DATE		DESCRIPTION	POST. REF.	DEBIT	CREDIT	
31	Dec.	31	Patricia Simpson, Capital	301	27 600 00		31
32			Patricia Simpson, Drawing	302		27 600 00	32

POSTING THE CLOSING ENTRIES

The closing entries are posted from the general journal to the general ledger. The word *Closing* is entered in the Description column of each account that is closed. After the closing entry is posted, each temporary account balance is zero.

Preparing a Postclosing Trial Balance

▶ 6. OBJECTIVE
Prepare a postclosing trial balance.

After the closing entries have been posted, prepare a postclosing trial balance to confirm that the general ledger is in balance. Only the accounts that have balances—the asset, liability and owner's capital accounts—appear on the postclosing trial balance. The postclosing trial balance matches the amounts reported on the balance sheet. To verify this, compare the postclosing trial balance, Figure 13.5 on page 468, with the balance sheet, Figure 13.3 on page 460.

If the postclosing trial balance shows that the general ledger is out of balance, find and correct the error or errors immediately. Any necessary correcting entries must be journalized and posted so that the general ledger is in balance before any transactions can be recorded for the new period.

FIGURE 13.5

Postclosing Trial Balance

Simpson Antiques
Postclosing Trial Balance
December 31, 2007

ACCOUNT NAME	DEBIT	CREDIT
Cash	13 1 3 6 00	
Petty Cash Fund	1 0 0 00	
Notes Receivable	1 2 0 0 00	
Accounts Receivable	32 0 0 0 00	
Allowance for Doubtful Accounts		1 0 5 0 00
Interest Receivable	3 0 00	
Merchandise Inventory	47 0 0 0 00	
Supplies	1 3 2 5 00	
Prepaid Insurance	4 9 0 0 00	
Prepaid Interest	7 5 00	
Store Equipment	30 0 0 0 00	
Accumulated Depreciation—Store Equipment		2 4 0 0 00
Office Equipment	5 0 0 0 00	
Accumulated Depreciation—Office Equipment		7 0 0 00
Notes Payable—Trade		2 0 0 0 00
Notes Payable—Bank		9 0 0 0 00
Accounts Payable		24 1 2 9 00
Interest Payable		2 0 00
Social Security Tax Payable		1 1 5 8 40
Medicare Tax Payable		2 6 7 40
Employee Income Taxes Payable		9 9 0 00
Federal Unemployment Tax Payable		9 60
State Unemployment Tax Payable		6 4 80
Salaries Payable		1 2 0 0 00
Sales Tax Payable		6 9 8 4 00
Patricia Simpson, Capital		84 7 9 2 80
Totals	134 7 6 6 00	134 7 6 6 00

Interpreting the Financial Statements

Interested parties analyze the financial statements to evaluate the results of operations and to make decisions. Interpreting financial statements requires an understanding of the business and the environment in which it operates as well as the nature and limitations of accounting information. Ratios and other measurements are used to analyze and interpret financial statements. Three such measurements are used by Simpson Antiques.

The **gross profit percentage** reveals the amount of gross profit from each sales dollar. The gross profit percentage is calculated by dividing gross profit by net sales. For Simpson, for every dollar of net sales, gross profit was almost 40 cents.

$$\frac{\text{Gross profit}}{\text{Net sales}} = \frac{\$219{,}030}{\$549{,}150} = 0.3988 = 39.9\%$$

The **current ratio** is a relationship between current assets and current liabilities that provides a measure of a firm's ability to pay its current debts. Simpson has $2.15 in current assets for every dollar of current liabilities. The current ratio is calculated in the following manner.

$$\frac{\text{Current assets}}{\text{Current liabilities}} = \frac{\$98{,}716.00}{\$45{,}823.20} = 2.15 \text{ to } 1$$

important!

Current Ratio

Banks and other lenders look closely at the current ratio of each loan applicant.

Caterpillar Inc. reported current assets of $20.9 billion and current liabilities of $16.2 billion on December 31, 2004. The current ratio shows that the business has $1.29 of current assets for each dollar of current liabilities.

Inventory turnover shows the number of times inventory is replaced during the accounting period. Inventory turnover is calculated in the following manner.

$$\text{Inventory turnover} = \frac{\text{Cost of goods sold}}{\text{Average inventory}}$$

$$\text{Average inventory} = \frac{\text{Beginning inventory} + \text{Ending inventory}}{2}$$

$$\text{Average inventory} = \frac{\$52,000 + \$47,000}{2} = \$49,500$$

$$\text{Inventory turnover} = \frac{\$330,120}{\$49,500} = 6.67 \text{ times}$$

For Simpson Antiques the average inventory for the year was $49,500. The inventory turnover was 6.67; that is, inventory was replaced about seven times during the year.

Journalizing and Posting Reversing Entries

▶ 7. OBJECTIVE
Journalize and post reversing entries.

Some adjustments made at the end of one period can cause problems in the next period. **Reversing entries** are made to reverse the effect of certain adjustments. This helps prevent errors in recording payments or cash receipts in the new accounting period.

Let's use adjustment **(f)** as an illustration of how reversing entries are helpful. On December 31 Simpson Antiques owed $1,200 of salaries to its part-time sales clerks. The salaries will be paid in January. To recognize the salaries expense in December, adjustment **(f)** was made to debit **Salaries Expense—Sales** for $1,200 and credit **Salaries Payable** for $1,200. The adjustment was recorded and posted in the accounting records.

By payday on January 3, the part-time sales clerks have earned $1,700:

$1,200   earned in December
$ 500   earned in January

The entry to record the January 3 payment of the salaries is a debit to **Salaries Expense—Sales** for $500, a debit to **Salaries Payable** for $1,200, and a credit to **Cash** for $1,700. This entry recognizes the salary expense for January and reduces the **Salaries Payable** account to zero.

recall

Accrual Basis
Revenues are recognized when earned, and expenses are recognized when incurred or used, regardless of when cash is received or paid.

Salaries Expense—Sales				Cash			
1/3	500			12/31	13,136	1/3	1,700
				Bal.	11,436		

Salaries Payable			
1/3	1,200	12/31	1,200
		Bal.	0

To record this transaction, the accountant had to review the adjustment in the end-of-period records and divide the amount paid between the expense and liability accounts. This review is time consuming, can cause errors, and is sometimes forgotten.

COMPUTERS IN ACCOUNTING   <<

TOOLS FOR SUCCESS: DECISION SUPPORT SYSTEMS

Executives and managers use financial statements to make decisions about the future. Transportation of goods might be moved from trucking vendors to air vendors. Staff reductions or increases might be in order. These managerial decisions are made while keeping in mind the goals of the company.

Computerized decision support systems help managers make the best possible decisions. *Decision support system (DSS)* is a term used to describe computer software designed to assemble, arrange, and analyze data in order to find the most profitable plan of action. For example, an automobile manufacturing company might use the software to determine the most cost-efficient manufacturing method. In this case the decision support system would extract information from the manufacturing, engineering, accounting information, and production planning systems. The various costs associated with different techniques for body formation, engineering models, and assembly processes would be assembled and combined in potential groupings.

Then the DSS would make projections based on "what-if" scenarios, calculating outcome on profits or operational costs. For example, would costs decrease if manufacturing of glass components were completed by an outside firm? Would profits increase if steel fabrication contained different composite materials? A DSS can provide executives a vision of the integrated relationships between manufacturing processes and the bottom line.

A computerized decision support system, however, cannot integrate the human elements into decisions. For example, a DSS might reveal a change in the production process that positively affects the bottom line, but doesn't reveal its impact on employees. How will the change affect job satisfaction or stress levels? Is retraining required? A business that uses DSS in combination with human element considerations will have the information to make decisions that positively impact not only the bottom line, but also the entire organization.

THINKING CRITICALLY

Companies select among a variety of transportation methods when moving goods from suppliers to warehouses or to retail locations. Describe how you think a decision support system could be used to evaluate the various shipping methods.

INTERNET APPLICATION

Using a search engine on the Internet, find a decision support system used in the farming, aviation, robotics, or natural or biological resources management industry. Write a one-page report on the decision support system. Describe the goal of the software, the types of data needed, and the benefits provided.

Reversing entries provide a way to guard against oversights, eliminate the review of accounting records, and simplify the entry made in the new period. As an example of a reversing entry, we will analyze the same transaction (January 3 payroll of $1,700) if reversing entries are made.

First, record the adjustment on December 31. Then record the reversing entry on January 1. Note that the reversing entry is the exact opposite (the reverse) of the adjustment. After the reversing entry is posted, the **Salaries Payable** account shows a zero balance and the **Salaries Expense—Sales** account has a credit balance. This is unusual because the normal balance of an expense account is a debit.

GENERAL JOURNAL   PAGE 25

	DATE		DESCRIPTION	POST. REF.	DEBIT	CREDIT	
1	2007		*Adjusting Entries*				1
35			*(Adjustment f)*				35
36	Dec.	31	Salaries Expense—Sales	602	1 2 0 0 00		36
37			Salaries Payable	229		1 2 0 0 00	37

GENERAL JOURNAL   PAGE 29

	DATE		DESCRIPTION	POST. REF.	DEBIT	CREDIT	
1	2008		*Reversing Entries*				1
2	Jan.	1	Salaries Payable	229	1 2 0 0 00		2
3			Salaries Expense—Sales	602		1 2 0 0 00	3

ACCOUNT __Salaries Payable__   ACCOUNT NO. __229__

DATE		DESCRIPTION	POST. REF.	DEBIT	CREDIT	BALANCE DEBIT	BALANCE CREDIT
2007							
Dec.	31	Adjusting	J25		1 2 0 0 00		1 2 0 0 00
2008							
Jan.	1	Reversing	J29	1 2 0 0 00			—0—

ACCOUNT __Salaries Expense—Sales__   ACCOUNT NO. __602__

DATE		DESCRIPTION	POST. REF.	DEBIT	CREDIT	BALANCE DEBIT	BALANCE CREDIT
2007							
Dec.	31	Balance				78 4 9 0 00	
	31	Adjusting	J25	1 2 0 0 00		79 6 9 0 00	
	31	Closing	J28		79 6 9 0 00	—0—	
2008							
Jan.	1	Reversing	J29		1 2 0 0 00		1 2 0 0 00

On January 3 the payment of $1,700 of salaries is recorded in the normal manner. Notice that this entry reduces cash and increases the expense account for the entire $1,700. It does not allocate the $1,700 between the expense and liability accounts.

GENERAL JOURNAL   PAGE __30__

	DATE		DESCRIPTION	POST. REF.	DEBIT	CREDIT	
1	2008						1
2	Jan.	3	Salaries Expense—Sales	602	1 7 0 0 00		2
3			Cash	101		1 7 0 0 00	3

After this entry is posted, the expenses are properly divided between the two periods: $1,200 in December and $500 in January. The **Salaries Payable** account has a zero balance. The accountant did not have to review the previous records or allocate the payment between two accounts when the salaries were paid.

ACCOUNT __Salaries Expense—Sales__   ACCOUNT NO. __602__

DATE		DESCRIPTION	POST. REF.	DEBIT	CREDIT	BALANCE DEBIT	BALANCE CREDIT
2007							
Dec.	31	Balance				78 4 9 0 00	
	31	Adjusting	J25	1 2 0 0 00		79 6 9 0 00	
	31	Closing	J28		79 6 9 0 00	—0—	
2008							
Jan.	1	Reversing	J29		1 2 0 0 00		1 2 0 0 00
	3		J30	1 7 0 0 00		5 0 0 00	

IDENTIFYING ITEMS FOR REVERSAL

Not all adjustments need to be reversed. Normally, reversing entries are made for accrued items that involve future payments or receipts of cash. Reversing entries are not made for uncollectible accounts, depreciation, and prepaid expenses—if they are initially recorded as assets. However, when prepaid expenses are initially recorded as expenses (the alternative method), the end-of-period adjustment needs to be reversed.

Simpson Antiques makes reversing entries for:

- accrued salaries—adjustment (**f**),
- accrued payroll taxes—adjustments (**g**) and (**h**),
- interest payable—adjustment (**i**),
- interest receivable—adjustment (**m**).

JOURNALIZING REVERSING ENTRIES

We just analyzed the reversing entry for accrued salaries, adjustment (**f**). The next two reversing entries are for accrued payroll taxes. Making these reversing entries means that the accountant does not have to review the year-end adjustments before recording the payment of payroll taxes in the next year.

GENERAL JOURNAL PAGE 29

	DATE		DESCRIPTION	POST. REF.	DEBIT	CREDIT	
1	2008						1
6	Jan.	1	Social Security Tax Payable	221	7 4 40		6
7			Medicare Tax Payable	223	1 7 40		7
8			Payroll Taxes Expense	665		9 1 80	8
9			To reverse adjusting entry				9
10			(g) made Dec. 31, 2007				10
11							11
12		1	Federal Unemployment Tax Payable	225	9 60		12
13			State Unemployment Tax Payable	227	6 4 80		13
14			Payroll Taxes Expense	665		7 4 40	14
15			To reverse adjusting entry				15
16			(h) made Dec. 31, 2007				16

The next reversing entry is for accrued interest expense. The reversing entry that follows prevents recording difficulties when the note is paid on February 1.

GENERAL JOURNAL PAGE 29

	DATE		DESCRIPTION	POST. REF.	DEBIT	CREDIT	
18	Jan.	1	Interest Payable	216	2 0 00		18
19			Interest Expense	695		2 0 00	19
20			To reverse adjusting entry				20
21			(i) made Dec. 31, 2007				21

In addition to adjustments for accrued expenses, Simpson Antiques made two adjustments for accrued income items. The next reversing entry is for accrued interest income on the note receivable. Simpson will receive cash for the note and the interest on March 1. The reversing entry eliminates any difficulties in recording the interest income when the note is paid on March 1.

GENERAL JOURNAL PAGE 29

	DATE		DESCRIPTION	POST. REF.	DEBIT	CREDIT	
23	Jan.	1	Interest Income	491	3 0 00		23
24			Interest Receivable	116		3 0 00	24
25			To reverse adjusting entry				25
26			(m) made Dec. 31, 2007				26

After the reversing entry has been posted, the ***Interest Receivable*** account has a zero balance and the ***Interest Income*** account has a debit balance of $30. This is unusual because the normal balance of ***Interest Income*** is a credit.

On March 1 Simpson Antiques received a check for $1,260 in payment of the note ($1,200) and the interest ($60). The transaction is recorded in the normal manner as a debit to ***Cash*** for $1,260, a credit to ***Notes Receivable*** for $1,200, and a credit to ***Interest Income*** for $60.

Refer to the ***Interest Income*** general ledger account below. After this entry has been posted, interest income is properly divided between the two periods, $30 in the previous year and $30 in the current year. The balance of ***Interest Receivable*** is zero. The accountant does not have to review the year-end adjustments before recording the receipt of the principal and interest relating to the note receivable on March 1.

ACCOUNT _Interest Receivable_   ACCOUNT NO. _116_

DATE		DESCRIPTION	POST. REF.	DEBIT	CREDIT	BALANCE DEBIT	BALANCE CREDIT
2007							
Dec.	31	Adjusting	J27	3 0 00		3 0 00	
2008							
Jan.	1	Reversing	J29		3 0 00	–0–	

ACCOUNT _Interest Income_   ACCOUNT NO. _491_

DATE		DESCRIPTION	POST. REF.	DEBIT	CREDIT	BALANCE DEBIT	BALANCE CREDIT
2007							
Dec.	31	Balance					1 3 6 00
	31	Adjusting	J27		3 0 00		1 6 6 00
	31	Closing	J28	1 6 6 00			–0–
2008							
Jan.	1	Reversing	J29	3 0 00		3 0 00	
Mar.	1		CR3		6 0 00		3 0 00

Notice that the adjustment for sales tax commission, adjustment **(n),** is not reversed. Since no cash will be received in the new year when the sales tax return is filed, there is no need to reverse the adjustment.

Review of the Accounting Cycle

In Chapters 7, 8, and 9, The Style Shop was used to introduce accounting procedures, records, and statements for merchandising businesses. In Chapters 12 and 13, Simpson Antiques was used to illustrate the end-of-period activities for merchandising businesses. Underlying the various procedures described were the steps in the accounting cycle. Let's review the accounting cycle.

1. ***Analyze transactions.*** Transaction data comes into an accounting system from a variety of source documents—sales slips, purchase invoices, credit memorandums, check stubs, and so on. Each document is analyzed to determine the accounts and amounts affected.

2. ***Journalize the data about transactions.*** Each transaction is recorded in either a special journal or the general journal.

3. ***Post the data about transactions.*** Each transaction is transferred from the journal to the ledger accounts. Merchandising businesses typically maintain several subsidiary ledgers in addition to the general ledger.

4. ***Prepare a worksheet.*** At the end of each period, a worksheet is prepared. The Trial Balance section of the worksheet is used to prove the equality of the debits and credits in the general

ABOUT ACCOUNTING

Professional Conduct

In September 1998 the Securities and Exchange (SEC) defined improper professional conduct by accountants. The new rule allowed the SEC to censure, suspend, or bar accountants who violate it. The American Institute of Certified Public Accountants (AICPA) supported the rule. The rule led to the dissolution of one of the nation's "big five" accounting firms (Arthur Andersen) in 2003 following the imposition of severe sanctions of the firm in the "Enron Affair," in which Arthur Andersen was the auditor for Enron. The Sarbanes-Oxley Act has further strengthened the SEC's power over professional conduct by accountants.

ledger. Adjustments are entered in the Adjustments section so that the financial statements will be prepared using the accrual basis of accounting. The Adjusted Trial Balance section is used to prove the equality of the debit and credits of the updated account balances. The Income Statement and Balance Sheet sections are used to arrange data in an orderly manner.

5. ***Prepare financial statements.*** A formal set of financial statements is prepared to report information to interested parties.

6. ***Journalize and post adjusting entries.*** Adjusting entries are journalized and posted in the accounting records. This creates a permanent record of the changes shown on the worksheet.

7. ***Journalize and post closing entries.*** Closing entries are journalized and posted in order to transfer the results of operations to owner's equity and to prepare the temporary accounts for the next period. The closing entries reduce the temporary account balances to zero.

8. ***Prepare a postclosing trial balance.*** The postclosing trial balance confirms that the general ledger is still in balance and that the temporary accounts have zero balances.

9. ***Interpret the financial information.*** The accountant, owners, managers, and other interested parties interpret the information shown on the financial statements and other less formal financial reports that might be prepared. This information is used to evaluate the results of operations and the financial position of the business and to make decisions.

In addition to the nine steps listed here, some firms record reversing entries. Reversing entries simplify the recording of cash payments for accrued expenses and cash receipts for accrued income.

Figure 13.6 on page 475 shows the flow of data through an accounting system that uses special journals and subsidiary ledgers. The system is composed of subsystems that perform specialized functions.

The accounts receivable area records transactions involving sales and cash receipts and maintains the individual accounts for credit customers. This area also handles billing for credit customers.

The accounts payable area records transactions involving purchases and cash payments and maintains the individual accounts for creditors.

The general ledger and financial reporting area records transactions in the general journal, maintains the general ledger accounts, performs the end-of-period procedures, and prepares financial statements. This area is the focal point for the accounting system because all transactions eventually flow into the general ledger. In turn, the general ledger provides the data that appear on the financial statements.

MANAGERIAL IMPLICATIONS

FINANCIAL STATEMENTS

- Managers carefully study the financial statements to evaluate the operating efficiency and financial strength of the business.

- A common analysis technique is to compare the data on current statements with the data from previous statements. This can reveal developing trends.

- In large businesses, financial statements are compared with the published financial reports of other companies in the same industry.

- In order to evaluate information on classified financial statements, managers need to understand the nature and significance of the groupings.

- Management ensures that closing entries are promptly made so that transactions for the new period can be recorded. Any significant delay means that valuable information, such as the firm's cash position, will not be available or up to date.

- The efficiency and effectiveness of the adjusting and closing procedures can have a positive effect on the annual independent audit. For example, detailed descriptions in the general journal make it easy for the auditor to understand the adjusting entries.

THINKING CRITICALLY

How can managers use the financial statements to learn about a company's operating efficiency?

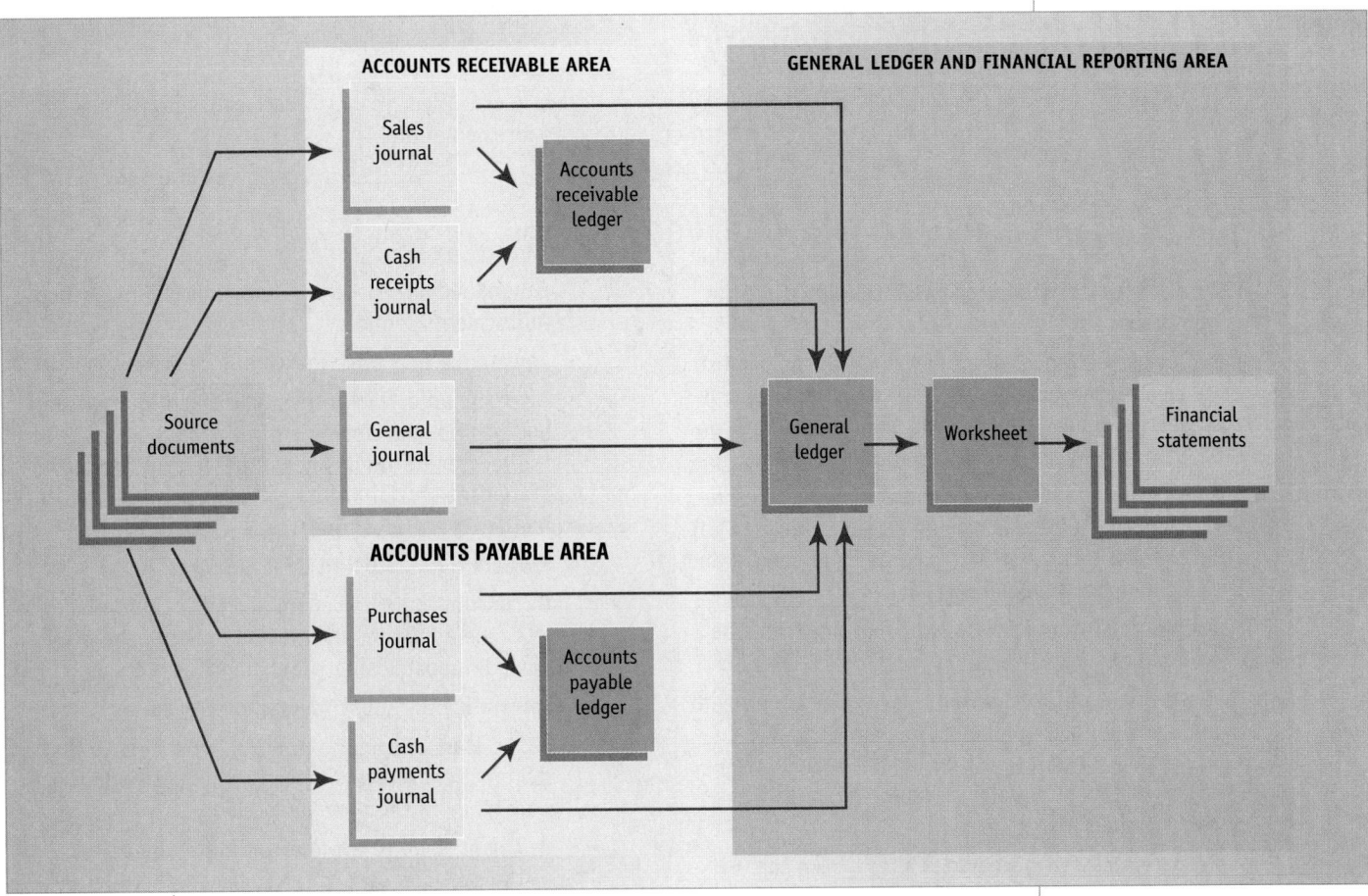

FIGURE 13.6 | Flow of Financial Data through an Accounting System

Section 2: **Self Review**

QUESTIONS

1. Which adjusting entries should be reversed?

2. Why do adjusting entries need detailed explanations in the general journal?

3. What do the four steps in the closing process accomplish?

EXERCISES

4. A reversing entry is made for an end-of-period adjustment that recorded

   a. estimated bad debts for the period.

   b. an accrued expense that involves future cash payments.

   c. a transfer of an amount from a prepaid expense account to an expense account.

   d. the change in merchandise inventory.

5. The current ratio is

   a. current liabilities divided by current assets,

   b. the sum of Cash, Accounts Receivable and Notes Receivable, divided by Current Liabilities.

   c. current assets divided by total liabilities.

   d. current assets divided by current liabilities.

ANALYSIS

6. At the end of the previous accounting period, an adjusting entry to record accrued employer's payroll taxes was made. Reversing entries were not made for the current accounting period. What effect will this have on the current period's financial statements?

(Answers to Section 2 Self Review are on page 495.)

REVIEW Chapter Summary

In this chapter, you have learned how to prepare classified financial statements from the worksheet and how to close the accounting records for the period.

Learning Objectives

1 Prepare a classified income statement from the worksheet.

- A classified income statement for a merchandising business usually includes these sections: Operating Revenue, Cost of Goods Sold, Gross Profit on Sales, Operating Expenses, and Net Income.
- To make the income statement even more useful, operating expenses may be broken down into categories, such as selling expenses and general and administrative expenses.

2 Prepare a statement of owner's equity from the worksheet.

A statement of owner's equity is prepared to provide detailed information about the changes in the owner's financial interest during the period. The ending owner's capital balance is used to prepare the balance sheet.

3 Prepare a classified balance sheet from the worksheet.

- Assets are usually presented in two groups—current assets, and plant and equipment. Current assets consist of cash, items to be converted into cash within one year, and items to be used up within one year. Plant and equipment consists of property that will be used for a long time in the operations of the business.
- Liabilities are also divided into two groups—current liabilities and long-term liabilities. Current liabilities will normally be paid within one year. Long-term liabilities are due in more than one year.

4 Journalize and post the adjusting entries.

When the year-end worksheet and financial statements have been completed, adjusting entries are recorded in the general journal and posted to the

general ledger. The data comes from the worksheet Adjustments section.

5 Journalize and post the closing entries.

After the adjusting entries have been journalized and posted, the closing entries should be recorded in the records of the business. The data in the Income Statement section of the worksheet can be used to journalize the closing entries.

6 Prepare a postclosing trial balance.

To confirm that the general ledger is still in balance after the adjusting and closing entries have been posted, a postclosing trial balance is prepared.

7 Journalize and post reversing entries.

At the start of each new period, most firms follow the practice of reversing certain adjustments that were made in the previous period.

- This is done to avoid recording problems with transactions that will occur in the new period.
- Usually, only adjusting entries for accrued expenses and accrued income need be considered for reversing. Of these, usually only accrued expense and income items involving future payments and receipts of cash can cause difficulties later and should therefore be reversed.
- The use of reversing entries is optional. Reversing entries save time, promote efficiency, and help to achieve a proper matching of revenue and expenses in each period.
- With reversing entries, there is no need to examine each transaction to see whether a portion applies to the past period and then divide the amount of the transaction between the two periods.

8 Define the accounting terms new to this chapter.

Glossary

Classified financial statement (p. 456) A format by which revenues and expenses on the income statement, and assets and liabilities on the balance sheet, are divided into groups of similar accounts and a subtotal is given for each group

Current assets (p. 459) Assets consisting of cash, items that normally will be converted into cash within one year, or items that will be used up within one year

Current liabilities (p. 461) Debts that must be paid within one year

Current ratio (p. 468) A relationship between current assets and current liabilities that provides a measure of a firm's ability to pay its current debts (current ratio = current assets ÷ current liabilities)

Gross profit (p. 458) The difference between net sales and the cost of goods sold (gross profit = net sales − cost of goods sold)

Gross profit percentage (p. 468) The amount of gross profit from each dollar of sales (gross profit percentage = gross profit ÷ net sales)

Inventory turnover (p. 469) The number of times inventory is purchased and sold during the accounting period (inventory turnover = cost of goods sold ÷ average inventory)

Liquidity (p. 460) The ease with which an item can be converted into cash

Long-term liabilities (p. 461) Debts of a business that are due more than one year in the future

Multiple-step income statement (p. 456) A type of income statement on which several subtotals are computed before the net income is calculated

Plant and equipment (p. 460) Property that will be used in the business for longer than one year

Reversing entries (p. 469) Journal entries made to reverse the effect of certain adjusting entries involving accrued income or accrued expenses to avoid problems in recording future payments or receipts of cash in a new accounting period

Single-step income statement (p. 456) A type of income statement where only one computation is needed to determine the net income (total revenue − total expenses = net income)

Comprehensive **Self Review**

1. Explain the difference between a single-step income statement and a multiple-step income statement. Which is normally favored?
2. What journal entry(ies) is (are) made in the adjustment column for beginning and ending inventories?
3. Why would a fax machine used in the office not be considered a current asset?
4. Immediately after closing entries are posted, which of the following types of accounts will have zero balances?
   a. asset accounts
   b. expense accounts
   c. liability accounts
   d. owner's drawing account
   e. *Income Summary* account
   f. owner's capital account
   g. revenue accounts
5. Give the sequence in which the following journal entries are posted to the accounts.
   a. adjusting entries
   b. entries to close expense accounts
   c. entries to close revenue accounts
   d. reversing entries
6. Describe the entry that would be made to close the *Income Summary* account in each of the following cases. The owner of the firm is Dorothy Hitt.
   a. There is net income of $38,000.
   b. There is a net loss of $18,000.

7. Which of the following accounts should have debit balances in the adjusted trial balance?

   a. *Sales Returns and Allowances*

   b. *Purchases Discounts*

   c. *Salaries Payable*

   d. *Unearned Rental Income*

(Answers to Comprehensive Self Review are on page 495.)

Discussion Questions

1. What is the difference, if any, between the classification Other Revenue and Expense and the classification Extraordinary Gains and Losses?

2. What are operating expenses?

3. Which section of the income statement contains information about the purchases made during the period and the beginning and ending inventories?

4. What is the purpose of the balance sheet?

5. What are current assets that usually are classified as Current Assets on the balance sheet?

6. How do current liabilities and long-term liabilities differ?

7. What information is provided by the statement of owner's equity?

8. What account balances or other amount are included on two different financial statements for the period? Which statements are involved?

9. What is the purpose of the postclosing trial balance?

10. What accounts appear on the postclosing trial balance?

11. If the totals of the adjusted trial balance Debit and Credit columns are equal, but the postclosing trial balance does not balance, what are likely causes of the problem?

12. What types of adjustments are reversed?

13. On December 31, Klien Company made an adjusting entry debiting *Interest Receivable* and crediting *Interest Income* for $300 of accrued interest. What reversing entry, if any, should be recorded for this item on January 1?

14. Various adjustments made at Acres Company are listed below. Which of the adjustments would normally be reversed?

   a. Adjustment for accrued payroll taxes expense

   b. Adjustment for supplies used

   c. Adjustment for depreciation on the building

   d. Adjustment for estimated uncollectible accounts

   e. Adjustment for accrued interest income

   f. Adjustment for beginning inventory

   g. Adjustment for estimated uncollectible accounts

   h. Adjustment to record portion of insurance premiums that have expired

15. What are the steps in the accounting cycle?

16. If the owner invests additional capital in the business during the month, how would that new investment be shown in the financial statements?

APPLICATIONS

Exercises

Classifying income statement items.

◄ **Exercise 13.1**
Objective 1

The following accounts appear on the worksheet of Odds and Ends Craft Store. Indicate the section of the classified income statement in which each account will be reported.

SECTIONS OF CLASSIFIED INCOME STATEMENT

a. Operating Revenue

b. Cost of Goods Sold

c. Operating Expenses

d. Other Income

e. Other Expenses

ACCOUNTS

1. Rent Expense

2. Depreciation Expense—Store Equipment

3. Sales

4. Interest Expense

5. Merchandise Inventory

6. Interest Income

7. Purchases

8. Sales Returns and Allowances

9. Utilities Expense

10. Purchases Returns and Allowances

Classifying balance sheet items.

◄ **Exercise 13.2**
Objective 3

The following accounts appear on the worksheet of Odds and Ends Craft Store. Indicate the section of the classified balance sheet in which each account will be reported.

SECTIONS OF CLASSIFIED BALANCE SHEET

a. Current Assets

b. Plant and Equipment

c. Current Liabilities

d. Long-Term Liabilities

e. Owner's Equity

ACCOUNTS

1. Rent Payable

2. Cash

3. Raja Julia, Capital

4. Merchandise Inventory

5. Accounts Payable

6. Store Supplies

7. Sales Tax Payable

8. Prepaid Insurance

9. Delivery Van

10. Accounts Receivable

CHAPTER 13: Review and Applications

Exercise 13.3
Objective 1

▶ **Preparing a classified income statement.**

The worksheet of Bowie Office Supply contains the following revenue, cost, and expense accounts. Prepare a classified income statement for this firm for the year ended December 31, 2007. The merchandise inventory amounted to $58,125 on January 1, 2007, and $51,300 on December 31, 2007. The expense accounts numbered 611 through 617 represent selling expenses, and those numbered 631 through 646 represent general and administrative expenses.

ACCOUNTS

401	Sales	$246,000	Cr.
451	Sales Returns and Allowances	4,200	Dr.
491	Miscellaneous Income	220	Cr.
501	Purchases	102,000	Dr.
502	Freight In	1,800	Dr.
503	Purchases Returns and Allowances	3,000	Cr.
504	Purchases Discounts	1,600	Cr.
611	Salaries Expense—Sales	44,200	Dr.
614	Store Supplies Expense	2,200	Dr.
617	Depreciation Expense—Store Equipment	1,400	Dr.
631	Rent Expense	12,000	Dr.
634	Utilities Expense	2,800	Dr.
637	Salaries Expense—Office	20,000	Dr.
640	Payroll Taxes Expense	5,000	Dr.
643	Depreciation Expense—Office Equipment	400	Dr.
646	Uncollectible Accounts Expense	640	Dr.
691	Interest Expense	520	Dr.

Exercise 13.4
Objective 2

▶ **Preparing a statement of owner's equity.**

The worksheet of Bowie Office Supply contains the following owner's equity accounts. Use this data and the net income determined in Exercise 13.3 to prepare a statement of owner's equity for the year ended December 31, 2007. No additional investments were made during the period.

ACCOUNTS

301	Sumit Patel, Capital	$61,200	Cr.
302	Sumit Patel, Drawing	40,200	Dr.

Exercise 13.5
Objective 3

▶ **Preparing a classified balance sheet.**

The worksheet of Bowie Office Supply contains the following asset and liability accounts. The balance of the **Notes Payable** account consists of notes that are due within a year. Prepare a balance sheet dated December 31, 2007. Obtain the ending capital for the period from the statement of owner's equity completed in Exercise 13.4.

ACCOUNTS

101	Cash	$11,780	Dr.
107	Change Fund	400	Dr.
111	Accounts Receivable	5,040	Dr.
112	Allowance for Doubtful Accounts	760	Cr.
121	Merchandise Inventory	51,300	Dr.
131	Store Supplies	1,000	Dr.
133	Prepaid Interest	80	Dr.
141	Store Equipment	10,200	Dr.
142	Accum. Depreciation—Store Equipment	1,080	Cr.
151	Office Equipment	3,200	Dr.

ACCOUNTS (CONT.)

152	Accum. Depreciation—Office Equipment	400	Cr.
201	Notes Payable	5,400	Cr.
203	Accounts Payable	5,625	Cr.
216	Interest Payable	60	Cr.
231	Sales Tax Payable	1,840	Cr.

◀ **Exercise 13.6**
Objective 5

Recording closing entries.

On December 31, 2007, the Income Statement section of the worksheet for Tompkins Company contained the following information. Give the entries that should be made in the general journal to close the revenue, cost of goods sold, expense, and other temporary accounts.

INCOME STATEMENT SECTION

	Debit	Credit
Income Summary	$ 38,000	$ 40,000
Sales		254,300
Sales Returns and Allowances	3,100	
Sales Discounts	2,300	
Interest Income		100
Purchases	134,300	
Freight In	1,700	
Purchases Returns and Allowances		1,900
Purchases Discounts		1,740
Rent Expense	8,400	
Utilities Expense	2,875	
Telephone Expense	1,450	
Salaries Expense	65,000	
Payroll Taxes Expense	5,150	
Supplies Expense	1,600	
Depreciation Expense	2,400	
Interest Expense	350	
Totals	$266,625	$298,040

Assume further that the owner of the firm is Bobby Tompkins and that the **Bobby Tompkins, Drawing** account had a balance of $26,000 on December 31, 2007.

◀ **Exercise 13.7**
Objective 7

Journalizing reversing entries.

Examine the following adjusting entries and determine which ones should be reversed. Show the reversing entries that should be recorded in the general journal as of January 1, 2008. Include appropriate descriptions.

2007	(Adjustment a)		
Dec. 31	Uncollectible Accounts Expense	3,600.00	
	Allowance for Doubtful Accounts		3,600.00
	To record estimated loss from uncollectible accounts based on 0.5% of net credit sales, $720,000		
	(Adjustment b)		
Dec. 31	Supplies Expense	4,640.00	
	Supplies		4,640.00
	To record supplies used during the year		

(Adjustment c)

| 31 | Insurance Expense | 1,350.00 | |
| | Prepaid Insurance | | 1,350.00 |

To record expired insurance on 1-year
$5,400 policy purchased on Oct. 1

(Adjustment d)

| 31 | Depreciation. Exp.—Store Equipment | 14,300.00 | |
| | Accum. Depreciation—Store Equip. | | 14,300.00 |

To record depreciation

(Adjustment e)

| 31 | Salaries Expense—Office | 2,600.00 | |
| | Salaries Payable | | 2,600.00 |

To record accrued salaries for Dec. 29–31

(Adjustment f)

31	Payroll Tax Expense	198.90	
	Social Security Tax Payable		161.20
	Medicare Tax Payable		37.70

To record accrued payroll taxes on accrued
salaries: social security, 6.2% $\times$ 2,600 =
$161.20; Medicare, 1.45% $\times$ 2,600 = $37.70

(Adjustment g)

| 31 | Interest Expense | 240.00 | |
| | Interest Payable | | 240.00 |

To record accrued interest on a 4-month,
6% trade note payable dated Nov. 1:
$24,000 $\times$ 0.06 $\times$ $\frac{2}{12}$ = $240

(Adjustment h)

| 31 | Interest Receivable | 200.00 | |
| | Interest Income | | 200.00 |

To record interest earned on 6-month,
10% note receivable dated Oct. 1:
$8,000 $\times$ 0.10 $\times$ $\frac{3}{12}$ = $200

Exercise 13.8 ▶ **Preparing a postclosing trial balance.**
Objective 6

The Adjusted Trial Balance section of the worksheet for Harmon Farm Supply follows. The owner made no additional investments during the year. Prepare a postclosing trial balance for the firm on December 31, 2007.

ACCOUNTS

	Debit	Credit
Cash	$ 18,600	
Accounts Receivable	59,800	
Allowance for Doubtful Accounts		$ 120
Merchandise Inventory	186,200	
Supplies	7,140	
Prepaid Insurance	3,060	
Equipment	51,000	
Accumulated Depreciation—Equipment		17,800
Notes Payable		9,500
Accounts Payable		8,700
Social Security Tax Payable		1,392
Medicare Tax Payable		324

ACCOUNTS (CONT.)

	Debit	Credit
Ken Harmon, Capital		267,964
Ken Harmon, Drawing	74,000	
Income Summary	180,000	186,200
Sales		773,000
Sales Returns and Allowances	14,400	
Purchases	486,900	
Freight In	5,400	
Purchases Returns and Allowances		8,500
Purchases Discounts		5,300
Rent Expense	33,800	
Telephone Expense	6,246	
Salaries Expense	123,140	
Payroll Taxes Expense	11,734	
Supplies Expense	6,600	
Insurance Expense	1,560	
Depreciation Expense—Equipment	8,100	
Uncollectible Accounts Expense	1,120	
Totals	$1,278,800	$1,278,800

PROBLEMS

Problem Set A

Preparing classified financial statements.

Hotwire Company distributes electronic components to small manufacturers. The adjusted trial balance data given below is from the firm's worksheet for the year ended December 31, 2007.

◀ **Problem 13.1A**
Objectives 1, 2, 3

eXcel

INSTRUCTIONS

1. Prepare a classified income statement for the year ended December 31, 2007. The expense accounts represent warehouse expenses, selling expenses, and general and administrative expenses.
2. Prepare a statement of owner's equity for the year ended December 31, 2007. No additional investments were made during the period.
3. Prepare a classified balance sheet as of December 31, 2007. The mortgage and the loans extend for more than a year.

ACCOUNTS

	Debit	Credit
Cash	$ 28,630	
Petty Cash Fund	400	
Notes Receivable	10,800	
Accounts Receivable	55,400	
Allowance for Doubtful Accounts		$ 5,000
Merchandise Inventory	228,325	
Warehouse Supplies	2,760	
Office Supplies	1,510	

ACCOUNTS (CONT.)

	Debit	Credit
Prepaid Insurance	7,200	
Land	36,000	
Building	172,000	
Accumulated Depreciation—Building		47,800
Warehouse Equipment	32,000	
Accumulated Depreciation—Warehouse Equipment		14,400
Delivery Equipment	44,200	
Accumulated Depreciation—Delivery Equipment		17,600
Office Equipment	20,000	
Accumulated Depreciation—Office Equipment		8,500
Notes Payable		19,200
Accounts Payable		42,000
Interest Payable		480
Mortgage Payable		56,000
Loans Payable, Long-term		12,000
Se Ri Pak, Capital (Jan. 1)		379,460
Se Ri Pak, Drawing	124,600	
Income Summary	234,000	228,325
Sales		1,763,400
Sales Returns and Allowances	17,200	
Interest Income		1,480
Purchases	769,700	
Freight In	12,800	
Purchases Returns and Allowances		7,440
Purchases Discounts		11,600
Warehouse Wages Expense	198,740	
Warehouse Supplies Expense	7,600	
Depreciation Expense—Warehouse Equipment	7,800	
Salaries Expense—Sales	270,800	
Travel and Entertainment Expense	28,750	
Delivery Wages Expense	91,650	
Depreciation Expense—Delivery Equipment	8,800	
Salaries Expense—Office	77,600	
Office Supplies Expense	3,550	
Insurance Expense	5,200	
Utilities Expense	9,600	
Telephone Expense	6,520	
Payroll Taxes Expense	62,500	
Property Taxes Expense	4,600	
Uncollectible Accounts Expense	4,800	
Depreciation Expense—Building	11,000	
Depreciation Expense—Office Equipment	6,000	
Interest Expense	11,650	
Totals	$2,614,685	$2,614,685

Analyze: What is the current ratio for this business?

Preparing classified financial statements.

Good to Go Auto Products distributes automobile parts to service stations and repair shops. The adjusted trial balance data that follows is from the firm's worksheet for the year ended December 31, 2007.

◀ Problem 13.2A
Objectives 1, 2, 3

eXcel

INSTRUCTIONS

1. Prepare a classified income statement for the year ended December 31, 2007. The expense accounts represent warehouse expenses, selling expenses, and general and administrative expenses.

2. Prepare a statement of owner's equity for the year ended December 31, 2007. No additional investments were made during the period.

3. Prepare a classified balance sheet as of December 31, 2007. The mortgage and the long-term notes extend for more than one year.

ACCOUNTS

	Debit	Credit
Cash	$ 98,000	
Petty Cash Fund	500	
Notes Receivable	10,000	
Accounts Receivable	139,200	
Allowance for Doubtful Accounts		$ 2,800
Interest Receivable	100	
Merchandise Inventory	127,500	
Warehouse Supplies	2,300	
Office Supplies	600	
Prepaid Insurance	3,640	
Land	15,000	
Building	102,000	
Accumulated Depreciation—Building		16,200
Warehouse Equipment	18,800	
Accumulated Depreciation—Warehouse Equipment		9,000
Office Equipment	8,400	
Accumulated Depreciation—Office Equipment		3,400
Notes Payable—Short-Term		14,000
Accounts Payable		55,900
Interest Payable		300
Notes Payable—Long-Term		12,000
Mortgage Payable		15,000
Colin O'Brien, Capital (Jan. 1)		317,020
Colin O'Brien, Drawing	69,650	
Income Summary	130,400	127,500
Sales		1,090,300
Sales Returns and Allowances	7,400	
Interest Income		480
Purchases	453,000	
Freight In	8,800	
Purchases Returns and Allowances		12,650
Purchases Discounts		8,240
Warehouse Wages Expense	107,600	
Warehouse Supplies Expense	4,800	

CHAPTER 13: Review and Applications

ACCOUNTS (CONT.)

	Debit	Credit
Depreciation Expense—Warehouse Equipment	2,400	
Salaries Expense—Sales	150,700	
Travel Expense	23,000	
Delivery Expense	36,425	
Salaries Expense—Office	84,000	
Office Supplies Expense	1,120	
Insurance Expense	8,875	
Utilities Expense	7,000	
Telephone Expense	3,180	
Payroll Taxes Expense	30,600	
Building Repairs Expense	2,700	
Property Taxes Expense	15,400	
Uncollectible Accounts Expense	2,580	
Depreciation Expense—Building	4,600	
Depreciation Expense—Office Equipment	1,520	
Interest Expense	3,000	
Totals	$1,684,790	$1,684,790

Analyze: What percentage of total operating expenses is attributable to warehouse expenses?

Problem 13.3A ▶

Objectives 4, 5, 7

Journalizing adjusting, closing, and reversing entries.

Obtain all data that is necessary from the worksheet prepared for Healthy Habits Company in Problem 12.4A. Then follow the instructions to complete this problem.

INSTRUCTIONS

1. Record adjusting entries in the general journal as of December 31, 2007. Use 25 as the first journal page number. Include descriptions for the entries.

2. Record closing entries in the general journal as of December 31, 2007. Include descriptions.

3. Record reversing entries in the general journal as of January 1, 2008. Include descriptions.

Analyze: Assuming that the firm did not record a reversing entry for salaries payable, what entry is required when salaries of $5,000 are paid in January?

Problem 13.4A ▶

Objectives 4, 7

Journalizing adjusting and reversing entries.

The data below concerns adjustments to be made at Vaughn Company.

INSTRUCTIONS

1. Record the adjusting entries in the general journal as of December 31, 2007. Use 25 as the first journal page number. Include descriptions.

2. Record reversing entries in the general journal as of January 1, 2008. Include descriptions.

ADJUSTMENTS

a. On October 1, 2007, the firm signed a lease for a warehouse and paid rent of $17,700 in advance for a six-month period.

b. On December 31, 2007, an inventory of supplies showed that items costing $1,840 were on hand. The balance of the **Supplies** account was $11,120.

c. A depreciation schedule for the firm's equipment shows that a total of $8,200 should be charged off as depreciation for 2007.

d. On December 31, 2007, the firm owed salaries of $4,400 that will not be paid until January 2008.

e. On December 31, 2007, the firm owed the employer's social security (6.2 percent) and Medicare (1.45 percent) taxes on all accrued salaries.

f. On September 1, 2007, the firm received a five-month, 8 percent note for $4,500 from a customer with an overdue balance.

Analyze: After the adjusting entries have been posted, what is the balance of the **Prepaid Rent** account on January 1, 2008?

Problem Set B

Preparing classified financial statements.

The Floppy Disk Store is a retail store that sells computers and computer supplies. The adjusted trial balance data given below is from the firm's worksheet for the year ended December 31, 2007.

◀ **Problem 13.1B**
Objectives 1, 2, 3

INSTRUCTIONS

1. Prepare a classified income statement for the year ended December 31, 2007. The expense accounts represent warehouse expenses, selling expenses, and general and administrative expenses.

2. Prepare a statement of owner's equity for the year ended December 31, 2007. No additional investments were made during the period.

3. Prepare a classified balance sheet as of December 31, 2007. The mortgage and the loans extend for more than one year.

ACCOUNTS

	Debit	Credit
Cash	$ 9,842	
Petty Cash Fund	100	
Notes Receivable	3,200	
Accounts Receivable	16,326	
Allowance for Doubtful Accounts		$ 2,250
Merchandise Inventory	35,400	
Warehouse Supplies	775	
Office Supplies	780	
Prepaid Insurance	2,200	
Land	7,642	
Building	48,500	
Accum. Depr.—Building		13,000
Warehouse Equipment	8,000	
Accumulated Depreciation—Warehouse Equipment		2,300
Delivery Equipment	16,400	
Accumulated Depreciation—Delivery Equipment		3,600
Office Equipment	6,000	
Accumulated Depreciation—Office Equipment		2,500
Notes Payable		5,000
Accounts Payable		11,700
Interest Payable		240
Mortgage Payable		15,950
Loans Payable		4,000
Franz Ulrich, Capital (Jan. 1)		60,940

ACCOUNTS (CONT.)

	Debit	Credit
Franz Ulrich, Drawing	24,000	
Income Summary	33,125	35,400
Sales		431,100
Sales Returns and Allowances	3,150	
Interest Income		462
Purchases	186,600	
Freight In	2,200	
Purchases Returns and Allowances		2,520
Purchases Discounts		2,350
Warehouse Wages Expense	38,900	
Warehouse Supplies Expense	1,790	
Depreciation Expense—Warehouse Equipment	1,400	
Salaries Expense—Sales	67,200	
Travel and Entertainment Expense	6,300	
Delivery Wages Expense	24,642	
Depreciation Expense—Delivery Equipment	2,440	
Salaries Expense—Office	15,900	
Office Supplies Expense	1,150	
Insurance Expense	1,500	
Utilities Expense	2,800	
Telephone Expense	1,380	
Payroll Taxes Expense	15,250	
Property Taxes Expense	1,750	
Uncollectible Accounts Expense	1,050	
Depreciation Expense—Building	3,000	
Depreciation Expense—Office Equipment	1,020	
Interest Expense	1,600	
Totals	$593,312	$593,312

Analyze: What is the gross profit percentage for the period ended December 31, 2007?

Problem 13.2B ▶   **Preparing classified financial statements.**
Objectives 1, 2, 3   Hog Wild is a retail firm that sells motorcycles, parts, and accessories. The adjusted trial balance data given below is from the firm's worksheet for the year ended December 31, 2007.

INSTRUCTIONS

1. Prepare a classified income statement for the year ended December 31, 2007. The expense accounts represent warehouse expenses, selling expenses, and general and administrative expenses.

2. Prepare a statement of owner's equity for the year ended December 31, 2007. No additional investments were made during the period.

3. Prepare a classified balance sheet as of December 31, 2007. The mortgage and the long-term notes extend for more than one year.

ACCOUNTS

	Debit	Credit
Cash	$ 14,350	
Petty Cash Fund	200	
Notes Receivable	6,000	

ACCOUNTS (CONT.)	Debit	Credit
Accounts Receivable	54,600	
Allowance for Doubtful Accounts		$ 5,000
Interest Receivable	200	
Merchandise Inventory	87,915	
Warehouse Supplies	3,700	
Office Supplies	1,800	
Prepaid Insurance	6,900	
Land	20,400	
Building	53,100	
Accumulated Depreciation—Building		8,400
Warehouse Equipment	24,000	
Accumulated Depreciation—Warehouse Equipment		4,000
Office Equipment	12,800	
Accumulated Depreciation—Office Equipment		1,800
Notes Payable—Short-Term		8,000
Accounts Payable		32,500
Interest Payable		1,800
Notes Payable—Long-Term		6,000
Mortgage Payable		35,875
Nick Henry, Capital (Jan. 1)		198,710
Nick Henry, Drawing	56,000	
Income Summary	88,980	87,915
Sales		608,417
Sales Returns and Allowances	9,400	
Interest Income		720
Purchases	230,050	
Freight In	9,600	
Purchases Returns and Allowances		6,420
Purchases Discounts		5,760
Warehouse Wages Expense	64,300	
Warehouse Supplies Expense	4,300	
Depreciation Expense—Warehouse Equipment	2,400	
Salaries Expense—Sales	78,900	
Travel Expense—Sales	21,000	
Delivery Expense	35,400	
Salaries Expense—Office	57,500	
Office Supplies Expense	1,360	
Insurance Expense	9,500	
Utilities Expense	6,912	
Telephone Expense	4,370	
Payroll Taxes Expense	19,200	
Building Repairs Expense	3,100	
Property Taxes Expense	11,700	
Uncollectible Accounts Expense	2,900	
Depreciation Expense—Building	3,200	
Depreciation Expense—Office Equipment	1,680	
Interest Expense	3,600	
Totals	$1,011,317	$1,011,317

Analyze: What is the inventory turnover for Hog Wild?

Problem 13.3B ▶   **Journalizing adjusting, closing, and reversing entries.**

Objectives 4, 5, 7   Obtain all data that is necessary from the worksheet prepared for Whatnots in Problem 12.4B. Then follow the instructions to complete this problem.

CONTINUING >>>
Problem

INSTRUCTIONS

1. Record adjusting entries in the general journal as of December 31, 2007. Use 29 as the first journal page number. Include descriptions for the entries.
2. Record closing entries in the general journal as of December 31, 2007. Include descriptions.
3. Record reversing entries in the general journal as of January 1, 2008. Include descriptions.

Analyze: Assuming that the company did not record a reversing entry for salaries payable, what entry is required when salaries of $2,600 are paid in January? (Ignore payroll taxes withheld.)

Problem 13.4B ▶   **Journalizing adjusting and reversing entries.**

Objectives 4, 7   The data below concerns adjustments to be made at Ramos Company.

INSTRUCTIONS

1. Record the adjusting entries in the general journal as of December 31, 2007. Use 25 as the first journal page number. Include descriptions.
2. Record reversing entries in the general journal as of January 1, 2008. Include descriptions.

ADJUSTMENTS

a. On August 1, 2007, the firm signed a one-year advertising contract with a trade magazine and paid the entire amount, $9,000, in advance. **Prepaid Advertising** had a balance of $9,000 on December 31, 2007.

b. On December 31, 2007, an inventory of supplies showed that items costing $1,300 were on hand. The balance of the **Supplies** account was $8,690.

c. A depreciation schedule for the firm's store equipment shows that a total of $6,250 should be charged off as depreciation for 2007.

d. On December 31, 2007, the firm owed salaries of $3,400 that will not be paid until January 2008.

e. On December 31, 2007, the firm owed the employer's social security (6.2 percent) and Medicare (1.45 percent) taxes on all accrued salaries.

f. On October 1, 2007, the firm received a five-month, 8 percent note for $4,400 from a customer with an overdue balance.

Analyze: Assuming that the company did not make a reversing entry for salaries payable, what entry would be required to record the payment of salaries of $3,800 in January? (Ignore payroll tax deductions.)

Challenge Problem

Year-End Processing

Programs Plus is a retail firm that sells computer programs for home and business use. On December 31, 2007, its general ledger contained the accounts and balances shown below.

ACCOUNTS	BALANCES	
Cash	$ 15,280	Dr.
Accounts Receivable	26,600	Dr.
Allowance for Doubtful Accounts	95	Cr.

ACCOUNTS (CONT.)	BALANCES	
Merchandise Inventory	62,375	Dr.
Supplies	6,740	Dr.
Prepaid Insurance	2,380	Dr.
Equipment	34,000	Dr.
Accumulated Depreciation—Equipment	10,100	Cr.
Notes Payable	7,264	Cr.
Accounts Payable	6,500	Cr.
Social Security Tax Payable	560	Cr.
Medicare Tax Payable	130	Cr.
Yasser Tousson, Capital	93,620	Cr.
Yasser Tousson, Drawing	50,000	Dr.
Sales	514,980	Cr.
Sales Returns and Allowances	9,600	Dr.
Purchases	319,430	Dr.
Freight In	3,600	Dr.
Purchases Returns and Allowances	7,145	Cr.
Purchases Discounts	5,760	Cr.
Rent Expense	14,500	Dr.
Telephone Expense	2,164	Dr.
Salaries Expense	92,000	Dr.
Payroll Taxes Expense	7,300	Dr.
Interest Expense	185	Dr.

The following accounts had zero balances:

> Interest Payable
> Salaries Payable
> Income Summary
> Supplies Expense
> Insurance Expense
> Depreciation Expense—Equipment
> Uncollectible Accounts Expense

The data needed for the adjustments on December 31 are as follows:

a.–b. Ending merchandise inventory, $67,850.

c. Uncollectible accounts, 0.5 percent of net credit sales of $245,000.

d. Supplies on hand December 31, $1,020.

e. Expired insurance, $1,190.

f. *Depreciation Expense—Equipment,* $5,600.

g. Accrued interest expense on notes payable, $325.

h. Accrued salaries, $2,100.

i. *Social Security Tax Payable* (6.2 percent) and *Medicare Tax Payable* (1.45 percent) of accrued salaries.

INSTRUCTIONS

1. Prepare a worksheet for the year ended December 31, 2007.

2. Prepare a classified income statement. The firm does not divide its operating expenses into selling and administrative expenses.

3. Prepare a statement of owner's equity. No additional investments were made during the period.

4. Prepare a classified balance sheet. All notes payable are due within one year.

5. Journalize the adjusting entries.

6. Journalize the closing entries.

7. Journalize the reversing entries.

Analyze: By what percentage did the owner's capital account change in the period from January 1, 2007, to December 31, 2007?

Critical Thinking Problem

Classified Balance Sheet

Lea Simone is the owner of Sweaters Galore, a store specializing in women's and children's sweaters. During the past year, in response to increased demand, Lea doubled her selling space by expanding into the vacant building space next door to her store. This expansion has been expensive because of the need to increase inventory and to purchase new store fixtures and equipment, including carpeting and state-of-the-art built-in fixtures. Lea notes that the company's cash position has gone down and she is worried about future demands on cash to finance the growth.

Lea presents you with a statement showing the assets, liabilities, and her equity for year-end 2006 and 2007, and asks your opinion on the company's ability to pay for the recent expansion. She did not have income and expense data available at the time. She commented that she had not made any new investment in the business in the past two years and was not financially able to do so presently. The information presented is shown below.

	December 31, 2006		December 31, 2007	
Assets				
Cash	$150,000		$ 30,000	
Accounts Receivable	45,000		91,500	
Inventory	105,000		234,000	
Prepaid Expenses	6,000		9,000	
Store Fixtures and Equipment	180,000		390,000	
Total Assets		$486,000		$754,500
Liabilities and Owner's Equity				
Liabilities				
Notes Payable (due in 4 years)	$ 90,000		$240,000	
Accounts Payable	132,000		171,000	
Salaries Payable	18,000		19,500	
Total Liabilities		$240,000		$430,500
Owner's Equity				
Lea Simone, Capital		246,000		324,000
Total Liabilities and Owner's Equity		$486,000		$754,500

INSTRUCTIONS

1. Prepare classified balance sheets for Sweaters Galore for December 31, 2006, and December 31, 2007. (Ignore depreciation.)

2. Based on the information presented in the classified balance sheets, what is your opinion of Sweaters Galore's ability to pay its current bills in a timely manner?

3. What is the advantage of a classified balance sheet over a balance sheet that is not classified?

BUSINESS CONNECTIONS

Understanding Financial Statements

Managerial | **FOCUS**

1. Why should management be concerned about the efficiency of the end-of-period procedures?

2. Spector Company had an increase in sales and net income during its last fiscal year, but cash decreased and the firm was having difficulty paying its bills by the end of the year. What factors might cause a shortage of cash even though a firm is profitable?

3. For the last three years, the balance sheet of Desai Hardware Center, a large retail store, has shown a substantial increase in merchandise inventory. Why might management be concerned about this development?

4. Why is it important to compare the financial statements of the current year with those of prior years?

5. Should a manager be concerned if the balance sheet shows a large increase in current liabilities and a large decrease in current assets? Explain your answer.

6. The latest income statement prepared at Wilkes Company shows that net sales increased by 10 percent over the previous year and selling expenses increased by 25 percent. Do you think that management should investigate the reasons for the increase in selling expenses? Why or why not?

7. Why is it useful for management to compare a firm's financial statements with financial information from other companies in the same industry?

Helping Your Boss May Be Wrong

Ethical | **DILEMMA**

It is standard accounting procedures, or GAAP, to make an adjusting entry to remove the current year's principle from the long-term liabilities. This entry reduces the long-term liabilities and increases the current liabilities. You are the bookkeeper for Biker's Business. Biker's Business has a bank loan that requires a current ratio of 1.5 times. The owner has asked that you do not make the adjusting entry to take the current portion from the long-term liabilities. You know if you make the adjusting entry Biker's Business' loan will need to be repaid immediately (or the loan called). What should you do?

Financial Performance

STREETWISE:
Questions from the
REAL WORLD

Refer to The Home Depot, Inc. 2004 *Annual Report* in Appendix A.

1. Locate the consolidated statements of earnings. What gross profit was reported for the year ended January 30, 2005? For February 1, 2004? If the company had targeted a 20 percent increase in gross profit between the fiscal years ended February 1, 2004, and January 30, 2005, respectively, was the goal achieved?

2. Using the financial statements, calculate the following measurements of financial performance and condition for The Home Depot, Inc. as of January 30, 2005.

   a. Gross profit percentage

   b. Current ratio

Balance Sheet

Financial Statement
| **ANALYSIS**

The following excerpts were taken from the Mattel, Inc. 2004 *Annual Report*.

Consolidated Balance Sheets

	December 31	
(in thousands)	*2004*	*2003*
Assets		
Current Assets		
Cash and short-term investments	$ 1,156,835	$ 1,152,681
Accounts receivable, less allowances of		
$229.2 million at December 31, 2003,		
and $125.1 million at December 31, 2002	759,033	543,888
Inventories	418,633	388,658
Prepaid expenses and other current assets	302,649	309,629
Total current assets	2,637,150	2,394,856

Liabilities and Stockholders' Equity		
Current Liabilities		
Short-term borrowings	$ 28,995	$ 19,590
Current portion of long-term liabilities	189,130	52,274
Accounts payable	349,159	289,680
Accrued liabilities	880,038	852,978
Income taxes payable	279,849	253,224
Total current liabilities	1,727,171	1,467,746

Analyze:

1. What is the current ratio for 2004? For 2003?

2. Has the ratio improved from 2003 to 2004? Why or why not?

3. The company reported net sales of $4,960,100,000 and gross profit of $2,429,483 for the period ended December 31, 2003. What is the gross profit percentage for this period?

Analyze Online: On the Mattel, Inc. Web site (**www.mattel.com**), find the investor relations section. Locate the consolidated statements of operations and the consolidated balance sheets within the most recent annual report. Answer the following questions.

4. What is the current ratio?

5. What is the gross profit percentage?

6. Compare these calculations with your calculations for 2004. Based on these two measurements, do you think the company is in a better financial position than it was in 2004? Why or why not?

Annual Report

Extending | THE THOUGHT

Once the year-end financial statements have been prepared, companies often publish an annual report, containing both financial and nonfinancial information about the company's operation over the past fiscal year.

In addition to the financial statements for the period, the report frequently includes

- a letter to its shareholders,

- management's discussion and analysis of the company's performance,

- notes that accompany the financial statements.

Although there is no comprehensive list of items that should be disclosed in an annual report, the accountants of the business must use their best professional judgment when deciding what information to include. What types of information do you think should be included in a company's annual report? Why?

Memo

Business | COMMUNICATION

You have been placed in charge of the closing process for Magnolia Tree Services for the period ending December 31. Time is short, and you must delegate the closing tasks to three accountants in your department: Brenda Calhoun, Sean Miele, and Cassandra Wilson. Write an e-mail to your co-workers, assigning each of them specific tasks to complete by the end of the week. In the e-mail, list the required closing tasks and identify which employee is responsible for each task. Make sure that your co-workers understand the order of the tasks that they are to perform.

Analyzing Home Depot

TEAMWORK

Ratios are an important part of financial analysis. Divide into groups of two or three. Each person should choose one year from the Home Depot *Annual Report* in Appendix A. Calculate the current ratio, gross profit percentage, and inventory turnover. Is Home Depot doing better or worse than the previous year? What account is causing this change?

Using Financial Statements from the Internet

Internet | CONNECTION

Choose the Web site of a corporation. You can find most corporation Web sites by typing the corporation's name after www., then .com. Find the 10K or annual report. Locate the Income Statement, Balance Sheet, and Cash Flow statements for the corporation. Notice the current assets and current liabilities. Calculate the current ratio, gross profit percentage, and inventory turnover.

Answers to **Self Reviews**

Answers to Section 1 Self Review

1. Classified statements permit users to better interpret the statements and analyze operations and financial conditions.
2. Current liabilities are those that fall due within one year. Long-term liabilities are those that will be due in more than one year.
3. Gross profit is the difference between net sales and the cost of goods sold.
4. **b.** A note receivable due in 13 months
5. **b.** As a deduction from the delivered cost of purchases
6. Net delivered cost of purchases is understated. Operating expenses are overstated. The net income from operations is unchanged.

Answers to Section 2 Self Review

1. Adjustments that include entries in asset and liability accounts that have not been used during the period.
2. So that anyone who needs to examine the entries at a later date will understand how and why the adjustments were made.
3. They provide a systematic and uniform method for closing all accounts that affect profit or loss for the period and transferring that profit or loss, adjusted for owner's withdrawals to the owner's capital account.
4. **b.** an accrued expense that involves future cash payments.
5. **d.** current assets divided by current liabilities.
6. If the accountant correctly allocates the entire future payment to the payroll taxes expense account and the accrued liability account, there will be no effects on the proper allocation of expense between periods. If the accountant debits the payment in the subsequent month to the payroll taxes expense account, payroll tax expense will be correctly stated in the earlier period and overstated in the current period. **Payroll Taxes Payable** will be overstated during the later period.

Answers to Comprehensive Self Review

1. Single-step: all revenues listed in one section and all related costs and expenses in another section. Multiple-step: various sections in which subtotals and totals are computed in arriving at net income. Multi-step statements are generally preferred.
2. An entry in the debit column on the **Income Summary** line and a credit to **Merchandise Inventory** for the amount of beginning inventory closes the beginning inventory. A debit on the **Merchandise Inventory** line and a credit to **Income Summary** for the amount of ending inventory sets up the ending inventory.
3. It generally has a life of more than one year and is used in carrying on the business.
4. **b.** expense accounts   **e.** **Income Summary** account
   d. owner's drawing account   **g.** revenue accounts
5. **a.** adjusting entries; **c.** entries to close revenue accounts; **b.** entries to close expense accounts; **d.** reversing entries
6. **a.** Debit **Income Summary** and credit **Dorothy Hitt, Capital** for $38,000.
   b. Debit **Dorothy Hitt, Capital** for $18,000 and credit **Income Summary** for $18,000.
7. **a.** **Sales Returns and Allowances**

Mini-Practice Set 2

Merchandising Business Accounting Cycle

Bargain Buys

Bargain Buys is a retail merchandising business that sells brand-name clothing at discount prices. The firm is owned and managed by Jennifer Jackson who started the business on May 1, 2007. This project will give you an opportunity to put your knowledge of accounting into practice as you handle the accounting work of Bargain Buys during the month of October 2007.

INTRODUCTION

Bargain Buys has a monthly accounting period. The firm's chart of accounts is shown below and on page 497. The journals used to record transactions are the sales journal, purchases journal, cash receipts journal, cash payments journal, and general journal. Postings are made from the journals to the accounts receivable ledger, accounts payable ledger, and general ledger. The employees are paid at the end of the month. A computerized payroll service prepares all payroll records and checks.

INSTRUCTIONS

1. Open the general ledger accounts and enter the balances for October 1, 2007. Obtain the necessary figures from the postclosing trial balance prepared on September 30, 2007, which is shown on page 499. (If you are using the *Study Guide & Working Papers,* you will find that the general ledger accounts are already open.)

2. Open the subsidiary ledger accounts and enter the balances for October 1, 2007. Obtain the necessary figures from the schedule of accounts payable and schedule of accounts receivable prepared on September 30, 2007, which appear on page 500. (If you are using the *Study Guide & Working Papers,* you will find that the subsidiary ledger accounts are already open.)

3. Analyze the transactions for October and record each transaction in the proper journal. (Use 10 as the number for the first page of each special journal and 16 as the number for the first page of the general journal.)

4. Post the individual entries that involve customer and creditor accounts from the journals to the subsidiary ledgers on a daily basis. Post the individual entries that appear in the general journal and in the Other Accounts sections of the cash receipts and cash payments journals to the general ledger on a daily basis.

5. Total, prove, and rule the special journals as of October 31, 2007.

6. Post the column totals from the special journals to the general ledger accounts.

Bargain Buys Chart of Accounts			
Assets		**Liabilities**	
101	Cash	203	Accounts Payable
111	Accounts Receivable	221	Social Security Tax Payable
112	Allowance for Doubtful Accounts	222	Medicare Tax Payable
121	Merchandise Inventory	223	Employee Income Tax Payable
131	Supplies	225	Federal Unemployment Tax Payable
133	Prepaid Insurance	227	State Unemployment Tax Payable
135	Prepaid Advertising	229	Salaries Payable
141	Equipment	231	Sales Tax Payable
142	Accumulated Depreciation—Equipment		

Bargain Buys
Chart of Accounts (continued)

Owner's Equity	Expenses
301 Jennifer Jackson, Capital	611 Advertising Expense
302 Jennifer Jackson, Drawing	614 Depreciation Expense—Equipment
399 Income Summary	617 Insurance Expense
Revenues	620 Uncollectible Accounts Expense
401 Sales	623 Janitorial Services Expense
402 Sales Returns and Allowances	626 Payroll Taxes Expense
Cost of Goods Sold	629 Rent Expense
501 Purchases	632 Salaries Expense
502 Freight In	635 Supplies Expense
503 Purchases Returns and Allowances	638 Telephone Expense
504 Purchases Discounts	644 Utilities Expense

MINI PRACTICE SET 2

7. Check the accuracy of the subsidiary ledgers by preparing a schedule of accounts receivable and a schedule of accounts payable as of October 31, 2007. Compare the totals with the balances of the **Accounts Receivable** account and the **Accounts Payable** account in the general ledger.

8. Check the accuracy of the general ledger by preparing a trial balance in the first two columns of a 10-column worksheet. Make sure that the total debits and the total credits are equal.

9. Complete the Adjustments section of the worksheet. Use the following data. Identify each adjustment with the appropriate letter.

   a. During October the firm had net credit sales of $9,435. From experience with similar businesses, the previous accountant had estimated that 0.8 percent of the firm's net credit sales would result in uncollectible accounts. Record an adjustment for the expected loss from uncollectible accounts for the month of October.

   b. On October 1 an inventory of the supplies showed that items costing $2,710 were on hand. Record an adjustment for the supplies used in October.

   c. On September 30, 2007, the firm purchased a one-year insurance policy for $8,400. Record an adjustment for the expired insurance for October.

   d. On October 31 the firm signed a four-month advertising contract for $2,800 with a local radio station and paid the full amount in advance. Record an adjustment for the expired advertising for October.

   e. On May 1, 2007, the firm purchased equipment for $83,000. The equipment was estimated to have a useful life of five years and a salvage value of $12,500. Record an adjustment for depreciation on the equipment for October.

   f.–g. Based on a physical count, ending merchandise inventory was determined to be $81,500.

10. Complete the Adjusted Trial Balance section of the worksheet.

11. Determine the net income or net loss for October and complete the worksheet.

12. Prepare a classified income statement for the month ended October 31, 2007. (The firm does not divide its operating expenses into selling and administrative expenses.)

13. Prepare a statement of owner's equity for the month ended October 31, 2007.

14. Prepare a classified balance sheet as of October 31, 2007.

15. Journalize and post the adjusting entries using general journal page 17.

16. Prepare and post the closing entries using general journal page 18.

17. Prepare a postclosing trial balance.

DATE		TRANSACTIONS
Oct.	1	Issued Check 601 for $3,500 to pay City Properties the monthly rent.
	1	Signed a four-month radio advertising contract with Radio KTTT for $2,800; issued Check 602 to pay the full amount in advance.
	2	Received $520 from Megan Greening, a credit customer, in payment of her account.
	2	Issued Check 603 for $17,820 to remit the sales tax owed for July through September to the State Tax Commission.
	2	Issued Check 604 for $7,673.22 to Super Styles, a creditor, in payment of Invoice 9387 ($7,880.00), less a cash discount ($156.78).
	3	Sold merchandise on credit for $2,480 plus sales tax of $124 to Emile Sahliveh, Sales Slip 241.
	4	Issued Check 605 for $1,150 to AMX Supply Co. for supplies.
	4	Issued Check 606 for $8,594.60 to Today's Threads, a creditor, in payment of Invoice 5671 ($7,830), less a cash discount ($175.40).
	5	Collected $1,700.00 on account from Jong Han Yoon, a credit customer.
	5	Accepted a return of merchandise from Emile Sahliveh. The merchandise was originally sold on Sales Slip 241, dated October 3; issued Credit Memorandum 18 for $630, which includes sales tax of $30.
	5	Issued Check 607 for $1,666 to Classy Clothes Inc., a creditor, in payment of Invoice 3292 ($1,700), less a cash discount ($34).
	6	Had cash sales of $17,200 plus sales tax of $860 during October 1–6.
	8	Received a check from James Bautista, a credit customer, for $832 to pay the balance he owes.
	8	Issued Check 608 for $1,884 to deposit social security tax ($702), Medicare tax ($162), and federal income tax withholding ($1,020) from the September payroll.
	9	Sold merchandise on credit for $1,975 plus sales tax of $98.75 to Dagmar Radin, Sales Slip 242.
	10	Issued Check 609 for $2,000 to pay *The Ames Daily* for a newspaper advertisement that appeared in October.
	11	Purchased merchandise for $4,820 from Super Styles, Invoice 9422, dated October 8; the terms are 2/10, n/30.
	12	Issued Check 610 for $300 to pay freight charges to Ace Freight Company, the trucking company that delivered merchandise from Super Styles on September 27 and October 11.
	13	Had cash sales of $12,290 plus sales tax of $614.50 during October 8–13.
	15	Sold merchandise on credit for $1,940 plus sales tax of $97 to James Batista, Sales Slip 243.
	16	Purchased discontinued merchandise from Akron Jobbers; paid for it immediately with Check 611 for $4,750.
	16	Received $510 on account from Emile Sahliveh, a credit customer.
	16	Issued Check 612 for $4,723.60 to Super Styles, a creditor, in payment of Invoice 9422 ($4,820.00), less cash discount ($96.40).
	18	Issued Check 613 for $6,000 to Jennifer Jackson as a withdrawal for personal use.

Continued

DATE		TRANSACTIONS
Oct.	20	Had cash sales of $12,800 plus sales tax of $640 during October 15–20.
	22	Issued Check 614 to City Utilities for $805 to pay the monthly electric bill.
	24	Sold merchandise on credit for $820 plus sales tax of $41 to Megan Greening, Sales Slip 244.
	25	Purchased merchandise for $3,380 from Classy Clothes Inc., Invoice 3418, dated October 23; the terms are 2/10, n/30.
	26	Issued Check 615 to Regional Telephone for $480 to pay the monthly telephone bill.
	27	Had cash sales of $12,240 plus sales tax of $612 during October 22–27.
	29	Received Credit Memorandum 175 for $430 from Classy Clothes Inc. for defective goods that were returned. The original purchase was made on Invoice 3418, dated October 23.
	29	Sold merchandise on credit for $2,820 plus sales tax of $141 to Jong Han Yoon, Sales Slip 245.
	29	Recorded the October payroll. The records prepared by the payroll service show the following totals: earnings, $10,800; social security, $702.00; Medicare, $162.00; income tax, $1,020; and net pay, $8,916. The excess withholdings corrected an error made in withholdings in September.
	29	Recorded the employer's payroll taxes, which were calculated by the payroll service: social security, $702; Medicare, $162; federal unemployment tax, $118; and state unemployment tax, $584. This, too, reflects an understatement of taxes recorded in September and corrected in this month.
	30	Purchased merchandise for $2,140 from Today's Threads, Invoice 5821, dated October 26; the terms are 1/10, n/30.
	31	Issued Checks 616 through 619, totaling $8,916.00, to employees to pay October payroll. For the sake of simplicity, enter the total of the checks on single line.
	31	Issued Check 620 for $200 to Handy Janitors for October janitorial services.
	31	Had cash sales of $1,590 plus sales tax of $79.50 for October 29–31.

Bargain Buys
Postclosing Trial Balance
September 30, 2007

ACCOUNT NAME	DEBIT	CREDIT
Cash	59 8 0 0 00	
Accounts Receivable	6 2 1 0 00	
Allowance for Doubtful Accounts		4 2 0 00
Merchandise Inventory	88 9 9 6 00	
Supplies	4 1 0 0 00	
Prepaid Insurance	8 4 0 0 00	
Equipment	83 0 0 0 00	
Accumulated Depreciation—Equipment		7 0 5 0 00
Accounts Payable		18 3 0 0 00
Social Security Tax Payable		7 0 2 00
Medicare Tax Payable		1 6 2 00
Employee Income Tax Payable		1 0 2 0 00
Federal Unemployment Tax Payable		5 1 2 00
State Unemployment Tax Payable		1 2 6 8 00
Sales Tax Payable		17 8 2 0 00
Jennifer Jackson, Capital		203 2 5 2 00
Totals	250 5 0 6 00	250 5 0 6 00

Bargain Buys

Schedule of Accounts Payable

September 30, 2007

Super Styles		7	8	3	0	00
Classy Clothes Inc.		1	7	0	0	00
Today's Threads		8	7	7	0	00
Total	18	3	0	0	00

Bargain Buys

Schedule of Accounts Receivable

September 30, 2007

Emily Clough			7	9	5	00
Megan Greening			5	2	0	00
James Bautista			8	3	2	00
Dagmar Radin			2	3	2	00
John Flanagan		1	6	2	1	00
Emile Sahliyeh			5	1	0	00
Jong Han Yoon		1	7	0	0	00
Total		6	2	1	0	00

Appendix A

Excerpts from The Home Depot, Inc., 2004 Annual Report

To Our Customers, Suppliers, Shareholders and Associates

Looking back at 2004, our strong performance was the result of focusing on our core purpose: **Improve Everything We Touch**. This core purpose, which we shared with our associates at our 25th anniversary celebration last summer, captures both who we are as a company and how we came together as a team in 2004 to build on our proud past and create an even brighter future.

Driven by our core purpose, we focused on the execution of our unwavering strategy to **enhance** the core, **extend** the business and **expand** our markets. As a result, we delivered record financial performance, with sales growth of 12.8% to $73 billion. To put that into perspective, from 2000 to 2004, we have grown our top line sales by more than $27 billion, roughly the sales of a company ranking among the top 60 in the Fortune 500.

Earnings per diluted share grew 20.2% to $2.26 in 2004. Average ticket reached $54.89, gross margin climbed to 33.4% and operating margin increased to 10.8% – all company records. We also drove comparable store sales of 5.4%, our best comparable store sales performance since 1999.

At the same time, we maintained one of the strongest balance sheets in retail, ending the year with shareholders' equity of $24 billion; $39 billion in assets, including $2.2 billion in cash and short-term investments; and a debt-to-equity ratio of 8.9%.

We had a great year when measured across virtually every key metric. Our outstanding financial performance allowed us to continue reinvesting in our business and return approximately $4 billion of cash to our shareholders last year through share repurchases and dividends. Over the past four years, total share repurchases and dividends returned to shareholders equated to $3.90 per diluted share, or approximately 56% of our cumulative earnings.

I could not be more proud of what our 325,000 associates achieved from both an operational and a financial perspective. In 2004, we accomplished something even more meaningful: building a foundation for continued growth and profitability well into the future.

Enhancing the Core
In 2004, we continued our focus to improve the customer experience in our stores by investing approximately $1 billion in store remodels and refreshes.

At the center of these efforts were continued performance improvements from major merchandising resets in core areas such as lighting, flooring, kitchen and appliances, to name a few. We also launched a steady stream of innovative and distinctive new products that received a record number of accolades from leading consumer publications. We continued to use technology, installing human resource and financial systems, to improve our operating systems and enable future growth. And, in all U.S. stores, we completed our installation of POS systems, which allowed us to roll out cordless scan guns to all stores and have over 1,000 self-checkout systems in place. These technologies shorten checkout times and enhance the customer experience.

We invested heavily not only in our physical assets, but also in our associates, through more than 23 million hours in learning, which helped our associates deliver better customer service. We enhanced our compensation and rewards programs with record Success Sharing payouts of approximately $90 million. We launched exciting new hiring partnerships with AARP and the Departments of Defense, Veterans Affairs and Labor, and we added new benefits programs that are available to full- and part-time associates, making us an employment practices leader in the retail industry.

Extending the Business
We opened 183 net new stores, including several new and exciting store formats in Manhattan, New York and Park Royal, West Vancouver. These stunning new urban formats represent the best of The Home Depot when it comes to innovation in design, merchandising, product selection and service delivery, and have opened up future revenue opportunities for The Home Depot.

You can do it. We can help.℠

We also continued to focus on services, with 23 national programs handling more than 11,000 installations per weekday. Our services revenue increased by 28% in 2004.

Responding to the growing demand for online shopping, we revamped our homedepot.com site, making dramatic improvements in the overall navigability of the site with more than 15,000 product SKUs for sale online, including appliances.

All of these extensions to our business are proof positive that our market-back customer approach is allowing us to successfully offer the right products and services to meet the changing needs of our diverse customer base.

Expanding the Market

We also made several important moves to expand our global market presence. With the acquisition of Home Mart in Mexico, we have become the largest home improvement retailer in that market in less than three years with 44 stores at year-end. In Canada, we celebrated our 10-year anniversary in 2004 and opened 15 stores, bringing our total there to 117. We also announced plans to expand our presence in China, capitalizing on our learning from our two merchandising offices, to enter the retail sector in this rapidly growing market.

We made several important acquisitions within the professional customer market: most notably White Cap Construction Supply, in June 2004, a leading professional distribution business; Creative Touch Interiors, in January 2004, a leading national design center partner for production homebuilders, which is now part of The Home Depot Supply, Builder Solutions; and Litemor, in February 2005, Canada's largest national commercial lighting distributor. These acquisitions give us strong entry points into the $400+ billion professional market. We intend to continue growing in the market both organically and through future acquisitions.

Improve Everything We Touch

We celebrated our 25th anniversary in 2004 and used this year to reaffirm the values that have made this company so special.

We rejuvenated our Team Depot volunteer program by creating our first annual Week of Service, contributing more than 260,000 volunteer hours in just seven days through more than 1,600 projects in our communities.

That same spirit of giving back and supporting our communities vividly came to life as four hurricanes struck the Southeastern U.S., and The Home Depot mobilized to deliver the largest relief and resupply effort in our company's history. In total, we donated more than $4 million in contributions to rebuilding efforts throughout the impacted areas.

We also stepped up and recommitted to our troops serving overseas, with a $1 million tool donation to support their rebuilding efforts in Iraq.

Finally, we witnessed our own Olympic Job Opportunity Program associates pursue their dreams of winning as they participated in the Olympics and Paralympics in Athens, Greece, bringing home a record 41 medals.

These and other efforts reflecting our values earned us prestigious recognition, including the 2004 Citizenship in Action Award from the U.S. Chamber of Commerce and the Freedom Award from the U.S. Department of Defense.

2005: A Turning Point

We have built an impressive track record of performance and success over the past several years and have a tremendous amount of momentum as we move into 2005.

Capitalizing on that momentum will require continued discipline and focus on execution. As we open 175 new stores in 2005 and continue to invest in the modernization of our stores, it is customer satisfaction, customer conversion and average ticket that will be key to driving growth in our core retail business. With approximately 1.3 billion customer transactions a year, even slight improvements in these key metrics can drive exponential gains in our financial performance. At the same time, we will stay focused on developing multiple platforms for sustainable, profitable growth in exciting new customer markets, product and service categories, and new geographies.

2005 is a turning point in our history: a year to build on our strong momentum and proven strategy, to continue to execute on our plan and to continually improve the customer shopping experience. This is a company with a proud past and increasingly bright future and we recognize that our associates are our competitive advantage.

In the four years I have been here, our 325,000 orange-blooded associates have proven to me time and again that when we set our minds on something, we always get it done – the right way – and that is exactly what we intend to do in 2005.

Thank you for your continued support, which was instrumental in helping us deliver on our core purpose to Improve Everything We Touch in 2004. I hope you are as excited as I am about the opportunities that lie ahead for our great company.

Sincerely,

Bob

Bob Nardelli
Chairman, President & Chief Executive Officer
March 28, 2005

Management's Discussion and Analysis of Results of Operations and Financial Condition

The Home Depot, Inc. and Subsidiaries

FORWARD-LOOKING STATEMENTS

Certain statements of The Home Depot's expectations made herein, including those regarding Net Sales growth, increases in comparable store sales, impact of cannibalization, commodity price inflation and deflation, implementation of store initiatives, Net Earnings performance, including depreciation expense and stock-based compensation expense, store openings, capital allocation and expenditures, the effect of adopting certain accounting standards, strategic direction and the demand for our products and services, constitute "forward-looking statements" as defined in the Private Securities Litigation Reform Act of 1995. These statements are based on currently available information and are subject to risks and uncertainties that could cause actual results to differ materially from our historical experience and expectations. These risks and uncertainties include economic conditions in North America, changes in our cost structure, the availability of sourcing channels consistent with our strategy of differentiation, conditions affecting new store development, conditions affecting customer transactions and average ticket, the success of our technology initiatives in improving operations and customers' in-store experience, our ability to identify and respond to evolving trends in demographics and consumer preferences, the relative success of our expansion strategy, including our ability to integrate acquisitions and create appropriate distribution channels for key sales platforms, our ability to attract, train and retain highly-qualified associates, the impact of new accounting standards and the impact of competition, decisions by management related to possible asset impairments, regulation and litigation matters. Undue reliance should not be placed on such forward-looking statements as they speak only as of the date made. Additional information regarding these and other risks is contained in our periodic filings with the Securities and Exchange Commission.

EXECUTIVE SUMMARY AND SELECTED CONSOLIDATED STATEMENTS OF EARNINGS DATA

For fiscal year ended January 30, 2005 ("fiscal 2004"), we reported Net Earnings of $5.0 billion and Diluted Earnings per Share of $2.26 compared to Net Earnings of $4.3 billion and Diluted Earnings per Share of $1.88 in fiscal year ended February 1, 2004 ("fiscal 2003"). Net Sales for fiscal 2004 increased 12.8% over fiscal 2003 to $73.1 billion. This growth in our business was achieved through the continued execution of our strategy of enhancing the core, extending the business and expanding the market. In the execution of our strategy, we invested $3.9 billion back into our business and invested $727 million for acquisitions of new businesses during fiscal 2004.

We enhanced our business by maintaining an aggressive pace of introducing innovative and distinctive new merchandise, supported by continued investments in store modernization and technology, including major merchandising resets that reflect emerging consumer trends. In fiscal 2004, we continued to invest in technology through the installation of human resource and financial systems to improve our operating systems and enable future growth. Our technological enhancements also included the conversion onto a new single point-of-sale platform in all stores in the United States ("U.S."), which allowed us to roll out cordless scan guns to all U.S. stores and self-checkout registers to over 1,000 stores. These enhancements streamlined the front-end of our stores and eliminated redundant tasks, allowing our associates to spend more time with our customers. These investments in our core business are paying off as evidenced by certain key operating performance measurements, including comparable store sales, which increased 5.4% in fiscal 2004 and sales per square foot which increased 1.2% to $375.26. Average ticket also increased 7.3% in fiscal 2004 to $54.89, a company record, with growth in every selling department. We achieved a record operating margin of 10.8% for fiscal 2004.

We extended our business by opening new stores and by offering a variety of installation and home maintenance programs through our Home Depot and EXPO Design Center stores. We currently offer 23 national installation programs that provide products and services to our do-it-for-me customers. We also arrange for the provision of flooring, countertop and window coverings installation services to production homebuilders through HD Builder Solutions Group, Inc. Our services revenue increased 28% to $3.6 billion in fiscal 2004, and we saw sustained growth in categories such as carpet, countertops, kitchens, windows, HVAC, roofing and sheds. We opened 183 net new stores during fiscal 2004, including three new urban format stores, two in New York City and one in Park Royal, West Vancouver, British Columbia, bringing our total store count to 1,890. We also continued the expansion of several initiatives including our Tool Rental Centers, Professional Business Customer ("Pro"), Appliance and Designplace℠ initiatives. In response to the growing demand for online shopping, we revamped our website, homedepot.com, making improvements in the overall navigability of the site with more than 15,000 products for sale, including appliances.

We have expanded our market by capturing a growing share of the professional residential, commercial and heavy construction markets which operate under our Home Depot Supply brand and by continuing our expansion outside of the U.S. As part of this expansion in 2004, we acquired White Cap Industries, Inc. ("White Cap"), a leading distributor of specialty hardware, tools and materials to construction contractors. In fiscal 2004, we made several important moves to expand our market and global presence. We opened 15 new stores in Canada, bringing the total to 117, and increased our footprint significantly in Mexico to 44 stores through both organic growth and the acquisition of 20 Home Mart Mexico, S.A. de C.V. ("Home Mart") stores. In fiscal 2004, we also announced our intention to enter the retail market in China.

APPENDIX A

Management's Discussion and Analysis of Results of Operations and Financial Condition (continued)

The Home Depot, Inc. and Subsidiaries

We generated $6.9 billion of cash flow from operations in fiscal 2004. In addition to the aforementioned investments of $3.9 billion in capital expenditures and $727 million for acquisitions, we also returned $3.8 billion to our shareholders in the form of dividends and share repurchases. Our financial condition remains strong as evidenced by our $2.2 billion in Cash and Short-Term Investments at January 30, 2005. At the end of fiscal 2004, our total debt-to-equity ratio was 8.9% and our return on invested capital (computed on beginning Long-Term Debt and Equity for the trailing four quarters) was 21.5% compared to 20.4% at the end of fiscal 2003, a 110 basis point improvement.

We believe the selected sales data, the percentage relationship between Net Sales and major categories in the Consolidated Statements of Earnings and the percentage change in the dollar amounts of each of the items presented below is important in evaluating the performance of our business operations. We operate in one business segment and believe the information presented in our Management's Discussion and Analysis of Results of Operations and Financial Condition provides an understanding of our business segment, our operations and our financial condition.

| | % of Net Sales | | | % Increase (Decrease) In Dollar Amounts | |
| | Fiscal Year[1] | | | | |
	2004	2003	2002	2004 vs. 2003	2003 vs. 2002
NET SALES	100.0%	100.0%	100.0%	12.8%	11.3%
Gross Profit	33.4	31.8	31.1	18.7	13.7
Operating Expenses:					
Selling and Store Operating	20.7	19.4	19.4	20.0	11.6
General and Administrative	1.9	1.8	1.7	22.1	14.4
Total Operating Expenses	22.6	21.2	21.1	20.2	11.9
OPERATING INCOME	10.8	10.6	10.0	15.8	17.4
Interest Income (Expense):					
Interest and Investment Income	0.1	0.1	0.1	(5.1)	(25.3)
Interest Expense	(0.1)	(0.1)	(0.0)	12.9	67.6
Interest, net	–	–	0.1	366.7	(107.1)
EARNINGS BEFORE PROVISION FOR INCOME TAXES	10.8	10.6	10.1	15.6	16.5
Provision for Income Taxes	4.0	4.0	3.8	14.7	15.0
NET EARNINGS	6.8%	6.6%	6.3%	16.2%	17.5%
SELECTED SALES DATA					
Number of Customer Transactions (000s)[2]	1,295,185	1,245,721	1,160,994	4.0%	7.3%
Average Ticket[2]	$ 54.89	$ 51.15	$ 49.43	7.3	3.5
Weighted Average Weekly Sales per Operating Store[2]	$ 766,000	$ 763,000	$ 772,000	0.4	(1.2)
Weighted Average Sales per Square Foot[2]	$ 375.26	$ 370.87	$ 370.21	1.2	0.2
Comparable Store Sales Increase (%)[3]	5.4%	3.8%	0%	N/A	N/A

(1) Fiscal years 2004, 2003 and 2002 refer to the fiscal years ended January 30, 2005, February 1, 2004 and February 2, 2003, respectively. Fiscal years 2004, 2003 and 2002 include 52 weeks.

(2) Excludes all subsidiaries operating under The Home Depot Supply brand (Apex Supply Company, Inc., The Home Depot Supply, Inc., Your Other Warehouse, LLC, White Cap Industries, Inc. and HD Builder Solutions Group, Inc.) since their inclusion may cause distortion of the data presented due to operational differences from our retail stores. The total number of the excluded locations and their total square footage are immaterial to our total number of locations and total square footage.

(3) Includes net sales at locations open greater than 12 months, including relocated and remodeled stores, and net sales of all the subsidiaries of The Home Depot, Inc. Stores and subsidiaries become comparable on the Monday following their 365th day of operation. We believe comparable store sales is a meaningful measurement of our operating performance and is a common measurement of operating performance in the retail industry. This measurement is intended only as supplemental information, and is not a substitute for net sales or net earnings presented in accordance with generally accepted accounting principles.

Management's Discussion and Analysis of
Results of Operations and Financial Condition (continued)

The Home Depot, Inc. and Subsidiaries

RESULTS OF OPERATIONS

For an understanding of the significant factors that influenced our performance during the past three fiscal years, the following discussion should be read in conjunction with the Consolidated Financial Statements and the Notes to Consolidated Financial Statements presented in this Annual Report.

Fiscal 2004 Compared to Fiscal 2003

Net Sales

Net Sales for fiscal 2004 increased 12.8% to $73.1 billion from $64.8 billion for fiscal 2003. Fiscal 2004 Net Sales growth was driven by an increase in comparable store sales of 5.4%, sales from the 183 net new stores opened during fiscal 2004, sales from the 175 net new stores opened during fiscal 2003 and sales from our newly acquired businesses. We plan to open 175 new stores during the fiscal year ending January 29, 2006, ("fiscal 2005"). We expect sales growth of 9% to 12% for fiscal 2005, driven by comparable store sales growth, sales from new stores opened during fiscal 2004 and fiscal 2005 and sales from newly acquired businesses.

The increase in comparable store sales in fiscal 2004, our best performance since 1999, reflects a number of factors. Our average ticket, which increased 7.3% to a company record of $54.89, increased in all selling departments and our comparable store sales growth in fiscal 2004 was positive in all selling departments. We experienced strong comparable store sales increases in building materials due in part to the impact of several hurricanes in the Southeastern U.S. Lumber was another strong category during fiscal 2004, driven primarily by commodity price inflation. Additionally, we had strong sales growth in our kitchen and bath categories, driven by appliances, bath fixtures, vanities and sinks. Finally, our comparable store sales growth in fiscal 2004 reflects the impact of cannibalization.

In order to meet our customer service objectives, we strategically open stores near market areas served by existing stores ("cannibalize") to enhance service levels, gain incremental sales and increase market penetration. As of the end of fiscal 2004, certain new stores cannibalized approximately 17% of our existing stores and we estimate that store cannibalization reduced fiscal 2004 comparable store sales by approximately 2.2%. Additionally, we believe that our sales performance has been, and could continue to be, negatively impacted by the level of competition that we encounter in various markets. However, due to the highly-fragmented U.S. home improvement industry, in which we estimate our market share is approximately 12%, measuring the impact on our sales by our competitors is extremely difficult.

Comparable store sales in fiscal 2005 are estimated to increase 4% to 7%. We expect our comparable store sales to be favorably impacted by the introduction of innovative and distinctive new merchandise as well as positive customer reaction to our ongoing store modernization program. Increased customer traffic, traffic conversion and higher average ticket are key to our 2005 sales growth forecast. This forecast of comparable store sales growth is net of an estimated cannibalization impact of about 2%. We do not believe that changing prices for commodities will have a material effect on Net Sales or results of operations in fiscal 2005.

The growth in Net Sales for fiscal 2004 reflects growth in services revenue, which increased 28% to $3.6 billion for fiscal 2004 from $2.8 billion for fiscal 2003, driven by strength in a number of areas including countertops, HVAC, kitchens and our flooring companies. We continued to drive our services programs, which focus primarily on providing products and services to our do-it-for-me customers. These programs are offered through Home Depot and EXPO Design Center stores. We also arrange for the provision of flooring, countertop and window coverings installation services to production homebuilders through HD Builder Solutions Group, Inc. Our services revenue is expected to benefit from the growing percentage of mature customers as they rely more heavily on installation services.

During fiscal 2004, we continued the implementation or expansion of a number of in-store initiatives. We believe these initiatives will enhance our customers' shopping experience as they are fully implemented in our stores. The Pro initiative adds programs to our stores like job lot order quantities of merchandise and a dedicated sales desk for our Pro customer base. Our Appliance initiative offers customers an assortment of in-stock name brand appliances, including General Electric® and Maytag®, and offers the ability to special order over 2,300 additional related products through computer kiosks located in the stores. Our Designplace℠ initiative offers our design and décor customers personalized service from specially-trained associates and provides distinctive merchandise in an attractive setting. Our Tool Rental Centers, which are located inside our stores, provide a cost effective way for our do-it-yourself and Pro customers to rent tools to complete home improvement projects. During fiscal 2004, we opened our 1,000th Tool Rental Center, making us the largest in the industry as measured by number of locations.

Management's Discussion and Analysis of Results of Operations and Financial Condition (continued)

The Home Depot, Inc. and Subsidiaries

The following table provides the number of stores with these initiatives:

	Fiscal Year 2005 Estimate	Fiscal Year		
		2004	2003	2002
Store Count	2,065	1,890	1,707	1,532
Initiatives:				
Pro	1,728	1,563	1,356	1,135
Appliance	1,952	1,787	1,569	743
Designplace^SM	1,952	1,787	1,625	873
Tool Rental Centers	1,186	1,061	825	601

Gross Profit

Gross Profit increased 18.7% to $24.4 billion for fiscal 2004 from $20.6 billion for fiscal 2003, an increase of 167 basis points. Gross Profit as a percent of Net Sales was 33.4% for fiscal 2004, the highest annual rate in our company's history, compared to 31.8% for fiscal 2003. The adoption of Emerging Issues Task Force ("EITF") 02-16, "Accounting by a Customer (Including a Reseller) for Certain Consideration Received from a Vendor" ("EITF 02-16"), reduced our Cost of Merchandise Sold by co-op advertising allowances of $891 million, or 122 basis points, in fiscal 2004 and $40 million, or 6 basis points, in fiscal 2003. See section "Impact of the Adoption of EITF 02-16." Excluding the impact of the adoption of EITF 02-16, our gross margin would have been 32.2% for fiscal 2004 compared with 31.7% for fiscal 2003. Improved inventory management, which resulted in lower shrink levels, contributed 18 basis points of our increase in gross profit. Finally, 33 basis points resulted from benefits arising from a change in merchandising mix, offset by the cost of our deferred interest programs, as the cost of these programs is reflected in our gross margin. Our deferred interest programs offer no interest and no payment programs over a six or twelve-month period through our private label credit card. We believe these programs deliver long-term benefits, including higher average tickets and customer loyalty.

Operating Expenses

Operating Expenses increased 20.2% to $16.5 billion for fiscal 2004 from $13.7 billion for fiscal 2003. Operating Expenses as a percent of Net Sales were 22.6% for fiscal 2004 compared to 21.2% for fiscal 2003.

Selling and Store Operating Expenses, which are included in Operating Expenses, increased 20.0% to $15.1 billion for fiscal 2004 from $12.6 billion for fiscal 2003. As a percent of Net Sales, Selling and Store Operating Expenses were 20.7% for fiscal 2004 compared to 19.4% for fiscal 2003. The increase in Selling and Store Operating Expenses in fiscal 2004 includes $1.0 billion of advertising expense related to the adoption of EITF 02-16. Excluding the impact of EITF 02-16, Selling and Store Operating Expenses increased 12.1% to $14.1 billion, or 19.2% of Net Sales, in fiscal 2004 compared with 19.4% of Net Sales in fiscal 2003.

The decrease in Selling and Store Operating Expenses as a percent of Net Sales for fiscal 2004, excluding the impact of EITF 02-16, was due to an increase in labor productivity and benefits from our private label credit card, which carries a lower discount rate than other forms of credit, like bank cards. Labor productivity, as measured by sales per labor hour, reached an all-time high in fiscal 2004, as we moved our associates from tasking to selling activities. This reduction in costs was partially offset by higher expenses associated with incentive programs, like our success sharing program and our management incentive plan. In addition, our planned investment in store modernization and technology caused remodel and repair expenses as well as depreciation expense to rise at a faster rate than our sales growth.

General and Administrative Expenses, which are included in Operating Expenses, increased 22.1% to $1.4 billion for fiscal 2004 from $1.1 billion for fiscal 2003. General and Administrative Expenses as a percent of Net Sales were 1.9% for fiscal 2004 and 1.8% for fiscal 2003. The increase in fiscal 2004 was primarily due to expenses associated with incentive programs and stock-based compensation expense.

While we will continue to drive productivity, our expenses will be under pressure in fiscal 2005 for two primary reasons. Given our continued reinvestment in our business in prior years and our capital expenditure forecast of $3.7 billion for fiscal 2005, our total depreciation expense is estimated to increase by approximately $250 million to approximately $1.6 billion for fiscal 2005, of which approximately $1.3 billion and $300 million are included in Selling and Store Operating Expenses and General and Administrative Expenses, respectively. Stock-based compensation expense is estimated to increase by $125 million in fiscal 2005 with approximately $65 million of the increase due to the adoption of Statement of Financial Accounting Standards ("SFAS") No. 123(R), "Share-Based Payment" ("SFAS 123(R)"). See section "Recent Accounting Pronouncements."

Interest, net

In fiscal 2004, we recognized $14 million of net Interest Expense compared to $3 million in fiscal 2003. Net Interest Expense as a percent of Net Sales was less than 0.1% for both fiscal 2004 and fiscal 2003. Interest Expense increased 12.9% to $70 million for fiscal 2004 from $62 million for fiscal 2003 primarily due to an increase in outstanding indebtedness and a reduction in the amount of capitalized interest. Interest Expense also increased due to the addition of $38 million in capital leases during the year. Interest and Investment Income decreased 5.1% to $56 million for fiscal 2004 from $59 million for fiscal 2003 primarily due to a lower interest rate environment.

Management's Discussion and Analysis of
Results of Operations and Financial Condition (continued)

The Home Depot, Inc. and Subsidiaries

Provision for Income Taxes

Our combined federal and state effective income tax rate decreased to 36.8% for fiscal 2004 from 37.1% for fiscal 2003. The majority of this reduction was due to the reversal of a $31 million valuation allowance as we were able to recognize previous capital losses for which no tax benefit had been recorded at the time the capital loss was incurred.

Diluted Earnings per Share

Diluted Earnings per Share were $2.26 and $1.88 for fiscal 2004 and fiscal 2003, respectively. The adoption of EITF 02-16 negatively impacted Diluted Earnings per Share for fiscal 2004 by $0.04 per share. Diluted Earnings per Share were favorably impacted in fiscal 2004 as a result of the repurchase of shares of our common stock in fiscal 2003 and fiscal 2004. Over the past three fiscal years, we have repurchased 200.5 million shares of our common stock for a total of $6.7 billion. In fiscal 2005, we estimate Diluted Earnings per Share growth of 10% to 14%.

Fiscal 2003 Compared to Fiscal Year Ended February 2, 2003 ("Fiscal 2002")

Net Sales

Net Sales for fiscal 2003 increased 11.3% to $64.8 billion from $58.2 billion for fiscal 2002. Fiscal 2003 Net Sales growth was driven by an increase in comparable store sales of 3.8%, sales from the 175 net new stores opened during fiscal 2003 and sales from the 203 net new stores opened during fiscal 2002.

The increase in comparable store sales in fiscal 2003 reflects a number of factors. Comparable store sales growth in fiscal 2003 was positive in all selling departments. Our lawn and garden category was the biggest driver of the increase in comparable store sales for fiscal 2003, reflecting strong sales in outdoor power equipment, including John Deere* tractors and walk-behind mowers, as well as snow throwers and snow blowers. Lumber was another strong category during fiscal 2003, driven primarily by commodity price inflation. Additionally, we had strong sales growth in our kitchen and bath categories and in our paint department reflecting the positive impact of new merchandising initiatives. During fiscal 2003, we added our Appliance initiative to 826 of our stores bringing the total number of stores with our Appliance initiative to 1,569 as of the end of fiscal 2003. Additionally, during fiscal 2003, each store was set with our new Color Solutions Center, which drove sales growth in interior and exterior paint, as well as pressure washers. Finally, our comparable store sales growth in fiscal 2003 reflects the impact of cannibalization.

As of the end of fiscal 2003, certain new stores cannibalized approximately 17% of our existing stores and we estimate that store cannibalization reduced fiscal 2003 comparable store sales by approximately 2.7%.

The growth in Net Sales for fiscal 2003 reflects growth in services revenue, which increased 40% to $2.8 billion in fiscal 2003 from $2.0 billion in fiscal 2002, driven by strength in a number of areas including countertops, HVAC, kitchens and our flooring companies.

Gross Profit

Gross Profit increased 13.7% to $20.6 billion for fiscal 2003 from $18.1 billion for fiscal 2002. Gross Profit as a percent of Net Sales was 31.8% for fiscal 2003 compared to 31.1% for fiscal 2002. The increase in the gross profit rate was attributable to changing customer preferences and continuing benefits arising from our centralized purchasing group. Improved inventory management, which resulted in lower shrink levels, increased penetration of import products, which typically have a lower cost, and benefits from Tool Rental Centers also positively impacted the gross profit rate. The adoption of EITF 02-16 also contributed to the increase in Gross Profit in fiscal 2003. The one-month impact of EITF 02-16 in fiscal 2003 resulted in a reduction of Cost of Merchandise Sold of $40 million.

Operating Expenses

Operating Expenses increased 11.9% to $13.7 billion for fiscal 2003 from $12.3 billion for fiscal 2002. Operating Expenses as a percent of Net Sales were 21.2% for fiscal 2003 compared to 21.1% for fiscal 2002.

Selling and Store Operating Expenses, which are included in Operating Expenses, increased 11.6% to $12.6 billion for fiscal 2003 from $11.3 billion for fiscal 2002. As a percent of Net Sales, Selling and Store Operating Expenses were 19.4% for fiscal 2003 and fiscal 2002. The increase in Selling and Store Operating Expenses in fiscal 2003 included $47 million of advertising expense related to the adoption of EITF 02-16. During fiscal 2003, we experienced rising workers' compensation and general liability expense, due to rising medical costs. We also experienced incremental expense associated with our store modernization program. These rising costs were offset, however, by increasing levels of sales productivity by our associates and benefits from our new private label credit program.

General and Administrative Expenses, which are included in Operating Expenses, increased 14.4% to $1.1 billion for fiscal 2003 from $1.0 billion for fiscal 2002. General and Administrative Expenses as a percent of Net Sales were 1.8% for fiscal 2003 and 1.7% for fiscal 2002. The increase in fiscal 2003 was primarily due to increased spending in technology and other growth initiatives.

Interest, net

In fiscal 2003, we recognized $3 million of net Interest Expense compared to $42 million of net Interest and Investment Income in fiscal 2002. Net Interest Expense as a percent of Net Sales was less than 0.1% for fiscal 2003 and net Interest and Investment Income as a percent of Net Sales was 0.1% for fiscal 2002. Interest Expense increased 67.6% to $62 million for fiscal 2003 from $37 million for fiscal 2002 primarily due to lower capitalized interest expense

APPENDIX A

Management's Discussion and Analysis of Results of Operations and Financial Condition (continued)

The Home Depot, Inc. and Subsidiaries

as we had fewer stores under development in fiscal 2003 as compared to fiscal 2002. Interest Expense also increased due to the addition of $47 million in capital leases during the year. Interest and Investment Income decreased 25.3% to $59 million for fiscal 2003 from $79 million for fiscal 2002 primarily due to lower average cash balances and a lower interest rate environment.

Provision for Income Taxes

Our combined federal and state effective income tax rate decreased to 37.1% for fiscal 2003 from 37.6% for fiscal 2002. The decrease in our effective tax rate in fiscal 2003 from fiscal 2002 was primarily due to the utilization of certain federal, state and foreign tax benefits not previously recognized.

Diluted Earnings per Share

Diluted Earnings per Share were $1.88 and $1.56 for fiscal 2003 and fiscal 2002, respectively. Diluted Earnings per Share were favorably impacted in fiscal 2003 as a result of the repurchase of shares of our common stock in fiscal 2002 and fiscal 2003.

IMPACT OF THE ADOPTION OF EITF 02-16

In fiscal 2003, we adopted EITF 02-16 which states that certain cash consideration received from a vendor is presumed to be a reduction of the prices of the vendor's products or services and should, therefore, be recorded as a reduction of Cost of Merchandise Sold when recognized in our Consolidated Statements of Earnings. That presumption is overcome when the consideration is either a reimbursement of specific, incremental and identifiable costs incurred to sell the vendor's products or a payment for assets or services delivered to the vendor. We received consideration in the form of advertising co-op allowances from our vendors pursuant to annual agreements, which are generally on a calendar year basis. As permitted by EITF 02-16, we elected to apply its provisions prospectively to all agreements entered into or modified after December 31, 2002. Therefore, the impact of us adopting EITF 02-16 in fiscal 2003 was limited to advertising co-op allowances earned pursuant to vendor agreements entered into in late 2003, which became effective in January 2004.

The one-month impact of the adoption of EITF 02-16 in fiscal 2003 resulted in a reduction of Cost of Merchandise Sold of $40 million, an increase in Selling and Store Operating Expenses of $47 million and a reduction of Earnings before Provision for Income Taxes of $7 million. The impact on our Diluted Earnings per Share was immaterial. Merchandise Inventories in our accompanying Consolidated Balance Sheets as of February 1, 2004 were also reduced by $7 million.

The impact of the adoption of EITF 02-16 in fiscal 2004 resulted in a reduction of Cost of Merchandise Sold of $891 million, an increase in Selling and Store Operating Expenses of $1.0 billion and a reduction of Earnings before Provision for Income Taxes of $158 million.

The impact on our Diluted Earnings per Share for fiscal 2004 was a reduction of $0.04 per share. We do not expect any further impact on our Diluted Earnings per Share from the adoption of EITF 02-16. Merchandise Inventories in our accompanying Consolidated Balance Sheets as of January 30, 2005 were also reduced by $158 million.

Prior to the adoption of EITF 02-16 in fiscal 2003, the entire amount of advertising co-op allowances received was offset against advertising expense and resulted in a reduction of Selling and Store Operating Expenses. In fiscal 2002, advertising co-op allowances exceeded gross advertising expense by $30 million. This excess amount was recorded as a reduction of Cost of Merchandise Sold in the accompanying Consolidated Statements of Earnings. We continue to earn certain advertising co-op allowances that are recorded as an offset against advertising expenses as they are reimbursements of specific, incremental and identifiable costs incurred to promote vendors' products. In fiscal 2004 and fiscal 2003, net advertising expense was $1.0 billion and $58 million, respectively, which was recorded in Selling and Store Operating Expenses.

The following table illustrates the full-year effect on Cost of Merchandise Sold, Gross Profit, Selling and Store Operating Expenses, Operating Income and Diluted Earnings per Share as if advertising co-op allowances had always been treated as a reduction of Cost of Merchandise Sold in accordance with EITF 02-16 (amounts in millions, except per share data):

	Fiscal Year Ended		
	January 30, 2005	February 1, 2004	February 2, 2003
Cost of Merchandise Sold			
As Reported	$48,664	$44,236	$40,139
Pro Forma	48,524	43,295	39,284
Gross Profit			
As Reported	24,430	20,580	18,108
Pro Forma	24,570	21,521	18,963
Selling and Store Operating Expenses			
As Reported	15,105	12,588	11,276
Pro Forma	15,105	13,529	12,157
Operating Income			
As Reported	7,926	6,846	5,830
Pro Forma	8,066	6,846	5,804
Diluted Earnings per Share			
As Reported	$ 2.26	$ 1.88	$ 1.56
Pro Forma	$ 2.30	$ 1.88	$ 1.56

Management's Discussion and Analysis of Results of Operations and Financial Condition (continued)

The Home Depot, Inc. and Subsidiaries

LIQUIDITY AND CAPITAL RESOURCES

Cash flow generated from operations provides us with a significant source of liquidity. For fiscal 2004, Net Cash Provided by Operating Activities increased to $6.9 billion from $6.5 billion for fiscal 2003. This increase was primarily driven by stronger Net Earnings and an increase in non-cash charges, such as depreciation and amortization.

Net Cash Used in Investing Activities increased to $4.5 billion for fiscal 2004 from $4.2 billion for fiscal 2003. This increase was primarily the result of $727 million used to purchase White Cap and Home Mart. In May 2004, we acquired all of the common stock of White Cap, a leading distributor of specialty hardware, tools and materials to construction contractors, and in June 2004, we acquired all of the common stock of Home Mart, the second largest home improvement retailer in Mexico. Capital Expenditures increased to $3.9 billion for fiscal 2004 from $3.5 billion for fiscal 2003. This increase was due to a higher investment in store modernization, technology and other initiatives. The increase in Net Cash Used in Investing Activities also reflects lower proceeds from the sale of property and equipment. In December 2003, we exercised an option to purchase certain assets under a lease agreement at an original cost of $598 million. There was no similar transaction in fiscal 2004. As of January 30, 2005, we own 86% of our stores. We believe our real estate ownership strategy is a competitive advantage.

We plan to open 175 stores in fiscal 2005, including 19 stores in Canada and 10 in Mexico, and estimate total Capital Expenditures to be approximately $3.7 billion, allocated as follows: 64% for new stores, 13% for store modernization, 12% for technology and 11% for other initiatives.

Net Cash Used in Financing Activities for fiscal 2004 was $3.1 billion compared with $1.9 billion for fiscal 2003. During fiscal 2004, 2003 and 2002, the Board of Directors authorized total repurchases of our common stock of $7.0 billion pursuant to a Share Repurchase Program. Over the past three fiscal years, we have repurchased 200.5 million shares of our common stock for a total of $6.7 billion. During fiscal 2004, we repurchased approximately 84 million shares of our common stock for $3.1 billion and during fiscal 2003 we repurchased 47 million shares of our common stock for $1.6 billion. As of January 30, 2005, approximately $300 million remained under our previously authorized Share Repurchase Program. In February 2005, our Board of Directors authorized an additional $2.0 billion in our Share Repurchase Program, bringing the total remaining authorization to $2.3 billion.

In September 2004, we issued $1.0 billion of 3¾% Senior Notes (see Note 2 in "Notes to Consolidated Financial Statements") at a discount of $5 million. The net proceeds of $995 million were used in part to repay our $500 million 6½% Senior Notes with the remainder used for general corporate purposes. During fiscal 2004, we also increased dividends paid by 21% to $719 million from $595 million in fiscal 2003.

In the second quarter of fiscal 2004, we increased the maximum capacity for borrowing under our commercial paper program to $1.25 billion as well as increased the related back-up credit facility with a consortium of banks to $1.0 billion. As of January 30, 2005, there were no borrowings outstanding under the program. The credit facility, which expires in May 2009, contains various restrictive covenants, none of which are expected to impact our liquidity or capital resources.

We use capital and operating leases to finance a portion of our real estate, including our stores, distribution centers and store support centers. The net present value of capital lease obligations is reflected in our Consolidated Balance Sheets in Long-Term Debt. In accordance with generally accepted accounting principles, the operating leases are not reflected in our Consolidated Balance Sheets. As of the end of fiscal 2004, our total debt-to-equity ratio was 8.9% compared to 6.1% at the end of fiscal 2003. This increase was due in part to the net increase in Senior Notes of $495 million. The increase in our total debt-to-equity ratio also reflects the consolidation of a variable interest entity in accordance with the revised version of Financial Accounting Standards Board ("FASB") Interpretation No. 46, "Consolidation of Variable Interest Entities," which increased Long-Term Debt by $282 million during the first quarter of fiscal 2004 but had no economic impact on our financial condition (see Note 5 in "Notes to Consolidated Financial Statements"). If the estimated net present value of future payments under the operating leases were capitalized, our total debt-to-equity ratio would increase to 30.8%.

As of January 30, 2005, we had $2.2 billion in Cash and Short-Term Investments. We believe that our current cash position and cash flow generated from operations should be sufficient to enable us to complete our capital expenditure programs and any required long-term debt payments through the next several fiscal years. In addition, we have funds available from the $1.25 billion commercial paper program and the ability to obtain alternative sources of financing if required.

Consolidated Statements of Earnings

The Home Depot, Inc. and Subsidiaries

	Fiscal Year Ended [1]		
amounts in millions, except per share data	January 30, 2005	February 1, 2004	February 2, 2003
NET SALES	$73,094	$64,816	$58,247
Cost of Merchandise Sold	48,664	44,236	40,139
GROSS PROFIT	24,430	20,580	18,108
Operating Expenses:			
Selling and Store Operating	15,105	12,588	11,276
General and Administrative	1,399	1,146	1,002
Total Operating Expenses	16,504	13,734	12,278
OPERATING INCOME	7,926	6,846	5,830
Interest Income (Expense):			
Interest and Investment Income	56	59	79
Interest Expense	(70)	(62)	(37)
Interest, net	(14)	(3)	42
EARNINGS BEFORE PROVISION FOR INCOME TAXES	7,912	6,843	5,872
Provision for Income Taxes	2,911	2,539	2,208
NET EARNINGS	$ 5,001	$ 4,304	$ 3,664
Weighted Average Common Shares	2,207	2,283	2,336
BASIC EARNINGS PER SHARE	$ 2.27	$ 1.88	$ 1.57
Diluted Weighted Average Common Shares	2,216	2,289	2,344
DILUTED EARNINGS PER SHARE	$ 2.26	$ 1.88	$ 1.56

(1) Fiscal years ended January 30, 2005, February 1, 2004 and February 2, 2003 include 52 weeks.

See accompanying Notes to Consolidated Financial Statements.

Consolidated Balance Sheets

The Home Depot, Inc. and Subsidiaries

amounts in millions, except per share data	January 30, 2005	February 1, 2004
ASSETS		
Current Assets:		
Cash and Cash Equivalents	$ 506	$ 1,103
Short-Term Investments	1,659	1,749
Receivables, net	1,499	1,097
Merchandise Inventories	10,076	9,076
Other Current Assets	450	303
Total Current Assets	14,190	13,328
Property and Equipment, at cost:		
Land	6,932	6,397
Buildings	12,325	10,920
Furniture, Fixtures and Equipment	6,195	5,163
Leasehold Improvements	1,191	942
Construction in Progress	1,404	820
Capital Leases	390	352
	28,437	24,594
Less Accumulated Depreciation and Amortization	5,711	4,531
Net Property and Equipment	22,726	20,063
Notes Receivable	369	84
Cost in Excess of the Fair Value of Net Assets Acquired, net of accumulated amortization of $56 at January 30, 2005 and $54 at February 1, 2004	1,394	833
Other Assets	228	129
TOTAL ASSETS	$38,907	$34,437
LIABILITIES AND STOCKHOLDERS' EQUITY		
Current Liabilities:		
Accounts Payable	$ 5,766	$ 5,159
Accrued Salaries and Related Expenses	1,055	801
Sales Taxes Payable	412	419
Deferred Revenue	1,546	1,281
Income Taxes Payable	161	175
Current Installments of Long-Term Debt	11	509
Other Accrued Expenses	1,578	1,210
Total Current Liabilities	10,529	9,554
Long-Term Debt, excluding current installments	2,148	856
Other Long-Term Liabilities	763	653
Deferred Income Taxes	1,309	967
STOCKHOLDERS' EQUITY		
Common Stock, par value $0.05; authorized: 10,000 shares; issued 2,385 shares at January 30, 2005 and 2,373 shares at February 1, 2004; outstanding 2,185 shares at January 30, 2005 and 2,257 shares at February 1, 2004	119	119
Paid-In Capital	6,650	6,184
Retained Earnings	23,962	19,680
Accumulated Other Comprehensive Income	227	90
Unearned Compensation	(108)	(76)
Treasury Stock, at cost, 200 shares at January 30, 2005 and 116 shares at February 1, 2004	(6,692)	(3,590)
Total Stockholders' Equity	24,158	22,407
TOTAL LIABILITIES AND STOCKHOLDERS' EQUITY	$38,907	$34,437

See accompanying Notes to Consolidated Financial Statements.

APPENDIX A

Consolidated Statements of Stockholders' Equity and Comprehensive Income

The Home Depot, Inc. and Subsidiaries

amounts in millions, except per share data	Common Stock Shares	Common Stock Amount	Paid-In Capital	Retained Earnings	Accumulated Other Comprehensive Income (Loss)[1]	Unearned Compensation	Treasury Stock Shares	Treasury Stock Amount	Total Stockholders' Equity	Comprehensive Income[2]
BALANCE, FEBRUARY 3, 2002	2,346	$117	$5,412	$12,799	$(220)	$ (26)	–	$ –	$18,082	
Net Earnings	–	–	–	3,664	–	–	–	–	3,664	$3,664
Shares Issued Under Employee Stock Plans	16	1	366	–	–	(40)	–	–	327	
Tax Effect of Sale of Option Shares by Employees	–	–	68	–	–	–	–	–	68	
Translation Adjustments	–	–	–	–	109	–	–	–	109	109
Realized Loss on Derivative	–	–	–	–	29	–	–	–	29	18
Stock Options, Awards and Amortization of Restricted Stock	–	–	12	–	–	3	–	–	15	
Repurchase of Common Stock	–	–	–	–	–	–	(69)	(2,000)	(2,000)	
Cash Dividends ($0.21 per share)	–	–	–	(492)	–	–	–	–	(492)	
Comprehensive Income										$3,791
BALANCE, FEBRUARY 2, 2003	2,362	$118	$5,858	$15,971	$ (82)	$ (63)	(69)	$(2,000)	$19,802	
Net Earnings	–	–	–	4,304	–	–	–	–	4,304	$4,304
Shares Issued Under Employee Stock Plans	11	1	249	–	–	(26)	–	–	224	
Tax Effect of Sale of Option Shares by Employees	–	–	24	–	–	–	–	–	24	
Translation Adjustments	–	–	–	–	172	–	–	–	172	172
Stock Options, Awards and Amortization of Restricted Stock	–	–	53	–	–	13	–	–	66	
Repurchase of Common Stock	–	–	–	–	–	–	(47)	(1,590)	(1,590)	
Cash Dividends ($0.26 per share)	–	–	–	(595)	–	–	–	–	(595)	
Comprehensive Income										$4,476
BALANCE, FEBRUARY 1, 2004	2,373	$119	$6,184	$19,680	$ 90	$ (76)	(116)	$(3,590)	$22,407	
Net Earnings	–	–	–	5,001	–	–	–	–	5,001	5,001
Shares Issued Under Employee Stock Plans	12	–	340	–	–	(54)	–	–	286	
Tax Effect of Sale of Option Shares by Employees	–	–	26	–	–	–	–	–	26	
Translation Adjustments	–	–	–	–	137	–	–	–	137	137
Stock Options, Awards and Amortization of Restricted Stock	–	–	100	–	–	22	–	–	122	
Repurchase of Common Stock	–	–	–	–	–	–	(84)	(3,102)	(3,102)	
Cash Dividends ($0.325 per share)	–	–	–	(719)	–	–	–	–	(719)	
Comprehensive Income										$5,138
BALANCE, JANUARY 30, 2005	2,385	$119	$6,650	$23,962	$ 227	$(108)	(200)	$(6,692)	$24,158	

(1) Balance at January 30, 2005 consists primarily of foreign currency translation adjustments.

(2) Components of Comprehensive Income are reported net of related income taxes.

See accompanying Notes to Consolidated Financial Statements.

Consolidated Statements of Cash Flows

The Home Depot, Inc. and Subsidiaries

	Fiscal Year Ended[1]		
amounts in millions	January 30, 2005	February 1, 2004	February 2, 2003
CASH FLOWS FROM OPERATING ACTIVITIES:			
Net Earnings	$ 5,001	$ 4,304	$ 3,664
Reconciliation of Net Earnings to Net Cash Provided by Operating Activities:			
Depreciation and Amortization	1,319	1,076	903
Stock-Based Compensation Expense	125	67	15
Changes in Assets and Liabilities, net of the effects of acquisitions:			
(Increase) Decrease in Receivables, net	(266)	25	(38)
Increase in Merchandise Inventories	(849)	(693)	(1,592)
Increase in Accounts Payable and Accrued Liabilities	917	790	1,394
Increase in Deferred Revenue	263	279	147
Increase (Decrease) in Income Taxes Payable	2	(27)	83
Increase in Deferred Income Taxes	319	605	173
Increase in Other Long-Term Liabilities	119	33	66
Other	(46)	86	(13)
Net Cash Provided by Operating Activities	6,904	6,545	4,802
CASH FLOWS FROM INVESTING ACTIVITIES:			
Capital Expenditures, net of $38, $47 and $49 of non-cash capital expenditures in fiscal 2004, 2003 and 2002, respectively	(3,948)	(3,508)	(2,749)
Purchase of Assets from Off-Balance Sheet Financing Arrangement	–	(598)	–
Payments for Businesses Acquired, net	(727)	(215)	(235)
Proceeds from Sales of Businesses, net	–	–	22
Proceeds from Sales of Property and Equipment	96	265	105
Purchases of Investments	(25,890)	(38,649)	(38,367)
Proceeds from Sales and Maturities of Investments	25,990	38,534	38,623
Net Cash Used in Investing Activities	(4,479)	(4,171)	(2,601)
CASH FLOWS FROM FINANCING ACTIVITIES:			
Proceeds from Long-Term Borrowings, net of discount	995	–	1
Repayments of Long-Term Debt	(510)	(9)	–
Repurchase of Common Stock	(3,106)	(1,554)	(2,000)
Proceeds from Sale of Common Stock, net	285	227	326
Cash Dividends Paid to Stockholders	(719)	(595)	(492)
Net Cash Used in Financing Activities	(3,055)	(1,931)	(2,165)
(Decrease) Increase in Cash and Cash Equivalents	(630)	443	36
Effect of Exchange Rate Changes on Cash and Cash Equivalents	33	20	8
Cash and Cash Equivalents at Beginning of Year	1,103	640	596
Cash and Cash Equivalents at End of Year	$ 506	$ 1,103	$ 640
SUPPLEMENTAL DISCLOSURE OF CASH PAYMENTS MADE FOR:			
Interest, net of interest capitalized	$ 78	$ 70	$ 50
Income Taxes	$ 2,793	$ 2,037	$ 1,951

(1) Fiscal years ended January 30, 2005, February 1, 2004 and February 2, 2003 include 52 weeks.

See accompanying Notes to Consolidated Financial Statements.

APPENDIX A

Notes to Consolidated Financial Statements

The Home Depot, Inc. and Subsidiaries

1 | SUMMARY OF SIGNIFICANT ACCOUNTING POLICIES

Business, Consolidation and Presentation

The Home Depot, Inc. and subsidiaries (the "Company") operate Home Depot stores, which are full-service, warehouse-style stores averaging approximately 106,000 square feet in size. The stores stock approximately 40,000 to 50,000 different kinds of building materials, home improvement supplies and lawn and garden products that are sold primarily to do-it-yourself customers but also to home improvement contractors, tradespeople and building maintenance professionals. In addition, the Company operates EXPO Design Center stores, which offer products and services primarily related to design and renovation projects, Home Depot Landscape Supply stores, which service landscape professionals and garden enthusiasts with lawn, landscape and garden products and Home Depot Supply stores serving primarily professional customers. The Company also operates The Home Depot Floor Stores, which offer primarily flooring products and installation services. At the end of fiscal 2004, the Company was operating 1,890 stores in total, which included 1,657 Home Depot stores, 54 EXPO Design Center stores, 11 Home Depot Landscape Supply stores, 5 Home Depot Supply stores and 2 Home Depot Floor Stores in the United States ("U.S."); 117 Home Depot stores in Canada and 44 Home Depot stores in Mexico.

The consolidated results include five wholly-owned subsidiaries that operate under The Home Depot Supply brand. The five subsidiaries are Apex Supply Company, Inc., The Home Depot Supply, Inc., Your Other Warehouse, LLC, White Cap Industries, Inc. and HD Builder Solutions Group, Inc. The Company offers plumbing, HVAC and other professional plumbing products through wholesale plumbing distributors, Apex Supply Company, Inc. and Your Other Warehouse, LLC. The Home Depot Supply, Inc. supplies maintenance, repair and operating products serving primarily the multi-family housing and lodging facilities management market. White Cap Industries, Inc. distributes specialty hardware, tools and materials to construction contractors. The Company arranges for flooring, countertops and window treatment installation services to production homebuilders through HD Builder Solutions Group, Inc. The Consolidated Financial Statements include the accounts of the Company and its wholly-owned subsidiaries. All significant intercompany transactions have been eliminated in consolidation.

Fiscal Year

The Company's fiscal year is a 52 or 53-week period ending on the Sunday nearest to January 31. Fiscal years ended January 30, 2005 ("fiscal 2004"), February 1, 2004 ("fiscal 2003") and February 2, 2003 ("fiscal 2002") include 52 weeks.

Use of Estimates

Management of the Company has made a number of estimates and assumptions relating to the reporting of assets and liabilities, the disclosure of contingent assets and liabilities, and reported amounts of revenues and expenses in preparing these financial statements in conformity with generally accepted accounting principles. Actual results could differ from these estimates.

Fair Value of Financial Instruments

The carrying amounts of Cash and Cash Equivalents, Receivables and Accounts Payable approximate fair value due to the short-term maturities of these financial instruments. The fair value of the Company's investments is discussed under the caption "Short-Term Investments" in this Note 1. The fair value of the Company's debt is discussed in Note 2.

Cash Equivalents

The Company considers all highly liquid investments purchased with maturities of three months or less to be cash equivalents. The Company's Cash and Cash Equivalents are carried at fair market value and consist primarily of high-grade commercial paper, money market funds, U.S. government agency securities and tax-exempt notes and bonds.

Short-Term Investments

Short-Term Investments are primarily auction rate securities. The interest rates on these securities are typically reset to market prevailing rates every 35 days or less, and in all cases every 90 days or less, but have longer stated maturities. Short-Term Investments are classified as available-for-sale and changes in the fair value are included in Accumulated Other Comprehensive Income (Loss), net of applicable taxes in the accompanying Consolidated Financial Statements. Prior to the end of fiscal 2004, the Company classified auction rate securities in Cash and Cash Equivalents. Prior period information was reclassified, including the impact on Cash Flow from Investing Activities, to conform to the current year presentation. There was no impact on Net Earnings or Cash Flow from Operating Activities as a result of the reclassification.

Accounts Receivable

The Company's valuation reserve related to accounts receivable was not material as of January 30, 2005 and February 1, 2004. The Company has an agreement with a third-party service provider who manages the Company's private label credit card program and directly extends credit to customers.

Merchandise Inventories

The majority of the Company's Merchandise Inventories are stated at the lower of cost (first-in, first-out) or market, as determined by the retail inventory method.

Notes to Consolidated Financial Statements (continued)

The Home Depot, Inc. and Subsidiaries

Certain subsidiaries and distribution centers record Merchandise Inventories at the lower of cost (first-in, first-out) or market, as determined by the cost method. These Merchandise Inventories represent approximately 11% of the total Merchandise Inventories balance.

Independent physical inventory counts are taken on a regular basis in each store and distribution center to ensure that amounts reflected in the accompanying Consolidated Financial Statements for Merchandise Inventories are properly stated. During the period between physical inventory counts, the Company accrues for estimated losses related to shrink on a store by store basis based on historical shrink results and current trends in the business. Shrink is the difference between the recorded amount of inventory and the physical inventory. Shrink (or in the case of excess inventory, "swell") may occur due to theft, loss, improper records for the receipt of inventory or deterioration of goods, among other things.

Income Taxes

The Company provides for federal, state and foreign income taxes currently payable, as well as for those deferred due to timing differences between reporting income and expenses for financial statement purposes versus tax purposes. Federal, state and foreign tax benefits are recorded as a reduction of income taxes. Deferred tax assets and liabilities are recognized for the future tax consequences attributable to differences between the financial statement carrying amounts of existing assets and liabilities and their respective tax bases. Deferred tax assets and liabilities are measured using enacted income tax rates expected to apply to taxable income in the years in which those temporary differences are expected to be recovered or settled. The effect of a change in income tax rates is recognized as income or expense in the period that includes the enactment date.

The Company and its eligible subsidiaries file a consolidated U.S. federal income tax return. Non-U.S. subsidiaries and certain U.S. subsidiaries, which are consolidated for financial reporting purposes, are not eligible to be included in the Company's consolidated U.S. federal income tax return. Separate provisions for income taxes have been determined for these entities.

The American Jobs Creation Act of 2004 ("AJC Act") provides a one-time 85 percent dividends-received deduction that would apply to qualified cash dividends received from controlled foreign corporations if the funds are reinvested in the U.S. The deduction can result in an effective income tax rate of 5.25 percent on the repatriation of foreign earnings, a rate much lower than the normal statutory income tax rate of 35 percent. At this time, the Company is evaluating whether some or all of its unrepatriated foreign earnings will be repatriated under this new law. Since the Company currently intends to reinvest the unremitted earnings of its non-U.S. subsidiaries and postpone their remittance indefinitely, no provision for U.S. income taxes for non-U.S. subsidiaries was recorded in the accompanying Consolidated Statements of Earnings.

The AJC Act also provides a new deduction for qualified domestic production activities. When fully phased-in, the deduction will be up to nine percent of the lesser of qualified production activities income or taxable income. Pursuant to Statement of Financial Accounting Standards ("SFAS") No. 109, "Accounting for Income Taxes," the deduction will be accounted for as a special deduction, not as a tax-rate reduction, because the deduction is contingent on performing activities identified in the AJC Act. The Company is currently assessing the potential impact of the AJC Act on its Provision for Income Taxes.

Depreciation and Amortization

The Company's Buildings, Furniture, Fixtures and Equipment are depreciated using the straight-line method over the estimated useful lives of the assets. Leasehold Improvements are amortized using the straight-line method over the original term of the lease or the useful life of the improvement, whichever is shorter. The Company's Property and Equipment is depreciated using the following estimated useful lives:

	Life
Buildings	10–45 years
Furniture, Fixtures and Equipment	3–20 years
Leasehold Improvements	5–30 years

Capitalized Software Costs

The Company capitalizes certain costs related to the acquisition and development of software and amortizes these costs using the straight-line method over the estimated useful life of the software, which is three years. These costs are included in Furniture, Fixtures and Equipment in the accompanying Consolidated Balance Sheets. Certain development costs not meeting the criteria for capitalization are expensed as incurred.

Revenues

The Company recognizes revenue, net of estimated returns, at the time the customer takes possession of merchandise or receives services. The liability for sales returns is estimated based on historical return levels. When the Company receives payment from customers before the customer has taken possession of the merchandise or the service has been performed, the amount received is recorded as Deferred Revenue in the accompanying Consolidated Balance Sheets until the sale or service is complete.

Services Revenue

Net Sales include services revenue generated through a variety of installation and home maintenance programs. In these programs, the customer selects and purchases material for a project and the Company provides or arranges professional installation. These programs are offered through Home Depot and EXPO Design Center

Notes to Consolidated Financial Statements (continued)

The Home Depot, Inc. and Subsidiaries

stores and focus primarily on providing products and services to our do-it-for-me customers. The Company also arranges for the provision of flooring, countertop and window coverings installation services to production homebuilders through HD Builder Solutions Group, Inc. Under certain programs, when the Company provides or arranges the installation of a project and the subcontractor provides material as part of the installation, both the material and labor are included in services revenue. The Company recognizes this revenue when the service for the customer is complete.

All payments received prior to the completion of services are recorded in Deferred Revenue in the accompanying Consolidated Balance Sheets. Services revenue, including the impact of deferred revenue, was $3.6 billion, $2.8 billion and $2.0 billion for fiscal 2004, 2003 and 2002, respectively.

Self-Insurance

The Company is self-insured for certain losses related to general liability, product liability, automobile, workers' compensation and medical claims. The expected ultimate cost for claims incurred as of the balance sheet date is not discounted and is recognized as a liability. The expected ultimate cost of claims is estimated based upon analysis of historical data and actuarial estimates.

Prepaid Advertising

Television and radio advertising production costs along with media placement costs are expensed when the advertisement first appears. Included in Other Current Assets in the accompanying Consolidated Balance Sheets are $33 million at the end of both fiscal 2004 and 2003 relating to prepayments of production costs for print and broadcast advertising.

Vendor Allowances

The Company currently receives two types of vendor allowances: volume rebates that are earned as a result of attaining certain purchase levels and advertising co-op allowances for the promotion of vendors' products that are typically based on guaranteed minimum amounts with additional amounts being earned for attaining certain purchase levels. All vendor allowances are accrued as earned, and those allowances received as a result of attaining certain purchase levels are accrued over the incentive period based on estimates of purchases.

In fiscal 2003, the Company adopted Emerging Issues Task Force No. 02-16, "Accounting by a Customer (Including a Reseller) for Certain Consideration Received from a Vendor" ("EITF 02-16"), which states that cash consideration received from a vendor is presumed to be a reduction of the prices of the vendor's products or services and should, therefore, be characterized as a reduction of Cost of Merchandise Sold when recognized in the Company's Consolidated Statements of Earnings. That presumption is overcome when the consideration is either a reimbursement of specific, incremental and identifiable costs incurred to sell the vendor's product or a payment for assets or services delivered to the vendor.

The Company received consideration in the form of advertising co-op allowances from its vendors pursuant to annual agreements, which are generally on a calendar year basis. As permitted by EITF 02-16, the Company elected to apply the provisions of EITF 02-16 prospectively to all agreements entered into or modified after December 31, 2002.

The impact of EITF 02-16 in fiscal 2004 and fiscal 2003 resulted in a reduction of Cost of Merchandise Sold of $891 million and $40 million, an increase to Selling and Store Operating Expenses of $1.0 billion and $47 million and a reduction to Earnings before Provision for Income Taxes of $158 million and $7 million, respectively. The impact on the Company's Diluted Earnings per Share was a reduction of $0.04 in fiscal 2004. There was no material impact on the Company's Diluted Earnings per Share in fiscal 2003. Merchandise Inventories in the accompanying Consolidated Balance Sheets were also reduced by $158 million and $7 million as of January 30, 2005 and February 1, 2004, respectively.

Volume rebates and advertising co-op allowances earned are initially recorded as a reduction in Merchandise Inventories and a subsequent reduction in Cost of Merchandise Sold when the related product is sold. Prior to the adoption of EITF 02-16 in January 2004, advertising co-op allowances earned had been offset against advertising expense to the extent of advertising costs incurred, with the excess treated as a reduction of Cost of Merchandise Sold.

The Company continues to earn certain advertising co-op allowances that are recorded as an offset against advertising expense as they are reimbursements of specific, incremental and identifiable costs incurred to promote vendors' products. In fiscal 2002, advertising co-op allowances exceeded gross advertising expense by $30 million. In fiscal 2004 and 2003, net advertising expense was $1.0 billion and $58 million, respectively, which was recorded in Selling and Store Operating Expenses.

Cost of Merchandise Sold

Cost of Merchandise Sold includes the actual cost of merchandise sold and services performed, the cost of transportation of merchandise from vendors to the Company's stores, locations or customers, the operating cost of the Company's distribution centers and the cost of deferred interest programs offered through the Company's private label credit card program.

The cost of handling and shipping merchandise from the Company's stores, locations or distribution centers to the customer is classified as Selling and Store Operating Expenses. The cost of shipping and handling, including internal costs and payments to third parties, classified as Selling and Store Operating Expenses, was $427 million, $387 million and $341 million in fiscal 2004, 2003 and 2002, respectively.

Notes to Consolidated Financial Statements (continued)

The Home Depot, Inc. and Subsidiaries

Cost in Excess of the Fair Value of Net Assets Acquired

Goodwill represents the excess of purchase price over fair value of net assets acquired. In accordance with SFAS No. 142, "Goodwill and Other Intangible Assets," the Company stopped amortizing goodwill effective February 4, 2002. The Company assesses the recoverability of goodwill at least annually by determining whether the fair value of each reporting entity supports its carrying value. The fair values of the Company's identified reporting units were estimated using the expected present value of discounted cash flows. The Company recorded no impairment charges for fiscal 2004 or fiscal 2003 and $1.3 million for fiscal 2002.

Impairment of Long-Lived Assets

The Company evaluates the carrying value of long-lived assets when management makes the decision to relocate or close a store, or when circumstances indicate the carrying amount of an asset may not be recoverable. Losses related to the impairment of long-lived assets are recognized to the extent the sum of undiscounted estimated future cash flows expected to result from the use of the asset are less than the asset's carrying value. If the carrying value is greater than the future cash flows, a provision is made to write down the related assets to the estimated net recoverable value. Impairment losses were recorded as a component of Selling and Store Operating Expenses in the accompanying Consolidated Statements of Earnings. When a location closes, the Company also recognizes in Selling and Store Operating Expenses the net present value of future lease obligations, less estimated sublease income.

Stock-Based Compensation

Effective February 3, 2003, the Company adopted the fair value method of recording stock-based compensation expense in accordance with SFAS No. 123, "Accounting for Stock-Based Compensation" ("SFAS 123"). The Company selected the prospective method of adoption as described in SFAS No. 148, "Accounting for Stock-Based Compensation – Transition and Disclosure" and accordingly, stock-based compensation expense was recognized related to stock options granted, modified or settled and expense related to the Employee Stock Purchase Plan ("ESPP") after the beginning of fiscal 2003. The fair value of stock options and ESPP as determined on the date of grant using the Black-Scholes option-pricing model is being expensed over the vesting period of the related stock options and ESPP. As such, the Company recognized $86 million and $40 million of stock-based compensation expense related to stock options and ESPP in fiscal 2004 and 2003, respectively.

Prior to February 3, 2003, the Company elected to account for its stock-based compensation plans under Accounting Principles Board Opinion No. 25, "Accounting for Stock Issued to Employees" ("APB 25"), which requires the recording of stock-based compensation expense for some, but not all, stock-based compensation. Pursuant to APB 25, no stock-based compensation expense related to stock option awards and ESPP was recorded in fiscal 2002.

The per share weighted average fair value of stock options granted during fiscal 2004, 2003 and 2002 was $13.57, $9.79 and $17.34, respectively. The fair value of these options was determined at the date of grant using the Black-Scholes option-pricing model with the following assumptions:

	Fiscal Year Ended		
	January 30, 2005	February 1, 2004	February 2, 2003
Risk-free interest rate	2.6%	3.0%	4.0%
Assumed volatility	41.3%	44.6%	44.3%
Assumed dividend yield	0.8%	1.0%	0.5%
Assumed lives of options	5 years	5 years	5 years

The following table illustrates the effect on Net Earnings and Earnings per Share as if the Company had applied the fair value recognition provisions of SFAS 123 to all stock-based compensation in each period (amounts in millions, except per share data):

	Fiscal Year Ended		
	January 30, 2005	February 1, 2004	February 2, 2003
Net Earnings, as reported	$5,001	$4,304	$3,664
Add: Stock-based compensation expense included in reported Net Earnings, net of related tax effects	79	42	10
Deduct: Total stock-based compensation expense determined under fair value based method for all awards, net of related tax effects	(237)	(279)	(260)
Pro forma net earnings	$4,843	$4,067	$3,414
Earnings per Share:			
Basic – as reported	$ 2.27	$ 1.88	$ 1.57
Basic – pro forma	$ 2.19	$ 1.78	$ 1.46
Diluted – as reported	$ 2.26	$ 1.88	$ 1.56
Diluted – pro forma	$ 2.19	$ 1.78	$ 1.46

APPENDIX A

Notes to Consolidated Financial Statements (continued)

The Home Depot, Inc. and Subsidiaries

Derivatives

The Company measures its derivatives at fair value and recognizes these assets or liabilities on the Consolidated Balance Sheets. The Company's primary objective for entering into derivative instruments is to manage its exposure to interest rates, as well as to maintain an appropriate mix of fixed and variable rate debt. At January 30, 2005, the Company had several outstanding interest rate swaps with a notional amount of $475 million that swap fixed rate interest on the Company's $500 million 5⅜% Senior Notes for variable interest rates equal to LIBOR plus 30 to 245 basis points and expire on April 1, 2006. At January 30, 2005, the fair market value of these agreements was $6 million, which is the estimated amount that the Company would have received to sell similar interest rate swap agreements at current interest rates.

Comprehensive Income

Comprehensive Income includes Net Earnings adjusted for certain revenues, expenses, gains and losses that are excluded from Net Earnings under generally accepted accounting principles. Examples include foreign currency translation adjustments and unrealized gains and losses on certain derivatives.

Foreign Currency Translation

Assets and Liabilities denominated in a foreign currency are translated into U.S. dollars at the current rate of exchange on the last day of the reporting period. Revenues and Expenses are generally translated at a daily exchange rate and equity transactions are translated using the actual rate on the day of the transaction.

Segment Information

The Company operates within a single operating segment within North America. Net Sales for Canada and Mexico were $4.2 billion, $3.4 billion and $2.6 billion during fiscal 2004, 2003 and 2002, respectively. Long-lived assets in Canada and Mexico totaled $1.7 billion and $1.2 billion as of January 30, 2005 and February 1, 2004, respectively.

Reclassifications

Certain amounts in prior fiscal years have been reclassified to conform with the presentation adopted in the current fiscal year.

2 | LONG-TERM DEBT

The Company's Long-Term Debt at the end of fiscal 2004 and fiscal 2003 consisted of the following (amounts in millions):

	January 30, 2005	February 1, 2004
3¾% Senior Notes; due September 15, 2009; interest payable semi-annually on March 15 and September 15	$ 995	$ –
6½% Senior Notes; due September 15, 2004; interest payable semi-annually on March 15 and September 15	–	500
5⅜% Senior Notes; due April 1, 2006; interest payable semi-annually on April 1 and October 1	500	500
Capital Lease Obligations; payable in varying installments through January 31, 2045	351	318
Other	313	47
Total Long-Term Debt	2,159	1,365
Less current installments	11	509
Long-Term Debt, excluding current installments	$2,148	$ 856

In the second quarter of fiscal 2004, the Company increased the maximum capacity for borrowing under its commercial paper program to $1.25 billion as well as increased the related back-up credit facility with a consortium of banks to $1.0 billion. As of January 30, 2005, there were no amounts outstanding under the program. The credit facility, which expires in May 2009, contains various restrictive covenants, none of which are expected to materially impact the Company's liquidity or capital resources.

In September 2004, the Company issued $1.0 billion of 3¾% Senior Notes due September 15, 2009 at a discount of $5 million with interest payable semi-annually on March 15 and September 15 of each year. The net proceeds of $995 million were used in part for the repayment of the Company's outstanding 6½% Senior Notes due September 2004 in the aggregate principal amount of $500 million. The remainder of the net proceeds was used for general corporate purposes.

Notes to Consolidated Financial Statements (continued)

The Home Depot, Inc. and Subsidiaries

The $5.0 million discount associated with the issuance is being amortized over the term of the 3¾% Senior Notes using the effective interest rate method. Issuance costs of $6.6 million are being amortized over the term of the 3¾% Senior Notes using the straight-line method. The Company also had $500 million of unsecured 5⅜% Senior Notes outstanding as of January 30, 2005, collectively referred to as "Senior Notes."

The Senior Notes may be redeemed by the Company at any time, in whole or in part, at a redemption price plus accrued interest up to the redemption date. The redemption price is equal to the greater of (1) 100% of the principal amount of the Senior Notes to be redeemed, or (2) the sum of the present values of the remaining scheduled payments of principal and interest to maturity. The Company is generally not limited under these indentures in its ability to incur additional indebtedness nor required to maintain financial ratios or specified levels of net worth or liquidity. However, the indentures governing the Senior Notes contain various restrictive covenants, none of which are expected to impact the Company's liquidity or capital resources. The Senior Notes are not subject to sinking fund requirements.

Interest Expense in the accompanying Consolidated Statements of Earnings is net of interest capitalized of $40 million, $50 million and $59 million in fiscal 2004, 2003 and 2002, respectively. Maturities of Long-Term Debt are $11 million for fiscal 2005, $517 million for fiscal 2006, $12 million for fiscal 2007, $296 million for fiscal 2008, $1.015 billion for fiscal 2009 and $313 million thereafter.

As of January 30, 2005, the market values of the publicly traded 3¾% Senior Notes and 5⅜% Senior Notes were approximately $989 million and $515 million, respectively. The estimated fair value of all other long-term borrowings, excluding capital lease obligations, was approximately $316 million compared to the carrying value of $313 million. These fair values were estimated using a discounted cash flow analysis based on the Company's incremental borrowing rate for similar liabilities.

3 | INCOME TAXES

The components of Earnings before Provision for Income Taxes for fiscal 2004, 2003 and 2002 are as follows (amounts in millions):

	Fiscal Year Ended		
	January 30, 2005	February 1, 2004	February 2, 2003
United States	$7,508	$6,440	$5,571
Foreign	404	403	301
Total	$7,912	$6,843	$5,872

The Provision for Income Taxes consisted of the following (amounts in millions):

	Fiscal Year Ended		
	January 30, 2005	February 1, 2004	February 2, 2003
Current:			
Federal	$2,153	$1,520	$1,679
State	279	307	239
Foreign	139	107	117
	2,571	1,934	2,035
Deferred:			
Federal	304	573	174
State	52	27	1
Foreign	(16)	5	(2)
	340	605	173
Total	$2,911	$2,539	$2,208

The Company's combined federal, state and foreign effective tax rates for fiscal 2004, 2003 and 2002, net of offsets generated by federal, state and foreign tax benefits, were approximately 36.8%, 37.1% and 37.6%, respectively.

The reconciliation of the Provision for Income Taxes at the federal statutory rate of 35% to the actual tax expense for the applicable fiscal years is as follows (amounts in millions):

	Fiscal Year Ended		
	January 30, 2005	February 1, 2004	February 2, 2003
Income taxes at federal statutory rate	$2,769	$2,395	$2,055
State income taxes, net of federal income tax benefit	215	217	156
Foreign rate differences	(17)	(29)	(1)
Change in valuation allowance	(31)	–	–
Other, net	(25)	(44)	(2)
Total	$2,911	$2,539	$2,208

Notes to Consolidated Financial Statements (continued)

The Home Depot, Inc. and Subsidiaries

The tax effects of temporary differences that give rise to significant portions of the deferred tax assets and deferred tax liabilities as of January 30, 2005 and February 1, 2004, were as follows (amounts in millions):

	January 30, 2005	February 1, 2004
Deferred Tax Assets:		
Accrued self-insurance liabilities	$ 185	$ 205
Other accrued liabilities	213	196
Net operating losses	41	19
Net loss on disposition of business	–	31
Total gross deferred tax assets	439	451
Valuation allowance	(23)	(50)
Deferred tax assets, net of valuation allowance	416	401
Deferred Tax Liabilities:		
Accelerated depreciation	(1,425)	(1,114)
Accelerated inventory deduction	(234)	(218)
Other	(66)	(36)
Total gross deferred tax liabilities	(1,725)	(1,368)
Net deferred tax liability	$(1,309)	$ (967)

At January 30, 2005, the Company had foreign net operating loss carry-forwards to reduce future taxable income of certain foreign subsidiaries of $18 million, which will expire at various dates from 2008 to 2014. Management has concluded that it is more likely than not that these tax benefits related to the net operating losses will be realized and hence no valuation allowance has been provided. The Company has not provided for U.S. deferred income taxes on $772 million of undistributed earnings of international subsidiaries because of its intention to indefinitely reinvest these earnings outside the U.S. The determination of the amount of the unrecognized deferred U.S. income tax liability related to the undistributed earnings is not practicable; however, unrecognized foreign income tax credits would be available to reduce a portion of this liability.

At January 30, 2005 and February 1, 2004, the Company had a valuation allowance against certain deferred tax assets totaling $23 million and $50 million, respectively. During fiscal 2004, $31 million of deferred tax assets previously reserved were realized due to the Company's ability to fully utilize capital losses. The remainder of the valuation allowance relates to certain deferred tax assets in jurisdictions where it is management's opinion that it is more likely than not that the benefit of the deferred tax assets will not be realized. The likelihood of realizing the benefit of deferred tax assets is assessed on an ongoing basis. Consequently, future changes in the valuation allowance are possible.

4 | EMPLOYEE STOCK PLANS

The Home Depot, Inc. 1997 Omnibus Stock Incentive Plan ("1997 Plan") provides that incentive stock options, non-qualified stock options, stock appreciation rights, restricted shares, performance shares, performance units and deferred shares may be issued to selected associates, officers and directors of the Company. The maximum number of shares of the Company's common stock authorized for issuance under the 1997 Plan includes the number of shares carried over from prior plans and the number of shares authorized but unissued in the prior year, plus one-half percent of the total number of issued shares as of the first day of each fiscal year. As of January 30, 2005, there were 113 million shares available for future grants under the 1997 Plan.

Under the 1997 Plan, as of January 30, 2005, the Company had granted incentive and non-qualified stock options for 183 million shares, net of cancellations (of which 99 million had been exercised). Incentive stock options and non-qualified stock options are priced at the fair market value of the Company's stock on the date of the grant and typically vest at the rate of 25% per year commencing on the first anniversary date of the grant and expire on the tenth anniversary date of the grant. The Company recognized $86 million and $40 million of stock-based compensation expense in fiscal 2004 and 2003, respectively, related to stock options granted, modified or settled and expense related to the ESPP after the beginning of 2003 (see Note 1 under the caption "Stock-Based Compensation").

Under the 1997 Plan, as of January 30, 2005, 4 million shares of restricted stock had been issued net of cancellations (the restrictions on 294,400 shares have lapsed). Generally, the restrictions on the restricted stock lapse according to one of the following schedules: (1) the restrictions on 25% of the restricted stock lapse upon the third and sixth year anniversaries of the date of issuance with the remaining 50% of the restricted stock lapsing upon the associate's attainment of age 62, or (2) the restrictions on 100% of the restricted stock lapse at three or five years. The fair value of the restricted stock is expensed over the period during which the restrictions lapse. The Company recorded stock-based compensation expense related to restricted stock of $22 million, $13 million and $3 million in fiscal 2004, 2003 and 2002, respectively.

Notes to Consolidated Financial Statements (continued)

The Home Depot, Inc. and Subsidiaries

8 | COMMITMENTS AND CONTINGENCIES

At January 30, 2005, the Company was contingently liable for approximately $1.2 billion under outstanding letters of credit issued for certain business transactions, including insurance programs, trade and construction contracts. The Company's letters of credit are primarily performance-based and are not based on changes in variable components, a liability or an equity security of the other party.

The Company is involved in litigation arising from the normal course of business. In management's opinion, this litigation is not expected to materially impact the Company's consolidated results of operations or financial condition.

9 | ACQUISITIONS

The following acquisitions completed by the Company were all accounted for under the purchase method of accounting. Pro forma results of operations for fiscal 2004, 2003 and 2002 would not be materially different as a result of these acquisitions and therefore are not presented.

In June 2004, the Company acquired all of the common stock of Home Mart Mexico, S.A. de C.V. ("Home Mart"), the second largest home improvement retailer in Mexico. The purchase of 20 Home Mart stores increased the total numbers of stores in Mexico to 44 as of the end of fiscal 2004. This acquisition was part of the Company's strategy to expand into new markets.

In May 2004, the Company acquired all of the common stock of White Cap Industries, Inc. ("White Cap"), a leading distributor of specialty hardware, tools and materials to construction contractors. Since the Company's acquisition of White Cap, White Cap has completed three small additional acquisitions. These acquisitions were part of the Company's strategy to expand the Company's professional customer base with value-added products and services.

In January 2004, the Company acquired substantially all of the assets of Creative Touch Interiors, a flooring installation company primarily servicing the production homebuilder industry.

In December 2003, the Company acquired all of the common stock of Economy Maintenance Supply Company ("EMS") and all of the common stock of RMA Home Services, Inc. ("RMA"). EMS is a wholesale supplier of maintenance, repair and operating products. RMA is a replacement windows and siding installed services business. In October 2003, the Company acquired substantially all of the assets of Installed Products U.S.A., a roofing and fencing installed services business.

In October 2002, the Company acquired substantially all of the assets of FloorWorks, Inc. and Arvada Hardwood Floor Company and all of the common stock of Floors, Inc., three flooring installation companies primarily servicing the production homebuilder industry. In June 2002, the Company acquired the assets of Maderería Del Norte, S.A. de C.V., a four-store chain of home improvement stores in Juarez, Mexico.

The total aggregate purchase price for acquisitions in fiscal 2004, 2003 and 2002 was $729 million, $248 million and $202 million, respectively. Accordingly, the Company recorded Cost in Excess of the Fair Value of Net Assets Acquired related to the acquisitions of $554 million, $231 million and $109 million for fiscal 2004, 2003 and 2002, respectively, in the accompanying Consolidated Balance Sheets.

Notes to Consolidated Financial Statements (continued)

The Home Depot, Inc. and Subsidiaries

10 | QUARTERLY FINANCIAL DATA (UNAUDITED)

The following is a summary of the quarterly consolidated results of operations for the fiscal years ended January 30, 2005 and February 1, 2004 (dollars in millions, except per share data):

	Net Sales	Increase (Decrease) in Comparable Store Sales[1]	Gross Profit	Net Earnings	Basic Earnings per Share	Diluted Earnings per Share
Fiscal Year Ended January 30, 2005:						
First Quarter	$17,550	7.7%	$ 5,768	$1,098	$0.49	$0.49
Second Quarter	19,960	4.8%	6,661	1,545	0.70	0.70
Third Quarter	18,772	4.5%	6,252	1,317	0.60	0.60
Fourth Quarter	16,812	4.6%	5,749	1,041	0.48	0.47
Fiscal Year	$73,094	5.4%	$24,430	$5,001	$2.27	$2.26
Fiscal Year Ended February 1, 2004:						
First Quarter	$15,104	(1.6)%	$ 4,829	$ 907	$0.40	$0.39
Second Quarter	17,989	2.2%	5,605	1,299	0.57	0.56
Third Quarter	16,598	7.8%	5,193	1,147	0.50	0.50
Fourth Quarter	15,125	7.6%	4,953	951	0.42	0.42
Fiscal Year	$64,816	3.8%	$20,580	$4,304	$1.88	$1.88

Note: The quarterly data may not sum to fiscal year totals due to rounding.

(1) Includes net sales at locations open greater than 12 months, including relocated and remodeled stores, and net sales of all the subsidiaries of The Home Depot, Inc. Stores and subsidiaries become comparable on the Monday following their 365th day of operation. We believe comparable store sales is a meaningful measurement of our operating performance and is a common measurement of operating performance in the retail industry. This measurement is intended only as supplemental information, and is not a substitute for net sales or net earnings presented in accordance with generally accepted accounting principles.

Management's Responsibility for Financial Statements

The financial statements presented in this Annual Report have been prepared with integrity and objectivity and are the responsibility of the management of The Home Depot, Inc. These financial statements have been prepared in conformity with U.S. generally accepted accounting principles and properly reflect certain estimates and judgments based upon the best available information.

The financial statements of the Company have been audited by KPMG LLP, an independent registered public accounting firm. Their accompanying report is based upon an audit conducted in accordance with the standards of the Public Company Accounting Oversight Board (United States).

The Audit Committee of the Board of Directors, consisting solely of outside directors, meets five times a year with the independent registered public accounting firm, the internal auditors and representatives of management to discuss auditing and financial reporting matters. In addition, a telephonic meeting is held prior to each quarterly earnings release. The Audit Committee retains the independent registered public accounting firm and regularly reviews the internal accounting controls, the activities of the independent registered public accounting firm and internal auditors and the financial condition of the Company. Both the Company's independent registered public accounting firm and the internal auditors have free access to the Audit Committee.

Management's Report on Internal Control over Financial Reporting

Our management is responsible for establishing and maintaining adequate internal control over financial reporting, as such term is defined in Exchange Act Rules 13a–15(f). Under the supervision and with the participation of our management, including our principal executive officer and principal financial officer, we conducted an evaluation of the effectiveness of our internal control over financial reporting based on the framework in *Internal Control – Integrated Framework* issued by the Committee of Sponsoring Organizations of the Treadway Commission (COSO). Based on our evaluation, our management concluded that our internal control over financial reporting was effective as of January 30, 2005. Our management's assessment of the effectiveness of our internal control over financial reporting as of January 30, 2005 has been audited by KPMG LLP, an independent registered public accounting firm, as stated in its report which is included herein.

Robert L. Nardelli
Chairman, President &
Chief Executive Officer

Carol B. Tomé
Executive Vice President &
Chief Financial Officer

Kelly H. Barrett
Vice President
Corporate Controller

Reports of Independent Registered Public Accounting Firm

The Board of Directors and Stockholders
The Home Depot, Inc.:

We have audited management's assessment, included in the accompanying Management's Report on Internal Control over Financial Reporting, that The Home Depot, Inc. and subsidiaries maintained effective internal control over financial reporting as of January 30, 2005, based on criteria established in *Internal Control – Integrated Framework* issued by the Committee of Sponsoring Organizations of the Treadway Commission (COSO). The Company's management is responsible for maintaining effective internal control over financial reporting and for its assessment of the effectiveness of internal control over financial reporting. Our responsibility is to express an opinion on management's assessment and an opinion on the effectiveness of the Company's internal control over financial reporting based on our audit.

We conducted our audit in accordance with the standards of the Public Company Accounting Oversight Board (United States). Those standards require that we plan and perform the audit to obtain reasonable assurance about whether effective internal control over financial reporting was maintained in all material respects. Our audit included obtaining an understanding of internal control over financial reporting, evaluating management's assessment, testing and evaluating the design and operating effectiveness of internal control and performing such other procedures as we considered necessary in the circumstances. We believe that our audit provides a reasonable basis for our opinion.

A company's internal control over financial reporting is a process designed to provide reasonable assurance regarding the reliability of financial reporting and the preparation of financial statements for external purposes in accordance with generally accepted accounting principles. A company's internal control over financial reporting includes those policies and procedures that (1) pertain to the maintenance of records that, in reasonable detail, accurately and fairly reflect the transactions and dispositions of the assets of the company; (2) provide reasonable assurance that transactions are recorded as necessary to permit preparation of financial statements in accordance with generally accepted accounting principles, and that receipts and expenditures of the company are being made only in accordance with authorizations of management and directors of the company; and (3) provide reasonable assurance regarding prevention or timely detection of unauthorized acquisition, use, or disposition of the company's assets that could have a material effect on the financial statements.

APPENDIX A

Reports of Independent Registered Public Accounting Firm (continued)

Because of its inherent limitations, internal control over financial reporting may not prevent or detect misstatements. Also, projections of any evaluation of effectiveness to future periods are subject to the risk that controls may become inadequate because of changes in conditions, or that the degree of compliance with the policies or procedures may deteriorate.

In our opinion, management's assessment that The Home Depot, Inc. and subsidiaries maintained effective internal control over financial reporting as of January 30, 2005, is fairly stated, in all material respects, based on criteria established in *Internal Control–Integrated Framework* issued by the Committee of Sponsoring Organizations of the Treadway Commission (COSO). Also, in our opinion, The Home Depot, Inc. and subsidiaries maintained, in all material respects, effective internal control over financial reporting as of January 30, 2005, based on criteria established in *Internal Control–Integrated Framework* issued by the Committee of Sponsoring Organizations of the Treadway Commission (COSO).

We also have audited, in accordance with the standards of the Public Company Accounting Oversight Board (United States), the Consolidated Balance Sheets of The Home Depot, Inc. and subsidiaries as of January 30, 2005 and February 1, 2004, and the related Consolidated Statements of Earnings, Stockholders' Equity and Comprehensive Income, and Cash Flows for each of the fiscal years in the three-year period ended January 30, 2005, and our report dated March 11, 2005 expressed an unqualified opinion on those consolidated financial statements.

KPMG LLP

KPMG LLP
Atlanta, Georgia
March 11, 2005

**The Board of Directors and Stockholders
The Home Depot, Inc.:**

We have audited the accompanying Consolidated Balance Sheets of The Home Depot, Inc. and subsidiaries as of January 30, 2005 and February 1, 2004, and the related Consolidated Statements of Earnings, Stockholders' Equity and Comprehensive Income, and Cash Flows for each of the fiscal years in the three-year period ended January 30, 2005. These Consolidated Financial Statements are the responsibility of the Company's management. Our responsibility is to express an opinion on these Consolidated Financial Statements based on our audits.

We conducted our audits in accordance with the standards of the Public Company Accounting Oversight Board (United States). Those standards require that we plan and perform the audit to obtain reasonable assurance about whether the financial statements are free of material misstatement. An audit includes examining, on a test basis, evidence supporting the amounts and disclosures in the financial statements. An audit also includes assessing the accounting principles used and significant estimates made by management, as well as evaluating the overall financial statement presentation. We believe that our audits provide a reasonable basis for our opinion.

In our opinion, the Consolidated Financial Statements referred to above present fairly, in all material respects, the financial position of The Home Depot, Inc. and subsidiaries as of January 30, 2005 and February 1, 2004, and the results of their operations and their cash flows for each of the fiscal years in the three-year period ended January 30, 2005, in conformity with U.S. generally accepted accounting principles.

As discussed in Note 1 to the Consolidated Financial Statements, effective February 3, 2003, the Company changed its method of accounting for cash consideration received from a vendor to conform to Emerging Issues Task Force No. 02-16 and adopted the fair value method of recording stock-based compensation expense in accordance with Statement of Financial Accounting Standards No. 123.

We also have audited, in accordance with the standards of the Public Company Accounting Oversight Board (United States), the effectiveness of The Home Depot, Inc. and subsidiaries' internal control over financial reporting as of January 30, 2005, based on criteria established in *Internal Control–Integrated Framework* issued by the Committee of Sponsoring Organizations of the Treadway Commission (COSO), and our report dated March 11, 2005 expressed an unqualified opinion on management's assessment of, and the effective operation of, internal control over financial reporting.

KPMG LLP

KPMG LLP
Atlanta, Georgia
March 11, 2005

Corporate and Stockholder Information

The Home Depot, Inc. and Subsidiaries

STORE SUPPORT CENTER

The Home Depot, Inc.
2455 Paces Ferry Road, NW
Atlanta, GA 30339-4024
Telephone: (770) 433-8211

THE HOME DEPOT WEB SITE

www.homedepot.com

TRANSFER AGENT AND REGISTRAR

EquiServe Trust Company, N.A.
P.O. Box 43010
Providence, RI 02940-3016
Telephone: (800) 577-0177
Internet address: www.equiserve.com

INDEPENDENT REGISTERED PUBLIC ACCOUNTING FIRM

KPMG LLP
Suite 2000
303 Peachtree Street, NE
Atlanta, GA 30308

STOCK EXCHANGE LISTING

New York Stock Exchange
Trading symbol – HD

ANNUAL MEETING

The Annual Meeting of Stockholders will be held at 10:00 a.m., Eastern Time, May 26, 2005, at the Philharmonic Center for the Arts in Naples, Florida.

NUMBER OF STOCKHOLDERS

As of March 28, 2005, there were approximately 200,000 stockholders of record and approximately 2,200,000 individual stockholders holding stock under nominee security position listings.

DIVIDENDS DECLARED PER COMMON SHARE

	First Quarter	Second Quarter	Third Quarter	Fourth Quarter
Fiscal 2004	$0.085	$0.085	$0.085	$0.100
Fiscal 2003	$0.060	$0.070	$0.070	$0.070

DIRECT STOCK PURCHASE/DIVIDEND REINVESTMENT PLAN

New investors may make an initial investment, and stockholders of record may acquire additional shares, of The Home Depot, Inc.'s common stock through the Company's direct stock purchase and dividend reinvestment plan. Subject to certain requirements, initial cash investments, cash dividends and/or additional optional cash purchases may be invested through this plan.

To obtain enrollment materials, including the prospectus, access The Home Depot web site, or call (877) HD-SHARE. For all other communications regarding these services, contact the Transfer Agent and Registrar.

FINANCIAL AND OTHER COMPANY INFORMATION

Our Annual Report on Form 10-K for the fiscal year ended January 30, 2005 is available on our web site at www.homedepot.com under the Investor Relations section. In addition, financial reports, recent filings with the Securities and Exchange Commission, news releases and other Company information are available on The Home Depot web site.

For a printed copy of Form 10-K (without exhibits), please contact:
The Home Depot, Inc.
Investor Relations
2455 Paces Ferry Road, NW
Atlanta, GA 30339-4024
Telephone: (770) 384-4388

The Home Depot, Inc. has included as exhibits to its Annual Report on Form 10-K for the fiscal year ended January 30, 2005 certificates of The Home Depot's Chief Executive Officer and Chief Financial Officer certifying the quality of The Home Depot's public disclosures. The Home Depot's Chief Executive Officer has also submitted to the New York Stock Exchange (NYSE) a certificate certifying that he is not aware of any violations by The Home Depot of the NYSE corporate governance listing standards.

QUARTERLY STOCK PRICE RANGE

	First Quarter	Second Quarter	Third Quarter	Fourth Quarter
Fiscal 2004				
High	$37.84	$36.30	$41.50	$44.30
Low	$35.01	$32.34	$32.39	$40.28
Fiscal 2003				
High	$28.76	$34.72	$37.84	$37.89
Low	$20.18	$27.85	$30.10	$31.93

About this report
Consistent with The Home Depot's commitment to the environment, this report was printed on paper that was manufactured in accordance with the Principles and Criteria of the Forest Stewardship Council (FSC). This certification ensures that the fiber from which the paper is manufactured comes partially from certified forests that are managed in a way that is socially beneficial, environmentally responsible and economically viable. The paper in this report contains at least 26% FSC-certified fiber and at least 20% post-consumer reclaimed fiber. The paper was also manufactured using wind generated electric power. The printing plant has been certified as an FSC-certified printer by SmartWood.

APPENDIX A

Appendix B

Combined Journal

Most small businesses have just a few employees and can devote only a limited amount of time to the preparation of accounting records. To serve the needs of these businesses, accountants have developed certain types of record systems that have special time-saving and labor-saving features but still produce all the necessary financial information for management. One example of such a system is the combined journal discussed in this appendix.

Small firms play an important role in our economy today. In fact, almost one-half of the businesses in the United States are classified as small firms. Despite their limited size, these businesses need good accounting systems that can produce accurate and timely information.

Systems Involving the Combined Journal

The **combined journal**, also called the *combination journal,* provides the cornerstone for a simple yet effective accounting system in many small firms. As its name indicates, this journal combines features of the general journal and the special journals in a single record.

If a small business has enough transactions to make the general journal difficult to use but too few transactions to make it worthwhile to set up special journals, the combined journal offers a solution. It has many of the advantages of special journals but provides the simplicity of a single journal. Like the special journals, the combined journal contains separate money columns for the accounts used most often to record a firm's transactions. This speeds up the initial entry of transactions and permits summary postings at the end of the month. Most transactions can be recorded on a single line, and the need to write account names is minimized.

Other Accounts columns allow the recording of transactions that do not fit into any of the special columns. These columns are also used for entries that would normally appear in the general journal, such as adjusting and closing entries.

Some small firms just use a combined journal and a general ledger in their accounting systems. Others need one or more subsidiary ledgers in addition to the general ledger.

DESIGNING A COMBINED JOURNAL

To function effectively, a combined journal must be designed to meet the specific needs of a firm. For a new business, the accountant first studies the proposed operations and develops an appropriate chart of accounts. Then the accountant decides which accounts are likely to be used often enough in recording daily transactions to justify special columns in the combined journal.

Consider the combined journal on the next page which belongs to the Quality Lawn Care and Landscaping Services, a small business that provides lawn and landscaping services. In designing this journal before the firm opened, the accountant established a Cash section with Debit and Credit columns because it was known that the business would constantly be receiving cash from customers and paying out cash for expenses and other obligations. Debit and Credit columns were also set up in Accounts Receivable and Accounts Payable sections because the firm planned to offer credit to qualified customers and would make credit purchases of supplies and other items.

After further analysis it was realized that the business would have numerous entries for the sale of services, the payment of employee salaries, and the purchase of supplies. Therefore, columns were established for recording credits to *Sales,* debits to *Salaries Expense,* and debits to *Supplies.* Finally, a column was set up for an Other Accounts section to take care of transactions that cannot be entered in the special columns.

COMBINED JOURNAL

	DATE	CK. NO.	DESCRIPTION	POST. REF.	CASH DEBIT	CASH CREDIT	ACCOUNTS RECEIVABLE DEBIT	ACCOUNTS RECEIVABLE CREDIT
1	2007							
2	Jan. 3	711	Rent for month			1 0 5 0 00		
3	5		Treschell Seymore	✓			2 5 0 00	
4	6		C & M Garden Supply	✓				
5	7		Cash sales		2 3 0 0 00			
6	7	712	Payroll			7 8 0 00		
7	10		Annie McGowan	✓	1 5 0 00			1 5 0 00
8	12		The Greenery	✓				
9	13		Allen Clark	✓	4 4 0 00			4 4 0 00
10	14		Cash sales		2 7 7 0 00			
11	14	713	Payroll			7 8 0 00		
12	17		Jessica Savage	✓			1 7 5 00	
13	18		Lawn and Garden Supply	✓				
14	19	714	Telephone service			2 0 1 00		
15	20		Ned Jones	✓	1 2 5 00			1 2 5 00
16	20		Starlene Neal	✓			1 1 0 00	
17	21		Cash sales		2 5 4 0 00			
18	21	715	Payroll	✓		7 8 0 00		
19	24		Lawn and Garden Supply	✓				
20	25		Jeraldine Wells	✓			2 2 5 00	
21	26	716	Ace Garden Supply			4 6 0 00		
22	28		Cash sales		2 2 0 0 00			
23	28	717	Payroll			7 8 0 00		
24	30		Note issued for purchase					
25			of landscape equipment					
26	31		Juanda Fischer	✓			9 8 00	
27	31		Totals		10 5 2 5 00	4 8 3 1 00	8 5 8 00	7 1 5 00
28					(101)	(101)	(111)	(111)

FIGURE B.1 | **Combined Journal**

RECORDING TRANSACTIONS IN THE COMBINED JOURNAL

The combined journal shown in Figure B.1 contains the January 2007 transactions of Quality Lawn Care and Landscaping Services. Notice that most of these transactions require only a single line and involve the use of just the special columns. The entries for major types of transactions are explained in the following paragraphs.

Payment of Expenses During January, Quality Lawn Care and Landscaping Services issued checks to pay three kinds of expenses: rent, telephone service, and employee salaries. Notice how the payment of the monthly rent on January 3 was recorded in the combined journal. Since there is no special column for rent expense, the debit part of this entry appears in the Other Accounts section. The offsetting credit appears in the Cash Credit column. The payment of the monthly telephone bill on January 19 was recorded in a similar manner. However, when employee salaries were paid on January 7, 14, 21, and 28, both parts of the entries could be made in special columns. Because the firm has a weekly payroll period, a separate column in the combined journal was set up for debits to Salaries Expense.

| ACCOUNTS PAYABLE | | SALES CREDIT | SUPPLIES DEBIT | SALARIES EXPENSE DEBIT | OTHER ACCOUNTS | | | | | |
DEBIT	CREDIT				ACCOUNT TITLE	POST REF.	DEBIT		CREDIT	
										1
					Rent Expense	511	1 0 5 0 00			2
		2 5 0 00								3
	4 5 0 00		4 5 0 00							4
		2 3 0 0 00								5
				7 8 0 00						6
										7
	2 2 5 00		2 2 5 00							8
										9
		2 7 7 0 00								10
				7 8 0 00						11
		1 7 5 00								12
	1 2 0 0 00				Equipment	131	1 2 0 0 00			13
					Telephone Exp.	514	2 0 1 00			14
										15
		1 1 0 00								16
		2 5 4 0 00								17
				7 8 0 00						18
	2 9 0 00		2 9 0 00							19
		2 2 5 00								20
4 6 0 00										21
		2 2 0 0 00								22
				7 8 0 00						23
					Equipment	131	8 5 0 0 00			24
					Notes Payable	201		8 5 0 0 00		25
										26
		9 8 00								26
4 6 0 00	2 1 6 5 00	10 6 6 8 00	9 6 5 00	3 1 2 0 00			10 9 5 1 00	8 5 0 0 00		27
(202)	(202)	(401)	(121)	(517)			(X)	(X)		28

FIGURE B.1 (concluded) Combined Journal

Sales on Credit On January 5, 17, 20, 25, and 31, Quality Lawn Care and Landscaping Services sold services on credit. The necessary entries were made in two special columns of the combined journal—the Accounts Receivable Debit column and the Sales Credit column.

Cash Sales Entries for the firm's weekly cash sales were recorded on January 7, 14, 21, and 28. Again, special columns were used—the Cash Debit column and the Sales Credit column.

Cash Received on Account When Quality Lawn Care and Landscaping Services collected cash on account from credit customers on January 10, 13, and 20, the transactions were entered in the Cash Debit column and the Accounts Receivable Credit column.

Purchases of Supplies on Credit Because the firm's combined journal includes a Supplies Debit column and an Accounts Payable Credit column, all purchases of supplies on credit can be recorded in special columns. Refer to the entries made on January 6, 12, and 24.

Purchases of Equipment on Credit On January 18, Quality Lawn Care and Landscaping Services bought some store equipment on credit. Since there is no special column for equipment, the debit part of the entry was made in the Other Accounts section. The offsetting credit appears in the Accounts Payable Credit column.

Payments on Account Any payments made on account to creditors are recorded in two special columns—Accounts Payable Debit and Cash Credit, as shown in the entry of January 26.

Issuance of a Promissory Note On January 30 the business purchased new cleaning equipment and issued a promissory note to the seller. Notice that both the debit to Equipment and the credit to Notes Payable had to be recorded in the Other Accounts section.

POSTING FROM THE COMBINED JOURNAL

One of the advantages of the combined journal is that it simplifies the posting process. All amounts in the special columns can be posted to the general ledger on a summary basis at the end of the month. Only the figures that appear in the Other Accounts section require individual postings to the general ledger during the month. Of course, if the firm has subsidiary ledgers, individual postings must also be made to these ledgers.

Daily Postings The procedures followed at Quality Lawn Care and Landscaping Services will illustrate the techniques used to post from the combined journal. Each day any entries appearing in the Other Accounts section are posted to the proper accounts in the general ledger. For example, refer to the combined journal shown on pages B-2 and B-3. The five amounts listed in the Other Accounts Debit and Credit columns were posted individually during the month. The account numbers recorded in the Posting Reference column of the Other Accounts section show that the postings have been made.

Because Quality Lawn Care and Landscaping Services has subsidiary ledgers for accounts receivable and accounts payable, individual postings were also made on a daily basis to these ledgers. As each amount was posted, a check mark was placed in the Posting Reference column of the combined journal.

End-of-Month Postings At the end of the month, the combined journal is totaled, proved, and ruled. Then the totals of the special columns are posted to the general ledger. Proving the combined journal involves a comparison of the column totals to make sure that the debits and credits are equal. The following procedure is used:

Proof of Combined Journal	
	Debits
Cash Debit Column	10,525
Accounts Receivable Debit Column	858
Accounts Payable Debit Column	460
Supplies Debit Column	965
Salaries Expense Debit Column	3,120
Other Accounts Debit Column	10,951
	26,879
	Credits
Cash Credit Column	4,831
Accounts Receivable Credit Column	715
Accounts Payable Credit Column	2,165
Sales Credit Column	10,668
Other Accounts Credit Column	8,500
	26,879

After the combined journal is proved, all column totals except those in the Other Accounts section are posted to the appropriate general ledger accounts. As each total is posted, the account number is entered beneath the column in the journal. Notice that an X is used to indicate that the column totals in the Other Accounts section are not posted, since the individual amounts were posted on a daily basis.

TYPICAL USES OF THE COMBINED JOURNAL

The combined journal is used most often in small professional offices and small service businesses. It is less suitable for merchandising businesses but is sometimes used in firms of this type if they are very small and have only a limited number of transactions.

Professional Offices The combined journal can be ideal to record the transactions that occur in a professional office, such as the office of a doctor, lawyer, accountant, or architect. However, special journals are more efficient if transactions become very numerous or are too varied.

Service Businesses The use of the combined journal to record the transactions of Quality Lawn Care and Landscaping Services has already been illustrated. The combined journal may be advantageous for a small service business, provided that the volume of transactions does not become excessive and the nature of the transactions does not become too complex.

Merchandising Businesses The combined journal can be used by a merchandising business, but only if the firm is quite small and has a limited number and variety of transactions involving few accounts. However, even for a small merchandising business, the use of special journals might prove more advantageous.

Disadvantages of the Combined Journal

If the variety of transactions is so great that many different accounts are required, the combined journal will not work well. Either the business will have to set up so many columns that the journal will become unwieldy, or it will be necessary to record so many transactions in the Other Accounts columns that little efficiency will result. As a general rule, if the transactions of a business are numerous enough to merit the use of special journals, any attempt to substitute the combined journal is a mistake. Remember that each special journal can be designed for maximum efficiency in recording transactions.

Glossary

G

Absorption costing The accounting procedure whereby all manufacturing costs, including fixed costs, are included in the cost of goods manufactured

Accelerated method of depreciation A method of depreciating asset cost that allocates greater amounts of depreciation to an asset's early years of useful life

Account balance The difference between the amounts recorded on the two sides of an account

Account form balance sheet A balance sheet that lists assets on the left and liabilities and owner's equity on the right (*see also* Report form balance sheet)

Accounting The process by which financial information about a business is recorded, classified, summarized, interpreted, and communicated to owners, managers, and other interested parties

Accounting cycle A series of steps performed during each accounting period to classify, record, and summarize data for a business and to produce needed financial information

Accounting system A process designed to accumulate, classify, and summarize financial data

Accounts Written records of the assets, liabilities, and owner's equity of a business

Accounts payable Amounts a business must pay in the future

Accounts payable ledger A subsidiary ledger that contains a separate account for each creditor

Accounts receivable Claims for future collection from customers

Accounts receivable ledger A subsidiary ledger that contains credit customer accounts

Accounts receivable turnover A measure of the speed with which sales on account are collected; the ratio of net credit sales to average receivables

Accrual basis A system of accounting by which all revenues and expenses are matched and reported on financial statements for the applicable period, regardless of when the cash related to the transaction is received or paid

Accrued expenses Expense items that relate to the current period but have not yet been paid and do not yet appear in the accounting records

Accrued income Income that has been earned but not yet received and recorded

Acid-test ratio A measure of immediate liquidity; the ratio of quick assets to current liabilities

Adjusting entries Journal entries made to update accounts for items that were not recorded during the accounting period

Adjustments *See* Adjusting entries

Aging the accounts receivable Classifying accounts receivable balances according to how long they have been outstanding

Allowance method A method of recording uncollectible accounts that estimates losses from uncollectible accounts and charges them to expense in the period when the sales are recorded

Amortization The process of periodically transferring the acquisition cost of an intangible asset to an expense account

Appropriation of retained earnings A formal declaration of an intention to restrict dividends

Articles of partnership *See* Partnership agreement

Asset turnover A measure of the effective use of assets in making sales; the ratio of net sales to total assets

Assets Property owned by a business

Audit trail A chain of references that makes it possible to trace information, locate errors, and prevent fraud

Auditing The review of financial statements to assess their fairness and adherence to generally accepted accounting principles

Auditor's report An independent accountant's review of a firm's financial statements

Authorized capital stock The number of shares authorized for issue by the corporate charter

Average collection period The ratio of 365 days to the accounts receivable turnover; also called the number of days' sales in receivables

Average cost method A method of inventory costing using the average cost of units of an item available for sale during the period to arrive at cost of the ending inventory

Average method of process costing A method of costing that combines the cost of beginning inventory for each cost element with the costs during the current period

Balance ledger form A ledger account form that shows the balance of the account after each entry is posted

Balance sheet A formal report of a business's financial condition on a certain date; reports the assets, liabilities, and owner's equity of the business

Bank draft A check written by a bank that orders another bank to pay the stated amount to a specific party

Bank reconciliation statement A statement that accounts for all differences between the balance on the bank statement and the book balance of cash

Banker's year A 360-day period used to calculate interest on a note

Bill of lading A business document that lists goods accepted for transportation

Blank endorsement A signature of the payee written on the back of the check that transfers ownership of the check without specifying to whom or for what purpose

Bond indenture A bond contract

Bond issue costs Costs incurred in issuing bonds, such as legal and accounting fees and printing costs

Bond retirement When a bond is paid and the liability is removed from the company's balance sheet

Bond sinking fund investment A fund established to accumulate assets to pay off bonds when they mature

Bonding The process by which employees are investigated by an insurance company that will insure the business against losses through employee theft or mishandling of funds

GLOSSARY

Bonds payable Long-term debt instruments that are written promises to repay the principal at a future date; interest is due at a fixed rate payable over the life of the bond

Book value That portion of an asset's original cost that has not yet been depreciated

Book value The total equity applicable to a class of stock divided by the number of shares outstanding

Brand name *See* Trade name

Break even A point at which revenue equals expenses

Budget An operating plan expressed in monetary units

Budget performance report A comparison of actual costs and budgeted costs

Business transaction A financial event that changes the resources of a firm

Bylaws The guidelines for conducting a corporation's business affairs

Call price The amount the corporation must pay for the bond when it is called

Callable bonds Bonds that allow the issuing corporation to require the holder to surrender the bonds for payment before their maturity date

Callable preferred stock Stock that gives the issuing corporation the right to repurchase the preferred shares from the stockholders at a specific price

Canceled check A check paid by the bank on which it was drawn

Capacity A facility's ability to produce or use

Capital Financial investment in a business; equity

Capital stock ledger A subsidiary ledger that contains a record of each stockholder's purchases, transfers, and current balance of shares owned; also called stockholders' ledger

Capital stock transfer journal A record of stock transfers used for posting to the stockholders' ledger

Capitalized costs All costs recorded as part of an asset's costs

Carrying value of bonds The balance of the *Bonds Payable* account plus the *Premium on Bonds Payable* account minus the *Discount on Bonds Payable* account; also called book value of bonds

Cash In accounting, currency, coins, checks, money orders, and funds on deposit in a bank

Cash discount A discount offered by suppliers for payment received within a specified period of time

Cash equivalents Assets that are easily convertible into known amounts of cash

Cash payments journal A special journal used to record transactions involving the payment of cash

Cash receipts journal A special journal used to record and post transactions involving the receipt of cash

Cash register proof A verification that the amount of currency and coins in a cash register agrees with the amount shown on the cash register audit tape

Cash Short or Over account An account used to record any discrepancies between the amount of currency and coins in the cash register and the amount shown on the audit tape

Cashier's check A draft on the issuing bank's own funds

Certified public accountant (CPA) An independent accountant who provides accounting services to the public for a fee

Charge-account sales Sales made through the use of open-account credit or one of various types of credit cards

Chart of accounts A list of the accounts used by a business to record its financial transactions

Check A written order signed by an authorized person instructing a bank to pay a specific sum of money to a designated person or business

Check register The record of cash payments of vouchers

Chronological order Organized in the order in which the events occur

Classification A means of identifying each account as an asset, liability, or owner's equity

Classified financial statement A format by which revenues and expenses on the income statement, and assets and liabilities on the balance sheet, are divided into groups of similar accounts and a subtotal is given for each group

Closing entries Journal entries that transfer the results of operations (net income or net loss) to owner's equity and reduce the revenue, expense, and drawing account balances to zero

Collateral trust bonds Bonds secured by the pledge of securities, such as stocks or bonds of other companies

Combined journal A journal that combines features of the general journal and the special journals in a single record

Commercial draft A note issued by one party that orders another party to pay a specified sum on a specified date

Commission basis A method of paying employees according to a percentage of net sales

Common costs Costs not directly traceable to a specific segment of a business

Common-size statements Financial statements with items expressed as percentages of a base amount

Common stock The general class of stock issued when no other class of stock is authorized; each share carries the same rights and privileges as every other share. Even if preferred stock is issued, common stock will also be issued

***Common Stock Dividend Distributable* account** Equity account used to record par, or stated, value of shares to be issued as the result of the declaration of a stock dividend

Comparative statements Financial statements presented side by side for two or more years

Compensation record *See* Individual earnings record

Compound entry A journal entry with more than one debit or credit

Conceptual framework A basic framework developed by the FASB to provide conceptual guidelines for financial statements. The most important features are statements of qualitative features of statements, basic assumptions underlying statements, basic accounting principles and modifying constraints

Conservatism The concept that revenue and assets should be understated rather than overstated if GAAP allows alternatives. Similarly, expenses and liabilities should be overstated rather than understated

Contingent liability An item that can become a liability if certain things happen

Contra account An account with a normal balance that is opposite that of a related account

Contra asset account An asset account with a credit balance, which is contrary to the normal balance of an asset account

Contra revenue account An account with a debit balance, which is contrary to the normal balance for a revenue account

Contribution margin Gross profit on sales minus direct expenses; revenues minus variable costs

Control account An account that links a subsidiary ledger and the general ledger since its balance summarizes the balances of the accounts in the subsidiary ledger

Controllable fixed costs Costs that the segment manager can control

Convertible bonds Bonds that give the owner the right to convert the bonds into common stock under specified conditions

Convertible preferred stock Preferred stock that conveys the right to convert that stock to common stock after a specified date or during a period of time

Copyright An intangible asset; an exclusive right granted by the federal government to produce, publish, and sell a literary or artistic work for a period equal to the creator's life plus 70 years

Corporate charter A document issued by a state government that establishes a corporation

Corporation A publicly or privately owned business entity that is separate from its owners and has a legal right to own property and do business in its own name; stockholders are not responsible for the debts or taxes of the business

Correcting entry A journal entry made to correct an erroneous entry

Cost basis principle The principle that requires assets to be recorded at their cost at the time they are acquired

Cost-benefit test If accounting concepts suggest a particular accounting treatment for an item but it appears that the theoretically correct treatment would require an unreasonable amount of work, the accountant may analyze the benefits and costs of the preferred treatment to see if the benefit gained from its adoption is justified by the cost

Cost center A business segment that incurs costs but does not produce revenue

Cost of goods sold The actual cost to the business of the merchandise sold to customers

Cost of production report Summarizes all costs charged to each department and shows the costs assigned to the goods transferred out of the department and to the goods still in process

Cost variance The difference between the total standard cost and the total actual cost

Coupon bonds Unregistered bonds that have coupons attached for each interest payment; also called bearer bonds

Credit An entry on the right side of an account

Credit memorandum (accounts receivable) A note verifying that a customer's account is being reduced by the amount of a sales return or sales allowance plus any sales tax that may have been involved

Credit memorandum (banking) A form that explains any addition, other than a deposit, to a checking account

Creditor One to whom money is owed

Cumulative preferred stock Stock that conveys to its owners the right to receive the preference dividend for the current year and any prior years in which the preference dividend was not paid before common stockholders receive any dividends

Current assets Assets consisting of cash, items that normally will be converted into cash within one year, or items that will be used up within one year

Current liabilities Debts that must be paid within one year

Current ratio A relationship between current assets and current liabilities that provides a measure of a firm's ability to pay its current debts (current ratio = current assets current liabilities)

Debentures Unsecured bonds backed only by a corporation's general credit

Debit An entry on the left side of an account

Debit memorandum A form that explains any deduction, other than a check, from a checking account

Declaration date The date on which the board of directors declares a dividend

Declining-balance method An accelerated method of depreciation in which an asset's book value at the beginning of a year is multiplied by a percentage to determine depreciation for the year

Deferred expenses *See* Prepaid expenses

Deferred income *See* Unearned income

Deferred income taxes The amount of taxes that will be payable in the future as a result of the difference between taxable income and income for financial statement purposes in the current year and in past years

Departmental income statement Income statement that shows each department's contribution margin and net income from operations after all expenses are allocated

Depletion Allocating the cost of a natural resource to expense over the period in which the resource produces revenue

Deposit in transit A deposit that is recorded in the cash receipts journal but that reaches the bank too late to be shown on the monthly bank statement

Deposit slip A form prepared to record the deposit of cash or checks to a bank account

Depreciation Allocation of the cost of a long-term asset to operations during its expected useful life

Differential cost The difference in cost between one alternative and another

Direct charge-off method A method of recording uncollectible account losses as they occur

Direct costing The accounting procedure whereby only variable costs are included in the cost of goods manufactured, and fixed manufacturing costs are written off as expenses in the period in which they are incurred

Direct expenses Operating expenses that are identified directly with a department and are recorded by department

Direct labor The costs attributable to personnel who work directly on the product being manufactured

Direct materials All items that go into a product and become a part of it

Direct method A means of reporting sources and uses of cash under which all revenue and expenses reported on the income statement appear in the operating section of the statement of cash flows and show the cash received or paid out for each type of transaction

Discount on bonds payable The excess of the face value over the price received by the corporation for a bond

Discounting Deducting the interest from the principal on a note payable or receivable in advance

Discussion memorandum An explanation of a topic under consideration by the Financial Accounting Standards Board

Dishonored check A check returned to the depositor unpaid because of insufficient funds in the drawer's account; also called an NSF check

Dissolution The legal termination of a partnership

Distributive share The amount of net income or net loss allocated to each partner

Dividends Distributions of the profits of a corporation to its shareholders

Donated capital Capital resulting from the receipt of gifts by a corporation

Double-declining-balance method A method of depreciation that uses a rate equal to twice the straight-line rate and applies that rate to the book value of the asset at the beginning of the year

Double-entry system An accounting system that involves recording the effects of each transaction as debits and credits

Draft A written order that requires one party (a person or business) to pay a stated sum of money to another party

Drawee The bank on which a check is written

Drawer The person or firm issuing a check

Drawing **account** A special type of owner's equity account set up to record the owner's withdrawal of cash from the business

Economic entity A business or organization whose major purpose is to produce a profit for its owners

Employee A person who is hired by and works under the control and direction of the employer

Employee's Withholding Allowance Certificate, Form W-4 A form used to claim exemption (withholding) allowances

Employer's Annual Federal Unemployment Tax Return, Form 940 or 940-EZ Preprinted government form used by the employer to report unemployment taxes for the calendar year

Employer's Quarterly Federal Tax Return, Form 941 Preprinted government form used by the employer to report payroll tax information relating to social security, Medicare, and employee income tax withholding to the Internal Revenue Service

Endorsement A written authorization that transfers ownership of a check

Entity Anything having its own separate identity, such as an individual, a town, a university, or a business

Equity An owner's financial interest in a business

Equivalent production The estimated number of units that could have been started and completed with the same effort and costs incurred in the department during the same time period

Exempt employees Salaried employees who hold supervisory or managerial positions who are not subject to the maximum hour and overtime pay provisions of the Wage and Hour Law

Expense An outflow of cash, use of other assets, or incurring of a liability

Experience rating system A system that rewards an employer for maintaining steady employment conditions by reducing the firm's state unemployment tax rate

Exposure draft A proposed solution to a problem being considered by the Financial Accounting Standards Board

Extraordinary, nonrecurring items Transactions that are highly unusual, clearly unrelated to routine operations, and that do not frequently occur

Face interest rate The contractual interest specified on the bond

Face value An amount of money indicated to be paid, exclusive of interest or discounts

Fair market value The current worth of an asset or the price the asset would bring if sold on the open market

Federal unemployment taxes (FUTA) Taxes levied by the federal government against employers to benefit unemployed workers

Financial statements Periodic reports of a firm's financial position or operating results

Financing activities Transactions with those who provide cash to the business to carry on its activities

Finished goods inventory The cost of completed products ready for sale; corresponds to the Merchandise Inventory account of a merchandising business

Finished goods subsidiary ledger A ledger containing a record for each of the different types of finished products

First in, first out (FIFO) method A method of inventory costing that assumes the oldest merchandise is sold first

Fixed budget A budget representing only one level of activity

Fixed costs Costs that do not change in total as the level of activity changes

Flexible budget A budget that shows the budgeted costs at various levels of activity

Footing A small pencil figure written at the base of an amount column showing the sum of the entries in the column

Franchise An intangible asset; a right to exclusive dealership granted by a governmental unit or a business entity

Freight In **account** An account showing transportation charges for items purchased

Full disclosure principle The requirement that all information that might affect the user's interpretation of the profitability and financial position of a business be disclosed in the financial statements or in footnotes to the statements

Full endorsement A signature transferring a check to a specific person, firm, or bank

Fundamental accounting equation The relationship between assets and liabilities plus owner's equity

Gain The disposition of an asset for more than its book value

General journal A financial record for entering all types of business transactions; a record of original entry

General ledger A permanent, classified record of all accounts used in a firm's operation; a record of final entry

General partner A member of a partnership who has unlimited liability

Generally accepted accounting principles (GAAP) Accounting standards developed and applied by professional accountants

Going concern assumption The assumption that a firm will continue to operate indefinitely

Goodwill An intangible asset; the value of a business in excess of the value of its identifiable assets

Governmental accounting Accounting work performed for a federal, state, or local governmental unit

Gross profit The difference between net sales and the cost of goods sold

Gross profit method A method of estimating inventory cost based on the assumption that the rate of gross profit on sales and the ratio of cost of goods sold to net sales are relatively constant from period to period

Gross profit percentage The amount of gross profit from each dollar of sales (gross profit percentage 5 gross profit 4 net sales)

High-low point method A method to determine the fixed and variable components of a semivariable cost

Historical cost basis principle *See* Cost basis principle

Horizontal analysis Computing the percentage change for individual items in the financial statements from year to year

Hourly rate basis A method of paying employees according to a stated rate per hour

Impairment A situation that occurs when the asset is determined to have a market value or a value in use less than its book value

Income statement A formal report of business operations covering a specific period of time; also called a profit and loss statement or a statement of income and expenses

Income Summary account A special owner's equity account that is used only in the closing process to summarize the results of operations

Independent contractor One who is paid by a company to carry out a specific task or job but is not under the direct supervision or control of the company

Indirect expenses Operating expenses that cannot be readily identified and are not closely related to activity within a department

Indirect labor Costs attributable to personnel who support production but are not directly involved in the manufacture of a product; for example, supervisory, repair and maintenance, and janitorial staff

Indirect materials and supplies Materials used in manufacturing a product that do not become a part of the product

Indirect method A means of reporting cash generated from operating activities by treating net income as the primary source of cash in the operating section of the statement of cash flows and adjusting that amount for changes in current assets and liabilities associated with net income, noncash transactions, and other items

Individual earnings record An employee record that contains information needed to compute earnings and complete tax reports

Industry averages Financial ratios and percentages reflecting averages for similar companies

Industry practice constraint In a few limited cases unusual operating characteristics of an industry, usually based on risk, special accounting principles and procedures have been developed. These may not conform completely with GAAP for other industries

Intangible assets Assets that lack a physical substance, such as goodwill, patents, copyrights, and computer software, although software has, in a sense, a physical attribute

Interest The fee charged for the use of money

Internal control system A system designed to safeguard assets, achieve efficient processing of transactions, and ensure accuracy and reliability of financial records

International accounting The study of accounting principles used by different countries

Interpret To understand and explain the meaning and importance of something (such as financial statements)

Inventory sheet A form used to list the volume and type of goods a firm has in stock

Inventory turnover The number of times inventory is purchased and sold during the accounting period (inventory turnover = cost of goods sold average inventory)

Investing activities Transactions that involve the acquisition or disposal of long-term assets

Invoice A customer billing for merchandise bought on credit

Job order A specific order for a specific batch of manufactured items

Job order cost accounting A cost accounting system that determines the unit cost of manufactured items for each separate production order

Job order cost sheet A record of all manufacturing costs charged to a specific job

Journal The record of original entry

Journalizing Recording transactions in a journal

Just-in-time system An inventory system in which raw materials are ordered so they arrive just in time to be placed into production

Labor efficiency variance *See* Labor time variance

Labor rate variance The difference between the actual labor rate per hour and the standard labor rate per hour multiplied by the actual number of hours worked on the job

Labor time variance The difference between the actual hours worked and the standard labor hours allowed for the job multiplied by the standard cost per hour

Last in, first out (LIFO) method A method of inventory costing that assumes that the most recently purchased merchandise is sold first

Ledger The record of final entry

Leveraged buyout Purchasing a business by acquiring the stock and obligating the business to pay the debt incurred

Leveraging Using borrowed funds to earn a profit greater than the interest that must be paid on the borrowing

Liabilities Debts or obligations of a business

Limited liability company (LLC) Provides limited liability to the owners, who can elect to have the profits taxed at the LLC level or on their individual tax returns

Limited liability partnership (LLP) A partnership that provides some limited liability for all partners

Limited partner A member of a partnership whose liability is limited to his or her investment in the partnership

Limited partnership A partnership having one or more limited partners

Liquidation Termination of a business by distributing all assets and discontinuing the business

Liquidation value Value of assets to be applied to preferred stock, usually par value or an amount in excess of par value, if the corporation is liquidated

Liquidity The ease with which an item can be converted into cash; the ability of a business to pay its debts when due

List price An established retail price

Long-term liabilities Debts of a business that are due more than one year in the future

Loss The disposition of an asset for less than its book value

Lower of cost or market rule The principle by which inventory is reported at either its original cost or its replacement cost, whichever is lower

Management advisory services Services designed to help clients improve their information systems or their business performance

Managerial accounting Accounting work carried on by an accountant employed by a single business in industry; the branch of accounting that provides financial information about business segments, activities, or products

Manufacturing business A business that sells goods that it has produced

Manufacturing cost budget A budget made for each manufacturing cost

Manufacturing margin Sales minus the variable cost of goods sold

Manufacturing overhead All manufacturing costs that are not classified as direct materials or direct labor

Manufacturing overhead ledger A subsidiary ledger that contains a record for each overhead item

Manufacturing Summary account The account to which all items on the statement of cost of goods manufactured are closed; similar to the Income Summary account

Marginal income The manufacturing margin minus variable operating expenses

Markdown Price reduction below the original markon

Market interest rate The interest rate a corporation is willing to pay and investors are willing to accept at the current time

Market price The price the business would pay to buy an item of inventory through usual channels in usual quantities

Market value The price per share at which stock is bought and sold

Markon The difference between the cost and the initial retail price of merchandise

Markup A price increase above the original markon

Matching principle The concept that revenue and the costs incurred in earning the revenue should be matched in the appropriate accounting periods

Materiality constraint The significance of an item in relation to a particular situation or set of facts

Materials price variance The difference between the actual price and the standard cost for materials multiplied by the actual quantity of materials used

Materials quantity variance The difference between the actual quantity used and the quantity of materials allowed multiplied by the standard cost of the materials

Materials requisition A form that describes the item and quantity needed and shows the job or purpose

Materials usage variance *See* Materials quantity variance

Maturity value The total amount (principal plus interest) that must be paid when a note comes due

Medicare tax A tax levied on employees and employers to provide medical care for the employee and the employee's spouse after each has reached age 65

Memorandum entry An informational entry in the general journal

Merchandise inventory The stock of goods a merchandising business keeps on hand

Merchandising business A business that sells goods purchased for resale

Merit rating system *See* Experience rating system

Minute book A book in which accurate and complete records of all meetings of stockholders and directors are kept

Monetary unit assumption It is assumed that only those items and events that can be measured in monetary terms are included in the financial statements. An inherent part of this assumption is that the monetary unit is stable

Mortgage loan A long-term debt created when a note is given as part of the purchase price for land or buildings

Multiple-step income statement A type of income statement on which several subtotals are computed before the net income is calculated

Mutual agency The characteristic of a partnership by which each partner is empowered to act as an agent for the partnership, binding the firm by his or her acts

Negotiable A financial instrument whose ownership can be transferred to another person or business

Negotiable instrument A financial document containing a promise or order to pay that meets all requirements of the Uniform Commercial Code in order to be transferable to another party

Net book value The cost of an asset minus its accumulated depreciation, depletion, or amortization, also known as book value

Net income The result of an excess of revenue over expenses

Net income line The worksheet line immediately following the column totals on which net income (or net loss) is recorded in two places: the Income Statement section and the Balance Sheet section

Net loss The result of an excess of expenses over revenue

Net of discount The invoice amount minus the cash discount offered

Net price The list price less all trade discounts

Net sales The difference between the balance in the Sales account and the balance in the *Sales Returns and Allowances* account

Net salvage value The salvage value of an asset less any costs to remove or sell the asset

Neutrality concept The concept that information in financial statements cannot be selected or presented in a way to favor one set of interested parties over another

Noncumulative preferred stock Stock that conveys to its owners the stated preference dividend for the current year but no rights to dividends for years in which none were declared

Nonparticipating preferred stock Stock that conveys to its owners the right to only the preference dividend amount specified on the stock certificate

No-par-value stock Stock that is not assigned a par value in the corporate charter

Normal balance The increase side of an account

Note payable A liability representing a written promise by the maker of the note (the debtor) to pay another party (the creditor) a specified amount at a specified future date

Note receivable An asset representing a written promise by another party (the debtor) to pay the note holder (the creditor) a specified amount at a specified future date

Objectivity assumption The idea that financial reports are unbiased and fair to all parties

On account An arrangement to allow payment at a later date; also called a charge account or open-account credit

Open-account credit A system that allows the sale of services or goods with the understanding that payment will be made at a later date

Operating activities Routine business transactions—selling goods or services and incurring expenses

Operating assets and liabilities Current assets and current liabilities

Opportunity cost Potential earnings or benefits that are given up because a certain course of action is taken

Organization costs The costs associated with establishing a corporation; an intangible asset account

Outstanding checks Checks that have been recorded in the cash payments journal but have not yet been paid by the bank

Overapplied overhead The result of applied overhead exceeding the actual overhead costs

Overhead application rate The rate at which the estimated cost of overhead is charged to each job

Owner's equity The financial interest of the owner of a business; also called proprietorship or net worth

Paid-in capital Capital acquired from capital stock transactions

Par value An amount assigned by the corporate charter to each share of stock for accounting purposes

Participating preferred stock Stock that conveys the right not only to the preference dividend amount but also to a share of other dividends paid

Partnership A business entity owned by two or more persons who carry on a business for profit and who are legally responsible for the debts and taxes of the business

Partnership agreement A legal contract forming a partnership and specifying certain details of operation

Patent An intangible asset; an exclusive right given by the U.S. Patent Office to manufacture and sell an invention for a period of 17 years from the date the patent is granted

Payee The person or firm to whom a check is payable

Payment date The date that dividends are paid

Payment voucher *See* Voucher

Payroll register A record of payroll information for each employee for the pay period

Periodic inventory Inventory based on a periodic count of goods on hand

Periodicity of income assumption The concept that income should be reported in certain time periods

Permanent account An account that is kept open from one accounting period to the next

Perpetual inventory Inventory based on a running total of number of units

Perpetual inventory system An inventory system that tracks the inventories on hand at all times

Petty cash analysis sheet A form used to record transactions involving petty cash

Petty cash fund A special-purpose fund used to handle payments involving small amounts of money

Petty cash voucher A form used to record the payments made from a petty cash fund

Physical inventory An actual count of the number of units of each type of good on hand

Piece-rate basis A method of paying employees according to the number of units produced

Plant and equipment Property that will be used in the business for longer than one year

Postclosing trial balance A statement that is prepared to prove the equality of total debits and credits after the closing process is completed

Postdated check A check dated some time in the future

Posting Transferring data from a journal to a ledger

Preemptive right A shareholder's right to purchase a proportionate amount of any new stock issued at a later date

Preference dividend A basic or stated dividend rate for preferred stock that must be paid before dividends can be paid on common stock

Preferred stock A class of stock that has special claims on the corporate profits or, in case of liquidation, on corporate assets

Premium on bonds payable The excess of the price paid over the face value of a bond

Prepaid expenses Expense items acquired, recorded, and paid for in advance of their use

Price-earnings ratio The ratio of the current market value of common stock to earnings per share of that stock

Principal The amount shown on the face of a note

Private sector The business sector, which is represented in developing accounting principles by the Financial Accounting Standards Board (FASB)

Process cost accounting A cost accounting system whereby unit costs of manufactured items are determined by totaling unit costs in each production department

Process cost accounting system A method of accounting in which costs are accumulated for each process or department and then transferred on to the next process or department

Production order *See* Job order

Profit center A business segment that produces revenue

Promissory note A written promise to pay a specified amount of money on a specific date

Property, plant, and equipment Long-term assets that are used in the operation of a business and that are subject to depreciation (except for land, which is not depreciated)

Public accountants Members of firms that perform accounting services for other companies

Public sector The government sector, which is represented in developing accounting principles by the Securities and Exchange Commission (SEC)

Purchase allowance A price reduction from the amount originally billed

Purchase invoice A bill received for goods purchased

Purchase order An order to the supplier of goods specifying items needed, quantity, price, and credit terms

Purchase requisition A list sent to the purchasing department showing the items to be ordered

Purchase return Return of unsatisfactory goods

Purchases **account** An account used to record cost of goods bought for resale during a period

Purchases discount A cash discount offered to customers for payment within a specified period

Purchases journal A special journal used to record the purchase of goods on credit

Qualitative characteristics Traits necessary for credible financial statements: usefulness, relevance, reliability, verifiability, neutrality, understandability, timeliness, comparability, and completeness

Quick assets Cash, receivables, and marketable securities

Ratio analysis Computing the relationship between various items in the financial statements

Raw materials The materials placed into production

Raw materials ledger card A record showing details of receipts and issues for a type of raw material

Raw materials subsidiary ledger A ledger containing the raw materials ledger cards

Real property Assets such as land, land improvements, buildings, and other structures attached to the land

Realization principle The concept that revenue occurs when goods or services, merchandise, or other assets are exchanged for cash or claims to cash

Receiving report A form showing quantity and condition of goods received

Recognition The determination of the period in which to record a business transaction

Record date The date on which the specific stockholders to receive a dividend are determined

Recoverability test Test for possible impairment that compares the asset's net book value with the estimated net cash flows from future use of the asset

Registered bonds Bonds issued to a party whose name is listed in the corporation's records

Registrar A person or institution in charge of the issuance and transfer of a corporation's stock

Reinstate To put back or restore an accounts receivable amount that was previously written off

Relevant range of activity The different levels of activity at which a factory is expected to operate

Replacement cost *See* Market price

Report form balance sheet A balance sheet that lists the asset accounts first, followed by liabilities and owner's equity

Residual value The estimate of the amount that could be obtained from the sale or disposition of an asset at the end of its useful life; also called salvage or scrap value

Responsibility accounting The process that allows management to evaluate the performance of each segment of the business and assign responsibility for its financial results

Restrictive endorsement A signature that transfers a check to a specific party for a stated purpose

Retail business A business that sells directly to individual consumers

Retail method A method of estimating inventory cost by applying the ratio of cost to selling price in the current accounting period to the retail price of the inventory

Retained earnings The cumulative profits and losses of the corporation not distributed as dividends

Return on common stockholders' equity A measure of how well the corporation is making a profit for its shareholders; the ratio of net income available for common stockholders to common stockholders' equity

Revenue An inflow of money or other assets that results from the sales of goods or services or from the use of money or property; also called income

Revenue recognition principle Revenue is recognized when it has been earned and realized

Reversing entries Journal entries made to reverse the effect of certain adjusting entries involving accrued income or accrued expenses to avoid problems in recording future payments or receipts of cash in a new accounting period

Salary basis A method of paying employees according to an agreed-upon amount for each week or month

Sales allowance A reduction in the price originally charged to customers for goods or services

Sales discount A cash discount offered by the supplier to customers for payment within a specified period

Sales invoice A supplier's billing document

Sales journal A special journal used to record sales of merchandise on credit

Sales return A firm's acceptance of a return of goods from a customer

Salvage value An estimate of the amount that could be received by selling or disposing of an asset at the end of its useful life

Schedule of accounts payable A list of all balances owed to creditors

Schedule of accounts receivable A listing of all balances of the accounts in the accounts receivable subsidiary ledger

Schedule of operating expenses A schedule that supplements the income statement, showing the selling and general and administrative expenses in greater detail

Schedule of vouchers payable A list of all amounts owed for unpaid vouchers

Scrap value *See* Residual value

Secured bonds Bonds for which property is pledged to secure the claims of bondholders

Semidirect expenses Operating expenses that cannot be directly assigned to a department but are closely related to departmental activities

Semivariable costs Costs that vary with, but not in direct proportion to, the volume of activity

Separate economic entity assumption The concept that a business is separate from its owners; the concept of keeping a firm's financial records separate from the owner's personal financial records

Serial bonds Bonds issued at one time but payable over a period of years

Service business A business that sells services

Service charge A fee charged by a bank to cover the costs of maintaining accounts and providing services

Shareholder A person who owns shares of stock in a corporation; also called a stockholder

Sight draft A commercial draft that is payable on presentation

Single-step income statement A type of income statement where only one computation is needed to determine the net income (total revenue − total expenses = net income)

Slide An accounting error involving a misplaced decimal point

Social entity A nonprofit organization, such as a city, public school, or public hospital

Social Security Act A federal act providing certain benefits for employees and their families; officially the Federal Insurance Contributions Act

Social security tax (FICA) A tax imposed by the Federal Insurance Contributions Act and collected on employee earnings to provide retirement and disability benefits

Sole proprietorship A business entity owned by one person who is legally responsible for the debts and taxes of the business

Special journal A journal used to record only one type of transaction

Specific identification method A method of inventory costing based on the actual cost of each item of merchandise

Standard cost card A form that shows the per-unit standard costs for materials, labor, and overhead

Standard costs A measure of what costs should be in an efficient operation

State unemployment taxes (SUTA) Taxes levied by a state government against employers to benefit unemployed workers

Stated value The value that can be assigned to no-par-value stock by a board of directors for accounting purposes

Statement of account A form sent to a firm's customers showing transactions during the month and the balance owed

Statement of cash flows A financial statement that provides information about the cash receipts and cash payments of a business

Statement of cost of goods manufactured A financial report showing details of the cost of goods completed for a manufacturing business

Statement of owner's equity A formal report of changes that occurred in the owner's financial interest during a reporting period

Statement of partners' equities A financial statement prepared to summarize the changes in the partners' capital accounts during an accounting period

Statement of retained earnings A financial statement that shows all changes that have occurred in retained earnings during the period

Statement of stockholders' equity A financial statement that provides an analysis reconciling the beginning and ending balance of each of the stockholders' equity accounts

Statements of Financial Accounting Standards Accounting principles established by the Financial Accounting Standards Board

Stock Certificates that represent ownership of a corporation

Stock certificate The form by which capital stock is issued; the certificate indicates the name of the corporation, the name of the stockholder to whom the certificate was issued, the class of stock, and the number of shares

Stock dividend Distribution of the corporation's own stock on a pro rata basis that results in conversion of a portion of the firm's retained earnings to permanent capital

Stock split When a corporation issues two or more shares of new stock to replace each share outstanding without making any changes in the capital accounts

Stockholders The owners of a corporation; also called shareholders

Stockholders of record Stockholders in whose name shares are held on date of record and who will receive a declared dividend

Stockholders' equity The corporate equivalent of owners' equity; also called shareholders' equity

Stockholders' ledger *See* Capital stock ledger

Straight-line amortization Amortizing the premium or discount on bonds payable in equal amounts each month over the life of the bond

Straight-line depreciation Allocation of an asset's cost in equal amounts to each accounting period of the asset's useful life

Subchapter S corporation (S corporation) An entity formed as a corporation that meets the requirements of Subchapter S of the Internal Revenue Code to be treated essentially as a partnership, so that the corporation pays no income tax

Subscribers' ledger A subsidiary ledger that contains an account receivable for each stock subscriber

Subscription book A list of the stock subscriptions received

Subsidiary ledger A ledger dedicated to accounts of a single type and showing details to support a general ledger account

Sum-of-the-years'-digits method A method of depreciating asset costs by allocating as expense each year a fractional part of the asset's depreciable cost, based on the sum of the digits of the number of years in the asset's useful life

Sunk cost A cost that has been incurred and will not change as a result of a decision

T account A type of account, resembling a T, used to analyze the effects of a business transaction

Tangible personal property Assets such as machinery, equipment, furniture, and fixtures that can be removed and used elsewhere

Tax accounting A service that involves tax compliance and tax planning

Tax-exempt wages Earnings in excess of the base amount set by the Social Security Act

Temporary account An account whose balance is transferred to another account at the end of an accounting period

Tickler file *See* Unpaid voucher file

Time and a half Rate of pay for an employee's work in excess of 40 hours a week

Time draft A commercial draft that is payable during a specified period of time

Time ticket Form used to record hours worked and jobs performed

Total equities The sum of a corporation's liabilities and stockholders' equity

Trade acceptance A form of commercial time draft used in transactions involving the sale of goods

Trade discount A reduction from list price

Trade name An intangible asset; an exclusive business name registered with the U.S. Patent Office; also called brand name

Trademark An intangible asset; an exclusive business symbol registered with the U.S. Patent Office

Trading on the equity *See* Leveraging

Transfer agent A person or institution that handles all stock transfers and transfer records for a corporation

Transfer price The price at which one segment's goods are transferred to another segment of the company

Transmittal of Wage and Tax Statements, Form W-3 Preprinted government form submitted with Forms W-2 to the Social Security Administration

Transparency Information provided in the financial statements and notes accompanying them should provide a clear and accurate picture of the financial affairs of the company

Transportation In **account** *See Freight In* account

Transposition An accounting error involving misplaced digits in a number

Treasury stock A corporation's own capital stock that has been issued and reacquired; the stock must have been previously paid in full and issued to a stockholder

Trend analysis Comparing selected ratios and percentages over a period of time

Trial balance A statement to test the accuracy of total debits and credits after transactions have been recorded

Underapplied overhead The result of actual overhead costs exceeding applied overhead

Unearned income Income received before it is earned

Unemployment insurance program A program that provides unemployment compensation through a tax levied on employers

Units-of-output method *See* Units-of-production method

Units-of-production method A method of depreciating asset cost at the same rate for each unit produced during each period

Unlimited liability The implication that a creditor can look to all partners' personal assets as well as the assets of the partnership for payment of the firm's debts

Unpaid voucher file A file to hold vouchers until they are due to be paid, filed by due date

Updated account balances The amounts entered in the Adjusted Trial Balance section of the worksheet

Valuation **account** An account, such as *Allowance for Doubtful Accounts,* whose balance is revalued or reappraised in light of reasonable expectations

Variable costing *See* Direct costing

Variable costs Costs that vary in total in direct proportion to changes in the level of activity

Variance analysis Explains the difference between standard cost and actual cost

Vertical analysis Computing the relationship between each item on a financial statement to some base amount on the statement

Voucher A form used to authorize payment of an obligation

Voucher register A journal used to record liabilities arising from business transactions

Voucher system A method of controlling liabilities and cash payments based on vouchers

Wage and Tax Statement, Form W-2 Preprinted government form that contains information about an employee's earnings and tax withholdings for the year

Wage-bracket table method A simple method to determine the amount of federal income tax to be withheld using a table provided by the government

Weighted average method *See* Average cost method

Wholesale business A business that manufactures or distributes goods to retail businesses or large consumers such as hotels and hospitals

Withdrawals Funds taken from the business by the owner for personal use

Withholding statement *See* Wage and Tax Statement, Form W-2

Workers' compensation insurance Insurance that protects employees against losses from job-related injuries or illnesses, or compensates their families if death occurs in the course of the employment

Work in process Partially completed units in the production process

Work in process subsidiary ledger A ledger containing the job order cost sheets

Working capital The measure of the ability of a company to meet its current obligations; the excess of current assets over current liabilities

Worksheet A form used to gather all data needed at the end of an accounting period to prepare financial statements

GLOSSARY

Credits

CREDITS

Chapter 1

pages 2–3 Rogan MacDonald/Bloomberg/News/Landov
page 3 Tom Wagner/Corbis

Chapter 2

pages 22–23 Joseph Kaczmareck/AP Wide World
page 23 Scott Olson/Getty Images

Chapter 3

pages 54–55 Layne Kennedy/Corbis
page 55 Photodisc/Getty Images; Company Logo: Adobe and the Adobe logo are either registered trademarks or trademarks of Adobe Systems Incorporated in the United States and/or other countries.

Chapter 4

pages 94–95 David Frazier/The Image Works
page 95 Kim Steele/Getty Images

Chapter 5

pages 130–131 Courtesy Johnson Space Center/NASA
page 131 Royalty Free/Corbis

Chapter 6

pages 164–165 Andy Newman/Carnival Cruise Lines/Getty Images
page 165 Tony Freeman/Photoedit; Company Logo: Used with permission of Carnival Cruise Lines.

Chapter 7

pages 198–199 Danny Johnston/AP Wide World
page 199 Tim Boyle/Getty Images

Chapter 8

pages 246–247 Tim Boyle/Getty Images
page 247 Daniel Acker/Bloomberg News/Landov

page 279 Company Logo: Amazon, Amazon.com and the Amazon.com logo are registered trademarks of Amazon.com, Inc. or its affiliates.

Chapter 9

pages 282–283 Joe Raedle/Getty Images
page 283 Keith Brofsky/Getty Images
page 334 Company Logo: The Dell logo is a trademark of Dell Inc.

Chapter 10

pages 338–339 Jeff Greenberg/Photoedit
page 339 Tim Boyle/Getty Images; Company Logo: Adobe and the Adobe logo are either registered trademarks or trademarks of Adobe Systems Incorporated in the United States and/or other countries.

Chapter 11

pages 376–377 Stephen Chernin/Getty Images
page 377 Michael Newman/Photoedit; Company Logo: used with the permission of Inter IKEA Systems B.V.

Chapter 12

pages 414–415 Tim Boyle/Getty Images
page 415 Allana Wesley White/Corbis

Chapter 13

pages 454–455 Justin Sullivan/Getty Images
page 455 C Squared Studios/Getty Images
page 493 Company Logo: MATTEL® & AMERICAN GIRL® are trademarks owned by and used with permission from Mattel, Inc. © 2005 Mattel, Inc. All Rights Reserved.

Index

A

Accountants, 4–5
Account balances, 62–64, 432
  changes in, 133
  journalizing and posting, 72
  updated, 429
Account form balance sheet, 143–145
Accounting, 4
  accrual basis, 415–416, 469
  careers in, 5
  computer use, 60
  educational requirements, 5
  government regulation of, 7–8
  history, 26
  international, 13
  as language of business, 4
  for law enforcement, 63
  professional conduct, 474
Accounting clerks, 5
Accounting cycle, 96, 178
  for accounting information, 175
  completing, 462–473
  illus., 178, 180
  merchandising business, 496–500
  review of, 473–475
  service business, 196–197
  steps, 174, 178–180
Accounting equation; *see* Fundamental accounting equation
Accounting information; *see* Financial information
Accounting principles; *see* Generally accepted accounting
    principles
Accounting process, 10
  business transactions, 24
Accounting scandals, 474
  regulatory response, 7–8
Accounting services, 5
Accounting system, 4
  and business type, 200
  computerized, 136
  double-entry, 71
  flow of data, 179–180
  flow of financial data, 474–475
  managerial implications, 110
Accounts, 56
  chart of, 75
  classification of, 56
  order of, 109
  payroll, 357–358
  permanent, 75
  purpose, 56
  temporary, 75
  types of, 56–62
Accounts payable, 26
  determining cost of purchases, 259–261
  incurred debt as, 26
  managerial implications, 262

Accounts payable—*Cont.*
  voucher system, 261
Accounts payable ledger, 256
  format, 256–257
  function, 256
  illus., 257, 260, 296
  posting cash paid on account, 257
  posting cash payments, 295–296
  posting credit purchases, 256–257
  purchase returns and allowances, 257–259
Accounts receivable, 31
  credit card sales, 221
  journalizing and posting, 66–67
  and uncollectible accounts, 420
Accounts receivable account, *illus.,* 214
Accounts receivable conversion, 305
Accounts receivable ledger, 207, 207–215; *illus.,* 212–213
  posting cash received on account, 208
  posting credit sales, 207–208
  posting sales returns and allowances, 210–211
  posting to, 288
  recording sales returns and allowances, 210
  reporting net sales, 211
  sales returns and allowances, 208–214
Accrual basis of accounting, 415–416, 469
Accrued expenses, 421–423
  adjustments, 421–423
Accrued income, 424–425
  adjustments, 424–425
Accrued interest, 422–423, 424–425
Accrued payroll taxes, 421–422
Accrued salaries, 421
AccuBooks, 60
Accumulated depreciation, 137
Additional investment by owner, 286
Adelphia Communications, 7
Adjusted book balance, 307
Adjusted trial balance, 139–140, 428–429
Adjusting entries, 133
  in accounting cycle, 179
  illus., 146, 463–465
  journalizing, 462–465
  posting, 465
Adjustments, 133
  accrued expenses, 421–423
  accrued income, 424–425
  in contra account, 137
  depreciation, 136–138, 420–421
  expired rent, 135–137
  to financial records, 307–309
  loss from uncollectible accounts, 419–420
  managerial implications, 429
  merchandise inventory, 417–419
  prepaid expenses, 423–424
  and reversing entries, 469–473
  supplies used, 133–135
  unearned income, 426

INDEX

Adjustments—*Cont.*
 on worksheet, 416–426
Adobe Acrobat software, 291
Adobe Portable Document Format, 339
Adobe Reader, 339
Adobe Systems, 90, 179, 339
ADP, Inc., 343
Advertising, 66
After-closing trail balance, 175
Allowance for doubtful accounts, adjustments, 419–420
Allstate Corporation, 103
Alternative accrual method, 424, 426
Amazon.com, 170, 279
American Accounting Association, 13
American Bankers Association transit number, 303
American Eagle Outfitters, 19, 36, 415, 423
American Express, 220
American Institute of Certified Public Accountants, 13, 474
American Institute of Professional Bookkeepers, 195
American Payroll Association, 381, 396
Analysis; *see* Transaction analysis
Annual report, 90
 Home Depot, Inc., A1–A25
Application software, 60
Arthur Andersen, 7, 18, 474
Assets, 28; *see also* Current assets
 analysis of transactions, 30–35
 book value, 137
 fair market value, 38
 long-term, 460
 transactions affecting, 56–62
Auditing, 5
Auditor's report, 13
Audit trail, 97
 and accounting systems, 101
 accounts payable ledger, 296
 cash payments journal, 296
 checking account, 262
 check numbers for, 99
 function, 97
 petty cash, 298
 posting references, *illus.*, 106–107
 sales journal, 206
 supplier's invoice number, *illus.*, 101
Automated teller machines, 285
Avery Denison Corporation, 59

B

Balance ledger form, **105,** 207; *illus.*, 208
Balance sheet, 28
 account form, 143–145
 analysis of transactions, 30–35
 assets on, 28
 classified, 459–461
 illus., 39, 144
 liabilities on, 28
 preparation of, 143–145
 report form, 143–145
 section of worksheet, 429
 and statement of owners' equity, 37–40
 uncollectible accounts, 419
 worksheet section, 140–142

Balance sheet accounts, 75
Bank credit cards, 218, 219–220; *illus.*, 219
Bank fraud, 305
Banking procedures
 adjusting financial records, 307–309
 deposit slips, 303
 endorsing checks, 301
 and identity theft, 305
 internal control, 309–310
 for postdated checks, 303
 reconciling bank statements, 303–307
 writing checks, 301
Bank reconciliation statement, 306; *illus.*, 307
Banks
 online banking, 291
 service charges, 304–305
 use of financial information, 6–7
Bank statement reconciliation, 303–307; *illus.*, 304
 changes in account balance, 304–305
 demonstration of process, 305–307
Bartlett, Colleen, 23
Ben & Jerry's Homemade, Inc., 26
Best, C. L., 95
Best, Daniel, 95
Big Four accounting firms, 5, 7
Blank endorsement, 302
Bloch, Henry, 283
Bloch, Richard, 283
Bloomingdale's, 211
Boeing Company, 131, 145
Bonding, 299
Book balance of cash, 305–306
Bookkeepers, 5
Bookkeeping, double-entry, 71
Book value, 137, 460
 versus market value, 143
Bottom line, 210
Break even, 36
Bush, George W., 7
Business administration, 425
Business credit cards, 219
Business entities, *illus.*, 12
 corporations, 11–12
 partnerships, 10–11, 12
 separate entity assumption, 11
 sole proprietorships, 10, 12
 by type of business, 200
Business etiquette, 37
Business transactions, 24; *see also* Transaction analysis
 on balance sheet, 30–35

C

California State Board of Equalization, 222
Cancelled checks, 304
Capital, 25, 171–172
Capital accounts, drawing account, 69–70, 171–174; *illus.*, 172–174
Capone, Al, 63
Careers
 in accounting, 5–6
 business administration, 425
 hospitality and tourism, 37

Careers—*Cont.*
  in human services, 343
  information technology, 176
  legal and protective services, 107
  in merchandising, 253
Carnival Corporation, 165
Carrs stores, 455
Cash, 284
  book balance, 305–306
  internal control, 298–300
  managerial implications, 308
  purchase of equipment, 58
  purchase of supplies, 59–60
  purchases for, 25–26
  services sold for, 31, 65–66
Cash account, 56–57
Cash balance, *illus.*, 308
Cash discount, 253, 286
Cash investment, 56–57
Cash paid on account, 257
Cash payments, 291–300
  control of, 299–300
  internal control, 298–299
  petty cash fund, 296–298
Cash payments journal, 291, 293, 295, 296
  advantages, 296
  illus., 295, 298, 360
  posting from, 294–296
  proof of, 294
  recording transactions, 291–294
Cash purchases
  equipment and supplies, 292
  merchandise, 292
Cash receipts, 284–290
  control of, 299
Cash receipts journal, 284
  accounts in, 284–285
  advantages, 290
  credit card sales, 221
  illus., 285, 288, 289
  posting from, 287–289
  posting to, 208
  proof of, 287
  recording transactions, 284–287
Cash received on account, 208, 286
Cash refund, 286, 292–293
Cash register proof, 285
Cash sales, 285
Cash short or over account, 285–286
Caterpillar, Inc., 28, 95, 469
Certified public accountants, 5
  independent, 13, 19
Charge account, 26
Charge-account sales, 219
Chart of accounts, 75
  retail, 217
  types, 201
Check, 301; *illus.*, 302
  accounts receivable conversion, 305
  cancelled, 304
  dishonored, 305
  endorsing, 301–302
  negotiable, 301, 357

Check—*Cont.*
  not-sufficient-funds, 304
  outstanding, 306
  paying employees by, 356–358
  point-of-purchase conversion, 305
  postdated, 303
  writing, 301
  written on payroll account, 357–358
  written on regular account, 357
Check Clearing for the 21st Century Act, 305
Checking account balance, 304–305
Chronological order, 96
Classification, 56
Classified balance sheet, 459–461; *illus.*, 460
Classified financial statements, 456
Classified income statement, 456–459; *illus.*, 457
Closely held corporations, 11
Closing entries, 166–174; *illus.*, 466
  in accounting cycle, 179
  journalizing, 465–467
  posting, 467
Closing process
  income summary account, 166–167
  merchandising business, 166–174
  steps, 167
CNA Financial Corporation, 103
Coca-Cola Company, 456
Cohen, Ben, 26
Combined journal, B1; *illus.*, B2-B3
  designing, B1
  disadvantages, B5
  posting from, B4–B5
  recording transactions, B2–B4
  systems involving, B1
  uses of, B5
Commission basis, 345
Compensation record, 358
Compound entry, 102–104
Computerized financial statements, 145
Computers
  in accounting, 136
  decision support systems, 470
  for general journal, 98
  hardware, 60
  order processing systems, 211
  payroll applications, 396
  software, 60
Conoco, Inc., 137
Consumer preferences, 250
Contra account, 137, 210, **259**
Contra asset account, 137
Contra revenue account, 209
Control account, 214
Corporations, 11
  advantages and disadvantages, 18
  characteristics, 11–12
Correcting entry, 110
Cost of goods sold, 250
  closing entries, 466
  on income statement, 458
Credit, 71, 73; *see also* Rules of debit and credit
  in compound entry, 102–104
  services sold on, 31–32, 66–67

INDEX

Credit card companies, 220
Credit card sales, 221; *illus.*, 221
Credit department, 218
Credit investigation, 218
Credit memorandum, 208, 304; *illus.*, 209
Creditors, 10, 26
    paying, 27
    recording payment to, 60–61
Credit policies
    accounting for sales, 221
    bank credit cards, 219–220
    business credit cards, 219
    credit card companies, 220
    open-account, 219
    significance of, 218
    types, 218
    and uncollectible accounts, 218
Credit purchases, 26, 58–59, 250, 256–257; *illus.*, 251
Credit sales
    journalizing and posting, 202
    managerial implications, 224
    posting, 204–205, 207–208
    recorded in sales journal, 203–204
    uncollectible accounts, 419–420
CSX Corporation, 194
Currency, 292, 303
Current assets, 459–460
Current liabilities, 461
Current ratio, 468–469
Customers
    commitment to, 23
    users of financial information, 8

D

Debit, 71, 73; *see also* Rules of debit and credit
    in compound entry, 102–104
Debit cards, 292
Debit memorandum, 304–305; *illus.*, 306
Decision support systems, 470
Deferred expenses, 423
Deferred income, 426
Dell Computer, 334
Deloitte & Touche, 5
Delta Air Lines, 37
Department of Health and Human Services, 343
Department of Justice, 107, 305
Deposit in transit, 306
Deposit slip, 303; *illus.*, 303
Depreciable base, 420
Depreciation, 136
    accumulated, 137
    adjustments, 136–138, 420–421
    and book value, 137
    long-term assets, 138
    office equipment, 421
    salvage value, 136, 420
    store equipment, 420
    straight-line, 136, 420
Depreciation expense, 420–421
Diners Club, 220
Direct deposit, 358

Discount, 220, 221
Discount Store News, 199
Discount terms, 292
Discussion memorandum, 12–13
Dishonored check, 305
Disney College Program, 37
Dominick's stores, 455
Double-entry system, 71
Drawee, 301
Drawer, 301
Drawing account, 69
    closing entries, 171–172, 467
    purpose, 69–70
Dun & Bradstreet, 461
DuPont Corporation, 160–161, 450

E

Earnings
    hourly employees, 346–352
    payroll information, 352–354
    quarterly summary, 382
    salaried employees, 352
    ways of computing, 345–346
    withholding requirements, 347–349
    withholdings not required, 349–352
E-commerce, 134
Economic entity, 10
Electric power differences, 68–79
Electronic Federal Tax Payment System, 348, 378
Electronic filing, 387
Employee fraud, 262
Employees, 340
    calculating total earnings, 345–346
    commission basis, 345
    commitment to, 23
    exempt, 352
    and Fair labor Standards Act, 340–341
    federal income tax, 341
    hourly basis, 345
    individual earnings records, 358–359
    Medicare tax, 341
    overseas workers, 384
    paid by check, 356–358
    paid by direct deposit, 358
    pay for hourly employees, 346–352
    pay for salaried employees, 352
    payroll records, 343
    piece-rate basis, 345
    recording payroll information, 352–354
    records management, 348
    salaries, 33
    salary basis, 345
    self-employment, 352
    Social Security taxes, 341
    state and local taxes, 341
    unemployment compensation taxes, 390–398
    users of financial information, 9
    withholding requirements, 347–349
    withholdings not required, 349–352
    workers' compensation, 342
Employee's Withholding Allowance Certificate, 348; *illus.*, 349

Employers
    Medicare tax expense, 380–381
    payroll taxes/insurance costs, 341–342
    quarterly federal tax return, 382–383
    Social Security tax expense, 380–381
    tax deposits, 378–380, 393–396
Employer's Annual Federal Unemployment Tax Return,
    394–396; *illus.,* 395
Employer's Quarterly Federal Tax Return, 382–383; *illus.,* 383
Employer's Quarterly Report, 391; *illus.,* 392
Employers' tax liabilities, 387
End-of-month financial statements, *illus.,* 177
End-of-the-month posting, *illus.,* 205
Endorsement, 301–302
Enron Corporation, 7, 17, 474
Entity, 10
Equifax, 218
Equipment; *see also* Property, plant, and equipment
    cash purchase, 58, 292
    purchases of, 25–26
Equity, 25
Ernst & Young, 5
Errors
    finding and correcting, 109–111, 176
    locating, 141
    in making change, 286
    slide, 74
    transposition, 74
    trial balance, 73–74
Ethics, 211
Euro, 179
European Economic Community, 179
European Union, 179
Exempt employees, 352
Expense accounts
    normal balance, 70
    salaries expense, 67–68
    transactions affecting, 65–69
    utilities expense, 68–69
Expense recognition, in accrual accounting, 416
Expenses, 31, 67, 169
    accrual basis, 416, 419, 420, 421–424
    cash payments for, 291
    closing entries, 466
    journalizing and posting, 168–170
    matching principle, 416
    operating, 458
    owner withdrawals, 34
    prepaid rent, 27–28
    for purchases, 25–27
    rules of credit and debit, 137
    salaries, 33
    transportation, 458
    utilities, 33–34
Experience rating system, 390
Expired insurance, 423
Exposure draft, 13

F

Facilities, prepaid rent, 27–28
Fair Labor Standards Act, 340–341
Fair market value, 38

FASB; *see* Financial Accounting Standards Board
Federal Bureau of Investigation, 6, 63
Federal employee earnings and withholding laws, 340–342
Federal income tax, 341
    computing withholding, 348–349
    Form 941, 384–387
    Form W-2, 387
    Form W-3, 387–388
    Form W-4, 348
    pay-as-you-go tax, 347–348
    required withholding, 347–349
    withholding allowances, 348
    withholding tables, *illus.,* 350–351
Federal Insurance Contributions Act, 341
Federal Reserve Bank, 378
Federal Tax Deposit Coupon, 378, 382, 393
    illus., 379
Federal Trade Commission, 211
Federal unemployment insurance; *see* Unemployment insurance
        program
Federal Unemployment Tax Act, 342, 496
Federal unemployment taxes, 342
Federal Withholding Tax Tables, *illus.,* 350–351
Federated Department Stores, 52, 214, 253
Fees income account, 65–66
FICA; *see* Federal Insurance Contributions Act
FICA tax, 341
    withholding requirements, 347
Filo, David, 3
Financial Accounting Standards Board
    guiding principles, 13
    publications, 12–13, 14
Financial information
    in accounting cycle, 178–180
    interpreting financial statement, 176–177
    managerial implications, 13, 179
    need for, 4
    postclosing trial balance, 175–176
Financial information users
    banks, 6–7
    customers, 8
    employees and unions, 9
    illus., 8
    investors, 7–8
    owners and managers, 6
    regulatory agencies, 7–8
    suppliers, 6
    tax authorities, 7
Financial interest, 24–28, 29
    equity, 25
    terminology, 28–29
Financial records, adjusting, 307–309
Financial reports, 460
Financial statements, 4, 36; *see also specific statements*
    in accounting cycle, 178
    adjusted trial balance section, 139–140
    auditing, 13
    classified, 456–461
    computerized, 145
    effect of adjustments, 429
    end-of-month, 177
    illus., 144
    importance of, 40

Financial statements—*Cont.*
    interpreting, 176–177, 468–469
    managerial implications, 73, 474
    posting adjusting entries, 145
    preparation of, 74, 142–145, 456–461
Flow of financial data, 179–180, 474–475; *illus.*, 475
Footing, 62
Form 8109, 393
Form 8109-B, 378
Form 940/940 EZ, 394–396; *illus.*, 395
Form 941, 380, 384–387; *illus.*, 385-386
Form W-2, 387; *illus.*, 388
Form W-3, 387–388, *illus.*, 389
Form W-4, 348; *illus.*, 349
Fortune, 36
Freight charges, 250, 292
Freight In, 250
Full endorsement, 302
Fundamental accounting equation, 30–35, 56, 57
FUTA; *see* Federal unemployment taxes

G

GAAP; *see* Generally accepted accounting principles
General Agreement on Tariffs and Trade (GATT), 103
General and administrative expenses, 458
General journal, 96
    adjusting entries, 462–465
    audit trail, 97
    cash balance, 308
    closing entries, 168–172, 465–467
    compared to general ledger, 105
    computerized entries, 98
    credit purchases, 250
    error correction, 109–111
    format, 96–97
    illus., 172–174, 202, 226
    merchandising, 202
    payroll expense, 361
    payroll tax expense, 381–382
    payroll transactions, 355–356
    preparing compound entries, 102–104
    recording transactions, 97–102
    record of sales, 225
    reversing entries, 469–473
    sales returns and allowances, 209, 210
    sales tax payable, 226
    unemployment insurance, 391–394
    workers' compensation, 397–398
General ledger, 105
    account analysis, 110
    account forms, 105, 106
    accounts receivable account, 214
    compared to general journal, 105
    computerized, 136
    credit card sales, 221
    error correction, 109–111
    format, 106
    notes receivable, 287
    order of accounts, 109
    posting to, 105–109, 253–255
    purchase allowances, 257–258
    returns and allowances, 258–259

General ledger—*Cont.*
    for sales returns and allowances, 210
    wholesale business, 217
Generally accepted accounting principles, 12, 493; *illus.*, 14
    development of, 12–13
    use of, 13
Genuardi's stores, 455
Google, 161
Governmental accounting, 6
Greenfield, Jerry, 26
Gross earnings, 352
Gross pay, 346
Gross profit, 458
Gross profit percentage, 468

H

H&R Block, 283, 411–412
Hardware, 60
Holt, Benjamin, 95
Home Depot, Inc., 19, 51–52, 90, 126, 160, 193, 242, 248, 278,
    333–334, 373, 411, 450, 493, 494
    acquisitions, A21
    capital resources, A9
    cash balance in 2004, 176
    commitments and contingencies, A21
    consolidated balance sheets, A11
    consolidated statement of cash flows, A13
    consolidated statement of earnings, A10
    consolidated statements of stockholders' equity and
        comprehensive income, A12
    corporate stockholders' information, A25
    earnings data, A3–A4
    employee stock plans, A20
    income taxes, A19–A20
    letter to customers, suppliers, shareholders and associates,
        A1–A2
    liquidity, A9
    long-term debt, A18–A19
    management responsibilities, A23
    management's discussion and analysis, A2–A9
    notes to consolidated financial statements, A14–A22
    quarterly financial data, A22
    report of independent registered public accounting firm,
        A23–A24
    report on internal control, A23
    significant accounting practices, A14–A18
    use of financial statements, 176
Homeland Security Department, 6
Hospitality industry, 37
Hourly employees, 346–352
Hourly rate basis, 345
Hours worked, 346, 352
Human services, 343

I

Identity theft, 305
Identity Theft and Assumption Deterrence Act, 305
IKEA, 371
Income, 31
Income statement, 36
    classified, 456–459
    illus., 39, 144

Income statement—*Cont.*
  items on, 36
  multiple-step, 456
  preparation of, 142
  section of worksheet, 429
  single-step, 456
  worksheet section, 140–142
Income statement accounts, 75
Income summary, 417, 429
  closing entries, 466–467
Income summary account, 166–171, 429, 467
Independent contractor, 340
Independent CPAs, 13
Individual earnings records, 358–359; *illus.,* 359, 383
Information technology, careers in, 176
Institute of Certified Professional Managers, 425
Insurance, prepaid, 424
Interest
  accrued, 424–425
  computing, 293
  prepaid, 424
  promissory note, 286–287, 293–294
  reversing entries, 473
Interest expense, 429
Interest income account, 424–425, 473
Interest receivable account, 425
Internal control systems
  banking procedures, 309–310
  bonding, 299
  for cash, 298–300
  for employee fraud, 262
  payroll operations, 398–399
  petty cash fund, 297–298
  for purchases, 261–262
Internal Revenue Code, on Subchapter S corporations, 11
Internal Revenue Service, 348
  Form W-4, 348
  Publication 15, Circular E, 348, 382
  tax treaties, 384
  use of financial information, 7
International accounting, 13
International Accounting Standards, 13
International Accounting Standards Committee, 13
International business
  European Union, 179
  GATT, 103
  national preferences, 250
  trade agreements, 103
International Space Station, 131
Internet
  e-commerce, 132
  information technology, 176
  online banking, 291
Internet, information searches, 3
Interpret, 176
  in accounting cycle, 179
Inventory sheet, 417
Inventory turnover, 469
Investment, fair market value, 38
Investors, use of financial information, 7–8
Invoice, 217; *illus.,* 249
  on-time payment, 461

J

JC Penney Company, Inc., 450
Johnson, James Wood, 55
Johnson, Robert Mead, 55
Johnson, Robert Wood, 55
Johnson & Johnson, 55
Journal, 96
  for merchandising, 201
Journalizing, 96
  in accounting cycle, 178
  adjusting entries, 145–146, 462–465
  closing entries, 166, 167, 465–467
  credit sales, 202
  illus., 146
  payroll data, 359–360
  payroll transactions, 355–356
  reconciling entries, 306
  reversing entries, 469–473
  unemployment insurance, 391–394
  workers' compensation, 397–398

K

Kampad, Ingvar, 371
Kelleher, Herb, 23
King, Rollin, 23
KPMG, 5

L

Land, 138, 420
Law enforcement professionals, 107
Ledger, 105
  for merchandising, 201
  posting for sales tax, *illus.,* 222
Left-right rules, 57, 58, 59, 61, 62, 66, 67, 68, 69, 70, 71
Legal careers, 107
Liabilities, 28
  analysis of transactions, 30–35
  long-term, 461
  payroll, 356
  transactions affecting, 56–62
Limited Liability Partnership Act, 11
Limited liability partnerships, 11
Liquidity, 460
List price, 216
Local taxes, 341, 349–352
Long-term assets, 145, 460
Long-term liabilities, 461
Lookback period, 379
Loss from uncollectible accounts, 419–420

M

Macy's, 211
Magnetic ink character recognition, 303
Management advisory services, 5
Management letter, 90
Managerial accounting, 6
Managerial implications
  accounting for purchases, 262
  accounting systems, 110

Managerial implications—*Cont.*
    adjustments, 429
    cash, 308
    credit sales, 224
    financial information, 13, 179
    financial statements, 13, 40, 73, 474
    payroll records, 358
    payroll taxes, 398
    worksheet, 147
Managers, 6
Manufacturing business, 200
Market value, 143
MasterCard, 219
Matching principle, 416, **422**
Mattel, Inc., 493–494
Medical First Responder certification test, 107
Medicare tax, 341
    employee contribution, 341
    employer contribution, 342
    employer deposits, 378
    employer expense, 380–381
    required withholding, 347
Merchandise inventory, 200
    adjusted trial balance, 429
    adjustments, 417–419
    cash purchases, 292
    on financial statements, 458
    turnover, 469
Merchandising, 200
Merchandising business, 200
    accounting cycle, 496–500
    accounting for purchases, 248–255
    accounts receivable, 207–215
    adjustments, 416–426
    careers in, 253
    cash payments, 291–294
    cash receipts, 284–290
    closing process, 166–174
    combined journal, B5
    computerized order processing, 211
    credit policies, 218–221
    credit sales for wholesalers, 216–217
    sales journal, 200–206
    sales taxes, 222–226
    special journal, 200
    subsidiary journal, 200
    types of journals and ledgers, 201
Merit rating system, 390
Minimum wage law, 340–341
Miscellaneous income, 424–425
Monthly Deposit Schedule, 380
Multiple-step income statement, 456

N

Nardelli, Robert, 19
National Aeronautics and Space Administration, 131
National preferences, 250
National Retail Federation, 253
Negotiable, 301
Net amount, 145
Net income line, 432

Net income/loss, **36, 142,** 459
    calculating, 432
    closing entries, 170–171
    from operations, 459
Net price, 216
Net sales, reporting, 211
Net worth, 28
Nominal accounts, 75
Normal balances, 63, 70, 106
Northwest Airlines, 37
Note payable, 103
    accrued interest, 422–423
    prepaid interest, 424
Note receivable, accrued interest, 424–425
Notes to consolidated financial statements, 19
Not-sufficient-funds check, 304

O

Old Age, Survivors, and Disability Insurance, 383
On account, 26
Online banking, 291
Open-account credit, 26, **219**
Operating expenses, 458
Operating revenue, 456–458
Order of accounts, 109
Order processing systems, 211
Other income, 459
Outstanding check, 306
Overseas workers, 346, 384
Overtime pay, 341
Overtime premium, 346
Owners, use of financial information, 6
Owners' equity, 25, 29
    analysis of transactions, 30–35
    on balance sheet, 461
    closing entries, 170–171
    in corporations, 11–12
    decreases in, 67–68
    drawing account, 69–70
    effect of expenses, 31
    effect of revenue, 31
    increased by net income, 432
    and net income, 142
    in partnerships, 10–11
    in sole proprietorship, 10
    transactions affecting, 56–62
    withdrawals, 34, 346

P

Pacioli, Luca, 26
Partnerships, 10–11
    advantages and disadvantages, 18
    limited liability, 11
Pay-as-you-go tax, 347–348
Payee, 301
Payment
    to creditors, 27, 60–61
    on-time, 461
    of salaries, 33
    utilities expense, 33–34

Payroll
  computerized, 396
  deductions not required, 349–352
  federal laws, 340–343
  internal control, 398–399
  journalizing, 359–361
  managerial implications, 358
  paid by check, 356–358
  paid by direct deposit, 358
  posting expense, 361
  recording, 355–356
Payroll account, 357–358
Payroll data, *illus.*, 359–360
Payroll liabilities, 356
Payroll records, 343, 382
Payroll register, 352–354, 355, 358, 378
  illus., 352–353, 379
Payroll taxes
  accrued, 421–422
  employer contribution, 341–342
  federal income tax, 341
  FICA tax, 341
  managerial implications, 398
  Medicare tax, 341
  paid by employers, 341–342
  payment of, 378–387
  records management, 348
  Social Security tax, 341
  state and local taxes, 341
  tax treaties, 384
  withholding requirements, 347–348
Payroll transactions, *illus.*, 356
Peachtree software, 60, 176, 279
Permanent account, 75
Petty cash analysis sheet, 297; *illus.*, 298
Petty cash fund, 284, 296–298
  establishing, 297
  internal control, 297–298
  making payments from, 297
  replenishing, 297
Petty cash voucher, 297
Piece-rate basis, 345
Pier 1 Imports, 247
Plant and equipment, 460–461; *see also* Property, plant, and
    equipment
Point-of-purchase conversion, 305
Postclosing trial balance, 175–176, 467–468
  in accounting cycle, 179
  finding errors, 176
  illus., 175, 468
Postdated check, 303
Posting, 105, 205; *illus.*, 108–109
  in accounting cycle, 178
  to accounts payable ledger, 295–296
  to accounts receivable ledger, 288
  adjusting entries, 143, 465
  cash paid on account, 257
  from cash payments journal, 294–295
  from cash receipts journal, 287–288
  cash received on account, 208
  closing entries, 166, 167, 467
  from combined journal, B4–B5
  by computer, 136

Posting—*Cont.*
  credit purchases, 256–257
  credit sales, 202, 207–208
  end-of-the-month, 205
  to general ledger, 105–109
  payroll expense, 361
  from purchases journal, 254
  returns and allowances, 258–259
  for sales journal, 204–205
  sales returns and allowances, 210–211
  for sales tax, 222
Prepaid expenses, 133
  adjustments, 423–424
  recording, 135
  rent, 27–28
Prepaid insurance, 423
Prepaid interest, 424
Prepaid rent, 61–62
Presidential Management Internship Program, 343
PricewaterhouseCoopers, 5
Pricing, 288
Private accounting, 6
Privately held corporations, 11
Professional conduct, 474
Profit and loss statement, 35; *see also* Income statement
Promissory note, 286–287; *illus.*, 286
  interest, 293–294
Proof of cash payments journal, 294
Proof of combined journal, B4
Proof of purchases journal, 287
Proof of sales journal, 204
Proper names, 141
Property, equal to financial interest, 24, 26, 28, 29
Property, plant, and equipment, 420
  depreciation adjustments, 420–421
Proprietorship, 28
Protective services, 107
Public accountants, 5
Publication 15, Circular E (IRS), 348, 382
Public Company Accounting Oversight Board, 7
Public Company Accounting Reform and Investor Protection Act,
    7–8, 17–18; *see also* Sarbanes-Oxley Act
Publicly owned corporations, 11
Purchase allowance, 257–259
Purchase invoice, 248
Purchase order, 247, 249
Purchase requisition, 247, 249
Purchase return, 257–259
Purchase returns and allowances account, 257–259; *illus.*,
    258–259
Purchases
  determining cost of, 259–261
  of equipment, 25–26
  freight charges, 250
  internal control, 261–262
  source document management, 252
  of supplies, 26–27
Purchases account, 250, 259–261
Purchases account number, 251
Purchases discount, 253, 292
Purchases journal, 250–252; *illus.*, 254
  recording transactions, 252–253
Purchasing procedures, 248

Q

Quickbooks, 279

R

Randalls stores, 455
Ratio analysis
current ratio, 468–469
gross profit percentage, 468
inventory turnover, 469
Ratios, 469–471
Real accounts, 75
Receivables, collecting, 32
Receiving report, 247
Record of final entry, 105
Record of original entry, 96
Regulatory agencies, use of financial information, 7–8
Rent
adjustments for expired, 135–136
of facilities, 27–28
prepaid, 61–62, 424
Report form balance sheet, 143–145
Restrictive endorsement, 302
Retail business, 200
Retail business careers, 253
Retail chart of account, 217
Revenue, 31, 169
cash for services, 65–66
closing entries, 466
from collecting receivables, 32
collections from accounts receivable, 67
journalizing and posting, 167–168
matching principle, 416
operating, 456–458
from selling services, 31–32
services sold for credit, 66–67
varying kinds of, 66
Revenue accounts
multiple, 66
transactions affecting, 65–69
Revenue recognition, 469
in accrual accounting, 416
Reversing entries, 469
identifying items, 472–473
illus., 471–473
journalizing and posting, 469–473
Rules of debit and credit
bank reconciliation, 308
depreciation, 137
drawing account, 171
expense accounts, 169
expenses, 134, 135, 137
net income/loss, 170
payroll expense, 355
payroll tax expense, 381
returns and allowances, 258
revenue accounts, 168
salaries and wages, 357
sales journal, 204
sales returns and allowances, 209

S

Safeway, Inc., 168, 455
Salaried employees
gross earnings, 352
gross pay, 348
hours worked, 352
overseas workers, 346
withholding requirements, 352
Salaries
accrued, 421
payment of, 33
reversing entries, 469–471
Salaries expense, 68
Salary basis, 345
Sales account, 225–226; *illus.,* 225
Sales allowance, 208–211
Sales discount, 253, 286
Sales drafts, 220
Sales invoice, 220, 248
Sales journal, 200–206
advantages, 205–206
credit card sales, 221
illus., 202, 203, 217
posting from, 204–205
purpose, 200–201
recording transactions, 203–204
wholesale business, 217
Sales return, 208–211
Sales returns and allowances journal, 210; *illus.,* 210
Sales slip, 220; *illus.,* 204, 219
Sales tax
in cash receipts journal, 285
recorded in sales account, 225–226
state sales tax returns, 222–225
Sales tax audits, 204
Sales vouchers, 220
Salvage value, 420
Sam's Clubs, 199, 345–346
Sarbanes-Oxley Act, 7–8, 474
Schedule of accounts payable, 259; *illus.,* 261
Schedule of accounts receivable, 214–215; *illus.,* 215
S corporations; *see* Subchapter S Corporations
Securities Act of 1933, 7
Securities and Exchange Commission, 6, 474
functions, 7
on GAAP, 12
Securities Exchange Act of 1934, 7
Self-employment, 352
Selling expenses, 458
Separate entity assumption, 10, 11
Series of trade discounts, 216
Service business, 196–197, **200**
Service charges, 304–305
Services, 65–67
selling, 31–32
Shareholders, 12; *see also* Stockholders
Single-step income statement, 456
Single trade discount, 216
Skuggs, M. B., 455
Skuggs stores, 455
Slide, 74

INDEX

Small business, combined journal, B4
Social entities, 10
Social Security Act, 341
Social Security Administration, 381, 383
Social Security tax, 341
   employee contribution, 341
   employer contribution, 342
   employer expense, 380–381
   required withholding, 347
   wage base limit, 341
Software, 60
Sole proprietorship, 10
   advantages and disadvantages, 18
   example, 24–28
Source document management, 252
Southwest Airlines, 23, 51–52, 136, 356, 373–374, 425
Special journal, 200
Statement of account, 259, **286**
Statement of financial condition, 52; *see also* Balance sheet
Statement of financial position, 28
Statement of income and expenses, 35; *see also* Income
   statement
Statement of operations, 36
Statement of owners' equity, 37
   illus., 39, 143, 459
   items on, 37–40
   preparation of, 143
Statements of Financial Accounting Standards, 12
States
   reporting and paying unemployment taxes, 391–393
   unemployment insurance, 390
   unemployment insurance programs, 346
   withholding taxes, 349
State sales tax returns, 222–225; *illus.,* 224
State taxes, 341
   income taxes, 341
   workers' compensation, 342
State unemployment taxes, 342
Stock, 11
Stockholders, 12
Straight-line depreciation, 420
Subchapter S Corporations, 11
Subscription income, 426
Subsidiary journal, 200
Subsidiary ledger, 257
Supplemental Security Income Program, 383
Suppliers, use of financial information, 6
Supplies
   adjustments for used, 133–135, 423
   cash purchase, 59–60
   cash purchases, 292
   purchase of, 26–27
SUTA; *see* State unemployment taxes
Systems software, 60

T

T-accounts, 56, 105, 134–135, 137, 168, 169, 170, 171, 209,
   258, 308, 356, 381
   for drawing account, 69–71
   for revenue and expenses, 65–69
   trial balance, 71–74

Tax accounting, 5
Tax authorities, use of financial information, 7
Tax calculations, 384
Tax compliance, 5
Taxes
   payment of, 292
   Subchapter S corporations, 11
   unemployment insurance, 390–398
Tax evasion, 63
Tax-exempt wages, 347
Tax Foundation, 371
Tax planning, 5
Tax returns, 371
Tax treaties, 384
Temporary account, 75
Time and a half, 341
Tom Thumb stores, 455
Tourism industry, 37
Trade agreements, 103
Trade discount, 216
   series of, 216–217
   single, 216
Transaction analysis
   in accounting cycle, 178
   balance sheet transactions, 30–35
   bank reconciliation, 308
   collecting receivables, 32–33
   drawing accounts, 68–71
   effect of owner withdrawals, 34
   illus., 35
   income statement transactions, 35–36
   paying creditors, 27
   payroll expense, 355–356
   payroll tax expense, 380–381
   renting facilities, 27–28
   returns and allowances, 258
   revenue and expense accounts, 65–69
   salaries and wages, 357
   salary payments, 33–34
   sales returns and allowances, 208–211
   selling services, 31–32
   service business, 196–197
   sole proprietorship, 24–28
   starting a business, 24–28
   summary of, 34–35
   T-accounts for, 56–64
   utilities expenses, 33–34
Transactions
   in cash payments journal, 291–294
   in cash receipts journal, 284–287
   in combined journal, B2–B4
   recorded in general journal, 97–102
   recorded in purchases journal, 252–253
   in sales journal, 203–204
   ways of recording, 426
Transmittal of Wage and Tax Statement, 387–388
Transportation expense, 458
Transportation In account, 250
Transposition, 73–74
Trial balance, 71; *illus.,* 72, *see also* Postclosing trial balance
   accounts, 132, 133
   errors, 73–74

Trial balance—*Cont.*
   merchandise inventory, 417
   preparation, 71–72
   for preparing financial statements, 139–140
TWA, 37

U

Uncollectible accounts, 218
   adjustments, 419–420
   write-off, 420
Unearned income, 426
Unemployment benefits, 391
Unemployment insurance program, 390
   computing and recording taxes, 391
   employer tax deposits, 393–394
   federal-state coordination, 390
   Form 940/940EZ, 394–396
   reporting and paying by states, 391–393
   reporting and paying federal tax, 393–396
Unions, users of financial information, 9
United States Chamber of Commerce, 262
Updated account balances, 429
Use tax, 222
Utilities expense, 33–34, 68

V

Verschoor, Curtis, 211
Visa International, 219
Vons stores, 455
Voucher system, 261

W

Wage and Hour Laws, 340
Wage and Tax Statement, 387
Wage base limit, 341
Wage-bracket table method, 348
Wal-Mart Stores, 126–127, 199, 242–243, 250, 345–346
Walt Disney Company, 136

Walton, Sam, 199
Wholesale business, 216
   careers, 253
   sales journal, 217
   trade discounts, 216–217
Wholesale chart of accounts, 217
Withdrawals, 34, 171
   owners' equity, 346
Withholding allowances, 348
Withholding statement, 387
Withholding taxes, 341
   computing, 349
   employer deposits, 378–380
   Form 941, 384–387
   for hourly employees, 347–349
   recording, 381–382
   salaried employees, 352
Workers' compensation insurance, 342
   deposit and monthly premium, 398
   estimated annual premium in advance, 396–398
Worksheet, 132
   accounting cycle, 132–138, 178
   adjusted trial balance section, 139–140, 428–429
   adjustments section, 133–138, 145–146, 416–426, 428, 462
   balance sheet section, 140–142, 429
   format, 132, 133
   illus., 134, 140–143, 166–167, 418–419, 420–433
   income statement section, 140–142, 429
   managerial implications, 147
   net income/loss, 432
   preparation steps, 416–417
   ten-column, *illus.*, 132, 430–433
   trial balance section, 132
WorldCom, 7, 17
Worldspan reservation system, 37

Y

Yahoo!, 3
Yang, Jerry, 3

INDEX